*~ Introduction to Scholarship
in Modern Languages
and Literatures*

∼ Introduction to Scholarship in Modern Languages and Literatures

THIRD EDITION

EDITED BY DAVID G. NICHOLLS

THE MODERN LANGUAGE ASSOCIATION OF AMERICA
NEW YORK   2007

© 2007 by The Modern Language Association of America
All rights reserved
Printed in the United States of America

For information about obtaining permission to reprint material from MLA
book publications, send your request by mail (see address below), e-mail
(permissions@mla.org), or fax (646 458-0030).

Library of Congress Cataloging-in-Publication Data

Introduction to scholarship in modern languages and literatures / edited
by David G. Nicholls. — 3rd ed.
    p. cm.
  Includes bibliographical references and index.
  ISBN: 978-0-87352-597-8 (hardcover : alk. paper)
  ISBN: 978-0-87352-598-5 (pbk. : alk. paper)
  1. Philology, Modern—History.   I. Nicholls, David, 1965–
PB29.I58 2007
407.2—dc22   2006033017

Cover illustration of the paperback edition: *Silent Shapes in Space and Time*,
by Thomas Ingmire. 1998. © Thomas Ingmire. Used by permission of the
artist and the City of Mountain View Public Library.

Printed on recycled paper

Published by The Modern Language Association of America
26 Broadway, New York, New York 10004-1789
www.mla.org

⁓ Contents

~ Preface

"Any formulation of aims and methods currently adopted in the fields of modern language scholarship in America must of necessity appear too limited to do justice to the ideals of a learned profession and too rigid to reflect the convictions and interests of its individual members" (MLA Committee on Research Activities 3). So begins the first of a series of publications issued by the Modern Language Association of America that identify key areas of scholarly concern for our field and elucidate basic methodological assumptions. The first, "The Aims, Methods, and Materials of Research in the Modern Languages and Literatures," was prepared by the Committee on Research Activities (later incorporated into the Publications Committee) in response to a 1948 request from the Executive Council. Published in 1952, the report immediately gives a provisional cast to the whole enterprise. Its authors not only anticipate that readers may find the publication "too limited" and "too rigid" but also note that it is written "at a time when the very foundations of these [humanistic] studies have been subject to criticism." Tellingly, a footnote indicates that the report is based on "the not always unanimous opinions" of the committee members (3).

The tentativeness of the first report provides a key to understanding the transformation of scholarship in modern languages and literatures over more than five decades. As practitioners continue to question the very foundations of their scholarly work, they devise new methods and develop new interests. It was clear from the beginning that a periodic report of this kind has lessons to teach. In the introduction to the second iteration, *The Aims and Methods of Scholarship in Modern Languages and Literatures*, James Thorpe writes that the volume "is about becoming and being a scholar." With an emphasis on *becoming*, he chooses students as the primary audience for the 1963 publication. Subsequent volumes would continue to address students even as the books served, in Thorpe's words, "any members of the scholarly community who would like to read a review of some current ideas on the aims and methods of scholarship" (vii). This, the sixth publication in the series, addresses students in particular and the scholarly community more generally. It seeks to provide an orientation for future scholars and to take stock of trends in the field over the past decade and a half.

The present volume is designed to highlight relations among languages and forms of discourse. In recent years, many scholars in modern languages and literatures have questioned the conceptual coherence of national literatures and have sought new ways to understand the circulation of languages and literatures both transnationally and within national contexts. At the same time, scholars have taken a broad array of texts as the basis for study. After consulting with the Publications Committee and MLA staff members on these and other developments in the field, I drew up a list of topics and invited prominent scholars to prepare essays on them. Authors conceived their task in a variety of ways. Because most provide an extensive survey of key works on their topic, the accompanying lists of works cited offer readers paths to further study.

The book is organized into three sections. The first, "Understanding Language," begins with Doris Sommer's investigation of multilingual aesthetics in "Language, Culture, and Society," provides an extensive survey of the field of linguistics by Paul J. Hopper, and concludes with Heidi Byrnes's exploration of what it means to become a competent user of a language—especially a second or foreign language. The second section,

"Forming Texts," places new emphasis on the role of speakers and writers in the creation of meaning; essays on rhetoric, composition, and poetics (by Susan C. Jarratt, David Bartholomae, and Charles Bernstein, respectively) view the formation and interpretation of texts from three distinct but interrelated intellectual perspectives. The third and longest section, "Reading Literature and Culture," starts with Leah S. Marcus's review of textual scholarship, which concerns "the specific forms in which written texts reach readers." Jerome McGann then offers a meditation on the difficulties of interpretation. Catherine Gallagher follows with an analytic account of the historical turn in literary criticism. J. Michael Holquist outlines the conceptual history of comparative literature, a field that has long questioned the very idea of a national literature. In her review of cultural studies, Jean Franco goes beyond the familiar terrain of British and American scholarship to include Latin American contributions. Anne Donadey studies, with Françoise Lionnet, the interdisciplinary scholarship in feminisms, genders, and sexualities, showing that work in this area looks increasingly at intersections among categories of identity (including race and ethnicity) and situates analysis transnationally. In his essay on race and ethnicity, Kenneth W. Warren sets out "to account for and critique the appeal of race to literary critics over the past two decades and to suggest reasons we ought to modify or resist aspects of that appeal." Susan Stanford Friedman takes on the broad topic of migrations, diasporas, and borders, considering the conceptual rubrics organizing work in these areas and demonstrating the ways in which population movement matters for students of language and literature. The section closes with Lawrence Venuti's essay on transla-

tion studies, a key topic for understanding the relations among languages, literatures, and cultures both in the past and in our increasingly globalized economy. In the volume's epilogue, "The Scholar in Society," Bruce Robbins reflects on the conflicted status of the humanistic scholar today, highlighting our collective need for national recognition and support even as we frequently strive to understand and engage with the world beyond our borders—and in contradiction with national agendas.

In the tradition of this series of publications, I close my prefatory remarks with a caveat and a promise. No book of this kind can fully cover a field as large and various as ours; there must be gaps in the coverage of topics, even as there is inevitable overlapping among the essays. So while I note that this volume is as provisional as the first, I also predict that it will act as a catalyst for future inquiry and argument in the study of modern languages and literatures. As a community, we will continue to ask questions about the foundations of our work, to trouble assumptions, and to chart new territory for analysis and debate. By fostering our collective reflection on the work of becoming and being scholars, this book promises yet another cycle of intellectual renewal.

DGN

WORKS CITED

MLA Committee on Research Activities. "The Aims, Methods, and Materials of Research in the Modern Languages and Literatures." *PMLA* 67.6 (1952): 3–37.

Thorpe, James, ed. *The Aims and Methods of Scholarship in Modern Languages and Literatures*. New York: MLA, 1963.

~ Acknowledgments

The development of this volume involved several stages of planning and evaluation and required the input of members of the association and of the MLA staff. In the initial planning stage, I consulted with the staff members Phyllis Franklin, Joseph Gibaldi, Judy Goulding, Sonia Kane, David E. Laurence, and Elizabeth B. Welles to prepare several models for evaluation by the Publications Committee, which oversees the development of the MLA's nonperiodical publications. The committee members who participated in the review of the initial models, an interim prospectus, or the manuscript are Judith H. Anderson, Dudley Andrew, Patricia Lynn Bizzell, Jeannine Blackwell, Debra Ann Castillo, Lynn Enterline, Simon E. Gikandi, Amy Katz Kaminsky, Jacques Lezra, Cristanne Miller, James A. Miller, Ross C. Murfin, Sandy Petrey, Timothy James Reiss, C. P. Haun Saussy, Dennis Tedlock, and Susan Wells. Other MLA members who offered expert advice and consultation on various parts of the manuscript are Daniel Balderston, Michael F. Bérubé, Diane W. Birckbichler, David Damrosch, Morris E. Eaves, Elizabeth Stone Freeman, Myra Jehlen, Steven G. Kellman, Jill Suzanne Kuhnheim, Eric William Lott, Susan Passler Miller, and Irmengard Rauch. My staff colleagues who provided editorial and administrative assistance in seeing the volume into print are Judith H. Altreuter, Rosemary G. Feal, Jeremy James George, Marcia Henry, Elizabeth Holland, and Michael Kandel. I am grateful to all these people for lending their intelligence and support toward the completion of this project.

~ Understanding Language

～ Language, Culture, and Society

DORIS SOMMER

GOOD DAY

To listen to the world now is to wake up from a romantic enchantment whose spell cast human subjects into vessels of one language, made language seem almost identical to nation, and made nation practically indistinguishable from state. By this magic of correspondences, the audible world projected, to use a visual correlative, a cultural product map on which particular spaces represented particular sounds, tastes, and literary textures. England was English, Germany German, France French, Spain Spanish. The redundancy of a single word that named both language and territory performed a kind of enchanted stability that felt like a dependable home.

But today, *home* often means not a here but a there, somewhere else, a loss for migrant parents and a lack for the children. It is not dependably "the place where, when you have to go there, / They have to take you in," as Robert Frost assured, certainly not for the many and multiplying numbers of displaced and dispossessed people. Newcomers aren't at home even at home. The effect of movement can also disconcert, to say the least, stable native neighbors when the

sounds of local streets and shops and services sound strange. Maybe they have always sounded a bit strange, especially in new countries of immigration such as those of the Americas, or in old countries with stubborn dialectal differences or in colonies where natives and newcomers clashed. The magic of correspondences reduced the sound of clashes to background noise and raised the volume for monolingual voice-overs of modern progress. By now, strangeness is the norm in many big cities worldwide, where urban life is recovering the heterogeneous and dynamic qualities that once defined the medieval metropolis (Sassen).

Today the push of peoples from poor countries to richer ones and the pull of market logic beyond national economies into regional and even broader arrangements affect more than money and markets. The effects of globalization include reshuffling the cultural map of languages and literatures. Hardly any spaces are left to the tidy coincidence that some of us imagined between national culture and sovereign state. Today, countries depend on one another for everything from markets to tribunals and terrorist grids. Countries and national cultures depend on immigrant workers or on the remittances

> **The redundancy of a single word that named both language and territory performed a kind of enchanted stability.**

3

sent back home, and they depend on news and books written in one place, published in another, and marketed to a world of readers. Reading, writing, and speaking—verbal creativity in general—often cross national boundaries and thereby transgress the lines of proper (or proprietary) language. And the continuing movement, sometimes in shuttles from home to host and back, makes more than one country, culture, and code familiar for many families. Between one code and another, migrants can switch, artfully, to play games of odd man out with monolinguals. One related game, in different registers of English, is "signifying," when African American players multiply the meanings of words to keep others in the dark (Gates). In a variation of the game, an inner-city teenager plays "lame" to win advantages while bridging two worlds (Labov). But multilingual games increase the range of differences; they increase the added values that difference brings to literature and to language in general every time strangeness defamiliarizes habitual use.

More than one language is a supplement, not a deficiency. It is a dangerous supplement for monolingualism, whether the addition amounts to two languages or to many. Bilingualism overloads a monosystem; multilingualism overloads it more. Both make similar mischief with meaning. The underlying goal of thinking about these overloads as intellectual, artistic, and ethical enhancements will be to open up academic and public debates beyond the failing standard of monolingual assimilation.

Unfortunately, for newcomers and also for host countries such as the United States, assimilation has been a powerful practice that reduces languages to one common denominator. Second-generation immigrants are often out of linguistic touch with their parents' countries of origin. Along with home languages, economic opportunities in global markets are lost in that squeeze; it cramps careers, deletes intimate connections in transnational families, and even reduces respect for one's parents and oneself. The sociologists Alejandro Portes and Lingxin Hao therefore recommend language maintenance—that

is, a "selective acculturation" option that adds languages instead of subtracting them (910)—because forced forgetfulness and the corollary disrespect of parents cannot produce strong societies. "The price of uniformity" is too high, they conclude.[1] Subtraction is an alarming trend not only in individual speakers but also among world languages. The number of currently existing languages is being reduced to roughly half, announcing present and future losses that we can hardly calculate (Nettle and Romaine). The reduction does not necessarily signal extermination of peoples, because people typically speak more than one language, but it does mean the simplification of their linguistic (aesthetic, cognitive, political) lives. Additive acculturation would acknowledge the pleasures and self-respect that code switchers earn by dint of their virtuosity, though they make embarrassing mistakes. Mistakes can brighten speech with a *sunrisa* (a mistake that puns on the Spanish word for "smile" [Hernández Cruz, "You Gotta"]) or give the pleasure of a found poem. Always, they mark communication with a cut or a tear that comes close to producing an aesthetic effect.[2] The risk and thrill of speaking or writing anything can sting, every time language fails us. Knowing how language can fail makes success feel like a small miracle. In other words, attention to a bilingual aesthetics can cast the precarious subjects as self-authorizing and original agents, even in the face of monolingual nativists such as Samuel Huntington, author of *Who Are We?*

If bilingual arts used to be a sideline for linguists and social scientists, the new attention to transnational circuits has made code switching a main attraction.[3] Skeptics about so much current attention to globalization will point out that the grids are old news. Early modern history in the West practically begins with the conquest of the Americas and Africa, with far-flung routes of trade, plunder, voluntary and forced migration, and the consolidation of hegemonic vernaculars at home to make metropolitan cultures more portable if not user-friendly abroad. Users often continued to speak their own home languages, both in Europe, where many regional dialects refused to die, and in colonial settings, where recent postcolonial cultures sometimes revive native traditions. The skeptics are right, of course. Modernity has never been a tidy map of cultural monads. But that impossible map has long served as a kind of mirage of modernity's promised land, where the self and the state dreamed of each other as ideal partners. A related and recurring dream, as resistant as the nation-state to wake-up calls from statistical evidence, is the vision of nuclear families as the only normal option for private life while others seem sick. These are romantic, rather dangerous daydreams, and it's time to wake up now.

A JEALOUS SPIRIT

Johann Gottfried Herder (1744–1803, in Prussia) continues to inspire many dreams of spiritual coherence between one's consciousness and one's country, ever since he published "Essay on the Origin of Language" in 1770. Writing against the Enlightenment internationalism of his mentor, Immanuel Kant, Herder argued that a particular language is the core of a particular *Volk*, a people or ethnic group, and that to mix languages is to lose one's core. For him, language does much more than simply give expression to thought; it determines thought. And since languages are different, molding the world in distinct and incommensurable ways, truth is not universal for Herder but plural and contradictory (Zammito; Brady). Along this line of attributing single linguistic identities to ideally coherent nations, the philosopher Wilhelm von Humboldt (1776–1835, in Germany) established research in the first modern university, founded by him in Berlin. Humboldt's cultural relativism assumed the value of every language as a *Versuch* ("attempt" or "search") among the many available ways of perceiving the world, though he believed that some languages, such as Greek and Latin, were more valuable attempts than others. Herder was less concerned with comparisons and more fixed on the fit between the folk and

its language. He is generally considered the father of ethnic nationalism, which identifies the political nation with a single ethnic essence.[4] Nazism is a glaring example of the conflation of a particular people and a political state.

Herder warned universalists, "against pure reason," that crossing cultural lines and speaking foreign languages would unravel body from soul. Human nature, he insisted, thrived on one vernacular per person and would not tolerate the foreign contamination that plagued Enlightened globalization. (That internationalist mind-set described the delegates to the Continental Congress in Philadelphia, who considered several alternatives to the language spoken by their British oppressors [Kellman].) When the single and unified spirit of a people was identified with its pure spirit of language, or *Sprachgeist*, two languages were clearly too many for Herder; "The age that wanders toward the desires and hopes of foreign lands is already an age of disease, flatulence, unhealthy opulence, approaching death!" (*Against Pure Reason* 43).

I reported this diagnosis in Mexico once, thinking it laughable enough to merit a mention. But the joke improved considerably among the Maya listeners, to judge from the volume of their laughter. I learned later that the Spanish word for fart (*pedo*) means kiss in Mayan.[5] Bilinguals will know that sometimes wit, as in this case, is an effect of displaced reception rather than clever expression and that part of the fun is to locate speakers at the butt of their own unintentional jokes. Herder would not be laughing. Could he have imagined that the "malady" of many languages might sound funny in a foreign language? Probably. He worried that high-mindedness foundered on dangerous foreign supplements. Could he have wanted to kiss off a problem with a perverse joke that cures gas cramps with laughing gas? Hardly. He was dead serious.

The deadliness should caution humanists. So much seriousness forfeits the creativity that sustains both art and democracy. Abraham Lincoln, for one, wasn't worried about deviating from expectations and playing the fool once in a while. He worried instead about people who refused to lighten up.[6] Lincoln knew that jokes interrupt single-minded zeal and intolerance. Democracy, like art, thrives on strangeness, surprise, on risk and the dangerous rub of conflict.[7] Tellingly, political theory about the relation between democracy and the foreigner come very close to art criticism for the political scientist Bonnie Honig, specifically to literary genre theory. She notes that theories of liberalism today address urgent issues raised by mass migration, generally cosidering it a problem to be solved. The concern is to safeguard a constitutional tradition from other, sometimes premodern, practices. But Honig balances the concern with an appreciation for foreigners who refresh the spirit of liberal democracy. She takes liberalism's fundamental respect for personal autonomy and its corollary precaution against thinking for others to a logical consequence: "It is important to rethink democracy in non-kinship terms, as a politics among strangers" (72). We have been telling ourselves the wrong kind of story about politics, she says. It is not a projected romance of reconciliation and cozy intimacy, though the desired happy endings of "foundational fictions" still keep most political theorists in thrall (Sommer, *Foundational Fictions*). Instead, democracy reads like the genre of the gothic thriller, in which the lover is as mysterious, possibly dangerous, as he is attractive. It is a double-edged adventure, full of uncertainties about the immigrant hero's character and about the law that might protect the national heroine (Honig, ch. 5). In fact, creative risk is a condition of democracy, as Theodor Adorno took care to explain. If we managed to banish risk altogether, and be rid of the "negative" moments of disagreement and doubt, there would be little democracy left to defend (172).[8] The risk brings linguistic dissonance and democracy close to art, if you consider that the practice of choosing and combining among conflicting options describes techniques, rather than outcomes, associated with liberal politics and with art (selection, recombination, judgment).

By contrast to Herder's linguistic hygiene

Democracy, like art, thrives on strangeness, surprise, on risk and the dangerous rub of conflict.

campaign, the great American tradition of linguistic anthropology in the early twentieth century avoided essentialism and pursued egalitarian—which also means antiracist—investigations. Franz Boas was the founder; both German and Jewish, he studied Native American languages at Columbia University. Though Boas agreed with Humboldt and Herder that linguistic categories reflect culturally specific perceptions of reality, he concluded that all languages are equally equipped to describe human experience. Then his student, Edward Sapir, went beyond observations about how language reflects cultural perceptions to revive the argument that language actually shapes them.[9] The difference between this position and Herder's is that for Sapir, living in two languages doesn't damage the speakers but doubles their resources for handling experience. Sapir's student and collaborator, Benjamin Lee Whorf, put it this way:

> the "linguistic relativity principle" . . . means, in informal terms, that users of markedly different grammars are pointed by the grammars toward different types of observations and different evaluations of externally similar acts of observation, and hence are not equivalent as observers but must arrive at somewhat different views of the world. (221)

These differences bring life to learning and to politics (not to mention the added economic value of thinking outside a single box). So we do well to keep a first language while learning others. Nevertheless, some liberal defenses of multilingualism stay stuck in a romantic ecology of language that equates a people with a single linguistic culture.

Let me mention one example of this Herderian axiom about different strokes for different folks; it represents a range of examples that, paradoxically, follow the same broad strokes. Speakers of Lakota object to a "thingness" about English, because for them English reifies spiritual meanings into objects. "Sweat house," for example, is a wooden translation for the mystical ceremony called *iníkagapi* ("with it they make life" [Bunge 378–79]). But the contrast between sacred Lakota and secular English is bogus. It ignores the heated mystical tradition in Standard English, where, for instance, *communion* means much more than wafer eating. The Lakota case shows only that one tradition doesn't easily understand another. More significant for me is that the case performs a cultural-political desire to value a particular language for its inherent qualities. Difference becomes content (paradoxically, the thingness that was dismissed as objectionable) rather than the effect of opacity for outsiders and satisfaction for insiders.

Herder had hypostatized that effect of difference into a solid monolingual core of national feeling (*Against Pure Reason*). His legacy continues to inspire some multiculturalists to make politically and aesthetically risky appeals to an essential quality of cultural particularity (see, e.g., Taylor; Flores; Pan). Herder's heirs may mix words and grammar, to the horror of linguistic purists like the master himself, but their goal is to create a stable *Sprachgeist* from creole speech, defending it as the authentic expression of its newly consolidated people (see Chaudenson; DeGraff; Thomason and Kaufman). Take Spanglish. To read Miguel Algarín's manifesto prologue to *Nuyorican Poetry* of 1975, the goal of Latino creativity was to harness a "disruptive, tense, informal street talk" in order "to arrive at an organized respectability" (Algarín and Piñero 19). Defenders of Spanglish as a single language make that appeal to respectability (Stavans), but some Nuyoricans prefer to understand Spanglish as the syncopation between languages, a disruptive and risky rhythm. "Worlds exist simultaneously, flashes of scenarios, linguistic stereo; they conflict, they debate," Víctor Hernández Cruz writes, "Spanish and English constantly breaking into each other like ocean waves" (*Red Beans* 89).

DIFFERENCE, IN ESSENCE OR AS EFFECT

Today the logic of language rights sometimes uses Herder's equation of one people equals one language. Consider the philosopher Charles Taylor's "Politics of Recognition" as a contemporary milestone here. Admirably, the essay defends cultural autonomy in French Canada, among other beleaguered cultural communities. But his logic of the long-standing cultural content that thrives in a linguistically unified group is grounds for recognition that come uncomfortably close to political quicksand. This reasoning is only a step away from insisting that the Serbian language be distinguished from Croatian as Yugoslavia broke up into competing nations. While the united country still existed, the minor differences in speech between its two main ethnic groups did not amount to distinct languages. Serbs and Croats understood each other quite well. But once civil war broke out, the language differences hardened rather artificially as one justification for continued fighting (Greenberg; Bugarski).

Members of undervalued groups suffer, say Taylor and other defenders of minority cultures, when their collective rights to resources and representation fail to win debates because those members are not recognized as such but are treated instead as individual, autonomous, liberal subjects. The complaint seems unobjectionable, because all individuals identify themselves as members of a group (among other forms of identification), but the remedy of group solidarity and autonomy has insalubrious side effects. One is intolerance for internal difference, since the cultural dynamic to be defended is not debate and reform but a particular and untranslatable spirit of a people, a Romantic, Herderian coziness of one compact culture threatened by contamination from others.[10]

Authenticity, the right to live "*my* way," keeps a straight and narrow course in Taylor's politics of recognition, as if sidetracks lead us astray (30). Disrespected people seem pitifully damaged and distant in Taylor's third person plural rather than interestingly doubled and resilient: "Their first task ought to be to purge themselves of this imposed and destructive identity" (the way Herder prescribed purging as a cure for cultural flatulence), lest they share the "crushing" fate of

Caliban (26). Caliban crushed? It is as if Taylor preferred to overlook the complexity of *The Tempest*, not to mention the many Caribbean sequels that turn the tide on Prospero's Eurocentrism. Readers and theatergoers will know that Caliban is not crushed. Shakespeare gave him credit for vengeful creativity; and Caribbeans, in French, Spanish, and English, continue to claim Caliban as the mixed man who maneuvers inside and alongside master codes. Aimé Césaire's *A Tempest*, Roberto Fernández Retamar's "Caliban," and Edward Kamau Brathwaite's "Letter Sycora X," among many other sequels to Shakespeare, defend difference, not by purging harmful elements but by incorporating a range of foreign and autochthonous sources into contemporary, hybrid identities (see also Henry). Difference and minoritarian rights become internal and dynamic effects instead of essences to defend from contamination. "In Praise of Créolité," by Jean Bernabé, Patrick Chamoiseau, and Raphaël Confiant, is a manifesto from Martinique that embraces complicated identities and resists assimilation into one universalist French culture. "School teachers of the great period of French assimilation were the slave traders of our artistic impulse." But this resistance doesn't substitute universalism for a more authentic *Sprachgeist*. It won't do, say the authors, to purge the languages of slavery and thereby sacrifice room to maneuver in the arts, in markets, and in politics. A single hybrid Creole would forfeit the real authenticity of creative freedom. Choose and lose, is the warning against monolingual nationalism.

> Our primary richness, we the Creole writers, is to be able to speak several languages: Creole, French, English, Portuguese, Spanish, etc. Now we must accept this perpetual bilingualism and abandon the old attitude we had toward it. Out of this compost, we must grow our speech.   (104)

In Brazil, the compost would surely evoke similar images from "The Cannibalist Manifesto" (1928) by Oswald de Andrade, which celebrates the country's enormous cultural appetite to consume foreign elements from Europe, Africa, and from everywhere else. A more defensive authenticity would eliminate foreign influences; this strategy is to be "national by subtraction," to borrow Roberto Schwarz's ironic label for the nativism that requires immigrants and indigenous peoples to leave their differences behind in order to enter a coherent monocultural compact. Schwarz contrasts this cultural anemia to the cannibalism that has long nourished Brazilian culture. What makes Brazil special is not a particular ingredient or spirit but the clever and canny ways in which many elements are mixed and remixed. Technique makes the country a collective work of art composed from a wealth of foreign loot and languages.

Technique is the focus of observations by the anthropologist Néstor García Canclini on the arts of hybrid cultures as they enter and exit modernity. It is also the focus of art criticism in general for the Russian formalists writing in the 1910s and 1920s. The formalists reminded critics who had forgotten classics such as Aristotle and Longinus that language arts depend on how words are put together, not on some supposedly spiritual meaning, including the meaning of a *Sprachgeist*. Standard Romantic approaches admired poetry as a shorthand for transcendent values—the shorter hand the better, since the spirit allegedly spoke through images. "Images belong to no one: they are 'the Lord's,' " Viktor Shklovsky intones mockingly ("Art" 7). Such loftiness and laziness provoked him to be naughty and unequivocal in "Art as Technique" (1917). He illustrated the technical quality of literary art in 1921 with a commentary on the naughtiest pages of *Tristram Shandy*, Lawrence Sterne's 1759–67 experimental English novel ("Sterne's *Tristram Shandy*"). Literariness as effect rather than literature as thing should be the subject of aesthetics.[11] Disturbance is aesthetic, he insisted. A good stylist gets something wrong just right, just as wit with a clever twist makes something right that might otherwise seem offensively wrong. Easy communication or habitual knowledge is death to the senses. "And so life is reckoned as nothing. Ha-

Easy communication or habitual knowledge is death to the senses.

bitualization devours works, clothes, furniture, one's wife, and the fear of war. And art exists that one may recover the sensation of life" ("Art" 12). "Not talking straight" is Mikhail Bakhtin's paraphrase; this indirection is a property of parody, of verbal masquerade, and of the complex artistic forms in great novels ("Discourse" 275).

Wordplay, distractions, detours, *foreign words* are among the devices of deliberate roughness that make up literary technique for Shklovsky and that Roland Barthes would pursue with pleasure (see also Shklovsky, "Art" 22). Roughing it, let's not forget, is a reliable English recipe for pleasure by way of discomfort. Ironically, and in the same spirit of Shklovsky's provocations, the delays or difficulties that English-only readers may encounter in a multilingual text probably make them better target readers than those who don't stop to struggle. Roughness can irritate the senses pleasantly enough to make the reader notice both the artist at work and a refreshed world that may have grayed from inattention.

THIS LANGUAGE THAT IS NOT ONE

Mikhail Bakhtin followed the formalists and wrote during the Stalinist period. They had cleared the decks of literary criticism of what they considered to be extraneous spiritual or political content, and he recovered some space to engage politics, indirectly. Bakhtin developed the formalist lesson of stylistics into his point of departure for a general critique of monological Western culture and for an implied critique of Stalinism. His study of discourse in the novel works like a hinge that opens up, from the stylistic model of simultaneous competing languages in a good novel to the multilingual complexities in the real world that should complicate all discursive practices. Style is his fulcrum of analysis that fanned out to cover the entire range of discourses from art and politics to philosophy and science. All these efforts to know the world, without exception, suffered from the same debilitating stylistic tic: they proceeded one language at a time. Wanting to focus

closely on an object of investigation, the discourses narrowed their vision to block out interference. A self-defeating result of chronic squinting and blocking has been to exclude living language along with the objects that language might investigate. The pretense of universality and univocity in the human sciences narrowed the sights of scholarship to ideal, lifeless abstractions. Here is one of many passages from Bakhtin that blame the murderous blockage on the monolingualism of philosophy, politics, linguistics, literary criticism:

> Aristotelian poetics, the poetics of Augustine, the poetics of the medieval church, of "the one language of truth," the Cartesian poetics of neoclassicism, the abstract grammatical universalism of Leibniz (the idea of a "universal grammar"), Humboldt's insistence on the concrete—all these, whatever their differences in nuance, give expression to the same centripetal forces in sociolinguistic and ideological life; they serve one and the same project of centralizing and unifying the European languages. The victory of one reigning language [dialect] over the others, the supplanting of languages, their enslavement, the process of illuminating them with the True Word, the incorporation of barbarians and lower social strata into a unitary language of culture and truth, the canonization of ideological systems, philology with its methods of studying and teaching dead languages, languages that were by that very fact "unities," Indo-European linguistics with its focus of attention, directed away from language plurality to a single proto-language—all this determined the content and power of the category of "unitary language," . . . in the midst of heteroglossia.
>
> ("Discourse" 271; see also 273)

Life, Bakhtin observed, occurs in clusters of competing voices, through different registers of one language but also in alien alternatives. *Heteroglossia* is the word he coined to describe the normally multifarious condition of any one language, because of the variety of social and regional styles that make it more than one.[12] Therefore it is almost impossible for anyone to be truly monolingual.[13] But the stronger linguistic difference is not internal; it is foreign, which does not mean uncommon. Bakhtin coined the companion word *polyglossia* to describe the normal and healthy interruption of one language by other languages that may be incomprehensible for some fictional characters and for some readers. Polyglossia pushes discursive practices past the limits of subtractive patriotism, even past the inclusive appetite of "cannibalistic" heteroglossia in a home language. Together, a capacious home language and transportable foreign codes combine to create compelling performances in literary prose. They also set the stage for liberal politics where democracy and the foreigner go together.

The aesthetic and political advantages of bi- and multilingualism (in terms of flexibility, creativity, agility) suggest cognitive advantages too. In fact, people who speak more than one language develop greater problem-solving capacity, a talent close to artistic creativity, than do monolinguals of comparable social and economic status (Breton 257). From the end of the nineteenth through the beginning of the twentieth century, bilingualism was treated as a liability for immigrants and a burden for receiving countries. But by the 1960s, Canadian investigators were beginning to show that bilinguals were intellectually better off and to suggest that their bilingual country was worth saving from both francophone separatists and anglophone assimilationists. In Montreal, bilingual children outperformed their monolingual peers in "divergent intelligence," the knack for knowing different names and possible uses for the same objects or situations, while they scored comparably to monolinguals in standard IQ tests that measure "convergent intelligence," which gets answers simply right or wrong.[14] The finding is a promise of superior education through bilingualism for native children as well as immigrants, but the promise is hardly heard in policy debates. Nor are the psychological arguments in favor of bilingualism taken sufficiently into account. The emotional advantages are clear too, since bilinguals develop a "metaconsciousness" to coordinate (Bakhtin might say orchestrate, as an artist orchestrates a novel) alternative ego positions and to withstand shocks with more outlets and defense mechanisms than monolinguals deploy.

With two or more languages, expression has more than one field in which to maneuver; in case one language gets blocked by fear or frustration, a sidetrack into another can avoid explosions. If bilingualism represents a problem for mental health, it is not that two languages add up to an overload of voices called schizophrenia, as professionals assumed in the first half of the twentieth century. The difficulty is not for speakers but for the doctors themselves, who may well be outmaneuvered in sophisticated games. How, for example, do you tell a defense mechanism from "rhetorical devices used to create a dramatic or a comic effect" (Titone 63).[15]

Gloria Anzaldúa called this skill to maneuver a special *facultad* for shifting perception. The virtuosity, as she tirelessly complained, comes at the price of pain for "those who do not feel psychologically or physically safe in the world" (*Borderlands* 38–39).[16] For her, that pain is felt more by Latinas than by Latinos.[17] But think also of Junot Díaz's male title character in the first story of *Drown*. Ysrael's Hebrew name starts with a "Greek i," as the letter is called in Spanish and in French. Doubled by the two ancient sources of Western culture, Greek and Hebrew, the young man is also divided by a childhood disaster.[18] He has only half a face, covered by a blue cloth mask, ever since a pig pulled off the other half. Maybe Díaz designed this double and divided Ysrael as an emblem for the bilingual bind of being too much and not enough. Early researchers would have read his condition as not competent enough, perhaps pitying the youth as semilingual, since anyone who had more than one face or tongue lacked competence in either (for a review of early studies, see Romaine 114–15). But since the 1960s linguists have grown used to what Mary Louise Pratt has called the creative contact zone between languages. They are more likely to admire the verbal agility that comes, in Ysrael's image, from an extra layer of prosthetic persona over the natural one.

> —I wonder how much of Ysrael's face is gone, Rafa said.
> —He has his eyes.
> —That's a lot, he assured me.   (8)

Local children warn them, "he's *ugly* and . . . that face of his would make you *sick!*" (8). But the narrator notices that Ysrael "was about a foot bigger than either of us" (15) and that he was so agile, you couldn't catch him: "coño, could he run" (7).

George Steiner, for another example, turns out to be so agile a theorist in English, German, and French, he can hardly catch up with himself. Maybe, he speculates, the agility comes from one language interfering in another. Having tried unsuccessfully (even under hypnosis!) to determine his "first language," Steiner wonders:

> Is there a discernible, perhaps measurable sense in which the options I exercise when uttering words and sentences in English are both enlarged and complicated by the "surrounding presence or pressure" of French and German? If it truly exists, such tangential action might subvert my uses of English, making them in some degree unsteady, provisional, off-centre. This possibility might underlie the pseudo-scientific rumour that multilingual individuals or children reared simultaneously in "too many" languages (is there a critical number?) are prone to schizophrenia and disorders of personality. Or might such "interference" from other languages on the contrary render my use of any one language richer, more conscious of specificity and resource? Because alternative means lie so very near at hand, the speech forms used may be more animate with will and deliberate focus.   (124)

For an English-French bilingual, as recorded by François Grosjean in *Life with Two Languages*, interference amounts to moments of freedom from the prison house of language. Side-stepping from one system of constraints into another can be an opportunity for relief and fresh air (as stutterers also tell us [Shell]).

> It is often liberating to speak a language that is not one's mother tongue because it is easier to speak of taboo subjects. I find it easier to speak of anything connected with the emotions in French, whereas in an emotional situation in English I am rather tongue-tied, the affective content of the words is so much greater. I can also swear much more easily in French and have a wider range of "vulgar" vocabulary. . . . I am finding that gradually the way I use French is influencing the way I use English—I can now say "shit" and "fuck off." Perhaps one day I'll even manage "I love you."   (Grosjean 277)

Immigrants may be the objects of uninformed and visceral responses; they may also be the laughingstock of ethnic jokes for not knowing the standard language. But the bilinguals who laugh at these jokes can take pride in getting them at that deep level of self-reflexive humor that Freud located close to wisdom (701). Error is a part of meaning, not apart from it.[19] From this perspective, knowing more than one language is humbling, because two languages make either one precarious and also because adding one to one leads to a mathematically sublime world of languages where two or three or more are never enough.

United States Anglos (or the French in France, Germans in Germany, Hispanophones in Spanish America) may not notice the invitation to this sublime depth of humor, but they can learn to read the exhilarating signs in one language too. If monolinguals miss particular foreign words, that's understandable. But hardly noticing that they missed something is comic, to use Freud's distinction between this slapstick and the mature mechanisms of wit (762–70). African Americans also know how silly white people can seem when they don't get the difference between an inside reference and the fact that it's for insiders (Gates 52; Morgan). Concern about the self-deprecation of migrants, who both incite and enjoy ethnic humor, sounds paradoxical and paternalist, as if the underprivileged newcomers didn't take pride in the wisdom of their self-irony, as if they didn't know better than to laugh at themselves (García Canclini, *Consumers* 71). Does it occur to critics that migrants have a knack for abstraction (literally distancing themselves from home and host rigidities) that might deflect the ridicule from ad hominem into a role to play? Is it also possible that migrants

Knowing more than one language is humbling, because two languages make either one precarious.

get pleasure from the attention and from the chance to turn jokes back on the jokesters?

Today we urgently need to follow Bakhtin's advice and admit that discourse (stylistic, philosophical, scientific, and political) proceeds in more than one language at a time. Unhinging everyday observations from the scientific pretension to unify knowledge will free his followers to notice that a single character in a novel can be the site of internal conflict. Bakhtin had generally assumed that each discourse would have a particular vehicle and that hybridity happens when different characters represent different registers or languages. But now common characters are likely to negotiate among more than one code. Even Bakhtin, by the time he wrote *Rabelais and His World*, was touting the delightfully mixed man. It is not possible, he repeated throughout the long book, to get any perspective from inside one's culture. Only on the multilinguistic borders, where Rabelais (among others) wrote, are true reason, humor, and wisdom available.[20]

BILINGUAL PROSTHESIS

Other writers who are now classics of their language traditions were borderline cases of correct usage: Ernest Hemingway, Ezra Pound, Franz Kafka, William Carlos Williams, Vladimir Nabokov, Kamala Das, Ngũgĩ wa Thiong'o, Chinua Achebe, Ha Jin, Junot Díaz. The charm of straddling and pulling particular codes beyond their tired shapes can be lost on universalists. True to Bakhtin's point about univocity missing the object of analysis, some of our best theorists cripple their work by forcing it into models where one size fits all. Universalism—and here Herder was right—is a denial of living particularities in the classical and neoclassical traditions he resisted. He was wrong, though, to think that particularities live in isolation one from another. You can tell one particularity from another because they do not match up; otherwise what is the difference? Particularism, in other words, is not an essence but an effect of comparison (Sommer, *Proceed*).

Paradoxically, Ernesto Laclau and others argue that today universalism is a capacious ground for inclusion and that it depends on difference to keep the space open and flexible. If, for example, religious freedom is a universal right, it makes sense only where there are many (competing, incommensurable, probably antagonistic) religions. If there were only one or none, the universality would be a constraint that delegitimates heretics. The universal has survived classical philosophy's dismissal of particularity as deviation; it has outlived the medieval collapse of universality into Christ, and it has veered past a European Enlightenment that conflated the universal (subject, class, culture) with particular (French) incarnations. Today's universalism is an ironic inversion of past definitions, because it is anchored in particularist demands. These demands unmoor universalism from any fixed cultural essence and keep it open to contrasting effects in an "always receding horizon" (107).[21] The corollary paradox of democracy, Laclau admits without embarrassment, is that democracy requires unity but depends on diversity. Tension and ambiguity make up the negativity that keeps modern societies dynamic and that Adorno defended against the scientific thinking that prefers to eliminate contradictions.[22] Freud is an example of a canny scientific observer who tried to force heterogeneous data into homogeneous universality. The best joke of his book about jokes is that his touted universal science of humor is based on Jewish jokes that non-Jews are forbidden to tell (657).

Jacques Derrida is funny too when he folds all language difference into the same monolingual mold, reluctant to face up to real breaks and breakdowns when different languages block (or unlock) each other. This reluctance is worth considering, given Derrida's enormous relevance for contemporary language and literary studies. For him, all language is cobbled together with provisional prosthetics, and it hobbles along in the same universally unsettling way. This consciousness dawned on Derrida, he says, through the childhood trauma of being denationalized and disconnected from his home language during

World War II. The French had closed fascist ranks against Jews in Algeria even tighter than the Germans required; "they must have been dreaming about it all along" (*Monolingualism* 16). Without the historical trauma, would Derrida have known how treacherous language can be? Bilinguals know the treachery, one way *and* another. Often they are victims of historical catastrophe; and even in peacetime they endure the risks and doubts of living in two languages. But Derrida universalizes a particular historical anxiety about language, turning the difference between history and structural fault lines into just another undecidable slippage.[23] For others, though, monolingualism is not the unmarked norm that contains all anxieties and exhilarations, as he claims. To the protests of Abdelkebir Khatibi about belonging to Arabic and therefore not being at ease in French, Derrida says he protests too much. Khatibi's *Amour bilingue* is written in French, after all. If the book chafes against the language, so do other books, inexorably, says Derrida. But despite his chuckles at Khatibi's performative contradiction of writing in French and claiming to belong to Arabic, Arabic words do rub into the wounds of French to irritate more acutely than Derrida's (narcissistic) folds and routes can describe (*Monolingualism* 26, 60).

Why object to Khatibi's performative contradiction, after Derrida himself dismissed the same objection when it referred to his own work? "Stop; don't play that trick of performative contradiction; only German or Anglo-American theorists like that strategy, a childish armory" (3–4). In fact, Khatibi's novel is an extended performance of the contradiction between languages that Hernández Cruz described as "flashes of scenarios, linguistic stereo; they conflict, they debate, Spanish and English constantly breaking into each other like ocean waves" (*Red Beans* 89). The Algerian novelist announces the theme in a kind of allegorical preface:

> And in French—his foreign language—the word for "word," *mot*, is close to the one for "death," *la mort*; only one letter is missing: the succinctness of the impression, a syllable, the ecstasy of a sti-

fled sob. Why did he believe that language is more beautiful, more terrible, for a foreigner?

> He calmed down instantly when an Arabic word, *kalma*, appeared, *kalma* and its scholarly equivalent, *kalima*, and the whole string of its diminutives which had been the riddles of his childhood: *klima*. . . . The diglossal *kal(i)ma* appeared again without *mot*'s having faded away or disappeared. Within him, both words were observing each other.   (4)

Languages foreign to one another—anthropomorphized as an Arabic lover and his French beloved—are the protagonists of the tangle that follows. The mutual attraction and repulsion of the couple go as deep as the difference between Muslim monotheism and Catholic idolatry:

> He very quickly saw an old emigrant woman beneath a statue of Mary; she was murmuring, *Allah akbar! Allah akbar!*

> He observed her without stating who he was. Mildly sleepy. Was he dreaming? The statues crumbled at his feet. He picked up a few fragments and offered them to the old woman. She hesitated, then grabbed one piece and kissed it. Now, he stumbled forward, in the midst of poor people praying. He was bathed in light from the central stained-glass window. At his back, the columns had left their straight lines. He picked up the face of Christ and shattered it.   (35)

Derrida rushes past scenes like this. After all, he reasons, the words are mostly French. But why reason this way in order to defend an equal insertion of all speakers into French or any other language? Maybe Derrida's residual universalism survives (like Freud's and Wittgenstein's) in a denial of linguistic-cultural differences. But since when have Jews, as a particular minority people, felt secure enough in one language to forfeit escape routes into others?

Derrida does lament the loss of "safe-home" languages like Yiddish or Ladino, but he revels in the purity of his French, as if it depended on the loss of home (48, 54). The impossible dream of going back to one coherent language provokes a romantic anxiety that Derrida considers universal. Listen to this reverie:

> One can, of course, speak several languages. There are speakers who are competent in more

than one language. Some even write several languages at a time (prostheses, grafts, translation, transposition). But do they not always do it with a view to an absolute idiom? And in the promise of a still unheard-of-language? Of a sole poem previously inaudible? (67)

No, not always, is a plausible answer. When bilinguals pause to worry about missing pieces, it may be to poach a patch from a parallel code. Sometimes the sutures flaunt their seams, to make worry an aesthetic or ideological effect. Artifice is a trace of art.

Bilingual prosthetics can't help but expose the nuts and bolts that try to hold words to the world, unlike more-private, monolingual attachments. Ludwig Wittgenstein was another model of inspired denial. He normally slid between German and English, sure only that words had circumstantial, not fixed, meanings; but he never described bilanguage games. Maybe they didn't seem to be the stuff of a universal philosophy of language.

"Bilingual prosthesis" was the inspired mistake that my student Dale Shuger made when she meant to say "bilingual aesthetics" as the subject of our course one semester. When a concept is lacking, prosthetic borrowings—like Sylvia Molloy's English teatime *cucharite* that stirred up Spanish into her underdeveloped French (296), or like the word *kosher* and the expression "He's good people"—can patch up a few holes in English, while "imeliar" or "baipasear" keep Spanish from crippling (see Véliz 36–38).

The borders between regional and national languages and between home and host languages map onto people as well as territories. This mapping is bad only when one is forced to take sides in a conflict, which is why patriots prefer monolingual and centripetal loyalties. What can a country expect from double-talking, dual nationals in times of conflict? It can expect, I want to suggest, a level of ambivalence between two intimate but precarious codes that is so unbearable, it might help deter conflict. Double consciousness is surely a dis-ease of bad fits, but the cure of reducing two minds to one of the two

can be catastrophically narrow. For all his complaints against double consciousness, W. E. B. Du Bois refused to cure it by "bleaching" his black soul (215).

Those who don't feel strained by the split may object that bilingualism doesn't necessarily lead to double consciousness, which is true for some privileged subjects. Or they may object, more likely, that monolingualism is a better standard for communication. Such objections sound prescriptive and deaf to existing differences of class, color, and location. One reason the English and the Irish don't get along even in the same language, Terry Eagleton taunts, is that one assumes it to be for communication and the other knows it's for performance:

> Indeed the conflict has been not just between two languages, but between two quite different conceptions of language, since the English empiricist conception of language as representational has never had much appeal to the more linguistically performative Irish. The Irish have, on the whole, in the manner of subaltern peoples, tended to see language as strategic, conative, rhetorical rather than cognitive. (131)

Living in two or more competing languages troubles the assumption that communication should be easy, and it upsets the desired coherence of romantic nationalism and ethnic essentialism. This troubling can be a good thing, since confusion and even anxiety about conflicting identities cause vigilance and insomnia; they interrupt the dangerous dream of single-minded loyalty. But the condition is volatile and will demand solutions: double loyalty can seek purgative cures that eliminate difference and induce more dreams of uniformity, or it can develop a new, aesthetic, and almost perverse taste for anxiety and irritation as stimuli for gradual and partial relief.

Not fitting easily or well, being both too much and not enough, can make ESL migrants aware of grammar (or relational) trouble with themselves and with their neighbors even after several generations. How is one to identify, when one is more than one? Two languages (often more than two) and loyalties that bind them to a home country and to their hosts can seem intolerable to patriots on either side of the border—and on both sides of their own divided selves. In 1937, at the banks of a river that marked Haiti's territorial limits, General Rafael Trujillo's Dominican troops commanded the border people to say *perejil*, to spare the real Dominicans, who pronounced "parsley" with a national accent. The other thirty thousand souls were slaughtered at a river already called the Massacre to commemorate a long history of racial and linguistic intolerance.[24] Speak English without an accent, parents advise children in the United States, just to be safe. My parents too tell me stories of language tests along the divided lines of Europe in World War II, where passing or failing pronunciation led to life or death.

But saying "shibbolet" with the accents of both Israel and Ephraim raises suspicions on both sides. To switch codes is to enter or leave one nation for another, by merely releasing a foreign sound, a word, a grammar tic, letting them slip into an always borrowed and precarious language. Ten American countries now recognize and even encourage dual citizenship, along with the generous remittances sent by United States–based nationals (Jones-Correa). But the United States remains suspicious of disloyalty, because military campaigns and economic competitions demand single-mindedness. Is belonging to two like bigamy, and is living in two languages a pathology?[25] Throughout this country and many others, monolingualism is losing its descriptive power for literary and cultural studies. It would claim that United States citizens normally speak English (after a long history of multilingualism that apparently ended during the paranoia of World War I) but doesn't add that many speak more than English. Visitors will hear several languages in any big city, such as New York, London, Paris, Toronto, Tel Aviv, Berlin, Kuala Lumpur, including the Boston that Grosjean described more than twenty years ago.[26] Maybe

> **Throughout this country and many others, monolingualism is losing its descriptive power for literary and cultural studies.**

the denial of diversity is predictable, to follow the ironic core of his book: "there is probably a larger proportion of bilinguals in monolingual nations than in bilingual and multilingual countries" (11). Are we waking up now to more candid and capacious expectations?

NOTES

I'm very grateful to Steven G. Kellman for his painstaking advice for rewriting this essay, also to David G. Nicholls and Mary Jepson. Many of the issues presented here are developed in my *Bilingual Aesthetics*.

1. See Alejandro Portes's summary in "English Only Triumphs."
2. Roland Barthes develops this approach to aesthetics in *The Pleasure of the Text*.
3. See the excellent book by Steven G. Kellman, *The Translingual Imagination*. Standard reviews of the educational and cognitive research on code switching are in Romaine (107–99) and also Hamers and Blanc (47–59).
4. To promote his concept of the *Volk*, Herder published letters and collected folk songs. The songs were published in 1773 as *Voices of the People in Their Songs* ("Stimmen der Voelker in ihren Liedern"). See Herder's "Essay." He believed in the many but not the many in the one (unless you count God as the unifier).
5. I thank Raquel Araújo of Mérida for this translation at the Performance and Politics Conference, Monterrey, June 2001.
6. This is Saul Bellow's frame for *Ravelstein*. "Anyone who wants to govern the country has to entertain it. During the civil war people complained about Lincoln's funny stories. Perhaps he sensed that strict seriousness was far more dangerous than any joke" (1). Robert R. Provine rues gaps in Lincoln's legacy: "John F. Kennedy was unusual among U.S. presidents in having both a presence of command and an excellent sense of humor" (32).
7. Democracy, as Adam Przeworski has argued cogently, is a desirable means for making decisions about public affairs precisely because societies are characterized by conflict. Absent conflict, there would be no need for democracy, for there would be no disputes that require resolution in a manner that is simultaneously authoritative and legitimate.
8. The paradox of striving for complete understanding is that it misunderstands the particularity of its object. To understand is to establish identity, which requires conceptualization that generalizes away otherness. Identifying, therefore, turns out to be a

trap at two levels (see Cornell): empathic identification violates the other person, and ontological identification eliminates particularity for the sake of unity. The greedy subject is Freud's formulation. See Fuss.

9. For a good overview, see Foley. See also Hymes; Boas; Sapir, *Language* and *Selected Writings*.

10. As Taylor writes, "Herder put forward the idea that each of us has an original way of being human . . . that is my way. . . . Just like individuals, a *Volk* should be true to itself, that is, its own culture" (30–31).

11. From a worried Anglo-American tradition, Michael Clark conflates the two: "Literature as such simply disappears against a general background of material action or symbolic determination, and with the disappearance of literature—the possibility of productive independence, individual autonomy, effective resistance, and difference itself disappears as well" (5–6).

12. Peter Elbow argues for the "bilingual" double-take effect of etymology (Letter). I am grateful for the observation but add that the effect depends on class and education rather than on linguistic migrancy and unsettledness.

13. See Holquist. The classic studies of code switching, alternating between one kind of speech and another, focus on this type of difference internal to a language. See Blom and Gumperz.

14. Romaine 133, referring to Scott and to Lambert 15. Romaine quotes Joshua Fishman (38) and Kenji Hakuta (43) regarding the inappropriateness of narrow intelligence testing for bilinguals (118). See also Hamers and Blanc 55. All refer to the influential 1962 Canadian study by Peal and Lambert that found superior performance of bilingual children on both verbal and nonverbal intelligence tests.

15. See also Titone 57–60. "It is not facetious to add that this defense mechanism may pose an obstacle to psychotherapy or psychoanalysis, but that this problem is not so much the bilingual patient's as it is the psychiatrist's. . . . Moreover, if code-switching is the potentially adaptive device this author believes it to be, it might account for the further impression that there is a low incidence of reactive schizophrenia in bilingual populations, despite epidemiological studies" (55).

16. Moya writes: "As a survival skill, *la facultad* allows such people to adjust quickly and gracefully to changing (and often threatening) circumstances. With origins in experiences of pain and trauma, *la facultad* involves a loss of innocence and an initiation into an awareness of discrimination, fear, depression, illness, and death" (469).

17. See Baron; Cameron; Coates; Eckert and McConnell-Ginet; Goodwin; Moore; Ortner and Whitehead; Philips, Steele, and Tanz; Strathern.

18. For a formulation of these conflicting but inseparable strands, see Derrida, "Violence."

19. *Différance* is what Derrida calls this constitutive contamination of meaning by the alternatives it necessarily conjures ("Différance"). From another vantage point, Elbow defends error in Standard English—to enable free writing for speakers of Ebonics, for example ("Inviting").

20. "The link of these forms with a multilingual world, . . . seems to us extremely important. . . . [I]t is impossible to overcome through abstract thought alone, within the system of a unique language, that deep dogmatism hidden in all the forms of this system. The completely new, self-criticizing, absolutely sober, fearless, and gay life of the image can start only on linguistic borders" (472).

21. Judith Butler cautiously agrees that universality can be a site of translation. "The universal is always culturally articulated, and . . . the complex process of learning how to read that claim is not something any of us can do outside of the difficult process of cultural translation. . . . [T]he terms made to stand for one another are transformed in the process, and where the movement of that unanticipated transformation establishes the universal as that which is yet to be achieved and which, in order to resist domestication, may never be fully or finally achievable" (Benhabib, Butler, Cornell, and Fraser 130).

22. Jürgen Habermas appreciated Adorno's point but pursued moments of symmetry through communicative action. Jean-François Lyotard despaired that the negativity invariably ended in unfairness, since societies have to make practical, positive decisions.

23. See, among many examples, the slide from particular to universal: "I do not doubt either that such 'exclusions' come to leave their mark upon this belonging or non-belonging of language, this affiliation *to* language, this assignation to what is peacefully called a language. But who exactly possesses it? . . . What of this being-at-home in language toward which we never cease returning?" (16–17).

24. The event recurs in novels of the area. It opens the historical novel by the Dominican Freddy Prestol Castillo, *El masacre se pasa a pie*, and, more recently, it haunts the Haitian American Edwidge Danticat's *The Farming of Bones*.

25. "The bigamy analogy comes up a lot among critics of dual nationality" (Jones-Correa 20n41). This statement suggests the nineteenth-century "foundational fictions" motif of sliding from eros to polis that I considered in *Foundational Fictions*.

26. My thanks to Steven Kellman for some of these examples. See also Arjun Appadurai's theorization of transnational cityscapes.

WORKS CITED AND SUGGESTIONS FOR
FURTHER READING

Adorno, Theodor W. *Negative Dialektik*. Frankfurt: Suhrkamp, 1966.

Algarín, Miguel, and Miguel Piñero, eds. *Nuyorican Poetry: An Anthology of Puerto Rican Words and Feelings*. New York: Morrow, 1975.

Andrade, Oswald de. "Oswald de Andrade's Cannibalist Manifesto." Trans. Leslie Bary. *Latin American Literary Review* 19.38 (1991): 35–47.

Anzaldúa, Gloria. *Borderlands / La Frontera: The New Mestiza*. San Francisco: Aunt Lute, 1987.

Appadurai, Arjun. "Global Ethnoscapes: Notes and Queries for a Transnational Anthropology." *Recapturing Anthropology: Working in the Present*. Ed. Richard G. Fox. Santa Fe: School of Amer. Research, 1991. 191–210.

Bakhtin, Mikhail. "Discourse in the Novel." *The Dialogic Imagination: Four Essays*. Ed. Michael Holquist. Trans. Caryl Emerson and Holquist. Austin: U of Texas P, 1981. 259–422.

———. *Rabelais and His World*. Trans. Helene Iswolsky. Bloomington: Indiana UP, 1984.

Baron, Dennis. *Grammar and Gender*. New Haven: Yale UP, 1986.

Barthes, Roland. *The Pleasure of the Text*. 1973. Trans. Richard Miller. New York: Hill, 1975.

Bellow, Saul. *Ravelstein*. New York: Penguin, 2000.

Benhabib, Seyla, Judith Butler, Drucilla Cornell, and Nancy Fraser. *Feminist Contentions: A Philosophical Exchange*. Introd. Linda Nicholson. New York: Routledge, 1995.

Bernabé, Jean, Patrick Chamoiseau, and Raphaël Confiant. *Éloge de la créolité / In Praise of Creoleness*. Bilingual ed. Trans. M. B. Taleb-Khyar. Paris: Gallimard, 1989.

Blom, Jan-Petter, and John J. Gumperz. "Social Meaning in Linguistic Structures: Code-Switching in Norway." *Directions in Sociolinguistics*. Ed. Gumperz and Dell Hymes. New York: Holt, Rinehart, 1972. 407–34.

Boas, Franz. Introduction. 1911. *Introduction to Handbook of American Indian Languages: Indian Linguistic Families of America North of Mexico*. By Boas and J. W. Powell. Ed. Preston Holder. Lincoln: U of Nebraska P, 1991. 1–79.

Brady, Ivan. Rev. of *Kant, Herder and the Birth of Anthropology*, by John Zammito. *Philosophy Now* Jan.–Feb. 2005. 5 Jan. 2006 <http://www.philosophynow.org/issue49/49brady.htm>.

Brathwaite, Kamau. "Letter Sycora X." *Middle Passages*. New York: New Directions, 1993. 97–98.

Breton, Albert, ed. *Economic Approaches to Language and Bilingualism*. Ottawa: Canadian Heritage, 1998.

Bugarski, Ranko. "Language, Nationalism, and War in Yugoslavia." *International Journal of the Sociology of Language* 151 (201): 69–87.

Bunge, Robert. "Language: The Psyche of a People." *Language Loyalties: A Source-Book on the Official English Controversy*. Ed. James Crawford. Chicago: U of Chicago P, 1992. 376–80.

Cameron, Deborah, ed. *The Feminist Critique of Language: A Reader*. New York: Routledge, 1990.

Césaire, Aimé. *A Tempest*. Trans. Richard Miller. New York: Ubu Repertory Theater, 1992.

Chaudenson, Robert. *Creolization of Language and Culture*. Ed. Salikoko S. Mufwene. Trans. Sheri Pargman, Mufwene, and Michelle Aucoin. London: Routledge, 2001.

Clark, Michael P., ed. *The Revenge of the Aesthetic*. Berkeley: U of California P, 2000.

Coates, Jennifer. *Women, Men and Language: A Sociolinguistic Account of Gender Differences in Language*. 2nd ed. London: Longman, 1993.

Cornell, Drucilla. *The Philosophy of the Limit*. New York: Routledge, 1992.

Danticat, Edwidge. *The Farming of Bones*. New York: Soho, 1998.

DeGraff, Michael, ed. *Language Creation and Language Change: Creolization, Diachrony, and Development*. Cambridge: MIT P, 1999.

Derrida, Jacques. "Différance." *Margins of Philosophy*. Trans. Alan Bass. Chicago: U of Chicago P, 1982. 3–27.

———. *Monolingualism of the Other; or, The Prosthesis of Origin*. Trans. Patrick Mensah. Stanford: Stanford UP, 1998.

———. "Violence and Metaphysics: An Essay on the Thought of Emmanuel Levinas." *Writing and Difference*. Trans. Alan Bass. Chicago: U of Chicago P, 1978. 79–153.

Díaz, Junot. "Ysrael." *Drown*. New York: Riverhead, 1996. 3–20.

Du Bois, W. E. B. *The Souls of Black Folk*. 1903. *Three Negro Classics*. Introd. John Hope Franklin. New York: Avon, 1965. 207–390.

Eagleton, Terry. "Postcolonialism: The Case of Ireland." *Multicultural States: Rethinking Difference and Identity*. Ed. David Bennett. London: Routledge: 1998. 125–34.

Eckert, Penelope, and Sally McConnell-Ginet. *Language and Gender*. Cambridge: Cambridge UP, 2003.

Elbow, Peter. "Inviting the Mother Tongue: Beyond 'Mistakes,' 'Bad English,' and 'Wrong Language.' " *Everyone Can Write: Essays Toward a Hopeful Theory of Writing and Teaching Writing*. New York: Oxford UP, 2000. 323–50.

———. Letter to the author. 21 Aug. 2002.

Fishman, Joshua A., ed. *Advances in the Creation and Revision of Writing Systems*. The Hague: Mouton, 1977.

Flores, Juan. "Reclaiming Left Baggage: Some Early Sources for Minority Studies." *Cultural Critique* 59 (2005): 187–206.

Foley, William A. *Anthropological Linguistics: An Introduction*. Malden: Blackwell, 1997.

Freud, Sigmund. "Wit and Its Relation to the Unconscious." 1905. *The Basic Writings of Sigmund Freud*. Trans. and ed. A. A. Brill. New York: Modern Lib., 1995. 601–774.

Frost, Robert. "The Death of the Hired Man." *North of Boston*. New York: Henry Holt, 1915. Bartleby.com. 1999. 21 Sept. 2006 <http://www.bartleby.com/118/3.html>.

Fuss, Diana. *Identification Papers*. New York: Routledge, 1995.

García Canclini, Néstor. *Consumers and Citizens: Globalization and Multicultural Conflicts*. Trans. and introd. George Yúdice. Minneapolis: U of Minnesota P, 2001.

———. *Hybrid Cultures: Strategies for Entering and Leaving Modernity*. Fwd. Renato Rosaldo. Trans. Christopher L. Chiappari and Silvia L. López. Minneapolis: U of Minnesota P, 1995.

Gates, Henry Louis, Jr. *The Signifying Monkey*. Oxford: Oxford UP, 1988.

Goodwin, Marjorie Harness. *He-Said-She-Said: Talk as Social Organization among Black Children*. Bloomington: Indiana UP, 1990.

Greenberg, Robert. "Language, Nationalism, and the Yugoslav Successor States." *Language, Ethnicity, and the State: Volume 2: Minority Languages in Eastern Europe Post-1989*. Ed. Camille O'Reilly. New York: Palgrave, 2001. 17–42.

Grosjean, François. *Life with Two Languages*. Cambridge: Harvard UP, 1982.

Habermas, Jürgen. *On the Pragmatics of Social Interaction: Preliminary Studies in the Theory of Communicative Action*. Trans. Barbara Fultner. Cambridge: Polity, 2001.

Hakuta, Kenji. *Mirror of Language: The Debate on Bilingualism*. New York: Basic, 1986.

Hamers, Josiane F., and Michael H. A. Blanc. *Bilinguality and Bilingualism*. 2nd ed. Cambridge: Cambridge UP, 2002.

Henry, Paget. *Caliban's Reason: Introducing Afro-Caribbean Philosophy*. New York: Routledge, 2000.

Herder, Johann Gottfried. *Against Pure Reason: Writings on Religion, Language, and History*. Trans. and ed. Marcia Bunge. Minneapolis: Fortress, 1993.

———. "Essay on the Origin of Language." 1770. *On the Origin of Language: Two Essays*. By Jean-Jacques Rousseau and Herder. Trans. John H. Moran and Alexander Gode. Chicago: U of Chicago P, 1990. 87–166.

Hernández Cruz, Víctor. *Red Beans: Poems*. Minneapolis: Coffee House, 1991.

———. "You Gotta Have Your Tips on Fire." *Mainland: Poems*. New York: Random, 1973. 3–4.

Holquist, Michael. "What Is the Ontological Status of Bilingualism?" *Bilingual Games: Some Literary Investigations*. Ed. Doris Sommer. New York: Palgrave, 2004. 21–34.

Honig, Bonnie. *Democracy and the Foreigner*. Princeton: Princeton UP, 2001.

Huntington, Samuel P. *Who Are We? The Challenges to America's National Identity*. New York: Simon, 2004.

Hymes, Dell, ed. *Language in Culture and Society: A Reader in Linguistics and Anthropology*. New York: Harper, 1964.

Jones-Correa, Michael. *Dual Nationality in Latin America and Its Consequences for the United States*. David Rockefeller Center for Latin Amer. Studies, Harvard U. Working Papers. Paper 1999-2000-3. 2004. 25 Sept. 2006 <http://drclas.fas.harvard.edu/working_papers/?entity_id=12>. Path: Download PDF Version.

Kellman, Steven G. *The Translingual Imagination*. Lincoln: U of Nebraska P, 2000.

Khatibi, Abdelkebir. *Love in Two Languages*. Trans. Richard Howard. Minneapolis: U of Minnesota P, 1990. Trans. of *Amour bilingue*. 1983.

Labov, William. "The Linguistic Consequences of Being a Lame." *Language in the Inner City: Studies in the Black English Vernacular*. Philadelphia: U of Pennsylvania P, 1972. 255–92.

Laclau, Ernesto. "Universalism, Particularism, and the Question of Identity." *The Identity in Question*. Ed. John Rajchman. New York: Routledge, 1995. 93–108.

Lambert, Wallace E. "The Effects of Bilingualism on the Individual: Cognitive and Sociocultural Consequences." *Bilingualism: Psychological, Social, and Educational Implications*. Ed. Peter A. Hornby. New York: Academic, 1977. 15–27.

Lyotard, Jean-François. *The Differend: Phrases in Dispute*. Trans George van den Abbeele. Minneapolis: U of Minnesota P, 1992.

Molloy, Sylvia. "Bilingual Scenes." Sommer, *Bilingual Games* 289–96.

Moore, Henrietta L. *Feminism and Anthropology*. Cambridge: Polity, 1988.

Morgan, Marcyliena. "More than a Mood or an Attitude: Discourse and Verbal Genres in African-American Culture." *African American English: Structure, History and Use*. Ed. Salikolo S. Mufwene, John R. Rickford, Guy Bailey, and John Baugh. New York: Routledge, 1988. 251–81.

Moya, Paula M. L. "Chicana Feminism and Postmodernist Theory." *Signs* 26 (2001): 441–83.

Nettle, Daniel, and Suzanne Romaine. *Vanishing Voices: The Extinction of the World's Languages*. New York: Oxford UP, 2000.

O'Donnell, Guillermo, Philippe C. Schmitter, and Laurence Whitehead, eds. *Transitions from Authoritarian Rule: Comparative Perspectives*. Baltimore: Johns Hopkins UP, 1986.

Ortner, Sherry B., and Harriet Whitehead, eds. *Sexual Meanings: The Cultural Construction of Gender and Sexuality*. Cambridge: Cambridge UP, 1981.

Pan, David. "J. G. Herder, the Origin of Language, and the Possibility of Transcultural Narrative." *Language and Intercultural Communication* 4.1–2 (2004): 1–10.

Peal, Elizabeth, and Wallace E. Lambert. "The Relation of Bilingualism to Intelligence." *Psychological Monographs* 76 (1962): 1–23.

Philips, Susan U., Susan Steele, and Christine Tanz, eds. *Language, Gender, and Sex in Comparative Perspective*. Cambridge: Cambridge UP, 1987.

Portes, Alejandro. "English Only Triumphs, but the Costs Are High." *Contexts* 1.1 (2002): 10–15.

Portes, Alejandro, and Lingxin Hao. "The Price of Uniformity: Language, Family, and Personality Adjustment in the Immigrant Second Generation." *Ethnic and Racial Studies* 25 (2002): 889–912.

Pratt, Mary Louise. "Arts of the Contact Zone." *Profession 91*. New York: MLA, 1991. 33–40.

Prestol Castillo, Freddy. *El masacre se pasa a pie*. Santo Domingo: Taller, 1973.

Provine, Robert R. *Laughter: A Scientific Investigation*. London: Faber, 2000.

Przeworski, Adam. "Some Problems in the Study of the Transition to Democracy." O'Donnell, Schmitter, and Whitehead 47–63.

Retamar, Roberto Fernández. *"Caliban" and Other Essays*. Trans. Edward Baker. Minneapolis: U of Minnesota P, 1989.

Romaine, Suzanne. *Bilingualism*. 2nd ed. Oxford: Blackwell, 1995.

Russian Formalist Criticism: Four Essays. Trans. Lee T. Lemon and Marion J. Reis. Lincoln: U of Nebraska P, 1965.

Sapir, Edward. *Language: An Introduction to the Study of Speech*. New York: Harcourt, 1921.

———. *Selected Writings*. Berkeley: U of California P, 1949.

Sassen, Saskia. *The Global City: New York, London, Tokyo*. 1991. 2nd ed. Princeton: Princeton UP, 2001.

Schwarz, Roberto. "Brazilian Culture: Nationalism by Elimination." Trans. Linda Briggs. *New Left Review* 167 (1988): 77–90. Rpt. in *Misplaced Ideas: Essays on Brazilian Culture*. By Schwarz. Ed. John Gledson. London: Verso, 1992. 1–18. Trans. of "Nacional por subtração."

Scott, S. "The Relation of Divergent Thinking to Bilingualism: Cause or Effect?" Report. McGill U, 1973.

Shell, Marc. *Stutter*. Cambridge: Harvard UP, 2006.

Shklovsky, Victor. "Art as Technique." *Russian Formalist Criticism* 3–24.

———. "Sterne's *Tristram Shandy*: Stylistic Commentary." *Russian Formalist Criticism* 25–60.

Sommer, Doris. *Bilingual Aesthetics: A New Sentimental Education*. Durham: Duke UP, 2004.

———, ed. *Bilingual Games: Some Literary Investigations*. New Directions in Latino Amer. Culture. New York: Palgrave, 2003.

———. *Foundational Fictions: The National Romances of Latin America*. Berkeley: U of California P, 1991.

———. *Proceed with Caution, When Engaged by Minority Writing in the Americas*. Cambridge: Harvard UP, 1999.

Springfield, Consuelo López, ed. *Daughters of Caliban: Caribbean Women in the Twentieth Century*. Bloomington: Indiana UP, 1997.

Stavans, Ilan. *Spanglish: The Making of a New American Language*. New York: Harper, 2003.

Steiner, George. *After Babel: Aspects of Language and Translation*. Oxford: Oxford UP, 1998.

Strathern, Marilyn. *The Gender of the Gift*. Berkeley: U of California P, 1988.

Taylor, Charles. "The Politics of Recognition." *Multiculturalism*. Ed. Amy Guttmann. Princeton: Princeton UP, 1994. 25–74.

Thomason, Sarah Grey, and Terrence Kaufman. *Language, Contact, Creolization, and Genetic Linguistics*. Berkeley: U of California P, 1988.

Titone, Renzo. "The Bilingual Personality as a Metasystem: The Case of Code Switching." *On the Bilingual Person*. Ed. Titone. Biblioteca de Quaderni d'Italianistica 7. Ottawa: Canadian Soc. for Italian Studies, 1989. 55–64.

Véliz, Claudio. *The New World of the Gothic Fox: Culture and Economy in English and Spanish America*. Berkeley: U of California P, 1994.

Whorf, Benjamin Lee. *Language, Thought, and Reality: Selected Writings of Benjamin Lee Whorf*. Ed. John B. Carroll. Cambridge: MIT P, 1956.

Zammito, John H. *Kant, Herder, and the Birth of Anthropology*. Chicago: U of Chicago P, 2002.

ᵔ Linguistics

PAUL J. HOPPER

BACKGROUND

Recent Linguistics

In the mid-1980s it was still possible for the president of the Linguistic Society of America to speak for the membership as a whole in summing up the state of the art in the field of linguistics for the *Chronicle of Higher Education*: "In human speech production and comprehension, the speaker-hearer accesses not only the mentally represented language system, but also other cognitive systems and knowledge of the world" (Fromkin 13).

In this statement we can discern the major themes and assumptions of late-twentieth-century linguistics: speech production and comprehension are distinguished from a "mentally represented language system," and this language system is "access[ed]" when we speak. The language system that is represented in the mind is identical for all speakers and hearers. They possess in addition to the language system a cognitive system, or rather several cognitive systems, and furthermore when they speak, they appeal to worldly and social knowledge, which itself is neither linguistic nor cognitive in nature.

The statement implicitly lays out a research agenda for linguists. Central to it is the structure of the mentally represented language system.

This system underlies production and comprehension, the study of which overlaps with the physics of sound, psychology, and physiology. The language system is also fundamental for cognitive systems, with which it must be calibrated and which introduce neurophysiology in a project that has come to be known as neurolinguistics. Finally, the speaker's general knowledge about the world, culture, and society must be invoked to fill out the explanations arrived at from the study of the language system and the associated cognitive systems: enter anthropology, sociology, and encyclopedic knowledge. These secondary areas are not viewed by linguists as anything but supplementary to the task of laying out the language system itself, the grammar.

For the time being we must accept this standard picture, without which a survey of the field of linguistics in recent years would be quite impossible. While other academic disciplines are also crucially involved with questions of language, linguistics alone claims as its exclusive province the architecture of the system. I later refer to challenges that have been offered at various times to the idea of a language system as well as to the exclusive claim of linguistics. Meanwhile, a useful place to start is the notion of the linguistic code. A language is viewed by linguists as a symbolic code that mediates between thoughts and utterances, and linguistics is a scientific research field that studies and describes the properties of this code. Modern linguistics is held to be a descriptive field. *Descriptive* contrasts with *prescriptive*, an adjective that captures the idea of regulating correct usage and identifying incorrect usage. Linguistics accepts as its goal the production of an objective description of a language and the development of a comprehensive theory of language; it is not concerned with standardizing or normalizing the speaking and writing practices of a speech community.

> **Linguistics accepts as its goal the production of an objective description of a language and the development of a comprehensive theory of language.**

It might be thought that a descriptive field of language would arrive at its theories through study of the activity of speaking. Yet until recently mainstream linguistics resisted the idea that the data of language should be taken from observations of actual usage. Instead, linguists have drawn data from their intuitions about their native languages or by a process of interrogating a native-speaker consultant ("How would you say in your language, *The man has bitten the dog*?"). There is an implicit assumption that a language is a complete entity fully resident in the individual's mind. With this assumption, the linguist's task is to find ways to exteriorize (i.e., to write down) the covert internal system of grammar and sound units that make up the language code.

Linguists differ among themselves, sometimes sharply, about the most appropriate way to represent the structure of a language.

The Linguistic Code

The linguistic code is conventionally divided into three major components: phonology, semantics, and grammar (comprising syntax and morphology).

PHONOLOGY

Phonology is the study of the distribution and patterning of the sound units of the language. It is closely linked to phonetics, the science that studies the physical nature of the speech sounds—their articulatory sources in human physiology and their acoustic effects through characteristic sound-wave structures. Phonology is the reduction of the very great variety of speech sounds in a language to groups of recurring sounds that function as linguistic units called phonemes. In English, the vowel in *bead* is longer in duration than the otherwise identical vowel in *beat*. This difference in vowel length is apparent even to the untrained ear. But because it is attributable to a difference in the nature of the following consonant (*d* is a voiced sound, whereas *t* is unvoiced), the two vowels are said to be only phonetically different, not phonologically different. In fact, the drawled vowel is heard before all voiced sounds, not merely *d*.

It should be noted that phonological and phonetic representations are independent of ordinary orthography. During the twentieth century, a standard set of special phonetic symbols, the International Phonetic Alphabet (IPA), was developed in order to encourage uniformity in transcribing speech sounds. This alphabet is not a fixed list of symbols and can be expanded to accommodate newly discovered sounds. For example, the symbol *B* was recently added to denote a bilabial trill (vibration of the lips, as in *brrr* to express cold) that came to light in previously undescribed languages of South America and Southeast Asia. Most of the so-called phonetic representations found in dictionaries are guides to the pronunciation of written words for the benefit of English speakers rather than phonological analyses. They should not be confused with IPA standard transcriptions of words. Teaching students the distinction between orthographic practice and standard phonetic and phonemic representations is the first pedagogical challenge of the linguistics classroom.

SEMANTICS

Semantics is the study of the meanings signaled by words and word combinations. It includes the questions of reference, both to objects or situations in the speech context and to items in the speech stream itself. Semantics includes, for example, problems in classifying and categorizing such words as *tomato*, *platypus*, and *shrub* and problems in the choice of referential forms such as *she*, *this*, *the*, *a*, *all*, and *some*. Semantics proper does not include the social uses of words and expressions. Thus, from the point of view of semantics, the utterance *It's drafty in here* is to be explained purely in terms of ambient airflow and deixis (i.e., place) rather than in terms of how such an expression might be used in practice (e.g., to suggest that the window be closed). The study of the social uses of linguistic expressions is a distinct subdiscipline known as pragmatics. The restriction to language sets linguistics apart methodologically from the more inclusive field of semiotics, the general study of sign systems, both linguistic and nonlinguistic.

GRAMMAR

The central area of linguistics is grammar, a domain that includes morphology and syntax. Morphology is the study of the structure of words—their roots and affixes (prefixes and suffixes). It merges with phonology on one side and syntax on the other. For example, a suffix may be obscured through phonological processes, as when the French noun *animal*, on receiving the plural suffix-s, must be pronounced *animaux*. On the syntactic side, case suffixes are governed by syntactic role, as when, in Latin, *Ariovistum Caesar vicit* tells us unambiguously that Caesar (nominative case) defeated Ariovistus (accusative case) and not the other way around. Affixes may be derivational, serving to create a new word, as *-ly* creates the adverb *heavily* from the adjective *heavy*, or inflectional, serving to indicate a changed function of the same word, such as the *'s* of the possessive *children's*. The derivational-inflectional distinction is not always easy to make. Morphology plays a more important role in some languages than others. English and Chinese are especially poor

The distinction between orthographic practice and standard phonetic and phonemic representations is the first challenge of the linguistics classroom.

in inflectional affixes, Turkish and Latin are moderately rich, Finnish and Georgian spectacularly so.

SYNTAX

Syntax is the study of the structure of sentences. Structure includes statements not merely about word order but also about the hierarchical arrangement of words. Hierarchical structure tells us, for example, that in a sentence like *We had a view from the summit of the mountain of the entire city and its suburbs*, the words *of the mountain* modify the noun *summit* and that the words *of the entire city and its suburbs* modify the noun *view* rather than the noun *mountain*. Syntactic analysis likewise tells us that there is in this sentence no syntactic phrase consisting of the words *the mountain of the entire city* even though these words occur next to one another. An important concept of syntax is construction. Syntactic relations are more than merely hierarchical; they also involve habitual groupings of words and phrases, known as constructions, such as the passive (as in *The game was being observed by scouts from the major leagues*), the cleft (as in *It was his colossal arrogance that amazed us the most*), and the pseudocleft (as in *What we noticed was an abundance of wealthy patrons*), which in some theories would be held to be transforms of more basic constructions (i.e., *Scouts from the major leagues were observing the game*, *His colossal arrogance amazed us the most*, and *We noticed an abundance of wealthy patrons*).

DIACHRONIC LINGUISTICS

The preceding account of linguistics adopts an exclusively synchronic perspective, that is to say, it aims to describe a set of facts that prevails at one single point in time. A second possible perspective is a diachronic (i.e., historical) account that studies the nature of changes in the linguistic system. (Larry Trask's *Historical Linguistics* and Jean Aitchison's *Language Change: Progress or Decay?* are scholarly and informative accounts of this field.) Diachronic phonology is the study of phonetic changes, as when Proto-Indo-European *p*, *t*, and *k* show up in the Germanic languages as *f*, *th*, and *h* (in the terminology of the field, voiceless stops become voiceless fricatives), and also of structural adjustments in which, while no actual change in the sounds themselves occurs, the phonological status of a sound is altered. For example, in Old English the phoneme *f* was pronounced as either voiceless [f] or voiced [v], the [v] variant being found between vowels. But if one of these vowels was lost, as when Old English *on life* (pronounced [on lívə]) "alive" lost its ə and became *on lif* [on lív], the segment [v] was promoted to full phonemic status, being no longer simply the way [f] was pronounced between vowels but a fully independent speech sound. (Later, when more words containing this sound were introduced from French, the spelling with the letter *v* was adopted.) This process, whereby a sound that was once a mere phonetic variant comes to be an autonomous phonological unit, is known as phonologization.

Diachronic syntax traces the adjustments among categories over time, such as when the participle *considering*, from the verb *to consider*, comes to be used as a preposition in *considering his age*, and also when changes occur in grammatical construction. One well-studied problem is the shift in English from a dative indirect object in expressions such as *me thinketh*, *me liketh* to a subject in *I think*, *I like*. Word order changes have also been much studied, such as the change from an earlier verb-final word order in Old English (as in *ond þa Deniscan sige hæfdon* "and the Danes had [*hæfdon*] a victory [*sige*]") to one in which the verb is placed immediately after the subject in Modern English (as in *The attorneys agreed on a compromise*). Changes may affect not merely the linear order of words but also the structure of sequences. Reanalysis is the starting point for other changes. When Shakespeare wrote ". . . letters to my friends, / And I am going to deliver them" (*TGV* 3.1), he most likely meant his listeners to understand [I am going] [to deliver them]—that is, "I am on my way to deliver

them." But at a later period of the language, such sentences were often understood as if they were structured: [I am going to] [deliver them]. Here, "going to" has become reanalyzed as a future tense; it eventually became *gonna* in casual speech.

Comparative linguistics is the study of language families, such as Indo-European and Austronesian (a family of languages spoken in Southeast Asia and the Pacific islands). The individual languages in a language family are related through regular sound correspondences that can be traced back to the unitary protolanguage of the family, such as Proto-Indo-European or Proto-Austronesian. Thus English (an Indo-European language of the Germanic branch) is related to Latin (an Indo-European language of the Italic branch) through such sound correspondences as Latin *piscis* "fish" to English *fish*, Latin *tres* "three" to English *three*, and Latin *centum* "hundred" to English *hundred*. The initial consonants of these words reflect Proto-Indo-European *p*, *t*, and *k*, respectively.

LANGUAGE TYPOLOGY

Language typology, the study of the different types of structure found in the world's languages and the study of the evolution of those types, straddles synchronic and diachronic linguistics. It is, in name at least, a new field, dating from the work of Joseph Greenberg in the 1960s; Bernard Comrie's *Language Universals and Linguistic Typology* is a good survey of recent concepts and results. As suggested by the title of Comrie's book, the study of typology goes hand in hand with the study of language universals, features that are found in all languages. Such features can be lexical (e.g., all languages have a word for *moon*), phonological (e.g., all languages have a consonant similar to the English consonant *k* in *kin*), or syntactic (e.g., all languages have a way of forming negative sentences). Such universals are absolute; they apply across the board. There are very few of them, and they are for the most part not all that interesting. But in his highly influential study of universals of word order, ("Some

Universals"), Greenberg introduced the idea of an implicational universal, a universal that is present in a language only when some other feature is also present. While not every language has the phoneme [s] (for example, Hawaiian lacks this sound), and many (including Swedish) that have the phoneme [s] lack the phoneme [z], no language has been found that has [z] but not [s]. So the presence of [z] implies the presence of [s]. Greenberg drew up a list of such implicational universals.

Greenberg also found that languages could be classified in one of three groups according to the position of the verb in the basic sentence. Using the abbreviations S, V, and O for subject, verb, and object, these three types were VSO, SVO, and SOV. Examples of these three types (taken from Edward Finegan's *Language* 235–39) are as follows:

Type 1 (VSO): Tongan (Pacific island
    language)
Na'e taa'i 'e Hina 'a Vaka
Past hit Subject Hina Object Vaka
"Hina hit Vaka"

Type 2 (SVO): English
Mary hit John

Type 3 (SOV): Japanese
Akiko ga Taroo o butta
Akiko Subject Taroo Object hit
"Akiko hit Taroo"[1]

This classification is more than a mere categorization into three groups. It is a typology, because other features follow from membership in each group, that is to say, word-order patterns form implicational universals. Just as languages that have the phoneme [z] can be predicted to also have the phoneme [s], so type 3 (SOV) languages can be predicted—with somewhat less certainty, admittedly—to have postpositions (i.e., "prepositions" that follow their noun) and to have auxiliary verbs that follow the main verb. Type 1 (VSO) languages are just the opposite: they have prepositions, and the auxiliary verbs precede the main verb. In type 3 languages, the possessor precedes the possessed noun; in type 1 languages, the possessor follows the possessed

noun. In these and several other respects, type 1 and type 3 languages are structurally mirror images of each other. Type 2 (SVO) languages, the class to which English belongs, are less consistent and often have features of both type 1 and type 3 languages. We see this inconsistency clearly in the coexistence in English of two ways of indicating possession:

As in a type 3 language, the possessor may precede the possessed noun: *the mail carrier's uniform*. Compare Japanese:
    Taroo no imooto
    Taroo of sister
    "Taroo's sister / the sister of Taroo"

As in a type 1 language, the possessor may follow the possessed noun: *the skill of the surgeon*. Compare Tongan:
    ko'e tuonga'ane 'o Vaka
    the sister of Vaka
    "Vaka's sister / the sister of Vaka"

Greenberg's paper started a deluge of studies, both historical and synchronic. Many of the historical papers dealt with questions of how word order changed. Was the mixed character of type 2 languages like English due to an earlier history as a type 3 language? If so, by what processes did change come about? Descriptive linguists also seized on Greenberg's results. Were there other types of language, especially VOS (in which the object of the verb preceded the subject)? Indeed there were. What was the status of languages in which word order was to a high degree flexible?

In the 1970s and 1980s, investigations of these questions gave rise to a new style of linguistics, one based on typology and the relation between usage and structure in language. As I show in the next section, during this time mainstream linguistics was Chomskian and was dedicated to the idea that the visible facts about languages were the superficial tip of a much more significant iceberg of invisible rules and processes that gave rise to them. This perspective tended to suppress some very interesting facts about how speakers of a language used the different resources of their languages, such as word order. Greenberg's work stimulated interest in these visible facts. For example, in Spanish a simple sentence like *Juan canta* "John sings" has an alternative form *Canta Juan*. We might think of the first of these as an answer to the question "What does John do?" and the second as answering the question "Who sings?" In Spanish, as in all languages, word order reflects differences in how information is being presented: as old or as new to the discourse.[2] Key events in the functionalism that emerged in the 1970s and 1980s were the publication of two edited volumes by Charles Li, *Word Order and Word Order Change* and *Subject and Topic*, and the Linguistics Institute organized by the Linguistics Society of America in the summer of 1976, which introduced many of the new ideas to the field.

DEVELOPMENTS SINCE 1990

In this survey of recent developments in linguistics, we refer to the current period as the 1990s, which includes writing up to 2005. The bibliographic references are not necessarily the earliest or most recent discussion or proposal of a topic, and they are not necessarily the work of the major proponents of an idea; they are mostly chosen because they offer a readable, informative, and up-to-date account. They are intended to serve as an entrée into the literature of a topic, not as a substitute for a full bibliography.

Formalism and Functionalism

A prominent feature of recent years has been the effort by many linguists to transcend the restrictions of narrowly practiced formalism. By the 1990s, it was possible to discern several distinct styles of doing linguistics. These styles break down into two large domains that have come to be known as formalism, or generativism, and functionalism (see Frederick Newmeyer's *Language Forms and Language Function*).

FORMALISM OR GENERATIVISM

Briefly, formalists assign absolute theoretical priority to the abstract structure of the linguistic code and view anything external to form, such as real-world or psychological conditions that affect form, as secondary. This is the autonomy postulate: linguistic structure is regarded for theoretical purposes as hermetically sealed from other aspects of linguistic communication.

The term *generativism*, sometimes used as an alternative to *formalism*, refers to the doctrine that a language system must be approached by specifying the rules through which grammatical sentences are produced or generated. A word of caution is necessary. To an outsider the words *rule*, *grammatical*, and *produce* may suggest a quite different picture from the one intended here. It should be remembered that because linguistics is a descriptive, not a prescriptive, field, the rules are not maxims of socially accepted linguistic behavior (such as "Don't say *ain't*"), *grammatical* does not mean in accordance with approved canons of good writing and good speaking, and *produce* does not refer to something a speaker does in going from an idea to an audible or written utterance. Rather, these terms are to be understood in their logical sense. A *rule* is an abstract formula, *grammatical* means conforming to the set of constructive rules that define the language, and *produce* means applying the formulas (rules) to a string in such a way that the output is a well-formed sentence. The formalist is interested first and foremost in the logical properties of the linguistic code itself, not in what its speakers do or when, why, and how they do it. An assumption made by most formalists is that language is innate (i.e., a human-specific genetic endowment)[3] and a mental-cerebral module that is separate from other human capacities and must therefore be studied in isolation from them. For recent discussion of this claim, I recommend Steven Pinker's *The Language Instinct* and Geoffrey Sampson's *Educating Eve* and its update, *The "Language Instinct" Debate*.

> **A prominent feature of recent years has been the effort by many linguists to transcend . . . narrowly practiced formalism.**

FUNCTIONALISM

Functionalists hold a variety of positions but in general argue, unlike formalists, that factors external to the language system are inseparable from linguistic structure. For some functionalists, language structure comes about through the settling or sedimentation of speech patterns; therefore a study of speech patterns is a prerequisite to even talking about structure. For others, linguistic structure is a result of natural human habits of thought, perception, and communication. Defenders of both these explanations, which are not necessarily incompatible, see language as a reflection of something much deeper and larger, seeking its sources and its very nature either in sociocultural interaction or in cognition.

While there is some overlap between formalism and functionalism, linguists in the 1990s generally came to identify with one or the other of these two styles, and during the decade sharp divergences in goals and approaches between the two became evident. Formalists continued to give priority to grammatical and phonological structure as a logical abstraction that must be explicated before attention is turned to applications of structure such as the study of usage. Formalists in the 1990s were interested in usage and psychology but insisted that such extraneous aspects of language must always be secondary to the goal of placing the formal theory of language on a sound footing. But formal linguists were reaching out to psycholinguistics and artificial intelligence.

Formal Linguistics

Since shortly after the middle of the twentieth century, syntactic theory was dominated by the ideas of Noam Chomsky. In his earlier, highly influential work, Chomsky argued that an approach to syntax that focused exclusively on word order and groupings of words could not account for crucial facts about the grammars of languages. One of these facts was that sentences were often manifested in ways that suggested a hidden ("deep") structure that was different from the apparent ("surface") structure. Examples would be sentences like *This violin is difficult to play sonatas on*, which depended for its meaning on a structure that was closer to *To play sonatas on this violin is difficult*, or passive sentences like *These dams were built by beavers*, which appeared to have *beavers* as a deep-structure subject. Complexities of this kind led Chomsky to suggest that instead of inductively finding the correct analysis of a sentence by sorting and classifying its superficial structures, it is necessary to posit or hypothesize an abstract level of structure and derive the surface structures deductively from it. This procedure, when extended to the entire field of syntax, came to be known as generative grammar, a term more properly applied to any method that aims to generate (i.e., discover and formulate the rules for constructing), rather than analyze, sentences. A generative grammar that includes different levels of structure and rules for moving between them (such as from active to passive) is moreover a transformational generative grammar or, more simply, a transformational grammar.

Since its inception in the 1950s, the generative grammar project went through several incompatible theories or through several stages of development—which of these depends on one's perspective. There has been since the 1970s in all schools of linguistics a tendency to seek a more comprehensive view of linguistic structure that incorporates language universals, a topic that came into prominence through the work of Greenberg.

THE CHOMSKIAN SCHOOL IN THE 1900S

In the 1990s, Chomskian linguistics underwent theoretical changes that moved it to new levels of abstraction and increasingly distanced it from the general functionalist and formalist mainstream. The concept of deep structure that Chomsky and his school developed in the 1960s was fairly intuitive. Sentences containing the same words and having basically equivalent meanings could yet differ in form, and it seemed natural to posit a single abstract form (a deep structure) that underlay the different superficial versions of a sentence. The "principles and parameters" model that Chomsky announced in the 1980s (*New Horizons in the Study of Language and the Mind*) added to earlier models an explicit commitment to the study of language universals and child language acquisition. Language structure, Chomsky insisted, was so complex that simple exposure to speech did not suffice to account for the quick and accurate learning accomplished by small children. How children acquired language was inexplicable without some reckoning of a prior (i.e., innate) linguistic knowledge that the child brought to the task. The principles and parameters model postulated, as part of the innate equipment possessed by all human beings, an array of parameters, a small number of alternative sets of available linguistic structures from which the child instinctively selected the set prompted by the language in his environment. Language arrived, so to speak, with open parameters; the basic stuff was there, and how it was arranged in any given language was a question of which parameters were selected. In the computer-age terminology much loved by the Chomsky school, the parameters were said to be switched in a certain way. One parameter, for example, is said to assign the basic verb position in a language to the first, middle, or final position. A child exposed to Japanese as his first language would hear verb-final sentences, think "Aha! A verb-final language!," and switch on the verb-final language parameter.

Parameter setting provided a theoretical accommodation to the radically differing ground plans for language structure that had been discerned. As we saw in the discussion of Greenberg's word order typology, placing the verb at the end of the sentence is more than the simple question of where to put the verb. Other grammatical features go along with it. As we saw, these grammatical features are markedly different for languages like Tongan, Arabic, and Irish that place the verb at the beginning of the sentence and whose grammar seems in many respects to be

the mirror image of verb-final languages. How could language structure be said to be universal when the differences among languages were apparently so profound? Parameter setting supplied an answer. Grammatical differences reflected divergences from the basic ground plan that resulted from choices among a small number of intrinsic possibilities. Once children identify the language spoken around them as a verb-final language, they do not have to learn separately all its other grammatical rules; the rules follow automatically when the verb-position parameter has been switched from open (its neutral setting) to verb-final.

RECENT REVISIONS TO GENERATIVE THEORY

Until the 1990s, then, much of Chomskian generative grammar was accessible to linguists in general, who could take from it any facets they found relevant to their own work. The minimalist program changed all that. The term *program* was intended to suggest a preliminary project rather than a theory. It was a map of an agenda for a scientific field. It was called minimalist because Chomsky, in his 1995 formulation of it (*Minimalist Program*), recognized only two perceptible levels: logical form and phonetic form. Logical form is the set of meanings, phonetic form the set of sounds. The interface between them is the subject matter of linguistics. The minimalist program thus makes explicit a reliance on the standard definition of a language as a system of rules that relates the sounds of words to their meanings.

Missing from Chomsky's new formulation is a hard-won concept of grammar that has been weaving in and out of Chomskian theory for the past thirty or forty years: the distinction between deep and surface structure. I cannot pursue in detail the arguments for dispensing with these two levels, except to say that the term *minimalist* implies an extreme simplification of the theory. This project therefore requires that every concept of the theory be rigorously questioned in the face of the presumption that it can be dispensed with.

> **How children acquired language was inexplicable without some reckoning of a prior (i.e., innate) linguistic knowledge.**

Deep structure and surface structure do not, Chomsky argues, pass muster and must be rejected. Another grammatical concept that must be set aside is that of movement. Many traditional grammatical rules make use of the notion that an element in a sentence owes its position to a movement. (A simple example is a sentence like *The desserts which he prepared were delicious*, where *which*, the direct object of *prepared*, has migrated from its position after the verb.) Movement, minimalists claim, can be eliminated, since the sort of displacement of words that seemed to require it falls out as a by-product of two more general principles, merge and copy. Merge puts new structures together to form a larger phrase; copy, as the name suggests, places a duplicate of a phrase somewhere in the developing sentence, leaving a trace in place of the original phrase, a trace that is then deleted.

The concepts of the minimalist program are difficult to illustrate without recourse to a complex apparatus of symbolic conventions. Indeed, much of the internal discussion of minimalism is conducted through esoteric abbreviations like BOC (bare output condition) and FI (full interpretation), abbreviations that are rarely expanded and that frequently render the progress of an argument obscure and inaccessible to all but a small band of insiders. The rhetoric of minimalism includes the claim that the project is scientific (i.e., difficult) and has led to progress in understanding the true nature of language. It should be borne in mind, however, that the database of the Chomskian school has not changed in fifty years. Far-reaching conclusions about the nature of language are, in this school, still founded on fantastic, mentally constructed sentences like *John thinks that it is believed that shaving himself is important*, whose grammatical status is, to the objective outsider, extremely dubious and that we may be confident never occur in natural speech. A number of commentators see the minimalist program as Chomsky's late-life radical revision of his thinking, a revision that essentially sets aside every achievement of the generative grammar project from the 1950s to the 1990s.

Systemic Linguistics

Systemic linguistics (more properly, systemic-functional linguistics) has its origins in the thought of the British linguist J. R. Firth, who insisted that the study of language is a social science and that language must always be viewed as contextualized speech. Systemic linguists look at how language both acts on and is constrained by its social contexts. Language is analyzed in terms of four strata: lexico-grammar, phonology (including writing), semantics, and context. Each of these strata is further subdivided into aspects. For example, context includes field (the topic), tenor (the people talking and their interrelationships), and mode (the channel of communication. such as dialogue, speech, writing). M.A.K. Halliday's *Introduction to Functional Grammar* is a detailed yet accessible introduction to systemic linguistics by its leading theorist and practitioner. Systemic linguistics has become very widely taught around the globe, especially in institutions of British genealogy where the English language has to be taught to nonnative speakers and where courses in systemic linguistics are often built into degree requirements. Its rather naive partitions of language simplify a complex field of study and so offer a strong appeal to language learners who need a quick grasp of elementary concepts.

Perhaps the most important contribution to the study of language by systemic linguists has been their pioneering research in corpus linguistics and their work on text analysis. One result of this research has been an increasing sense of the inseparability of grammar from lexicon. Offshoots of this school have also moved in the direction of critical linguistics. The term *critical* here has its origins in the Continental critical theory movement, whose leaders include the German sociologist Jürgen Habermas. The term refers to a set of ethical questions concerning how language is exploited by power structures for illegitimate ends. Norman Fairclough's *Critical Discourse Analysis* and Fairclough and Ruth Wodak's "Critical Discourse Analysis" give a good idea of the concepts, methods, and directions of this branch of linguistics.

Optimality Theory

At the end of the twentieth century, many linguists were turning to an approach to language that is known as optimality theory. Optimality theory (see Archangeli) starts from the idea of universal grammar, the hypothesis that languages in general draw their grammatical rules from a pool (perhaps genetically prescribed) of universal structures, all of which are in principle available but in practice limited to a small number in any given language. These structures are understood to be constraints, that is, preferences that limit grammatical and phonological choices. They are not absolute prohibitions; rather, one constraint can be stronger than another and override it. When conflicts between constraints occur, there is said to be a violation, and one constraint wins out. For example, a universal constraint is that a morpheme (the linguist's cover term for prefixes, stems, and suffixes) should keep a single form and not vary. (This is the "one form, one meaning" principle.) A morpheme should not have forms that diverge too widely from one another. Another constraint is that a nasal consonant such as *n* or *m* will preferably adapt its articulation to a following consonant. Both *intolerant* and *impossible* contain the negative prefix in-/im-: the im- form in *impossible* has a labial nasal *m* because the next consonant, *p*, is also labial. The first of these constraints, that forms of the same morpheme not proliferate, violates the second one, that nasals conform to a following consonant, since the second constraint brings about two distinct forms of the prefix. In English (and perhaps all languages), the preference to adapt nasal consonants to the next consonant is stronger than and overrides the preference to keep the form of morphemes constant.

Differences in the choice of constraints and in the order in which they are applied lead to the characteristic phonological structure of a language. Optimality theory is basically a proposal for mediating between language-specific structure and an observed set of language universals. These universals are understood as tendencies rather than as absolutes. Much of the interest in optimality theory lies in its liberation of linguists from the largely unproductive work of bottom-up cataloging of actual exceptionless universals and from the general despair of explaining exceptions. Instead, observed tendencies are postulated as universals, and failure to manifest them completely is made into the basis of an explanatory linguistic description. For example, the universal that a word should have two syllables explains rules of insertion of vowels and consonants (epenthesis), deletion (ellipsis), and compounding (as when in Chinese two-syllable words are created by adding more or less meaningless monosyllables to monosyllabic words). There is a loss of universality if changes result in a reduction of length from two to one syllable. The enormous success of optimality theory can be gauged by its domination of the programs of the Linguistics Society of America and the regional linguistics societies during the 1990s. The theory continues to be a highly visible paradigm and was recently extended into syntax.

Functional Linguistics

The theories discussed so far have in common a deference to quite traditional ideas about sentence syntax in which it is assumed that the core grammar of a language dwells in a unit known as the sentence and that the goal of linguistics is to discover the set of grammatical rules for forming sentences and, eventually, to relate these rules to language universals and cognition. The methods, procedures, and formalisms of this kind of linguistics suggest a view of language as something autonomous and bounded; the study of language may have applications that are not purely linguistic (such as providing a basis for the study of social variation or for children's acquisition of the linguistic system), but in essence language consists exclusively of phonological, morphological, syntactic, and semantic structures, on which nothing external can be brought to bear as direct evidence for theory construction.

LINGUISTICS AND COGNITION

For the formal linguist, cognition, insofar as language is concerned, can be seriously studied only on the basis of explicitly stated grammatical rules. But a major constituency in the field of linguistics is cognitive linguists who start with the premise that linguistic rules are themselves a product of how we perceive and think about the world and communicate with others. The prior task is therefore to relate linguistic rules to cognitive structures and cognitive processes. In actual practice, since the data of language are the primary source of knowledge about these cognitive structures, cognitive linguists generally work both sides together, seeking to find sufficient examples of a particular linguistic structure to justify confidence in a general statement about the accompanying thought process.

Consider the following example, which has been frequently discussed in the literature. Expressions of time in all languages are overwhelmingly couched in terms that suggest a natural apprehension of time in terms of spatial dimensions, in particular length. Illustrated with English forms, pairings of time words with length words include *a long time*, *a short time*, *from Monday to Friday* (cf. *from Saint Louis to Chicago*), *the film went on for two hours* (cf. *we went on for two miles*), *a stretch of time*, *an extent of time*, *a length of time*, and many others. (*Light-year* is thus anomalous in stating distance in terms of time, which is perhaps why many people find the term confusing.) Phrases like *at this point in time*, *in this era*, *by this time*, and others in which time words are construed with locative prepositions show that not only length but also point (*at*) and area (*in*) relations can be converted into time expressions. Even grammatical forms involving tense and temporal relations can often be shown to have evolved out of spatial expressions. A crosslinguistically common example is

the equivalent of the English progressive aspect, as in *they are hunting wild boar*. Frequently the origin of this construction is found in a preposition with a nominalized form of the verb (i.e., a verb that has been made into a noun). A rough translation is something like *they are at [the] hunting [of the] wild boar*. Although this account is not universally accepted for English, it is seen clearly in other languages, for example, the German *sie ist am Schreiben* "she is writing" (literally, "she is at the writing"). The independent rise of this construction in numerous languages has led some linguists to postulate a universal cognitive association between time and space, with time expressions being organized and having their historical origin in spatial terms.

METAPHOR

The cognitive relation between space and time revealed by such analysis is often viewed as a metaphoric one. Metaphor has played an important role in cognitive linguistics since the 1980s, and this role was strengthened in the 1990s. In the 1980s, George Lakoff and Mark Johnson argued that communication occurs through large-scale metaphors with which we understand our cultural world. They pointed to many groups of expressions organized around a common abstract theme: *life is a journey*, with a *way*, a *direction*, *obstacles*, *turning points*, and so on and questioned whether there was any limit to this perspective—whether, in other words, it might not be the case that language is metaphor "all the way down." During the 1990s, there was some tendency to replace the term *metaphor*, the substitution of one concept with another, with *metonymy*, the symbolization of a concept by an adjacent or included part. In particular, those linguists interested in language change recognized the relevance of metaphor and metonymy for a theory of how meanings shift over time. For example, *can* in earlier English meant "know how to," but its meaning shifted to one of general ability through a chain of adjacent concepts (inferences): *knowing how* strongly implies *being able to*. In her influential book *From Etymology to Pragmatics*, Eve Sweetser described metaphoric meaning transfers—for example, between the notion of physically grasping and that of understanding, between seeing and knowing—that were pervasive in Indo-European and other language families. The work of Elizabeth Traugott was also an influential force in the 1990s. Traugott's focus was on grammar rather than lexicon. She traced a number of Old English lexical items that had come to serve grammatical functions—for example, the noun *hwíl* "a period of time," which became the modern English subordinating conjunction *while*—and postulated general principles that governed lexical changes. I return to Traugott's work later.

The space-time conversion is only a small segment of the widely used approach to language that is now a distinct and complex subdiscipline known as cognitive linguistics. A central concept of this field, and one that governs much thinking and research, is the notion of a prototype, as elaborated in the work of the psychologist Eleanor Rosch. Our concepts, in this view, have their sources not in particular instances nor in platonic ideas nor in exclusionary lists of features but rather in typical instances of a phenomenon. Concepts are organized into central (prototypical) and marginal instances. My central idea of a bird is likely to be a sparrow or a crow rather than a swan or an ostrich. Swans and ostriches are marginal instances of the category "bird." My central idea of a fruit includes apples and strawberries (and mangoes and papayas) but not tomatoes and eggplants (aubergines). No general (e.g., botanical) definition excludes tomatoes and eggplants from the category "fruit" or swans and ostriches from the category "bird," but we don't immediately think of these items when asked to name a member of the category. They are included in the category but as marginal instances. Extended to the linguistic notion of syntactic or grammatical categories, it can be said that there are prototypical and marginal nouns, verbs, adjectives, and so on; thus *chair* would be a prototypical noun, while *dancing* and *headway* are more marginal nouns. It is characteristic of the marginal instances that they compete in some way and overlap with neighboring cate-

gories; thus the noun *dancing* competes with the category verb (*dancing is fun / they are dancing*) in much the same way that tomatoes have features that overlap with both fruits and vegetables.

An early application in linguistics to prototypes was the work of Brent Berlin and Paul Kay on universal color categories (*Basic Color Terms*). Berlin and Kay found that there were a small number of focal colors, such as *red, blue, black*, from which different languages made a selection. To a large extent the selection made in a given language could be predicted from the number of such focal color names available in the language. For instance, a language that had five names would choose *white, black, red, green*, and *yellow*, and if a sixth color was added to these five, it would be blue. The theory was highly touted throughout the 1970s and 1980s as an example of a linguistic universal with roots in human physiology and cognition, but in the 1990s some linguists were raising questions about it. Sampson, for example, criticizes the authors' methods and data and notes important exceptions (65–69). He cites premodern Japanese described in an article by Noriko McNeill ("Colour and Colour Terminology"). Japanese in this earlier time was a five-color language where the basic color terms were not *white, black, red, green*, and *yellow*, as predicted, but *white, black, orange, turquoise*, and *yellow*. The example is significant because it suggests that cultural environment is a weightier factor than natural human propensities: these colors are the ones yielded by the most easily available dyestuffs of the period.

The application of prototypes to syntax can be exemplified in the analysis of transitive sentences, sentences that contain a direct object, as in *He broke the toy*. The simple transitive-intransitive dichotomy overlooks the fact that there are several degrees of transitivity. *He broke the toy* (transitive) contrasts not only with *He was crying* (intransitive) but also with sentences that are in one of many different ways less transitive, such as *Garbage attracts raccoons, We could hear the bells*, and others where the grammatical subject-verb-object sequence does not mean that an agent is acting on an object. While *I killed him* and *I caused him to die* might come down to the same thing, there is a difference in the way the two actions are understood. Killing is more direct, more sudden, more deliberate, and more final than causing to die. One way to characterize the difference is to say that *to kill* is a prototypical action verb, while *to cause to die* is more a marginal action verb. Put another way, we might say that *I killed the preacher* is closer to the prototype of a transitive sentence, and *I caused the preacher to die* is more distant from the transitive prototype. The example must be understood in the context of a theory, well known since the 1970s, that equated *kill* with *cause to die*. For a short discussion, see Paul Hopper and Sandra Thompson.

Another important idea in current cognitive linguistics is the notion of iconicity (Simone). In many ways linguistic structure reflects thought proportionally. Complex linguistic structure is calibrated with complex conceptual structure. *I killed the preacher* suggests a simpler and more direct thought than *I caused the preacher to die*; it indicates a short action with an immediate result. *I caused the preacher to die* suggests a slower and more complex event, perhaps involving a third party or some other remote cause, and the action is not necessarily intentional. This difference is reflected in the structure of the two utterances. We would not expect the slower and more complex event to be represented by a briefer and simpler syntax. The principle of iconicity has many applications. Noun plurals, in all languages that have them, are more complex than noun singulars; the comparatives and superlatives of adjectives are always more complex than the positives (e.g., *wetter* and *wettest* are more complex than *wet*); polite requests are more complex than peremptory ones (*Would you mind not smoking?* vs. *stop smoking!*).

In syntax, different degrees of necessity and obligation are expressed in many languages by looser versus tighter syntactic

Complex linguistic structure is calibrated with complex conceptual structure.

structure (see Noonan). English examples of this difference would be:

1. They made John leave.
2. They asked John to leave.
3. They expected that John would leave.

The complexity of the verb phrase (*made . . . leave, asked . . . to leave, expected that . . . would leave*) reflects iconically the degree of control over the action that the phrase signals: the more control, the shorter and simpler the verb and the shorter the conceptual distance between agent and action. In example 1, the simple form *made . . . leave* corresponds to complete control: the subject *they* has fully carried out the action and John did in fact leave; in example 2, *asked to leave* indicates that the subject *they* is not fully in control and that John still technically has the option to remain; in example 3, the subject *they* has no control at all over John's leaving. Moreover, the sentences are graded from more to less immediate (shorter to greater conceptual distance): in the first, John's leaving is presented as an unmediated effect of the verb; in the second, John has some choice—his leaving is separated from the asking by the possibility of refusing; in the third, John's leaving is unrelated to the verb *expected*—he may be unaware of their expectation. In one form or another such iconic syntactic patterns have been found in all languages investigated.

COGNITIVE GRAMMAR

One of the most visible developments of the 1990s was the movement known as cognitive grammar, associated especially with Ronald Langacker ("Conceptualization"), Leonard Talmy, and Mark Turner and Gilles Fauconnier. While in a general way cognitive grammar is part of the cognitive linguistics movement, it has a distinctive methodology and set of concepts. Linguistic expressions are seen as integrated amalgams of form and meaning (remember that for most other theories, forms and meanings are not integrated; they are separate entities combined by rules). This cognitive grammar principle of the inseparability of form and meaning applies in the realms of both syntax and individual words. Cognitive grammarians attach importance to visualization. The forms and meanings of language are seen as image schemas, that is, schematic maps or diagrams of concepts. Typically, image schemas are represented as squares, circles, lines, and directional arrows. Consider, for example, the trio of words *advise*, *adviser*, and *advisee* as presented in Langacker (fig. 1).

The concept linking these words must be specified as a relation. Two entities are connected in some way, and the concept cannot be understood without simultaneous reference to both. It is an experiential relation rather than a physical one, a feature that is represented by a dotted line. Moreover, one of the entities is presented in the discourse as a primary participant,

FIG. 1

~

An example of image schemas,
in Langacker, "Conceptualization" 10.

(a)   *advise*

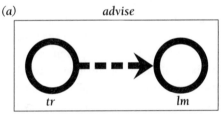

(b)   *adviser*

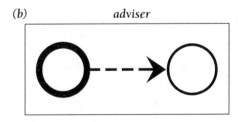

(c)   *advisee*

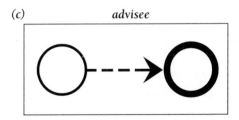

called the trajector (tr), and the other as a secondary participant, called the landmark (lm). Finally, some aspect of the relation is profiled, that is, understood as the starting point or the most prominent aspect. In *She advises me*, the verb *advises* is profiled. In *She is my adviser*, the trajector *she* is profiled. In *I am her advisee*, the landmark *I* is profiled. Notice that in the representation of figure 1, the basic array of lines, circles, and arrows is identical for all three schemes. The only thing that differs is the prominence of one or the other participant in the relation. The profiling is represented by thicker lines.

The two prepositions *above* and *below* also differ only in the selection of one or another entity as trajector (fig. 2). In *Our apartment is above the common room*, the trajector is *our apartment* and the landmark is *the common room*. In *The common room is below our apartment*, it is the reverse: the trajector is *the common room*, and the landmark is *our apartment*. The spatial (i.e., conceptual) relations are thus identical, and only the selection of one or the other participants as trajector triggers the choice of *above* or *below*.

During the 1990s, cognitive grammar in one form or another gained a significant following among linguists.

GRAMMATICALIZATION

Another, not necessarily distinct, direction of functional linguistics in the 1990s has been the exploration of the origins of grammatical forms in earlier lexical forms. The idea of grammaticalization, which challenges the fixed code theory that dominates linguistics, is an old one. Consider, as an example, the English future tense expressed by *be going to*, as in *He is going to get married*. We could understand such a sentence either as a declaration of a future event or as an answer to the question, "Why is he going?" The verb form *going* can have the concrete lexical sense of a verb of motion comparable to *traveling* or the more abstract, grammatical sense of a future tense. But in other contexts there is no such ambiguity. *If you turn off the air conditioner, the ice carvings are going to melt* has only the future meaning. The phrase *be going to* has become

FIG. 2

~

Image schemas for *above* and *below*, in Langacker, "Conceptualization" 11.

(a)   *above*

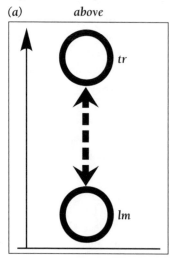

(b)   *below*

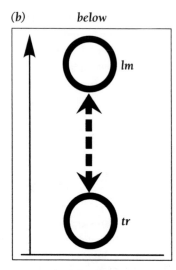

nite and indefinite), prepositions, and pronouns. Major categories are nouns, verbs, adjectives, and adverbs. In English some prepositions rise out of the present participles of verbs: *concerning your proposal* comes from *to concern*, *considering her age* comes from *to consider*. A more exotic example is from the Asian language Yao Samsao:

(a) nĩn pun péw yie
    he give axe me
    "He gave me an axe"
(b) maa cáp bùdò'-gwăy pun fù'-cúey
    mother cut fingernails give child
    "The mother cut the child's nails for him"
    (Heine and Kuteva 150)

We see that, as in many other languages, the verb meaning "give" (here, *pun*) has become grammaticalized in certain contexts as a preposition meaning "for."

This process can go quite far, as when the grammaticalized verb shrinks to a mere ending on the main verb. A well-known case of this is the development of future-tense inflections in Romance languages, where the Latin verb meaning "have" is now a suffix: Latin *cantare habeo* "I have to sing" becomes in French *chanter-ai* "[I] shall sing." A second kind of grammaticalization is the fixing of looser combinations of words into syntactic constructions. Usually such constructions center around a change in one key word, for example the verb *do* in English, which comes to be an essential element in negation (*He didn't clean the stove top*), in questions (*Did he clean the stove top?*), and in emphasis (*He did clean the stove top*). In a number of languages, including most European ones, the verb *have* has come to be used as a past-tense auxiliary, apparently starting from a past participle used as an adjective: *Caesar urbem captam habet* "Caesar has/holds the captured city," which eventually becomes *has captured the city*.

The changes in meaning that take place in grammaticalization are often described in terms of metaphor or metonymy. When *give* is used as a preposition meaning "for," there is said to be a (metonymic) transfer of the sense from a literal meaning of *give* to one of direction or benefit.

grammaticalized as an auxiliary verb, adding the meaning "future tense" to the main verb. While there is no distinct definition of grammaticalization (because there is not always agreement about which forms are to be called grammatical and which ones lexical), there are some typical examples.

One example is the emergence of a minor category or an affix (i.e., prefix or suffix) out of a major category or a full word. Minor categories are such things as auxiliary verbs, articles (defi-

The precise nature of the semantic changes has been studied by Traugott, who concludes that meanings come to be more subjective over time; the term *subjective* includes both the speaker's point of view and references to the act of speaking in which the speaker is involved. In our previous example of *He is going to get married*, where a verb of motion comes to be understood as a future tense, the objective action of visible movement is replaced by a more subjective one of imputed intention. The process is metonymic, in that some inferential part of the meaning of the verb of movement is fastened on as the new central meaning: if he is going in order to get married, it is likely that the event of marrying is a future one.

Recently, grammaticalization has been a much discussed topic; some linguists question its validity altogether. They do so on the grounds that although nouns and verbs may become prepositions, for example, they do not have to and that there are occasional examples of the reverse change, as when prepositions become verbs (e.g., *We quickly downed our drinks*). Opponents of grammaticalization have used such examples to reject the argument that linguistic change is subject to general tendencies (the so-called directionality question). Proponents of grammaticalization argue that despite a few counterexamples, change, when it occurs, generally proceeds along certain identifiable paths, such as Traugott's "subjectification" mentioned above, and that a counterexample like *down* used as a verb does not constitute a reversal of direction, only the creation of a new word from an old preposition. For a discussion of the issues, see Hopper and Traugott.

While grammaticalization could be understood as a simple question of the origins of grammatical forms, for some linguists (see, e.g., Hopper, "Emergent Grammar" [1987]), grammaticalization was not a process that led to a fixed conclusion but rather an ongoing and never-ending movement toward structure. Grammar in this view was emergent, its structure constantly adapting to ongoing interactions. This perspective gained some importance in the 1990s.

THE STUDY OF SPOKEN LANGUAGE

A prominent theme in the linguistics of the 1990s has been an intense focus on the properties of spoken language. This focus challenged many of the standard assumptions about linguistic data and indirectly raised new questions about the goals and nature of the field.

One of these questions concerns the status of the sentence as a basic unit. While this or that theory might have things to say about discourse, the general assumption is always that a discourse text consists of an array of sentences, each of which can stand alone as the staging area for grammar. Discourse context may require adaptations of sentence structure—for example, by requiring that a noun be replaced by a pronoun or that a landmark rather than a trajector be the subject of its sentence—but syntactic explanation is held to reside exclusively in the isolated sentence. Discourse is how sentences are used in practice; sentences are, in a frequently used analogy, the building blocks of discourse, and discourse considerations do not enter into sentence-internal analysis. This philosophy informs all purely syntactic theories, even those that claim to extend their explanations into discourse (for some critical discussion, see Hopper, "Emergent Grammar" [1988]; Linell).

A diagnostic feature that unites and distinguishes most linguistic theories, both formalist and functionalist, is a dependence on constructed examples. Constructed examples are sentences that are made up out of one's head or, to put it more politely, are derived from intuition, the philosopher's term for introspection. It does not matter whether anyone actually uttered the sentence *Mulder believes the rumor that Scully hid the files* (typical of many found in recent articles). The important point is that the speaker's internal grammar permits this combination to be said (or, more likely, written), no matter how improbable it might be in practice. Again, this is the "can say" principle: linguistics is concerned with what speakers can say, not with what they in practice do say.

As long as the data of language are either written or derivative of written forms, this postulate is not hard to sustain. But from the 1970s on, the technology for recording and analyzing speech communication became more sophisticated, especially through the tape recorder and the sound spectograph. Without question the most significant development in the 1990s was the low-cost personal computer, with its potential for detailed studies of phonation in long utterances (the older sound spectographs were limited to two or three seconds) and especially very large data storage and fast search software. Linguists now have on their desktops the capacity for accessing immensely large bodies of linguistic data. The personal computer has in effect brought into existence an entirely new subdiscipline of linguistics which for some linguists has raised broad new questions about the nature of grammar.

> **The personal computer has in effect brought into existence an entirely new subdiscipline of linguistics.**

One by-product of these developments has been a close attention to the distinctive features of spoken language and the refinement of techniques of transcription of spoken language (Du Bois, Schuetze-Coburn, Paolino, and Cumming). Although linguists have always insisted on the primacy of spoken over written language, a principle stated explicitly by Ferdinand de Saussure in *Course in General Linguistics* (1922), in practice the database of linguistics has tended to be either written or, as argued in Per Linell's *The Written Language Bias in Linguistics*, unconsciously dependent on written texts. This attitude changed with the growing recognition of fundamental differences between the language of speech and the language of writing, differences that for some amounted to a cognitive chasm, characterized by Walter Ong as a "restructuring of consciousness" (78). In a less radical vein, Wallace Chafe and Jane Danielewicz, on the basis of a study of conversations, drew up lists of typical features of the grammars of speech and writing—finding, for example, that the *-ing* participle that follows a noun, as in *students registering for this course*, was rare in spoken discourse but common in writing.

A number of linguists in the 1990s found congeners in a corner of sociology that dealt with local interactions and that had turned its attention to the language used in them. The conversation analysis (CA) paradigms in linguistics and sociology share a common origin and a common vocabulary but have different goals (Pomerantz and Fehr). The linguists' preoccupation with the question of the nature of grammar contrasts with the sociologists' concern for the joint construction of social reality in small-scale interactions, but there are rich and to some extent competitive exchanges between the two orientations. The basis of CA is the fact of turn taking: conversation is a dialogic process that exists by virtue of principles governing how the roles of speaker and hearer are alternately assigned. Because turn taking is fundamental, the basic unit of conversation analysis is not the sentence but a unit known as the turn constructional unit, or TCU. A brief example from Emanuel Schegloff illustrates this unit:

> Pam: 'hh *Oh* yeah you've gotta tell Mike tha:t.
> Uh-cuz they want that on fi:lm   (59)

Spellings like *gotta* and *cuz* and the transcription of a drawl by a colon after a vowel (*tha:t, fi:lm*), are standard in this kind of work, as is the representation of exhalations ('hh) and hesitations (*uh*). What from a more conventional linguistic standpoint look like irrelevant vocalizations may be important clues to the organization of talk. Schegloff notes that a linguist making a conventional syntactic analysis of the utterance would start by editing out the "nonlinguistic" components and creating a complex sentence with a main and a subordinate clause: *You've got to tell Mike that, because they want that on film.* From the CA perspective such an analysis misses the point. The lengthened vowel in *tha:t*, together with the intonation contour and the possibility of syntactic completion, show that *you've gotta tell Mike tha:t* is pragmatically complete (i.e., it is a complete turn constructional unit). The hearer could, on picking up on the terminal drawl of *tha:t*, infer that the speaker had finished her turn, and that he could now "legally" come in with his own turn to talk. (Notice that it is immaterial to the definition of a TCU whether the hearer does or does not actually take his turn. The TCU is defined by intonation contours, syntactic completion, and the potential of signaling a change of turn to the hearer.) So the subsequent utterance *cuz they want that on film* must be interpreted either as an increment to the already completed TCU or as a new TCU, each of which would have different implications for further analysis. I return later to another hot topic of the 1990s, the question of how linguistic structure (grammar) relates to the TCU.

Conversation analysis in linguistics belongs to a broad category of approaches to the study of language that make the assumption that linguistic data should be collected for some purpose other than the intended analysis. To the outsider, this point is often puzzling, since it seems obvious. To start with, there seems something unscientific about your making up data and then analyzing the very data you made up. Then there is the question of the goals of linguistics. Why would a linguist not be interested in studying how people talk to one another and communicate through language?

To understand the premises of mainstream linguistics, one must look back at a long tradition that is reflected in a distinction made by Chomsky between linguistic performance, what people actually do when they talk, and linguistic competence, the mental ability or linguistic knowledge that talking presupposes. The immediate task of linguistics, some would say, is to expound this mental ability: without understanding the ability, it is meaningless to study how people use it in verbal interactions. Some would go even further, as does Chomsky, and insist that language is exclusively a matter of expression by an individual speaker, not of communication between speakers. This firm denial of the relevance of the social dimension makes language a purely internal affair; everything comes down not to what people do in fact say but to what they can say, which usually is measured against the investigator's own intuitions about what is and what is not grammatical.

Sentences thus qualify as either grammatical (e.g., *We regretted his leaving*) or ungrammatical (e.g., **We persuaded his leaving*). The asterisk marks a sequence of words that does not pass muster grammatically in the investigator's self-interrogation. Such sequences may or may not be meaningless. The issues raised here are beyond the scope of a survey of the discipline, but the reader should be aware that the competence/performance distinction is quite controversial, as is the denial of recorded utterances as a source of relevant data.

CORPUS LINGUISTICS

One reason for a reliance on intuition is that the database is unproblematic. In most sciences the process of gathering data is tightly controlled and subject to many independent checks. The data drawn from intuition are not subject to such scrutiny. Consequently, conventional linguists are free to spend their time composing theories. Indeed, to a degree inconceivable in most sciences, data gathering and theory building are blurred into a single operation. As long as intuition was the only source of data, this procedure was acceptable. The invention of large electronic storage, especially the CD and the Internet (which could be described as the corpus's natural habitat), together with high-speed search software, changed this situation and led in the 1990s to a new subdiscipline of linguistics known as corpus linguistics.

The term *corpus* (its plural is *corpora*) refers to a collection of texts of various kinds. The texts may be randomly chosen, with an emphasis on size, or they may be selected by genre, period, or some other criterion. The associated search software typically yields a concordance, in which the target string appears in all the contexts found for it in the corpus. Concordances are not themselves new, of course; concordances for the Bible, the works of Shakespeare, and other texts were compiled by hand in the nineteenth century. An example of a large corpus is COBUILD, standing for Collins–Birmingham University International Language Database, which includes in its 200 million words eleven subcorpora with

FIG. 3

~

Occurrences of *deathly* in a trial using COBUILD, to find the word's collocations.

Keitel, with his camera, to tail a deathly ill human. His third film set in
no strength left and my face turned deathly pale and I was helpless. Now if
terrify you that you know you look deathly sick and would fall to the ground
Roses. "I Think You're Cool" is a deathly accurate take on the Axl whine
except in repose, when she looked deathly ill. Once, even, late on an
aren't. The festival president, a deathly pale high-caste man in red-and-
softly. Mrs. Madrigal looked deathly ill. "Are you thinking what I'm
and beans—of which my mother was deathly afraid because of botulism and
coming here. I know that you are deathly sick; and yet, Sick as you
You are sick, Creon! You are deathly sick! Creon: As you say:
is the reason Bernadette turned deathly pale, her lips and cheeks
something was wrong. The theatre was deathly silent. Then Nicol simply

such rubrics as spoken texts, books, popular newspapers, and learned publications. In a trial with COBUILD, the word *deathly* was elicited to find its collocations, the families of other words whose company it keeps (fig. 3).

Each occurrence of *deathly* appears in the middle of a single line of text, which can be expanded to five lines if needed. The lines in the output are numbered (not shown here), so that if the entire context is needed, the location of each item in the text of the corpus can be recovered. It can be seen from this example that:

The word *deathly* collocates with *ill* (3), *sick* (3), *pale* (3), and *afraid* (1), words suggesting fear and infirmity.

Although there are only twelve lines of data, the linking verbs *be* (five occurrences), *look* (three occurrences), and *turn* (two occurrences) account for ten of the verbs. This finding suggests that there is a family of formulas (fixed expressions) parallel to *turn deathly pale*. The study of such fixed expressions is an important direction in corpus linguistics; some would go so far as to say that a language is nothing but a vast store of these expressions.

A part-of-speech problem arises: *deathly* appears to be an adverb modifying the adjectives *ill*, *pale*, *sick*, and so on, and to be parallel in formation to *incredibly* and *awfully*, where the suffix *-ly* has been added to the adjectives *incredible* and *awful*. The problem is that the stem *death-* is

not an adjective but a noun. If you consulted only your intuition, you would be inclined to say that when *-ly* is added to a noun, the result is not an adverb but an adjective (*queenly*, *kingly*, *friendly*, etc.).

Corpus linguists frequently offer this kind of challenge to those who rely on imagined language rather than examples taken from usage. For an enlightening and readable discussion, see Michael Stubbs's *Text and Corpus Analysis: Computer-Assisted Studies of Language and Culture*.

Examples of more-specialized corpora are the Santa Barbara Corpus of Spoken American English (Du Bois, *Santa Barbara Corpus*) and the Corpus of Spoken Professional American English (Barlow). Transcriptions of spoken texts in such corpora range from closely detailed ones, such as the Santa Barbara Corpus, to normal orthography, with minimal attention to pauses, comparable to the way talk is represented in a novel, such as the spoken parts of COBUILD. The following extract from the Santa Barbara Corpus gives an idea of its content and transcriptional style:

13.25 14.05	KATHY:	.. Juice in the morning,
14.05 14.75		.. makes you sick?
14.75 16.50		. . . You know [it gets me too].
15.42 17.67	CAROLYN:	[You know what's good is] .. hibiscus cooler.

17.67 18.82		. . . <P That stuff is great.
18.82 20.37	KATHY:	Maybe it doesn't have as much s[ugar in it.
19.97 21.02	CAROLYN:	[Stuff is P> so good].
20.27 22.30	KATHY:	But .. or][2ange juice has so much su2]gar in it.
21.02 22.00	PAM:	[2X XX XX2].
22.30 22.95	WARREN:	.. It's okay,
22.95 23.45		I used this one.
23.45 23.95	CAROLYN:	[It does (Hx)]?
23.50 23.95	SHARON:	[!Cooper],
23.95 25.35		<L2 Lle[2nar L2> .. is to fill2]?
24.28 26.38	KATHY:	[2Just .. makes me feel like I2] ate a candy bar.

Each line is a TCU. The numbers column at the left gives the time in seconds of each interactions. It illustrates an approach taken to a major technical problem in transcription: how to represent simultaneous utterances. Thus Sharon's utterance *"llenar* is to fill" lasts from 23.95 to 25.35 seconds into the recording, and the overlapping utterance by Kathy "Just makes me feel like I ate a candy bar" lasts from 24.28 to 26.38, giving 1.07 seconds of overlap, from 24.28 to 25.35. Square brackets in the text likewise identify overlapping utterances, which may involve not just two but several speakers, sometimes (as here) engaged in separate dialogues. Simply sorting out and comprehending simultaneous utterances and assigning them to the right speakers on the basis of a purely audio recording can be a formidable task for the transcriber. A few more of the many transcriptional conventions used in the Santa Barbara Corpus also appear in this excerpt. The notation L2 in <L2Llenar L2> identifies *"llenar"* as a foreign language form. Utterances that could not be heard distinctly enough to be transcribed are represented with Xs. Dots signify pauses of various lengths. The exclamation point marks a proper name that has been altered in the text and obscured in the audio recording so as to protect the speaker's identity. A sharp exhalation of breath is represented with (Hx). Matching overlaps are indicated with a number beside a square bracket ([2ange juice and [2Just .. makes). Voice qualities are indicated by < > with various letters at each end of the angled brackets; for example, <P . . . P> encloses an utterance spoken softly ("piano"). Transcription is a difficult but important skill and is increasingly considered an indispensable part of a linguist's training. In the first decade of the twenty-first century, video recording, with its even more complex transcriptional demands, was moving out of the experimental stage.

The application of a text like the Santa Barbara Corpus in conversational analysis is clear: the precise phonetic and timing details allow the mechanisms of turn taking to be studied reliably. For example, in the above excerpt, Carolyn's "It does?" is seen by the timing to be a reaction to Kathy's "But orange juice has so much sugar in it," even though three TCUs intervene in the transcript. The exhalation Hx following Carolyn's "It does?" signals the end of a turn.

An important line of research in recent years has been the search for sources of grammar in interactions (see the excellent survey of this research in Ochs, Schegloff, and Thompson). We have seen that standard theories of grammar either refrain altogether from seeking explanations outside structure or appeal to presumed cognitive mechanisms that do not require an actual interaction between two or more speakers. By contrast, conversation analysis sees grammar as the product of an interaction. A starting point was the recognition that the sentence of written discourse could not be simply transferred without further ado to the spoken language.

Conversation analysis sees grammar as the product of an interaction.

It has long been recognized that natural conversational speech proceeds not in well-formed sentences but in short bursts, each lasting two or three seconds. The name for these short utterances has varied over the years according to the criteria used to define them. They have been called intonation units, breath units, idea units, thought units, turn constructional units, and, more recently, transition-relevant places. While each of these terms refers to something a little different and results in a slightly different emphasis, the basic idea is the same. Discourse proceeds by short jumps separated by hesitations that Chafe, in a lecture, called perches, the analogy being to a sparrow that flies from branch to branch, settling briefly at each point. The idea unit (to choose, arbitrarily, one of the terms) roughly matches the clause of standard structural linguistics, a minimal sequence having a meaning and a syntactic structure. Could it be that the clause of standard linguistics and school grammar is simply the transfer to the written language of a unit that is imposed on natural speech through physiology (breath control) and cognition (short-term storage)?

One indication of this equation was found in an important feature shared by the clause and the idea unit: a strong discourse tendency to deliver significant pieces of information one at a time. In theory, clauses like the following—typical of many such examples in published work—are possible: *Scully did not show the photo to Mulder at the office yesterday.* But in practice both speakers and writers tend to formulate utterances so that only one new item occurs in each clause (see Pawley and Syder for a recent discussion). The clause just cited has too much in it to be authentic: four nouns, a verb, and a new-information adverb. It requires unpacking. More natural is the technique of introducing each piece of significant information in a separate unit, as in the following excerpt from the Santa Barbara Corpus:

230.20 231.43	MARCI:	. . . Myra's your friend,
231.43 231.90		[right]?
231.43 231.85	KENDRA:	[Mhm].
231.90 235.15	MARCI:	.. I thought she told me .. at .. somebody's shower.
235.15 236.10		.. Becky's shower—
236.10 236.60		.. No.
236.60 238.80		.. Somebody's shower at Becky's house.
238.80 239.35	X:	(H)

239.35 242.65	MARCI:	. . . That she was pregnant again.
242.65 244.35		. . . Like two weeks pregnant.
244.35 244.68	KENDRA:	.. [No,
244.53 245.00	MARCI:	[<X Or one X>]—
244.68 245.40	KENDRA:	that was] Trish.
245.40 246.73	MARCI:	.. That was Tr=ish[2=.
246.52 246.90	KENDRA:	[2Mhm2].
246.73 247.18	MARCI:	O2]kay.
247.18		So we already knew Trish was preg[nant].

It can be seen that the information is dribbled in a bit at a time, each piece in its own TCU: somebody's *shower*, *Becky's* shower, somebody's shower at Becky's *house*, that she was *pregnant* again, like *two weeks* pregnant. Moreover, significant information is typically introduced in nouns and prepositional phrases, with pronouns (*she*, *somebody's*) glossing over less important information and functioning to provide continuity between successive utterances.

Such observations bear on one of the most significant projects of recent linguistic studies of spoken discourse, the attempt to explain how grammar comes about. Most linguists take for granted a sharp separation between facts of discourse and facts of grammar, seeing grammar as the a priori basis on which utterances are given consistent form. But for some, this order of priorities—first grammar, then discourse—is the wrong one. Grammar, some argue, is the result of historical processes that are rooted in everyday usage. It seems to follow that grammar should not be segregated from usage but instead understood as always motivated by usage.

The project of seeking the motivations for grammar in usage has been understood in different ways. One of them, the cognitive grammar approach, sees stable mental structures (thought) as mediating between usage and grammar. Because these structures are held to reside more or less permanently in the head of the speaker, linguists of this school see no reason to study actual discourse; they are content to assert that cognitive structures necessarily reflect usage.

Cognitive linguistics in this style is therefore part of the "can say" rather than the "do say" movement, seeing the goal of linguistics as being to explicate what speakers *can* in theory say rather than what they in practice *do* say. It emphasizes "the crucial role of conceptualization in social interaction" and analyzes language "in terms of more basic systems and abilities (e.g., perception, attention, categorization)" (Langacker, "Conceptualization" 1). Recent surveys of some of the issues are found in Langacker's "Conceptualization" and *Concept, Image, and Symbol.*

Many in the cognitive grammar movement describe their project as usage-based grammar. Yet for the most part cognitive grammar is not usage-based in the sense of studying usage for direct explanations of grammatical structure. (Two of the papers in an edited volume with the title *Usage-Based Models of Language* [Barlow and Kemmer], by Sidney Lamb and by Langacker, contain not one item of data drawn from usage!) But starting in the 1980s and increasingly in the 1990s, linguists turned their attention to the relation between discourse and grammar with a view to discovering the sources of grammatical structure in common usage.

One well-known study of a language from this perspective was John Du Bois's 1987 study "The Discourse Basis of Ergativity," based on discourse data from the Maya language Sacapultec. Du Bois looked at Sacapultec discourses, especially sentences that had both an agent and an object, such as *The boys stole the pears.* A statistical count of agents and objects in the text revealed an interesting asymmetry: agents were almost always pronouns, while nouns were more likely to occur in the object position. Nouns also often occurred as subject of a verb that had no object, as in *The boys were sleeping.* It seemed that the agent of a clause that had an object was almost always a pronoun. Du Bois referred to this distribution as the preferred argument structure. It explained a feature of the grammar of Sacapultec, that nouns have a special grammatical case precisely when they are not agents. Furthermore, this kind of case marking (known as the absolutive case) is by no means a peculiarity of an obscure Indian language of Guatemala; it is widespread in the world's languages.[4]

Du Bois's study of Sacapultec was typical of a number of studies in the 1980s that linked together discourse, grammatical structure, and linguistic typology. This kind of work gave a significant impetus to a major project of functionalism in the 1990s, the search for discourse motivations for grammatical structure.

Du Bois's studies of the statistical relation between grammatical structure and discourse usage were part of a movement that gained prominence in the 1990s, attention to frequency. Grammar began to be seen by many as probabilistic rather than purely categorical. The claims made by formalists of precision and scientificity were, in this view, sustainable only so long as data were drawn from intuition, where a great deal of unconscious preediting had taken place, or from edited written texts. Spoken texts pointed to a more gradated and variable picture of grammar. This stochastic trend went hand in hand with the increasing sophistication of electronic corpora and techniques of transcription. Frequency came into its own as an important methodological and theoretical factor in linguistics, and in the 1990s it was routinely used by most functionalists (see the articles in Bybee and Hopper). Much of this work was along the lines of Du Bois's study of case marking in Sacapultec: the objective was to show that commonly described structural types in language emerged through aggregation, as a natural result of discourse. This kind of investigation, by looking at the motivations for forms and their discourse distributions, ran counter to the common assumption of formal linguists that grammatical constructions were either purely optional or fully categorical—that is, either random or one hundred percent implemented. Rather, the picture was one of preferences and movement toward structure. Consider the case of English *I think*, discussed by Sandra Thompson and Anthony Mulac. From a sentence-level perspective it might seem that *I think that the game is over* and *I think the game is over* are identical, that adding *that* after *I think* is simply a randomly chosen option of the speaker. Thompson and Mulac showed that in casual spoken discourse these are in fact two different constructions: the version without *that* is evidential, that is, a construction that quantifies the degree of certainty with which something is asserted. (In a number of languages the evidential is a verbal category that is obligatory in every statement.) *I think* is different not only from *I think that* but also from *you think*, *he thinks*, and so on. The same is true of *I guess*. The text study of Thompson and Mulac showed that *I think* is followed by *that* only 9% of the time, and *I guess* only 1% of the time. Moreover, the verbs *think* and *guess* are construed 95% of the time with the first-person subject *I*. This kind of study places the notion of grammar as a fixed code in a new light; it shows, as Thompson and Mulac note, a pattern of usage becoming a pattern of structure. It is in line with the proposal that I made (see Hopper, "Emergent Grammar" [1987] and "Emergent Grammar" [1988]) that grammar should be seen not as something rigid and ready-made out of which discourses are composed but as the residue of usage, which therefore was in constant reformation by its speakers. This emergent-grammar postulate had some influence among functionalists in the 1990s.

A similar, though not identical, view of linguistic structure was being developed at this time by Joan Bybee, whose work in the 1990s looked to text frequency as a direct motivator of emergent structure. Frequent collocations such as *we'll*, *he'd* lead to a fixing of habitual sequences as grammar. Languages consist of arrays of such sequences, some more deeply embedded in history than others. Paths of change, such as a verb of wishing that becomes a future tense (e.g., the English *will*), can be identified across many languages (Bybee, Perkins, and Pagliuca).

COMPARATIVE, TYPOLOGICAL, AND
HISTORICAL LINGUISTICS

The subdisciplines of linguistics that deal with historical relations among languages and with the study of change were also vigorous in the

> **The comparative field was dominated by an acrimonious debate between lumpers and splitters.**

1990s. Like much of linguistics during the past decade or so, these fields responded to the emerging global perspectives on language that characterized the latter half of the twentieth century, which manifested themselves as an interest in language universals, in the results of fieldwork in out-of-the-way languages, and in wider historical relations among language families.

The comparative field was dominated by an acrimonious debate between lumpers and splitters. The lumpers, who sometimes called themselves Long Rangers, wished to reduce the very large number of known human language families to a smaller number of families that united what had previously been recognized as separate families or isolates (an isolate is an orphan language that has no known historical affinities). Joseph Greenberg, who made linguistic headlines in the 1980s by arguing that all the Native languages of North America could be subsumed under just three families (Eskimo, Amerindian, and Na-Dene), turned his attention to Indo-European. When he died in 2002 (lamenting in his final weeks, some say, that he had not been able to reconstruct Proto-World), he had published two volumes on the lexicon and grammar of what he called the Eurasiatic language family (*Indo-European . . . Grammar* and *Indo-European . . . Lexicon*). He included in this macrofamily Indo-European, Uralic, Altaic, Japanese, Ainu, Korean, and Eskimo. His work had a counterpart of sorts in an older but still ongoing comparative project started by the Russians, known as the Nostratic theory. The Nostraticists (who do not agree among themselves which languages are members of this family) garnered some public attention in the 1990s for their dramatic claim to have reconstructed human language as it was twenty-five millennia ago.

The splitters were hard-line methodologists, raised on the ideal of strict comparison supported by reference to documented sound changes. They pointed out that the macrofamilies being proposed were not based on the rigorous point-by-point reconstruction of earlier forms, as required by standard methodology, but on look-alikes, words bearing only a superficial similarity. The lumpers' response (see Greenberg, "Concept") has generally been twofold. First, they argue that the methodology of comparative linguistics is based on a two-hundred-year experience with a single language family, Indo-European, that is of relatively shallow time depth and richly supported by ancient texts; it is therefore unrealistic to expect similar results from less well documented language families. Second, if one has enough examples, mere look-alikes, given consistent correspondences among the sounds of the words, build up to a convincing picture that compensates for the lack of the kind of minutely analyzed evidence available in Indo-European. The implication by Greenberg that decades of scholarship in Amerindian linguistic classification was based on tenuous data inflamed a number of specialists in this field, and the quarrel became extremely bitter in the 1990s, with accusations of bias on the part of publishers and sloppy scholarship on the part of certain authors flying around. Lyle Campbell's *American Indian Languages* (2000), besides offering a highly regarded survey of the state of the art in Native American linguistics, presented in detail the case against Greenberg's classification.

Linguistic typology was an assiduously pursued subdiscipline in the 1990s. The Association for Linguistic Typology was founded in 1994, and the association's journal, *Linguistic Typology*, was launched in 1997. The proposal that there are types of language has been around for a long time (often packaged with ideas about superior and inferior languages—and their speakers), but it came into its own in the 1960s with the work of Greenberg.

I have already discussed Greenberg's study of word order (Greenberg, "Some Universals"), which shows the existence of three broad types of language according to the position of the verb with respect to the subject and object (VSO, SVO, and SOV). In the 1990s the search for types of language had moved from a search for universals to a more realistic search for cross-linguistic tendencies and recurrent features.

Many typological studies in the 1990s were small-scale and local, dealing with such topics as verbal morphology. Often the authors presented an analysis of an unusual linguistic phenomenon in a single language with some sort of reference to parallels in other languages.

Grammatical constructions in individual languages are analyzed always with an eye on comparable structures in other languages. One feature of 1990s typological studies has been an almost geometric increase in the quantity and quality of linguistic data.[5] This burgeoning of descriptions of obscure languages was due in part to perestroika, which opened up little known research areas in the Eurasian continent to Western linguists and also made available significant research already done by Russian linguists. Yet by and large typology was aloof from the important developments in discourse studies, and its database remained confined to simple isolated sentences.

Linguistics in the 1990s: An Overview

The 1990s saw important developments in the academic organization of linguistics. One of these was a weakening of American hegemony. Largely because of the Chomsky wave in the 1960s and 1970s, the United States had come to be seen as far ahead of the rest of the world in linguistic theory and methodology. Its influence is still strong in Europe and elsewhere. But if generativism in Europe is still derivative of American thought, in the areas of grammaticalization, typology, cognitive grammar, and functionalism generally the European and Australian presence expanded throughout the 1980s, and by the 1990s the standard east-to-west direction of transatlantic academic pilgrimages had been well-nigh reversed. Well-financed research projects on the languages of Europe and on linguistic typology, applied linguistics, and cognitive linguistics spawned numerous workshops and conferences in lovely old cities (and some not-so-lovely new ones). In Australia the first serious endeavor to describe its rapidly dying native languages was undertaken in the 1960s by Robert Dixon. By the 1990s Australia had planted a disproportionately influential footprint on the worldwide field of linguistic theory and descriptive practice and a major center for both Aboriginal and Pacific linguistics and linguistic typology. In the 1990s also the Max Planck Institutes in Nijmegen (psycholinguistics) and Leipzig (evolutionary anthropology) attracted funding and full-time research scholars, largely in the areas of cross-linguistic analysis, typology, and cognitive linguistics. Japanese linguists also made important contributions in all subdisciplines of linguistics in the 1990s.

Integrational Linguistics

We expect that any academic field will be contested. But linguistics may be unique in that there are those within it who dispute its very legitimacy as a discipline. During the 1980s and 1990s a small but perceptive and articulate group of scholars, following the lead of Roy Harris, who had retired from his chair at Oxford in the 1980s, turned a withering gaze on the entire project of linguistics as it was generally practiced. Harris objects that we do not communicate through reference to prior fixed abstract forms; rather, "we create language as we go, both as individuals and as communities, just as we create our social structures, and our forms of artistic expression, our moral values, and everything else in the great complex we call civilization." He calls for a movement "away from a study based on the hypothesis of fixed monolithic structures called 'languages' which somehow exist independently of whether or how they are brought into use," and in its place he appeals for

> a science in which a language is envisaged, not as something which exists as a system over and above the communication situations in which it is manifested, but as a cumulative product of such situations which can be variously exploited to provide a basis for their subsequent renewal.
> ("Communication" 149–50)

It was a direct challenge to basic assumptions of the sort pronounced by Victoria Fromkin as cited in the opening paragraph of this article: the fixed code; the uniformity of linguistic knowledge; a language as a distinct, mentally represented system. At first this confrontation was deconstructive, questioning the validity of the enterprise of classifying and analyzing utterances. The flavor of the integrationist critique is nicely captured in Nigel Love's witty and devastating review of Neil V. Smith's *The Twitter Machine*, a Chomsky-worshiping popularization of linguistics that enjoyed some currency at this time.

During the 1990s Harris developed a program that he called integrationism or integrational linguistics. Mainstream linguistics, he maintained, was segregational in its ideology, in that it identified language as an entity distinct from other aspects of the communicative situation. The goal of integrationism is to develop an account of language in which speech is merged with other things happening in communication. The intellectual posture of the integrationists is much influenced by the later Ludwig Wittgenstein: they view language as something external that happens among speakers rather than as an invisible internal mechanism. In practice much of integrationist scholarship is an erudite and literate celebration of freedom from the idea of a language as a fixed mental code. It shows the implications of this liberation for the study of such topics as individual motivations, variation, stylistics, standards, and national languages. The compilation *Integrational Linguistics*, edited by Roy Harris and George Wolf, contains representative articles, each with an introduction by the editors. Michael Toolan's *Total Speech* provides a wide-ranging survey of the ideas surrounding the integrationalist movement.

~

We started with a statement by a leading linguist written in 1985 proclaiming linguistics as what looked like a pre-Copernican science; a central sphere of language structure around which orbited an unnumbered assortment of subordinate spheres with labels like "cognition," "semantics," and "pragmatics," each of which was accessible or available to the speaker on demand. No doubt for many linguists this picture is not merely adequate but a necessary strategy for approaching the enormous complexity of human communication through speech. But for others it was a constraining image. In the 1990s, serious scholars strove to free themselves from it. The tensions these movements have engendered continue to make linguistics a thrilling and engrossing discipline.

NOTES

The assistance of Hilary Franklin and Ludmila Selemeneva, graduate students at Carnegie Mellon, is gratefully acknowledged.

1. The format presented here is standard in linguistics. The foreign language sentence is written out on line 1, here in italics; line 2 is a word-by-word gloss; and line 3 is an equivalent English translation.

2. The relevance of new and old information to language structure was by no means a fresh discovery, having been studied quite intensively by many linguists in the 1930s and 1940s. The novelty lay in its integration with language universals and the syntactic typology developed by Greenberg. A survey of the present kind, which focuses on developments in the 1990s, perforce glosses over many important achievements by earlier linguists.

3. The innateness of language properly refers to a very specific hypothesis, namely, that the principles of linguistic structure (i.e., of abstract grammar) are genetically prescribed. It does not mean that only humans have the unique combination of faculties that make language possible (which probably all linguists would subscribe to). For a full discussion of the issues involved, see Geoffrey Sampson's *"Language Instinct" Debate*.

4. Languages that manifest a special case for the subject of the transitive verb are known as ergative languages, and the case in question is called the ergative case. For some accessible discussions, see Comrie.

5. The index to Finegan's introductory textbook of linguistics, *Language: Its Structure and Use*, references over 350 languages.

WORKS CITED AND SUGGESTIONS FOR FURTHER READING

Aitchison, Jean. *Language Change: Progress or Decay?* 3rd ed. Cambridge: Cambridge UP, 2001.

Archangeli, Diana. "Optimality Theory: An Introduction to Linguistics in the 1990s." *Optimality Theory: An Overview.* Ed. Archangeli and D. T. Langendoen. Cambridge: Blackwell, 1997. 1–32.

Barlow, Michael. *Corpus of Spoken Professional American English.* Houston: Athelstan, 1998.

Barlow, Michael, and Suzanne Kemmer, eds. *Usage-Based Models of Language.* Stanford: Center for the Study of Lang. and Information, 2001.

Berlin, Brent, and Paul Kay. *Basic Color Terms: Their Universality and Evolution.* Berkeley: U of California P, 1969.

Bybee, Joan, and Paul Hopper, eds. *Frequency and the Emergence of Linguistic Structure.* Typological Studies in Lang. 45. Amsterdam: Benjamins, 2001.

Bybee, Joan, Revere Perkins, and William Pagliuca. *The Evolution of Grammar: Tense, Aspect, and Modality in the Languages of the World.* Chicago: U of Chicago P, 1994.

Campbell, Lyle. *American Indian Languages: The Historical Linguistics of Native America.* Oxford: Oxford UP, 2000.

Chafe, Wallace, and Jane Danielewicz. "Properties of Spoken and Written Language." *Comprehending Oral and Written Language.* Ed. R. Horowitz and S. J. Samuels. New York: Academic, 1987. 83–113.

Chomsky, Noam. *The Minimalist Program.* Cambridge: MIT P, 1995.

———. "A Minimalist Program for Linguistic Theory." *The View from Building 20.* Ed. K. Hale and S. J. Keyser. Cambridge: MIT P, 1993. 1–52.

———. *New Horizons in the Study of Language and the Mind.* Cambridge: Cambridge UP, 2000.

Comrie, Bernard. *Language Universals and Linguistic Typology.* 2nd ed. Oxford: Blackwell, 1989.

Du Bois, John W. "The Discourse Basis of Ergativity." *Language* 63 (1987): 805–55.

———. *The Santa Barbara Corpus of Spoken American English.* CD-ROM. Philadelphia: Linguistic Data Consortium, 2000.

Du Bois, John W., Stephan Schuetze-Coburn, Danae Paolino, and Susanna Cumming. "Outline of Discourse Transcription." *Talking Data: Transcription and Coding in Discourse.* Ed. Jane A. Edwards and Martin D. Lampert. Hillsdale: Erlbaum, 1993. 45–89.

Fairclough, Norman. *Critical Discourse Analysis: The Critical Study of Language.* London: Longman, 1995.

Fairclough, Norman, and Ruth Wodak. "Critical Discourse Analysis." *Discourse as Social Interaction.* Ed. Teun van Dijk. London: Sage, 1997. 258–84.

Finegan, Edward. *Language: Its Structure and Use.* 2nd ed. Fort Worth: Harcourt, 1994.

Fromkin, Victoria. "Major Trends in Research: Twenty-two Leading Scholars Report on Their Fields: Linguistics." *Chronicle of Higher Education* 4 Sept. 1985: 12–13.

Greenberg, Joseph H. "The Concept of Proof in Genetic Linguistics." *Reconstructing Grammar: Comparative*

Linguistics and Grammaticalization. Typological Studies in Lang. 43. Ed. Spike Gildea. Amsterdam: Benjamins, 2000. 161–76.

———. *Indo-European and Its Closest Relatives: The Eurasiatic Language Family: Grammar.* Stanford: Stanford UP, 2000.

———. *Indo-European and Its Closest Relatives: The Eurasiatic Language Family: Lexicon.* Stanford: Stanford UP, 2002.

———. "Some Universals of Language with Particular Reference to the Order of Meaningful Elements." *Universals of Language.* 2nd ed. Ed. Greenberg. Cambridge: MIT P, 1966. 73–113.

Halliday, M. A. K. *Introduction to Functional Grammar.* 2nd ed. London: Arnold, 1994.

Harris, Roy. "Communication and Language." Love, *Foundations* 136–50.

———. *The Language Myth.* London: Duckworth, 1981.

Harris, Roy, and George Wolf. *Integrational Linguistics: A First Reader.* Language and Communication Lib. 18. Oxford: Elsevier, 1998.

Heine, Bernd, and Tania Kuteva. *World Lexicon of Grammaticalization.* Cambridge: Cambridge UP, 2002.

Hopper, Paul J. "Emergent Grammar." *Proceedings of the Thirteenth Annual Meeting of the Berkeley Linguistics Society.* Vol. 13. Berkeley: U of California P, 1987. 139–57.

———. "Emergent Grammar and the *A Priori* Grammar Postulate." *Linguistics in Context: Connecting Observation and Understanding.* Collected General Lectures from the 1985 LSA Linguistics Inst., Georgetown U. Ed. D. Tannen. Englewood Cliffs: Ablex, 1988. 117–34.

Hopper, Paul J., and Sandra Thompson. Introduction. *Studies in Transitivity.* Syntax and Semantics 15. Ed. Hopper and Thompson. New York: Academic, 1982. 1–5.

Hopper, Paul J., and Elizabeth Traugott. *Grammaticalization.* Cambridge Textbooks in Linguistics. 2nd ed. Cambridge: Cambridge UP, 2003.

Lakoff, George, and Mark Johnson. *Women, Fire, and Dangerous Things: What Categories Reveal about the Mind.* Chicago: U of Chicago P, 1987.

Langacker, Ronald W. *Concept, Image, and Symbol: The Cognitive Basis of Grammar.* Berlin: Mouton de Gruyter, 1990.

———. "Conceptualization, Symbolization, and Grammar." *The New Psychology of Language: Cognitive and Functional Approaches to Language Structure.* Ed. Michael Tomasello. Mahwah: Erlbaum, 1998. 1–39.

———. *Foundations of Cognitive Grammar: Volume I: Theoretical Prerequisites.* Stanford: Stanford UP, 1987.

The LDC Corpus Catalog. Linguistic Data Consortium, U of Pennsylvania. 1992–2004. 16 Jan. 2005. 7 June 2006 <http://www.ldc.upenn.edu/Catalog/index.jsp>.

Li, Charles N., ed. *Subject and Topic.* London: Academic, 1975.

———, ed. *Word Order and Word Order Change.* Austin: U of Texas P, 1974.

Linell, Per. *The Written Language Bias in Linguistics.* London: Routledge, 2005.

Love, Nigel, ed. *The Foundations of Linguistic Theory: Selected Writings of Roy Harris.* London: Routledge, 1990.

———. Rev. of *The Twitter Machine,* by Neil Smith. *Journal of Literary Semantics* 19 (1990): 193–97.

McNeill, Noriko. "Colour and Colour Terminology." *Journal of Linguistics* 8 (1972): 21–33.

Newmeyer, Frederick. *Language Forms and Language Function.* Cambridge: MIT P, 1998.

Noonan, Mickey. "Complementation." *Language Typology and Syntactic Description.* Vol. 3. Ed. Tim Shopen. Cambridge: Cambridge UP, 1985. 42–140.

Ochs, Elinor, Emanuel A. Schegloff, and Sandra A. Thompson, eds. *Interaction and Grammar.* Studies in Interactional Sociolinguistics 13. Cambridge: Cambridge UP, 1996.

———. Introduction. Ochs, Schegloff, and Thompson, *Interaction* 1–51.

Ong, Walter. *Orality and Literacy: The Technologizing of the Word.* London: Routledge, 1982.

Pawley, Andrew, and Frances Syder. "The One Clause at a Time Hypothesis." *Perspectives on Fluency.* Ed. Heidi Riggenbach. Ann Arbor: U of Michigan P, 2000. 163–99.

Pinker, Steven. *The Language Instinct: The New Science of Language and Mind.* New York: Morrow, 1994.

Pomerantz, Anita, and B. J. Fehr. "Conversation Analysis: An Approach to the Study of Social Action as Sense-Making Practices." *Discourse as Social Interaction.* Ed. Teun van Dijk. London: Sage, 1997. 64–91.

Rosch, Eleanor. "On the Internal Structure of Perceptual and Semantic Categories." *Cognitive Psychology* 7 (1975): 573–605.

Sampson, Geoffrey. *Educating Eve: The "Language Instinct" Debate.* London: Cassell, 1997.

———. *The "Language Instinct" Debate.* New York: Continuum, 2005.

Saussure, Ferdinand de. *Course in General Linguistics.* Trans. and ed. Roy Harris. La Salle: Open Court, 1986. Trans. of *Cours de linguistique générale,* 2nd ed., 1922.

Schegloff, Emanuel. "Turn Organization: One Intersection of Grammar and Interaction." Ochs, Schegloff, and Thompson, *Interaction* 52–133.

Simone, Raffaele, ed. *Iconicity in Language.* Current Issues in Linguistic Theory 110. Amsterdam: Benjamins, 1995.

Stubbs, Michael. *Text and Corpus Analysis: Computer-Assisted Studies of Language and Culture.* Language in Soc. 23. Oxford: Blackwell, 1996.

Sweetser, Eve. *From Etymology to Pragmatics; Metaphorical and Cultural Aspects of Semantic Structure.* Cambridge Studies in Linguistics. Cambridge: Cambridge UP, 1990.

Talmy, Leonard. "The Relation of Grammar to Cognition." *Topics in Cognitive Linguistics*. Ed. B. Rudzka-Ostyn. Amsterdam: Benjamins, 1988. 165–205.

Thompson, Sandra, and Anthony Mulac. "A Quantitative Perspective on the Grammaticization of Epistemic Parentheticals in English." *Grammaticalization*. Vol. 2. Ed. Elizabeth Traugott and Bernd Heine. Amsterdam: Benjamins, 1991. 313–39.

Toolan, Michael. *Total Speech: An Integrational Linguistic Approach to Language*. Durham: Duke UP, 1996.

Trask, R. Larry. *Historical Linguistics*. New York: St. Martin's, 1996.

Traugott, Elizabeth. "Subjectification in Grammaticalization." *Subjectivity and Subjectivisation in Language*. Ed. Dieter Stein and Susan Wright. Cambridge: Cambridge UP, 1995. 31–54.

Turner, Mark, and Gilles Fauconnier. "Conceptual Integration and Formal Expression." *Metaphor and Symbolic Activity* 10 (1995): 183–204.

Language Acquisition and Language Learning

HEIDI BYRNES

FRAMING THE TOPIC ANEW

When, in 1992, "Language Acquisition and Language Learning" appeared for the first time in the lineup of essays that circumscribed scholarship in modern languages and literatures, Claire Kramsch presented the topic by strongly linking it to teaching. Assuming that most readers were either seeking or already following a career focused on linguistic or literary scholarship, she argued that knowledge about how people learn a language as the knowledge is presented in the fields of linguistics, psychology, sociology, and education would enable scholars to understand better something they also do, namely, teach a language.

As I revisit the topic, I share her assumption. However, in the intervening time the nature of that knowledge and its applicability to language learning and teaching have become considerably more expansive, considerably more sophisticated and thus less transparent, and also considerably more contested. The concluding reflections by the guest editor Lourdes Ortega in a recent special issue of the *Modern Language Journal* on research dimensions of instructed second language acquisition (SLA) corroborate that assessment. Her proposal of three principles that should guide further discussion appears merely

to assert the commonsensical: the value of research is to be judged by its social utility; value-free research is impossible; epistemological diversity is a good thing (430). And yet, in foregrounding social and ethical dimensions for SLA research and reflecting on how they might reposition both research and praxes in teaching and learning second languages, Ortega provides both a critical summary of recent developments and a challenging proposal for the future.

At issue are problems that anyone has encountered who ever learned a foreign language or endeavored to teach others how to learn one. How do we relate innate abilities of human beings, members of the only languaging species, to environmental, particularly instructional influences? How do individual and social factors help explain the observable variation in accomplishing language learning in both first (L1) and second (L2) languages? How is language as a formal system related to language as a flexible meaning-making system that resides within and shapes cultural contexts? How are we to imagine the relation between language and culture, between knowing and social being, and how does a classroom, perhaps located in a totally different cultural context, negotiate that relation? Furthermore, what of stability in language, what of change? What conceptual constructs are available to help us understand the nature of tutored language learning? How might we organize language education in such a fashion as to make instructed language learning more efficient, more effective, and ultimately more successful, particularly for adult learners? Finally, what aspects of language learning are amenable to generalized statements in what we consider to be rigorous scientific inquiry, and what aspects fundamentally elude such abstraction and might better be understood as socially embedded choices by individual language users in a particular communicative context of situation that, in turn, resides in a larger context of culture?

In sum, the central question is, What does it mean to become and be a competent user of a language and, more specifically, of a second or foreign language, especially for adult learners? In this overview, I attempt to answer this question through two interrelated arguments. I first look at theoretical approaches in terms of their influence on current thinking about language learning. I hasten to add that, in using the term *theory*, I am less concerned with the specifics of a particular theory of language and more interested in conveying the underlying assumptions that drive major approaches to capturing the nature of language. Acquisitional phenomena are indisputably central to such assumptions. In that sense, nothing is more practical than theory, nor is there a dichotomy between, much less a hierarchy of, theoretical knowledge and its application or utilization.

I then explore how SLA theorizing has imagined the acquisition process in a more applied way, for L1 learning and, more extensively, instructed L2 learning. Generally the field has undergone a gradual shift from more formalist to more functionalist to more individually and psycholinguistically driven to more socially contextualized ways of understanding language, understanding human knowing and learning, and describing the relational acts of teaching and learning. For each of these approaches, and for the reality of the classroom, one attempts to

What does it mean to become and be a competent user of a language . . . ?

specify how learners' contributions in interaction with teachers' roles and stances support long-term L2 learning.

In the final section I relate those findings to evolving programmatic praxes in collegiate foreign language departments. I interpret recent developments in SLA that help overcome the unproductive structural and intellectual split that characterizes nearly all departments: between language courses and content courses. Suggestions for reading that offers additional generalist discussion and also focused treatments complete my presentation of the field of SLA.

THEORIZING THE NATURE OF LANGUAGE ACQUISITION

Nearly fifty years after their first publication, Noam Chomsky's representations regarding a scientifically rigorous approach for the study of language and the human capacity for language continue to influence much linguistic theorizing. More important, they continue to influence the way in which L1 and L2 learning are conceptualized and translated into teaching and learning praxes—despite Chomsky's often-referenced statement that insights from linguistics, before they are presumed useful for the language teacher, should be validated by language practitioners (43).

If Chomsky is right, then the contemporary situation in SLA might provide that necessary validation, for the benefit not only of practitioners but for the entire foreign language education community as it grapples with diverse discontinuities, even incongruities, in recent scholarship and practice.

Accordingly, I begin the journey by first probing the central tenets of a cognitively oriented approach to theorizing language and language acquisition generally referred to as universal grammar or UG. Thereafter, I examine current challenges to that approach, which range from minor adjustments to wholesale refutation.

The Problem of Language Learning and Solutions in Universal Grammar

As a theoretical model, UG identifies and proposes explanations for a number of language phenomena, particularly in the context of L1 acquisition. First, for the phenomenon that children learn languages in a remarkably short period of time, UG theory postulates an innate universal grammar that is characterized by specifically linguistic rather than general psychological predispositions for handling language data. Second, because children achieve this feat in a fashion that is remarkably similar across languages and is remarkably forgiving of incomplete and even flawed data—fractured syntax, false starts and disfluencies, and incoherencies of spoken language, referred to as the poverty-of-stimulus phenomenon—UG postulates a system of universal principles and parameters that place constraints on the handling or processing of the data. Third, constraints are necessary because a language system cannot be learned only by positive evidence (what can be said); negative evidence (what cannot be said) is also required. In other words, one assumes that such negative evidence is generally not provided in the language-learning environment (e.g., through caretakers) and discounts the possibility that the nonlinguistic context may provide negative evidence as a corrective for language use in comprehension and production.

UG also foregrounds the fact that language does not arrange sequences of words in simple linearity but creates groupings of words, strings, of different length, complexity, and continuity or discontinuity. These strings form constituents that are hierarchically arranged. For example, the string of words that makes up a noun phrase ("The species-specific fact of language learning . . .") contrasts with the string of words that makes up a verb phrase (". . . continues to puzzle researchers and practitioners"). In UG grammar, the competence for detecting such constituents is described in terms of logical rules that are imagined metaphorically both as mental representations and as processing mechanisms that enable acquisition of only those strings of speech or written text that are permissible in a particular language. Strong emphasis on an innate capacity, referred to as nativism, postulates a language instinct triggered by input, a position Steven Pinker has taken in his popularizing book *The Language Instinct*.

Theoretical Challenges to the UG Model

Since its first presentation and development in the 1960s and 1970s, the UG approach to language and language acquisition has been challenged on theoretical grounds and on the basis of learner data. Scholars refute in particular the formal and innatist stance of UG, which often goes hand in hand with a focus on syntax and rules, and they replace UG with various functional approaches.

FROM SYNTACTIC NATIVISM TO COGNITIVE NATIVISM

William O'Grady, a UG theorist, questions the UG assumption that a universal, innate computational structure separate from meaning provides the most appropriate description of the phenomenon of language. Replacing UG's general nativism, he proposes a "cognitive nativism" where "the entire grammar is the product of the interaction of the language acquisition device with experience; no grammatical knowledge is inborn" (58). In other words, accounting for why language is the way it is involves recognizing that the posited symbolic representations cannot exhaust themselves in purely grammatical, innate categories; they must also consider cognitive features that interact with our physical and linguistic environment.

THE CHALLENGE FROM FUNCTIONALIST APPROACHES: COGNITIVE LINGUISTICS AND COGNITIVE GRAMMAR

From outside UG theory comes a more fundamental critique, in an approach that is functionalist, not formalist cognitive—namely, cognitive linguistics. The disagreement between UG grammarians and cognitive linguists is not that one side believes in a biological basis for language while the other does not. The split is over whether "both cultural artifacts [e.g., language] and biological structures are understood primarily in terms of their functions" (Tomasello, "Introduction" xii) and, more pointedly, whether the functional quality of language is crucial to the understanding of language or merely a subsidiary aspect.

For functionalists, the symbol system of language is not operated by a mind conceived of as a logical, nonprobabilistic computational machine that carries out rules; it is, instead, an integral part of human cognition. Linguistic phenomena must therefore be grounded in what we know about general human cognitive abilities, which psychology explores from a social science perspective and philosophy from a humanities perspective. Such basic abilities of the human mind as perception, attention, and categorization must be investigated for their role in a language capacity. Similarly, salience and perspective taking, reflections of the processes of vision and attention, can be expected to affect the acquisition of both general and specific features of language. In other words, at the heart of the issue is meaning making done by embodied minds that are grounded in experience, not done by the abstract processing of formal structures.

But how does a cognitive grammar differ from a formalist grammar? And how does it differ from a psychological approach? All three study syntax, morphology, lexicon, and discourse. How do cognitive grammarians pursue their dual aim of accounting for linguistic evidence and being psychologically plausible? Answers to these questions establish critical dispositions for the nature of language and language learning.

For Ronald Langacker, a key representative of the functionalist approach, a cognitive grammar captures language as a "symbolic phenomenon, consisting of patterns of imposing and symbolizing particular schemes of conceptual structuring" (2). As highlighted by John Taylor (8–16), among our facilitative capacities is the ability to categorize both the external world of things and events and the internal world of beliefs, hopes, and fears; to visualize things in a figure-ground relation, foregrounding some things and backgrounding others, an ability that is intimately connected to attention; to construe a given reality from different perspectives and in alternative ways; to construe one thing in terms of another (according to George Lakoff and Mark Johnson a feature that permeates all our thinking and is fundamental to what we call metaphors); to work with conceptual archetypes that lie somewhere between full-fledged and fixed inbuilt structures and the notion of the mind as a blank slate; to inference—that is, to fill in incomplete information; to variously automatize routines; to apply learned rules; to draw on large amounts of data available in memory and to move among them; to delight in forms in themselves, language forms in particular, as in language play; to further the social aspect of the human condition through language; and finally, and most important, to engage in symbolic behavior, to "represent to ourselves the contents of our thoughts, in a form that is independent of the external circumstances that occasioned the thoughts" (16) and communicate them to others. Cognitive grammar specifies these capacities in relation to both the structure of languages and our ability to learn them. This specification is beginning to echo in contemporary approaches to SLA and might be seen as part of the challenge for future directions as laid out by Ortega.

Another functionalist variant, connectionism, begins with an even stronger use-and-development orientation in order to separate what is considered universal from what is individual and variable. To that end the competition model (Bates and MacWhinney; MacWhinney) works with constructs such as cue validity and cue strength with the goal of specifying how language is acquired, in what order, and what its final acquisitional state is. Cue validity is the objective property of a cue in relation to a human being who is in tune with the information value of cues because of their ecology of occurrence.

For example, use of the relative pronouns *who* or *which* has high cue validity for indicating an animate versus an inanimate referent. Cue strength is a subjective property that learners attach to data in line with their intentions. Both constructs continuously unite language form and function and account for variation in a principled way. Indeed, one could think of connectionism as taking variation in learning very seriously.

RETHINKING THE NATURE AND PLACE OF GRAMMAR: EMERGENTISM

When the functional quality of language, the lifelong development of language use, and variation receive primary focus, standard assumptions about grammar can become so compromised as to be invalidated. That invalidating position is taken by emergentism. In the debate about the nature and role of grammar, Paul Hopper considers grammar to be the by-product of communicating in and understanding language (155–56): any regularity that one observes is the result of the regularity of discourse. Grammar in this view is "simply the name for certain categories of observed repetitions in discourse" (156). In other words, instead of being the precondition for language development, grammar becomes a consequence; instead of being fixed and innate, it is emergent. The result is a fundamental rethinking of the nature of the linguistic sign: the sign does not exist a priori, as claimed in formalist approaches and tacitly presupposed in functionalist approaches. Instead, emergentism "makes the sign itself subject to the exigencies of communication and assigns ontological priority to the fact of communication itself." Therefore it "refers to the essential incompleteness of a language, and sees lability between form and meaning as a constant and as a natural situation" (157). In the continuum from formalist to functionalist to sociocultural approaches for understanding language and language learning, emergentism is a particularly significant theoretical step.

> **Instead of being the precondition for language development, grammar becomes a consequence; instead of being fixed and innate, it is emergent.**

Data-Based Challenges to UG Theories of Language

Beyond theoretically argued concerns about formalist notions of language capacity, the field has produced rich data-driven studies that challenge those notions. For adult L2 acquisition a particularly puzzling phenomenon is that past a certain age, generally postpuberty, few learners seem to be able to attain native levels of ability, especially with regard to pronunciation but also in morphology and syntax. Attributing the phenomenon to maturational constraints on L2 learning, the strong version of what is called the critical period hypothesis has recently been stated less categorically: findings revealed more of a decrease than a breakdown in ultimate attainment and also modest evidence of native-like performance on the part of adult L2 learners along with some postmaturational effects (Birdsong).

For L1 acquisition some of the richest data-based work relies on crosslinguistic studies of language learning. Dan Slobin, a lead crosslinguistic researcher, concludes that, instead of positing universal characteristics of languages as innate in human beings, one should assume that language itself has a structuring and focusing role. Reminiscent of cue strength and validity phenomena is his observation that language draws "the child's attention to the possibility of dividing nouns on the basis of animacy; or verbs on the basis of duration, or determinacy, or validity; or pronouns on the basis of social status, and the like" ("Origins" 318).

We can see this power of language to structure our world in the difference between content words (verbs, nouns, adjectives), which relate to experiences and events in the world, and functors (sometimes actual function words), which relate these content words to one another or to the discourse perspectives of the speaker. Functors can be grammatical forms that express tense, mood, person, number, case, or gender of participant; they can be prepositions that show relations. Functors are a closed rather than an unlimited class and express only certain notions, the "grammaticizable notions," while ignoring others. As Slobin notes, "there is no direct and universal mapping between the ways in which human beings experience events and express them in language" (267). L2 learners have experienced this phenomenon—for example, when learning prepositions. As markers of relations in real and metaphoric space, prepositions surely ought to be universal; but, alas, they are not. There is no uniform way in which languages handle what is grammaticized and what is not and in which languages decide what categories are obligatory in a language (e.g., cases, grammatical gender assignments) and what are not.

Those facts challenge learners with two very different semantic tasks. "If one class [the content words] draws on prespecified meanings, its acquisition consists of lookup and elimination, while the acquisition of meanings in the other class requires some kind of more general learning abilities." In the spirit of Hopper's emergentism, Slobin concludes that both nativists and functionalists

> have erred in attributing the origins of structure to the mind of the child, rather than to the interpersonal communicative and cognitive processes that everywhere and always shape language in its peculiar expression of content and relations.
>
> (267)

To explicate further this phenomenon—and the idea that language shapes our ways of viewing the world—Slobin uses the term "thinking for speaking" ("From 'Thought' "). Mental processes during speaking require us to observe what aspects of the event a grammar makes available to us for expression or even obliges us to express as we verbalize events. In English, the speaker must determine whether an event is seen primarily as ongoing or as completed ("Chomsky is speaking this afternoon; Chomsky speaks this afternoon"). With certain variable prepositions (e.g., "in") German speakers must

decide whether the event in question is more about direction and process or more about location and stasis. Speakers of Japanese express a particularly rich array of interpersonal relationships through the system of honorifics. As Slobin states, "we encounter the contents of the mind in a special way when they are being accessed for *use.* . . . *I propose that, in acquiring a native language, the child learns particular ways of thinking for speaking*" ("From 'Thought' " 76; emphasis in original). Just how real and long-lasting such language-shaped habits of thinking for speaking are has been observed by researchers (e.g., Carroll and Lambert; Dimroth and Starren), who found that even very advanced L2 learners tend to structure the information pertaining to a particular event in terms of their native language information structures and categories rather than in terms of those of the L2.

The challenges for all language learning have thus been reconfigured from a formalist to a functionalist to a complex cognitive-linguistic enterprise that is rooted in human social experience at the intersection of thought, language, and culture.

A Social-Semiotic Theory of Language: Hallidayan Systemic Functional Linguistics

I began with theoretical considerations and traced a number of approaches that emphasized formal features of language and assumed a logical computational model inspired by Chomsky. Given that structuralist and UG approaches owe their prominence in the United States to certain disciplinary and cultural predispositions, it is not surprising that their most comprehensive challenge has arisen outside the country. As systemic-functional linguistics (SFL) enters United States discussions, after its development and elaboration by M. A. K. Halliday and his followers for over forty years, primarily in Australia, its major tenets are being appropriated into L1 teaching and learning, gradually as well into L2 literacy-oriented instruction (Byrnes, "Toward

. . . Abilities" and *Advanced Language Learning*; Byrnes and Sprang; Schleppegrell; Schleppegrell and Colombi).

Already in the early 1970s, Halliday extended a mostly psychological or ethnographic functionalism in two ways: by combining it with the British linguist Alan Firth's emphasis on a notion of system as "a set of options in a stated environment; in other words, a choice, together with a condition of entry" (Halliday, "Place" 45) and by combining it with the underlying tenets of Prague school linguistics with its emphasis on texts as related to language, culture, and cognition. The result is an understanding of language as a social semiotic that both derives from social contexts and actively construes them. Instead of seeing language as a code, the preferred metaphor of behaviorists and generativists, or as a system of arbitrary signs, as Ferdinand de Saussure's language analysis did, SFL focuses on the meaning potentialities of language in use. In Halliday's words, language is functional "in its interpretation (1) of texts, (2) of the system, and (3) of the elements of linguistic structures" and has evolved in order "to satisfy human needs. . . . It is not arbitrary." Its metafunctions refer to two kinds of meanings that underlie language: "(i) to understand the environment (ideational), and (ii) to act on the others in it (interpersonal). Combined with these is a third metafunctional component, the 'textual,' which breathes relevance into the other two" (*Introduction* xiii). While a focus on syntax privileges forms to which meanings are subsequently attached, "in a functional grammar . . . language is interpreted as a system of meanings, accompanied by forms through which the meanings can be realized" (xiv). The aim is to construct a grammar "for purposes of text analysis" (xv), since language consists of oral and written text or discourse in various contexts. Gordon Wells summarizes Halliday's focus like this:

> Only some of the features of the situation are relevant in categorizing situation-types . . . and these can be captured under three headings, or dimensions: "field," "tenor," and "mode." Field concerns the social action that is involved . . . what is going on; in the case of certain types of event, this semiotic content may be referred to as the "subject matter." Tenor is concerned with the who of the event—the participants and their relationship to each other, considered from the point of view of status and their roles in the event. Mode refers to the choice of channel on the spoken-written continuum and to the role assigned to language in the event. (48)

If one takes seriously the notion of text in situation, language learning would then be a kind of appropriation of culture, and culture would be not a fixed but a dynamic social given. Language learning would also be a kind of enculturation, akin to Slobin's notion of thinking for speaking, with knowledge of the language and the culture itself culturally situated.

SPECIFYING THE ACQUISITION PROCESS

On the basis of this framing discussion I now begin to specify more closely the actual acquisition process. Overall, UG-oriented SLA research (e.g., by Towell and Hawkins or by White) has had only limited direct impact on the bulk of classroom-based research in SLA and nearly no presence in classroom praxes. But its metaphors about how we are to imagine language powerfully influence much of the talk in SLA and also the talk about teaching. For the most part, the influence is indirect, through the work of Steven Krashen and the central role in language acquisition that he accords to comprehensible input (as contrasted with rules) and his distinction between teaching and learning. There is a close link among the focus on comprehensible input, content-based instruction (CBI), and communicative language teaching. Similarly, the acquisition/learning opposition can readily morph into the distinction between implicit learning, through exposure to language data and through inductive hypothesis formation, and explicit learning, through the provision of rules (e.g., in teaching) that are deductively applied. Krashen privileges implicit learning as natural, not only for its seemingly straightforward accounting of how children learn their native language but also in the context of tutored L2 learning.

Not surprisingly, that stance to this day leads to suspicion of explicit teaching, which is equated with "drill and kill" grammar teaching. In contrast, CBI and communicative language teaching are seen as noninterventionist, a teaching that naturally leads to learning of both content and language.

Cognitive Approaches to Language Learning

From these explicitly learner-centered notions about instructed learning, a psycholinguistically oriented cognitive approach developed three major constructs: focus on form (FonF), input processing, and task. What unites all three is an understanding of language learning as an individualist, rationalist, and positivist enterprise best described through psycholinguistic notions of cognition—that is, in terms of the processing of language data (see Long and Doughty). Language learning is "ultimately a matter of change in an individual's internal mental state" (Doughty and Long, "Scope" 3).

EXPLICIT TEACHING: FOCUS ON FORM,
INPUT PROCESSING, AND TASKS

The psycholinguistic view of language learning provides the context in which Catherine Doughty's data-based 1991 claim that instruction does make a difference became so significant: it helped gradually rehabilitate explicit teaching and reshape language learning as a favorable response to instructional data manipulated by the teacher in ways that often echo the manipulation prescribed in experimental SLA research design.

One prominent manifestation of such explicit teaching are FonF instructional treatments. In contrast with the explicit grammar teaching of yesteryear, FonF presupposes a focus on mean-

ing as a precondition for its recommendations: "meaning and use must already be evident to the learner at the time that attention is drawn to the linguistic apparatus needed to get the meaning across" (Doughty and Williams, "Issues" 4). With their processing focus, FonF pedagogies (Doughty and Williams, "Pedagogical Choices") wish to retain the advantages of naturalistic L2 acquisition, CBI, or immersion L2 learning while ensuring targetlike formal abilities in learners. But because the vast majority of United States L2 classrooms are not meaning- but structure-driven, the focus-on-form agenda can easily be misread as a reaffirmation of old-style grammar teaching. This misinterpretation is aided by the agenda's very name.

Another line of development that builds on Krashen's comprehensible input hypothesis aims to determine just how input becomes intake and ultimately output. In metaphoric language reminiscent of the computer world, language teaching here is all about "processing instruction" (VanPatten), an attempt to alter students' ways of attending to the L2 in language classrooms. Teachers provide metalinguistic information (raise awareness about form-meaning links) and structure their pedagogies according to psycholinguistic principles—for instance, through increasing the frequency of occurrence of a particular grammatical feature, thereby raising its saliency and presumably its learnability.

Finally, psycholinguistically oriented L2 instruction has become inseparable from two nearly ubiquitous notions, task and interaction. I treat them in this and the subsequent section, respectively. At heart, the notion of task is about engaging learners in worthwhile activities for their own sake. As Robert Sternberg notes, the method is "having students do tasks, or at least meaningful simulations, that experts do in the various disciplines. Second, it means teaching them to think in ways that experts do when they perform these tasks" (5). Beyond that general orientation, however, the task method is used differently by different practitioners. Martin Bygate,

A psycholinguistically oriented cognitive approach developed three major constructs: focus on form, input processing, and task.

Peter Skehan, and Merrill Swain explain that for many teachers and teacher educators, *task* has superseded the broader term *communicative language teaching* because of the new method's potential to create well-motivated pedagogies and because of its perceived usefulness for curriculum building (see Long and Crookes). In linking meaning and form, task seems particularly suited to overcoming the focus on structure and grammar and to move toward thematically oriented material. Specific pedagogical tasks turn into interlinked activity sequences that foster learner autonomy, collaboration, and authenticity of language use. For researchers, task is attractive because it specifies how input influences L2 development and how negotiation for meaning during task performance influences learner processing and, by extension, L2 performance and learning. Finally, the assessment community uses task as a way to operationalize various aspects of language performance, be it for formative, summative, or diagnostic purposes. Teachers' and curriculum developers' use of the notion of task receive additional treatment in the next section.

ATTENTION, AWARENESS, NOTICING, AND THEIR RELATION TO IMPLICIT AND EXPLICIT LEARNING

As new research techniques (including computer simulation) and the use of large searchable databases have become possible, processing-oriented approaches have been extended into analysis of learner attention, awareness, and noticing and their relation to implicit and explicit learning. That focus appears to move some closer to general psychology studies than to those dealing with instructed L2 learning.

In the nexus of attention and awareness, memory, and fluency, Richard Schmidt ("Attention") distinguishes among the raw data of input (e.g., sounds, intonations), what is apperceived by a human being (e.g., utterances or parts of utterances as strings of words), and what is actually processed (e.g., lexical strings as exemplars of categories in the linguistic system; see also the previous Slobin discussion). At issue is how learners focus their attention in a way that

data become "relevant for a particular domain, i.e., that attention must be specifically focused and not just global" (Schmidt, "Attention" 30).

To Schmidt, noticing, a kind of conscious awareness, is understood as "the necessary and sufficient condition for converting input to intake." While incidental learning, an unintentional paying attention, does take place, its facilitative role for learning depends on "whether the demands of a task focus attention on what is to be learned" ("Role" 129). But one should not assume

> that incidental instructions trigger implicit learning processes, that rule-search instructions result in explicit knowledge, that uninstructed second language learners learn implicitly or that learners in form-focused classes do not learn implicitly.
> ("Implicit Learning" 199)

In any case, claims regarding implicit and explicit learning refer to learner-internal processes and require the investigation of learner awareness through self-reporting, a controversial issue because verbalization might in fact distort the nature of the processes. Finally, assuming that awareness and attention do facilitate learning, "the important question is . . . whether more attention results in more learning" ("Attention" 30). That question can be resolved only with longitudinal studies that determine

> whether restructuring in the underlying grammar [a short-hand descriptor for language acquisition] is closely associated with changes in awareness or happens independently of any conscious reflection on the target language
> ("Implicit Learning" 198)

MEMORY, THE ALLOCATION OF ATTENTIONAL RESOURCES, AND TASK-BASED LEARNING

Task-based learning has also been used for linked global statements about pedagogy and curriculum. Thus, Peter Robinson distinguishes among task complexity, the task-dependent cognitive demands of tasks; task difficulty, which depends on learner factors such as aptitude, confidence, and motivation; and task conditions— for example, the interactiveness or noninteractiveness of a speaking task. By his definition, task complexity alone can serve as the basis for materials design and syllabus construction because it inheres in the task itself ("Task Complexity"). But such claims have been disputed through classroom observation, inasmuch as it is less the task that becomes an occasion for learning through interaction and more the demands that a teacher's staging of a task makes on learners. Different learners then take that original task in often unforeseen directions (see, e.g., Swain and Lapkin).

FLUENCY

While fluency has typically been thought of as an ever more automatic application of rules, which leads to fewer unacceptable pauses or fractured and flawed syntax or morphology, Andrew Pawley and Frances Syder take a very different approach. They state that linguistic theory, not just a performance theory, must account for two puzzles in language use and, more specifically, language learning: nativelike selection, the ability to form grammatical sentences, the generative aspect; and nativelike fluency, the performative aspect. In order to address both concerns, one needs to recognize the importance of a stock of lexicalized sentences ("I don't care") or semilexicalized sequences ("I'd rather . . . "), a kind of instance-based learning, and a continuum between fully productive rules of sentence formation and rules of low productivity. For that reason, researchers such as Halliday see a continuum between syntax and lexicon, a fact expressed in the term *lexicogrammar*. In a perspective reminiscent of the above discussion on grammaticization, they refer to some features of the lexical inventory of a language as a most delicate grammar (Hasan). If such a continuum exists, a valid notion of L2 learning would have to admit both rule-based and instance-based processing along with the relation between them (for an extended discussion, see Skehan).

From Input to Interaction to Output: The Interactionist Framework

The most dynamic extension of such considerations is the so-called interaction hypothesis. Stated in various stages by Michael Long, its 1996 version refocuses L2 learning in two directions. First, the interaction hypothesis moves L2 learning from intramental psycholinguistic processes into interpersonal and intermental interactions and negotiations in native and nonnative speakers as well as into communicative situations among only nonnative speakers. At the same time it retains its solid psycholinguistic grounding. Long identifies the role of the linguistic environment primarily "in terms of the positive and negative evidence speakers and writers provide learners about the target language" ("Role" 413), a clear echo of the learning problems first identified by UG.

Second, although Long considers comprehensible input as the source of acquisition, he moves toward an explicit accounting of acquisition as involving "output" or speech. He writes:

> Negotiation for meaning, and especially negotiation work that triggers *interactional* adjustments by the NS [native speaker] or more competent interlocutor, facilitates acquisition because it connects input, internal learner capacities, particularly selective attention, and output in productive ways.
> (451–52)

The fecundity of both moves is apparent from the fact that most current research studies address issues foregrounded in the interaction paradigm (see excellent overviews provided by Gass; Gass and Selinker; and the focused journal treatment guest-edited by Gass and Mackey).

For example, Rod Ellis and Xien He investigate how modifications of input and output (through task modification) affect the incidental acquisition of vocabulary; Long, S. Inagaki, and Lourdes Ortega specify how particular interactional features, such as recasts (reformulation by teachers of incorrect or inappropriate learner answers) affect language acquisition; and Alison Mackey explores how conversational interaction affects language development. A huge research effort has concentrated in great detail on how corrective feedback and learner uptake are related in the communicative classroom (Lyster; Lyster and Ranta). Nevertheless, the most recent summary by Howard Nicholas, Patsy Lightbown, and Nina Spada concludes that, in the special case of recasts as feedback, "it is not yet possible to draw general conclusions about the contribution that recasts make in language development" (748), not least because research mostly hails from experimental contexts (for L1 learning) or laboratory settings (for L2), not from classrooms. In that less than resounding assessment the recast literature only echoes what interactionist researchers also acknowledge: the interaction hypothesis remains a promise until broadly situated evidence for learning supports it.

Challenging the Framework: Voices from the Classroom

Not surprisingly, researcher educators who value the dynamics of classrooms in and of themselves and maintain strong connections to them and to teachers offer among the most trenchant critiques of the central constructs of grammar, interaction, and task.

Beginning with notions of grammar, Diane Larsen-Freeman highlights four dynamics of language through the new term *grammaring*: the dynamism of language change over time; the real-time dynamism captured by the distinction of product and process, akin to Slobin's thinking for speaking; the organic dynamism between the system as a whole and individual variation; and a dynamism in the evolving learner language, the interlanguage. As a result she replaces the "acquisition metaphor" and the notion of a "target language" with a "participation metaphor," a term she borrows from Anna Sfard (33). Similarly, the papers in Claire Kramsch's volume *Language Acquisition and Language Socialization*, with its subtitle *Ecological Perspectives*, propose a language ecology metaphor.

Regarding the treatment of repair strategies in the interactionist paradigm, Leo van Lier invites a new look at classroom interaction as typically summarized in terms of the three components of a so-called IRF exchange: initiation, response, feedback. To him, classrooms should be examined for the kinds of affordances a particular communicative situation makes accessible to learners and for an underlying orientation toward success in interaction, described as "the achievement of mutual understanding, contingency and intersubjectivity" (173). Accordingly, he highlights two features of interaction :

> first, the signaling of relations between a current utterance and previous utterances, either directly (utterance to utterance) or through shared knowledge or shared affordances in the environment; second, the raising of expectations and the crafting of deliberate ambiguities so that future utterances can find a conversational home.   (169)

With such a refocused notion of interaction as fundamentally social interaction, it is neither "comprehensible input" nor "meaning negotiation" that constitutes the necessary and sufficient condition for language development but "the organic, self-regulating process of contingent interaction" (175).

Finally, Henry Widdowson takes up the "dogma of the authentic" that is embedded in the advocacy of tasks (27). The primary role of tasks in the L2 classroom is not to replicate the user reality of the other culture but to enable learners to begin to acquire and use the meaning-making potential of the code. Framed beyond oral transactional language, that potential is particularly expansive in the literate language of textuality. It is also well accommodated in writing development that takes a literacy orientation and creates genre-based writing tasks (see Byrnes, "Role"; Crane; Ryshina-Pankova).

TOWARD A SOCIOCULTURAL UNDERSTANDING OF LANGUAGE LEARNING AND TEACHING

I have followed a trajectory of developments—in theory, SLA research, and classroom practice—from decontextualized positivist to sociocultural notions of language and language acquisition. The sociocultural notions currently yield some of the most interesting impulses for the field. I focus on the influence this burgeoning literature on a general understanding of the individual as language learner as well as on specific aspects of the instructed environment and the learning-teaching process.

The source of deep and often undetected miscommunication may not be flawed language knowledge.

tity itself can be framed in different ways: social identity, sociocultural identity, voice, cultural identity, and ethnic identity (Pierce). Language plays a differential role in each case. For example, identity construction may reflect the consequences of differential access to and influence in private and public fora for social action and therefore for language use, consequences that are frequently tied to gender.

Sociocultural Approaches to the Individual as Language Learner

Among the impulses for rethinking the instructed learner is earlier observation of language learners in cross-cultural and crosslinguistic communication in multilingual and multicultural societies. A fundamental insight from that research is that social and sociolinguistic phenomena are coconstructed by all participants (Jacoby and Ochs). The source of deep and often undetected miscommunication may not be flawed language knowledge. It may instead lie in lack of topical or sociopragmatic knowledge, in different social orientations, in different forms of discourse socialization or conversational styles, or in different assignments of roles. In such cases, L2 performances are not most interestingly described in relation to native-speaker standards, and the learner is not the permanently deficient nonnative speaker but a multicompetent user at various stages of bilingualism (Cook, "Evidence" and *Portraits*). Indeed, the primary designation as "learner of an L2" may be insufficiently rich, inasmuch as it suggests a one-way transfer from the L1 to the L2 (usually a negative transfer) instead of a potential two-way street and, in any case, an expansion of resources (Cook, *Effects*).

The process is not one of "acquiring" or coming to know the other language in native speaker–like perfection but one of mutually accomplishing conversation or, more broadly, of creating meaning. A readily observable phenomenon is code switching (see Zentella for an example of Spanish-English code switching in the Puerto Rican community in New York), which turns out to be a central means of identity construction across linguistic and cultural divides rather than a symptom of deficiencies. But iden-

In sum, a local understanding of language capacity replaces a general communicative competence with a practice-specific, interactional competence that has both societal and linguistic perspectives and demands both macro and micro levels of analysis. Furthermore, the changing nature of these competencies suggests the need for a dynamic treatment, such as that captured by Nancy Hornberger's use of continua that are specified through contexts, development in the individual, and relations among the media being employed (e.g., oral and written language genre). For each of these continua, education plays a pivotal role.

Viewing the Instructed Learner from a Sociocultural Perspective

DEVELOPING A SOCIOCULTURAL THEORY OF LEARNING

The sociocultural theories of cognition and learning developed by the Russian psychologist Lev Vygotsky have come to exert a profound influence on contemporary views of language learning and teaching (Lantolf and Thorne). A key translator of Vygotskian insights into the SLA environment, James Lantolf, provides the following characterization of Vygotsky's fundamental theoretical insights:

> Higher forms of human mental activity are always, and everywhere, *mediated* by symbolic means. . . . Mediation, whether physical or symbolic, is understood to be the introduction of an auxiliary device into an activity that then links humans to the world of objects or to the world of mental behavior. Just as physical tools (e.g.,

hammers, bulldozer, computers, etc.) allow humans to organize and alter their physical world, Vygotsky reasoned that symbolic tools empower humans to organize and control such mental processes as voluntary attention, logical problem-solving, planning and evaluation, voluntary memory, and intentional learning. Included among symbolic tools are . . . most importantly, language. . . . Symbolic tools are the means through which humans are able to organize and maintain control over the self and its mental, and even physical, activity.   ("Sociocultural Theory" 418)

In other words, human beings attain the capacity to control or regulate their memory, attention, perception, planning, learning, and development—central areas also addressed in psycholinguistic discussions—in conjunction with their appropriation of mediating artifacts, including language, as human beings are brought into culturally specified and organized activities. The linkage between socioculturally formed environments and the nature and development of psychological abilities suggests that cognitive development begins in our material and social worlds (see also the emphasis on social cognition in Wertsch, "Sociocultural Approach"). Through a complex process of internalization of the social situations in which the use of tools and linguistic symbols occurred, human beings developed a kind of cognition that is not captured in terms of brain-based cognitive processes but better described in terms of a mind that reflects the cultural and social relationships that characterized the original embedded activities (see Wertsch, "Generalized Collective Dialogue").

Directly focusing on language learning, Dwight Atkinson highlights just how dramatically a sociocultural approach differs from psycholinguistic traditions when he juxtaposes these key terms: *input* as data suggests a trigger for a language-learning automaton as opposed to the sociocultural notion of a child being "input/inserted into an ongoing stream of social interaction that supports her language development at every turn" (528), an image he borrows from James Gee ("First Language Acquisition"); *interaction* is studied for its conditioning effect on input versus interaction as occurring in a context

of situation within a *context of culture*, a term used by Halliday ("Notion" 4); the scientific ambitions of SLA denigrate teaching as opposed to appreciation of the central role of the teacher who acts much as other members of a cultural community do when they help the community's less capable members solve problems; and the cognition that enables language learning is seen as lonely as opposed to the idea of language "providing an extremely powerful semiotic means of performing and participating in activity-in-the-world" (537). In sum, "thought, feeling, and activity in the social world are brought together in the form of human beings actively operating as part of that world" (539).

Lantolf adds to Atkinson's critique of psycholinguistically driven interpretations of language teaching and learning when he questions the often repeated assertion of a fixed acquisitional sequence ("Sociocultural . . . Research"). In Manfred Pienemann's learnability-teachability hypothesis, the central assumption is that learners progress along essentially immutable sequences or stages of development, at least with regard to their emergence if not their accurate control (Pienemann identified five major stages). In sociocultural theory such claims are unsustainable, not only because learners engage with language in very different environments and very different ways but also because the very nature of social learning, including language learning, precludes such notions of predictability in order to be able to say interesting *and* foundational things about language use and learning (see also Lantolf and Thorne).

LINKING SOCIOCULTURAL THEORY WITH FUNCTIONAL LINGUISTICS

A sociocultural approach to language learning has opened up a number of highly productive linkages. For example, there is the felicitous compatibility between Hallidayan systemic functional linguistics with Vygotsky's approach to understanding language development (Byrnes, *Advanced Language Learning*). Just that connection was made in Sydney public schools, which aimed to develop L1 literacy in disadvantaged children (see particularly Christie, *Pedagogy*; Martin, "Design," "Genre," and "Mentoring"). Wells points to the complementary contribution of Halliday and Vygotsky to a "language-based theory of learning":

> If Vygotsky's ultimate target is an explanation of individual mental functioning, Halliday's might be said to be the nature and organization of language as a resource for human social living. And it is this concern with the contribution of language to social living that provides the organizing principle in terms of which Halliday's larger program can best be understood.   (45)

In another connection, Lantolf relates Vygotskian understanding of psycholinguistic processes to the notions of emergent grammar by Hopper ("Sociocultural . . . Research" 348–49). Both linkages achieve what Langacker spelled out as characteristic for cognitive linguistics: its emphasis on "the semiological function of language and the crucial role of conceptualization in social interaction" (1).

SOCIOCULTURAL THEORY IN THE L2 CLASSROOM

Translating such considerations into methodology and classroom practice that engage both learners and teachers, Joan Kelly Hall recommends a set of general principles: (1) Language learning cannot be fully explained as "an innate process of acquiring and controlling a system of isolated, context-free linguistic structures" (*Methods* 38). (2) The process is inherently social and involves a dynamic site for learning, the so-called zone of proximal development (ZPD), in which experts (e.g., teachers) and learners jointly enact a situation in such a way that individuals can, over time, develop mastery of a particular skill or knowledge regarding a topic. (3) Teaching is a designing of learning opportunities in the zone of proximal development through scaffolding, a form of strategically guided assistance that involves imitation, repetition, and play. (4) There is an intrinsic link between the cognitive and affective dimensions of learning. (5) Familiarity, predictability, and routinization of communicative activities play an important role in the learning process, because they help students develop a shared knowledge base and strong interpersonal bonds. (6) Studying language learning means studying the processes by which "learners' involvement in their classroom activities is shaped, and how, over time, such involvement affects the development of their social and psychological identities both as learners and users of the target language" (41).

In other words, in a sociocultural agenda, explicit teaching is deeply embedded in a pedagogy that integrates four factors: situated practice, the immersion in meaningful practices in a community of learners; overt instruction, which refers to various scaffolding activities on the part of teachers or other experts, during the accomplishment of more complex activities than would be possible in solitary work; critical framing, the process whereby learners come to understand their growing competence and mastery of a skill or area of knowledge in relation to particular systems of knowledge and social practice; and transformed knowledge, in which students "transfer and re-create designs of meaning from one context to another" (New London Group 85–88).

Explicit teaching occupies a particularly assured place in the kind of genre-based literacy pedagogy inspired by Halliday and Vyotsky. To James Martin, explicit teaching is *"guidance through interaction in the context of shared experience"* for the purposes of fostering discourse competence ("Mentoring" 126; emphasis in original). Such discourse competence or literacy in both a first and second language is a way of making learners aware of the meaning repertoire of language by providing a kind of visible pedagogy that traces the relation between language and social practices at all levels of the language system ("Genre").

A pivotal construct in this approach is that of register or, more recently, genre. Though variation exists in the definition of genre, for example, as typification of rhetorical action (Miller); as regularities of staged, goal-oriented social processes (Martin, "Genre"); or as consistency of communicative purposes (Swales), the key characteristic of genres is that they reflect disciplinary cultures and focus on "conventionalised communicative events embedded within disciplinary or professional practices" (Bhatia 23). That conventionalization enables both an analysis of various textual genres and a genre-based pedagogy that powerfully links the prototypicality of textual organization, as it is represented in the notion of genre, to carefully scaffolded pedagogies (Christie, "Genres"; Hyland; Kalantzis and Cope; Paltridge; Richards and Nowicki, "In Search" [parts 1 and 2]; Rothery; Swales; and articles in the collection by Johns).

A further extension translates those insights into a linked curricular and pedagogical context in a unique four-year integrated collegiate curriculum at Georgetown (*Curriculum*): in this program, genre serves as the basis for selecting and sequencing curricular units, for making pedagogical choices that target advanced levels of L2 ability, and for devising assessment instruments and guidelines (Crane; Rinner and Weigert). It accomplishes that crucial programmatic advantage by linking tasks and entire task sequences that are themselves derived from the variety of genres included in instruction. In turn, each genre-based task in the curriculum requires learners to attend to the language features of the genre while addressing the genre's content foci. In progressing through the curriculum and performing genre-based tasks at each instructional level, learners follow an articulated trajectory that enables them to attain advanced literacy abilities in German, by continuously linking content, culture, and language use and by increasingly using the resources of the L2 to develop their own competent nonnative voice in German.

CODA: EVOLVING PRAXES, EMERGING DIRECTIONS

There is no doubt that current SLA research and much of language teaching and learning reflects a social science orientation. But current SLA research also offers much promise for providing an important link between language teaching

and learning and the humanities enterprise that is suitable for overcoming the institutionalized rift in foreign language departments (Byrnes, "Constructing").

Wording that opportunity negatively, one can state that foreign language departments as humanities enterprises must take note of developments in SLA in order to overcome the problematic consequences of language-independent theorizing that have all but removed their foreign languageness and foreign cultureness, the very characteristic that distinguishes them from other disciplinary and academic areas that also do othering and do culture (e.g., anthropology, English, history, sociology) and that constitutes their unique intellectual dynamic (Byrnes, "Cultural Turn").

But I prefer to express the opportunity positively, by highlighting two facts. First, engaging with contemporary SLA, research scholars in literary and cultural studies will find many sympathetic vibrations between their interests and those of a functionally oriented SLA. Particularly the text- and language-based functionalism of Hallidayan systemic-functional linguistics, along with the pedagogies both for content learning and language acquisition that such an approach can engender, offers a felicitous basis for joint construction of an entire program. Second, with well-thought-out models for action, departments will not merely meet their challenges but also thrive intellectually and programmatically as they reconceptualize their programs holistically. I conclude by mentioning a few particularly promising areas.

Focus on Literacy

Among the most important developments in SLA is the shift toward a textual and literacy orientation that embraces a socially and culturally embedded literacy; accommodates all modalities—speaking, listening, reading, and writing; and continually links them (Belcher and Hirvela). Even in delimited versions, it dramatically resituates the primarily oral interactional or transactional language use of beginning and intermediate levels of language instruction, the bulk of language teaching in the United States, including United States higher education (see Kern; Swaffar, "Doing"). A textual and literacy orientation also enables the kind of reflective practice in language use that can address key competencies for language-based social practices in contemporary multilingual and multicultural societies. More broadly, the shift involves the development of multiple literacies and proposes literacy as a framework that can address the development of culturally appropriate discursive abilities, from the beginning of language instruction to graduate study and professional-level language use (see Byrnes, "Content-Based . . . Instruction"; Byrnes and Sprang; Swaffar, "Template"; Swaffar and Arens), thereby enabling language users to be competent participants in various public and institutional settings.

A genre-based understanding of textuality can be remarkably supportive of the interests of literary scholars.

guage Learning; Byrnes and Maxim; and Byrnes, Weger-Guntharp, and Sprang). But the demands by heritage learner groups for maintaining, recovering, or expanding their linguistic and cultural heritage at high levels are commanding increased attention (Kagan and Dillon). Coupled with the realization that native-nonnative distinctions are often unable to specify how learners might acquire the desired competencies in public, professional, and institutional language use in a range of contexts and with a range of content foci, SLA has begun to turn to L1 literacy research that deals with the language of schooling and disciplinary knowledge (see particularly Gee, "Socio-cultural Approaches"; Schleppegrell) to chart new directions (see Byrnes, "Toward . . . Abilities").

Acknowledging the Special Role of Literature

Through a sophisticated understanding of register and genre, of authorial voice and heteroglossia, of intertextuality and intratextual features of coherence and cohesion, a genre-based understanding of textuality can be remarkably supportive of the interests of literary scholars (for an encompassing example, see Swaffar, "Template"). Both literary and language acquisitional interests are particularly well ensured through M. M. Bakhtin's notion of the fundamental dialogism of meaning making.

Focus on the Advanced Learner

With an interest in literacy, contemporary directions in SLA have begun to consider the construct of advancedness as well as the curricular, pedagogical, and assessment practices required to instantiate it. Granted, such considerations are still exceptional in the FL environment (see the contributions in Byrnes, *Advanced Lan-*

Curricular Proposals That Espouse Long-Term Acquisition

Directly connected to the possibility of learners' attaining advanced levels of ability is the need for curricular proposals that address the long-term nature of L2 learning. Because the United States educational system officially provides no curricular space for an extended sequence of language learning, well-developed proposals on how the available time might foster long-term acquisition are critically needed. Despite best intentions, the Standards framework, created collaboratively by a group of foreign language professional organizations, has been unable to fulfill that need, not least because it offers few curricular principles for attaining the desired learning goals (*Standards*). Developing viable curricular proposals is therefore a key task for the entire foreign language community (see *Curriculum*).

Acknowledging the Importance of the Educational Context

Collegiate foreign language instruction must recognize one of the central tenets of any successful teaching: careful attention to learners and the institutional context where learning takes place. For L2 teaching and learning of adults, that attention means building on the fact that these learners are literate users of their native languages (see Swaffar, Arens, and Byrnes for an early countermove) who wish to learn to use the L2 at a satisfying level of competence, despite many programmatic obstacles. To the extent possible, programs should respond to that desire by creating articulated curricula (e.g., *Curriculum*), pedagogies (e.g., Colombi), and assessment practices (e.g., Norris) with an eye toward efficacy, efficiency, and accountability. By embracing literacy as an encompassing conceptual framework, departments can begin to overcome the shortcomings of language instruction that is construed merely as communicative or transactional language of daily use (Byrnes, "Reconsidering" and "Perspectives").

New Models for Accomplishing the Goals of Language across the Curriculum and Content-Based Instruction

Socioculturally and textually oriented curricular and pedagogical practices in contemporary SLA are poised to accomplish the goals that earlier efforts in language across the curriculum projects (see Adams; Kecht and Hammerstein) or CBI were unable to reach (see Wesche and Skehan for an excellent review). They will do so through an integrated approach for linking content and language acquisition that recognizes language as a social semiotic and instructed L2 acquisition as the acquisition of a rich repertoire of expressive capabilities in a framework of linguistic-cultural choices (Byrnes, "Content-Based . . . Instruction").

Language for Professional or Special Purposes

The desire of many foreign language departments to offer individual courses, at times concentrations, or even entire programs that target

language use in particular professional environments can also be accommodated under a genre framework. Diverse courses can be set up with the same intellectual rigor and the same academic demands as other offerings in a department (see Weigert for such an approach for business language courses; Rinner and Weigert for business and culture courses).

A Pedagogy of Compatible Discursive Practices

With its focus on literacy and textuality, contemporary SLA offers a pedagogical discourse that can signal and sustain the kind of intellectual unity that collegiate foreign language departments require in order to overcome their existing structural and intellectual divisions, including the increasing practice of outsourcing language instruction to variously configured centers.

Constructivist Approaches

The effort to create intellectual unity will be the more successful, the more faculty members espouse constructivist frameworks for their scholarly work. To Mary McGroarty, "such approaches are marked by heightened attention to agency and subjectivity, to the generation and interpretation of meaning, and to the constant interplay between individual and group activity" (591).

Giving Voice to the Humanities in a Multicultural World

With this final point I return to the beginning. The dramatic shifts in SLA over the last decade can be described as a working through of fundamental considerations regarding language, cognition, culture, and society. As a field, SLA has experienced the same dynamics that have confronted other disciplines. Because its subject matter is language, the insights it has gained can contribute to making all humanities disciplines, as interpretive language-based fields, relevant again in a multicultural world.

The story I have told highlights this characteristic of recent work in the SLA field: just like language itself, contemporary SLA has begun to create an internally cohesive and coherent story that points outside itself to social realities. There it finds not only consonant developments in a range of human endeavors and forms of inquiry but also areas to which it can contribute insightfully and enthusiastically.

WORKS CITED AND SUGGESTIONS FOR FURTHER READING

This bibliography includes full references for works cited in the text and other works the student of language acquisition and language learning might want to consult. For collections of overview articles, I recommend the *Annual Review of Applied Linguistics*. This publication surveys research in applied linguistics in a thematically arranged fashion, covering a wide range of topics including those of interest to language teaching and learning, broadly interpreted.

There are numerous handbooks in this field (see Doughty and Long, *Handbook*; Kaplan; Ritchie and Bhatia; and Spolsky).

For recent overview books for language teaching and learning, see Byrnes, *Learning Foreign and Second Languages*; Dörnyei, *Teaching and Researching Motivation*; Ellis, *Task-Based Language Learning and Teaching*; Gass and Selinker, *Second Language Acquisition*; Hall, *Methods for Teaching Foreign Languages*; Johns, *Genre in the Classroom*; Kern, *Literacy and Language Teaching*; Lantolf, *Sociocultural Theory and Second Language Learning*; Lantolf and Thorne, *Sociocultural Theory and the Genesis of Second Language Development*; Larsen-Freeman, *Teaching Language*; McCarthy and Carter, *Language as Discourse*; Mitchell and Myles, *Second Language Learning Theories*; Schleppegrell, *The Language of Schooling*; Schleppegrell and Colombi, *Developing Advanced Literacy in First and Second Languages*; Skehan, *A Cognitive Approach to Language Learning*; Swaffar and Arens, *Remapping the Foreign Language Curriculum*.

For tracing recent developments in SLA, I recommend two works in particular. First, see Alan Firth and Johannes Wagner's "On Discourse, Communication, and (Some) Fundamental Concepts in SLA Research"; see articles in response by Michael Long, Joan Kelly Hall, and Ben Rampton. Second, see Barbara Seidlhofer's *Controversies in Applied Linguistics*, an excellent collection that includes both the original position paper and the responses, sometimes in several iterations. Seidlhofer provides an excellent context for each controversy.

Adams, Thomas M. "Languages across the Curriculum: Taking Stock." *ADFL Bulletin* 28.1 (1996): 9–19.

Atkinson, Dwight. "Toward a Sociocognitive Approach to Second Language Acquisition." *Modern Language Journal* 86 (2002): 525–45.

Bakhtin, M. M. "The Problem of Speech Genres." *M. M. Bakhtin: "Speech Genres" and Other Late Essays.* Ed. Caryl Emerson and Michael Holquist. Austin: U of Texas P, 1986. 60–102.

Bates, Elizabeth, and Brian MacWhinney. "Competition, Variation, and Language Learning." *Mechanisms of Language Acquisition.* Ed. MacWhinney. Hillsdale: Erlbaum, 1987. 157–93.

Belcher, Diane, and Alan Hirvela, eds. *Linking Literacies: Perspectives on L2 Reading-Writing Connections.* Ann Arbor: U of Michigan P, 2001.

Bhatia, Vijai K. "A Generic View of Academic Discourse." *Academic Discourse.* Ed. John Flowerdew. Harlow, Eng.: Longman, 2002. 21–39.

Birdsong, David, ed. *Second Language Acquisition and the Critical Period Hypothesis.* Mahwah: Erlbaum, 1999.

Bygate, Martin, Peter Skehan, and Merrill Swain. Introduction. *Researching Pedagogic Tasks: Second Language Learning, Teaching and Testing.* Ed. Bygate, Skehan, and Swain. Harlow, Eng.: Pearson Educ., 2001. 1–20.

Byrnes, Heidi, ed. *Advanced Language Learning: The Contribution of Halliday and Vygotsky.* London: Continuum, 2006.

———. "Constructing Curricula in Collegiate Foreign Language Departments." Byrnes, *Learning* 262–95.

———. "Content-Based Foreign Language Instruction." *Mind and Context in Adult Second Language Acquisition: Methods, Theory, and Practice.* Ed. Cristina Sanz. Washington: Georgetown UP, 2005. 282–302.

———. "The Cultural Turn in Foreign Language Departments: Challenge and Opportunity." *Profession 2002.* New York: MLA, 2002. 114–29.

———, ed. *Learning Foreign and Second Languages: Perspectives in Research and Scholarship.* New York: MLA, 1998.

———, ed. "Perspectives: Interrogating Communicative Competence as a Framework for Collegiate Foreign Language Study." *Modern Language Journal* 90 (2006): 244–66.

———. "Reconsidering Graduate Students' Education as Teachers: It Takes a Department!" *Modern Language Journal* 85 (2001): 512–30.

———. "The Role of Task and Task-Based Assessment in a Content-Oriented Collegiate FL Curriculum." *Language Testing* 19 (2002): 419–37.

———. "Toward Academic-Level Foreign Language Abilities: Reconsidering Foundational Assumptions, Expanding Pedagogical Options." *Developing Professional-Level Language Proficiency.* Ed. Betty Lou Leaver and Boris Shekhtman. Cambridge: Cambridge UP, 2002. 34–58.

Byrnes, Heidi, and Hiram H. Maxim, eds. *Advanced For-*

eign Language Learning: A Challenge to College Programs. AAUSC Issues in Lang. Program Direction. Boston: Heinle, 2004.

Byrnes, Heidi, and Katherine A. Sprang. "Fostering Advanced L2 Literacy: A Genre-Based Cognitive Approach." Byrnes and Maxim 47–85.

Byrnes, Heidi, Heather Weger-Guntharp, and Katherine A. Sprang, eds. *Educating for Advanced Foreign Language Capacities: Constructs, Curriculum, Instruction, Assessment.* Washington: Georgetown UP, 2006.

Carroll, Mary, and Monique Lambert. "Information Structure in Narratives and the Role of Grammaticised Knowledge: A Study of Adult French and German Learners of English." Dimroth and Starren 267–87.

Chomsky, Noam. "Linguistic Theory." *Language Teaching: Broader Contexts.* Ed. Robert G. Mead. Middlebury: Northeast Conf., 1966. 43–49.

Christie, Frances. "Genres as Choice." *The Place of Genre in Learning: Current Debates.* Ed. I. Reid. Geelong, Austral.: Deakin U, 1987. 22–34.

———. *Pedagogy and the Shaping of Consciousness: Linguistic and Social Processes.* London: Cassell, 1999.

Colombi, M. Cecilia. "Academic Language Development in Latino Students' Writing in Spanish." Schleppegrell and Colombi 67–86.

Cook, Vivian, ed. *Effects of the Second Language on the First.* Clevedon, Eng.: Multilingual Matters, 2003.

———. "Evidence for Multicompetence." *Language Learning* 42 (1992): 557–91.

———, ed. *Portraits of the L2 User.* Clevedon, Eng.: Multilingual Matters, 2002.

Cope, Bill, and Mary Kalantzis, eds. *Multiliteracies: Literacy Learning and the Design of Social Futures.* New York: Routledge, 2000.

———. "The Power of Literacy and the Literacy of Power." *The Powers of Literacy: A Genre Approach to Teaching Writing.* Ed. Cope and Kalantzis. Pittsburgh: U of Pittsburgh P, 1993. 63–89.

Crane, Cori. "Modeling a Genre-Based Foreign Language Curriculum." Byrnes, *Advanced Language Learning* 223–41.

Crookes, Graham, and Susan M. Gass, eds. *Tasks and Language Learning: Integrating Theory and Practice.* Clevedon, Eng.: Multilingual Matters, 1993.

———, eds. *Tasks in a Pedagogical Context: Integrating Theory and Practice.* Clevedon, Eng.: Multilingual Matters, 1993.

Curriculum "Developing Multiple Literacies": Introduction. German Dept., Georgetown U. 1997–2000. 4 Sept. 2004. 1 Feb. 2006 <http:www3.georgetown.edu/departments/german/programs/curriculum/index .html>.

Dimroth, Christine, and Marianne Starren, eds. *Information Structure and the Dynamics of Language Acquisition.* Amsterdam: Benjamins, 2003.

Dörnyei, Zoltan. *Teaching and Researching Motivation.* Harlow, Eng.: Longman, 2001.

Doughty, Catherine. "Second Language Instruction Does Make a Difference: Evidence from an Empirical Study of SL Relativization." *Studies in Second Language Acquisition* 13 (1991): 431–69.

Doughty, Catherine J., and Michael H. Long, eds. *The Handbook of Second Language Acquisition.* Malden: Blackwell, 2003.

———. "The Scope of Inquiry and Goals of SLA." Doughty and Long, *Handbook* 3–16.

Doughty, Catherine, and Jessica Williams, eds. *Focus on Form in Classroom Second Language Acquisition.* Cambridge: Cambridge UP, 1998.

———. "Issues and Terminology." Doughty and Williams, *Focus* 1–11.

———. "Pedagogical Choices in Focus on Form." Doughty and Williams, *Focus* 197–261.

Ellis, Rod. *Task-Based Language Learning and Teaching.* Oxford: Oxford UP, 2003.

Ellis, Rod, and Xien He. "The Roles of Modified Input and Output in the Incidental Acquisition of Word Meanings." *Studies in Second Language Acquisition* 21 (1999): 285–301.

Firth, Alan, and Johannes Wagner. "On Discourse, Communication, and (Some) Fundamental Concepts in SLA Research." *Modern Language Journal* 81 (1997): 285–300.

Gass, Susan M. *Input, Interaction, and the Second Language Learner.* Mahwah: Erlbaum, 1997.

Gass, Susan M., and Alison Mackey, eds. *The Role of Input and Interaction in Second Language Acquisition.* Spec. issue of *Modern Language Journal* 82 (1998): 299–386.

Gass, Susan M., and Larry Selinker. *Second Language Acquisition: An Introductory Course.* Mahwah: Erlbaum, 2001.

Gee, James. "First Language Acquisition as a Guide for Theories of Learning and Pedagogy." *Linguistics and Education* 6 (1995): 331–54.

———. "Socio-cultural Approaches to Literacy (Literacies)." *Annual Review of Applied Linguistics* 12 (1992): 31–48.

———. "What Is Literacy?" *Negotiating Academic Literacies: Teaching and Learning across Languages and Cultures.* Ed. Vivian Zamel and Ruth Spack. Mahwah: Erlbaum, 1998. 51–59.

Hall, Joan Kelly. "A Consideration of SLA as a Theory of Practice: A Response to Firth and Wagner." *Modern Language Journal* 81 (1997): 301–06.

———. *Methods for Teaching Foreign Languages: Creating a Community of Learners in the Classroom.* Upper Saddle River: Prentice, 2002.

Halliday, M. A. K. *An Introduction to Functional Grammar.* 2nd ed. London: Arnold, 1994.

———. "The Notion of 'Context' in Language Education." *Text and Context in Functional Linguistics.* Ed. Mohsen Ghadessy. Amsterdam: Benjamins, 1999. 1–24.

———. "The Place of 'Functional Sentence Perspective'

in the System of Linguistic Description." *Papers on Functional Sentence Perspective*. Ed. František Daneš. Prague: Academia, 1974. 43–53.

Hasan, Ruqaiya. "The Grammarian's Dream: Lexis as a Most Delicate Grammar." *Ways of Saying: Ways of Meaning: Selected Papers of Ruqaiya Hasan*. Ed. Carmel Cloran, David Butt, and Geoffrey Williams. London: Cassell, 1996. 73–103.

Hopper, Paul. "Emergent Grammar." Tomasello, *New Psychology* 155–75.

Hornberger, Nancy. "Continua of Biliteracy." *Literacy across Languages and Cultures*. Ed. Bernardo M. Ferdman, Rose-Marie Weber, and Arnulfo G. Ramírez. Albany: State U of New York P, 1994. 103–39.

Hyland, Ken. "Genre: Language, Context, and Literacy." *Annual Review of Applied Linguistics* 22 (2002): 113–35.

Jacoby, Sally, and Elinor Ochs. "Co-construction: An Introduction." *Research on Language and Social Interaction* 28 (1995): 171–83.

Johns, Ann M., ed. *Genre in the Classroom: Multiple Perspectives*. Mahwah: Erlbaum, 2002.

Kagan, Olga, and Kathleen Dillon. "Heritage Speakers' Potential for High-Level Language Proficiency." Byrnes and Maxim 99–12.

Kalantzis, Mary, and Bill Cope. "A Multiliteracies Pedagogy: A Pedagogical Supplement." Cope and Kalantzis, *Multiliteracies* 239–48.

Kaplan, Robert B., ed. *The Oxford Handbook of Applied Linguistics*. New York: Oxford UP, 2002.

Kecht, Maria-Regina, and Katharina von Hammerstein, eds. *Languages across the Curriculum: Interdisciplinary Structures and Internationalized Education*. Columbus: National East Asian Langs. Resource Center, 2000.

Kern, Richard. *Literacy and Language Teaching*. Oxford: Oxford UP, 2000.

Kramsch, Claire. "Language Acquisition and Language Learning." *Introduction to Scholarship in Modern Languages and Literatures*. Ed. Joseph Gibaldi. New York: MLA, 1992. 53–76.

———, ed. *Language Acquisition and Language Socialization: Ecological Perspectives*. London: Continuum, 2002.

———. "Social Discursive Constructions of Self in L2 Learning." Lantolf, *Sociocultural Theory* 133–53.

Krashen, Steven D. *The Input Hypothesis: Issues and Implications*. London: Longman, 1985.

Lakoff, George, and Mark Johnson. *Metaphors We Live By*. Chicago: U of Chicago P, 1980.

Langacker, Ronald. "Conceptualization, Symbolization, and Grammar." Tomasello 1–39.

Lantolf, James P. "Sociocultural and Second Language Learning Research: An Exegesis." *Handbook of Research in Second Language Teaching and Learning*. Ed. Eli Hinkel. Mahwah: Erlbaum, 2005. 335–53.

———, ed. *Sociocultural Theory and Second Language Learning*. Oxford: Oxford UP, 2000.

———. "Sociocultural Theory and Second Language Learning: Introduction." *Modern Language Journal* 78 (1994): 418–20.

Lantolf, James P., and Steven L. Thorne. *Sociocultural Theory and the Genesis of Second Language Development*. New York: Oxford UP, 2006.

Larsen-Freeman, Diane. *Teaching Language: From Grammar to Grammaring*. Boston: Thomson-Heinle, 2003.

Long, Michael H. "Construct Validity in SLA Research: A Response to Firth and Wagner." *Modern Language Journal* 81 (1997): 318–23.

———. "The Role of the Linguistic Environment in Second Language Acquisition." Ritchie and Bhatia 413–68.

Long, Michael H., and Graham Crookes. "Three Approaches to Task-Based Syllabus Design." *TESOL Quarterly* 26 (1992): 27–56.

Long, Michael H., and Catherine J. Doughty. "SLA and Cognitive Science." Doughty and Long, *Handbook* 866–70.

Long, Michael, S. Inagaki, and Lourdes Ortega. "The Role of Implicit Negative Feedback in SLA: Models and Recasts in Japanese and Spanish." *Modern Language Journal* 82 (1998): 357–71.

Lyster, Roy. "Recasts, Repetition, and Ambiguity in L2 Classroom Discourse." *Studies in Second Language Acquisition* 20 (1998): 51–81.

Lyster, Roy, and Leila Ranta. "Corrective Feedback and Learner Uptake: Negotiation of Form in the Communicative Classroom." *Studies in Second Language Acquisition* 19 (1997): 37–66.

Mackey, Alison. "Input, Interaction, and Second Language Development: An Empirical Study of Question Formation in ESL." *Studies in Second Language Acquisition* 21 (1999): 557–87.

MacWhinney, Brian. "The Competition Model: The Input, the Context, and the Brain." Robinson, *Cognition* 69–90.

Martin, James R. "Design and Practice: Enacting Functional Linguistics." *Annual Review of Applied Linguistics* 20 (2000): 116–26.

———. "Genre and Literacy—Modeling Context in Educational Linguistics." *Annual Review of Applied Linguistics* 13 (1993): 141–72.

———. "Mentoring Semogenesis: 'Genre-Based' Literacy Pedagogy." Christie, *Pedagogy* 123–55.

McCarthy, Michael, and Ronald Carter. *Language as Discourse: Perspectives for Language Teaching*. London: Longman, 1994.

McGroarty, Mary. "Constructive and Constructivist Challenges for Applied Linguistics." *Language Learning* 48 (1998): 591–622.

Miller, Carolyn R. "Genre as Social Action." *Quarterly Journal of Speech* 70 (1984): 151–67.

Mitchell, Rosamond, and Florence Myles. *Second Language Learning Theories*. London: Arnold, 1998.

New London Group. "A Pedagogy of Multiliteracies: Designing Social Futures." *Harvard Educational Review* 66.1 (1996): 60–92.

Nicholas, Howard, Patsy M. Lightbown, and Nina Spada. "Recasts as Feedback to Language Learners." *Language Learning* 51 (2001): 719–58.

Norris, John M. "Validity Evaluation in Foreign Language Assessment." Diss. U of Hawai'i, Manoa, 2004.

O'Grady, William. "The Radical Middle: Nativism without Universal Grammar." Doughty and Long, *Handbook* 43–62.

Ortega, Lourdes. "For What and for Whom Is Our Research? The Ethical as Transformative Lens in Instructed SLA." *Modern Language Journal* 89 (2005): 427–43.

Paltridge, Brian. *Genre and the Language Learning Classroom.* Ann Arbor: U of Michigan P, 2001.

Pawley, Andrew, and Frances Syder. "Two Puzzles for Linguistic Theory: Nativelike Selection and Nativelike Fluency." *Language and Communication.* Ed. Jack Richards and Richard Schmidt. London: Longman, 1983. 191–226.

Pienemann, Manfred. "Is Language Teachable? Psycholinguistic Experiments and Hypotheses." *Applied Linguistics* 10 (1989): 52–79.

Pierce, Bonny Norton. "Social Identity, Investment, and Language Learning." *TESOL Quarterly* 29 (1995): 9–31.

Pinker, Steven. *The Language Instinct.* New York: Morrow, 1994.

Rampton, Ben. "Second Language Research in Late Modernity: A Response to Firth and Wagner." *Modern Language Journal* 81 (1997): 329–33.

Richards, David, and Ursula Nowicki. "In Search of a Viable Learning Theory to Support Genre-Based Teaching to Adult Migrants: Part I." *Prospect* 13.1 (1998): 40–52.

———. "In Search of a Viable Learning Theory to Support Genre-Based Teaching to Adult Migrants: Part II." *Prospect* 13.2 (1998): 63–77.

Rinner, Susanne, and Astrid Weigert. "Integrating Content Courses via Genre: From Sports to the EU Economy." Byrnes, Weger-Guntharp, and Sprang 136–51.

Ritchie, William C., and Tej K. Bhatia, eds. *Handbook of Second Language Acquisition.* San Diego: Academic, 1996.

Robinson, Peter, ed. *Cognition and Second Language Instruction.* New York: Cambridge UP, 2001.

———. "Task Complexity, Cognitive Resources, and Second Language Syllabus Design: A Triadic Framework for Examining Task Influences on SLA." Robinson, *Cognition* 287–318.

Rothery, Joan. "Learning about Language." *Language Development: Learning Language, Learning Culture.* Ed. Ruqaiya Hasan and James R. Martin. Norwood: Ablex, 1989. 199–256.

Ryshina-Pankova, Marianna. "Creating Textual Worlds in Advanced Learner Writing: The Role of Complex Theme." Byrnes, *Advanced Language Learning* 164–83.

Schleppegrell, Mary J. *The Language of Schooling: A Functional Linguistics Perspective.* Mahwah: Erlbaum, 2004.

Schleppegrell, Mary J., and M. Cecilia Colombi, eds. *Developing Advanced Literacy in First and Second Languages: Meaning with Power.* Mahwah: Erlbaum, 2002.

Schmidt, Richard. "Attention." Robinson, *Cognition* 3–32.

———. "Implicit Learning and the Cognitive Unconscious: Of Artificial Grammars and SLA." *Implicit and Explicit Learning of Languages.* Ed. Nick Ellis. London: Academic, 1994. 165–209.

———. "The Role of Consciousness in Second Language Learning." *Applied Linguistics* 11 (1990): 129–58.

Seidlhofer, Barbara, ed. *Controversies in Applied Linguistics.* Oxford: Oxford UP, 2003.

Skehan, Peter. *A Cognitive Approach to Language Learning.* Oxford: Oxford UP, 1998.

Slobin, Dan I. "From 'Thought and Language' to 'Thinking for Speaking.' " *Rethinking Linguistic Relativity.* Ed. John J. Gumperz and Stephen C. Levinson. Cambridge: Cambridge UP, 1996. 70–96.

———. "The Origins of Grammaticizable Notions: Beyond the Individual Mind." *The Crosslinguistic Study of Language Acquisition.* Ed. Slobin. Vol. 5. Mahwah: Erlbaum, 1997. 265–323.

Spolsky, Bernard, ed. *Concise Encyclopedia of Educational Linguistics.* Amsterdam: Elsevier, 1999.

Standards for Foreign Language Learning: Preparing for the Twenty-First Century. Lawrence: Allen, 1996.

Sternberg, Robert J. "What Is an 'Expert Student'?" *Educational Researcher* 32. 8 (2003): 5–9.

Swaffar, Janet. "Doing Things with Language: Acquiring Discourse Literacy through Languages across the Curriculum." Kecht and von Hammerstein 119–49.

———. "A Template for Advanced Learner Tasks: Staging Genre Reading and Cultural Literacy through the Précis." Byrnes and Maxim 19–45.

Swaffar, Janet, and Katherine Arens. *Remapping the Foreign Language Curriculum: An Approach through Multiple Literacies.* New York: MLA, 2005.

Swaffar, Janet K., Katherine Arens, and Heidi Byrnes. *Reading for Meaning: An Integrated Approach to Language Learning.* Englewood Cliffs: Prentice, 1991.

Swain, Merrill, and Sharon Lapkin. "Interaction and Second Language Learning: Two Adolescent French Immersion Students Working Together." *Modern Language Journal* 82 (1998): 320–37.

Swales, John M. *Genre Analysis: English in Academic and Research Settings.* Cambridge: Cambridge UP, 1990.

Taylor, John R. *Cognitive Grammar.* Oxford: Oxford UP, 2002.

Tomasello, Michael. "Introduction: A Cognitive-Functional Perspective on Language Structure." Tomasello, *New Psychology* vii–xxiii.

———, ed. *The New Psychology of Language: Cognitive and Functional Approaches to Language Structure.* Vol. 1. Mahwah: Erlbaum, 1998.

Towell, Richard, and Roger Hawkins. *Approaches to Sec-*

ond Language Aquisition. Clevedon, Eng.: Multilingual Matters, 1994.

van Lier, Leo. "Constraints and Resources in Classroom Talk: Issues of Equality and Symmetry." Byrnes, *Learning* 157–82.

VanPatten, Bill. *Input Processing and Grammar Instruction in Second Language Acquisition*. Norwood: Ablex, 1996.

Vygotsky, Lev. *Thought and Language*. Ed. and trans. Alex Kozulin. Cambridge: MIT P, 1986.

Weigert, Astrid. "What's Business Got to Do with It? The Unexplored Potential of Business Language Courses for Advanced Foreign Language Learning." Byrnes and Maxim 131–50.

Wells, Gordon. "The Complementary Contribution of Halliday and Vygotsky to a 'Language-Based Theory of Learning.' " *Linguistics and Education* 6 (1994): 41–90.

Wertsch, James V. "Generalized Collective Dialogue and Advanced Foreign Language Capacities." Byrnes, *Advanced Language Learning* 60–72.

———. "A Sociocultural Approach to Socially Shared Cognition." *Perspectives on Socially Shared Cognition.* Ed. Lauren B. Resnick, John M. Levine, and Stephanie D. Teasley. Washington: Amer. Psychological Assn., 1991. 85–100.

Wesche, Marjorie B., and Peter Skehan. "Communicative, Task-Based, and Content-Based Language Instruction." Kaplan 207–28.

White, Lydia. "Second Language Acquisition and Universal Grammar." *Studies in Second Language Acquisition* 12 (1990): 121–33.

Widdowson, Henry G. "Object Language and the Language Subject: On the Mediating Role of Applied Linguistics." *Annual Review of Applied Linguistics* 20 (2000): 21–33.

Zentella, Ana Celia. *Growing Up Bilingual: Puerto Rican Children in New York*. Malden: Blackwell, 1997.

~ *Forming Texts*

∼ Rhetoric

SUSAN C. JARRATT

distinction[s] forever on the move

—Kenneth Burke, *Language as Symbolic Action*

Rhetoric's appearance on its own in this volume might be taken as evidence of the happy ending of a very old story. From its venerable origins in classical Greece, rhetoric becomes the cornerstone of Western European education, flourishing through the Middle Ages and the Renaissance; it falls from grace with the rise of science and Enlightenment reason but is reborn in the twentieth century. Numerous signs of professional success confirm the revival of rhetoric. In response to a recent survey, seventy-two doctoral programs in rhetoric and composition reported housing over a thousand students (Brown, Meyer, and Enos). The MLA supports two specifically rhetoric-related divisions, and scholarly publications on the subject abound.[1] And yet, while some of this recent scholarship serves to secure rhetoric's foundations, a great deal of it calls into question the familiar story, from the stability of the classical tradition at one end to rhetoric's apparent decline and rebirth at the other. The very proliferation of scholarship in rhetoric that has brought the field into this volume has unearthed disputes over its legitimacy, purposes, and effects.

Consider the following passage from *Hippolytos*, a tragedy written by the fifth-century BCE Athenian Euripides:

It's just these too seductive words
that make our teeming cities fall apart,
ruining homes and families.
It's crazy for us to tell each other
whatever charms the ear,
when what we need are words
that will keep honor in our lives!

(lines 750–56)

These lines are spoken by Phaidra, queen of Athens by virtue of her marriage to Theseus, a "man of splendid birth" (line 235). But because she came from Crete, she was considered an alien in Athenian culture. Theseus himself at the time of the play's action was temporarily exiled from Athens for killing legitimate heirs to the throne. The seductive words that trouble Phaidra are those of her practically minded nurse, who has just offered to solve the queen's problem, a shameful passion for her stepson, Hippolytos. The nurse promises to win the young man over by means of a *pharmakon*, a magical spell or cure. But as it turns out, the remedy she has in mind is simply an act of speech: the nurse tells Hippolytos of his stepmother's desire. Humiliated, Phaidra kills herself without ever speaking of her feelings but dies clutching a tablet on which she's written a false accusation of rape against Hippolytos. Theseus, enraged, refuses to listen to his

73

son's side of the story or to hold a legal proceeding, as the chorus urges, and wishes his son dead. Hippolytus, with right on his side, nonetheless gains little sympathy because of his priggishness and antisocial obsessions. The god Poseidon hears and acts on Theseus's misplaced curse, frightening Hippolytos's beloved horses with a terrifying phantasm of a bull so that they trample him. The dying young man is returned to the palace to be blessed by his patron goddess, Artemis, who assures him that he will be remembered in rituals of mourning and song.

Like the ancient Greeks, we fear the violent potential of language but, at the same time, have a sense that language can help us contain or master violent forces.

This story stages some of the competing impulses embedded in rhetoric at an early moment and anticipates definitional debates resurfacing in our own era. Phaidra's plaint gives voice to long-standing hopes for rhetoric: that sensible words will bind people together in cities and provide a mechanism for making orderly decisions; that resisting the temptations of pleasurable speech will set people (both citizens and others) on a path to earn good reputations (*eukleios*). Later in the play, Phaidra frames such hopes for her own sons:

> I want them to live openly and speak their
>   minds
> in the city famous for that, Athens,
> enhanced in their own fame
> because I was their mother.   (lines 646–49)

Here is a utopian vision of rhetoric: a political practice enabling free and open exchange of views by competent and authorized speakers for efficacious collective action. This rhetoric is the province of virtuous men, whose status is ensured by the appropriate behavior, and good reputations, of their subordinates—mothers, wives, daughters, slaves, and noncitizens—in a stable social hierarchy.

But the misappropriations and failures of speech and writing fatally undermine this vision. Rhetoric as the artful performance of recognized genres in public spaces by authorized speakers gives way to broken and misbegotten language acts in intimate or isolated settings by speakers whose gender, social class, and alien status cast doubt on their legitimacy (Goff). Rather than rhetoric's typical scene—a single person addressing an audience of quiet listeners—we see multiple actors using speech, writing, and embodied gestures in an array of combinations, in spaces both open and hidden. Speech grounded in publicly established norms collides with expressions of private yearning, impulses toward transgression, and idiosyncratic behavior.

Other questions lurk in the background of the action. Who taught Phaidra and the nurse to read and write? How did they compose their messages? Was there a conventional way to speak of love? To write a suicide note? To condemn a son to death? Here rhetoric concerns itself not only with political order and free speech but also with desire and fear, not only with speech but also with silence and the double-edged power of words as remedy and fatal dose. In rhetoric's realm, wise moderation (*sophrosune*) is met with antisocial excesses, and virtuous behavior in the interest of god-given moral codes is challenged by cunning tactics in the face of complex circumstances.

The passage from *Hippolytos* (lines 750–56) is appealing in its urgent mix of desperation and hope. The character speaks with a sense that things are about to fall apart—and in fact they are, both in the drama and in Athens of 428 BCE, the date of the play's production: a time when the achievements of the Periclean democracy were crumbling. The leaders of Athens were fatally divided as the city, in its imperialist enthusiasm, plunged further into war with Sparta. The end of that century and the first half of the next would give rise to an abundance of rhetorical theory and oratorical performance, while a shaky democracy struggled against the ultimately successful imperializing designs of the Macedonians: Philip and his son, Alexander.

Our time presents its own urgencies and moments of desperation. Like the ancient Greeks, we fear the violent potential of language but, at the same time, have a sense that language can help us contain or master violent forces.[2] Scholarship in rhetoric takes up these tensions and is invigorated by them in a time when terror, war, and states of emergency create an urgent need for analyses of public arguments; when manipulations of language cause grave concern and erode the legitimacy of government; and when global conflicts call attention to differences not only of language but also of that constellation of cultural codes, gestures, and performances that can be comprehended as rhetorical.

IN A WORD

Siting rhetoric in scenes ranging from intimate family drama to the realm of international conflict may suggest that it has no limits. The scope of the field, a controversial topic in the time of the ancient Greeks, reemerges in our time to provoke debate about what can be called rhetoric (Bender and Wellbery, "Rhetoricality"; Gross and Keith). According to a standard definition, rhetoric concerns itself with the ways human beings use speech to influence one another's attitudes and behavior, but theorists have extended every element of that definition. George Kennedy, for example, proposes that even nonhuman animals use language rhetorically (*Comparative Rhetoric* 11–27). Many rhetoricians consider that symbol systems other than speech, such as visual images, music, and even silence, are also phenomena of rhetorical interest (Barthes, "Rhetoric of the Image"; Glenn, *Unspoken*; Mitchell). Not all scholars work from a view of rhetoric as limited to persuasive or even communicative aims; some expand the term to take in all language in its figural or meaning-making power.[3] We've begun expansively, at the outer limits of the term and field, with definitional touch points that also serve as nodes of conflict—or *staseis* (*stasis* in the singular), to apply a term from the ancient Greek panoply of rhetorical resources.[4] A set of questions used in preparing legal arguments, the *staseis* can give shape to an unwieldy body of ma-

terial by asking four questions: Does it exist? If so, what is it? What value should it be assigned? And where does it reside (in whose jurisdiction does it fall)? Instead of bringing rhetoric to the bar, this inventional strategy suggests multiple angles of entry into our subject.

Questioning rhetoric's existence may seem an odd way to begin an inquiry, but it makes sense in the historiographical debates alluded to above. Is the rhetoric that has returned in the twentieth century anything like, or enough like, the practices, theories, and institutions of the past to warrant our use of the same term (Bender and Wellbery, "Rhetoricality"; Halloran, "On the End")? Or, to put the question into a different disciplinary context, does the current field of composition studies—the teaching of writing in United States schools and colleges—bear enough resemblance to the historical arts of oratorical performance to warrant an association of this field with rhetoric (see Bartholomae in this volume; S. Miller, *Rescuing*; North)? Whatever position one adopts toward this question, taking it up demands at least a passing knowledge of the widely reproduced story of rhetoric's origins in the civilizations of the ancient Mediterranean and its subsequent two-thousand-year history in the West. Here is a short version:

> In the city-states of Greece of the fifth century BCE the transition from a warrior-king system of rule to democracy demanded that newly enfranchised citizens acquire skill in public argumentation in order to defend their lives and property in the new courts and participate in decision making in the new assemblies. A group of itinerant teacher-performers called the first Sophists—including Gorgias, Protagoras, Prodicus, and Antiphon—offered training in these verbal arts, leaving fragments, some in a highly wrought prose style, suggesting that knowledge is a human product derived from debate in time- and culture-bound settings (Sprague). The gadfly philosopher Socrates was classed among them by some, and the whole realm of rhetorical activity became a subject for reflection in fifth-century drama. Plato's fourth-century dialogues found fault with the Sophists' reliance on common belief (*doxa*) and manipulation of democracy's ignorant mobs.

His dialogues about the Sophists (*Gorgias*, *Protagoras*, *Phaedrus*) demonstrate a dialectical method of exposing logical error and revealing the universal truths on which a genuine rhetoric, growing out of the teacher's love of a student's soul, must be based. Plato's student Aristotle modified the philosophy of his teacher, dividing realms of human knowledge and activity into theoretical, practical, and productive. His "art" of rhetoric was the most complete treatment of the subject to date, presenting a method for discovering in particular cases the available means of persuasion. Isocrates, Plato's and Aristotle's contemporary and competitor, laid out in pedagogical writings (e.g., "Antidosis") and demonstrated through political pamphlets (e.g., "Panegyricus") a different approach to rhetoric as a comprehensive *paideia* ("education") in public discourse, guided by the teacher's artful instruction but also dependent on the student's natural ability and regular practice. The program required broad knowledge of civic affairs and the exercise of moral judgment.

During the Hellenistic era, rhetorical categories were systematized, recorded, and eventually taken up by the Romans. The republican aristocrat, lawyer, and senator Cicero made a profound contribution to classical rhetoric in the first-century BCE through his youthful rhetoric text *De Inventione*; his eloquent legal speeches; and most notably in the extended dialogue of his later years, *De Oratore*. Following in the path of the first Sophists and Isocrates, Cicero articulated a broad view of rhetoric as the art of good judgment and civic engagement. Aiming to instruct and please audiences, as well as move them to action, his rhetoric required a lifelong commitment to virtuous conduct in public affairs. The advent of empire impeded the practice of political oratory, but Roman rhetoric survived in the schools. A complete course of study in language learning, reading, interpretation, translation, and rhetorical performance was presented by the first-century CE teacher Quintilian in his *Institutes of Oratory*, featuring a definition of the orator as the good man speaking well. Greek rhetoric (so this version of the story goes) declined into trivial exercises and performance pieces because of the absence of a democratic forum for debate.

Rhetoric nonetheless survived in the Byzantine East and remained important enough in the West to become the queen of arts in the medieval university. Strict social hierarchies and Christianity's suspicion of verbal persuasion constrained its scope, but Augustine found an accommodation in the usefulness of rhetoric for bringing uninformed listeners into the fold. The advent of the Renaissance, with its passion for ancient learning and eloquent style, marked a high point. But the new science—along with Cartesian rationality, the Enlightenment concept of clear reasoning unimpeded by language, and the Romantic focus on individual creativity—brought the two-thousand-year run of ancient rhetoric to a halt.

The argument of this narrative relies on a definition of rhetoric as a broadly accepted set of cultural assumptions and language practices systematized in European educational, legal, and religious institutions. Other narratives are possible, as we see below, but in order to circulate—that is, to argue with one another—they must in some way evoke the word itself. Thus we arrive at the second *stasis*: definition. *Rhetoric* comes from the Ancient Greek root *rhe*, meaning "speak," and the various forms of this root open onto multiple sites of rhetorical activity: rhetors are people who speak, especially those who have achieved recognition for their excellence of character and ability to use language artfully.[5] The speech itself, both its oral performance and its written version, is referred to as rhetoric, a composition crafted to fit a particular situation—perhaps in a formalized genre, such as a legal defense, a political argument, or a ceremonial speech of praise or blame. "Rhetorical situation" indexes the scene of address; the audience and context; the publicity of the speech; its location in a historical, social, political, or institutional setting. What prepares a rhetor for performance is a *paideia*, a system of training designed to cultivate natural capacity and taught through a system of rules or precepts (an "art," in the most common English translation of the Greek word *technē*). Thus a rhetoric is also a textbook containing such instructions. Such a work is sometimes referred to as a theory, a term also derived from an Ancient Greek verb, *theorein*, meaning "to see," or even as a science (Cole 1; Aune 50). Finally, we come to collections of such speeches or rhetorical theories, preserved in writing (later in print and electronically), constituting a canon of rhetoric. The study of rhetoric may entail any or all of these domains.

The third *stasis*—Of what value is it?—has persisted across rhetoric's history, from the epic praise of eloquent speech as a source of honor and fame to Plato's denigration of rhetoric as an unscrupulous knack of manipulation (unless preceded by a dialectical process of truth seeking) to Quintilian's vision of "the good man speaking well" (Kastely; Lanham, " 'Q' Question"; Weaver).[6] Despite the twentieth-century revival of rhetoric in the university as a serious subject of scholarly inquiry and pedagogical practice, the most commonplace use of the term in popular parlance and journalism persistently harks back to Plato's criticism: rhetoric is insubstantial or deceptive language covering over reality or substance. In what ways has contemporary rhetorical scholarship reproduced or sought to dislodge that evaluation? The fourth *stasis*, jurisdiction, poses questions about rhetoric's place. Does rhetoric concern public discourse only, or does it belong in social and intimate realms as well? Where in the academy does rhetoric belong? Does it make sense to apply the label to those scholars whose ideas have affinities with rhetoric but who do not adopt the term?

These introductory points are like handholds for a rock climber, offering a few well-placed propositions to prevent vertigo and temporary support for the newcomer to rhetoric: a terrain James L. Kinneavy described in 1990 as "unmanageable mountains of partially mapped information" ("Contemporary Rhetoric" 186). But definitions of rhetoric work best as transitive rather than propositional statements: sentences that speak about what rhetoric does, where it has been, how it has changed, and where it can be found. Propositions are more at home in classical philosophy, evoking the timeless and universal; to fix *rhetoric* in a proposition violates its nature. Approaching the subject dynamically, we place it in motion, locating rhetoric in circuits of contingency and change, the elements of historical inquiry.

Definitions of rhetoric work best as transitive rather than propositional statements.

We began with the ancient Greeks, an appropriate and indeed unavoidable locus. Rhetoric studies in the twenty-first-century academy are inevitably bound up with the terms, figures, and texts of its ancient Greek and Roman beginnings. The question is not whether to engage with its ancient roots but on what terms. But for most students and teachers in modern university departments of language and literature, the ancient Mediterranean is not a very familiar place. Although a student in English today may have read portions of the *Iliad* and perhaps a Greek tragedy or two as part of a general education curriculum, few scholars in English or communication study Greek and Latin languages and literatures as they would have a century and a half ago. To determine how this change occurred, we turn to a more recent history: the beginnings of the disciplines of English and speech communication, as well as the new field of literary theory, in United States higher education over the past two centuries.

FAMILY RELATIONS: RHETORIC, ENGLISH, AND SPEECH

"English" as a recognized academic subject was not self-begotten. . . . It is a normal and legitimate child. . . . Its mother, the eldest daughter of Rhetoric, was oratory—or what we now prefer to call public speaking. . . .

—William Riley Parker, "Where Do English Departments Come From?"

The MLA was formed in 1883 at a historical moment when the curriculum of a few influential United States universities began to shift away from the study of classical languages and from rhetoric (recitation, declamation, oratory, and debate) as the primary instructional activity. Institutional histories constitute an important area of rhetorical scholarship, and the story of the decline of rhetoric and rise of English has been told from several angles over the past twenty years or so. In William Riley Parker's fanciful analogy of disciplines in a nuclear family relationship (philology plays the father), English eventually grows to "vigorous manhood," alienated from both its parents. Rhetoric, in Parker's view, lost integrity and vitality by giving oratory away to elocution (a popular, nonacademic performance genre) and by its association with "that dismal, unflowering desert, freshman theme-writing" (349).

Historians in the field of rhetoric and composition have told the story with somewhat different points of emphasis. Tracing the history back to England, Thomas P. Miller, in *The Formation of College English: Rhetoric and Belles Lettres in the British Cultural Provinces*, offers a spirited case for eighteenth-century professors of rhetoric as the first teachers of English literature and composition. Hugh Blair in Edinburgh, John Witherspoon in the American colonies, and Thomas Sheridan in Ireland (among others) responded to the pressure placed on intellectuals in England's "cultural provinces" to assimilate to the language practices of the dominant class. But their "English studies" included attention to political exchange, the formation of moral judgments using popular values, and the production of written texts, along with the refinement of speech and writing according to the standards of elite English users and the cultivation of taste through criticism of nonfactual discourse. During the nineteenth century, English went through a process of reduction, Miller asserts, through which "rhetoric began to be marginalized as the discipline came to concentrate on philological studies and a few literary genres—poetry, drama, and fiction" (3).[7]

The decline of rhetoric leads to the rise of writing instruction in the nineteenth-century United States version of the story, told most vividly by Susan Miller (*Textual Carnivals* and *Rescuing the Subject*) and most recently by David R. Russell in *Writing in the Academic Disciplines* (see also Berlin, *Writing Instruction*; Crowley, *Composition* and *Methodical Memory*; Halloran, "Rhetoric in the American College Curriculum"; and Ohmann). As in England, the literatures of modern languages made their way into the United States college curricula as less demanding alternatives to the classics. French, German, and English poetry and fiction came to make up the "lady's course" in colleges such as Oberlin, in contrast with the more rigorous mainstream curriculum in ancient languages and oral performance.

James Berlin, Sharon Crowley, and Richard Ohmann all argue that the shifts in language study are evidence of economic change. Instead of educating a powerful elite to assume the role of decision makers, employing oratorical expertise in politics, law, and the ministry, the universities at the end of the nineteenth century needed to train the middle classes for the specialized writing tasks demanded by new industries and professions. Cultivating taste through reading great literature served to shape bourgeois subjects who would have less need for the civic participation anticipated by the course of study in rhetoric (Crowley, *Composition* 30–45). Simultaneously, modern languages were "territorialized as national literatures in separate departments" and taught as subjects for reading and criticism rather than as living languages, report Bruce Horner and John Trimbur in their study of composition as the outgrowth of a monolingual language policy (602). Departments of English as they took shape at the turn of the twentieth century offered a course of study dedicated to the reading and interpretation of imaginative genres (poetry, fiction, drama). By mid-century, the teaching of required, entry-level courses in composition came to be seen as a low-status and undesirable labor passed off to marginal members of the profession (Crowley, *Composition* 118–31).

The narrative of rhetoric's decline in the wake of English studies as outlined above has been seriously challenged by recent historical scholarship. New histories of rhetoric and writing instruction have identified rhetorically oriented teachers and theorists from the turn of the twentieth century to the 1960s, especially outside elite institutions. JoAnn Campbell argues for the rhetorical significance of Gertrude Buck's 1899 theory of metaphor, and Kathryn M. Conway has presented a vivid picture of rhetorically based pedagogy and performance in the Seven Sisters colleges at the turn of the century. Susan Kates and Karyn Hollis have both documented the rhetorical activities of activist educators from the 1890s through the 1950s. David Gold's dissertation identifies rhetorical theorizing and instruction in women's colleges and historically black colleges during the same period. James Berlin (*Rhetoric and Reality*), Greg Myers ("Reality"), and others have identified teachers inspired by the communist movements of the 1930s who adopted rhetorical methods in their scholarship and teaching. As the title of Gold's dissertation suggests ("Never Mind What Harvard Thinks"), a narrative constructed on evidence from elite institutions may not effectively stand in for curricular and scholarly activity across a wider range of institutional sites.

With the advent of cultural and performance studies over the past two decades, English may no longer stand in such sharp contrast to rhetoric in the terms offered above (see, e.g., Berlin, *Rhetorics, Poetics*). But how deeply and thoroughly changes have penetrated into teaching practices across the country, especially in secondary schools, is another question. There was, however, an adjacent discipline taking shape during the same period, in which students were able to continue with the active discourse practices left aside by English. It is to that discipline that I now turn.

RHETORIC AND SPEECH COMMUNICATION

An opportunity was now at hand for the speech discipline to pick up what English had abandoned.

—Herman Cohen, *The History of Speech Communication*

At the 1914 meeting of the National Association of Teachers of English, a small group of teacher-scholars broke with that organization and founded the National Association of Academic Teachers of Public Speaking.[8] In the standard narrative, the rhetoric that had been reduced to freshman composition in English found a home in the newly established discipline of speech communication. This division, however, has never been pure or thorough, nor has the narrative of a thriving speech-communication-

based rhetoric gone unchallenged. Thomas W. Benson makes a strong case for the influence of Cornell's "invisible college" of rhetoric, housed in the Department of Speech and Drama from the 1920s to the 1960s; he finds that key figures who studied at Cornell carried the study of rhetoric outward to colleges and universities across the country (1–2). Herman Cohen's detailed history of speech communication from 1914 to 1945 offers a different view. Although Cohen takes note of the work of Everett Lee Hunt and other notable rhetoric scholars at Cornell during this period, his conclusion, based on his reading of catalogs of scholarship and conference presentations as well as extensive records of professional organizations and editorial boards, is that rhetoric was overshadowed by public speaking in the first half of the century (186–274; see also Mailloux, "Disciplinary Identities").

According to the most current scholarship, it seems that rhetoric was neither totally absent from university departments of English and writing instruction nor particularly thriving across the spectrum of speech communication departments in the first half of the twentieth century. When we turn to the canonical texts of rhetorical theory before its mid-century revival, we find that the best-known figures from this period— I. A. Richards and Kenneth Burke—are both associated with English studies (although Burke had a tenuous relation with academic institutions for most of his life) and that both develop complex bodies of theory integrating literary critical and rhetorical issues. Richards's reflections on how words come to mean and on the sources of misunderstanding (*The Meaning of Meaning* [1923]; see Richards and Ogden) inspired the imaginative writing theories of Ann Berthoff, and Richards continues to appear in anthologies of literary criticism and rhetorical theory. But his influence has been minimal in comparison with that of Burke, whose monumental legacy almost equals his scholarly ambitions. Burke's first work, *Counter-statement*, published in 1931, was

a call to attend to the ways we use language to build social structures, a call to use rhetoric and communication as framing devices and intellectual foils for exploring the murky realm where language, philosophy, social life, and political ideology exist as one—before disciplines cleave them apart—and a call to see the extent to which language and politics are profoundly of a kind.

(Wolin 38)

The multivolume project of most sustaining interest to rhetoricians was announced in the introduction to Burke's 1945 *A Grammar of Motives*. Burke sought nothing less than to give an account of human motives: "the basic forms of thought . . . in accordance with the nature of the world as all men necessarily experience it" (xv). Through key terms of his dramatistic theory of motives—the pentad of act, scene, agent, agency, and purpose he undertook to explicate the symbolic action of literature, philosophy, and political discourse. A companion volume, *A Rhetoric of Motives*, introduced the concept of identification as an accessory to persuasion in the reclamation of rhetoric as a means of understanding how writers represent human change. Difficult to categorize, Burke moved across disciplines, exhorting anthropologists, psychologists, sociologists, and literary critics to recognize the influence of rhetoric, which he saw as "rooted in an essential function of language itself . . . ; the use of language as a symbolic means of inducing cooperation in beings that by nature respond to symbols" (43). Like Richards, Burke appears in anthologies of both literary criticism and theory, but the continuing stream of scholarship on his writings comes largely from rhetoricians (e.g., Biesecker, *Addressing*; Crusius; Quandahl, "More than Lessons"; Selzer).[9]

RHETORIC AND PHILOSOPHY'S LINGUISTIC TURN

In the worlds of Continental philosophy, human sciences, and linguistics, another story line was playing out over the same time period. With the invention of science in the seventeenth century,

> **Dramatic reconceptualizations of nature, economics, psychology, and language redirected the course of European intellectual history.**

nature had come to be seen as an ordered and knowable world of the real outside human consciousness, which had the power through empirical investigations guided by reason to discover and fix nature's meaning. Language was a sometimes intrusive but ideally transparent medium for communicating that meaning. Though people could reason with one another to arrive at decisions about, for example, new forms of government, like the democracies of the eighteenth century, each mind operated independently. But beginning with the publication of Charles Darwin's *Origins of the Species* in 1859 and through the turn of the twentieth century, dramatic reconceptualizations of nature, economics, psychology, and language redirected the course of European intellectual history, disrupting well-established relations among knowledge, language, social order, and human self-understanding. The revolutionary changes set in motion during this period were in some cases born out of the study of ancient rhetoric and would ultimately influence rhetoric's twentieth-century incarnation.

Soon after Darwin's blow to natural philosophy, Karl Marx, trained as a classicist, overturned German idealism by arguing that not soul or spirit but human relations in labor are determinants of history and consciousness. Although Marx himself had little to say about rhetoric (Aune describes him as a participant in the "antirhetoric" of modernity [27–30]), his concept of ideology as a determinant of knowledge and value has rich rhetorical implications.[10] In the realm of psychology, Sigmund Freud introduced a theory of the unconscious, access to which becomes possible through linguistic acts of narrating dreams in the rhetorical structure of analysis. The reach of these two thinkers extends far beyond the realm of rhetoric, but each argues (for different reasons) that people's words are not their own. In the realm of language, Friedrich Nietzsche's disruptions created a similar effect and mark the most significant point of departure for scholars of rhetoric, linguistics, and literary theorists. For these philosophers and their successors, as Samuel IJsseling writes, "The source from which speech proceeds is different from consciousness. In short man is not lord and master in his own house" (127).

Nietzsche takes classical philosophy around a "linguistic turn" (Rorty, *Linguistic Turn*), radically challenging the possibility of truth based on a logic of noncontradiction, the stability of ethics in a Judeo-Christian frame, and the correspondence of an internally derived knowledge to an external reality. Nietzsche studied and taught ancient Greek philosophy (as was typical in German universities in the 1870s). His notes for a series of lectures on ancient Greek rhetoric offered in 1872–73 at the University of Basel ("Description"), along with his seminal essay on the tropical essence of language, "On Truth and Lying in an Extra-moral Sense" (1873) are translated (the lectures including facing-page German) in Sander Gilman, Carole Blair, and David Parent's 1989 *Friedrich Nietzsche on Rhetoric and Language*. An important group of French literary theorists follow as heirs of Nietzsche, working from his insight that language does not represent the world but, through its tropes and figures, brings it into being. Ferdinand de Saussure's structural linguistics develops a compatible thesis derived from structural anthropology: meaning is generated through signs structured in a binary relation to each other rather than through a natural correspondence between signs and what they signify. Roland Barthes, who announced the death of the author and cataloged the meanings of popular cultural objects in a structure like mythology, made a serious engagement with ancient rhetoric in his seminar at the École Pratique des Hautes Études in 1964–65 ("Old Rhetoric"; see also Worsham, "Eating History"). Rearticulating the tropological or figurative origins of language ("White Mythology"), Jacques Derrida carried structuralism into new territory, demonstrating through a reading of Plato's *Phaedrus* his method of deconstruction: taking apart seemingly stable binary oppositions—in Plato's case, speech and writing—to expose hierarchies of value and occlusions of meaning structured in literary and cultural texts

("Plato's Pharmacy"; see also Neel). Rhetoric figures more prominently in the work of Derrida's contemporary, Paul de Man. Through a reading of Nietzsche's engagement with ancient rhetoric, de Man lays out a "process of reading in which rhetoric is a disruptive intertwining of trope and persuasion" (ix).

Two more French intellectuals may be introduced together because their projects, for all their differences, involve not the analysis of literary texts but the large-scale organization of knowledge and language use as a broad social system. Jean-François Lyotard in *The Differend: Phrases in Dispute* uses the conundrums of pre-Socratic logic along with a reading of Aristotle's logical principles as a historical background for demonstrating the incommensurability of competing versions of reality and history in the context of the twentieth-century's violent conflicts. Trained initially in the social sciences, Michel Foucault, through his intensive studies of clinics, prisons, and knowledge paradigms over history in disciplines such as economics and linguistics, arrives at a theory of discourse as a system with vast power over people's speech, actions, and self-understanding ("Discourse"). His essays on historiography (i.e., how history is written ["Nietzsche"]) and his studies of language, sexuality, and religion in ancient Greece have had a powerful influence in rhetoric and classics (*History of Sexuality* and *Fearless Speech*).

Coming of age during the most dramatic political revolution of the early twentieth century, Mikhail Bakhtin was a linguistic theorist and literary critic influenced both by Marxist economic and social theory and by the formalist aesthetic theory of his era. He argued eloquently that language in essence and in all forms, from ordinary speech to literary creations, functions as dialogue. In his attempt to account for the heteroglossia (the interplay of voices) that characterizes prose fiction from within a critical culture that privileged the more monologic genre of poetry, Bakhtin valued his encounter with ancient rhetoric:

> Once rhetorical discourse is brought into the study with all its living diversity, it cannot fail to have a deeply revolutionizing influence on

linguistics and on the philosophy of language. It is precisely those aspects of any discourse (the internally dialogic quality of discourse, and the phenomena related to it), not yet sufficiently taken into account and fathomed in all the enormous weight they carry in the life of language, that are revealed with great external precision in rhetorical forms, provided a correct and unprejudiced approach to those forms is used. Such is the general methodological and heuristic significance of rhetorical forms for linguistics and for the philosophy of language.   (268–69)

Another line of philosophical innovation with close relations to rhetoric can be traced back to such nineteenth-century German philosophers as Friedrich Schleiermacher and Wilhelm Dilthey and such twentieth-century German philosophers as Martin Heidegger and Hans-Georg Gadamer. Taking issue with a classical philosophy that purported to establish irrefutable truth, hermeneutics ultimately extended its reach to "all problems of understanding in the so-called human sciences" (Jost and Hyde xiii), offering what many scholars identify as rhetorical approaches to questions of time, truth, and authority in interpretive practice (Gadamer 568–69). Gadamer turns to Aristotle's development of moral reasoning as a knowledge of the self acting in concrete situations (*phronesis*) for an alternative to the "false objectification" of scientific interpretation (312–24).

On the other side of the Atlantic, another disruption of a metaphysically oriented philosophy occurs with the emergence of pragmatism. Eclectic thinkers such as Charles Sanders Peirce, William James, and John Dewey argue that basic philosophical problems of knowledge and ethics cannot be resolved outside the consideration of their practical consequences. Issues of interpretation and perspective, of the situated stances of thinkers and actors, thoroughly permeate any philosophical enterprise. Later in the century, Richard Rorty reintroduces and elaborates the pragmatic challenge to analytic philosophy in *Philosophy and the Mirror of Nature* and other works, undercutting the classical concept of language as a reflection of or conduit to truth with the idea of philosophy as a conversation (see Mailloux, *Rhetoric*).

At many points, these theorizations of language, culture, and knowledge can be understood as rhetorical, as William Keith has put it, "in all but name" (Gross and Keith 1), although few of the figures reviewed above place their work squarely in the disciplinary realm of rhetoric.[11] Because of the lack of interest in pedagogy and student writing in the United States on the part of Continental philosophers and literary theorists, as well as, in some cases, a disregard for the rhetorical situatedness of their own discourse, some rhetoricians and compositionists do not believe alliances with literary theory are productive. Despite this one-way-street effect, many other scholars in rhetoric have found in Continental philosophy and discourse theory important resources for their work. Some of the key figures appear in anthologies (Bizzell and Herzberg; Brummett; Enos and Brown, *Professing*; Foss, Foss, and Trapp) and are required reading for PhD examinations. A comprehensive account of the intersections between literary theory and new rhetoric studies since the linguistic turn has yet to be written (see essays in Clifford and Schilb), but I explore some sites of connection in the final section of this essay. For now, my narrative of the uneven development of rhetoric in English, speech communication, and Continental philosophy becomes an institutional backdrop for the emergence of a particular form of rhetorical scholarship and teaching in the distinctive institutional space of rhetoric and composition.

RHETORIC FOR WRITING

During the 1960s, an influx of new, underprepared students into the universities led to the inauguration of composition as a research field and, some believe, prepared for a turn to rhetoric as a historical and theoretical ground for the teaching of writing.[12] Not all compositionists adopted rhetoric as a foundation for writing instruction, but a few key scholars made the link persuasively and disseminated their vision of a newly constituted field of rhetoric through major publications and graduate programs.[13] The professional narratives of this generation of scholars, most of whom were trained in literary criticism or education, often feature the trope of seeking something missing or of experiencing a misfit between their training as scholars and the institutional demands they faced as academics. They were drawn to rhetoric not only because it offered a perspective on writing as a sophisticated and central rather than a remedial and marginal component of liberal education but also because it gave them resources for orienting their work with student writers to the pressing political, legal, and cultural problems of the era. Sharon Crowley narrates her turn toward rhetoric in these terms:

> I had found by painful experience that high school students had no use at all for instruction in lit-with-grammar. This was the 'sixties, after all, and what my urban students needed was instruction in how to construct an effective argument; that is, they needed rhetoric.
>
> ("Communications Skills" 98)[14]

Edward P. J. Corbett's *Classical Rhetoric for the Modern Student* and James Kinneavy's *Theory of Discourse* stand as pillars at this point on the historical path. The two books in their structures and emphases exemplify two functions of rhetoric: as instruction and theory. First published in 1965, Corbett's textbook presents a thorough course of study in ancient rhetorical formulas, including elements such as the topoi (common "places" for generating arguments about a topic), the three general forms of proof (based in logic, emotion, and the character of the speaker), and figures of speech.[15] The book also contains examples of persuasive speeches and print texts for analysis, along with a historical survey of the field. In his rationale, Corbett argues that rhetoric (for better or worse) permeates modern life and that an understanding of relevant parts of the ancient art will serve citizens as a bulwark against propaganda and demagoguery. Further, a rhetorical approach offers a "positive" aid to writing instead of the "negative" practices more common in the composition classroom of the day (29–31).

The resources for invention . . . hold great interest for scholarship in rhetoric during this period.

The resources for invention—a term rhetoricians adopt from the Latin *inventio*, referring to the discovery of materials to be used in an oration—hold great interest for scholarship in rhetoric during this period. In a turn away from the fixed formulas and error correction characteristic of many freshman composition courses in the 1960s (see Crowley, *Methodical Memory*), rhetoric scholars found resources in ancient Greek and Roman writing pedagogy and began to focus more attention on the ways writers compose. Aristotle's definition of rhetoric as a heuristic process—the faculty of discovering the available means of persuasion in each case—provided a key point of reference and inspiration for this line of scholarship (see Lauer, "Issues"; Young, Becker, and Pike).

Kinneavy likewise worked against the limited scope of composition instruction—its restriction to expository writing and the interpretation of literary texts—and cast his major work as a textbook for advanced students or teachers in training. But his *Theory of Discourse* reaches beyond the domain of composition by aspiring to "present a coherent and unified view of the field of English" (ix) and to provide a legitimate foundation for composition as a research field (1–3; see Bartholomae in this volume). Kinneavy built that foundation on a framework of communication. Citing as sources Aristotle's *On Rhetoric*, Peirce's semiotics, and M. H. Abrams's literary-criticism, he envisioned communication as a triangle of factors: the producer of a communication (a speaker or writer); the receiver (a listener or reader); and the message itself, including form and content. This triangle is set into a context or situation, constituting the fourth element to be considered in the production or analysis of any discourse.[16] In an article anticipating the longer work, Kinneavy vividly figures the four purposes of writing derived from the communication triangle:

> If a comparison may be drawn, it could be said that language is like a windowpane. I may throw bricks at it to vent my feelings about something; I may use a chunk of it to chase away an intruder;

I may use it to mirror or explore reality; and I may use a stained-glass window to call attention to itself as an object of beauty. Windows, like language, can be used expressively, persuasively, referentially, and esthetically.   ("Basic Aims" 303)

Both Corbett and Kinneavy conceived of rhetoric (or discourse) as a quintessentially human activity, its study rightfully at the center of the liberal arts curriculum. Each drew from rhetoric's ancient legacy, and most productively from Aristotle, a communicative purpose and a rich array of composing strategies for a practice that had become severely attenuated in the composition classes of their era.

The influence of Aristotle's work has been profound and persistent in late-twentieth-century rhetoric studies. The first text in the Western tradition to systematize, and some would say theorize, the practice of public speaking, *On Rhetoric* has served as both a source of materials for contemporary writing theory and practice and a point of entry into the larger world of ancient rhetoric. Scholars have sought to place Aristotle's rhetoric text in the wider context of his substantial body of work, especially his writings on ethics and poetics, and within the historical, political, and intellectual climate of his era. Investigations into the sources of Aristotle's approach to rhetoric led a number of scholars to the fragmentary but provocative writings of the first Sophists, who emerged as a particularly lively site of historical and historiographical debate in the 1990s (Jarratt, *Rereading*; J. Poulakos; Schiappa, *Protagoras*; Vitanza, "Notes"). Perhaps because of Aristotle's penchant for classification and definition, his work has given rise to multiple lines of scholarly inquiry leading out from key terms: the three modes of persuasion (*pisteis*)—ethos (Baumlin and Baumlin), pathos (Quandahl, "Feeling"; Worsham, "Going Postal"), and logos (Crosswhite; Fahnestock and Secor); the commonplaces of argument or topoi (C. Miller, "Aristotle's 'Special Topics' "); and the enthymeme, an informal mode of reasoning characteristic of rhetoric (Gage; Walker, *Rhetoric*), among many others.

The *Rhetoric* has more to say about the logic of speeches—the structure of argument—than about any other subject. Whether inspired by Aristotle, by later theories of argument, or by the opening up of writing instruction to purposes and forms other than the literary critical essay, rhetoricians have produced a rich body of work on the argumentative structure of texts in a variety of genres over the past three decades. Aristotle's topoi, lists of common modes of reasoning, are divided into a few general formulas and a much longer list of special or subject-specific topics. Recognizing that twentieth-century subjects for deliberation would of course differ from those of fourth-century Greece, Carolyn Miller nonetheless explored the possibility that Aristotle's special topics might suggest a way of getting at discipline-specific forms of reasoning ("Aristotle's 'Special Topics' "). Chaim Perelman and Lucie Olbrechts-Tyteca's monumental work on legal reasoning, as well as Thomas Kuhn's *Structure of Scientific Revolutions*, prepared the way for rhetorical analyses of knowledge claims in disciplines outside the humanities (Mailloux, "Disciplinary Identities"). As rhetoricians began developing undergraduate courses in technical and professional writing and in writing in the disciplines across the university, scholars such as Charles Bazerman, Jeanne Fahnestock, and Greg Myers (*Writing Biology*) took the lead in developing discipline-specific argument, the rhetoric of science, and text analysis as strong research fields (see also Nelson, Megill, and McCloskey).

Argument theory and analysis continue to develop in the humanities also, as rhetoricians elaborate systems of rhetorical reasoning for composition classes and draw on the work of philosophers such as Stephen Toulmin in the process. Although some research in technical and professional writing can become so instrumentally oriented as to lose its connection with the scholarly field of rhetoric, the investment in a historical tradition remains strong in the work of major figures. Fahnestock's recent *Rhetorical Figures in Science* takes readers "back over the epistemological watershed of the late eighteenth and early nineteenth centuries" by demonstrating how some of the lesser known figures of speech (antithesis, *gradatio*, *antimetabole*, etc.) function in contemporary scientific arguments (viii).

The rediscovery of a venerable two-thousand-year rhetorical tradition had a dual effect. Some saw in it a grounding for a contemporary discipline and a wealth of scholarly resources; others criticized the reach into a distant past as insufficiently attentive to historical differences. Three decades of historical work in rhetoric have unsettled the master narrative (offered in the opening section) without dispensing with it. Scholarly debate has focused on two historiographical issues. One concerns the question of parallels or the lack of them between ancient and contemporary cultures. In addition to transporting pedagogical techniques, historians have drawn connections between the uses of rhetoric in ancient and modern democracies (Jarratt, *Rereading*), exposed the roots of antifoundational philosophy in the epistemological conflict between Plato and the Sophists (Fish, *Doing*; Mailloux, *Reception Histories*), and found an adumbration of postmodern language play in the first sophistic (Ballif; Vitanza, *Negation*).

Others have argued that because of the differences in cultural and material conditions and because of the dramatic shifts in concepts of the self, the mind, and modes of apprehending the world since ancient times, building scholarly projects on such parallels is unwarranted (Halloran, "On the End"). In their 1990 essay "Rhetoricality: On the Modernist Return of Rhetoric," John Bender and David E. Wellbery make a case for a decisive break at the Enlightenment and argue that rhetoric has now been replaced by rhetoricality, a generalized condition of modern existence. Carolyn Miller counters this view in "Classical Rhetoric without Nostalgia":

> Although Bender and Wellbery emphasize the coherence and doctrinal "codification" in the classical tradition, and its connection with property and social position, we might just as easily emphasize the disagreements, the fissures, the possibilities for rabble-rousing and subversion, the differential interests and ideologies of Aristotelian and Isocratean rhetoric, of descriptive and nor-

mative conceptualizations. This is not to say that the tradition can be anything we like or that translation is unnecessary.   (160)[17]

A related issue has to do with how the story of the past is told. Is it appropriate to begin the story of rhetoric in fifth-century BCE Greece, or should earlier traditions of persuasive speaking and writing be included? Written texts—preserved on clay tablets, papyrus, and stone—offer evidence of what some historians would term rhetorical activity in ancient Sumer, Egypt, China, and India centuries before the Greeks invented the word *rhetoric*. In these lines from a collection of Sumerian poems about the goddess Inanna, composed around 2000 BCE, the goddess is thanking her father for giving her the extraordinary personal accomplishments suitable for her high station. Here she introduces many of the themes found in ancient Greek rhetoric:

> He gave me the art of forthright speech.
> He gave me the art of slanderous speech.
> He gave me the art of adorning speech.
> (Wolkstein and Kramer 17)

The value of "forthright speech," the epistemological problem of false speech, and the ethical problem of beautiful but seductive speech, all given voice by a powerful figure, suggest a concern for rhetorical issues in this very early Middle Eastern civilization 1,500 years before the invention of the term *rhetoric* (Lipson and Binkley 11–13). The problems of origins and naming crop up even in the Greek context. Did Greek rhetoric begin in the fifth century, or is it valid to speak of rhetoric in the much earlier forms of epic and archaic lyric (Jarratt "Sappho's Memory"; Walker, *Rhetoric*)? Did the first Sophists practice rhetoric, or is it more appropriate to describe their activities under the term *logos* (Cole; Schiappa, *Beginnings*)? Can the story of the past be related as it was without the intrusion of modern perspectives (Schiappa, "*Rhetorikē*")? If not, how will revisionary or postmodern histories be evaluated (Hariman, "Allegory"; T. Poulakos; Vitanza, *Writing Histories*)? These questions are far from settled.[18]

COUNTERNARRATIVES

I . . . am [a] colored woman that goes about to speak for the rights of the colored woman. I want to keep the thing stirring, now that the ice is cracked.

—Sojourner Truth

Constructing a narrative about rhetoric, as Nan Johnson has written,

> requires first the acknowledgment of the institutional role that rhetorical pedagogies play in inscribing discursive practices that maintain rather than destabilize status-quo relationships of gender, race, and class. If rhetoric did not have this kind of institutional force, rhetorical power could not have been held so long by so few.
>
> (*Gender* 1–2)

Troubling the standard story has led some scholars not only to note rhetoric's exclusionary force but also to search behind it for sites of rhetorical activity by outsiders: those not imagined by its theories or allowed in its traditional realms of participation. A flood of new scholarship recovering and analyzing such practices, as well as seeking to gauge their effects on traditional theory and practice, has been redrawing the rhetorical map.

Women have entered the picture through essay collections (Lunsford, *Reclaiming*; Sutherland and Sutcliffe; Wertheimer), monographs (Eldred and Mortensen; Glenn, *Rhetoric*), and anthologies of primary texts (Donawerth; Logan, *With Pen*; Ritchie and Ronald). Some efforts to recover women's rhetorical activities—sometimes involving the realignment of genres such as poetry, conduct books, memoir, and letter writing to capture their rhetorical force—have focused on such notable women in the western European tradition as Sappho, Aspasia, Christine de Pisan, Elizabeth I, and Mary Wollstonecraft. The oratory and political writing of nineteenth-century African American women has received particularly careful attention (Logan, *"We Are Coming"*; Royster). If Enlightenment theory invalidated

rhetoric at one level, its promises of citizenship and political enfranchisement opened the doors to a wealth of rhetorical practices in pursuit of those prizes at another. The "ice was cracked," in Sojourner Truth's figure (qtd. in Logan, *With Pen* 29), when Maria Stewart spoke in 1832 before a "promiscuous" audience (i.e., including both men and women) in Boston, inspired by David Walker's militant 1829 manifesto and followed by an impressive line of powerful orators and political writers through the rest of the century (see Foner and Branham).

One of the methodological questions driving this work asks to what extent rhetors from a particular group develop distinctive rhetorical techniques or rely on the modes of argumentation, emotional appeal, and self-presentation available in traditional sources (see, for example, Bacon; Ritchie and Ronald's introduction). Some rhetoric scholars have sought alternatives to the method of building histories around single, prominent figures—in effect recapitulating the movement by feminist historians more generally away from an additive model of women's history toward projects taking gender as a category of analysis (Ballif; Brody; Mattingly). It may be taken as a sign of the growing sophistication of the field that studies featuring achievements of extraordinary rhetors from marginalized groups are being joined by measured analyses of the complex interplay of forces determining rhetorical possibilities for rhetors who can be sited at the intersections of multiple social axes. Johnson's argument that middle-class white women on public podiums at the turn of the twentieth century are enmeshed in an ideology of domesticity, Shevaun E. Watson's reading of the violence wrought by African American slave testimonies in the Denmark Vesey trial early in the nineteenth century, and Steven Mailloux's tracing of tropes about slave bodies by southern proslavery writers through abolitionists including Frederick Douglass are examples of these newer styles of history writing ("Remarking"; see also Clark and

Troubling the standard story has led some scholars not only to note rhetoric's exclusionary force but also to search behind it for sites of rhetorical activity by outsiders.

Halloran; Lyons, "Rhetorical Sovereignty" and *X-Marks*).

The desire to pluralize rhetoric's history has led scholars outside the Western tradition and raised perplexing methodological questions (Bizzell and Jarratt). Scholars of East Asian rhetoric have taken a lead in producing new work (e.g., Liu; Lu; Mao, "Individualism," "Reclustering," *Reflective Encounters*, and "Rhetorical Borderlands") and debating the terms on which comparative rhetoric should proceed. The methodological challenge of describing rhetorically distinct practices under national identities was brought into question by Yoshihisa Itaba, Hideki Kakita, and Satoru Aonuma, on behalf of the Japan Society for Rhetorical Studies, at the 2003 meeting of the Alliance of Rhetoric Societies. Acknowledging that they were present under a national-linguistic term, they nonetheless declined to speak of Japanese rhetoric as a way of calling attention to "a sort of reverse Orientalism [that] should therefore be called Occidentalism" generated by such a category (Itaba, Kakita, and Aonuma).[19] Borrowing from anthropological methods a two-pronged approach to non-Western rhetorics somewhat mitigates the difficulty by multiplication. A study of, for example, Chinese rhetoric would first examine Chinese practices on their own terms and then consider them in relation with Western traditions (Mao, *Reflective Encounters*; see also Garrett).

From the time Romans adopted Greek rhetorical education, rhetoric has been a comparative practice. Quintilian recommended that young students begin with Greek because they will unavoidably learn Latin through its general use (1.1.12).[20] Bruce Horner and John Trimbur characterize the classically based college curriculum in the nineteenth century as multilingual, giving a new angle of vision to learning based in so-called dead languages. More recently, scholars have taken up the task of comparing rhetorical styles in modern languages, an enterprise that has undergone serious critique since its beginnings in the 1960s.[21] Nuanced treatments of speech and writing in scenes of transnational contact, such as Susan Romano's study of indig-enous people in Mexico during the Spanish colonial period and Scott Lyons's work on American Indian writing ("Rhetorical Sovereignty" and *X-Marks*), give evidence of the promising future for scholarship in comparative rhetoric (see also Abbott).

Although most of the research cited here comes from scholars in the United States, some of them have sought a wider perspective through association with the International Society for the History of Rhetoric (ISHR), founded in 1977. Aiming to

> [promote] the study of both the theory and practice of rhetoric in all periods and languages and the relationship of rhetoric to poetics, literary theory and criticism, philosophy, politics, religion, law, and other aspects of the cultural context
> (*Intl. Soc.*),

the ISHR holds a biennial conference and supports the journal *Rhetorica*, both of which operate in six official languages, five living and one dead (English, French, German, Italian, Spanish, and Latin). Despite the journal's strongly western European orientation, contributors have recently written on Byzantine rhetoric (Walker, "These Things") and ancient Egyptian rhetoric (Hutto). Investigations of Jewish rhetoric (Friedenberg) and Islamic rhetoric (Gaffney) are beginning to receive recognition. The relative paucity of scholarship on non-Western rhetorics suggests a wealth of research opportunities awaiting those just entering the field.

NEW DIRECTIONS IN RHETORICAL SCHOLARSHIP

[O]ld Rhetoric is *set in opposition to that* new *which may not yet have come into being: the world is incredibly full of old Rhetoric.*

—Roland Barthes, "The Old Rhetoric"

Proceeding under the mode of narrative, this account has attempted to track an unsettled but dynamic field, making a case for the vitality of rhetoric in the twenty-first century not as a reinstitution of an intact system of categories but through the capacity of those who take up its "ruins" (Hariman, "Allegory" 267) and use them to pursue questions such as those posed by the character Phaidra at the outset. Neither a single, widely accepted set of theoretical assumptions nor a common method inform the highly diverse practices of scholarship in rhetoric at the beginning of the twenty-first century. Nonetheless, we may set up a provisional framework for organizing some significant current projects in rhetorical scholarship by returning to the familiar terms of the communication triangle, not as a set of givens but as a set of questions. As we track the ratios between speaker and audience, audience and context, text and context, and so on, we find scholars testing, stretching, sometimes abandoning, but more often creatively reworking the conventional categories in response to new developments in theory, to the expansion of electronic media and accompanying pervasiveness of the image, and to the force of events on the global stage.

Who Speaks?

At its most literal, the communications model of rhetorical action presupposes autonomous speakers fully aware of their intentions and authors of their words: this figure of speaker we earlier saw deposed by Marx, Freud, Nietzsche, and their successors. Some scholars in rhetoric have moved decisively in the direction of redefining the speaker or author as subject—that is, a person subjected to the determinations of ideology, the unconscious, institutions, and systems of discourse (Biesecker, "Rethinking"; Vitanza, *Negation*; see also Clifford and Schilb). Others have taken a more qualified view of the issue, often discussed as a question of agency. Carolyn Miller, for example, suggests that

> rhetorical action [is] a function that is both intended and governed (and both imperfectly), a function for which neither the humanist ideology of agency nor the postmodern ideology of ventriloquism is sufficient explanation but for which both can offer insight.
>
> ("Classical Rhetoric" 159)

In her keynote address at the 2003 Alliance of Rhetoric Societies meeting, Karlyn Kohrs Campbell drew on the ancient concept of *technē*, an "art" in the sense of a thoughtful practice, guided but not wholly determined by learned principles. Citing the feminist theory of Judith Butler, Campbell explained how rhetors will repeat those words that come from elsewhere; but between the multiple iterations of discourse, differences arise, and it is in those differences, as well as in the spaces of articulation between rhetor and audience, that the potential for agency lies. Campbell's terms resonate with those of essays in a recent collection on ethos (Baumlin and Baumlin), some of which exploit the spatial associations of the ancient term in alliance with postmodern theories of the subject (see Jarratt and Reynolds).

The categories of agency and subjectivity have led rhetoricians to reexamine the long tradition of oratory as a practice of and reflection on bodies in space. Twenty-first-century theorists of rhetoric are focusing on the materiality of rhetorical performance and various modes of embodiment produced in rhetorical acts (Fleckenstein; Ratcliffe, "Material Matters"; Selzer and Crowley). Another line of research merging the question of subjectivity with a radical conception of practice moves further from the entanglements of the human. Janet Atwill's argument for Aristotelian rhetoric as a productive rather than practical art draws on the French cultural theorist Pierre Bourdieu, particularly his term *habitus*, a pattern of partly conscious, partly automatic cultural practice. Atwill's posthumanist rhetoric carries the classical concept of invention into new terrain.

Agency arises as a factor in contemporary studies of speaking and writing by people from marginalized social groups. The spaces of rhetorical engagement, as Johnson noted above, have historically been restricted to speakers and writers from privileged social groups. Agency becomes a more active concept when it defines the movement of excluded groups into formerly restricted arenas of speech and publication. Feminist scholars who have contributed to this line of work in various ways (in addition to the historians mentioned above) include Lisa Ede, Cheryl Glenn, and Andrea Lunsford ("Border Crossings"); Krista Ratcliffe (*Anglo-American Feminist Challenges*); and Lynn Worsham ("After Words"). A related issue is the problem of enfranchised speakers representing others (Alcoff; Spivak). The flourishing of feminist engagements with rhetoric is evident not only in publications but also in the Feminism(s) and Rhetoric(s) Conferences, which have been held biennially since 1997, and in the Coalition for Women Scholars in the History of Rhetoric and Composition.[22] Studies of race and rhetoric likewise take up questions of agency, embodiment, style (Gilyard; Olson and Worsham; Pough) as well as the rhetorical dimensions of whiteness (Keating; Ratcliffe, "Eavesdropping"). A new collection on postcolonial studies includes essays on rhetorics of *testimonio*, questions of representation, and linguistic styles (Lunsford and Ouzgane). Such issues will continue to occupy scholars of rhetoric in the twenty-first century.

The question, Who speaks?, is broached in the field of psychoanalysis, a discourse that has lurked with little visibility on the boundaries of the new rhetoric but has become more manifest in recent times. Earlier theorists raised the question without pursuing it very far. IJsseling, for example, includes in his brief discussion of Freud the comment that "Freudian psychoanalysis is more a rhetoric than an hermeneutic, more an analysis of hidden rhetorical structures than an interpretation of a hidden meaning" (96). Wayne Booth draws an analogy between the rhetorical situation and the analytic scene as systems for changing minds: ". . . when the analyst talks of transference he is dealing with the processes that underlie what we mean by ethical proof" ("Scope" 107–08; see also Fish, *Doing* 525–54; Quandahl, "More than Lessons"). A new body of work on the emotions, some of which draws on Aristotle, falls into this realm of study (Micciche and Jacobs; Quandahl, "Feeling"). The most thorough and impressive engagement

Despite the advent of writing, print, and electronic communications, the scene of the face-to-face public encounter maintains its hold on the imagination and scholarly energy of rhetoricians.

comes in Susan Wells's *Sweet Reason*, a study of rhetorics of modernity (specifically those of Jürgen Habermas and Jacques Lacan) as "temporally situated means of analyzing the discursive economies of rationality and desire" (132). This ambitious study outlines the possibilities for a rhetoric of intersubjectivity to organize approaches to language in action under the conditions of modernity, including the absence of a stable distinction between rationality and desire (140–41). Marshall Alcorn employs psychoanalytic concepts to make an argument about the modern divided self and rhetorical ethos (see Alcorn, "Self-Structure"). His *Changing the Subject in English Class* investigates resistance to change—the chief emotional impediment to learning—in terms of a rhetoric of mourning, an unconscious process of giving up a part of one's ego required by new learning. The implications and potential value of this study and others of its type are profound in a world riven by violently opposed and passionately held belief systems.

To Whom?

Despite the advent of writing, print, and electronic communications, the scene of the face-to-face public encounter maintains its hold on the imagination and scholarly energy of rhetoricians. The etymology of *audience* (from the Latin verb *audire* ["to hear"]) implies interlocutors located in a common time and place, as well as outcomes in action: a verdict in a trial, a vote by a deliberative body, or a religious conversion. Surrounding conditions such as silence (Glenn, *Unspoken*) and listening (Ratcliffe, "Eavesdropping"), as well as the specific conditions of print culture, under which an audience of strangers must be imagined and even invoked in the text, have posed provocative challenges to scholars in rhetoric and literary studies (Ede and Lunsford, "Audience Addressed"; Warner, *Letters*).

A related strand of scholarly activity arose in the mid–twentieth century and fixed on the concepts of space or spheres of discursive action as the organizing terms. Hannah Arendt's 1958 *Human Condition* drew on the ancient Greek admiration for excellent speech and action in the public realm as an inspiration for theorizing an alternative mode of life in the face of the destructive and alienating power of modern science and the loss of meaning in mass, industrial society. Jürgen Habermas's 1964 *Structural Transformation of the Public Sphere* touched similar themes in a work that, following its translation into English in 1989, has given rise to a new alliance of scholars from literary and political theory, philosophy, and rhetoric under the rubric of public sphere studies. With special attention to the conditions of print culture in the era of democratic revolutions, public sphere scholars analyze the conditions and effects of public speaking and writing in various historical, geographic, and cultural contexts (Black Public Sphere Collective; Eberly; Roberts-Miller). They also theorize about conditions under which publics and counterpublics become possible against the twenty-first-century constraints of expert-generated knowledge, bureaucracy, and corporate-owned mass media (Farrell, *Norms*; Hauser; Warner, *Public*; Wells). In a public lecture on the exploitation of developing nations under globalization, the Indian writer Arundhati Roy crystallizes the hopes that drive public sphere theory:

> I think it's time to de-professionalize the public debate on matters that vitally affect the lives of ordinary people. It's time to snatch our futures back from the "experts." Time to ask, in ordinary language, the public question and to demand, in ordinary language, the public answer.   (24)

The emphasis on rhetorical action in public sphere theory dovetails with another twentieth-century reconfiguration of audience. Speech act theory, initiated by J. L. Austin's *How to Do Things with Words* (delivered as William James Lectures at Harvard University in 1955), poses a challenge to analytic philosophy in arguing that "the truth or falsity of a statement depends not merely on the meanings of words but on what act you were performing in what circumstances"

(145). Initially distinguishing sentences that communicate information (constative) from those that have effects or perform action, Austin ultimately comes to the rhetorical conclusion that all speech has a performative force: "Once we realize that what we have to study is *not* the sentence but the issuing of an utterance in a speech situation, there can hardly be any longer a possibility of not seeing that stating is performing an act" (139; emphasis in original). Scholars in queer theory such as Judith Butler (*Gender Trouble*), Eve Kosofsky Sedgwick, and Michael Warner find in performativity an alternative to identity as a way of understanding subject formation. Rhetoric has conventionally been more focused on the potential effects of speech on listeners (what Austin would call a "perlocutionary" effect), but the move toward a more generalized concept of performativity blurs the speaker-audience distinction, placing all rhetorical acts in a discursive system guided by rules (conditions of felicity, in Austin's terminology), the adherence to which guarantees the efficacy of the speech or writing.

Moving from the sentence to discourse—large-scale networks of language organized by institutions, disciplines, or even whole cultures—we have moved even further from a communication model involving speakers and listeners. In "Discourse on Language," Michel Foucault argues that topics about which people speak are made available or excluded by discursive formations—such as the accepted reasoning about madness and sanity, crime, or sexuality—an arrangement that dramatically diminishes the potential for rhetorical agency imagined under a communications model. Nonetheless, Foucault's brilliant insights about the power of institutions have permeated rhetorical scholarship, leading teachers to reflect about the contradictions inherent in locating rhetoric as a civic practice in educational institutions (see Bartholomae in this volume). Not only words but bodies also are shaped by discourse, argues Foucault, bringing his work into dialogue with speech act and performance theory. Scholars in rhetoric studies have worked directly with speech act theory and performativity (Mao, "Individualism"; Flecken-stein) and more recently under the terms *materiality* and *embodiment* (see Selzer and Crowley). In this line of analysis, the body becomes a text and the text a body, propelling us on to the next pole in the communication triangle.

About What?

The "message" corner of the communications triangle invites us to consider a reality or content put into words—still a commonplace understanding in many sectors both inside and outside the academy. But in the humanities, the epistemological implications of post-Nietzschean philosophy have taken firm hold, and the idea that knowledge is shaped through language choices is widely accepted. The social or rhetorical construction of knowledge was embraced enthusiastically by scholars in rhetoric and composition in the 1970s and 1980s, especially those who found resonance between this position and discussions of communally agreed-on knowledge in ancient rhetoric (Berlin, "Poststructuralism"; Leff, "In Search of Ariadne's Thread"; Scott). Such a recognition places considerable weight on the tasks of composing and interpreting texts.

Because strategies of invention (composition, text production) were discussed above, we turn here to methods of interpretation, also called hermeneutics, rhetorical analysis, or text analysis. Methods of scholarship in rhetoric at present often blend interpretation with history and theory. But considered as a discrete practice, the rhetorical analysis of speeches has more often been undertaken by scholars in speech communication under categories such as political rhetoric or the rhetoric of social movements, or by classicists analyzing the rhetoric of the Attic orators (see Connor) and Ciceronian legal speeches (R. Enos). Literary criticism, another kind of analysis, through the middle of the century focused primarily on formal properties of poems and novels, paying little attention to their effects on readers. With his award-winning

1961 *Rhetoric of Fiction*, however, Wayne Booth bridged the gap between rhetoric and literary studies by asserting that aesthetic productions did in fact have designs on their readers and by exploring how those rhetorical purposes were pursued in the medium of fiction. Scholars at the intersection of literary and rhetorical studies have continued in Booth's path of reading literary texts rhetorically, drawing in some cases on the hermeneutic theory of Gadamer cited above (Fish, *Doing* and "Rhetoric"; Kastely; Mailloux, *Reception Histories* and *Rhetorical Power*; see also McGann's essay in this volume). Another point of connection between rhetorical and literary analysis occurs in the work of Terry Eagleton, who, in his study of Walter Benjamin, defines rhetoric as "the process of analyzing the material effects of particular uses of language in particular social conjunctures" (*Walter Benjamin* 101). In the final chapter of his widely adopted *Literary Theory*, Eagleton proposes rhetoric in the form of political criticism as the most useful approach to literary studies for our times.

For rhetorical scholars associated with writing, textual analysis has gained momentum lately, especially among those concentrating on disciplinary writing in the university beyond first-year composition. The focus of this new work is genre. Rather than empty forms, genres have come to be seen as sites of social action: places where students learn disciplinary conventions and become initiated into intellectual communities (Bawarshi; Bazerman; Dillon; C. Miller, "Genre").

Interest in the rhetoric of visual texts and of electronic media has grown over the past decade. Borrowing Rorty's language, W. J. T. Mitchell labels the new interest in images a "pictorial turn" (11–34), although rhetoric's history reveals a long-standing attention to word-image relations. Gorgias exemplifies the power of words with a visual parallel: soldiers experience fear on seeing an enemy not yet encountered. Aristotle dwells on the power of words to bring images before the eyes. The rhetorical handbooks from the Hellenistic era onward suggest the usefulness of ekphrasis, describing an art object or scene, the for developing rhetor. Juxtaposing parallel processes of representation—verbal and visual—has inspired critical reflection in many eras since (Hagstrum). Roman rhetoricians cultivated the ability to memorize a speech through a process of visualization attributed to the Greeks and carried into the Middle Ages (Yates). Although recent work in this area has been more the province of literary critics and theorists than rhetoricians (see, for example, Heffernan), Burke treats the relation of image and idea in *Rhetoric of Motives* (84–90) and, more recently, Don Paul Abbott reads the sixteenth-century mestizo Diego Valadés's masterwork, *Rhetorica Christiana*, in terms of the rhetorical power of the drawings.

The word-image relation has generated more excitement among rhetoricians in the realm of electronic media. In his *Electronic Word: Democracy, Technology, and the Arts*, Richard Lanham praises the rich perceptual field of the computer screen and makes the claim, by now questionable, for computer technology as a democratizing force in education. He finds a parallel between the forms of playful and open-ended expression possible in the digital realm and the rhetorical practice of the ancient Greeks. Considering not only word and image but also features such as speed, distance, technical skill, isolation, online personae, and the possibilities for persuasion, scholars have analyzed electronic media using rhetorical materials (see Faigley, "Material Literacy"; Welch). Laura J. Gurak, for example, in *Cyberliteracy: Navigating the Internet with Awareness*, examines the nature of persuasion and the constitution of information online, as well as gender differences in online communication and the role of government and business in new technologies. Although cast in terms of literacy rather than rhetoric, the essayscollected in Gail Hawisher and Cynthia L. Selfe's *Global Literacies and the World-Wide Web* well represent the ways rhetorical issues operate in new electronic media: the construction of knowledge in specific national, cultural, and eth-

nic contexts, and questions of power and access outside the First World.

Within What Context or Situation?

In shifting attention to visual images and electronic media as objects of analysis, we have moved far from the classic rhetorical situation.[23] To round out this disposition of new work in rhetoric, we turn finally to areas of scholarship that most vividly evoke rhetorical situations in both familiar and unexpected ways.

In a use of the term that marks a dramatic contrast with rhetoric's historical manifestations, a number of composition scholars have been conducting studies of what they term rhetorics of the everyday. Martin Nystrand and John Duffy, in the introduction to their collection *Toward a Rhetoric of Everyday Life*, explicitly set their method off against classical rhetoric with its focus on the arts of persuasion or the ornaments of elite discourse. Instead they take rhetoric to involve the ways individuals and groups use language to constitute their "social realities" and "create, manage, or resist ideological meanings." Borrowing methods from ethnography and critical discourse analysis, scholars in this group aim to "elucidat[e] the entanglements of writing and writers within their quotidian contexts" (ix). Rhetoric here finds a common boundary with literacy, so that the choice of the term calls attention to its force. For Ralph Cintron, whose eloquent study of a Mexican community near Chicago, *Angel's Town*, set a high standard for such studies, rhetorics of the everyday are those words used by people outside circuits of power and stability to mark out their place, to make their presence felt and recognizable to one another under conditions of struggle.

Global movements and power struggles occupy another set of rhetoricians, but at the other end of the geographic spectrum, setting the widest possible parameters for the rhetorical situation. Especially since the events of September 11

> **Occupying the spaces of street, schoolroom, and cyberspace, rhetoric can be as stable as a monument or as slippery as an octopus.**

in the United States, scholars have been tracking rhetorics of empire, globalization, and trans-nationality (Asen and Brouwer; Collins and Glover). Despite the millennia dividing them from their ancient precursors, they have found common topics with ancient Greeks in arguments about empire, domination, hegemony, and the use of military force (see, e.g., Mendelsohn). Analyzing physical monuments, memorials, and memories of traumatic world events of all types has become a preoccupation for rhetors at the end of the violent twentieth century, some of whom also turn to ancient rhetorical genres in their analyses (Bernard-Donals and Glejzer; Blair and Michel; Wiederhold). Classical formulations undergo dramatic reapplication in the situation of the new South Africa, where rhetorics of democracy inform the twentieth-century invention of truth commissions (Doxtader; Ross; Salazar). The public recounting of intimate memories of physical and psychic trauma, as well as acts of political violence, toward the end of nation formation makes strikingly new demands on rhetorical analysis as an ethical practice.

~

Distinctions are indeed on the move, opening a space for rhetoric in the modern languages and literatures of the twenty-first century. As this overview has shown, the distinctions within rhetoric are just as mobile. Occupying the spaces of street, schoolroom, and cyberspace, rhetoric can be as stable as a monument or as slippery as an octopus. The tensions between norm and transgression, rule and play, authority and exclusion keep it as taut as a drawn bow. If the institutional and disciplinary conditions of the 1960s found a need for rhetoric, the current circumstances are no less propitious for its flourishing.

NOTES

I would like to thank Katherine Mack for research assistance in the preparation of this essay. I'm grateful to Cezar Ornatowski, Kate Ronald, and John Trimbur for helpful conversations about this project, and especially to Katherine Mack, Steven Mailloux, Ellen Quandahl, and Shevaun Watson for their comments on early drafts.

1. The most important journals in rhetoric are the *Rhetoric Society Quarterly* (associated with the Rhetoric Society of America), *Rhetorica* (the publication of the International Society for the History of Rhetoric), *Philosophy and Rhetoric*, *Pre/Text*, *JAC: A Journal of Composition Theory*, and *Rhetoric Review*. Articles on rhetoric appear regularly in *College English* and *College Composition and Communication*. The primary journal of the National Communication Association, *Quarterly Journal of Speech*, also publishes articles about rhetoric.

2. Wars in the twentieth century have preceded surges of rhetorical activity: examples include I. A. Richards's address to misunderstanding after the First World War (see Conley 260–84), Kenneth Burke's attempt at the "purification of war" with his post–World War II project on human motives (*Grammar*), and various responses to the rhetoric of social protest during the Vietnam War era (e.g., Bitzer and Black 21–43; Booth, *Modern Dogma*; Corbett).

3. For an extended treatment of the scope of rhetoric, see Gross and Keith. Fleming's essay on rhetorical education is replete with definitions. The introductory essay in Covino and Jolliffe includes a glossary of terms and major figures. Jasinki offers substantive essays on key concepts in an encyclopedia format. For a list of some of the most famous and influential definitions of rhetoric, see Eidenmuller.

4. For a discussion of stasis theory, see Hermogenes; Corbett and Eberly.

5. Definitions and contexts for Greek and Latin terms are accessible through the *Perseus Digital Library*, an online reference tool at www.perseus.tufts.edu/.

6. Because the practice of rhetoric has been the exclusive province of men in so many eras and locales, I preserve the references to "man" and masculine pronouns where they occur in quoted materials in order to make those exclusions visible to readers who now expect nonsexist language.

7. A related study by Gauri Viswanathan explores "[t]he amazingly young history of English literature as a subject of study (it is less than a hundred and fifty years old) . . . [and] the irony that English literature appeared as a subject in the curriculum of the colonies long before it was institutionalized in the home country"—that is, as early as the 1820s (2–3). On the development of English literary studies in England, see also Court; Eagleton (*Literary Theory*).

8. The society incorporated in 1950 as the Speech Association of America changed its name to Speech Communication Association in 1970 and adopted its present name, the National Communication Association, in 1997.

9. A third figure who turned toward rhetoric from a literary background in the first half of the century

was Richard Weaver. His conservative, Christian approach to the ethics of rhetoric has not been taken up by contemporary scholars, although his commitment to the teaching of writing before such attention was institutionalized is notable.

10. Studies of the rhetorical performances of "anti-rhetorical" figures make up a significant and growing category of research. See, for example, Aune on Marx; J. Smith on Hegel; and Walmsley on Locke.

11. Perhaps the source of this disregard lies in what de Man calls the "ambivalent dignity" of rhetoric, which on the one hand "becomes the ground for the furthest-reaching dialectical speculations conceivable to the mind" and on the other "appears in the textbooks that have undergone little change from Quintilian to the present [as] the humble and not-quite-respectable handmaiden of the fraudulent grammar used in oratory." Between the two, de Man writes, "the distance is so wide as to be nearly un-bridgeable" (130–31). Seeking to bridge that gap, John Schilb creates a lively yet evenhanded overview of the evasions, antagonisms, and potential cross-fertilizations of rhetoric and literary theory by putting six high-profile compositionists and literary theorists into imagined dialogues: Edward P. J. Corbett in conversation with Roland Barthes, Wayne Booth with Jacques Derrida, and the linguist Francis Christensen with Jacque Lacan.

12. Lester Faigley narrates this period of political and academic turmoil with great effectiveness in the introduction to *Fragments of Rationality*. For a full treatment of composition studies, see Bartholomae in this volume.

13. Graduate programs in rhetoric were instituted in the late 1970s and early 1980s by James Kinneavy at the University of Texas, Austin; by Janice Lauer at Purdue University; by Edward P. J. Corbett at Ohio State University; by Ross Winterowd at the University of Southern California; and by Richard Young at Carnegie Mellon University.

14. Both Corbett and Kinneavy turned to rhetoric to help them understand and find alternatives to irrational, violent, or "deviant" modes of political expression (Kinneavy, "Basic Aims" 303) characteristic of the late 1960s. See Corbett's 1969 essay "The Rhetoric of the Open Hand and the Closed Fist" (in Connors) and Booth's *Modern Dogma*.

15. Corbett's text has continued in print through four editions, the most recent (1998) coauthored with Robert J. Connors. The quotations in this section are from the third edition (1990).

16. For Kinneavy, *discourse* is the more comprehensive term for any complete unit of symbolic communication. *Rhetoric* applies specifically to the aim of persuasion (*Theory* 3–4). For an overview of discourse theories, see Macdonell.

17. See also Ede and Lunsford, "On Distinctions"; Foucault, "Nietzsche"; Halloran, "Further Thoughts"; and Hariman, "Allegory."

18. This discussion has concentrated on reinterpretations of ancient Greek rhetoric but could well have taken up newer historical approaches to rhetoric in other periods. See, for example, Enders's study of the interactions among rhetoric, law, and drama in the Middle Ages; Streuver's exploration of sophistic elements in Renaissance historians; and Hariman's collection of essays on prudence (*Prudence*).

19. This material was presented at the Conference on the Status and Future of Rhetorical Studies, 11–14 September 2003, at Northwestern University; the conference was sponsored by the Alliance of Rhetoric Societies. As of August 2005, position papers continue to be available electronically at www .comm.umn.edu/ARS/. Keynote addresses from the conference can be found in the ARS archive at www .rhetoricalliance.org>. *Rhetoric Society Quarterly* devoted an issue to major statements from the conference (34.3 [2004]).

20. Although Quintilian gives credit to learned and eloquent women, the education he describes was restricted to boys.

21. For an overview of the movement and its controversies, see chapter 2 of Casanave's *Controversies in Second Language Writing*. Kennedy's 1998 *Comparative Rhetoric* contains a wealth of material on non-Western cultures but may be faulted for ethnocentrism in its reliance on the questionable oral-literacy framework (see Lyons, "Rhetorical Sovereignty").

22. Many points of connection between rhetoric and feminist theory remain to be explored. The contingency in Butler's "Contingent Foundations," the strategy in Spivak's strategic essentialism, the standpoint in Hartsock's feminist materialism: all these concepts have resonance with rhetoric and could be enriched through that recognition. In one notable exception, De Lauretis has made very direct engagements with rhetoric through her use of Peircian semiotics in *Technologies of Gender*.

23. Bitzer's "The Rhetorical Situation," leading the inaugural issue of *Philosophy and Rhetoric*, is the now canonical twentieth-century statement on the subject. Bitzer's position has been critiqued through the theoretical lenses of semiotics and poststructuralism, respectively, by Vatz and by Biesecker ("Rethinking").

WORKS CITED AND SUGGESTIONS FOR FURTHER READING

Abbott, Don Paul. *Rhetoric in the New World: Rhetorical Theory and Practice in Colonial Spanish America*. Columbia: U of South Carolina P, 1996.

Alcoff, Linda Martín. "The Problem of Speaking for Others." *Cultural Critique* 20 (1991–92): 5–32.

Alcorn, Marshall W., Jr. *Changing the Subject in English*

Class: Discourse and the Constructions of Desire. Carbondale: Southern Illinois UP, 2002.

——. "Self-Structure as a Rhetorical Device: Modern *Ethos* and the Divisiveness of the Self." Baumlin and Baumlin 3–36.

Arendt, Hannah. *The Human Condition.* Chicago: U of Chicago P, 1958.

Aristotle. *On Rhetoric: A Theory of Civic Discourse.* Trans. George A. Kennedy. New York: Oxford UP, 1991.

Asen, Robert, and Daniel C. Brouwer, eds. *Counterpublics and the State.* Albany: State U of New York P, 2001.

Atwill, Janet M. *Rhetoric Reclaimed: Aristotle and the Liberal Arts Tradition.* Ithaca: Cornell UP, 1998.

Augustine. *On Christian Teaching.* Trans. R. P. H. Green. New York: Oxford UP, 1999.

Aune, James Arnt. *Rhetoric and Marxism.* Boulder: Westview, 1994.

Austin, J. L. *How to Do Things with Words.* 2nd ed. Ed. J. O. Urmson and Marina Sbisà. Cambridge: Harvard UP, 1975.

Bacon, Jacqueline. *The Humblest May Stand Forth: Rhetoric, Empowerment, and Abolition.* Columbia: U of South Carolina P, 2002.

Bakhtin, M. M. *The Dialogic Imagination: Four Essays.* Trans. Caryl Emerson and Michael Holquist. Austin: U of Texas P, 1981.

Ballif, Michelle. *Seduction, Sophistry, and the Woman with the Rhetorical Figure.* Carbondale: Southern Illinois UP, 2001.

Barthes, Roland. "The Old Rhetoric: An Aide-Mémoire." *The Semiotic Challenge.* Trans. Richard Howard. New York: Hill, 1988. 11–93.

——. "The Rhetoric of the Image." *Image-Music-Text.* Trans. Stephen Heath. New York: Noonday, 1977. 32–51.

Baumlin, James S., and Tita French Baumlin, eds. *Ethos: New Essays in Rhetorical and Critical Theory.* Dallas: Southern Methodist UP, 1994.

Bawarshi, Anis. "The Genre Function." *College English* 62 (2002): 335–60.

Bazerman, Charles. *Shaping Written Knowledge: The Genre and Activity of the Experimental Article in Science.* Madison: U of Wisconsin P, 1988.

Bender, John, and David E. Wellbery, eds. *The Ends of Rhetoric: History, Theory, Practice.* Stanford: Stanford UP, 1990.

——. "Rhetoricality: On the Modernist Return of Rhetoric." Bender and Wellbery, *Ends* 3–39.

Benson, Thomas. "The Cornell School of Rhetoric: Idiom and Institution." *Communication Quarterly* 51 (2003): 1–56.

Berlin, James A. "Poststructuralism, Semiotics, and Social-Epistemic Rhetoric: Converging Agendas." Enos and Brown, *Defining* 137–53.

——. *Rhetoric and Reality: Writing Instruction in American Colleges, 1900–1985.* Carbondale: Southern Illinois UP, 1987.

——. *Rhetoric, Poetics, and Cultures: Refiguring College English Studies.* Urbana: NCTE, 1996.

——. *Writing Instruction in Nineteenth-Century American Colleges.* Carbondale: Southern Illinois UP, 1984.

Bernard-Donals, Michael F., and Richard Glejzer. *Between Witness and Testimony: The Holocaust and the Limits of Representation.* Albany: State U of New York P, 2001.

Berthoff, Ann E., ed. *Richards on Rhetoric: I. A. Richards; Selected Essays, 1927–74.* New York: Oxford UP, 1991.

Bialostosky, Don. *Booth, Bakhtin, and the Culture of Criticism.* Columbus: Ohio State UP. 1995.

Biesecker, Barbara A. *Addressing Postmodernity: Kenneth Burke, Rhetoric, and a Theory of Social Change.* Tuscaloosa: U of Alabama P, 1997.

——. "Rethinking the Rhetorical Situation from within the Thematic of *Différance.*" *Philosophy and Rhetoric* 22 (1989): 110–30.

Bitzer, Lloyd. "The Rhetorical Situation." *Philosophy and Rhetoric* 1 (1968): 1–14.

Bitzer, Lloyd, and Edwin Black, eds. *The Prospect of Rhetoric: A Report of the National Developmental Project.* Englewood Cliffs: Prentice, 1971.

Bizzell, Patricia, and Bruce Herzberg. *The Rhetorical Tradition.* 2nd ed. Boston: St. Martin's, 2001.

Bizzell, Patricia, and Susan Jarratt. "Rhetorical Traditions, Pluralized Canons, Relevant History, and Other Disputed Terms: A Report from the History of Rhetoric Discussion Groups at the ARS Conference." *Rhetoric Society Quarterly* 34.3 (2004): 19–25.

Black Public Sphere Collective, ed. *The Black Public Sphere: A Public Culture Book.* Chicago: U of Chicago P, 1995.

Blair, Carole, and Neil Michel. "Reproducing Civil Rights Tactics: The Rhetorical Performances of the Civil Rights Memorial." *Rhetoric Society Quarterly* 30 (2002): 31–55.

Booth, Wayne C. *Modern Dogma and the Rhetoric of Assent.* Chicago: U of Chicago P, 1974.

——. "The Revival of Rhetoric." *PMLA* 80 (1965): 8–12.

——. "The Rhetorical Stance." *College Composition and Communication* 14.3 (1963): 139–45.

——. *The Rhetoric of Fiction.* Chicago: Chicago UP, 1961.

——. "The Scope of Rhetoric Today: A Polemical Excursion." Bitzer and Black 93–114.

Bourdieu, Pierre. *Outline of a Theory of Practice.* Trans. Richard Nice. Cambridge: Cambridge UP, 1977.

Brereton, John C., ed. *The Origins of Composition Studies in the American College, 1875–1925: A Documentary History.* Pittsburgh: U of Pittsburgh P, 1995.

Brody, Miriam. *Manly Writing: Gender, Rhetoric, and the Rise of Composition.* Carbondale: Southern Illinois UP, 1993.

Brown, Stuart C., Paul R. Meyer, and Theresa Enos. "Doctoral Programs in Rhetoric and Composition: A

Catalog of the Profession." *Rhetoric Review* 12.2 (1994): 240+.

Brummett, Barry, ed. *Reading Rhetorical Theory*. Fort Worth: Harcourt, 2000.

Burke, Kenneth. *Counter-statement*. Los Altos: Hermes, 1953.

———. *A Grammar of Motives*. New York: Braziller, 1945.

———. *Language as Symbolic Action: Essays on Life, Literature, and Method*. Berkeley: U of California P, 1966.

———. *A Rhetoric of Motives*. New York: Prentice, 1952.

Butler, Judith. "Contingent Foundations." *Feminists Theorize the Political*. Ed. Butler and Joan W. Scott. New York: Routledge, 1992. 3–21.

———. *Excitable Speech: A Politics of the Performative*. New York: Routledge, 1997.

———. *Gender Trouble: Feminism and the Subversion of Identity*. New York: Routledge, 1990.

Campbell, JoAnn, ed. *Toward a Feminist Rhetoric: The Writing of Gertrude Buck*. Pittsburgh: U of Pittsburgh P, 1996.

Campbell, Karlyn Kohrs. *Agency: Promiscuous and Protean*. Conf. of Alliance of Rhetoric Societies. Evanston. 13 Sept. 2003. 13 July 2004 <http://www.rhetoricsociety.org/ARS/pdf/campbellonagency.pdf>.

Casanave, Christine Pearson. *Controversies in Second Language Writing: Dilemmas and Decisions in Research and Instruction*. Ann Arbor: U of Michigan P, 2004.

Cicero. *De Inventione*. Trans. H. M. Hubbell. Cambridge: Harvard UP, 1960.

———. *De Oratore*. Trans. E. W. Sutton and H. Rackham. 2 vols. Cambridge: Harvard UP, 1979.

Cintron, Ralph. *Angel's Town: Chero Ways, Gang Life, and Rhetorics of the Everyday*. Boston: Beacon, 1997.

Clark, Gregory, and S. Michael Halloran, eds. *Oratorical Culture in Nineteenth-Century America: Transformations in the Theory and Practice of Rhetoric*. Carbondale: Southern Illinois UP, 1993.

Clifford, John, and John Schilb, eds. *Writing Theory and Critical Theory*. New York: MLA, 1994.

Cohen, Herman. *The History of Speech Communication: The Emergence of a Discipline, 1914–45*. Annandale: Speech Communication Assn., 1994.

Cole, Thomas. *The Origins of Rhetoric in Ancient Greece*. Baltimore: Johns Hopkins UP, 1991.

Collins, John, and Ross Glover, eds. *Collateral Language: A User's Guide to America's New War*. New York: New York UP, 2002.

Conley, Thomas M. *Rhetoric in the European Tradition*. New York: Longman, 1990.

Connor, W. Robert, ed. *Greek Orations: Fourth Century B.C.* Prospect Heights: Waveland, 1966.

Connors, Robert J., ed. *Selected Essays of Edward P. J. Corbett*. Dallas: Southern Methodist UP, 1989.

Connors, Robert J., Lisa S. Ede, and Andrea A. Lunsford, eds. *Essays on Classical Rhetoric and Modern Discourse*. Carbondale: Southern Illinois UP, 1984.

Conway, Kathryn M. "Woman Suffrage and the History of Rhetoric at the Seven Sisters Colleges, 1865–1919." Lunsford, *Reclaiming* 203–26.

Corbett, Edward P. J. *Classical Rhetoric for the Modern Student*. 3rd ed. New York: Oxford UP, 1990.

Corbett, Edward P. J., and Robert J. Connors. *Classical Rhetoric for the Modern Student*. 4th ed. Oxford: Oxford UP, 1999.

Corbett, Edward P. J., and Rosa A. Eberly. *Elements of Reason*. 2nd ed. New York: Longman, 2000.

Court, Franklin E. *Institutionalizing English Literature: The Culture and Politics of Literary Study, 1750–1900*. Stanford: Stanford UP, 1992.

Covino, William A., and David A. Jolliffe. *Rhetoric: Concepts, Definitions, Boundaries*. Boston: Allyn, 1995.

Crosswhite, James. *The Rhetoric of Reason: Writing and the Attractions of Argument*. Madison: U of Wisconsin P, 1996.

Crowley, Sharon. "Communications Skills and a Brief Rapprochement of Rhetoricians." *Rhetoric Society Quarterly* 34 (2004): 89–103.

———. *Composition in the University: Historical and Polemical Essays*. Pittsburgh: U of Pittsburgh P, 1998.

———. *Methodical Memory: Invention in Current-Traditional Rhetoric*. Carbondale: Southern Illinois UP, 1990.

Crusius, Timothy W. *Kenneth Burke and the Conversation after Philosophy*. Carbondale: Southern Illinois UP, 1999.

De Lauretis, Teresa. *Technologies of Gender: Essays on Theory, Film, and Fiction*. Bloomington: Indiana UP, 1987.

de Man, Paul. *Allegories of Reading: Figural Language in Rousseau, Nietzsche, Rilke, and Proust*. New Haven: Yale UP, 1979.

Derrida, Jacques. "Plato's Pharmacy." *Dissemination*. Trans. and introd. Barbara Johnson. Chicago: U of Chicago P, 1981. 61–171.

———. "Structure, Sign, and Play in the Discourses of the Human Sciences." *Writing and Difference*. Trans. Alan Bass. Chicago: U of Chicago P, 1978. 278–93.

———. "White Mythology: Metaphor in the Text of Philosophy." Trans. F. C. T. Moore. *New Literary History* 6 (1974): 5–74.

Dillon, George L. *Contending Rhetorics: Writing in Academic Disciplines*. Bloomington: Indiana UP, 1991.

Donawerth, Jane, ed. *Rhetorical Theory by Women before 1900: An Anthology*. Lanham: Rowman, 2002.

Doxtader, Erik. "Making History in a Time of Transition: The Rhetorical Occasion, Constitution, and Representation of South African Reconciliation." *Rhetoric and Public Affairs* 4 (2001): 223–60.

Eagleton, Terry. *Literary Theory: An Introduction*. Minneapolis: U of Minnesota P, 1983.

———. *Walter Benjamin; or, Toward a Revolutionary Criticism*. London: Verso, 1981.

Eberly, Rosa A. *Citizen Critics: Literary Public Spheres*. History of Communication. Champaign: U of Illinois P, 2000.

Ede, Lisa, Cheryl Glenn, and Andrea Lunsford. "Border Crossings: Intersections of Rhetoric and Feminism." *Rhetorica* 13 (1995): 401–41.

Ede, Lisa, and Andrea Lunsford. "Audience Addressed / Audience Invoked: The Role of Audience in Composition Theory and Pedagogy." *College Composition and Communication* 35 (1984): 155–71.

———. "On Distinctions between Classical and Modern Rhetoric." Connors, Ede, and Lunsford 37–49.

Eidenmuller, Michael E. *Scholarly Definitions of Rhetoric.* Amer. Rhetoric. 7 July 2004. <http://www.american rhetoric.com/rhetoricdefinitions.htm>.

Eldred, Janet Carey, and Peter Mortensen. *Imagining Rhetoric: Composing Women of the Early United States.* Pittsburgh: U of Pittsburgh P, 2002.

Enders, Jody. *Rhetoric and the Origins of Medieval Drama.* Ithaca: Cornell UP, 1992.

Enos, Richard Leo. *The Literate Mode of Cicero's Legal Rhetoric.* Carbondale: Southern Illinois UP, 1988.

Enos, Theresa, and Stuart C. Brown, eds. *Defining the New Rhetorics.* Newbury Park: Sage, 1993.

———. *Professing the New Rhetorics: A Sourcebook.* Englewood Cliffs: Prentice, 1994.

Euripides. *Hippolytos.* Trans. Robert Bagg. New York: Oxford UP, 1973.

Fahnestock, Jeanne. *Rhetorical Figures in Science.* New York: Oxford UP, 1999.

Fahnestock, Jeanne, and Marie Secor. *A Rhetoric of Argument.* New York: Random, 1982.

Faigley, Lester. *Fragments of Rationality: Postmodernity and the Subject of Composition.* Pittsburgh: U of Pittsburgh P, 1992.

———. "Material Literacy and Visual Design." Selzer and Crowley 171–201.

Farrell, Thomas B., ed. *Landmark Essays on Contemporary Rhetoric.* Mahwah: Hermagoras, 1998.

———. *Norms of Rhetorical Culture.* New Haven: Yale UP, 1993.

Fish, Stanley. *Doing What Comes Naturally: Change, Rhetoric, and the Practice of Theory in Literary and Legal Studies.* Durham: Duke UP, 1989.

———. "Rhetoric." *Critical Terms for Literary Study.* 2nd ed. Ed. Frank Lentricchia and Thomas McLaughlin. Chicago: U of Chicago P, 1995. 203–22.

Fleckenstein, Kristie S. "Bodysigns: A Biorhetoric for Change." *JAC: A Journal of Composition Theory* 21 (2001): 761–90.

Fleming, David. "Rhetoric as a Course of Study." *College English* 61 (1998): 169–91.

Foner, Philip S., and Robert J. Branham, eds. *Lift Every Voice : African American Oratory, 1787–1900.* Tuscaloosa: U of Alabama P, 1998.

Foss, Sonja K., Karen A. Foss, and Robert Trapp, eds. *Contemporary Perspectives on Rhetoric.* 3rd ed. Prospect Heights: Waveland, 2002.

Foucault, Michel. "Discourse on Language." *Archaeology of Knowledge.* Trans. A. M. Sheridan Smith. New York: Pantheon, 1972. 215–37.

———. *Fearless Speech.* Ed. Joseph Pearson. Los Angeles: Semiotext(e), 2001.

———. *The History of Sexuality.* 3 vols. Trans. Robert Hurley. New York: Pantheon, 1978–87. Vol. 1: *Introduction* (1978); vol. 2: *The Use of Pleasure* (1985); vol. 3: *The Care of the Self* (1987).

———. "Nietzsche, Genealogy, History." *Language, Counter-memory, Practice: Selected Essays and Interviews.* Ed. Donald F. Bouchard. Trans. Bouchard and Sherry Simon. Ithaca: Cornell UP, 1977. 139–64.

Friedenberg, Robert V. *"Hear O Israel": The History of American Jewish Preaching, 1654–1970.* Tuscaloosa: U of Alabama P, 1989.

Fulkerson, Richard. "The Toulmin Model of Argument and the Teaching of Composition." *Argument Revisited, Argument Redefined: Negotiating Meaning in the Composition Classroom.* Ed. Barbara Emmel, Paula Resch, and Deborah Tenney. Thousand Oaks: Sage, 1996. 45–72.

Gadamer, Hans-Georg. *Truth and Method.* 1960. 2nd rev. ed. Trans. Joel Weinsheimer and Donald G. Marshall. New York: Crossroad, 1989.

Gaffney, Patrick D. *The Prophet's Pulpit: Islamic Preaching in Contemporary Egypt.* Berkeley: U of California P, 1994.

Gage, John. "An Adequate Epistemology for Composition: Classical and Modern Perspectives." Connors, Ede, and Lunsford 152–69.

Garrett, Mary. "Some Elementary Methodological Reflections on the Study of the Chinese Rhetorical Tradition." *International and Intercultural Communication Annual* 22 (1999): 53–63.

Genette, Gerard. "Rhetoric Restrained." *Figures of Literary Discourse.* Trans. Alan Sheridan. New York: Columbia UP, 1982. 103–26.

Gilman, Sander L., Carole Blair, and David J. Parent, eds. and trans. *Friedrich Nietzsche on Rhetoric and Language.* New York: Oxford UP, 1989.

Gilyard, Keith, ed. *Race, Rhetoric, and Composition.* Portsmouth: Boynton, 1999.

Glenn, Cheryl. *Rhetoric Retold: Regendering the Tradition from Antiquity through the Renaissance.* Carbondale: Southern Illinois UP, 1997.

———. *Unspoken: A Rhetoric of Silence.* Carbondale: Southern Illinois UP, 2004.

Goff, Barbara. *Noose of Words: Readings of Desire, Violence, and Language in Euripides' Hippolytos.* New York: Cambridge UP, 1999.

Gold, David. "Never Mind What Harvard Thinks: Alternative Sites of Rhetorical Instruction in American Colleges, 1873–1947." Diss. U of Texas, Austin, 2003.

Gorgias. "Encomium of Helen." Sprague 50–54.

Gross, Alan G., and William M. Keith, eds. *Rhetorical Hermeneutics: Invention and Interpretation in the Age of Science.* Albany: State U of New York P, 1997.

Gurak, Laura J. *Cyberliteracy: Navigating the Internet with Awareness.* New Haven: Yale UP, 1997.

Habermas, Jürgen. *The Structural Transformation of the*

Public Sphere: An Inquiry into a Category of Bourgeois Society. Trans. Thomas Burger. Cambridge: MIT P, 1989.

Hagstrum, Jean H. *The Sister Arts: The Tradition of Literary Pictorialism and English Poetry from Dryden to Gray*. Chicago: U of Chicago P, 1958.

Halloran, S. Michael. "Further Thoughts on the End of Rhetoric." Enos and Brown, *Defining* 109–19.

———. "On the End of Rhetoric, Classical and Modern." *College English* 6 (1975): 621–31.

———. "Rhetoric in the American College Curriculum and the Decline of Public Discourse." *Pre/Text* 3.3 (1982): 245–69.

Hariman, Robert. "Allegory and Democratic Public Culture in the Postmodern Era." *Philosophy and Rhetoric* 35 (2002): 267–96.

———. *Political Style: The Artistry of Power*. Chicago: U of Chicago P, 1995.

———, ed. *Prudence: Classical Virtue, Postmodern Practice*. University Park: Pennsylvania State UP, 2003.

Hartsock, Nancy C. M. *"The Feminist Standpoint Revisited" and Other Essays*. Boulder: Westview, 1998.

Hauser, Gerard A. *Vernacular Voices: The Rhetoric of Publics and Public Spheres*. Columbia: U of South Carolina P, 1999.

Hawisher, Gail E., and Cynthia L. Selfe, eds. *Global Literacies and the World-Wide Web*. New York: Routledge, 2000.

Heffernan, James A. W. *Museum of Words: The Poetics of Ekphrasis from Homer to Ashbery*. Chicago: U of Chicago P, 1993.

Hermogenes. *On Issues: Strategies of Argument in Later Greek Rhetoric*. Introd., trans., and ed. Malcolm Heath. Oxford: Clarendon, 1995.

Hobbs, Catherine L. *Rhetoric on the Margins of Modernity: Vico, Condillac, Monboddo*. Carbondale: Southern Illinois UP, 2002.

Hollis, Karyn. *Liberating Voices: Writing at the Bryn Mawr Summer School for Women Workers*. Carbondale: Southern Illinois UP, 2004.

Horner, Bruce, and John Trimbur. "English Only and U.S. College Composition." *College Composition and Communication* 53 (2002): 594–630.

Horner, Winifred Bryan, ed. *The Present State of Scholarship in Historical and Contemporary Rhetoric*. Rev ed. Columbia: U of Missouri P, 1990.

Howell, Wilbur Samuel. *Eighteenth-Century British Logic and Rhetoric*. Princeton: Princeton UP, 1971.

———. *Logic and Rhetoric in England, 1500–1700*. Princeton: Princeton UP, 1956.

Hutto, David. "Ancient Egyptian Rhetoric in the Old and Middle Kingdoms." *Rhetorica* 20 (2002): 213–33.

IJsseling, Samuel. *Rhetoric and Philosophy in Conflict: An Historical Survey*. Trans. Paul Dunphy. The Hague: Nijhoff, 1976.

International Society for the History of Rhetoric. 16 Dec. 2005. 11 Feb. 2006 <http://ishr.cua.edu>.

Isocrates. "Antidosis." Trans. George Norlin. *Isocrates*. Vol. 2. Cambridge: Harvard UP, 1929. 185–365.

———. "Panegyricus." Trans. George Norlin. *Isocrates*. Vol. 1. Cambridge: Harvard UP, 1982. 115–241.

Itaba, Yoshihisa, Hideki Kakita, and Satoru Aonuma. "Position Statement." *The Alliance of Rhetoric Societies (ARS) Conference on the Status and Future of Rhetoric Studies*. Northwestern U. 11–14 Sept. 2003. 8 June 2006 <http://www.comm.umn.edu/ARS/Tradition/Itaba,%20tradition.htm>.

Jackson, Ronald L., II, and Elaine B. Richardson, eds. *Understanding African-American Rhetoric: Classical Origins to Contemporary Innovations*. New York: Routledge, 2003.

Jaeger, Werner. *Paideia*. 3 vols. Trans. Gilbert Highet. New York: Oxford UP, 1939.

Jarratt, Susan C. *Rereading the Sophists: Classical Rhetoric Refigured*. Carbondale: Southern Illinois UP, 1991.

———. "Sappho's Memory." *Rhetoric Society Quarterly* 32.1 (2002): 11–43.

Jarratt, Susan C., and Nedra Reynolds. "The Splitting Image: Contemporary Feminisms and the Ethics of Ethos." Baumlin and Baumlin 37–63.

Jasinski, James. *Sourcebook on Rhetoric: Key Concepts in Contemporary Rhetorical Studies*. Thousand Oaks: Sage, 2001.

Johnson, Nan. *Gender and Rhetorical Space in American Life, 1866–1910*. Carbondale: Southern Illinois UP, 2002.

———. *Nineteenth-Century Rhetoric in North America*. Carbondale: Southern Illinois UP, 1991.

Jost, Walter, and Michael J. Hyde, eds. *Rhetoric and Hermeneutics in Our Time: A Reader*. New Haven: Yale UP, 1997.

Jost, Walter, and Wendy Olmsted, eds. *A Companion to Rhetoric and Rhetorical Criticism*. Oxford: Blackwell, 2004.

Kahn, Victoria. *Rhetoric, Prudence, and Skepticism in the Renaissance*. Ithaca: Cornell UP, 1985.

Kastely, James L. *Rethinking the Rhetorical Tradition from Plato to Postmodernism*. New Haven: Yale UP, 1997.

Kates, Susan. *Activist Rhetorics and American Higher Education, 1885–1937*. Carbondale: Southern Illinois UP, 2001.

Keating, Ana Louise. "Investigating 'Whiteness,' Eavesdropping on 'Race.'" *JAC: A Journal of Composition Theory* 20 (2000): 426–33.

Kennedy, George A. *Classical Rhetoric and Its Christian and Secular Traditions from Ancient to Modern Times*. 1980. 2nd ed. Chapel Hill: U of North Carolina P, 1999.

———. *Comparative Rhetoric: An Historical and Cross-Cultural Introduction*. New York: Oxford UP, 1998.

———. *Greek Rhetoric under Christian Emperors*. Princeton: Princeton UP, 1983.

Kent, Thomas. *Paralogic Rhetoric: A Theory of Communicative Interaction*. Lewisburg: Bucknell UP, 1993.

Kinneavy, James. "The Basic Aims of Discourse." *College Composition and Communication* 20 (1969): 297–304.

———. "Contemporary Rhetoric." Horner 186–246.

———. *Greek Rhetorical Origins of Christian Faith: An Inquiry.* New York: Oxford UP, 1987.

———. *A Theory of Discourse.* Englewood Cliffs: Prentice, 1971.

Kitzhaber, Albert R. *Rhetoric in American Colleges, 1850–1900.* Dallas: Southern Methodist UP, 1990.

Kuhn, Thomas S. *The Structure of Scientific Revolutions.* 2nd ed. Chicago: U of Chicago P, 1970.

Lanham, Richard A. *The Electronic Word: Democracy, Technology, and the Arts.* Chicago: U of Chicago P, 1993.

———. *A Handlist of Rhetorical Terms: A Guide for Students of English Literature.* 2nd ed. Berkeley: U of California P, 1991.

———. *Motives of Eloquence. Literary Rhetoric in the Renaissance.* New Haven: Yale UP, 1976.

———. "The 'Q' Question." *South Atlantic Quarterly* 87 (1988): 653–700.

Lauer, Janice. "Disciplinary Formation: The Summer Rhetoric Seminar." *JAC: A Journal of Advanced Composition* 18 (1998): 503–08.

———. "Issues in Rhetorical Invention." Connors, Ede, and Lunsford 127–39.

Leff, Michael C. "The Idea of Rhetoric as Interpretive Practice: A Humanist's Response to Gaonkar." Gross and Keith 89–100.

———. "In Search of Ariadne's Thread: A Review of the Recent Literature on Rhetorical Theory." Farrell, *Landmark Essays* 43–63.

Lipson, Carol S., and Roberta A. Binkley, eds. *Rhetoric before and beyond the Greeks.* Albany: State U of New York P, 2004.

Liu, Yameng. "Three Issues in the Argumentative Conception of Early Chinese Discourse." *Philosophy East and West: A Quarterly of Comparative Philosophy* 46.1 (1996): 33–58.

Logan, Shirley Wilson. *"We Are Coming": The Persuasive Discourse of Nineteenth-Century Black Women.* Carbondale: Southern Illinois UP, 1999.

———. *With Pen and Voice: A Critical Anthology of Nineteenth-Century African-American Women.* Carbondale: Southern Illinois UP, 1995.

Lu, Xing. *Rhetoric in Ancient China, Fifth to Third Century B.C.E.: A Comparison with Classical Greek Rhetoric.* Columbia: U of South Carolina P, 1998.

Lunsford, Andrea A., ed. *Reclaiming Rhetorica: Women in the Rhetorical Tradition.* Pittsburgh: U of Pittsburgh P, 1995.

———. "Rhetoric and Composition." *Introduction to Scholarship in Modern Languages and Literatures.* 2nd ed. Ed. Joseph Gibaldi. New York: MLA, 1992: 77–100.

Lunsford, Andrea A., and Lahoucine Ouzgane, eds.

Crossing Borderlands: Composition and Postcolonial Studies. Pittsburgh: U of Pittsburgh P, 2004.

Lyons, Scott Richard. "Rhetorical Sovereignty: What Do American Indians Want from Writing?" *College Composition and Communication* 51 (2000): 447–68.

———. *X-Marks: A Brief and True Report on American Indian Writing.* Carbondale: Southern Illinois UP, forthcoming.

Lyotard, Jean-François. *The Differend: Phrases in Dispute.* Trans. Georges Van Den Abbeele. Minneapolis: U of Minnesota P, 1988.

Macdonell, Diane. *Theories of Discourse: An Introduction.* New York: Blackwell, 1986.

Mack, Peter, ed. *Renaissance Rhetoric.* New York: St. Martin's, 1994.

Mailloux, Steven. "Disciplinary Identities: On the Rhetorical Paths between English and Communication Studies." *Rhetoric Society Quarterly* 30.2 (2000): 5–29.

———. *Reception Histories: Rhetoric, Pragmatism, and American Cultural Politics.* Ithaca: Cornell UP, 1998.

———. "Re-marking Slave Bodies: Rhetoric as Production and Reception." *Philosophy and Rhetoric* 35 (2002): 96–119.

———. *Rhetorical Power.* Ithaca: Cornell UP, 1989.

———, ed. *Rhetoric, Sophistry, Pragmatism.* New York: Cambridge UP, 1995.

Mao, Lu Ming. " 'Individualism' or 'Personhood': A Battle of Locution or Rhetorics." *Rhetoric, Cultural Studies, and Literacy.* Ed. John Fred Reynolds. Hillsdale: Erlbaum, 1995. 127–35.

———. "Re-clustering Traditional Academic Discourse: Alternating with Confucian Discourse." *ALT DIS: Alternative Discourses and the Academy.* Ed. Helen Fox, Christopher Schroeder, and Patricia Bizzell. Portsmouth: Boynton, 2002. 112–25.

———. *Reflective Encounters: The Making of Rhetorical Traditions.* U of Minnesota Dept. of Communication Studies. 7 Aug. 2005 <http://www.comm.umn.edu/ARS/Tradition/Mao,%20tradition.htm>.

———. "Rhetorical Borderlands: Chinese American Rhetoric in the Making." *College Composition and Communication* (2005): 426–69.

Marrou, Henri I. *A History of Education in Antiquity.* Trans. George Lamb. New York: Mentor, 1956.

Mattingly, Carol. *Appropriate(ing) Dress: Women's Rhetorical Style in Nineteenth-Century America.* Carbondale: Southern Illinois UP, 2002.

McGee, Michael Calvin. "The 'Ideograph': A Link between Rhetoric and Ideology." *Quarterly Journal of Speech* 66 (1980): 1–16.

Mendelsohn, Daniel. "Theatres of War." *New Yorker* 12 Jan. 2004: 79–84.

Micciche, Laura, and Dale Jacobs, eds. *A Way to Move: Rhetorics of Emotion and Composition Studies.* Portsmouth: Boynton, 2003.

Miller, Carolyn R. "Aristotle's 'Special Topics' in Rhetorical Practice and Pedagogy." *Rhetoric Society Quarterly* 17 (1987): 61–70.

———. "Classical Rhetoric without Nostalgia." Gross and Keith 156–71.

———. "Genre as Social Action." *Quarterly Journal of Speech* 70 (1984): 151–67.

Miller, Susan. *Rescuing the Subject: An Introduction to Rhetoric and the Writer.* Carbondale: Southern Illinois UP, 1989.

———. *Textual Carnivals: The Politics of Composition.* Carbondale: Southern Illinois UP, 1991.

Miller, Thomas P. *The Formation of College English: Rhetoric and Belles Lettres in the British Cultural Provinces.* Pittsburgh: U of Pittsburgh P, 1997.

Mitchell, W. J. T. *Picture Theory: Essays on Visual and Verbal Representation.* Chicago: U of Chicago P, 1994.

Moran, Michael G., and Michelle Ballif, eds. *Twentieth-Century Rhetorics and Rhetoricians.* Westport: Greenwood, 2000.

Murphy, James J. *Rhetoric in the Middle Ages: A History of Rhetorical Theory from St. Augustine to the Renaissance.* Berkeley: U of California P, 1974.

Murphy, James J., et al. *A Synoptic History of Classical Rhetoric.* 3rd ed. Mahwah: Erlbaum, 2003.

Myers, Greg. "Reality, Consensus, and Reform in the Rhetoric of Composition Teaching." *College English* 48 (1986): 154–74.

———. *Writing Biology: Texts in the Social Construction of Scientific Knowledge.* Madison: U of Wisconsin P, 1990.

Neel, Jasper P. *Plato, Derrida, and Writing.* Carbondale: Southern Illinois UP, 1988.

Nelson, John S., Allan Megill, and Donald N. McCloskey. *The Rhetoric of Human Sciences: Language and Argument in Scholarship and Public Affairs.* Madison: U of Wisconsin P, 1987.

Nietzsche, Friedrich. "Description of Ancient Rhetoric." Gilman, Blair, and Parent 2–193.

———. "On Truth and Lying in an Extra-moral Sense." Gilman, Blair, and Parent 246–57.

North, Stephen. *The Making of Knowledge in Composition.* Albany: State U of New York P, 1987.

Nystrand, Martin, and John Duffy, eds. *Toward a Rhetoric of Everyday Life: New Directions in Research on Writing, Text, and Discourse.* Madison: U of Wisconsin P, 2003.

Ohmann, Richard. *English in America: A Radical View of the Profession.* New York: Oxford UP, 1976.

Olson, Gary A., ed. *Philosopher, Rhetoric, Literary Criticism: (Inter)views.* Carbondale: Southern Illinois UP, 1994.

Olson, Gary A., and Lynn Worsham, eds. *Race, Rhetoric, and the Postcolonial.* Albany: State U of New York P, 1999.

Ong, Walter J. *Orality and Literacy: The Technologizing of the Word.* New York: Routledge, 2002.

———. *Ramus, Method, and the Decay of Dialogue: From the Age of Discourse to the Art of Reason.* Cambridge: Harvard UP, 1958.

Parker, William Riley. "Where Do English Departments Come From?" *College English* 38 (1967): 339–51.

Peirce, Charles S. *Peirce on Signs: Writings on Semiotic.* Ed. James Hoopes. Chapel Hill: U of North Carolina P, 1991.

Perelman, Chaim, and Lucie Olbrechts-Tyteca. *The New Rhetoric: A Treatise on Argumentation.* Trans. John Wilkinson and Purcell Weaver. South Bend: U of Notre Dame P, 1969.

Phelps, Teresa Godwin. *Shattered Voices: Language, Violence, and the Work of Truth Commissions.* Philadelphia: Pennsylvania Studies in Human Rights, 2004.

Plato. *Gorgias.* Trans. James H. Nichols, Jr. Ithaca: Cornell UP, 1998.

———. *Phaedrus.* Trans. James H. Nichols, Jr. Ithaca: Cornell UP, 1998.

———. *Protagoras.* Trans. C. C. W. Taylor. New York: Oxford UP, 1991.

Pough, Gwendolyn. *Check It While I Wreck It: Black Womanhood, Hip Hop Culture, and the Public Sphere.* Boston: Northeastern UP, 2004.

Poulakos, John. *Sophistical Rhetoric in Classical Greece.* Columbia: U of South Carolina P, 1995.

Poulakos, Takis, ed. *Rethinking the History of Rhetoric: Multidisciplinary Essays on the Rhetorical Tradition.* Boulder: Westview, 1993.

Quandahl, Ellen. "A Feeling for Aristotle: Emotion in the Sphere of Ethics." Micciche and Jacobs 11–22.

———. " 'More than Lessons in How to Read': Burke, Freud, and the Resources of Symbolic Transformation." *College English* 63 (2001): 633–54.

Quintilian. *Institutio Oratoria.* Trans. H. E. Butler. 4 vols. Cambridge: Harvard UP, 1980.

Ratcliffe, Krista. *Anglo-American Feminist Challenges to the Rhetorical Traditions: Virginia Woolf, Mary Daly, Adrienne Rich.* Carbondale: Southern Illinois UP, 1996.

———. "Eavesdropping as a Rhetorical Tactic: History, Whiteness, and Rhetoric." *JAC: A Journal of Composition Theory* 20 (2000): 87–119.

———. "Material Matters: Bodies and Rhetoric." *College English* 64 (2002): 613–23.

Richards, I. A., and C. K. Ogden. *The Meaning of Meaning: A Study of the Influence of Language upon Thought and of the Science of Symbols.* New York: Harcourt, 1956.

Ritchie, Joy, and Kate Ronald, eds. *Available Means: An Anthology of Women's Rhetoric(s).* Pittsburgh: U of Pittsburgh P, 2001.

———. "Introduction: Aspasia, Diotima, and Hortensia." Ritchie and Ronald, *Available Means* 1–19.

Roberts-Miller, Patricia. *Voices in the Wilderness: Public Discourse and the Paradox of Puritan Rhetoric.* Tuscaloosa: U of Alabama P, 1999.

Romano, Susan. "Tlaltelolco: The Grammatical-Rhetorical *Indios* of Colonial Mexico." *College English* 66 (2004): 9–29.

Rorty, Richard. *Contingency, Irony, and Solidarity.* New York: Cambridge UP, 1989.

———, ed. *The Linguistic Turn.* Chicago: U of Chicago P, 1968.

———. *Philosophy and the Mirror of Nature.* Princeton: Princeton UP, 1979.

Ross, Fiona. *Bearing Witness: Women and the Truth and Reconciliation Commission in South Africa.* London: Pluto, 2003.

Roy, Arundhati. *Power Politics.* Boston: South End, 2001.

Royster, Jacqueline Jones. *Traces of a Stream: Literacy and Social Change among African American Women.* Pittsburgh: U of Pittsburgh P, 2000.

Russell, David R. *Writing in the Academic Disciplines: A Curricular History.* 2nd ed. Carbondale: Southern Illinois UP, 2002.

Salazar, Philippe-Joseph. *An African Athens: Rhetoric and the Shaping of Democracy in South Africa.* Mahwah: Erlbaum, 2002.

Saussure, Ferdinand de. *Course in General Linguistics.* Ed. Charles Bally and Albert Sechehaye. Trans. Wade Baskin. New York: McGraw, 1966.

Schiappa, Edward. *The Beginnings of Rhetoric Theory in Classical Greece.* New Haven: Yale UP, 1999.

———. *Protagoras and Logos: A Study in Greek Philosophy and Rhetoric.* 2nd ed. Columbia: U of South Carolina P, 2003.

———. "*Rhetoriké*: What's in a Name? Toward a Revised History of Early Greek Rhetorical Theory." *Quarterly Journal of Speech* 78 (1992): 1–15.

Schilb, John. "Composition and Poststructuralism: A Tale of Two Conferences." *College Composition and Communication* 40 (1989): 422–43.

Scott, Robert L. "On Viewing Rhetoric as Epistemic." *Central States Speech Journal* 18 (1967): 9–16.

Sedgwick, Eve Kosofsky. "Socratic Raptures, Socratic Ruptures: Notes toward Queer Performativity." *English Inside and Out: The Places of Literary Criticism.* Ed. Susan Gubar and Jonathan Kamholtz. New York: Routledge, 1993. 122–36.

Selzer, Jack. *Kenneth Burke in Greenwich Village: Conversing with the Moderns, 1915–1931.* Madison: University of Wisconsin P, 1996.

Selzer, Jack, and Sharon Crowley, eds. *Rhetorical Bodies.* Madison: U of Wisconsin P, 1999.

Smith, Adam. *Lectures on Rhetoric and Belles Lettres: Delivered in the University of Glasgow by Adam Smith: Reported by a Student in 1762–63.* Ed. John M. Lothian. Carbondale: Southern Illinois UP, 1963.

Smith, John H. *The Spirit and Its Letter: Traces of Rhetoric in Hegel's Philosophy of Bildung.* Ithaca: Cornell UP, 1988.

Spivak, Gayatri Chakravorty. "Can the Subaltern Speak?" *Marxism and the Interpretation of Culture.* Ed.

Cary Nelson and Larry Grossberg. Urbana: U of Illinois P, 1988. 271–313.

Sprague, Rosamond Kent, ed. *The Older Sophists: A Complete Translation by Several Hands of the Fragments in Die Fragmente der Vorsokratiker.* Columbia: U of South Carolina P, 1972.

Streuver, Nancy S. *The Language of History in the Renaissance: Rhetoric and Historical Consciousness in Florentine Humanism.* Princeton: Princeton UP, 1970.

Sutherland, Christine Mason, and Rebecca Sutcliffe, eds. *The Changing Tradition: Women in the History of Rhetoric.* Calgary: U of Calgary P, 1999.

Todorov, Tzvetan. *Theories of the Symbol.* Trans. Catherine Porter. Ithaca: Cornell UP, 1982.

Toulmin, Stephen E. *The Uses of Argument.* New York: Cambridge UP, 1958.

Vatz, Richard. "The Myth of the Rhetorical Situation." *Philosophy and Rhetoric* 6 (1973): 154–61.

Viswanathan, Gauri. *Masks of Conquest: Literary Study and British Rule in India.* New York: Columbia UP, 1989.

Vitanza, Victor J. *Negation, Subjectivity, and the History of Rhetoric.* Albany: State U of New York P, 1997.

———. " 'Notes' towards Historiographies of Rhetorics; or, Rhetoric of the Histories of Rhetorics: Traditional, Revisionary, and Sub/Versive." *Pre/Text* 8 (1987): 63–115.

———, ed. *Writing Histories of Rhetoric.* Carbondale: Southern Illinois UP, 1994.

Walker, Jeffrey. *Rhetoric and Poetics in Antiquity.* Oxford: Oxford UP, 2000.

———. " 'These Things I Have Not Betrayed': Michael Psellos' Encomium of His Mother as a Defense of Rhetoric." *Rhetorica* 22 (2004): 49–101.

Walmsley, Peter. *Locke's Essay and the Rhetoric of Science.* Lewisburg: Bucknell UP, 2003.

Warner, Michael. *The Letters of the Republic: Publication and the Public Sphere in Eighteenth-Century America.* Cambridge: Harvard UP, 1990.

———. *Public and Counterpublic.* New York: Zone, 2002.

Warnick, Barbara. *The Sixth Canon: Belletristic Rhetorical Theory and Its French Antecedents.* Columbia: U of South Carolina P, 1993.

Watson, Shevaun E. "Unsettled Cities: Race and Rhetoric in the Early Republic." Diss. Miami U, 2004.

Weaver, Richard. *The Ethics of Rhetoric.* Chicago: Regenery, 1953.

Welch, Kathleen E. *Electric Rhetoric: Classical Rhetoric, Oralism, and a New Literacy.* Cambridge: MIT P, 1999.

Wells, Susan. *Sweet Reason: Intersubjective Rhetoric and the Discourses of Modernity.* Chicago: U of Chicago P, 1996.

Wertheimer, Molly Meijer. *Listening to Their Voices: The Rhetorical Activities of Historical Women.* Columbia: U of South Carolina P, 1997.

Wiederhold, Eve. "The Face of Mourning: Deploying Grief to Construct a Nation." *JAC: A Journal of Composition Theory* 22 (2002): 847–89.

Winterowd, W. Ross. *Rhetoric: A Synthesis*. New York: Holt, Rinehart, 1968.

Wolin, Ross. *The Rhetorical Imagination of Kenneth Burke*. Columbia: U of South Carolina P, 2001.

Wolkstein, Diane, and Samuel Noah Kramer. *Inanna: Queen of Heaven and Earth: Her Stories and Hymns from Sumer*. New York: Harper, 1983.

Worsham, Lynn. "After Words: A Choice of Words Remains." *Feminist and Composition Studies: In Other Words*. Ed. Susan C. Jarratt and Worsham. New York: MLA, 1998. 329–56.

———. "Eating History, Purging Memory, Killing Rhetoric." Vitanza, *Writing* 139–55.

———. "Going Postal: Pedagogic Violence and the Schooling of Emotion." *JAC: A Journal of Composition Theory* 18 (1998): 213–45.

Yates, Frances A. *The Art of Memory*. Chicago: U of Chicago P, 1966.

Young, Richard E., Alton L. Becker, and Kenneth L. Pike. *Rhetoric: Discovery and Change*. Fort Worth: Harcourt, 1970.

Young, Richard, and Maureen Daly Goggin. "Some Issues in Dating the Birth of the New Rhetoric in Departments of English: A Contribution to a Developing Historiography." Enos and Brown, *Defining* 22–43.

~ Composition

DAVID BARTHOLOMAE

Scholarly work in composition began with the very first language courses designed for undergraduates in the American university at the end of the eighteenth, the beginning of the nineteenth century. These courses typically combined training in rhetoric, oratory, and written composition. While my focus in this essay is on recent scholarship, let me provide a brief point of reference. In 1819, Edward Channing became the third Boylston Professor of Rhetoric and Oratory at Harvard, a position he held for thirty-two years. In 1856, after his retirement, he published his *Lectures Read to the Seniors at Harvard College*. The lectures address such topics as "Reasons for Preaching" and "Judicial Oratory," topics perhaps more appropriate for mention in a chapter on rhetorical scholarship, but he also wrote "A Writer's Preparation," "A Writer's Habits," and "The Study of Our Own Language." In "A Writer's Habits," Channing makes a claim for the teaching of writing that remains familiar:

> The confidence of teachers that their apparatus has not been applied in vain may be pardoned them. It is not arrogant. They can say truly that part of their instruction was most definite, and, though humble, it generally accomplished what it proposed. Perhaps they hope that more was taught than forms and proprieties, and that they led the mind to feel that there was some bond between the forms and proprieties and its own action. The process, after all, may have been more than mechanical. (187)

Although I deal here with scholarship beginning in the mid-1960s and early 1970s, more than a hundred years later, the period in between should not be seen as empty or insignificant. Much was happening, in fact, to change the purpose and structure of schooling in English. For example, after Channing's retirement, the Boylston chair at Harvard was awarded to Francis J. Child, who had little time or interest in student compositions and who helped create what we now take for granted as the study of literature. During Child's tenure at Harvard, composition became a freshman course, conceived as primarily remedial and taught by a more irregular and less distinguished faculty—and where the large numbers of students and the stacks and stacks of essays to be read seemed to justify methods, or an "apparatus," in Channing's terms, that could be little more than mechanical. This, too, sounds familiar. As English departments became more specialized and with the increase in the number (and range) of institutions and students, the freshman course—almost always referred to as necessary but unmanageable—was reinvented at colleges and universities across the country.

Some of the very best historical scholarship

in composition deals with the period 1850–1950, and an interested reader can turn to these books to fill in what I must leave out. For years, graduate students and scholars turned to Albert Kitzhaber's unpublished 1953 University of Washington dissertation, "Rhetoric in American Colleges, 1850–1900," to get a detailed sense of textbooks and pedagogical concerns and practices. This work is now available in print, with a fine introduction by John Gage. James Berlin, in *Writing Instruction in Nineteenth-Century American Colleges*, worked with many of the materials in Kitzhaber's dissertation to develop an argument about the ideological concerns of the American university, an argument that continues to shape discussions of past and current practice. John Brereton has collected and provided context for many primary documents from this period in *The Origins of Composition Studies in the American College, 1875–1925*. David Russell, in *Writing in the Academic Disciplines, 1870–1990*, considers the role and status of student writing beyond the introductory or freshman course. Perhaps the most readable of the histories of this period is Robert Connors's *Composition-Rhetoric: Backgrounds, Theory, and Pedagogy*. Connors has a great fondness for the everyday materials of classroom practice, and he provides a fine sense of the material conditions of composition instruction from 1760 to 1960. The most subtle, comprehensive, and carefully researched accounts of the intellectual context of the development of composition can be found in Nan Johnson's *Nineteenth-Century Rhetoric in North America* and Thomas P. Miller's *The Formation of College English: Rhetoric and Belles Lettres in the British Cultural Provinces*.

As I read through the materials from this period, the legacy of scholarship is represented by the work of those who felt the importance of the charge that was given to them—teaching writing to a broad and diverse population—and who turned their professional efforts to better understand their subject, a writing that was not necessarily literary, and the place of that writing in the college or university curriculum—or, more

Would composition courses work—could writing be taught and learned?

broadly, within the conventions and institutions of knowledge that defined the historical and cultural moment.

The subject raised fundamental questions. What was good writing, in the context of schooling, and for what purposes could it be valued as good? What topics and genres were appropriate for American undergraduates? How might one understand the relation between the actual languages of use and local or national standards (such as an idealized American English)? More specifically, what did students do when they sat down to write? How, that is, did they imagine and enact the work of writing? What were the appropriate exercises, assignments, courses, and curricula to shape a young writer's education? Would composition courses work—could writing be taught and learned? If writing could be taught, what were the appropriate goals—preparation for advanced education, for advanced thought? for citizenship and vocation? And how might scholars value and support that work, particularly in relation to the structures of value that had produced English departments and literature as an area of study?

～

The study of composition began with a course and its questions, but the problems of individual classrooms and the work of individual writers came to stand for fundamental questions of use, acquisition, pedagogy, and value as they pertained to writing outside or on the margins of literature and literary value. More recently, composition scholars have extended their reach to look at writing across the disciplines and across the grades—and to look, as well, at forms of ordinary or unauthorized writing, writing outside school. In the very best cases, the small and local problems of language and learning provided an occasion to ask questions that were significant and persistent.

This essay provides an introduction to current scholarship in composition—along with a list of representative or exemplary texts—for those new to the field. I begin my account in the

1960s and early 1970s for the sake of convenience, although this period is not an entirely arbitrary starting point, since it is at this time that composition begins again to demand attention as an area of professional-scholarly identification, with a history, with substantial careers as points of reference, with a surprising new prominence in the MLA *Job Information List*, with new venues for publication, and (by the mid-1970s) with new courses in PhD curricula at major research universities. As is often the case, the moment of renewal was defined (and experienced) as a moment of crisis.

I use books as my main references, but with misgivings. Between the 1960s and the 1980s the field did not rely on or support the book as a primary means of publication and circulation, and the essay or article remains an important and appropriate venue for scholarship in the field. Many of the important essays, however, have been reprinted in collections, referenced below.

I am pleased that this volume separates scholarship in composition from scholarship in rhetoric (see Jarratt in this volume). I believe that there are important and fundamental differences between the fields in history, object, and method. There are, of course, also important cross-references, and some should be evident in the two essays in this volume; others, unfortunately, may remain undocumented.

I want to mark the opening moment in my account of scholarship in composition by turning briefly to four books, all of which served to organize and direct the field. I will list them in the order that I discuss them below: *A Theory of Discourse*, by James Kinneavy (1971); *Research in Written Composition*, by Richard Braddock, Richard Lloyd-Jones, and Lowell Schoer (1963); *Themes, Theories, and Therapy: The Teaching of Writing in College*, by Albert B. Kitzhaber (1963); and *Uptaught*, by Ken Macrorie (1970). These will allow me to suggest four directions for research and scholarship. This is a loose ordering system, to be sure, and I don't want to claim too much for it, although I believe it allows me to make some useful distinctions in aims, methods, and goals. I am not suggesting that these four

books are the necessary starting points for a reader interested in learning about the field. In fact, my advice to such a reader would be to work backward, to read back to the work of the 1960s and 1970s from the more recent studies I gather under their names. The current work is more readable and recognizable, and it is through the current work that a reader can best understand and make use of the past. Once I've covered the areas of research indicated by these four texts, I'll take a moment to look at what I've left out.

TRAVELING THEORY

Each of these four books differently makes the same statement and the same call. The teaching of composition is ungoverned, generally uninformed, and poorly sponsored. A composition course is required of all students, and yet it has no consistent or compelling purpose, no way of accounting for itself and its success or failure. And in the face of such absence or anarchy, composition (the course, the faculty, the urgency coded into the curriculum) must establish a scholarly or experimental or theoretical base. Here, for example, are the opening paragraphs of Kinneavy's *Theory of Discourse*:

> The present anarchy of the discipline of what is commonly categorized as "composition," both in high schools and colleges, is so evident as scarcely to require proof.
>
> Composition is so clearly the stepchild of the English department that it is not a legitimate area of concern in graduate studies, is not even recognized as a subdivision of the discipline of English in a recent manifesto put out by the major professional association (MLA) of college English teachers, in some universities is not a valid area of scholarship for advancement in rank, and is generally the teaching province of graduate assistants or fringe members of the department.
>
> The present chaotic subsistence of freshman and upper-division courses in composition underscores their precarious claim to existence. The agenda of freshman composition vary from nothing to everything. . . .

Such a rich variety on the surface might suggest an underlying poverty. It does suggest one clear hypothesis: there is no definite concept of what the basic foundations of composition are. There is even the uneasy suspicion that there is no more to composition *as* composition than what could and should be covered in an adequate high school course.

On the contrary, it is the thesis of this work that the field of composition—or discourse as it will presently be termed—is a rich and fertile discipline with a worthy past which should be consulted before being consigned to oblivion, an exciting present, and a future that seems as limitless as either linguistics or literature.   (1–2)

Kinneavy's project was comprehensive, synthetic, and magisterial. Oddly, given its difficulty and range of reference, his book was designed as a textbook, presumably for undergraduates, but it has circulated primarily through the scholarly community. It is used frequently as a key text in the first graduate courses offered under the name of composition. The book is contingent with three other grand projects, two in and one out of composition: Northrop Frye's *Anatomy of Criticism* (1957); Richard Young, Alton Becker, and Kenneth Pike's *Rhetoric: Discovery and Change* (1970), like Kinneavy's *Theory* written as a textbook although seldom used as one; and James Moffett's *Teaching the Universe of Discourse* (1968), a book directly primarily at the K-12 curriculum. Kinneavy's book (like the others) represents the desire for a unifying theory. To this end, Kinneavy provides a "history of theory and practice and a survey of current theory in practice." The project is encyclopedic: its method is to read, classify, and appropriate everything that has been written on discourse in any field—linguistics, literary criticism, history, philosophy, psychology, rhetoric—in order to develop a theory and an "intelligible framework" that can be applied to the problems of writing and learning to write (5).

Perhaps the best way to provide a sense of the book's synthetic method is to look at the citations. The first chapter has a list of 117 references ranging among (alphabetically) M. H. Abrams's *The Mirror and the Lamp*, Alexander

Bain's *English Composition and Rhetoric*, Rudolph Carnap's *Logical Foundations of Probability*, Noam Chomsky's *Aspects of a Theory of Syntax*, Gustav Herdan's *Quantitative Linguistics*, Bronislaw Malinowski's *Coral Gardens and Their Magic*, H. L. Mencken's *The American Language*, Willard Quine's *From a Logical Point of View*, Quintilian's *Institutio Oratoria*, Ferdinand de Saussure's *Course in General Linguistics*, Joel Spingarn's "Creative Criticism," Denys Winstanley's *The University of Cambridge in the Eighteenth Century*, and Paul Ziff's *Semantic Analysis*. The list is at once inspiring and impossible—inspiring because of the range and seriousness of Kinneavy's learning; impossible because it assumes a figure of the scholar, no longer in circulation, perhaps no longer possible, and a figure with limited circulation in the 1970s—that is, the figure of the person who has read (and who can read) everything.

It is no surprise, then, that Kinneavy lamented the move to specialization in scholarship at the end of the twentieth century, and he lamented the move toward writing classes that would prepare students to write for the limited audience of the academic disciplines (see, e.g., "Writing"). A learned person, he argued, should be able and be free to draw on all areas of learning; a writing course should prepare a scholar to speak to the widest possible audience. While the field no longer has scholars attempting to write a book like his *Theory*, the desire remains among some to create a writing curriculum that can connect students to all areas of advanced knowledge and that can prepare them to write and to act on behalf of common concerns, a desire perhaps best represented by Kurt Spellmeyer's books, *Common Ground: Dialogue, Understanding, and the Teaching of Writing*, which addresses the purpose of the first-year course, and *Arts of Living: Reinventing the Humanities for the Twenty-First Century*, which is more strident and which addresses the humanities more generally.

A significant and influential scholar of Kinneavy's generation, one equally eager to establish precursors (although through a much shorter and more idiosyncratic reading list) and having a greater commitment to practice, is Anne Berthoff. Berthoff was an important figure for the next generation of composition scholars, particularly those who did not gather under the name of rhetoric or the methods of cognitive science. She had a philosopher's interest in questions of language and interpretation, and the figures she promoted as important to the work of composition were Samuel Coleridge, C. S. Peirce, Suzanne Langer, Kenneth Burke, I. A. Richards, and Paulo Freire. The best places to begin reading Berthoff are *The Making of Meaning: Metaphors, Models, and Maxims for Writing Teachers* and *The Sense of Learning*.

In my reading of composition scholarship, Kinneavy's *Theory* was more the end of something than it was a beginning, although Kinneavy and his students continued (and continue) to play an important role in the field. After 1971, there were a few similar attempts to create a unified, comprehensive theory applied to composition and teaching. There was *The Philosophy of Composition*, by E. D. Hirsch, Jr., before (or on his way to) his well-known and controversial work on "cultural literacy," and a response to that book by George L. Dillon, *Constructing Texts*. Still, Kinneavy's fundamental method as a scholar remains very much a part of work in the field, even if the range of that work is now more limited.

The turn to rhetoric and the history of rhetoric marks one possible line from Kinneavy to the present. (This will not be my concern here; see Jarratt in this volume.) For the connections of rhetoric to composition, the reading list would begin with Edward P. J. Corbett's *Classical Rhetoric for the Modern Student* (1965; Corbett and Connors).

I want to turn attention to other lines of inquiry. Following Kinneavy, composition scholars continue to survey the history of theory and practice, and scholars continue to study established fields of specialty, like linguistics, philosophy, or literary criticism, in order to bring them to bear on the problems of composition, usually represented as problems in the conception and design of the required writing course.

The history of theory and practice has been an active and compelling area of research. Several books mentioned above provide histories of composition as a school subject from the mid–nineteenth to the mid–twentieth century. For projects that work more closely with the material record of teaching (textbooks, exercises, teachers' materials), see Connors's *Selected Essays of Robert J. Connors*, Sharon Crowley's *Composition in the University: Historical and Polemical Essays* and *The Methodical Memory: Invention in Current-Traditional Rhetoric*, and Richard Ohmann's *English in America: A Radical View of the Profession*. Lucille Schultz, Stephen Carr, and Jean Ferguson Carr have done important work on the production, circulation, and use of textbooks (grammars, spellers, and rhetorics) in their *Archives of Instruction: Nineteenth-Century Rhetorics, Readers, and Composition Books in the United States*, a groundbreaking book that brings the history of the book to the history of rhetoric and composition.

Robin Varnum and Thomas Masters provide histories of significant composition programs on individual campuses in *Fencing with Words: A History of Writing Instruction on the Amherst Campus* and *Practicing Writing: The Postwar Discourse of Freshman English* (dealing with curricula at Wheaton, Northwestern, and the Univ. of Illinois). Stephen Parks traces an important moment in the history of the professional organization Conference on College Composition and Communication (CCCC) in *Class Politics: The Movement for Students' Rights to Their Own Language*.

Books that survey current scholarship in composition, examining its key terms and methods, are Stephen North's *The Making of Knowledge in Composition: Portrait of an Emerging Field*, Joseph Harris's *A Teaching Subject: Composition since 1966*, and Bruce Horner's *Terms of Work for Composition*. One of the most ambitious, widely cited, and influential accounts of the present is Susan Miller's *Textual Carnivals: The Politics of*

The turn to rhetoric and the history of rhetoric marks one possible line from Kinneavy to the present.

Composition. For a range of positions, I would recommend the collection of essays *Contending with Words: Composition and Rhetoric in a Postmodern Age*, edited by John Schilb and Patricia Harkin. In 2001, there was a large meeting to herald the new millennium, with much stocktaking and various predictions for the future, and these talks have been gathered in *Composition Studies in the New Millennium: Rereading the Past; Rewriting the Future* (Bloom, White, and Daiker).

I have been looking at histories of the field and of teaching. I want to also use Kinneavy to mark the desire to bring theory to composition, which has led those concerned with composition to turn elsewhere, to work that is not primarily directed toward composition, much of it rooted specifically in literary theory. One of the best books of this type is Kay Halasek's *A Pedagogy of Possibility: Bakhtinian Perspectives on Composition Studies*. That it has become increasingly common to turn to literary theory and literary history in such acts of translation is predictable, since the people preparing these studies are often trained and located in English departments. (The implications of using literary theory for student writing are usually unexamined, however.) The precariousness of the relation between these two areas of teaching is one of the concerns of Schilb's *Between the Lines: Relating Composition Theory and Literary Theory*. See also John Clifford and Schilb's *Writing Theory and Critical Theory*, Andrea Lunsford and Lahoucine Ouzgane's *Crossing Borderlands: Composition and Postcolonial Studies*, and Gary Olson's *Rhetoric and Composition as Intellectual Work*. Jasper Neel's *Plato, Derrida, and Writing* thinks from these key figures to the situation of writing in the undergraduate curriculum. Hephzibah Roskelly and Kate Ronald think about composition pedagogy through the work of Peirce, William James, John Dewey, and Freire in *Reason to Believe: Romanticism, Pragmatism, and the Teaching of Writing*. In *Changing the Subject in English Class: Discourse and the Constructions of Desire*, Marshall Alcorn uses Jacques Lacan to explain the role and value of desire in writing instruction.

Finally, Kinneavy identifies linguistics as a re-lated area of research. There is, in fact, a long history of interaction between research in composition and research in language acquisition and the teaching of English as a second or foreign language. Recent work with bearing on the classroom is well represented by Ulla Connor's *Contrastive Rhetoric: Cross-Cultural Aspects of Second-Language Writing* and by three recent essay collections: Diane Belcher and George Braine's *Academic Writing in a Second Language: Essays on Research and Pedagogy*, Vivian Zamel and Ruth Spack's *Negotiating Academic Literacies: Teaching and Learning across Languages and Cultures*, and Ken Hyland and Jack Richards's *Second Language Writing*. The most ambitious and wide-ranging work being done in this area is represented by Suresh Canagarajah's highly acclaimed *Resisting Linguistic Imperialism in English Teaching* and *A Geopolitics of Academic Writing*. Both books consider writing and teaching in the context of English as a global language.

There has not, however, been much recent exchange between linguistics and first language writing instruction in English. The early work of William Labov, while not directed specifically at composition instruction, was of enormous importance as composition tried to think through questions of standard language and local dialect: *The Study of Non-standard English* and *Language in the Inner City*. Work in sociolinguistics was central to Geneva Smitherman's crucially important work on Black English in the university curriculum and as the medium for intellectual work, *Talkin' and Testifyin': The Language of Black America*. There were early experiments in creating templates for the construction of sentences: Francis Christensen's *The Sentence and the Paragraph* and Frank O'Hare's *Sentence-Combining: Improving Student Writing without Formal Grammar Instruction*. Christensen's "generative rhetoric" of the sentence and the worksheets of sentence combining are of interest now only as part of the historical record. Joseph Williams, on the other hand, has created a useful and teachable grammar for the writing class (and with applications for writing in the professions), one with wide and lasting application. There are now several versions of this book available. The classroom version, *Style: Ten Lessons in Clarity and Grace*, provides a descriptive language and a method writers can use to read and revise sentences to make them more efficient for a reader to process. The pedagogy was developed in the writing program at the University of Chicago, the Little Red Schoolhouse. Michael Halliday's theory of a systemic functional grammar has inspired many to think about genre and context in writing and schooling. Perhaps the best place to begin would be with two collections: Bill Cope and Mary Kalantzis's *The Powers of Literacy: A Genre Approach to the Teaching of Writing* and John Swales's *Genre Analysis: English in Academic and Research Settings*.

CONTROLLED RESEARCH

In 1961, the Executive Committee of the National Council of Teachers of English appointed its Ad Hoc Committee on the State of Knowledge about Composition and, with the support of the United States Office of Education, commissioned a study to review "what is known and what is not known about the teaching and learning of composition and the conditions under which it is taught" (Braddock, Lloyd-Jones, and Schoer 1). It is worth noting that this study received federal funding, one of several studies to do so during this period. The problem of writing was understood, as it has often been since, as a national concern. The research to be reviewed was only that which used "scientific methods," like controlled experimentation or quantitative analysis. This moment, too, was perceived as a crisis in composition:

> Today's research in composition, taken as a whole, may be compared to chemical research as it emerged from the period of alchemy: some terms are being defined usefully, a number of procedures are being refined, but the field as a whole is laced with dreams, prejudices, and makeshift operations. Not enough investigators are really informing themselves about the procedures and results of previous research before embarking on

their own. Too few of them conduct pilot experiments and validate their measuring instruments before undertaking an investigation. . . . And far too few of those who have conducted an initial piece of research follow it with further exploration or replicate the investigations of others.   (5)

The report of this committee, *Research in Written Composition*, summarized selected research projects, reviewed available research methods, and gave a summary report on the "state of knowledge" in composition. Since then, there have been several important controlled studies of writing and learning to write, all of them determined to move beyond "dreams, prejudices, and makeshift operations." They have drawn on traditions of research in education, the social sciences, and cognitive science. And, although they have lost their central place in the journals and meetings of the composition community, similar research on writing continues under the sponsorship of schools of education and departments of psychology. I would like to look at three particularly impressive projects that were conducted by figures central to composition and its scholarship. Although their methods were drawn from the human sciences, their concern was not so much to find an absolute or objective truth as to develop forms of study that could be transported and replicated from case to case or campus to campus and to develop representations of writing and learning that could be generalized across individuals and across classrooms.

In 1971, Janet Emig published a relatively short pamphlet on a study she had conducted, *The Composing Process of Twelfth Graders*. She argued that while writing instruction was driven by a shared set of rules and assumptions (about planning and purpose, about preparation and organization, and about the process of writing itself), these had little to do with what actual writers did, whether they were experts or novices. Her study reviewed accounts by established writers (e.g., in *Paris Review* interviews) and surveyed student writers. Its methodological innovation, however, was a record of students "composing aloud" while composing on paper. This method gave rise to a series of studies of the "composing process," usually studies of individuals using a case-study approach or some form of talk-aloud protocol, and they had a substantial effect on how composition was (and is) taught and how student writing was understood and represented. Much of this work was reported in journals; the best way to review it is through collections: Lad Tobin and Tom Newkirk's *Taking Stock: The Writing Process Movement in the 90s*, Sondra Perl's *Landmark Essays on Writing Process*, Mike Rose's *When a Writer Can't Write: Studies in Writer's Block and Other Composing Process Problems*, and Ann Penrose and Barbara Sitko's *Hearing Ourselves Think: Cognitive Research in the College Writing Classroom*. Rose's work contributed significantly to the process movement (see his recent collection of essays *An Open Language*).

An important early essay in research on the composing process was Linda Flower and John Hayes's "A Cognitive Process Theory of Writing" (1981). Flower and her colleagues have conducted perhaps the most impressive, continuous research project in the field, one that relies on disciplined observation, experimentation, and report. This project has involved teams of researchers to carry out the data collection and review; it has required the conviction, determination, and support necessary to carry on an evolving line of inquiry, with many participants, through more than two decades. Flower began with a concern to study writing as a cognitive process and to apply a problem-solving approach to writing instruction. Over time (and with the turn of cognitive research to situated cognition), she began to organize research projects designed to investigate how "different writers and readers are constructing meaning" through the "interplay of shaping forces": personal intentions, social imperatives, prior knowledge, ability, and motivation. In Flower's work these questions are empirical. She says:

> By *empirical*, I do not mean as a matter that can be resolved by the simple accumulation of facts, but . . . as a question that calls for observation-based theory building grounded in the investi-

Research on the composing process set out to create a useful account of the writer at work.

gation of actual writers in specific contexts. . . . (*Construction* 43)

Her current projects include work with community literacy settings, the application of her developing theory to writers who are unschooled or out of school, and work in public settings to solve problems that require oral and written presentations that cross boundaries of race and class. You can trace her work across a series of important, multiauthored books, and you can find related projects in her citations and references: *Reading-to-Write: Exploring a Cognitive and Social Process*; *Problem-Solving Strategies for Writing* (a textbook); *Making Thinking Visible: Writing, Collaborative Planning, and Classroom Inquiry*; *Writers at Work: Strategies for Communicating in Business and Professional Settings* (a textbook); *The Construction of Negotiated Meaning: A Social Cognitive Theory of Writing*; *Problem-Solving Strategies for Writing in College and Community* (a revised edition of the earlier textbook); and *Learning to Rival: A Literate Practice for Intercultural Inquiry*.

Research on the composing process set out to create a useful account of the writer at work. There have also been controlled studies of curricula and of writing development as measured across time (longitudinal studies), studies of courses and curricula.

In 1975, James Britton and his colleagues published *The Development of Writing Abilities (11–18)*, the result of a study supported by the National Schools Council in England. The goal was to account for stages in the learning of writing, so that the school curriculum could better respond to and anticipate a curriculum (it was assumed) that was built into the learners. The study gathered 2,122 pieces of school writing from 500 children across the age range 11 to 18. The researchers realized that while there was an extensive literature on what children should write, there was little on what children did write, nor were there established methods for describing (let alone evaluating) differences in their written texts. The value of the study is the record of the work to establish a system of classification (with *audience* and *function* as the key organizing terms), a system that could be used by the research team to sort and identify students' written work in school. The study revealed much about the failures of schooling; and it is the terms of this argument, rather than a theory of development, that has kept the book in circulation.

In the opening of their study, Britton and his colleagues note:

> While we were working on our two major dimensions of function and audience we also did a good deal of preliminary thinking about a third dimension—the language resources that a child draws on in order to write—but we were not able to develop this area of inquiry fully.   (16)

One way of representing these language resources is to think about the effects of class difference on writing (or learning to write). Carolyn Steedman completed a significant study of class and children's writing in England, *The Tidy House* (see also her *Radical Soldier's Tale* and *Past Tenses*). That Steedman's work has never had much prominence among those working on composition on either side of the Atlantic is a shame, since class has been a neglected category of analysis in the study of writing and schooling in the United States.

More recently, Marilyn Sternglass completed a longitudinal study of writing development on a much smaller scale, one where class is an area of consideration, *Time to Know Them*. Sternglass tracked nine students through their degree program at City College in New York. Her book became a significant and controversial document in the political battles over the role of remediation in the CUNY system. The book is remarkable for the care it gives to the social, economic, and political contexts of student learning and achievement.

In addition, there are currently two large-scale longitudinal studies being conducted on United States campuses, one at Harvard, directed by Nancy Sommers, and one at Stanford, directed by Andrea Lunsford. These projects are just now being reported on at conferences. We will wait for the full reports. Each works from a substantial corpus of student writing, papers written for every course across a four-year curriculum, with interviews and surveys to support the analysis. Neither study is designed to make universal claims about writing development. I know the Harvard project best, so let me speak to its goals. It is designed to give a detailed and textured account of the practices and attitudes, the culture of writing, on the Harvard campus and to track those practices and attitudes along two axes—the work as it develops across the four undergraduate years and the work as it divides across academic disciplines. These are exciting and significant projects and promise not only a large-scale, text-based account of writing in the college curriculum but also, and for the first time, a corpus of student writing to be archived for further study.

DEFINING THE OBJECT OF STUDY

In 1963, Albert Kitzhaber completed and published the report of the Dartmouth College study of student writing, funded by the Carnegie Corporation. The study was begun to answer two questions: (1) Can English composition at Dartmouth be taught more effectively in the required freshman English course than it is now?; (2) Can anything be done to ensure that students will continue to write at least as well after they have left freshman English as they do while they are taking it? For purposes of this essay, I would like Kitzhaber's report, *Themes, Theories, and Therapy: The Teaching of Writing in College*, to stand as the critical, scholarly, philosophical, but decidedly unscientific counterpart to *Research in Written Composition*. Kitzhaber began with a review of the "present state of composition" in the United States university. His conclusion comes as no surprise: "Freshman English in the nation's colleges and universities is now so confused, so clearly in need of radical and sweeping reforms, that college English departments can continue to ignore the situation only at their increasing peril" (26).

The book is an extended report on their examination of writing on the Dartmouth campus, with recommendations for reform that were meant to be useful, even exemplary, for others with similar concerns. It begins with local practice, hard to locate and hard to define, and struggles to bring it into focus as an object of study. Kitzhaber and his colleagues ask the difficult questions that are always part of a study of writing and schooling: How might we value and understand student writing? What forms of knowledge does it represent? What is the relation between this knowledge and the goals of the institution?

For the work I am gathering together under Kitzhaber's name, local circumstances and local examples lead to fundamental questions about written language, questions (for example) about race, gender, representation, knowledge, value, acquisition, standardization, and learning. In composition scholarship, the questions are grounded in the particular conditions of undergraduate writing rather than in novels, poems, stories, plays, or work from the canons of writing that have served scholars in English more generally. On campuses across the country, for example, there are programs for the study of working-class literary production or the traditions of African American writing that rely on special collections and library archives; at the same time, composition programs support, manage, and promote opportunities for working-class and African American writers and for the close, regular study of their writing. The primary texts for composition are local, shifting, and ephemeral: student writing and revision, a discussion in class, the materials of a given semester. They are hard to grasp, hard to hang on to, difficult to document, difficult to know, and difficult to value. For these reasons the work I gather below has, to my mind, been the most varied, the most interesting, and the most unpredictable in the last three decades.

In the discussion that follows, I point to some key texts that have raised broad questions about student writing and about writing and schooling—they are exemplary in their efforts to place, locate, and define the object of study. Then I look at work that has focused on particular areas of concern, areas determined either by the curriculum (e.g., writing in the disciplines, for example, or writing for the professions) or by composition's stake in critical debates occupying the broader scholarly community (e.g., the relation of writing to technology; of writing to gender, race, or sexuality).

Perhaps the most important and widely circulated example of this work is Mina Shaughnessy's *Errors and Expectations*, which began as a study of a particular, local problem: How might teachers read and understand the writing of students who entered the CUNY system through open admissions, students whose writing seemed unreadable and whose lack of preparation seemed to make teaching impossible? The book provides a record of how Shaughnessy (and her colleagues) learned to read four thousand student essays written by incoming freshmen at City College between 1970 and 1974. The purpose of the study was to

> be precise about the types of difficulties to be found in basic writing (BW) papers at the outset and, beyond that, to demonstrate how the sources of those difficulties can be explained without recourse to such pedagogically empty terms as "handicapped" or "disadvantaged." (4)

The book contains many examples of student writing, each included to "deepen one's sense of pattern and thereby [develop] the ability to make swift assessments and classifications of writing difficulties" (5). The book was innovative and profound; it reorganized the field, provided new ways of reading student writing and teaching composition. It was read widely for the ways it allowed a broad audience to think, again, about the role of the American university, about the relation between standard and nonstandard language, about common knowledge and its relation to the academy. A surprising and worthwhile but forgotten book from this period at CUNY is *Beat Not the Poor Desk*, by Marie Ponsot and Rosemary Deen. For recent accounts of this period, of Shaughnessy's work and its legacy, see Bruce Horner and Min-Zhan Lu's *Representing the "Other": Basic Writers and the Teaching of Basic*

Writing and Mary Soliday's *The Politics of Remediation: Institutional and Student Needs in Higher Education.*

New York was a key site of research in composition in the early and mid-1970s. From the same decade, although from the other coast, came two books attempting to define, contextualize, and value student writing, both worth continued attention: Roger Sale's *On Writing* and Richard Lanham's *Style: An Anti-text.* Lanham's work continued through a series of books whose titles register the changing environment for student writing: *Revising Prose* (which was later accompanied by computer-assisted instruction), *Literacy and the Survival of Humanism*, and *The Electronic Word.*

There have been a number of outstanding books with a similar ambition to confront local materials and conditions, to approach the object of study as a fundamental problem, and to approach it with a care for language and method such that the thinking illuminates significant and urgent questions of writing and schooling. James Slevin's *Introducing English: Essays in the Intellectual Work of Composition* is exemplary in this regard. Slevin begins with the desire to extend Shaughnessy's work to think broadly about composition and writing in the university curriculum. His argument is that the

> radical action of "open admissions" was not admission but *attendance*, and what happened after that. It was not simply universities affording educational opportunities but what students chose and worked to make of those opportunities and the consequences of those choices and work, particularly the serious intellectual changes and disruptions arising from them. The most significant of these consequences was the unveiling within higher education of the arbitrariness of the symbolic violence of the entire educational system, and both the simultaneous and subsequent transformation of the work of composition, fundamentally challenging reading and writing practices in the academy. (55–56)

Open admissions, and Shaughnessy's work more specifically, had made students' intellectual

work present where before it had been absent, assumed, taken for granted. Slevin's argument is that this moment, seen through the lens of Shaughnessy's work, has called (or should call) all student writing into question. We need to learn again how to read it, particularly for the way it troubles conventional assumptions about writing and learning, about standard and nonstandard language, and about general education in relation to the advanced work of the university. It is not that students are ill prepared, Slevin argues, but that we are ill prepared to think of them as participating in the work of the academy. We are not prepared to read their work; to value it; to understand its origins, place, or consequences. To read, value, and understand, he argues, is the crucial work of composition. The object of study is the written record of students encountering the institution; to read it, one must reread the institution—its genres, traditions, values—as represented in the freshman course and in the academic disciplines. This project, perhaps to its credit, is still not well defined. Slevin says:

It is not that students are ill prepared . . . but that we are ill prepared to think of them as participating in the work of the academy.

> Composition is a discipline . . . that cannot know itself because we have lost our power to name what we do. Our discipline is about the encounter of different ways of reading and writing; our discipline arises in acts of interpretation and composing, in encounters with old and new student populations and different ways of reading and thinking and persuading brought into our classroom by students. Our disciplinary work in all its form, including research, arises from the need and the desirability of promoting and enriching this dialogue, already [under way]. (44)

I have chosen Slevin's *Introducing English* as exemplary for how it foregrounds the problem of defining the object of study and for its recognition that the work of students can provide access to fundamental problems of writing and difference, of knowledge and power, of tradition and change.

In the general category of work suggested by a line drawn through Kitzhaber, Shaughnessy, and Slevin, there are several other important and influential books of the last two decades. Lester Faigley, in *Fragments of Rationality: Postmodernity and the Subject of Composition*; Susan Miller, in *Rescuing the Subject: A Critical Introduction to Rhetoric and the Writer*; James Berlin, in *Rhetorics, Poetics, and Cultures: Refiguring College English Studies*; and Patricia Bizzell, in *Academic Discourse and Critical Consciousness* led the way in placing student writing and the work of the composition classroom in relation to the general critique of language, knowledge, and power central to postmodern critical study. I would list two of my own books as participating in the work of this project: *Facts, Artifacts, and Counterfacts* (with Anthony Petrosky) and *Writing on the Margins: Essays on Composition and Teaching*, and I would add Linda Brodkey's *Writing Permitted in Designated Areas Only*, which contains essays on the freshman course she designed for the University of Texas, Austin, and on the political controversy that shut it down.

Other scholars have worked closely with student writing and its relation to the institution and to traditions of learning. Among these, I recommend two widely read books of essays by Peter Elbow, *Embracing Contraries: Explorations in Learning and Teaching* and *Everyone Can Write: Essays toward a Hopeful Theory of Writing and Teaching Writing* and Gerald Graff's *Clueless in Academe: How Schooling Obscures the Life of the Mind*. Graff has written widely on the English curriculum. This book (and a later textbook) looks at how argument, as a standard protocol in academic discourse, is and is not represented in the composition curriculum. William E. Coles, Jr., and James Vopat published a collection of writing assignments, student papers, and commentary from leading composition scholars, *What Makes Writing Good: A Multiperspective*. David Bleich's *The Double Perspective: Language, Literacy, and Social Relations* looks closely at student writing and the writing classroom, as do Thomas Newkirk's *The Performance of Self in Student Writing*, Kathleen Blake Yancey's *Reflection in the Writing Classroom*, Russell Durst's *Collision Course*, and Candace Spigelman's *Personally Speaking: Experience as Evidence in Academic Discourse*.

Slevin's *Introducing English* is an important thinking through of composition (or students' writing); it is also surprising in its reach and range of reference, from early America to the *New Yorker* to the MLA. It represents a different way of thinking historically, looking not so much for a narrative as for the persistence of certain ways of thinking and feeling. It follows the tradition of cultural studies as exemplified in the work of Raymond Williams—for example, *Culture and Society* or *Keywords*. (Williams is a remarkable but generally ignored resource for research in composition.)

There are several books, some of which preceded Slevin's, that I admire for their similar reach and ambition. They work closely with composition as a current practice and yet set it in a complicated relations to cultural projects at other moments in history. Kathryn Flannery's *The Emperor's New Clothes: Literature, Literacy, and the Ideology of Style* traces the desire for a normative style from the seventeenth century to the twentieth. Richard Miller's *As If Learning Mattered: Reforming Higher Education* examines the institutions of schooling from Matthew Arnold through the Great Books program to current practice. Miller's new book, *Writing at the End of the World*, situates the writing classroom in relation to the violence of our current moment. Gwen Gorzelsky, in *The Language of Experience: Literate Practices and Social Change*, places contemporary urban literacy instruction in the context of social movements in the English Renaissance and in United States labor history. James Seitz, in *Motives for Metaphor: Literacy, Curriculum Reform, and the Teaching of English*, examines the deep ambivalence about metaphor (and the problems of figuration) across various moments in American schooling.

To represent a variety of projects concerned with critical pedagogy, or the possible relations between schooling and social justice, and with close attention to student writing and current practice, I recommend Judith Goleman's *Working Theory: Critical Composition Studies for Students and Teachers*, Geoffrey Sirc's *English Composition as a Happening*, and Xin Liu Gale's

Teachers, Discourses, and Authority in the Post-modern Composition Classroom.

The above books look at the particulars of writing and schooling. There are many that look either to specific areas of critical concern or to specific areas of the curriculum. A growing number of scholars are discussing the discourses of race, gender, and sexuality as they circulate in student writing and the composition classroom. The best places to begin reading in this area are Keith Gilyard's *Race, Rhetoric, and Composition* and *Let's Flip the Script: An African American Discourse on Language, Literature, and Learning*, Catherine Prendergast's *Literacy and Racial Justice: The Politics of Learning after* Brown v. Board of Education, Susan Jarratt and Lynn Worsham's *Feminism and Composition Studies*, Gesa Kirsch et al.'s *Feminism and Composition*, and Harriet Malinowitz's *Textual Orientations: Lesbian and Gay Students and the Making of Discourse Communities.*

And, as would be expected, there are many projects defined by acts of attention and inquiry directed at particular areas in the curriculum. I'll have to be quite selective in presenting examples. For writing instruction K-12, see Lucy Calkins's *The Art of Teaching Writing*; Jerome Harste, Kathy Short, and Carolyn Burke's *Creating Classrooms for Authors*; Nancie Atwell's *In the Middle*; and Harvey Daniels and Steven Zemelman's *A Community of Writers: Teaching Writing in the Junior and Senior High School*. For basic writing or courses designed for students who are unprepared for the college curriculum, I recommend Theresa Enos's *A Sourcebook for Basic Writing Teachers*. For the teaching of professional writing and the study of writing in the workplace, there are Nancy R. Blyler and Charlotte Thralls's *Professional Communication: The Social Perspective*, Charles Bazerman and James Paradis's *Textual Dynamics of the Professions*, and Rachel Spilka's *Writing in the Workplace: New Research Perspectives*. For writing across the curriculum or writing in the disciplines, see Art Young and Toby Fulwiler's *Writing across the Disciplines: Research into Practice* and Anne Herrington and Charles Moran's *Writing, Teaching, and Learning in the Disciplines*. Jonathan Monroe's *Local Knowledges, Local Practices: Writing in the Disciplines at Cornell* is an account of one of the most well articulated and influential writing-in-the-disciplines programs in the country.

The role of technology in writing and in the teaching of writing has been an area of considerable activity, and the subject invites speculation beyond the application of computers to the writing classroom. For recent work in this area, see Stephen Doheny-Farina's *The Wired Neighborhood*, Stuart Selber's *Multiliteracies for a Digital Age*, Gail Hawisher et al.'s *Computers and the Teaching of Writing in American Higher Education, 1979–1994*, Cynthia Selfe's *Technology and Literacy in the Twenty-First Century*, and David Kaufer and Brian Butler's *Designing Interactive Worlds with Words: Principles of Writing as Representational Composition*. For studies of writing centers or programs of tutorial support, see Jeanette Harris and Joyce Kinkead's *Writing Centers in Context: Twelve Case Studies* and Gary Olson's *Writing Centers: Theory and Administration*. Composition programs have always grappled with problems of assessment, including problems of placement or exit examinations. For work on assessment, see Edward White's *Teaching and Assessing Writing* and Kathleen Blake Yancey and Irwin Weiser's *Situating Portfolios: Four Perspectives*.

Finally, there has been attention in the last decade to the position of composition programs in relation to English departments and the contract categories available to tenure-stream faculty members. For work in this area, see Margaret O'Neill et al.'s *A Field of Dreams: Independent Writing Programs and the Future of Composition Studies* and Eileen E. Schell and Patricia Lambert Stock's *Moving a Mountain: Transforming the Role of Contingent Faculty in Composition Studies and Higher Education.*

REFIGURING THE SCENE OF INSTRUCTION

I began this discussion with Kinneavy's *Theory of Discourse* and the magisterial figure of the teacher-scholar. In the early 1970s, there were others whose impact on the field was defined, at least initially, by the alternative figures they provided, striking figures of the teacher and scholar—some of these we would now, looking back on the period, call countercultural—figures that also refigured the student writer and the writing classroom. The most significant of such books were Ken Macrorie's *Uptaught*, Peter Elbow's *Writing without Teachers*, and William E. Coles, Jr.'s, *The Plural I*. Macrorie begins his book with the following:

> At 10:48 p.m., April 3, 1969, I watched the president of my university leave his mansion and, followed by about thirty white-helmeted policemen carrying clubs and marching in tight formation behind him, stride across the street and up the walk to the Student Union to clear out any students who insisted on sitting in the Snack Bar after the eleven o'clock closing hour.
>
> I had been a professor more than twenty years. The sight was new, and it made me sick.
>
> Not because the president was acting irrationally.
>
> Not because the students were acting irrationally.
>
> But because the professors were not there. In the last five years, I had learned something about their responsibility in this affair. More than anyone else, they have made the university sick unto death.   (2)

The gesture is typical. The problems of writing and teaching are located in relation to the political-cultural climate of the late 1960s. (Elbow's *Writing without Teachers* begins, "Many people are now trying to become less helpless, both personally and politically: trying to claim more control over their own lives" [vii].) In Macrorie's account, freshman English played a central role in the death of the university through its deadening effect on students and faculty members alike. Freshman composition, in *Uptaught*, is where students learn to produce writing that is never read, because what is written matters neither to the writer nor to the reader; it enacts a fundamental disconnection between learning and experience. *Uptaught* is offered as a

journal of the writer's blindness and awakening; the figure at the center of the narrative learns to teach a course that matters. Macrorie coins the term "Engfish" to name a "language in which fresh truth is almost impossible to express"; "A feel-nothing, say-nothing language, dead like Latin, devoid of the rhythms of contemporary speech" (9, 18). And he provides accounts of students working to find a language that will allow them to be present to their moment in history.

Uptaught is dated, much more so than the other two books I've referenced, *Writing without Teachers* and *The Plural I*, but I want to insist on its importance at the time and I want to use it to stand at the head of a list of titles that, although not proposing to organize the field, significantly challenge the standard accounts of composition and teaching. The books on this list are written outside the usual genres of scholarship (often relying on some form of personal narrative), and they are written to provide a new figure for the teacher and a new way to imagine the student as writer. The most widely read and influential book is Elbow's *Writing without Teachers* (see also his *Writing with Power*), which is offered as a kind of antitextbook for the university without walls, as Adrienne Rich named those attempts to create and support alternate sites for learning. *Writing without Teachers* promoted freewriting as a method (writing all at once, with the internal editor turned off). The image Elbow provides of the student writing freely is one of the most powerful and pervasive figures in the contemporary writing classroom.

To my mind, however, the most interesting of these three authors is Coles, whose *Plural I* is a narrative account, with dialogue, of a freshman writing course he taught at Case Western Reserve in the late 1960s. For a reader, the distinction between fiction and report is blurred. One of the great pleasures of the book is that it reproduces student papers and class discussion and the striking, critical presence of the teacher, a figure active in the scene (as well as reflecting back on it). The narrative, shaped by evolving class

The image . . . of the student writing freely is one of the most powerful and pervasive figures in the contemporary writing classroom.

discussion and the progress of student writing from week to week, enacts the argument of a pedagogy (linked to the work of Theodore Baird, at Amherst) where students learn to perform close, critical readings of their own writing and where a sequence of assignments, one linked to the next, often in a revisionary spirit, leads them to question the relation between language and thought, language and experience, and language and identity. From one week to the next, students struggle to locate themselves and their thoughts within the regime of common sense and standard utterance. It is a remarkable book and, unfortunately, one of a kind.

The most interesting work that has followed these three has tended to be either autobiographical or a mix of personal narrative and academic reflection on issues and texts. Perhaps the most influential is Mike Rose's *Lives on the Boundary: The Struggles and Achievements of America's Underprepared*. Rose thinks through his experience as student and teacher to general issues of class and academic readiness. Gilyard's compelling book *Voices of the Self: A Study of Language Competence* effectively represents the difficult position of Black English in the nation's schools through personal narrative and a discussion of the available literature. There is a similar mix in Victor Villanueva's *Bootstraps: From an American Academic of Color*. Wendy Bishop, in *Teaching Lives* and in other works, simultaneously inhabits the positions of creative writer and composition teacher. One of the most unpredictable and compelling books of the last decade has been Paul Kameen's *Writing/Teaching: Essays toward a Rhetoric of Pedagogy*. The book is formally experimental, placing a narrative account of a writing course next to a series of reflections prompted by Platonic dialogues. It raises questions about the possibilities of dialogue in teaching and puts pressure on received notions of the Socratic method. There have been many narrative accounts of teaching in the last decade, the vast majority on the teaching of literature; Kameen's is one of the very few to resist the heroic narrative ("Once my students were blind, but now they can see").

THE EXTRACURRICULUM

An area of scholarly work not predicted by my opening four texts is the relatively recent one of literacy studies. A body of earlier work, to be sure, has made work in literacy possible, but it was located in anthropology and sociolinguistics (and only marginally present in Kinneavy's list of references). Some work in English, like Janice Radway's *Reading the Romance*, turned to common readers and ethnographic research methods. Composition came to literacy studies in the late 1980s and early 1990s as scholars were looking more to social, cultural, and political contexts for writing (and for its teaching).

Composition studies had an established tradition of casting attention to common, everyday, or unauthorized writers, so it was not surprising that students and scholars working in this area should extend this attention beyond the classroom and the college. Perhaps the most useful starting points for those interested in the composition work in this area are a collection gathered for use by scholars in composition, *Literacy: A Critical Sourcebook*, edited by Ellen Cushman, Eugene Kintgen, Barry Kroll, and Mike Rose, and Anne Gere's "Kitchen Table and Rented Rooms: the Extracurriculum of Composition," along with her later book-length study, *Writing Groups: History, Theory, and Implications*, both of which turned to uses of writing (and writing instruction) in local community and women's groups.

For all those doing work in literacy, the standard initial point of reference has been Shirley Brice Heath's *Ways with Words: Language, Life, and Work in Communities and Classrooms*. Heath was trained as an anthropologist, and this study, eloquent and enormously influential, is an ethnographic account of language development, including the development of writing in relation to schooling, in three North Carolina communities. Marcia Farr is another figure who, through her writing and her students, has had a deep and productive relation to composition. Farr, a sociolinguist, played an important role in the National Institute of Education. She has edited a number of volumes, including *Ethnolinguistic Chicago: Language and Literacy in the City's Neighborhoods* and *Literacy across Communities* (Moss and Farr).

Ethnographic method has become a standard tool in composition scholarship. Combined with the comparative projects of sociolinguistics, it has produced a productive line of work that continues to examine writing (and reading) in local settings, often as defined by race, class, or ethnicity. See for example Julie Lindquist's *A Place to Stand: Politics and Persuasion in a Working-Class Bar*, Ralph Cintron's *Angel's Town: Chero Ways, Gang Life, and Rhetorics of the Everyday*, Jabari Mahiri's *Shooting for Excellence*, John Trimbur's *Popular Literacy*, and Glynda Hull's *Changing Work / Changing Workers: Critical Perspectives on Language, Literacy, and Skills*. Gail Hawisher and Cynthia Selfe have completed *Literate Lives in the Information Age: Narratives on Literacy from the United States*. The most widely read and celebrated scholar in this area is Deborah Brandt, whose *Literacy as Involvement* and *Literacy in American Lives* have inspired a generation of younger scholars.

The work in literacy has also taken a historical turn, with attention to writing and to scenes of instruction that would otherwise be lost. Two important and influential studies are Jacqueline Jones Royster's *Traces of a Stream: Literacy and Social Change among African American Women* and Shirley Wilson Logan's *"We Are Coming": The Persuasive Discourse of Nineteenth-Century Black Women*. Susan Miller completed an impressive study of students' commonplace books written in the late eighteenth and early nineteenth centuries and held by the Virginia Historical Society, *Assuming the Positions: Cultural Pedagogy and the Politics of Commonplace Writing*. Susan Wells wrote on nineteenth-century women physicians and their writing as students and as scientists, in *Out of the Dead House*. Janet Carey Eldred and Peter Mortensen wrote on women's education, in *Imagining Rhetoric: Composing Women of the Early United States*.

BEYOND THE LIBRARY: ALTERNATIVE GENRES FOR SCHOLARSHIP IN COMPOSITION

More than any other field, composition invites (even requires) its scholars to consider their work a thing in practice, to make their arguments and reach audiences beyond the pages of a journal or monograph. The desire to think through a problem or argument by designing assignments or lessons, curricula or teacher training programs, may, in fact, be one of the defining characteristics of the scholar in composition.

Textbooks

While not all textbooks represent a scholarly intervention in the field, the best do, and they are written both to bring an argument to a broad audience (thousands, even hundreds of thousands of students) and to work out that argument in practice, by organizing the engagement of student writers over a course of instruction and by giving them an understanding, both theoretical and critical, of their work. Anyone interested in thinking about composition through its textbooks should look at the books that have dominated the market across time. The two most interesting are Cleanth Brooks and Robert Penn Warren's *Modern Rhetoric* and James McCrimmon's *Writing with a Purpose*. While their impact on American education has been great, the big sellers tend to be the least responsive to changes in scholarship and the least reflective.

There are, however, textbooks that have made serious interventions in the field but whose value is not necessarily reflected in sales. A few that I particularly admire are William E. Coles, Jr.'s, *Composing*; John Trimble's *Writing with Style*; Ann Berthoff's *Forming/Thinking/Writing*; Donald Hall's *Writing Well*; Winston Weathers's *An Alternative Style*; Robert Scholes, Nancy Comley, and Gregory Ulmer's *Text Book*; Donald McQuade and Nancy Sommers's *Student Writers at Work*; John Gage's *The Shape of Reason*; Mariolina

Salvatori and Patricia Donahue's *The Elements (and Pleasures) of Difficulty*; Joseph Comprone's *From Experience to Expression*; Patricia Bizzell and Bruce Herzberg's *Negotiating Difference*; Keith Hjortshoj's *The Transition to College Writing*; and Joseph Harris's *Rewriting*.

Programs and Curricula

It is also the case that scholarship in composition is articulated in programs and curricula, where an argument is developed through the organization of courses, teaching materials, and faculty. Programs and curricula are difficult if not impossible to read, reference, and archive, so they have a tenuous relation to the literature of composition. There are, to be sure, accounts of courses and programs. Monroe's *Local Knowledges, Local Practices*, for example, provides a history of an undergraduate writing program; a theoretically informed overview; and essays by its various teachers, including faculty members from across departments on the Cornell campus. I include "Programs and Curricula" as part of this essay not, however, to call for additional books but to make the case that such work should be valued by departments and by the profession, when deserving, as significant scholarly and intellectual labor. A report of the MLA Commission on Professional Service, "Making Faculty Work Visible," and a policy statement by the Council of Writing Program Administrators, "Evaluating the Intellectual Work of Writing Administration" both recommend that valuation. The MLA report argues on behalf of various forms of intellectual work, from published research to curriculum design and program development, and concludes, "The profession should work to establish the structures and processes for evaluating and rewarding such long-term investments and accomplishments" (177).

READING AROUND IN THE FIELD

A useful selected and annotated bibliography available from one of the largest textbook pub-

lishers in the field, *The Bedford Bibliography for Teachers of Writing*, is edited by Bizzell, Herzberg, and Nedra Reynolds. Careful and reliable, it is an excellent resource for anyone trying to understand the field by surveying its literature.

Another helpful index would be a list of books and articles that have been chosen by the field for its major awards. The major book awards serving composition are the MLA Mina Shaughnessy Award, the CCCC Outstanding Book Award, the NCTE David H. Russell Award, and the awards sponsored by the *Journal of Advanced Composition*. All these can be accessed online. Bedford Books has also published a collection of the Braddock Award winners; the award goes to the outstanding article each year in the journal *College Composition and Communication*. The collection is *On Writing Research* and edited by Lisa Ede. The more recent Braddock winners can be found on the CCCC Web site. There is the Landmark Essays series published by Lawrence Erlbaum; the quality varies among its texts, but they are a useful point of reference.

To search the journals, a good place to begin is the most representative and widely read, *College Composition and Communication* (*CCC*), the principal journal of the Conference on College Composition and Communication. Several other journals publish significant scholarship: *JAC: A Journal of Composition Theory*, *Journal of Basic Writing*, *Composition Studies*, *Computers and Composition*, *Journal of Business and Technical Communication*, *Pre/Text*, *Teaching English in the Two-Year College*, *Technical Communication Quarterly*, *Written Communication*, *Writing Center Journal*, *Writing on the Edge*, and *WPA: Writing Program Administration*. A fuller bibliography of journals can be found online at http://comppile.tamucc .edu/journals.htm.

WHAT'S NEXT

In the last decade, scholarship in composition was dominated by literacy studies, usually ethnographic, sometimes historical; by theory; and by histories of composition, rhetoric, and schooling. As the coeditor of a publication series, I see a fair share of dissertations and first books. It is clear that the new generation of scholars in composition is taking the most successful published work as models. The manuscripts we receive most often are histories or literacy studies. And why not? For either, the archive seems unlimited and therefore fertile ground for PhD students. There are always new neighborhoods or groups to study ethnographically. University libraries hold surprising numbers of books, textbooks, and documents related to composition programs and to the teaching of writing. The street and the archive hold the promise of something new, something new that can be treated with methods whose value to the scholarly community is already established.

I would prefer to see more manuscripts and dissertations dealing with the primary subject—that is, with student writing and the possibilities for student writing in the contemporary academy. I think a field can spend too much time looking at itself and its history, and I fear that this is the case with composition. There is still important historical work to be done, to be sure, some of it already under way, but as I see the new work, the periods and areas are becoming more limited and more local. The same can be said of literacy studies. The best of it has been powerful and important, but it is difficult to generalize from small cases, and the arguments to be made become repetitive and buried behind local detail. Theory in composition, like theory everywhere, is a difficult starting point for someone entering the field, and the day is past (I am pleased to say) when it was enough to translate the major texts for an audience of practitioners.

The important questions are persistent, and for me the most important have to do with student writing—its value and promise. Questions of value should be a constant source of debate and controversy. What is a good student paper? What makes it good? What is it good for? What genres of writing are appropriate for the college classroom? Are there emerging or possible genres

Questions of value should be a constant source of debate and controversy.

that we have not yet given appropriate attention? Can we establish a corpus of student writing for common reference? What are best practices for courses with varied goals and in varied settings? Such questions are worth a professional's time and energy.

Can a young scholar build a career around this work? Yes, but not easily and not without risk. Assistant professors at major research universities are less likely now to have a primary engagement with a freshman composition program than they once did, less likely to be charged to manage, organize, and value the writing of hundreds or thousands of students. More and more programs are being turned over to nontenure-stream faculty members, who are often quite brilliant teachers but who do not have the resources, the time, or the charge to think of the work as a scholarly enterprise. My sense is that departments are providing neither the motive nor the occasion for the "research" faculty to think about composition and teaching.

The motivation is there, however, to think about history, about literacy, about linguistics or genre or document design or technology. I know that I will continue to receive outstanding manuscripts that follow the tracks I've identified in the essay above, and I will be eager to receive them. The manuscript I'm most eager to receive is one that I can't easily predict or describe—this is every editor's dream. At the moment, it is always surprising to receive a manuscript with student writing at its center.

NOTE

I want to thank the students in my graduate seminar, Introduction to Composition Studies, where I first began to work out the structure of this essay. And I'd like to thank my colleagues at Pitt, who provided a colloquium where I could try out the argument. I particularly thank Kathryn Flannery, whose comments led to some substantial changes in the manuscript. I am grateful to the MLA's anonymous reviewer who provided important suggestions and corrections. And I'd like to thank Pat Bizzell, who gave the essay a careful and generous reading and whose work has helped all of us better understand the shape and promise of the field.

WORKS CITED AND SUGGESTIONS FOR
FURTHER READING

Alcorn, Marshall. *Changing the Subject in English Class: Discourse and the Constructions of Desire*. Carbondale: Southern Illinois UP, 2002.

Atwell, Nancie. *In the Middle: New Understandings about Writing, Reading, and Learning*. Portsmouth: Boynton, 1998.

Bartholomae, David. *Writing on the Margins: Essays on Composition and Teaching*. Boston: Bedford–St. Martin's, 2004.

Bartholomae, David, and Anthony Petrosky. *Facts, Artifacts, and Counterfacts: Theory and Method for a Reading and Writing Course*. Upper Montclair: Boynton, 1986.

Bazerman, Charles, and James Paradis, eds. *Textual Dynamics of the Professions: Historical and Contemporary Studies of Writing in Profession Communities*. Madison: U of Wisconsin P, 1991.

Belcher, Diane, and George Braine, eds. *Academic Writing in a Second Language: Essays on Research and Pedagogy*. Norwood: Ablex, 1995.

Berlin, James. *Rhetorics, Poetics, and Cultures: Refiguring College English Studies*. Urbana: NCTE, 1996.

———. *Writing Instruction in Nineteenth-Century American Colleges*. Carbondale: Southern Illinois UP, 1984.

Berthoff, Ann E. *Forming/Thinking/Writing*. Rochelle Park: Hayden, 1978. Portsmouth: Boynton, 1988.

———. *The Making of Meaning: Metaphors, Models, and Maxims for Writing Teachers*. Montclair: Boynton, 1981.

———. *The Sense of Learning*. Portsmouth: Boynton, 1990.

Bishop, Wendy. *Teaching Lives: Essays and Stories*. Logan: Utah State UP, 1997.

Bizzell, Patricia. *Academic Discourse and Critical Consciousness*. Pittsburgh: U of Pittsburgh P, 1992.

Bizzell, Patricia, and Bruce Herzberg. *Negotiating Difference: Cultural Case Studies for Composition*. Boston: Bedford–St. Martin's, 1996.

Bizzell, Patricia, Bruce Herzberg, and Nedra Reynolds, eds. *The Bedford Bibliography for Teachers of Writing*. 6th ed. Boston: St. Martin's, 2003.

Bleich, David. *The Double Perspective: Language, Literacy, and Social Relations*. New York: Oxford UP, 1988. Urbana: NCTE, 1993.

Bloom, Lynn Z., Edward M. White, and Donald A. Daiker, eds. *Composition Studies in the New Millennium: Rereading the Past, Rewriting the Future*. Carbondale: Southern Illinois UP, 2003.

Blyler, Nancy R., and Charlotte Thralls, eds. *Professional Communication: The Social Perspective*. Newbury Park: Sage, 1993.

Braddock, Richard, Richard Lloyd-Jones, and Lowell Schoer. *Research in Written Composition*. Champaign: NCTE, 1963. Natl. Conf. on Research in Lang, and Literacy. New York U Dept. of Teaching and Learning. 13 Feb. 2006 <http://education.nyu.edu/teachlearn/research/ncrll/Braddock_et_al.pdf>.

Brandt, Deborah. *Literacy as Involvement: The Acts of Writers, Readers, and Texts*. Carbondale: Southern Illinois UP, 1990.

———. *Literacy in American Lives*. Cambridge: Cambridge UP, 2001.

Brereton, John. *The Origins of Composition Studies in the American College, 1875–1925: A Documentary History*. Pittsburgh: U of Pittsburgh P, 1995.

Britton, James N., et al. *The Development of Writing Abilities (11–18)*. London: Macmillan, 1975.

Brodkey, Linda. *Writing Permitted in Designated Areas Only*. Minneapolis: U of Minnesota P, 1996.

Brooks, Cleanth, and Robert Penn Warren. *Modern Rhetoric*. 4th ed. New York: Harcourt, 1979.

Calkins, Lucy. *The Art of Teaching Writing*. Portsmouth: Heinemann, 1994.

Canagarajah, Suresh. *A Geopolitics of Academic Writing*. Pittsburgh: U of Pittsburgh P, 2002.

———. *Resisting Linguistic Imperialism in English Teaching*. New York: Oxford UP, 1999.

Channing, Edward. *Lectures Read to the Seniors at Harvard College*. Boston: Ticknor, 1856. Gainesville: Scholars' Facsims. and Rpts., 1997.

Christensen, Francis. *The Sentence and the Paragraph*. Urbana: NCTE, 1966.

Cintron, Ralph. *Angel's Town: Chero Ways, Gang Life, and Rhetorics of the Everyday*. Boston: Beacon, 1997.

Clifford, John, and John Schilb. *Writing Theory and Critical Theory*. New York: MLA, 1994.

Coles, William E., Jr. *Composing: Writing as a Self-Creating Process*. Upper Montclair: Boynton, 1974.

———. *The Plural I: The Teaching of Writing*. New York: Holt, Rinehart, 1978. Rpt. as *The Plural I—and After*. Upper Montclair: Boynton, 1988.

Coles, William E., Jr., and James Vopat. *What Makes Writing Good: A Multiperspective*. Lexington: Heath, 1985.

Comprone, Joseph. *From Experience to Expression: A College Rhetoric*. Boston: Houghton, 1981.

Connor, Ulla. *Contrastive Rhetoric: Cross-Cultural Aspects of Second-Language Writing*. Cambridge: Cambridge UP, 1996.

Connors, Robert. *Composition-Rhetoric: Backgrounds, Theory, and Pedagogy*. Pittsburgh: U of Pittsburgh P, 1997.

———. *Selected Essays of Robert J. Connors*. Ed. Lisa Ede and Andrea Lundsford. Boston: Bedford–St. Martin's, 2003.

Cope, Bill, and Mary Kalantzis, eds. *The Powers of Literacy: A Genre Approach to the Teaching of Writing*. Pittsburgh: U of Pittsburgh P, 1993.

Corbett, Edward P. J., and Robert J. Connors. *Classical Rhetoric for the Modern Student*. 1965. 4th ed. New York: Oxford UP, 1999.

Crowley, Sharon. *Composition in the University: Historical and Polemical Essays*. Pittsburgh: U of Pittsburgh P, 1998.

———. *The Methodical Memory: Invention in Current-Traditional Rhetoric*. Carbondale: Southern Illinois UP, 1990.

Cushman, Ellen, Eugene R. Kintgen, Barry M. Kroll, and Mike Rose, eds. *Literacy: A Critical Sourcebook*. Carbondale: Southern Illinois UP, 1988.

Daniels, Harvey, and Steven Zemelman. *A Community of Writers: Teaching Writing in the Junior and Senior High School*. Portsmouth: Heinemann, 1988.

Dillon, George L. *Constructing Texts: Elements of a Theory of Composition and Style*. Bloomington: Indiana UP, 1981.

Doheny-Farina, Stephen. *The Wired Neighborhood*. New Haven: Yale UP, 1996.

Durst, Russell. *Collision Course: Conflict, Negotiation, and Learning in a College Composition Course*. Urbana: NCTE, 1999.

Ede, Lisa, ed. *On Writing Research: The Braddock Essays, 1975–1998*. Boston: Bedford–St. Martin's, 1999.

Elbow, Peter. *Embracing Contraries: Explorations in Learning and Teaching*. New York: Oxford UP, 1986.

———. *Everyone Can Write: Essays toward a Hopeful Theory of Writing and Teaching Writing*. New York: Oxford UP, 2000.

———. *Writing without Teachers*. 1973. New York: Oxford UP, 1998.

———. *Writing with Power: Techniques for Mastering the Writing Process*. 1981. New York: Oxford UP, 1998.

Eldred, Janet Carey, and Peter Mortensen. *Imagining Rhetoric: Composing Women of the Early United States*. Pittsburgh: U of Pittsburgh P, 2002.

Emig, Janet A. *The Composing Process of Twelfth Graders*. Urbana: NCTE, 1971.

Enos, Theresa, ed. *A Sourcebook for Basic Writing Teachers*. New York: McGraw, 1987.

Evaluating the Intellectual Work of Writing Administration. Council of Writing Program Administrators. 1998. 12 Feb. 2006 <http://www.wpacouncil.org/positions/intellectualwork.html>.

Faigley, Lester. *Fragments of Rationality: Postmodernity and the Subject of Composition*. Pittsburgh: U of Pittsburgh P, 1992.

Farr, Marcia, ed. *Ethnolinguistic Chicago: Language and Literacy in the City's Neighborhoods*. Mahwah: Erlbaum, 2005.

Flannery, Kathryn T. *The Emperor's New Clothes: Literature, Literacy, and the Ideology of Style*. Pittsburgh: U of Pittsburgh P, 1995.

Flower, Linda. *The Construction of Negotiated Meaning: A Social Cognitive Theory of Writing*. Carbondale: Southern Illinois UP, 1994.

———. *Learning to Rival: A Literate Practice for Intercultural Inquiry*. Mahwah: Erlbaum, 2000.

———. *Making Thinking Visible: Writing, Collaborative Planning, and Classroom Inquiry*. Urbana: NCTE, 1994.

———. *Problem-Solving Strategies for Writing*. 1981. 5th ed. New York: Harcourt, 2003.

———. *Problem-Solving Strategies for Writing in College and Community*. Boston: Heinle, 1997.

———. *Reading-to-Write: Exploring a Cognitive and Social Process*. New York: Oxford UP, 1990.

———. *Writers at Work: Strategies for Communicating in Business and Professional Settings*. Boston: Heinle, 1994.

Flower, Linda, and John Hayes. "A Cognitive Process Theory of Writing." *College Composition and Communication* 32 (1981): 365–87.

Frye, Northrop. *The Anatomy of Criticism: Four Essays*. 1957. Updated ed. Princeton: Princeton UP, 2000.

Gage, John T. *The Shape of Reason: Argumentative Writing in College*. Needham Heights: Macmillan, 1991.

Gale, Xin Liu. *Teachers, Discourses, and Authority in the Postmodern Composition Classroom*. Albany: State U of New York P, 1996.

Gere, Anne Ruggles. "Kitchen Table and Rented Rooms: The Extracurriculum of Composition." *College Composition and Communication* 54 (1994): 75–107.

———. *Writing Groups: History, Theory, and Implications*. Carbondale: Southern Illinois UP, 1987.

Gilyard, Keith. *Let's Flip the Script: An African American Discourse on Language, Literature, and Learning*. Detroit: Wayne State UP, 1996.

———, ed. *Race, Rhetoric, and Composition*. Portsmouth: Boynton, 1999.

———. *Voices of the Self: A Study of Language Competence*. Detroit: Wayne State UP, 1991.

Goleman, Judith. *Working Theory: Critical Composition Studies for Students and Teachers*. Westport: Bergin, 1995.

Gorzelsky, Gwen. *The Language of Experience: Literate Practices and Social Change*. Pittsburgh: U of Pittsburgh P, 2005.

Graff, Gerald. *Clueless in Academe: How Schooling Obscures the Life of the Mind*. New Haven: Yale UP, 2003.

Halasek, Kay. *A Pedagogy of Possibility: Bakhtinian Perspectives on Composition Studies*. Carbondale: Southern Illinois UP, 1999.

Hall, Donald. *Writing Well*. Boston: Little, 1973. 9th ed. New York: Longman, 1997.

Harris, Jeanette, and Joyce Kinkead. *Writing Centers in Context: Twelve Case Studies*. Urbana: NCTE, 1993.

Harris, Joseph. *Rewriting: How to Do Things with Texts*. Logan: Utah State UP, 2006.

———. *A Teaching Subject: Composition since 1966*. Upper Saddle River: Prentice, 1997.

Harste, Jerome Charles, Kathy Short, and Carolyn Burke. *Creating Classrooms for Authors: The Reading-Writing Connection*. 1988. 2nd ed. Portsmouth: Heinemann, 1995.

Hawisher, Gail, et al. *Computers and the Teaching of Writing in American Higher Education, 1979–1994*. Norwood: Ablex, 1996.

Hawisher, Gail, and Cynthia Selfe. *Literate Lives in the Information Age: Narratives on Literacy from the United States.* Mahwah: Erlbaum, 2004.

Heath, Shirley Brice. *Ways with Words: Language, Life, and Work in Communities and Classrooms.* Cambridge: Cambridge UP, 1983.

Herrington, Anne, and Charles Moran, eds. *Writing, Teaching, and Learning in the Disciplines.* New York: MLA, 1992.

Hirsch, Eric Donald, Jr. *Cultural Literacy: What Every American Needs to Know.* New York: Vintage, 1988.

———. *The Philosophy of Composition.* Chicago: U of Chicago P, 1977.

Hjortshoj, Keith. *The Transition to College Writing.* Boston: St. Martin's, 2001.

Horner, Bruce. *Terms of Work for Composition: A Materialist Critique.* Albany: State U of New York P, 2000.

Horner, Bruce, and Min-Zhan Lu. *Representing the "Other": Basic Writers and the Teaching of Basic Writing.* Urbana: NCTE, 1999.

Hull, Glynda A. *Changing Work / Changing Workers: Critical Perspectives on Language, Literacy, and Skills.* Albany: State U of New York P, 1997.

Hyland, Ken, and Jack Richards, eds. *Second Language Writing.* Cambridge: Cambridge UP, 2003.

Jarratt, Susan C., and Lynn Worsham, eds. *Feminism and Composition Studies: In Other Words.* New York: MLA, 1998.

Johnson, Nan. *Nineteenth-Century Rhetoric in North America.* Carbondale: Southern Illinois UP, 1991.

Kameen, Paul. *Writing/Teaching: Essays toward a Rhetoric of Pedagogy.* Pittsburgh: U of Pittsburgh P, 2000.

Kaufer, David, and Brian Butler. *Designing Interactive Worlds with Words: Principles of Writing as Representational Composition.* Mahwah: Erlbaum, 2000.

Kinneavy, James. *A Theory of Discourse: The Aims of Discourse.* New York: Norton, 1980.

———. "Writing across the Curriculum." *Profession 83.* New York: MLA, 1983. 13–20.

Kirsch, Gesa, et al. *Feminism and Composition: A Critical Sourcebook.* Boston: Bedford–St. Martin's, 2003.

Kitzhaber, Albert Raymond. *Rhetoric in American Colleges, 1850–1900.* Ed. John Gage. Dallas: Southern Methodist UP, 1990.

———. *Themes, Theories, and Therapy: The Teaching of Writing in College.* New York: McGraw, 1963.

Labov, William. *Language in the Inner City: Studies in the Black English Vernacular.* Philadelphia: U of Pennsylvania P, 1972.

———. *The Study of Non-standard English.* Urbana: NCTE, 1970.

Lanham, Richard. *The Electronic Word: Democracy, Technology, and the Arts.* Chicago: U of Chicago P, 1993.

———. *Literacy and the Survival of Humanism.* New Haven: Yale UP, 1983.

———. *Revising Prose.* 1979. 4th ed. New York: Longman, 1999.

———. *Style: An Anti-text.* New Haven: Yale UP, 1974.

Lindquist, Julie. *A Place to Stand: Politics and Persuasion in a Working-Class Bar.* Oxford: Oxford UP, 2002.

Logan, Shirley Wilson. *We Are Coming: The Persuasive Discourse of Nineteenth-Century Black Women.* Carbondale: Southern Illinois UP, 1999.

Lunsford, Andrea, and Lahoucine Ouzgane. *Crossing Borderlands: Composition and Postcolonial Studies.* Pittsburgh: U of Pittsburgh P, 2004.

Macrorie, Ken. *Telling Writing.* 1970. 4th ed. Portsmouth: Boynton, 1985.

———. *Uptaught.* 1970. Portsmouth: Boynton, 1996.

Mahiri, Jabari. *Shooting for Excellence: African American and Youth Culture in New Century Schools.* Urbana: NCTE, 1998.

"Making Faculty Work Visible: Reinterpreting Professional Service, Teaching, and Research in the Fields of Language and Literature: A Report of the MLA Commission on Professional Service." *Profession 1996.* New York: MLA, 1996. 161–216.

Malinowitz, Harriet. *Textual Orientations: Lesbian and Gay Students and the Making of Discourse Communities.* Portsmouth: Boynton, 1995.

Masters, Thomas. *Practicing Writing: The Postwar Discourse of Freshman English.* Pittsburgh: U of Pittsburgh P, 2004.

McCrimmon, James McNab. *Writing with a Purpose.* 1950. 8th ed. Boston: Houghton, 1984.

McQuade, Donald, and Nancy Sommers, eds. *Student Writers at Work: The Bedford Prizes.* 1984. New York: Palgrave-Macmillan, 2000.

Miller, Richard Earl. *As If Learning Mattered: Reforming Higher Education.* Ithaca: Cornell UP, 1998.

———. *Writing at the End of the World.* Pittsburgh: U of Pittsburgh P, 2005.

Miller, Susan. *Assuming the Positions: Cultural Pegagogy and the Politics of Commonplace Writing.* Pittsburgh: U of Pittsburgh P, 1998.

———. *Rescuing the Subject: A Critical Introduction to Rhetoric and the Writer.* Carbondale: Southern Illinois UP, 1989, 2004.

———. *Textual Carnivals: The Politics of Composition.* Carbondale: Southern Illinois UP, 1991.

Miller, Thomas P. *The Formation of College English: Rhetoric and Belles Lettres in the British Cultural Provinces.* Pittsburgh: U of Pittsburgh P, 1997.

Moffett, James. *Teaching the Universe of Discourse.* 1968. Portsmouth: Boynton, 1987.

Monroe, Jonathan, ed. *Local Knowledges, Local Practices: Writing in the Disciplines at Cornell.* Pittsburgh: U of Pittsburgh P, 2003.

Moss, Beverly J. J., and Marcia Farr, eds. *Literacy across Communities.* Cresskill: Hampton, 1994.

Neel, Jasper. *Plato, Derrida, and Writing.* Carbondale: Southern Illinois UP, 1988.

Newkirk, Thomas. *The Performance of Self in Student Writing.* Portsmouth: Boynton, 1997.

North, Stephen M. *The Making of Knowledge in Compo-*

sition: Portrait of an Emerging Field. Upper Montclair: Boynton, 1987.

O'Hare, Frank. *Sentence-Combining: Improving Student Writing without Formal Grammar Instruction.* Urbana: NCTE, 1973.

Ohmann, Richard Malin. *English in America: A Radical View of the Profession.* 1976. Hanover: Wesleyan UP, 1996.

Olson, Gary A., ed. *Rhetoric and Composition as Intellectual Work.* Carbondale: Southern Illinois UP, 2002.

———, ed. *Writing Centers: Theory and Administration.* Urbana: NCTE, 1984.

O'Neill, Margaret N., et al., eds. *A Field of Dreams: Independent Writing Programs and the Future of Composition Studies.* Logan: Utah State UP, 2002.

Parks, Stephen. *Class Politics: The Movement for Students' Rights to Their Own Language.* Urbana: NCTE, 2000.

Penrose, Ann M., and Barbara Sitko, eds. *Hearing Ourselves Think: Cognitive Research in the College Writing Classroom.* New York: Oxford UP, 1993.

Perl, Sondra, ed. *Landmark Essays on Writing Process.* Mahwah: Erlbaum, 1995.

Ponsot, Marie, and Rosemary Deen. *Beat Not the Poor Desk.* Montclair: Boynton, 1982.

Prendergast, Catherine. *Literacy and Racial Justice: The Politics of Learning after* Brown v. Board of Education. Carbondale: Southern Illinois UP, 2003.

Radway, Janice A. *Reading the Romance: Women, Patriarchy, and Popular Literature.* Chapel Hill: U of North Carolina P, 1984.

Rose, Mike. *Lives on the Boundary: The Struggles and Achievements of America's Underprepared.* New York: Free, 1989.

———. *An Open Language: Selected Writing on Literacy, Learning, and Opportunity.* Boston: Bedford–St. Martin's, 2006.

———, ed. *When a Writer Can't Write: Studies in Writer's Block and Other Composing Process Problems.* New York: Guilford, 1985.

Roskelly, Hephzibah, and Kate Ronald. *Reason to Believe: Romanticism, Pragmatism, and the Teaching of Writing.* Albany: State U of New York P, 1998.

Royster, Jacqueline Jones. *Traces of a Stream: Literacy and Social Change among African American Women.* Pittsburgh: U of Pittsburgh P, 2000.

Russell, David R. *Writing in the Academic Disciplines, 1870–1990: A Curricular History.* 1991. 2nd ed. Carbondale: Southern Illinois UP, 2002.

Sale, Roger. *On Writing.* New York: Random, 1970.

Salvatori, Mariolina, and Patricia Donahue. *The Elements (and Pleasures) of Difficulty.* New York: Longman, 2004.

Schell, Eileen E., and Patricia Lambert Stock. *Moving a Mountain: Transforming the Role of Contingent Faculty in Composition Studies and Higher Education.* Urbana: NCTE, 2000.

Schilb, John. *Between the Lines: Relating Composition Theory and Literary Theory.* Portsmouth: Boynton, 1996.

Schilb, John, and Patricia Harkin, eds. *Contending with Words: Composition and Rhetoric in a Postmodern Age.* New York: MLA, 1991.

Scholes, Robert, Nancy Comley, and Gregory Ulmer. *Text Book: Writing through Literature.* Boston: Bedford–St. Martin's, 2002.

Schultz, Lucille M., Stephen L. Carr, and Jean Ferguson Carr. *Archives of Instruction: Nineteenth-Century Rhetorics, Readers, and Composition Books in the United States.* Carbondale: Southern Illinois UP, 2005.

Seitz, James E. *Motives for Metaphor: Literacy, Curriculum Reform, and the Teaching of English.* Pittsburgh: U of Pittsburgh P, 1999.

Selber, Stuart A. *Multiliteracies for a Digital Age.* Carbondale: Southern Illinois UP, 2004.

Selfe, Cynthia L. *Technology and Literacy in the Twenty-First Century: The Importance of Paying Attention.* Carbondale: Southern Illinois UP, 1999.

Shaughnessy, Mina P. *Errors and Expectations: A Guide for the Teacher of Basic Writing.* New York: Oxford UP, 1977.

Sirc, Geoffrey. *English Composition as a Happening.* Logan: Utah State UP, 2002.

Slevin, James F. *Introducing English: Essays in the Intellectual Work of Composition.* Pittsburgh: U of Pittsburgh P, 2001.

Smitherman, Geneva. *Talkin' and Testifyin': The Language of Black America.* Detroit: Wayne State UP, 1986.

Soliday, Mary. *The Politics of Remediation: Institutional and Student Needs in Higher Education.* Pittsburgh: U of Pittsburgh P, 2002.

Spellmeyer, Kurt. *Arts of Living: Reinventing the Humanities for the Twenty-First Century.* Albany: State U of New York P, 2003.

———. *Common Ground: Dialogue, Understanding, and the Teaching of Composition.* Englewood Cliffs: Prentice, 1993.

Spigelman, Candace. *Personally Speaking: Experience as Evidence in Academic Discourse.* Carbondale: Southern Illinois UP, 2004.

Spilka, Rachel. *Writing in the Workplace: New Research Perspectives.* Carbondale: Southern Illinois UP, 1993.

Steedman, Carolyn. *Past Tenses: Essays on Writing, Autobiography, and History.* London: Rivers Oram, 1992.

———. *The Radical Soldier's Tale.* London: Routledge, 1988.

———. *The Tidy House: Little Girls Writing.* London: Virago, 1982.

Sternglass, Marilyn S. *Time to Know Them: A Longitudinal Study of Writing and Learning at the College Level.* Mahwah: Erlbaum, 1997.

Swales, John M., ed. *Genre Analysis: English in Academic and Research Settings.* Cambridge: Cambridge UP, 1990.

Tobin, Lad, and Tom Newkirk, eds. *Taking Stock: The Writing Process Movement in the 90s.* Portsmouth: Boynton, 1994.

Trimble, John R. *Writing with Style: Conversations on the*

Art of Writing. 1975. 2nd ed. Englewood Cliffs: Prentice, 2000.

Trimbur, John, ed. *Popular Literacy: Studies in Cultural Practices and Poetics.* Pittsburgh: U of Pittsburgh P, 2001.

Varnum, Robin. *Fencing with Words: A History of Writing Instruction on the Amherst Campus.* Urbana: NCTE, 1996.

Villanueva, Victor. *Bootstraps: From an American Academic of Color.* Urbana: NCTE, 1993.

Weathers, Winston. *An Alternate Style: Options in Composition.* Rochelle Park: Hayden, 1980.

Wells, Susan. *Out of the Dead House: Nineteenth-Century Women Physicians and the Writing of Medicine.* Madison: U of Wisconsin P, 2001.

White, Edward Michael. *Teaching and Assessing Writing.* 1985. 2nd ed. San Francisco: Jossey-Bass, 1994.

Williams, Joseph M. *Style: Ten Lessons in Clarity and Grace.* 7th ed. New York: Longman, 2002.

Williams, Raymond. *Culture and Society, 1780–1950.* New York: Columbia UP, 1983.

———. *Keywords: A Vocabulary of Culture and Society.* New York: Oxford UP, 1985.

Yancey, Kathleen Blake. *Reflection in the Writing Classroom.* Logan: Utah State UP, 1998.

Yancey, Kathleen Blake, and Irwin Weiser, eds. *Situating Portfolios: Four Perspectives.* Logan: Utah State UP, 1997.

Young, Art, and Toby Fulwiler, eds. *Writing across the Disciplines: Research into Practice.* Upper Montclair: Boynton, 1986.

Young, Richard Emerson, Alton L. Becker, and Kenneth L. Pike. *Rhetoric: Discovery and Change.* New York: Harcourt, 1970.

Zamel, Vivian, and Ruth Spack, eds. *Negotiating Academic Literacies: Teaching and Learning across Languages and Cultures.* Mahwah: Erlbaum, 1998.

◇ *Poetics*

CHARLES BERNSTEIN

1

While poetics suggests a long history of laws of composition, poetics can also stress poiesis—the actual making or doing: poetry as process. Every doing carries the potential of something new, emergent, something not already predicated by poetics. Practice overtakes theory, practice changes theory. And not just writing practice but performance practice, the practice of sound.

To write is to produce meaning and not reproduce a preexisting meaning. To write is to progress and not remain subjected (by habits or reflexes) to the meaning that supposedly precedes language. To write is always first to rewrite, and to rewrite does not mean to revert to a previous form of writing, no more than an anteriority of speech, or of presence, or of meaning. The book creates meaning, and meaning creates life (and not vice versa). Fiction or poetry is never about something; it is something. Writing is not the living repetition of life. The author is that which gives the disquieting language of fiction or poetry its unities and disunities, its knot of coherence and chaos, its insertion into the real. All reading is done haphazardly. Now some people might say the situation (of poetry and fiction) is not very encouraging, but one must reply that it is not meant to encourage those who say that!

Poetics is "an unruly, multisubjective activity" (Clifford 52–53); the reading of poetry, just as the writing of poetry, is beyond the control of any authority. Poetics opens the space of a page to interplay and contradiction, to many voices, a complexity of words. A poet brushes scraps of themes against the continuum of history. Language surrounds chaos. Poetry brings similitude and representation to configurations waiting from forever to be spoken. A poet is writing from inside the opening where the writing subject disappeared without writing. The search for traces is a polyphony of stories.

Ethnopoetics is not simply the poetics of exotic others but calls attention to the ethnicity—the particularity and nongeneralizability—of all poetic practices. Oral poetry is best thought of as something not older than or prior to or simpler than the written but as something that goes on coexisting with, and interacting with, the written. We consider both alphabetic and nonalphabetic writing codes of the historical past and imaginary codes of a potential present.

Poetics stays grounded in the fact of making, the complex of that which has so made such "it," inside and out, the intimately present (oneself, like they say), else the vastness of all possible dimension. "To measure is all we know..." (Williams, *Paterson* 236). Such reference proposes world in all its times and places, in determined labors of common body, constructs of passage and echo. "Only the imagination is real . . ." (Williams, *Collected Poems* 2: 334). (As in New England—to work . . .).[1]

2

To practice poetics is to acknowledge the inevitability of metaphor, the linguisticality of perception, the boundedness of thought, the passion of ideas, the beauty of error, the chains of logic, the possibilities of intuition, and the uncanny delight of chance. In contrast to the syllogistic rationality of expository writing, poetics is situational, shifts with the winds, courts contradiction, feeds on inconsistency.

3

The profession is best that professionalizes least.

The sociologist C. Wright Mills got this just right when he wrote, "The aim of the college, for the individual student, is to eliminate the need in his life for the college; the task is to help him become a self-educating man. For only that will set him free" (368).[2]

4

In a culture that too often derides learning, complexity, and nuance, and where the demand for intelligibility is consistently used as a weapon to suppress unwelcome or difficult ideas, there is no higher aspiration than scholarship. But students caught up in the "major," just as faculty caught up in the "profession," often act as if scholarship requires adherence to a set of norms, either in subject matter or style, that define the field. Consistency of tone, standardization of documentation formats, and shopworn modes of analysis are more likely to anesthetize a required paper than allow entry for the aes-

Poetics is situational, shifts with the winds, courts contradiction, feeds on inconsistency.

thetic. Rewriting may be admirable but not if it means stating a rote idea more clearly: rewriting should add reflection to a paragraph, not strip it of its unresolved thoughts. Felt inconsistency is preferable to mandated rationalization.

To state the obvious: an unorganized (or "differently" organized) essay that suggests active thinking is often more useful in response to a literary work than a paper of impeccable logic that has little to say. I realize that I am setting up a false dichotomy: It is not a question of choosing logic versus thinking but rather understanding the value, and implications, of each. And yet, for the young scholar, the demands of expository normalcy may compete with the demands of poetics.[3] Shall we demand all students be extravagant? No doubt, this would be rash. But shall we continue to demand that all students curb their writing, as if composition were a dog and not a god?

I prize the adventure of learning: scholarship not as a predetermined ride to selected ports of call but an exploration by association, one perception leading to the next, a network of stoppages, detours, reconnaissance. Not double majors with extra requirements and ever more protocols but multicentered *minors*, connected by peripheral routes, less-traveled passages, hunches.

Art students used to be told that the fundamental requirement for drawing or painting was to accurately render figures. But this confused one modality of representation with the entire process of visual aesthesis. It might have been better to say: *you can't draw if you can't perceive.* Correlatively, we might say, you can't write if you can't think. Scholarship requires poetics.

Paratactic writing, thinking by association, is no less cogent or persuasive than hypotactic exposition, with its demands that one thought be subordinated to the next. Poetics reminds us that the alternate logics of poetry are not suited just for emotion or irrational expression; poetics lies at the foundation of all writing.

Poetry is a name we use to discount what we fear to acknowledge.

The accurate documentation of information used in a work is a vital principle of scholarship. Similarly, scholarship requires a writer to consider challenges to her or his views: but this too often is assumed to mean considering challenges to the content of what is being said while ignoring challenges to the style and form. The importance of poetics for scholarship is not to decree that anything goes but rather to insist that exposition is an insufficient guarantor of reason. Poetics makes scholarly writing harder, not easier: it complicates scholarship with an insistence that the way we write is never neutral, never self-evident.

Clarity in writing is a rhetorical effect not a natural fact. One man's eloquence can be another's poison; one woman's stuttering may be the closest approximation of truth that we will ever know.

I won't note that poetics can also take a form directly opposite to what I am proposing; like *politics*, *poetics* is plural.)

In some ways, literary theory, in its many forms, has displaced poetics as a model for scholarship. Anthologies of literary theory, while often including statements by poets from earlier centuries, largely turn their attention to literary theorists and related philosophers when they come to the twentieth century.[4] Perhaps this seems a more sensible choice as models for both scholarship and literary criticism. Poetics, in this system, becomes another form of poetry—something to be subjected to criticism and analysis but not the model for the practice of criticism, scholarship, or interpretation that it, nonetheless, continues to be.

5

As a literary genre, *poetics* refers to works on the philosophy of composition, from Aristotle's *Poetics* to many contemporary works on the poetics of one thing or another, from scholarship to architecture. *Poetics* also is the term used for works about poetry written by poets. There is a long and storied history of both kinds of poetics, but this is to be an account not of the history of a literary form but rather of the significance of poetics for literary scholarship. With that in mind, it is important to note a distinction among literary theory, philosophy, and poetics. Literary theory can be described as the application of philosophical, political, or psychoanalytical principles or methods to the study of literary or cultural works. Theory suggests a predilection for consistency and explanation and, like philosophy, may take the form of stand-alone arguments. Poetics, in contrast, is provisional, context-dependent, and often contentious. Theory will commonly take a scientific tone; poetics will sometimes go out of its way to seem implausible, to exaggerate, or even to be self-deprecating. (Since this is a work of poetics,

6

One of the two most important lessons of poetics is that the contemporary practice of poetry informs all readings of poetry. Poetry begins in the present moment and moves backward and forward from there. With no orientation in contemporary poetry and poetics, the young scholar will remain ungrounded, without a direct connection to how works of literature are engendered in her or his own time. Without this knowledge, it will be all the harder to understand the relation of older works to their own time or to ours, or, for that matter, future works to the times yet to come. The absence of this visceral connection to poetic practice may be disguised by the demeanor of disinterested or clinical professionalism, but it will be betrayed in the body of the text of any scholarship produced.

Literary works do not exist only, or even primarily, on the page.

The second fundamental lesson of poetics is that literary works do not exist only, or even primarily, on the page. Alphabetic writing in books remains the dominant medium for poetry in our time, as it has been over the past many hundreds of years; but there was poetry and poetics before the invention of the alphabet, just as new poetries and new poetics will emerge from our pos-talphabetic environment of digital and electronic language reproduction. Indeed, the *now*, as well as the archive of poetry, is as likely to be found on the Web as in books. Modern reproduction technologies have also made available recordings of poets reading their work. These recordings, together with live performances, are a crucial part of any critical or scholarly approach to po-etry over the past one hundred years.[5]

New poetry is being created and performed every day. All scholarship in poetry occurs against this backdrop. Poetry readings and po-etry on the Web are directly relevant to literary scholarship of any type and of all periods. In this sense, poetry and poetics, as I am imagining them here, are a core value of the literary acad-emy. It is exhilarating to see new poetics emerg-ing in literary magazines and small-press books, in local reading series and electronic discussion lists and Web sites and blogs. The ongoing cre-ation of new poetics offers us a glimpse into how literature is made in response to ever-changing conditions. And it offers us a chance not just to observe the unfolding story but to change it.

7

Read globally, write locally.

Narrowing down a field to one period, genre, or method inhibits one of the most important possibilities for scholarship: making connections across these divides. Lots of knowledge about a specific area of interest is admirable and some-times invaluable; knowledge about lots of differ-ent areas is invaluable and sometimes admirable. It is not a question of being eclectic but devel-oping your senses of association.

8

What is the aim of literary scholarship? What is the purpose of a literature class? For some, it may be the accumulation of verifiable information that can be extracted from the literary work—

social, political, historical, linguistic, or psycho-analytic. I have no wish to undermine such ap-proaches to scholarship and teaching. Rather, I want to suggest an equally significant, but dis-tinct, motivation for literary scholarship and teaching, a motivation for which thematic ap-proaches to interpretation may prove detrimen-tal. This "other" approach to reading centers on the aesthetic experience of the literary work; as such, it presents an epistemological dilemma for thematic criticism. For if a literary work is not experienced aesthetically, the reader will not ex-perience what makes it a work of art; this, in turn, will compromise any thematic reading. Po-etics is a prerequisite for literary study.

9

Everybody talks about the crisis in the humani-ties but nobody takes responsibility for it.

It is often lamented that humanists make a poor case for their values in the face of the pow-erful claims by those who advocate, on the one hand, invariant, often religiously derived, prin-ciples and those who advocate, on the other, technorationality—the idea that knowledge must be observer-independent and reproduc-ible. I want to propose poetics as the foundation for a realm of values that is neither scientistic nor moralistic.

Poetics is an ethical engagement with the shifting conditions of everyday life. If it is poetic license to contrast ethics, as a dialogic practice of response in civil society, with morality, as a fixed code of conduct and belief, then poetic license I will hap-pily claim.

Poetics is an activity, an informed response to emerging circumstances. As such, it cannot claim the high ground of morality or systematic theory. Poetics is tactical, not strategic. Indeed, it is the lack of strategy, the aversion to the high ground, that often causes poetics to appear weak or con-fused or inconsistent or relativistic.

Yet, in the struggle between ethics and mo-rality, ethics has the advantage even when it ap-pears to be wandering in the wilderness. This advantage is too rarely taken advantage of. What is needed is a *poetics of poetics*; that is, a defense of the ethical grounding of poetics. A poetics of poetics would allow for a greater self-awareness of the history and value of po-etics. In that sense, my approach is closely related to what George Lakoff argues in *Moral Politics*: that we must be as strong in our advocacy of our values, what he calls the values of nurturing parents, as the moralists are for their values, what he calls the values of the strict father.

> **I want a visceral poetics that articulates the value of the particular over and against the rule of the universal.**

A poetics of poetics refutes the charge of rel-ativism, just as a philosophy of aesthetic judg-ment refutes the idea that tastes are merely per-sonal.[6] Indeed, a poetics of poetics makes the case that value judgments are better when they take into account multiple, and often competing, factors and refuse the simple solution of preex-isting rule.

10

I want a visceral poetics that articulates the value of the particular over and against the rule of the universal; that refuses to sacrifice the local in the name of the national or corporate; that is dialect-ical rather than monologic, situational rather than objective; and that prizes knowing and truthfulness more than knowledge and truth.

I want a social poetics that is embodied rather than neutral, that actively acknowledges context dependence as a counter to the appearance of objectivity. Social poetics, like what Kenneth Burke calls "sociological criticism" (qtd. in Ad-ams 921), begins with a conception of the poem as an action to be read in relation to its social motivation, not its intention (see *Rhetoric*). The motive or design is the underlying reason for a work to come into being in the world, its ori-entation or trajectory; in contrast, intention is the calculated effect of style and technique. Social poetics acknowledges the agency of a work of art, not simply its historicity, where agency is recognized in the work's response to particular conditions.

11

How can such aesthetic or poetic readings be accomplished? So much literary training di-rects us toward the themes and content of a work as if they were the meaning, that we have al-most come to believe, against ourselves, that all the rest is window dressing. Perhaps we've lost the hang for listening; perhaps we just don't hang in long enough. Perhaps we've lost the hankering.

But maybe it is just a matter of practice.

The aim of a course in poetics is not the mem-orization of facts but the engagement with works—and not so much with the themes of work as with their material emanations as sound and form. Tests in such an environment are counterproductive. And the emphasis on under-graduate essays that mimic the style of profes-sional academic conference papers is replaced by interactive "wreadings" that echo, distort, trans-late, reform, and imitate the poems that are un-der active consideration. What is called for is not so much analysis as responsiveness, for it is only after the work has got under the skin that there is a basis for an analysis.

12

I have two research tools for an activist poetics of reading, where poetics is acknowledged as a prerequisite for scholarship. Call them *methods of poetics research for aesthetically informed schol-arship*. The first tool is the "wreading experi-ments"—a set of operations to be performed on the poems under consideration (see app. A).[7] This research tool requires sustained reflection on the results. Such research notes are an inte-gral part of the literary inquiry and subsequent scholarship.

The second poetics research tool for aesthet-ically informed scholarship is the Poem Profiler, meant to increase awareness of the nonthematic dimensions of the poem (see app. B). Essentially, the Poem Profiler is a list of rhetorical features of individual poems. Researchers rate the levels of these features on a one-to-ten scale, one being the lowest level and ten the highest.

READINGS

For the long history of Western poetics any short list is bound to be reductive and misleading. But certain works have, over time, become touchstones for any dialogue about poetics. Since poetics is more about this dialogue than formulating "correct" positions, a basic orientation in the history of poetics is necessary. For this reason, anthologies such as Hazard Adams's *Critical Theory since Plato* offer a good start; though, for poetics, it would be better to begin not with Plato but with Herakleitos, who already offers a response to Plato's banishment of poetics from the ideal republic.[8] Even the quickest tour of the Western canon of poetics would include stops for Longinus's "On the Sublime," which established one of the key terms for aesthetics, and Lucretius's *The Nature of Things*, which is exemplary as a work of both science and cosmology that is at the same time a poem. Defending the necessity for poetry is a long-standing approach for poetry; the classic examples are apologies for poetry by Philip Sidney and Percy Shelley. William Blake's *Marriage of Heaven and Hell* inaugurates a form of radical poetics that stands in opposition to the values of modern, industrialized societies; the full implications of Blake's poetics were first articulated in Algernon Charles Swinburne's *William Blake*. Two touchstone works of British Romantic poetry are William Wordsworth's Preface to *Lyrical Ballads*, which argues for a poetic diction that comes from everyday speech, and Samuel Taylor Coleridge's *Biographia Literaria*, which makes the case for Imagination. Consider these works alongside the epic derangement of Lautréamont's *Les chants de Maldoror* and that still-burning torch, Oscar Wilde's "The Decay of Lying," a manifesto for poetic artifice and against sincerity. On the North American side, Edgar Allan Poe's "The Poetic Principle" and Emily Dickinson's letters complement Ralph Waldo Emerson's essays and Henry David Thoreau's *Walden*.[9]

The long twentieth century begins, for poetics, in France, with Stéphane Mallarmé's "Crisis in Verse" and "The Book: A Spiritual Instrument" and their exquisite arguments for a pure poetry and an art for the sake of art. At the same time, for the Americas, in Cuba, José Martí's "Our America" is still the foundational essay for locating a New World poetics on a north-south axis. This is not the place to map out the vibrant field of European or Latin American, much less a global, poetics, apart from noting the extraordinary significance for American poetics of a set of challenging works that have redefined poetry in the process of reconceptualizing consciousness, perception, and the real. In France, consider the writings of Paul Valéry, who in many ways abandoned poetry for a poetics of active, wandering thought; Antonin Artaud, who struggled with the limits of the body in pain and of theatricality; Marcel Duchamp, who reframed the nature of the aesthetics by breaking down the distinction between the art object and the objects of everyday life (see esp. his interview with Pierre Cabanne); André Breton, the advocate of the political necessity of a surreality revealed through unexpected juxtaposition; Danielle Collobert and her poetics of the microtones of the daily; and Edmond Jabès, whose poetry and prose merge into an endless dialogue about writing and the book.

Then, from whatever country of the mind we want to claim for them, go on to Paul Celan, the great poet of the systematic extermination process of the Second World War, who eviscerates the language that he is bound to as subject and subjected; Ludwig Wittgenstein, a philosopher whose later work provides one of the key models for poetics (see his *Philosophical Investigations*); and Walter Benjamin, who essays explore the multivalent nature of connection among discrepant elements. From Russia, at the time of the revolution, there was Velimir Khlebnikov, the great futurist. In Great Britain, Basil Bunting and Hugh MacDiarmid both developed crucial approaches to dialect poetry; Veronica Forrest-Thomson argued for poetic artifice; and Allen

Fisher explored the relation of science and information to verse. There were Nicholas Guillén's syncreticism and José Lezama Lima's miscegenation in Cuba; Haroldo de Campos's work as a visual poet and "trancreator" (his term for a new approach to translation) in Brazil; César Vallejo's iconoclastic modernist revolution in Peru; Federico García Lorca's "Theory and Function of the Duende" in Spain; Aimé Césaire's "Poetry and Knowledge," Édouard Glissant's *Poetics of Relation*, and Kamau Brathwaite's "nation language" in the Caribbean; and Leopold Senghor's "negritude" in Senegal.[10]

Considering just North America, and the United States in particular, fundamental contribution to poetics was made by a number of modernists, including Ezra Pound, Wallace Stevens, T. S. Eliot, William Carlos Williams, and Gertrude Stein, whose "Composition as Explanation" is the foundational work of modernist poetics in its refusal of explanation in favor of composition. Somewhat later, consider also Laura (Riding) Jackson's *Anarchism Is Not Enough* and *The Telling*, Louis Zukofksy's *Prepositions*, and the essays of Langston Hughes and Mina Loy. The context for this work is provided by two very useful collections, not of poetics but of artists' writings and manifestos, *Art in Theory*, edited by Charles Harrison and Paul Wood, and *Manifesto: A Century of Isms*, edited by Mary Ann Caws. Melissa Kwasny's new anthology, *Toward the Open Field: Poets on the Art of Poetry, 1800–1950*, also provides many key texts.

During the years following the Second World War, there was a great outpouring of poetics by American poets, including Charles Olson's "Projective Verse" and "Proprioception" (full-body perception), Frank O'Hara's "Personism: A Manifesto," Adrienne Rich's *On Lies, Secrets, and Silence*, and Robert Creeley's *A Quick Graph*. Much of the spirit of the time is captured in *The Poetics of the New American Poetry*, edited by Don Allen and Warren Tallman (which includes O'Hara's essay); this book should be read alongside full collections of essays by Olson, Rich (*Arts* and *On Lies*), Creeley (*Collected Essays* and *Quick Graph*), Jack Spicer, Larry Eigner, Barbara Guest, Robert Duncan, Allen Ginsberg, Robin Blaser, and Jerome Rothenberg. Meanwhile, David Antin invented a new form of talking poetics—a mixed genre involving improvisation, philosophy, and autobiography, that he both performs live and subsequently transforms into work that extends the possibilities of both the essay and the poem (see his *Conversation* and *What It Means*).

The proliferation of politically engaged, socially informed, and aesthetically radical poetics in the period from 1975 to the present is charted by several anthologies, edited by Christopher Beach (*Artifice*); Mark Wallace and Stephen Marks; Claudia Rankine and Juliana Spahr; and Peter Baker; in addition to Bruce Andrews and my *The L=A=N=G=U=A=G=E Book* and my *The Politics of Poetic Form*. Collections edited by James McCorkle; Molly McQuade; and Donald Hall (*Claims*) provide other overviews of the poetics of the period, while Susan Bee and Mira Schor offer a highly relevant collection of writings by visual artists. Robert Sheppard's "The Necessity of Poetics" offers a good summary of many of the issues covered in this essay.

The period since 1975 has been marked by a profound shift from the dominance of male writers of poetics; by the turn of the twenty-first century, poetics was no longer a boy's club. A feminist approach to poetics is charted not only by Adrienne Rich but also by Kathleen Fraser, Rachel Blau DuPlessis, and Nicole Brossard.

The provocative and transformative poetics of Amiri Baraka have yet to be fully collected. Both Nathaniel Mackey and Lorenzo Thomas have published groundbreaking collections of essays on African American poetics, and Erica Hunt's "Notes for an Oppositional Poetics" in my *Politics of Poetic Form* offers a crucial intervention into that dialogue.

The connection between politics and form is at the heart of Bruce Andews's formally uncompromising essays, just as it informs Ron Silliman's *The New Sentence*. Hank Lazer undertakes the task of negotiating among the many audiences and ideologies for poetry. Leslie Scalapino pushes to erase the difference between her poetry and poetics, while articulating a distinct need for each (*How Phenomena* and *Public World*). Ann Lauterbach's collection of essays considers the relation of the flaw to the aesthetic. Rosmarie Waldrop offers a lifetime of thinking about translation, digression, appropriation, and form.

Probably the most philosophical and theoretically sophisticated approach to poetics is represented by Steve McCaffery's two, often mind-bogglingly comic, essay collections (*North* and *Prior to Meaning*). Christian Bök picks up on McCaffery's "pataphysics" (Alfred Jarry's science of imaginary answers to imaginary questions) with a tour-de-force work of poetics written with a number of severe constraints, including using the same number of words and sentences in each chapter. Joan Retallack, taking up themes of John Cage, has made an eloquent case for "poethics" (poetics conceived as an ethical activity). Related to poethics is ecopoetics—the way in which poetry reflects and refracts the environment that is its habitat. Ecopoetics is the focus of essays by Jed Rasula and of the magazine *Ecopoetics*, edited by Jonathan Skinner. Pierre Joris orients his poetics to wandering, to the nomad inside our poetic selves; Nick Piombino's poetics are both psychoanalytic and aphoristic (*Boundary* and *Theoretical Objects*); and Alan Davies is enigmatic in the pursuit of nothing less than the imaginary of everyday life. In his essays, Bob Perelman has interrogated many of the assumptions governing the poetics of the period, while Ben Friedlander has invented a new mode of doing poetics by transforming essays by Poe and others into contemporary commentaries. Johanna Drucker has explored, with wit and philosophical rigor, the visual dimensions of poetry and the book. Susan Stewart's study *Poetry and the Fate of the Senses* is an impassioned plea for the value of poetry in the fullness of its sentences. Lyn Hejinian is perhaps best known for her essay against closure, but her poetics provides wide-ranging accounts of the relation of poetry to consciousness, narrative, travel, and knowledge. Mean-

Over the past ten years, the Internet has become a homing ground for both poetry and poetics.

while, Susan Howe has undertaken the monumental work of undermining monumental histories, speaking of and for the cracks between victories in a style that merges historical scholarship and song.

Over the past ten years, the Internet has become a homing ground for both poetry and poetics. The best gateway to innovative poetry and poetics on the Web is the Electronic Poetry Center (http://epc.buffalo.edu), while the gateway for sound recordings of poets on the Web is Penn Sound (http://writing.upenn.edu/pennsound), which, for example, includes the lively poetics series Philly Talks. To experience poetics in the making, there is no better place to start than Ron Silliman's blog, which is updated daily. Joel Kuszai's collection *Poetics@* is a carefully shaped selection from a Web poetics forum that keeps the dialogue at the center of the action. The importance of the Web for poetry and poetics is explored in Jerome McGann's *Radiant Textuality* and Loss Pequeño Glazier's *Digital Poetics*.

Recent critical accounts of twentieth-century poetics worth noting here include those by Peter Quartermain, Michael Davidson (*Ghostlier Demarcations* and *Guys*), Charles Altieri, Maria Damon, Craig Dworken, Gerald Bruns, Susan Vanderborg, Hank Lazer, Christopher Beach (*Poetic Culture*), Barrett Watten, Juliana Spahr, Michael Magee, Stephen Fredman, Aldon Nielsen (*Black Chant* and *Integral Music*), James Longenbach, and above all Marjorie Perloff, whose many illuminating books have championed poets and poetics (*Poetics*, *Radical Artifice*, and *Twenty-First-Century Modernism*).

NOTES

1. The opening section of this essay is a collectively authored statement that I compiled, in 1991, from responses of the Core Faculty members of the just-founded Poetics Program of the Department of English at the State University of New York, Buffalo: Robert Creeley, Raymond Federman, Susan Howe, Dennis Tedlock, and myself.

2. Mills's essay is cited by Carl Davidson (9). Thanks

to Joel Kuszai for bringing this quotation to my attention. See also Williams, *Embodiment*.

3. Emerson's essays—in particular "The American Scholar," his address to the Phi Beta Kappa Society, at Cambridge on 31 August 1837 (*Nature*)—and "The Poet" remain foundational for American poetics (*Essays*). See especially Stanley Cavell's extensive writing on Emerson (e.g., *Conditions*). And behind Emerson, think, for the purposes of the brief for poetics, of Montaigne and Pascal.

4. For example, Hazard Adams's *Critical Theory since Plato*. Works of poetics (by poets) dominate the book up until the twentieth century, when the contribution by poets almost entirely disappears. Nonetheless, this collection remains a useful compendium of poetics and indeed of the twentieth-century critical theory that has been closely connected with the work of the most socially engaged and innovative poetics of the same period.

5. My *Close Listening: Poetry and the Performed Word* provides a set of essays on the significance of the poetry reading for poetry and poetics.

6. See Wittgenstein, *Lectures*. For a full account of the relation of Wittgenstein to poetics, see Marjorie Perloff's *Wittgenstein's Ladder*.

7. Jerome McGann and Lisa Samuels provide an essential account of wreading experiments in their essay "Deformance and Interpretation."

8. Many of the pre-twentieth-century works recommended in this essay are available both online and in numerous print editions. Note that items mentioned that are not in Works Cited are included in Adams's anthology or in one edited by Melissa Kwasny, which I mention later, or in both.

9. Dickinson's textual fragments are sometimes typed as letters, but Marta Werner, in her two editions, casts Dickinson as the progenitor of contemporary poetics (*Radical Scatters* and *Emily Dickinson's Open Folios*). Susan Howe's *My Emily Dickinson* is the key text for reading Dickinson in the context of poetics.

10. For further information on international poetics, see a special issue of *Boundary 2* that I edited, entitled *99 Poets / 1999: An International Poetics Symposium*. Ernesto Livon-Grosman was instrumental in my suggestions here regarding Latin American poetics. He recommends, also, Alejandra Pizarnik and Oliverio Girondo, from Argentina; however, their most relevant work has not yet been translated into English, a reminder of the limitations of an English-centered approach to poetics.

WORKS CITED AND SUGGESTIONS FOR FURTHER READING

Adams, Hazard, ed. *Critical Theory since Plato*. Rev. ed. Fort Worth: Harcourt, 1992.

Allen, Donald, and Warren Tallman. *The Poetics of the New American Poetry*. New York: Grove, 1973.

Altieri, Charles. *Postmodernisms Now: Essays on Contemporaneity in the Arts*. University Park: Pennsylvania State UP, 1998.

Andrews, Bruce. *Paradise and Method: Poetics and Praxis*. Evanston: Northwestern UP, 1996.

Andrews, Bruce, and Charles Bernstein, eds. *The L=A=N=G=U=A=G=E Book*. Carbondale: Southern Illinois UP, 1984.

Antin, David. *A Conversation with Charles Bernstein*. New York: Granary, 2002.

———. *What It Means to Be Avant-Garde*. New York: New Directions, 1993.

Artaud, Antonin. *Selected Writings*. Ed. Susan Sontag. Berkeley: U of California P, 1988.

Baker, Peter, ed. *Contemporary Poetry and Poetics*. New York: Lang, 1996.

Baraka, Amiri. *The Leroi Jones / Amiri Baraka Reader*. Ed. William J. Harris. New York: Thunder's Mouth, 1999.

Beach, Christopher, ed. *Artifice and Indeterminacy: An Anthology of New Poetics*. Tuscaloosa: U of Alabama P, 1998.

———. *Poetic Culture: Contemporary American Poetry between Community and Institution*. Evanston: Northwestern UP, 1999.

Bee, Susan, and Mira Schor, eds. *M/E/A/N/I/N/G: An Anthology of Artists' Writings, Theory, and Criticism*. Durham: Duke UP, 2000.

Benjamin, Walter. *Selected Writings*. 4 vols. Cambridge: Harvard UP, 1996–2003.

Bernstein, Charles, ed. *Close Listening: Poetry and the Performed Word*. New York: Oxford UP, 1998.

———, ed. *99 Poets / 1999: An International Poetics Symposium*. *Boundary 2* 26.1 (1999): 1–276.

———, ed. *The Politics of Poetic Form: Poetry and Public Policy*. New York: Roof, 1990.

Blake, William. *The Marriage of Heaven and Hell*. *Works in the William Blake Archive*. Ed. Morris Eaves, Robert Essick, and Joseph Viscomi. 1996–2005. 13 June 2006 <http://www.blakearchive.org/blake/indexworks.htm>.

Blaser, Robin. *Collected Essays*. Ed. Miriam Nichols. Berkeley: U of California P, forthcoming.

Bök, Christian. *'Pataphysics: The Poetics of an Imaginary Science*. Evanston: Northwestern UP, 2002.

Brathwaite, Kamau. *Roots*. Ann Arbor: U of Michigan P, 1999.

Breton, André. *Manifestos of Surrealism*. Trans. Richard Seaver and Helen R. Lane. Ann Arbor: U of Michigan P, 1969.

Brossard, Nicole. *Picture Theory*. Trans. Barbara Goddard. New York: Roof, 1990.

Bruns, Gerald. *The Material of Poetry: Sketches for a Philosophical Poetics*. Athens: U of Georgia P, 2005.

Bunting, Basil. *Basil Bunting on Poetry*. Ed. Peter Makin. Baltimore: Johns Hopkins UP, 1999.

Burke, Kenneth. *A Rhetoric of Motives*. New York: Prentice, 1950.

Cabanne, Pierre. *Dialogues with Marcel Duchamp*. New York: Da Capo, 1987.

Campos, Haroldo de. *Novas: Selected Writing*. Ed. A. S. Bessa and Odile Cisneros. Evanston: Northwestern UP, 2006.

Cavell, Stanley. *Conditions Handsome and Unhandsome: The Constitution of Emersonian Perfectionism*. Chicago: U of Chicago P, 1990.

———. *The Senses of* Walden. Chicago: U of Chicago P, 1992.

———. *This New Yet Unapproachable America: Essays after Emerson after Wittgenstein*. Albuquerque: Living Batch, 1988.

Caws, Mary Ann, ed. *Manifesto: A Century of Isms*. Lincoln: U of Nebraska P, 2001.

Celan, Paul. *Selections*. Ed. Pierre Joris. Berkeley: U of California P, 2005.

Césaire, Aimé. "Poetry and Knowledge." 1945. *Refusal of the Shadow: Surrealism and the Caribbean*. Ed. Michael Richardson. Trans. Richardson and Krzysztof Fijalkowski. New York: Verso, 1996. 134–45.

Clifford, James. *The Predicament of Culture: Twentieth-Century Ethnography, Literature, and Art*. Cambridge: Harvard UP, 1988.

Coleridge, Samuel Taylor. Excerpts from *Biographia Literaria*. Adams 476–80.

Collobert, Danielle. *It, Then*. Trans. Norma Cole. Oakland: O, 1989.

Creeley, Robert. *Collected Essays*. Berkeley: U of California P, 1989.

———. *A Quick Graph: Collected Notes and Essays*. Ed. Donald Allen. San Francisco: Four Seasons Foundation, 1970.

Damon, Maria. *The Dark End of the Street: Margins in American Vanguard Poetry*. Minneapolis: U of Minnesota P, 1993.

Davidson, Carl. *The New Radicals in the Multiversity: An Analysis and Strategy for the Student Movement*. Chicago: SDS Print Shop, 1968.

Davidson, Michael. *Ghostlier Demarcations: Modern Poetry and the Material Word*. Berkeley: U of California P, 1997.

———. *Guys like Us: Citing Masculinity in Cold War Poetics*. Berkeley: U of California P, 2003.

Davies, Alan. *Signage*. New York: Roof, 1987.

Dickinson, Emily. *Emily Dickinson's Open Folios: Scenes of Reading, Surfaces of Writing*. Ed. Marta L. Werner. Ann Arbor: U of Michigan P, 1995.

———. *Radical Scatters: Emily Dickinson's Fragments and Related Texts, 1870–1886*. Ed. Marta L. Werner. Electronic ed. U of Michigan P, 2000.

Drucker, Johanna. *Figuring the Word: Essays on Books, Writing, and Visual Poetics*. New York: Granary, 1998.

Duncan, Robert. *Fictive Certainties*. New York: New Directions, 1985.

DuPlessis, Rachel. *The Pink Guitar: Writing as Feminist Practice*. New York: Routledge, 1990.

Dworken, Craig. *Reading the Illegible*. Evanston: Northwestern UP, 2003.

Eigner, Larry. *Areas Lights Heights: Writings, 1954–1989*. Ed. Ben Friedlander. New York: Roof, 1990.

Emerson, Ralph Waldo. *Essays: Second Series*. Boston: Phillips, 1858.

———. *Nature: Addresses and Lectures*. Boston: Munroe, 1849.

Fisher, Allen. *Topological Shovel*. Willowdale, ON: Gig, 1999.

Forrest-Thomson, Veronica. *Poetic Artifice: A Theory of Twentieth-Century Poetry*. Manchester: Manchester UP, 1978.

Fraser, Kathleen. *Translating the Unspeakable: Poetry and the Innovative Necessity: Essays*. Tuscaloosa: U of Alabama P, 2000.

Fredman, Stephen. *The Grounding of American Poetry: Charles Olson and the Emersonian Tradition*. New York: Cambridge UP, 1993.

Friedlander, Ben. *Simulcast: Four Experiments in Criticism*. Tuscaloosa: U of Alabama P, 2004.

García Lorca, Federico. "Play and Theory of the Duende." *In Search of Duende*. Ed. and trans. Christopher Maurer. New York: New Directions, 1998. 48–62.

Ginsberg, Allen. *Deliberate Prose: Selected Essays, 1952–1995*. New York: Harper, 2000.

Glazier, Loss. *Digital Poetics*. Tuscaloosa: U of Alabama P, 2001.

Glissant, Édouard. *Poetics of Relation*. Trans. Betsy Wing. Ann Arbor: U of Michigan P, 1997.

Guest, Barbara. *Forces of Imagination: Writings on Writings*. Berkeley: Kelsey Street, 2003.

Guillén, Nicolas. *The Daily Daily*. Trans. Vera M. Kutzinski. Berkeley: U of California P, 1989.

Hall, Donald, ed. *Claims for Poetry*. Ann Arbor: U of Michigan P, 1983.

———. *Goatfoot Milktongue Twinbird: Interviews, Essays, and Notes on Poetry, 1970–76*. Ann Arbor: U of Michigan P, 1978.

Harrison, Charles, and Paul Wood. *Art in Theory, 1900–2000: An Anthology of Changing Ideas*. Malden: Blackwell, 2003.

Hejinian, Lyn. *The Language of Inquiry*. Berkeley: U of California P, 2000.

Herakleitos. Fragments. *Seven Greeks*. Trans. Guy Davenport. New York: New Directions, 1995. 158–71.

Howe, Susan. *The Birth-mark: Unsettling the Wilderness in American Literary History*. Middletown: Wesleyan UP, 1993.

———. *My Emily Dickinson*. Berkeley: North Atlantic, 1988.

———. *Pierce-Arrow*. New York: New Directions, 1999.

Hughes, Langston. *Langston Hughes and the* Chicago De-

fender: *Essays on Race, Politics, and Culture, 1942–62.*
Ed. Christopher C. De Santis. Urbana: U of Illinois P,
1995.

Hunt, Erica. "Notes for an Oppositional Poetics." Bernstein, *Politics* 197–212.

Hurlbert, Mark, et al. *Beyond English, Inc.* Portsmith:
Boynton, 2002.

Jabès, Edmond. *From the Book to the Book: An Edmond Jabès Reader.* Trans. Rosmarie Waldrop. Middletown:
Wesleyan UP, 1992.

Jackson, Laura (Riding). *Anarchism Is Not Enough.* Ed.
Lisa Samuels. Berkeley: U of California P, 2001.

———. *The Laura (Riding) Jackson Reader.* Ed. Susan
Friedmann. New York: Persea, 2005.

———. *The Telling.* New York: Harper, 1973.

Joris, Pierre. *A Nomad Poetics.* Middletown: Wesleyan
UP, 2003.

Khlebnikov, Velimir. *Letters and Theoretical Writings.*
Trans. Paul Schmidt, Ed. Charlotte Douglas. Cambridge: Harvard UP, 1987. Vol. 1 of *Collected Works.*

Kwasny, Melissa, ed. *Toward the Open Field: Poets on the
Art of Poetry, 1800–1950.* Middletown: Wesleyan UP,
2004.

Kuszai, Joel, ed. *Poetics@.* New York: Roof, 1999.

Lakoff, George. *Moral Politics: How Liberals and Conservatives Think.* Chicago: U of Chicago P, 2002.

Lauterbach, Ann. *The Night Sky: Writings on the Poetics of
Experience.* New York: Viking, 2005.

Lautréamont, Comte de. Maldoror *and the Complete
Works of the Comte de Lautréamont.* Trans. Alexis Lykiard. Cambridge: Exact Change, 1994.

Lazer, Hank. *Opposing Poetics.* 2 vols. Evanston: Northwestern UP, 1996.

Lezama Lima, José. *Selections.* Trans. James Irby, G. J.
Racz, Nathaniel Tarn, and Roberto Tejada. Ed. Ernesto Livon-Grosman. Berkeley: U of California P,
2005.

Longenbach, James. *The Resistance to Poetry.* Chicago: U
of Chicago P, 2004

Longinus. "On the Sublime." Adams 76–98.

Loy, Mina. *The Lost Lunar Baedeker: Poems.* Ed. Roger L.
Conover. New York: Farrar, 1997.

Lucretius. *On the Nature of Things.* Trans. William Ellery
Leonard. Internet Classics Archive. MIT. 1994–2000.
16 Feb. 2006 <http://classics.mit.edu/Carus/nature
_things.html>.

MacDiarmid, Hugh. *Selected Essays.* Berkeley: U of California P, 1970.

Mackey, Nathaniel. *Discrepant Engagements: Dissonance,
Cross-culturality, and Experimental Writing.* New York:
Cambridge UP, 1993.

Magee, Michael. *Emancipating Pragmatism: Emerson,
Jazz, and Experimental Writing.* Tuscaloosa: U of Alabama P, 2004.

Mallarmé, Stéphane. "The Book: A Spiritual [Instrument]." Adams 674–75.

———. "Crisis in Verse." *Symbolism: An Anthology.* Ed.
T. G. West. London: Methuen, 1980. 1–12.

Martí, José. *Selected Writings.* Trans. Esther Allen. New
York: Penguin, 2002.

McCaffery, Steve. *North of Intention: Critical Writings,
1973–1986.* New York: Roof, 1986.

———. *Prior to Meaning: The Protosemantic and Poetics.*
Evanston: Northwestern UP, 2001.

McCorkle, James. *Conversant Essays: Contemporary Poets
on Poetry.* Detroit: Wayne State UP, 1990.

McGann, Jerome. *Poetics of Sensibility: A Revolution in Literary Style.* Oxford: Oxford UP, 1996.

———. *Radiant Textuality: Literature after the World
Wide Web.* New York: Palgrave. 2001.

McGann, Jerome, and Lisa Samuels. *Deformance and Interpretation.* Inst. for Advanced Technology in the Humanities. U of Virginia. 11 Oct. 2004 <http://www
.iath.virginia.edu/~jjm2f/old/deform.html>.

McQuade, Molly, ed. *By Herself: Women Reclaim Poetry.*
Saint Paul: Graywolf, 2000.

Mills, C. Wright, "Mass Society and Liberal Education."
Power, Politics, and People. New York: Oxford UP,
1963. 353–73.

Nielsen, Aldon. *Black Chant: Languages of African-American Postmodernism.* New York: Cambridge UP,
1997.

———. *Integral Music: Languages of African American Innovation.* Tuscaloosa: U of Alabama P, 2004.

O'Hara, Frank. "Personism: A Manifesto." *The Collected
Poems of Frank O'Hara.* Ed. Donald Allen. Berkeley: U
of California P, 1995. 498–99.

Olson, Charles. *Collected Prose.* Ed. Donald Allen and
Ben Friedlander. Los Angeles: U of California P,
1997.

Perelman, Bob. *The Marginalization of Poetry: Language
Writing and Literary History.* Princeton: Princeton UP,
1996.

Perloff, Marjorie. *The Poetics of Indeterminacy: Rimbaud to
Cage.* Princeton. Evanston: Northwestern UP, 1999.

———. *Radical Artifice: Writing Poetry in the Age of Media.* Chicago: U of Chicago P, 1992.

———. *Twenty-First-Century Modernism: The "New" Poetics.* Malden: Blackwell, 2001.

———. *Wittgenstein's Ladder: Poetic Language and the
Strangeness of the Ordinary.* Chicago: U of Chicago P,
1999.

Piombino, Nick. *Boundary of Blur.* New York: Roof,
1993.

———. *Theoretical Objects.* Los Angeles: Green Integer,
1999.

Poe, Edgar Allan. "The Poetic Principle." Adams 575–
84.

Quartermain, Peter. *Disjunctive Poetics: From Gertrude
Stein and Louis Zukofsky to Susan Howe.* New York:
Cambridge UP, 1992.

Rankine, Claudia, and Juliana Spahr, eds. *American
Women Poets in the Twenty-First Century: Where Lyric
Meets Language.* Middletown: Wesleyan UP, 2002.

Rasula, Jed. *This Compost: Ecological Imperatives in American Poetry.* Athens: U of Georgia P, 2002.

Retallack, Joan. *Poethical Wager*. Berkeley: U of California P, 2004.

Rich, Adrienne. *Arts of the Possible: Essays and Conversations*. New York: Norton, 2002.

———. *On Lies, Secrets, and Silence: Selected Prose, 1966–1978*. New York: Norton, 1979.

Rothenberg, Jerome. *Pre-Faces and Other Writings*. New York: New Directions, 1981.

Scalapino, Leslie. *How Phenomena Appear to Unfold*. Elmwood: Potes and Poets, 1989.

———. *The Public World / Syntactically Impermanence*. Middletown: Wesleyan UP, 1999.

Senghor, Leopold. *Prose and Poetry*. Trans. John Reed and Clive Wake. London: Heinemann, 1976.

Shelley, Percy. "A Defense of Poetry." Adams 516–29.

Sheppard, Robert. "The Necessity of Poetics." *Pores* 1 (2001). 13 Aug. 2005 <http://www.pores.bbk.ac.uk/1>. Path: Robert Sheppard.

Sidney, Philip. "An Apology for Poetry." Adams 143–62.

Silliman, Ron. *The New Sentence*. New York: Roof, 1987.

———. *Silliman's Blog*. 11 Oct. 2004 <http://ronsilliman.blogspot.com>.

Spahr, Juliana. *Everybody's Autonomy: Connective Reading and Collective Identity*. Tuscaloosa: U of Alabama P, 2001.

Spicer, Jack. *The House That Jack Built: The Collected Lectures of Jack Spicer*. Ed. Peter Gizzi. Middletown: Wesleyan UP, 1998.

Stein, Gertrude. *Writings, 1903–1932*. Ed. Catherine R. Stimpson. New York: Lib. of Amer., 1998.

Stewart, Susan. *Poetry and the Fate of the Senses*. Chicago: U of Chicago P, 2001.

Swinburne, Algernon Charles. *William Blake: A Critical Essay*. 1868. New York: Bloom, 1986.

Tedlock, Dennis. *Breath on the Mirror: Mythic Voices and Visions of the Living Maya*. San Francisco: Harper, 1993.

Thomas, Lorenzo. *Extraordinary Measures: Afrocentric Modernism and Twentieth-Century American Poetry*. Tuscaloosa: U of Alabama P, 2000.

Thoreau, Henry David. *Walden*. eBooks@Adelaide. U of Adelaide Lib. 2004. 13 Aug. 2005 <http://etext.library.adelaide.edu.au/t/thoreau/henry_david/walden>.

Valéry, Paul. "Poetry and Abstract Thought." Adams 910–19.

Vallejo, César. *Aphorisms*. Trans. Stephen Kessler. Los Angeles: Green Integer, 2001.

Vanderborg, Susan. *Paratextual Communities: American Avant-Garde Poetry since 1950*. Carbondale: Southern Illinois UP, 2001.

Waldman, Ann, and Andrew Schelling, eds. *Disembodied Poetics: Annals of the Jack Kerouac School*. Albuquerque: U of New Mexico P, 1994.

Waldrop, Rosmarie. *Dissonance (If You Are Interested)*. Tuscaloosa: U of Alabama P, 2005.

Wallace, Mark, and Steven Marks, eds. *Telling It Slant:*

Avant-Garde Poetics of the 1990s. Tuscaloosa: U of Alabama P, 2002.

Watten, Barrett. *The Constructivist Moment: From Material Text to Cultural Poetics*. Middletown: Wesleyan UP, 2003.

Wilde, Oscar. "The Decay of Lying." Adams 658–70.

Williams, William Carlos. *Collected Poems*. Ed. Christopher MacGowan. 2 vols. New York: New Directions, 1986 and 1988.

———. *The Embodiment of Knowledge*. New York: New Directions, 1974.

———. *Paterson*. Rev. ed. Ed. Christopher MacGowan. New York: New Directions, 1992.

Wittgenstein, Ludwig. *Lectures and Conversations on Aesthetics, Psychology, and Religious Belief*. Ed. Cyril Barrett. Berkeley: U of California P, 1972.

———. *Philosophical Investigations*. Trans. G. E. M. Anscombe. New York: Macmillan, 1958.

Wordsworth, William. Preface. *Lyrical Ballads*. 1800. Ed. Bruce Graver and Ronald Tetreault. *Romantic Circles*. 24 Apr. 2006 <http://www.rc.umd.edu/editions/LB/>.

Zukofsky, Louis. *Prepositions*. Hanover: Wesleyan UP, 2001.

APPENDIX A:
WREADING EXPERIMENTS: A SAMPLER

Note: A full set of these experiments is available at http://writing.upenn.edu/bernstein/wreadiing-experiments.html.

1. Homophonic translation: Take a poem in a foreign language that you can pronounce but not necessarily understand and translate the sound of the poem into English (e.g., French "blanc" to "blank" or "toute" to "toot").

2. Jackson Mac Low's acrostic chance: Pick a book at random and use the title as an acrostic key phrase. For each letter of key phrase, go to the page number in the book that corresponds (a = 1, z = 26) and copy, as the first line of the poem, from the first word that begins with that letter to the end of line or sentence. Continue through all key letters, leaving stanza breaks to mark each new key word. Variations include using the author's name as a code for reading through her or his work, using your own or a friend's name, picking different kinds of books for this process, devising alternative acrostic procedures.

3. Substitution (1): "Mad libs." Take the poem or other source text and put blanks in place of three or four words in each line, noting the part of speech under each blank. Fill in the blanks, being sure not to recall the original context.

4. Dialectize: Translate the poem into one or several "dialects." Or do this just by the accent you give in reading the work out loud.

APPENDIX B: POEM PROFILER

STYLISTIC TEXTURES AND POETIC DICTION

Coefficient of weirdness (wackiness quotient)
Ambiguity
Ambivalence
Irreverence
Sobriety
Humor
Eloquence
Plainness
Sincerity
Smoothness (vs. roughness, bumpiness, striation)
Neat (vs. messy)
Pretentiousness
Subtlety (vs. bluntness)
Indirect (vs. straightforward)
Intelligence
Visual imagery
Dreaminess
Particularity (vs. generality) of details
Stylistic consistency
Innovation
Originality
Ornamental/decorative
Relevance
Tastefulness
Speechlike
Sampling (use of found or quoted material)
Comprehensibility
Coherence
Spontaneity
Exploratory
Density
Predictability
Abstractness
Sensuous
Unusual vocabulary
Complexity
Repetitiveness
Self-consciousness
Artifice (vs. "natural")
Difficulty
Modern/contemporary (vs. old-fashioned)

DEVELOPMENTAL/TEMPORAL/COMPOSITIONAL STRUCTURES (WHAT HOLDS THE POEM TOGETHER?)

Fragmentary/disjunctive/nonlinear/discontinuity [parataxis]
Logical/expository continuity (linear 1 / hypotaxis)
Narrative continuity (beginning, middle, and end) (linear 2 / hypotaxis)
Journey
Journal/diary
Stream of consciousness / thought process
Dreamlike/surreal
Closure

Symmetrical
Fast-paced
Jerky
Kinetic (moves from one thing to another) vs. static (continuous present)
Programmatic or procedural
Received form (sonnet, ballad, etc.)

DEVICES

Irony
Paradox
Exaggeration
Understatement
Simile
Metaphor
Personification
Symbolism
Allegory
Enjambment
Metonymy
Literary or historical allusion
Persona

MOOD/TONE

[rate the first term only]
Scary/reassuring
Dark/light
Impersonal/emotional
Engaged /disaffected (alienated)
Affirmative/skeptical/hostile
Elegiac (mournful) / celebratory (panegyric)
Hot/cold
Angry/friendly
Cool/uncool
Turbulent/calm
Disturbed/content
Reckless/cautious
Happy/sad
Depressed/elated
Bright/dull
Meditative/unreflective
Bubbly/sober
Elusive/explicit
Erotic/dispassionate
Mysterious/apparent

COUNTING

Syllables per line
Lines per stanza or for poem
Stanzas
Words per line
Programmatic or procedural structure

VISUAL SHAPE/FORM

Flush left, justified/ragged prose, overall "field" design, etc.

SOUND

Dissonance/cacophony (noisy, harsh)
Melodious/harmonious/mellifluous ("pleasing")
Assonance
Alliteration
Rhyme
Off-rhyme
Metrical patterns
Obtrusive (vs. not noticeable)

POINT OF VIEW

Direct POV of author as speaker (monologic/lyric)
Persona
Narrator (epic)
Multiple POVs (dialogic or polyvocal)
n/a

CONTENT

Political
Liberal/conservative/radical
Urban
Pastoral
Moral
Sexual

Religious
Spiritual
Mystical
Philosophical
Love
Family
Ethnic/racial
Nationalistic/patriotic
Gender
Mortality (death)
Illness
Conflict (war)
Discontent

CONTEXTS

Author's date of birth/death
Date of poem's composition
Place of composition
Relevant sociohistorical facts
Relevant biographical facts
Relevant ethnic, gender, national, sexual orientation
Place/context of original publication and significant
      subsequent publication
Variant versions, including performances

~ Reading Literature and Culture

~ Textual Scholarship

LEAH S. MARCUS

If *textual scholarship* is defined broadly enough, it encompasses almost everything that literary scholars do, except that the traditional associations of the phrase require it to be accompanied by a portentous aura of high seriousness and erudition. The phrase is used here to refer to those branches of literary study that analyze or determine the specific forms in which written texts reach readers. Such work includes the discovery and study of manuscripts and printed books as material artifacts; the analysis of changes in the materially embodied texts as they were shaped and reshaped by authors, scribes, printers, editors, and publishers; and the creation and critique of new textual embodiments in the form of new editions, whether printed or online. Such analytic processes are not, of course, unique to literary studies: similar endeavors are undertaken by historians, philosophers, art historians, media or film scholars, among others. Indeed, rudimentary textual scholarship is practiced by anyone who has ever noticed a typographic error in a newspaper headline or memo.

Over the past three decades, because of an infusion of poststructuralist methodology and computerized technology, textual scholarship

> **Textual scholarship has lost its dry-as-dust reputation and become one of the most exciting and contested areas of literary studies.**

has lost its dry-as-dust reputation and become one of the most exciting and contested areas of literary studies. Arguably, it has always been the most fundamental, in that textual scholarship determines the very shape in which the objects of literary studies reach the people who read and analyze them. Textual scholarship is itself a form of interpretation, and through editorial practice it sets the parameters within which we explicate a given literary text. It also plays a key role in defining the literary canon, insofar as texts that are discovered, edited, and published are given a currency that can lead to canonicity, while texts that are not so favored are not. The present essay offers a brief history and overview of the field but concentrates on the vexed and interesting matter of textual scholarship as interpretation. My examples come largely from Anglo-American and anglophone literature, because that is the area about which I know most, but similar trends are visible in other literatures (see, e.g., Chartier, *Forms* and *Order*; Gabler, Bornstein, and Pierce; Grésillon; and Greetham, *Scholarly Editing*, "Textual Scholarship," and *Textual Scholarship*). At present, the discipline of literary studies is faced with a catch-22. We depend on textual scholarship to give us reliable information about the composition, dissemination, and reception of literary and other texts, and to create editions that reliably communicate those texts and that information. At the same time, we are all too aware of the constructed nature of such activities and the extent to which they are subject to interpretive pressures of their own. Textual scholars today must strive for objectivity and uniformity in working with their materials, just as they have in the past. But today, perhaps more than in the past, they are painfully—or gleefully—cognizant that these goals are unattainable in practice.

TEXTUAL SCHOLARSHIP IN THE PAST

As D. C. Greetham pointed out in the 1992 MLA *Introduction to Scholarship* that preceded the present volume, contemporary trends in textual scholarship were anticipated by Western scholars as early as the sixth century BCE, when Peisistratus (c. 560–527 BCE) decided to stabilize the Homeric epic, which existed in his culture in many disparate oral forms, by having an official copy of Homer's work fixed in writing for the Panathena festival. The rivalry between the early libraries of Alexandria and Pergamum prefigured the modern textual debate between "new bibliographers" and what I like to call the "new philology," discussed below, in that Alexandrian textualists emphasized the combing of extant scrolls of the same work for comparative purposes with the goal of combining them to create an ideal text, while Pergamanians expressed skepticism about the Alexandrian enterprise and preferred to anchor their work in a single extant "best text" copy. Anticipating the canonizing activities of nineteenth- and twentieth-century editors, ancient librarians strictly limited the number of poets and dramatists whose work they collected, thereby consigning other classical writers to oblivion (Greetham, "Textual Scholarship" 105–07). Similarly, early compilers of the major religious texts—like the Hebrew and Christian Bibles and to some extent the Qur'an—

established canonicity in foundational religious texts by deciding which writings to include and which to reject as apocryphal or, in the Qur'an, which punctuation and ordering of the text to consider authoritative.

But all this earlier activity notwithstanding, there seems to be general agreement that modern textual scholarship dates back to the Renaissance, when scholars rediscovered numerous texts from the Greek and Roman past; attempted to edit them; and, beginning in the late fifteenth century, made them widely available internationally through a flood of printed editions that used the newly invented technology of movable type. To locate the origins of modern, "scientific" editing in the Renaissance is to associate it with other types of origin attributed to the same era: the rise of modern empiricism and of the modern Burkhardtian individual; of global exploration, vastly expanded international trade, and commercial development. Identification of textual scholarship as a Renaissance invention therefore tends to privilege those elements of modern textual scholarship that place emphasis on empirical techniques, standardization, and the authority of the individual author. In fact, like the history of science, textual scholarship in the Renaissance—or early modern era, to use today's preferred terminology—was as chaotic as it was intense and productive. Famously, Lorenzo Valla (1407–57) used philological principles to demonstrate that the Donation of Constantine, used by the Church to justify its wielding of secular power, was a forgery. Not all scholars were so scrupulous. The same Erasmus who did so much to establish the text of the Greek Bible on humanistic philological principles also forged at least one document when an original that took the tone he wanted was inconveniently unavailable (Grafton 43–45). Many of the early humanist printers used extraordinary care in producing the most accurate possible editions—the Aldine press kept a scholar in house to check typeset pages for errors—but such printers were often rewarded for their pioneering spirit by bankruptcy. And early printers regularly destroyed the manuscripts their editions had been based on once the book was in print: they did not have the concern of later philologists for the preservation of a literary text along the full gamut of its manuscript and printed history.

We can trace a path by which early modern textual scholarship gradually became regularized, but well into the eighteenth century it was, by present standards of textual accuracy, quite cavalier. In publishing his edition of Shakespeare, Alexander Pope saw no difficulty about demoting to the notes passages from the plays that he disapproved of. Even Samuel Johnson, the formidable lexicographer and critic, used eighteenth-century editions as base texts for his 1765 edition of Shakespeare instead of going back to earlier printed editions. However, in the course of the century, pre-eighteenth-century editions gradually received greater attention: when Johnson reedited Shakespeare in 1778, he increasingly consulted them. The eminent classicist Richard Bentley freely emended Milton in his 1732 edition of *Paradise Lost*, though his liberties with Milton's text were so outrageous that they were controversial even then.

During the nineteenth century, the genealogical methods of classical historical philology were increasingly applied to modern literatures. The name of Karl Lachmann (1793–1851) is particularly associated with this development. Lachmann's stemmatics, which Lachmann employed in editing Lucretius, but also medieval German literature like *Parzifal* and the Minnesingers, demonstrated how errors in textual transmission over many centuries could often be traced back methodically to their origin in a single miscopied version. He emphasized that literary texts needed to be studied (and recovered) through analysis of the historical accretions that altered them over time.

In the historical philology of the nineteenth and early twentieth centuries, Lachmann's methods gradually became standard. Yet the concerns of philologists did not permeate all aspects of the field of textual scholarship. Through much of the nineteenth century, the "history of the book" as we know it now did not exist. Just as editors tended to choose the last edition produced dur-

ing an author's lifetime as the definitive basis or copytext for their work, so most bibliographers, editors, and collectors tended to pass over the "original" form in which a writer's work was published in favor of later versions. Many an early binding in simple calf or soft vellum was sacrificed to collectors' desire for sumptuous modern replacements. Generally speaking, the version of a literary work that commanded the most respect (and price) among bibliographers and collectors was the last edition or the most elaborate one, not the first.

The new bibliography of the early and mid twentieth century brought radical change. Though the new bibliographers—scholars like W. W. Greg and Alfred Pollard in England and Fredson Bowers in the United States—kept some of the genealogical methods of nineteenth-century historical philology for the purpose of recovering authorial intent, they insisted on greater uniformity and accountability in editorial practice and created editions that sought to distinguish clearly between the literary text and ancillary historical materials. As much as possible, they sought to recover originals, the first or final version intended by the author, and tended to view mediating institutions like the printing house, the playhouse, or the schools as agents of corruption rather than contributors to the meaning of a given literary work. As has frequently been noted, the new bibliography in England and America was more or less contemporary with literary modernism. The new bibliographers were arguably antimodernist in their insistence on textual stability at a time that modernist poetics was dismantling so many received literary forms. The important editions produced by new bibliographers were designed to be definitive and to relieve future scholars of the painful task of consulting manuscript and early printed versions for themselves. Works like Fredson Bowers's *Principles of Bibliographical Description* set standards for the precise description of literary materials that are still followed today.

On the other hand, we can identify a clear methodological alliance among the approximately contemporaneous movements of the new bibliography, literary modernism, and the new criticism, in that all, at least in their dominant manifestations, tended to idealize literary texts and cordon them off from the polluting influence of what was defined as extraliterary. Not surprisingly, at about the same time, bibliographers and collectors reversed their earlier sense of priorities and began to value first editions more highly than later ones, creating a rage for first editions that transformed the book market. Textual scholarship in its various manifestations had assimilated the Romantic paradigm of the literary work as a brief, brilliant moment of incandescent creativity that, over time, could only lose its luminosity.

To offer a gross generalization, the purpose of textual scholarship as formulated by the new bibliography was to create printed texts that approached as nearly as possible the literary creation as it existed in that originary brilliance in the mind of its author. For that reason, all other things being equal, the practitioners of the new bibliography preferred manuscripts or early printed versions as copytexts. They needed to immerse themselves in historical research such as the recovery of printing-house practices, but they studied such institutions primarily to free the literary text from the corruptions that the institutions introduced. Herbert J. C. Grierson put the matter rather bluntly early in the century: for the lover of literature "literary history has an indirect value. He studies history that he may discount it" (2: v–vi).

As literary studies became professionalized in the mid–twentieth century, the field tended to bifurcate, with textual scholars and literary critics taking separate and irreconcilable tracks. Textual scholars established literary texts by using and further developing Greg's "rationale of copytext," by which editors selected a text to "copy" for their edition in all "accidentals" of spelling, capitalization, and so forth, while retaining the freedom to emend the copytext when it came to essential features of the text, or "substantives," so long as the editors could claim that such emendations followed the author's original or final intent. Critical editions

that followed or adapted Greg's rationale were usually meticulous in recording emendations, but not necessarily in a way that was accessible to the general public or even to other literary scholars. Lewis Mumford and Edmund Wilson both complained about the "barbed wire" of bristling, unintelligible textual variants that separated text and explanatory notes in the MLA's Center for Editions of American Authors (CEAA; the CEAA evolved into the MLA's present Committee on Scholarly Editions [CSE]). Textual scholars were the patient, hardworking technicians who worked behind the scenes to make close reading in a "new critical" vein possible and attractive for critics, who, for their part, as Bowers complained, seemed to "believe that texts are discovered under cabbage plants" (*Textual and Literary Criticism* 3).

During this period of bifurcation, textual scholars liked to point out the impoverishment of literary critics who operated without a sound sense of bibliography. Thus Bowers heaped scorn upon John Crowe Ransom for contending that Milton deliberately "roughed up" *Lycidas* during the process of composition, when a simple study of the transmission of the text would show the opposite to be true (3). Thus Alan Tate made an elaborate argument about the perfection of Emily Dickinson's "Because I could not Stop for Death," basing the argument on an outmoded edition of 1890 that titled the poem "The Chariot" (a title Dickinson had never used), omitted one entire stanza, and heavily emended several other lines (McGann, *Beauty* 123–26). If Tate had used a more recent edition available to him, would he have found a version closer to Dickinson's manuscript to be better or worse than the one he extolled for its perfection? Much of the bibliographers' scorn was justified, particularly given the penchant of the new criticism for close reading. It makes a great deal of interpretive difference, to mention only two of many famous textual cruxes, whether Herman Melville called the "fish of the sea" "coiled" or "soiled" in *White-Jacket* (Harkness 26) and whether D. H. Lawrence's Henry Morel "whimpers" or "whispers" the word "Mother!" at the end of *Sons and*

Lovers. Lawrence's manuscript and corrected galleys say "whimpers," but the Viking Press edition in the United States (1958) and the Heinemann Phoenix edition in London (1913; reset 1956) prefer "whispers" (Baron and Baron 464).

On the other side of the divide, literary critics could absolve themselves from worrying about issues of textual scholarship so long as they did not make undocumented claims that they could have checked against existing textual scholarship and so long as they used the best possible modern edition of an author's works. Many literary critics felt scorn for textual scholarship (and some still do)—it was the engineering branch of literary studies, forced to sully itself in enumerative work and investigation of historical processes and therefore compromised in a way that mainstream belletristic criticism was not. Literary critics were encouraged to use the same "standard" edition so that variant readings would not rear their ugly heads and destabilize the capacity for textual consensus that the new bibliography had provided. In the institution where I began my teaching career, one young scholar during the 1970s was allegedly denied tenure at least partly on grounds that she had cited eighteenth-century printings of her eighteenth-century authors rather than the standard modern scholarly editions! Since the 1980s, by contrast, textual stability has increasingly been sacrificed to other disciplinary goals, and the earlier divide between textual scholarship and literary criticism has eroded almost to the point of invisibility.

TEXTUAL SCHOLARSHIP IN THE PRESENT

The recovery of originary or final authorial intentions is a laudable goal: who would not find it valuable to know precisely what Victor Hugo, Chinua Achebe, Heinrich Kleist, Iris Murdoch, and Fyodor Dostoyevsky had in mind as they wrote and revised, or at least what printed version of their writings they might endorse as faithfully fulfilling their intentions? To put the matter so baldly is to highlight some of its internal complexities: What if authors were unclear about their intent, or changed their intent for a given text over time? What if there were multiple authors and each had a different intent for the same work (Stillinger)? What if the subsequent history of the work suggests that the author or authors were plain wrong in thinking that they knew what they intended? What if an editor or publisher, in the author's view, improved on what the author had intended? (We may think immediately of Ezra Pound and his intent for T. S. Eliot's *The Waste Land.*) Or what if authors deliberately overrode what might otherwise have been their intent—out of self-censorship, perhaps, or a strong sense of what would appeal to a targeted market of readers (Eaves)? And, for that matter, what is literary intent and how can it be separated from the welter of social and economic pressures that help determine the shape of any cultural production? As Michel Foucault put the matter at about the same time that Mumford and Wilson were grumbling about barbed wire, "What difference does it make who is speaking?" (160). Over time the cachet of the new bibliography has eroded as a result of shifting paradigms of authorship and altering perceptions of the discipline of literary studies. Meanwhile the new bibliography has itself evolved to meet some of the objections of poststructuralist and new-historicist critics (Tanselle, *Rationale*).

A number of forces have conspired to alter the climate for textual scholarship in the past twenty-five years. The new bibliography has come under attack for its emphasis on textual stability over process, its tendency in practice to construct the author's intent in ways that coincide with the editor's aesthetic or political preferences, its tendency to impose stemmatic ordering in textual situations where such imposition appears unwarranted, its encoding of patriarchal and colonial assumptions, and (occasionally) its faint aura of class privilege. The issue of textual stability is a vexed one because the field oscillates over time between the two poles of rigid fixity and chaotic indeterminacy. Confronted with an unexamined plenitude of manuscript and printed evidence about what an author may have written, many of us can share the new bibliographers' desire for order and codification. In fact, we continue to rely on standard editions and bibliographies of authors about whom we desire textual information without going to the trouble of replicating the painstaking research ourselves. Then again, confronted with too much rigidity in the stabilization of literary texts, which tends to appear tyrannical over time, most of us can understand the recent desire to deconstruct or otherwise undermine the standard editions in order to free literary texts to assume a range of forms and meanings that were precluded by those editions.

With the passage of time, some of the new bibliographers' editorial emendations that may have appeared judicious or even transparently obvious at the time the editions were first published have come to appear strangely arbitrary. For example, in the standard edition of Herman Melville's *Mardi: And a Voyage Thither*, the CEAA editors overrode both authorized editions published during Melville's lifetime and emended the numbering of 375 pillars that embellished Melville's "Temple of the Year, somewhere beyond Libya" to 365 pillars, because Melville states that the pillars "signify days." The author, they argued, must have intended a congruence between the number of pillars and the number of days in the year (Melville 228). But this conclusion relates more to the editors' desire for symmetry and closure than to anything we know about Melville's intent. What if he deliberately wanted to signal the number of days in the year plus ten, perhaps to satisfy some desire for symmetry of his own, or perhaps to disrupt readers' expectations of congruence between architecture and the calendar? Scholars who may wish to investigate the anomaly are ill served by an edition that corrects it without any supporting material evidence that the emended version of the passage represents Melville's intent.

Much of the recent dissatisfaction with twentieth-century editorial practice has to do

Poststructuralist ideas about textuality . . . prefer kinetic process over fixity, orphan status over filiation, and plurality over monovocality.

with its valorization of textual stability per se. In recent decades, the discipline of literary studies has assimilated poststructuralist ideas about textuality, which prefer kinetic process over fixity, orphan status over filiation, and plurality over monovocality. To the extent that standard editions encode the second of each of these contrasting terms by suppressing the first, they appear to us to fall short of the kinesis and plenitude that, as readers of Roland Barthes and Jean-François Lyotard, we have come to expect in our interaction with literary texts. Sometimes authors deliberately play with textual differences in order to create a tension between two or more versions of, say, a poem—as in Marianne Moore's "Poetry," which Moore first published in a thirty-line version (1935 and 1951) but which she pared down to three lines for the 1967 *Complete Poems*. The *Complete Poems* is therefore forever incomplete, forever in need of supplement. "The interplay of the two texts is at the centre of the reading experience" (McGann, *Beauty* 86–87). The playwright Tom Stoppard takes positive pleasure in altering his texts over time: the recurrent image of scattering pages in the film version of *Rosencrantz and Guildenstern Are Dead* aptly captures his position towards theatrical texts. Or, to take an earlier example, the English baroque poet Richard Crashaw published a cruciform poem in a different, perennially incomplete form every time it appeared, as a way of indicating humility towards his own creations before the plastic powers of God (Chambers). A single critical edition of one version could not capture the spirit of such designedly multiple texts.

During most of the twentieth century, it was seldom practical for economic reasons to offer parallel edited versions of a literary work that existed in numerous early forms, though it was theoretically possible for an individual reader to at least glimpse pieces of different early versions of the work through the textual notes in a good critical edition. Indeed, editors considered it an element of their responsibility to the profession and the public at large to override multiple texts in favor of a single definitive version of the literary work. Some innovators created special printed formats for displaying a text's transformation over time, as in Hans Gabler's synoptic edition of *Ulysses*, which incorporated various stages in the process of authorial revision as part of the experience of reading the work. In the synoptic *Ulysses*, the left side of each opening registers the "ineluctable modality of the visible" (1:74) by showing revisions seriatim in the text, while the right side offers the critical edition that results from the editorial process. Here is a passage chosen more or less at random from the synoptic text, with only Gabler's editorial superscriptions omitted:

> [Browbeaten Mr Bloom fell] Mr Bloom, chapfallen, drew behind a few paces so as not to overhear. Martin laying down the law. Martin could wind a [fellow] [fathead] sappyhead like that round his little finger, without his seeing it.
> (235)

The equivalent passage on the right-hand side (the critical edition) reads:

> Mr Bloom, chapfallen, drew behind a few paces so as not to overhear. Martin laying down the law. Martin could wind a sappyhead like that round his little finger, without his seeing it.   (236)

Despite the Joycean flow of the synoptic text, Gabler's edition was criticized for regularizing the novel too much. In Gabler's version, following the Rosenbach manuscript, Stephen Daedalus answers his own query earlier in the novel about the "word known to all men": "Love, yes. Word known to all men" (419). In the view of some vocal scholars at the time, this passage, as one that Joyce himself had suppressed, did not belong in a critical edition of the novel, which was too open-ended to admit such a self-defeating form of closure (Kidd). In addition to having other problems with emendation, at least in the view of his critics, Gabler's text of *Ulysses* pulled in two directions: the synoptic text in the direction of an emphasis on writing as process, as innovated in "genetic" European editions of Friedrich Hölderlin, Friedrich Klopstock, Franz Kafka, Gustave Flaubert, and Marcel Proust (Grésillon; Gabler, Bornstein, and Pierce; McGann, "*Ulysses*"), the critical edition in the direction of stasis and closure. If Gabler had begun his Joyce edition twenty years later, might he have pushed for an electronic format rather than print? The development of electronic editions has made it possible for textual scholars to achieve both goals simultaneously without an appearance of methodological confusion. Electronic editions can offer stable, searchable texts along with the ability to compare different manuscript and printed versions of a given work in a way that brings its composition to life as process, not only as product.

Objections to the inert quality of the standard critical edition are of course not based solely on aesthetic preference for multiplicity and multivocality over stasis and unity. There is also the question of the relation of a literary text over time to its surrounding culture, which is always, perforce, in flux. The new bibliography assumed for strategic purposes that an author's intentions could be regarded as single, but they may have been irreducibly plural; authors may have intended different versions of a work for different occasions and audiences. Sometimes pressure from readers or editors prompted authors to alter their creations, as in Charles Dickens's revised ending for *Great Expectations*, which conceded to readers' desires for a marriage between Pip and Estella by hinting that Pip would not again part from her. Richard Wright similarly revised *Native Son* to reject the bleak original ending that showed Bigger Thomas strapped in the electric chair and awaiting execution.

When revision is prompted by editorial pressure, does that mean it does not encode the author's intent? In any case, it represents the text as it was received in print by the original audience—a form that many critics today find considerably more interesting than what the author may have intended. Even when authors expressly stated that editorial interventions had improved their work over its prepublication form, the new bibliography did not necessarily regard the published version as definitive, as in G.

Thomas Tanselle's controversial CEAA edition of Melville's *Typee* (1968), which restored cuts made by the editor of the second edition even though Melville himself termed the cuts "beneficial" (Greetham, *Textual Scholarship* 336). Virginia Woolf revised her novels with a great deal of self-censorship and corrected them differently, depending on whether they were being issued for the British or for the American market. As she noted in the holograph manuscript of *Orlando*, "ink is excessively sensitive to environment" (Lee 5). Sometimes, paradoxically, writers may revise their novels for a new edition to try to achieve an effect similar to that the work had on its first readers years before, as in Joyce Carol Oates's recently updated version of *A Garden of Earthly Delights* (first published in 1967), which, as Judith Shulevitz lamented in the *New York Times Book Review*, sacrifices the "satisfying plainness" of the original opening for a twenty-first-century revision "with all the saturated color and kinescopic precision a writing workshop leader could ask for." Clearly, there are now not one but two versions of *A Garden of Earthly Delights*, one for the 1960s and one redesigned by the author for the present.

Since 1980, editorial practice has become increasingly sensitive to such forms of textual multiplicity, and literature has been increasingly reattached to the culture of which it forms a part. Led by Jerome G. McGann in the United States and Donald F. McKenzie in Britain, a movement to rehistoricize editorial practice has revolutionized textual scholarship. Critical editions are still being created, but alongside them readers now are increasingly exposed to what Donald Reiman has termed "versioning," an editorial method that produces a modern version of a single historically specific form, whether in manuscript or in print, of a given text or two or more versions printed separately for comparative purposes, instead of attempting a single definitive composite edition in the manner of the new bibliography. Reiman's interest in versioning stemmed from his dilemmas in attempting to edit Romantic texts that changed markedly over time, but the technique has also been adopted in many other

areas of scholarship, perhaps most notably in the editing of Shakespeare.

The editing of Shakespeare has been revolutionized over the past three decades by a revitalized interest in the Bard as a reviser of his own plays, perhaps in the direction of greater artistic perfection, but perhaps also with an eye to the tastes of different audiences. After pioneering work by Steven Urkowitz, Michael Warren, Gary Taylor, and Stanley Wells (see Taylor and Warren; Wells and Taylor, *William Shakespeare . . . Works* and *William Shakespeare . . . Companion*), it is now commonplace in Shakespeare criticism to regard early printed quarto and folio versions of the plays as encoding different intents geared to different times and audiences. Seduced by the fascinating problems of Shakespearean multiplicity, numerous scholars have turned to editing the plays: it is no longer possible to separate Shakespearean editors from critics. Even the "bad quartos" despised by new bibliographers as inferior, possibly pirated copies of what Shakespeare actually wrote, are now receiving editions of their own, and some scholars are exploring the hitherto heretical possibility that Shakespeare may have worked collaboratively more often than we think. There can be no question, at the very least, that he worked in collaboration with his theatrical company, so that all Shakespearean texts are "contaminated" by the early modern playhouse in a way that cannot be remedied through even the most careful editing.

Obviously, the potential of electronic editions is crucial in making the textual differences among different versions of Shakespeare's plays easily negotiable, as it is crucial for so many other cases of textual multiplicity. It is a sign of the times that early editions of Shakespeare are now readily available online through *Early English Books Online* (*EEBO*), the British Library, and smaller initiatives like Peter Donaldson's MIT *Shakespeare Electronic Archive*. Even seemingly traditionalist enterprises like the MLA-sponsored New Variorum Edition of Shakespeare have laid plans to make all their edited volumes of the plays available in CD-ROM or Web-based formats that will allow readers to retrieve all the major textual forms the plays have assumed over the four hundred–odd years since their original publication.

Recent editorial practice continues to use traditional stemmatics but frequently modifies it when that methodology does not apply. Created to track alterations in classical texts over centuries of recopying, stemmatics is less useful for cases of much more rapid transmission or for cases in which there may never have been a single written original. There are many such "open recensions": the oral epics of Homer, of South Slavic peoples, and of modern urban rap culture; biblical texts such as the creation story from Genesis or the four Gospels, which cannot be resolved into a single authoritative account of the events they describe; courtly lyrics, speeches, or sermons that may have been intended for oral delivery but were transcribed by auditors, either during or after their delivery, possibly in multiple versions, as is frequently the case with the sermons of John Donne or the speeches of Queen Elizabeth I. That a monarch's speeches or a Croatian oral epic or a rap artist's street performance can now be incorporated within the purview of literature indicates the degree to which the canon has expanded since the heady days of the new bibliography.

The matter of editing and canonicity is tricky: on the one hand, full-dress critical editing of an author's work has traditionally been one of the signs that the author has arrived; it has served to create a secure niche for an author in terms of future scholarship. We reasonably expect a similar level of editorial attention to works that we are in the process of making canonical, if only to ensure that they receive equal exposure and currency. On the other hand, as amply indicated above, the traditional ways of indicating canonicity through new bibliographical practice are ill suited to many of the forms that are coming to be included in the broadened field we now conceptualize as literary and cultural studies.

One of the things that is frequently obscured in traditional critical editions is a given text's en-

> **One of the things that is frequently obscured in traditional critical editions is a given text's engagement with issues of colonialism and race.**

gagement with issues of colonialism and race. For example, nearly all modern editors of Christopher Marlowe's *Tamburlaine* emend the first octavo's description of him as "snowy" in complexion to the preferred reading of "sinewy," on grounds that "snowy" is hardly likely as a description of a warrior-conqueror, even though it is the reading of all the early texts; one of the later octavos even amplifies the descriptive term to "snowy-white." In this case, editors have tacitly discounted the overwhelming likelihood that Tamburlaine, whom we have tended to think of as the paradigmatic Islamic other for the English in the sixteenth century, might instead be defined by Marlowe as light-skinned, like the English themselves. Similarly, editors of *The Tempest* have regularly glossed Shakespeare's description of Sycorax as a "blue-eyed hag" to mean "bleary eyed" or "blue around the eyes," confident that Shakespeare could not possibly have intended an Algerian witch to have eyes of such a quintessentially north European color (Marcus, *Unediting* 5–17).

Even more significantly, eclectic editions that freely emend their copytext to incorporate other materials deemed part of the author's intent can completely obscure a process of what we might call textual racialization, as in the first quarto of *The Merchant of Venice*, where the plot's gradual entrapment and alienation of Shylock is mirrored textually by an alteration in the identification of speakers. Shylock's speeches are headed "Shylock" early in the play but increasingly "Jew" toward the end as he collapses into a stereotype. Similarly, the first quarto (1622) and first folio (1623) versions of *Othello* encode very different conceptions of race, and nearly all the passages that critics use to discuss race in the play are in the folio only. To imagine Shakespeare as revising from a text resembling the quarto to a text resembling the folio version is to imagine a Shakespeare who participated in a gradual cultural process by which color came to be the chief marker of racial difference (Marcus, "Two Texts").

In all these cases, editorial constructions of textual stability have aligned with nineteenth- and early-twentieth-century colonial assumptions, which is to say that textual critics, like everyone else, are creatures of their times. The same tendency is quite visible in more recent work: we can, for example, trace a process by which the Faber and Faber editors of the Yoruba author Amos Tutuola's *Palm Wine Drinkard* (1952) regularized the language of his novel to bring it more nearly into line with standard English, though obviously they chose to prefer some Nigerian forms, like "Drinkard" instead of "Drunkard" in the title. In the view of some educated Nigerians, they did not standardize nearly enough. What is the effect of Faber's editorial intervention? It was the publisher and not the author who determined the degree of ethnicity allowed in the novel as it was published; it was the publisher who thereby defined a boundary between Anglo-American self and anglophone other. In such a formulation, editing can itself be a form of colonial or racial codification. Since the field of postcolonial studies has become active in textual scholarship, we can expect newly edited versions of literary texts that engage colonial issues, along with the discovery and editing of the works of previously unknown writers. The fields of Afro-American and Chicano studies have contributed enormously to the expansion and diversification of the canon through critiques of received editorial practice and the dissemination of previously unknown work, both in print and electronically.

Feminism and gender studies are two other areas that currently have a strong impact on the shape of textual scholarship. In the same way that scholars studying race and colonialism have shown how editorial practice can perpetuate assumptions of racial and ethnic superiority, feminist and queer theorists have posited an alignment between traditional editorial practice and the social control of women and sexual "deviance." Early humanist scholars frequently conceptualized the texts they were editing as unruly women whom they were bringing under patri-archal domination (Jed), and a similar implicit gendering of textual scholarship has endured for centuries. Even in a standard twentieth-century guide to research methodology, we find Richard Altick assenting to a definition of the driving force behind textual scholarship as an "incontinency of the Spirit" that "hath a pleasure in it like that of Wrestling with a fine Woman" (15).

It would, of course, be a mistake to assume that all regularizing impulses are by definition straight and patriarchal. Feminist scholars over the last several decades have worked to dissipate outmoded assumptions on the part of editors and bibliographers. But, like scholars in other canon-expanding areas of the discipline—postcolonial, Afro-American, Chicano studies—they have done codifying of their own, collecting and publishing editions of previously unknown or undervalued writers: Elizabeth Cary, Christine de Pisan, Maria Edgeworth, Zora Neale Hurston, Harriet Jacobs, and Zitkala-Sa (Gertrude Simmons Bonnin), to name only a few. The Brown University *Women Writers Project* has been an especially important venue for making women writers available in printed editions and online.

Feminist textual scholars have also attempted to disentangle cases of literary collaboration in which a woman author's contribution may have been eclipsed or reshaped by the man's; the genesis, publication, and revision of Mary Shelley's *Frankenstein* (1818 and 1831), for example, or Harriet Mill's role in the authorship of J. S. Mill's autobiography. They have studied women's roles as translators, collectors, printers and publishers of books and reevaluated evidence for women's authorship of anonymous materials previously attributed to men. The issue of textual collaboration and mixing is also of particular interest to the field of gender studies. For example, scholars have shown how queer the history of textual scholarship can be shown to be if sufficient attention is paid to questions of homosocial and homoerotic desire (Goldberg), as in the close friendship of the early modern playwrights Francis Beaumont and Phineas Fletcher, who were both collaborators and bedfellows and apparently even shared the same mistress (Masten 121–55).

Appropriately for a field as diverse as textual scholarship in the present, we have a wide array of textual presentations to choose from—a development that is very welcome but also potentially quite bewildering, especially to neophytes in the field. Would-be readers of a given author or literary text can often find a photographic reprint of the work in manuscript, typescript, copyedited or early printed versions, in print or online or both; a type facsimile, which records as faithfully as possible within the limits of modern typography the original appearance of a single text of a literary work; a diplomatic transcript, which reproduces the words, spelling, and punctuation of a single version but without attempting to reproduce the work's appearance in the original; an edited version of one among a number of possible early texts of a given work, like the 1608 quarto of *King Lear* or the 1850 version of Wordsworth's *Prelude*; and a gamut of synthesizing critical editions, which vary greatly, as we have seen. They vary in the amount of editorial intervention allowed; in the variety of textual evidence consulted; in the autonomy accorded to different early versions of a given text; and in the ways the author's intent, whether conceptualized as singular or plural, is reconstructed and incorporated into the editorial process (Greetham, *Textual Scholarship* 347–417).

Thirty years ago, literary critics could rely on the devalued but indispensable work of textual scholars to provide them with reliable texts. Today, with the breakdown of that convenient division of labor and a new recognition of the rhetorical power of the editorial process, more and more professors and students of literature are setting up shop as textual scholars themselves. The field is rich but also rife with problems: it has gradually marginalized the standardized practices associated with the new bibliography but is only in process of replacing them with a new uniform system, so that in some respects, mutatis mutandis, we have returned to the heady, chaotic days of traditional philology that

twentieth-century bibliographical practice was designed to reform. Hence the phrase "new philology" is sometimes applied to the revisionist work in textual scholarship today.

THE HISTORY OF THE BOOK

One key element in the new textual scholarship is a passionate interest in the materiality of texts: the forms in which they have been preserved since their creation (whether through inscription on stone, papyrus, parchment codex, loose manuscript leaves, printed book, or online edition), the ways in which alterations in those material forms correlate with or contribute to other elements of social and cultural change, the ways in which the forms in which they are disseminated correlate with changing conventions of copyright and intellectual property, and the ways in which the interpretation of a text is altered from one material presentation to another. Those interests are encompassed in the wide rubric of the "history of the book," a movement spearheaded in recent decades by scholars like Robert Darnton and Roger Chartier. The history of the book incorporates the traditional interests of descriptive and analytic bibliography and of publishing and copyright history, but with an added injection of theory, particularly the writings of Foucault.

Historians of the book study its format in formal terms but also in relation to environments of reading and writing. What difference does it make in terms of reading whether a given text is entered on a roll of parchment, as was standard in classical times, or in a codex, as is still standard for printed books today? (Anyone who has attempted to read a book online has become reacquainted with some differences between the two forms of reading.) How does the formal presentation of a book contribute to its meaning? We may think here of the appropriately green cover of Walt Whitman's virtually self-published *Leaves of Grass* (1855) or of the sinuous, sweeping giant S that begins *Ulysses* in most twentieth-century editions—but not in Gabler's, since that highly appealing graphic presentation was added by the designers of the United States Random House edition; it was not part of the author's intention. One of the major criticisms of the Gabler *Ulysses* has been that it did not respect early editions of *Ulysses* as material artifacts or attempt to preserve elements of syncopation between the book's design and Joyce's own alterations of the page proofs, which may have taken design elements into account. To take another example, if the 1633 duodecimo edition of George Herbert's *The Temple* was designed in size and ornamentation to resemble pocket editions of the Book of Common Prayer available at the same period, then that tells us something important about how the editors and publishers expected the edition to be received (Targoff 112–17). Are there formal features of printed books that have been specifically gendered feminine at certain periods or geared to readers of a specific race, class, or cultural group? And what about fake imprints, which are very common, for example, in French books under the censorship of the ancien regime? Not only typography and ornamentation but also prefatory material; dedicatory poems; illustrations; printed marginalia; title page decoration; information about publisher, printer, and place of publication; and even the internal organization of the volume are part of the interpretation of the book as a material artifact.

Historians of the book are also interested in how books have been altered by early owners or other readers. To take some medieval examples, if manuscript materials were bound up together as a unit, even if the contents were quite disparate, that may tell us something about habits of mind then. The existence of contemporary large compendiums or "great books" of chivalry may alert us to generic expectations readers brought to Sir Thomas Mallory's *Morte Darthur*. If a patron commissioned a special edition of a literary text to memorialize himself and his court, as in Heinrich II of Hesse's commission of the Kassel *Willehalm* Codex, how does the presence of the patron in the volume, through dedicatory inscriptions and illustrations, inflect the ways in which it was likely to be read and used (Holladay)? Manuscript marginalia in books of any period may be as interesting as the contents, in that they can offer clues about the book's reception by at least one reader. The Folger manuscript of *Merry Wives of Windsor*, which dates probably from the 1650s (Folger ms. V.A. 73), employs pointing fists in the margins to call attention to the topic of marrying for love instead of money—a sign that the subject was of particular interest to the transcriber or an early reader.

Of course, the malleability of material books to alteration at any time in their history can create pitfalls for scholars. Particularly in American libraries, choice editions of major writers often turn out to have been altered or even made up from pieces of other copies. Such tampering can be interesting in itself: the Harvard and University of Texas copies of the 1633 posthumous edition of John Donne's *Poems* both have Donne's signature pasted onto the title page—obviously an early enhancement that may well have been engineered by the same friends who saw the book through the press. But the Harvard copy also has a frontispiece portrait of Donne that was pasted in from a later edition: anyone who uses that copy to make a general argument about the appearance of the first edition of Donne's *Poems* is likely to go seriously astray. Similarly, reputable scholars have been misled in making arguments about portrait frontispieces in George Herbert's *Temple* and Ben Jonson's 1616 *Works*, to mention only two examples, simply because they used Huntington Library copies into which portraits from elsewhere had been pasted (Marcus, *Unediting* 199, 259n26). Most major American collections contain at least a few of what bibliographers term "sophisticated" copies of literary classics: that is, copies that have been altered in various ways from their original formatting and appearance, usually by enterprising book dealers. Not many libraries do enough to warn scholars about the nonrepresentative features of these copies.

> **The malleability of material books to alteration at any time in their history can create pitfalls for scholars.**

Sometimes new books are made up entirely. The Mayflower Bible at the University of Texas, said to have accompanied the Pilgrims to America on the Mayflower, was for many years one of Texas's prized possessions, acquired after a bitter bidding war with the Mayflower Society. However, it was the Mayflower Society who won: an alert Texas librarian noticed that the Book of Common Prayer included in the Mayflower Bible was in fact spliced together from two different editions, one of which dated from 1634, which was somewhat late for the first Mayflower crossing! Pages from the Mayflower Bible that derived from the 1634 prayerbook contained charming (forged) illustrations supposedly doodled by Pilgrim children who conveniently dated their drawings 1619 and 1623. The impossible dating revealed that all the illustrations, and in fact the whole production, had been faked (Thomas).

One of the greatest pitfalls to good scholarly work in the history of the book, as in textual scholarship more generally, is a lack of bibliographic training. Under the old regime of separated duties, literary scholars counted on bibliographers to do the bibliographic work for them. But now that literary scholars have set themselves up as students of the book, they need to learn the techniques that will enable them to distinguish sophisticated copies, they need to be wary about generalizing about an edition on the basis of any single copy, and they need to continue to rely on the expertise of trained bibliographers for matters they cannot investigate themselves.

Consider the following hermeneutic circle. The famous forger and bibliographer Thomas J. Wise (1859–1937) helped fuel the seemingly insatiable early-twentieth-century demand for first editions by creating numerous fakes: for example, a separate early printing of Elizabeth Barrett Browning's *The Runaway Slave at Pilgrim's Point*, which she had in fact never published separately (Collins 89–91; Todd 60–62). If curious scholars wanted verification of the book's genuineness, they had only to turn to what had long been the standard bibliography of Browning, which

happened also to be by Wise and which duly included the first edition of *The Runaway Slave*, even though Wise himself had manufactured it. One way for the average scholar to escape this circle of deceit would be to rely on a more recent bibliographer, Warner Barnes, who lists the edition correctly as a forgery and explains a bit of its provenance (65–68).

The history of the book is rife with similar stories of deception. That deception is part of its fascination and a worthy research topic in its own right but also a warning to scholars to take care in working with material artifacts. Which is not to say that any of us can be expected to take on the prodigious task of inventing the field anew on the basis of our own research. At a time when there are so many competing ideas about how textual scholarship should be done, we need to be quite clear about which elements of the field we are willing to take on trust from previous scholars and which areas of previous scholarship we wish to challenge and rework.

ELECTRONIC TEXTUAL SCHOLARSHIP

As anyone who has browsed the World Wide Web for literary authors and texts is well aware, there are already electronic editions in a wide variety of formats, from simple reprints of older printed scholarship to highly sophisticated hypertextual archives like the *Complete Writings and Pictures of Dante Gabriel Rossetti* and *The William Blake Archive*, both at the University of Virginia. In addition, scholars are increasingly choosing CD-ROM format for major editions. Some electronic archives aim eventually to bring a literary text to life in all its major transformations from manuscript through a range of printed editions, often with a generous selection of explanatory materials and related cultural documents also included in searchable form.

Electronic editions can claim many significant advantages over printed ones. As noted above, they allow for disparate forms of textual presentation that if placed to-gether in a printed edition might appear confused or im-possibly unwieldy. A stable critical edition, or more than one, might be presented along with a display of early manuscript and printed forms that allow the reader to examine and critique the processes by which the critical edition was arrived at. In some cases, readers can intervene in the editorial process and either revise an existing critical edi-tion for their own use or capture a single version of the text for further analysis. Electronic edi-tions are particularly well suited for presentation of material by authors who were perennial revis-ers, such as Joyce and Rosetti; they can also bring together collections of material (slave narratives, literature by women) in a form that is easily ex-pandable as new material is discovered. They en-able deep searches of a wide variety of primary texts and archival material, exceeding the capac-ities of most printed indexes and concordances. They facilitate multimedia presentations—al-lowing their creators, for example, to present au-dio materials to accompany the ballad poems of Robert Burns or present staged scenes on video to accompany the written text of Shakespeare's *Twelfth Night*. But they also introduce complex new questions about copyright and intellectual property, and not all copyright holders welcome them. An electronic edition of Joyce is unlikely anytime soon because of the anxieties of the copyright holders.

Insofar as the World Wide Web facilitates, or at least fails to police, rowdy, cheek-by-jowl jux-tapositions of disparate cultural materials, Web-based textual scholarship by the very nature of its medium further erodes the boundary between and implicit hierarchy of traditional canonical literature and other forms of cultural production. While revisionist textual scholars hail the rapid digitalization of the discipline over the past de-cade as helping dismantle assumptions about the potential for textual purity and integrity behind some earlier editorial and bibliographic prac-tices, many other scholars in the field are un-willing to concede that the altered medium

Electronic editions are particularly well suited for presentation of material by authors who were perennial revisers.

changes the ontological status of the literary text in any es-sential way (Burnard, O'Brien O'Keeffe, and Unsworth; McGann, *Radiant Textuality*).

As books published before 1500 are called *in-cunabula*, so we now find ourselves in the age of electronic incunabula—an area of textual schol-arship that is so new that its impact is almost impossible to assess. There are, however, several clear trends, the most obvious of which is elec-tronic editing's remarkable editorial eclecticism. If, as many scholars would contend, the idea of the authoritative edition is now for all purposes defunct, that erosion of authority is particularly evident on the World Wide Web, where multiple versions of a given literary text compete for reader attention without the usual credentializ-ing of providers that accompanies the scholarly publication of books. Much of the painstaking work of the most careful twentieth-century edi-tors has, in effect, been rolled back.

To return to the example of Emily Dickinson treated earlier, readers wishing to consult an on-line edition of her writings will most likely en-counter one of several postings of the 1890 edi-tion of her poems, which is out of copyright and therefore available for use. But as they consult an online edition of the 1890 *Poems*, will those read-ers recognize that "The Chariot" is not Dickin-son's title for "Because I could not Stop for Death," that the poem in her manuscript was longer and differently worded? Of course the version they are reading can be described as fairly definitive in terms of early audience re-sponse, because it approaches the form in which the printed poem reached the public in 1890, even if it differs in significant ways from the poem as Dickinson wrote it. We are back in the shadow of Foucault and of the deconstruction of received textual authority: "What difference does it make who is speaking?" And precisely what is being said? What if we unwittingly base our scholarly conclusions on a downloaded text that has been truncated or abridged or bowdlerized or otherwise revised? The textual indeterminacy that has appealed to so many scholars in theory is often exhilarating online, but it appears incommodious or worse when we find ourselves in need of something "authoritative."

The MLA's Committee on Scholarly Editions has for many years provided guidance on and articulated standards for the editing of scholarly editions in print. In recent years, the committee updated its "Guidelines and Guiding Questions for Editors of Scholarly Editions" to include electronic editions. These guidelines are a central feature of the MLA volume *Electronic Textual Editing* (Burnard, O'Brien O'Keeffe, and Unsworth), which is the result of a collaboration between the committee and the Text Encoding Initiative (TEI). The TEI is an international consortium that has created standards for encoding text in SGML (standard generalized markup language) and, more recently, in XML (extensible markup language). By using the TEI guidelines, editors and publishers make use of a set of standards for marking textual features that is designed to endure as software interfaces evolve. *Electronic Textual Editing* includes the TEI P4 guidelines along with advice on when (and when not) to use them. The book presents practical advice on editing and marking up texts representing a variety of genres and historical situations.

Electronic editions are delivered to users in several fashions, and the choice of delivery medium can have consequences for the durability of an edition. A number of recent endeavors, like the mammoth *Canterbury Tales Project*, which has already published massive compilations of early versions of Chaucer's "General Prologue" and "Wife of Bath's Prologue," have used CD-ROM. CD-ROMs are somewhat like the printed book in that they may be updated only through a new edition. Web-based editions, by contrast, allow for frequent updating. Indeed, to a certain extent electronic editions with links to other electronic sites require frequent updating, for links often change. Many a well-engineered edition has fallen into disrepair simply because its creators became busy with something else. We budget for maintenance of books in libraries but not always for the maintenance of electronic scholarly materials. How long can electronic editions remain useful without significant maintenance, and who will maintain them over time? The TEI guidelines anticipate this dilemma by offering an encoding scheme that is standard and that will endure as delivery platforms change. Nevertheless, humanists will need to continue addressing the significant problem of electronic textual vulnerability; and libraries are increasingly searching for ways to archive and preserve electronic materials.

By moving significant editing and archiving projects into electronic form, we have by no means solved the conundrum of silent editorial shaping of the literary text. Electronic textual scholarship is, perforce, a creature of its time, and with standardization and stabilization we are sure to create ideological effects as yet unknown that may hamper subsequent generations of scholars in the same way that the standardization offered by the new bibliography hampered postmodernist and new-historicist critics in the 1980s and 1990s. Setting aside the more visible forms of ideological intervention represented by site design and organization, hypertext markup languages have rhetorics of their own; they can premap and therefore constrict the ways in which we use electronic editions just as predigital editorial practice did. And, of course, electronic editions can never fully reproduce the material forms that a text has assumed at important points in its predigital history. The most careful photofacsimile may not distinguish adequately between pen strokes and age spotting on a manuscript and cannot give users a sense of the heft and feel of a binding. It is as important now as it has ever been for scholars to choose carefully among the array of available editions on the basis of the purposes that we need the edition to serve—which means that we all need to know more than a little about textual scholarship.

NOTE

The author warmly thanks Michael Winship, Warner Barnes, David G. Nicholls, and the anonymous MLA reviewer for their helpful corrections and suggestions.

WORKS CITED AND SUGGESTIONS FOR FURTHER READING

In addition to the works cited and suggested below, these journals are particularly prominent in the field: *Library: The Transactions of the Bibliographical Society* (1889–), *Papers of the Bibliographical Society of America* (1913–), *Studies in Bibliography* (Univ. of Virginia; 1948–), and *Text: An Interdisciplinary Annual of Textual Studies* (Soc. for Textual Scholarship; 1981–).

Altick, Richard D. *The Scholar Adventurers*. 1950. New York: Free, 1966.

Barnes, Warner. *A Bibliography of Elizabeth Barrett Browning*. Austin: U of Texas P, 1967.

Baron, Helen, and Carl Baron, eds. *Sons and Lovers*. By D. H. Lawrence. Cambridge: Cambridge UP, 1992.

Bergmann, Elizabeth Loizeaux, and Neil Fraistat, eds. *Reimagining Textuality: Textual Studies in the Late Age of Print*. Madison: U of Wisconsin P, 2002.

Bornstein, George, ed. *Editorial Theory and Literary Criticism*. U of Michigan P. 17 Feb. 2006 <http://www.press.umich.edu/series.do?id=UM77>.

———, ed. *Representing Modernist Texts: Editing as Interpretation*. Ann Arbor: U of Michigan P, 1991.

Bornstein, George, and Ralph G. Williams, eds. *Palimpsest: Editorial Theory in the Humanities*. Ann Arbor: U of Michigan P, 1993.

Bowers, Fredson. *Bibliography and Textual Criticism*. Oxford: Clarendon, 1964.

———. *Principles of Bibliographical Description*. Princeton: Princeton UP, 1949. New York: Russell, 1962.

———. *Textual and Literary Criticism*. Cambridge: Cambridge UP, 1959.

Brack, O M, Jr., and Warner Barnes, eds. *Bibliography and Textual Criticism: English and American Literature, 1700 to the Present*. Chicago: U of Chicago P, 1969.

Burnard, Lou, Katherine O'Brien O'Keeffe, and John Unsworth, eds. *Electronic Textual Editing*. New York: MLA, 2006.

The Canterbury Tales Project. Humanities Research Inst., U of Sheffield. 2000. 17 Feb. 2006 <http://www.shef.ac.uk/hri/canterbury.htm>.

Chambers, A. B. "Crooked Crosses in Donne and Crashaw." *New Perspectives on the Life and Art of Richard Crashaw*. Ed. John R. Roberts. Columbia: U of Missouri P, 1990. 157–73.

Chartier, Roger. *Forms and Meanings: Texts, Performances, and Audiences from Codex to Computer*. Philadelphia: U of Pennsylvania P, 1995.

———. *The Order of Books: Readers, Authors, and Libraries in Europe between the Fourteenth and Eighteenth Centuries*. Trans. Lydia G. Cochrane. Stanford: Stanford UP, 1994.

Cohen, Philip, ed. *Devils and Angels: Textual Editing and Literary Theory*. Charlottesville: UP of Virginia, 1991.

Collins, John. *The Two Forgers: A Biography of Harry Buxton Forman and Thomas James Wise*. New Castle: Oak Knoll, 1992.

The Complete Writings and Pictures of Dante Gabriel Rossetti. Ed. Jerome J. McGann. Inst. for Advanced Technology in the Humanities, U of Virginia. 17 Feb. 2006 <http://rossettiarchive.org>.

Darnton, Robert. "What Is the History of Books?" *Daedalus* 111 (1982): 65–83. Rpt. in *The Kiss of Lamourette*. New York: Norton, 1990. 107–35.

Eaves, Morris. " 'Why Don't They Leave It Alone?': Speculations on the Authority of the Audience in Editorial Theory." Ezell and O'Brien O'Keeffe 85–99.

Eisenstein, Elizabeth L. *The Printing Press as an Agent of Change*. 2 vols. Cambridge: Cambridge UP, 1979.

Ezell, Margaret J. M., and Katherine O'Brien O'Keeffe, eds. *Cultural Artifacts and the Production of Meaning: The Page, the Image, and the Body*. Ann Arbor: U of Michigan P, 1994.

Finneran, Richard J., ed. *The Literary Text in the Digital Age*. Ann Arbor: U of Michigan P. 1996.

Foucault, Michel. "What Is an Author?" 1969. Trans. Josué V. Harari. *Textual Strategies: Perspectives in Poststructuralist Criticism*. Ed. Harari. Ithaca: Cornell UP, 1979. 141–60.

Gabler, Hans Walter, ed. *Ulysses: A Critical and Synoptic Edition*. By James Joyce. 3 vols. New York: Garland, 1984.

Gabler, Hans Walter, George Bornstein, and Gillian Borland Pierce, eds. *Contemporary German Editorial Theory*. Ann Arbor: U of Michigan P, 1995.

Gaskell, Philip. *From Writer to Reader: Studies in Editorial Method*. Oxford: Clarendon, 1978.

———. *A New Introduction to Bibliography*. New York: Oxford UP, 1972.

Goldberg, Jonathan, ed. *Queering the Renaissance*. Durham: Duke UP, 1994.

Grafton, Anthony. *Forgers and Critics: Creativity and Duplicity in Western Scholarship*. Princeton: Princeton UP, 1990.

Greetham, D. C. *Scholarly Editing: A Guide to Research*. New York: MLA, 1995.

———. "Textual Scholarship." *Introduction to Scholarship in Modern Languages and Literatures*. Ed. Joseph Gibaldi. New York: MLA, 1992. 103–37.

———. *Textual Scholarship: An Introduction*. New York: Garland, 1992.

Greg, W. W. "The Rationale of Copy-Text." *Studies in Bibliography* 3 (1950–51): 19–36. Brack and Barnes 41–58.

Grésillon, Almuth. *Éléments de critique génétique: Lire les manuscrits modernes*. Paris: PUF, 1994.

Grierson, Herbert J. C., ed. *The Poems of John Donne*. 2 vols. Oxford: Clarendon, 1912.

Guidelines for Editors of Scholarly Editions. MLA. 15 Nov. 2005. 17 Feb. 2006 <http://www.mla.org/cse_guidelines>.

Harkness, Bruce. "Bibliography and the Novelistic Fallacy." Brack and Barnes 23–40.

Holladay, Joan A. *Illuminating the Epic: The Kassel Willehalm Codex and the Landgraves of Hesse in the Early Fourteenth Century.* Seattle: U of Washington P, 1996.

Jed, Stephanie H. *Chaste Thinking: The Rape of Lucretia and the Birth of Humanism.* Bloomington: Indiana UP, 1989.

Kidd, John. "The Scandal of *Ulysses.*" *New York Review of Books* 30 June, 1988: 32–39.

Kline, Mary-Jo. *A Guide to Documentary Editing.* 2nd ed. Baltimore: Johns Hopkins UP, 1998.

Lee, Hermione. "Orlando and Her Biographer." *Times Literary Supplement* 18 Mar. 1994: 5–6.

Marcus, Leah S. "The Two Texts of *Othello* and Early Modern Constructions of Race." *Textual Performances: The Modern Reproduction of Shakespeare's Drama.* Ed. Lukas Erne and Margaret Jane Kidnie. Cambridge: Cambridge UP, 2004. 21–36.

———. *Unediting the Renaissance: Shakespeare, Marlowe, Milton.* London: Routledge, 1996.

Martin, Henri-Jean, Roger Chartier, and Jean-Pierre Vivet, eds. *Histoire de l'édition française.* 4 vols. Paris: Promodis, 1982.

Masten, Jeffrey. *Textual Intercourse: Collaboration, Authorship, and Sexualities in Renaissance Drama.* Cambridge: Cambridge UP, 1997.

McGann, Jerome J. *The Beauty of Inflections: Literary Investigations in Historical Method and Theory.* Oxford: Clarendon, 1988.

———. *A Critique of Modern Textual Criticism.* Chicago: U of Chicago P, 1983.

———. *Radiant Textuality: Literature after the World Wide Web.* New York: Palgrave, 2001.

———. "*Ulysses* as Postmodern Text: The Gabler Edition." *Criticism* 27 (1985): 283–305.

McKenzie, D. F. *Bibliography and the Sociology of the Text: The Panizzi Lectures 1985.* London: British Lib., 1986.

McKenzie, D. F., David McKitterick, and I. R. Willison, eds. *The Cambridge History of the Book in Britain.* 7 vols. Cambridge: Cambridge UP, 2000– .

McKerrow, Ronald B., and David McKitterick. *An Introduction to Bibliography for Literary Students.* Winchester: Oak Knoll, 1995.

McLeod, Randall, ed. *Crisis in Editing: Texts of the English Renaissance.* New York: AMS, 1994.

Melville, Herman. *Mardi: And a Voyage Thither.* Ed. Harrison Hayford, Hershel Parker, and G. Thomas Tanselle. Evanston: Northwestern UP, 1970.

Mumford, Lewis. "Emerson behind Barbed Wire." *New York Review of Books* 18 Jan. 1968: 3–5.

The Perseus Digital Library. Ed. Gregory Crane. Dept. of the Classics, Tufts U. 17 Feb. 2006 <http://www.perseus.tufts.edu/>.

Reiman, Donald H. "'Versioning': The Presentation of Multiple Texts." *Romantic Texts and Contexts.* Columbia: U of Missouri P, 1987. 167–80.

Rosencrantz and Guildenstern Are Dead. Dir. Tom Stoppard. Brandenberg, 1990.

Shakespeare Electronic Archive. Ed. Peter Donaldson. MIT. 17 Feb. 2006 <http://shea.mit.edu>.

Shillingsburg, Peter. *Scholarly Editing in the Computer Age: Theory and Practice.* 3rd ed. Ann Arbor: U of Michigan P, 1996.

Shulevitz, Judith. "Get Me Rewrite." *New York Times Book Review* 6 Apr. 2003: 31.

Standard Generalized Markup Language (SGML). Cover Pages: Online Resource for Markup Language Technologies. Ed. Robin Cover. 12 July 2002. 17 Feb. 2006 <http://xml.coverpages.org/sgml.html>.

Stillinger, Jack. *Multiple Authorship and the Myth of the Author in Criticism and Textual Theory.* New York: Oxford UP, 1991.

Tanselle, G. Thomas. *A Rationale of Textual Criticism.* Philadelphia: U of Pennsylvania P, 1989.

———. *Selected Studies in Bibliography.* Charlottesville: UP of Virginia, 1979.

Targoff, Ramie. *Common Prayer: The Language of Public Devotion in Early Modern England.* Chicago: U of Chicago P, 2001.

Taylor, Gary, and Michael Warren, ed. *The Division of the Kingdoms: Shakespeare's Two Versions of* King Lear. Oxford: Clarendon, 1983.

TEI: Yesterday's Information Tomorrow. TEI: The Text Encoding Initiative. 18 Feb. 2006 <http://www.tei-c.org/>.

Thomas, John B., III. "Tales from the Vault: Our *Mayflower* Bible." *Common-Place* 1.3 (2001). 18 Feb. 2006 <http://www.historycooperative.org/journals/cp/vol-01/no-03/tales/>.

Todd, William B., ed. *Thomas J. Wise: Centenary Studies.* Austin: U of Texas P, 1959.

Urkowitz, Steven. *Shakespeare's Revision of* King Lear. Princeton: Princeton UP, 1980.

Wells, Stanley, and Gary Taylor, eds. *William Shakespeare: A Textual Companion.* Oxford: Clarendon, 1987.

———. *William Shakespeare: The Complete Works.* Oxford: Clarendon, 1986.

The William Blake Archive. Ed. Morris Eaves, Robert N. Essick, and Joseph Viscomi. Inst. for Advanced Technology in the Humanities. U of Virginia. 1996–2006. 17 Feb. 2006 <http://www.blakearchive.org/main.html>.

Wilson, Edmund. "The Fruits of the MLA: I. 'Their Wedding Journey,'" *New York Review of Books* 26 Sept. 1968: 7–10.

Wise, Thomas J. *A Bibliography of the Writings in Prose and Verse of Elizabeth Barrett Browning.* London: Clay, 1918.

Women Writers Online. Brown U. 17 Feb. 2006 <http://www.wwp.brown.edu/texts/wwoentry.html>.

Women Writers Project. Brown U. 17 Feb. 2006 <http://www.wwp.brown.edu/>.

⁓ Interpretation

JEROME McGANN

In *The Need for Roots*, Simone Weil criticizes historical thinking and its search for documentary foundations. "There are holes in documents," she points out, so that when we read documents, we want to ensure that "unfounded hypotheses be present to the mind." Reading documents requires

> reading between the lines, to transport oneself fully, with complete self-forgetfulness, into the events evoked there. . . . The so-called historical mind does not pass through the paper to flesh and blood; it consists of a subordination of thought to the document. (283–84)

I begin with this passage from Weil for three reasons. First, I want to set my introduction to interpretation in a serious context. Weil always felt reading to be, like all forms of human action, a spiritual emergency. Second, her critique of historicist method involves an insistence on the reader's share in any textual engagement. This insistence became such a critical commonplace during the past half century, however, that it was far more often followed in the letter than in the spirit. Readings that "pass through the paper to flesh and blood" are rare events—readings like, for instance, Weil's reading of *The Iliad*, Lautréamont's of gothic fiction, or Kathy Acker's outrageous travesty of *The Scarlet Letter* and other

classic nineteenth-century novels. The reading that Weil proposes involves what she sees as a transport and self-extinction, a passage to a human encounter "that is not me in any sense," as D. H. Lawrence once put the matter in his poem "Manifesto" (pt. 6, line 20).

That way of reading leads me to my third reason for beginning with this passage from Weil. Let me make my point by way of Joan Dargan's "readerly" interpretation of the Weil passage: "it is the reader who determines where to travel in the space between the lines, which details are significant, and where their complete meaning lies. For Weil, the discernment of the reader takes precedence over the dictates of the document" (6). That view of Weil's reading proposal seems to me inadequate in several important respects. The idea that an active reader can by determined effort discover a document's significant details and track them to their complete meaning is not just mistaken, it is a mistaken reading of Weil. In the first place, the illusory concept of a "complete meaning" was utterly foreign to Weil's thinking. Furthermore, when Weil speaks of the holes in documents, her words are figural, not literal. Do we think she is speaking of holes in paper or vellum? No, she is reading the readers of documents, and her critique applies as much to presentist historians, who settle on the authority of a current reader, as it does to traditional historicists, who think the documents speak for themselves as incarnations of a known past. But the documents do not contain possessable meanings; they are full of *wholes*, they leak with meaning. The past is no more given or unified than the present (or the future). Documents offer the possibility—as endless as living—of an encounter with the human unknown.

> **To find flesh and blood is the ultimate purpose of reading and its sophisticated partner, interpretation.**

To find flesh and blood is the ultimate purpose of reading and its sophisticated partner, interpretation. To achieve that engagement, it helps, I believe, to begin with Weil and her documents rather than with that immaterial reading matter called texts. For unlike texts, documents in fact do often have real holes in them, or are otherwise marked by marks of their actual historical passage. The physical object—the specific manuscript, the particular edition or printed object we read (like this very object you are reading now)—is coded and scored with human activity. An awareness of this fact is the premise for interpreting material culture, and the awareness is particularly imperative for literary interpretation, where linguistic "message" regularly invisibilizes the codependent and equally meaningful "medium" that codes all messages.

The power of D. F. McKenzie's "sociology of texts" project rests in the thoroughness of his understanding of "the primacy of the physical artifact (and the evidence it bears of its own making)" (*Making Meaning* 271). As the literary work passes on through time and other hands, to other readers besides ourselves, it bears along with and as itself the gathered history of all its engagements. Sometimes some of these codes appear explicitly in the documents—as inscriptions, for instance, or marginalia, or bookplates or labels or other physical transformations, like book damage or ornamental additions. Secret and multiplying histories lie concealed in those tracings. Often, perhaps even more often, those multiplying histories have to be pursued in other, less direct ways: who were the readers of the book, when was it read, when wasn't it read,

where is/was it located, how was it produced, why and how has it survived?

Those flesh-and-blood questions need flesh-and-blood answers. Why? Because interpretation is a social act—a specific deed of critical reflection made in a concert of related moves and frames of reference (social, political, institutional) that constitute the present as an interpreted inheritance from a past that has been fashioned by other interpreting agents. All these multiple agencies leave the documents marked with their diverse intentions and purposes, many of which were unapparent even to those who executed those purposes. Those three governing temporalities (past, present, future) are subject to an unlimited number of redeterminations, and every interpretational move is an instance of such a redetermination (itself subject to interpretation within the ancient idea of the hermeneutic circle, reinvigorated more recently by Hans-Georg Gadamer and Martin Heidegger and their legacy [Coltman]). Themselves embedded in the circle (at "an inner standing point," as Dante Gabriel Rossetti called it ["Stealthy School" 337]), the interpreting agents can be at most partially aware of this impinging and dynamic concert of reflection. The ideal interpreting agent can know the presence of the whole but never the sum of the parts.

PERFORMATIVE INTERPRETATION

In that general field of dynamic reflection we may usefully distinguish two kinds of interpretive action: a mode oriented to performative models, of which translation and parody are perhaps the master types, and a mode oriented to scholarship, which is our customary exemplar of interpretation. Although this essay focuses on scholarly interpretive models, I want to give close attention to performative models for a couple of important reasons.

Scholarly models regularly operate under a horizon of truth and the idea of its accessibility.

This truth may be either normative (like Aristotle's rules [Halliwell]) or positive (the scientific method for determining facts) or some combination of both. The most advanced forms of interpretive scholarship—the production of scholarly editions—exhibit this hankering for truth in their common attachment to the idea of what has been called the definitive edition: the edition that, if properly done, would obviate the need for further scholarly editions. When we speak of the meaning of a work (*the* meaning!), we are invoking the same fundamental ideological commitment. The spell of that (literally charming) ideal gets broken when one realizes (a) that scholarship is itself a historical performance executed in the framework of a certain limited (and limiting) set of protocols and (b) that the scholar's interpretive intervention alters the object of interpretation and the fields that organize those objects. Scholarship, like science, is committed basically not to truth but to rigor (as to method), thoroughness (as to empirical evidence), and accuracy (in the treatment of its facts and data).

Scholarship and interpretation, therefore, are too narrowly conceived when they are imagined as being about something—as one might say that this essay is about interpretation or that the essay over there is about *Don Juan*. Rather, scholarship and interpretation are procedures that *do something about something*. The significance of that fact may become more clear if we shift our attention briefly to performative modes of interpretation per se.

In the nineteenth century, the appreciation and study of literature began as recitation. Readers (like the famous McGuffey series of schoolbooks) compiled prose and poem texts for training people in oral performance and articulation. This ancient interpretive model lost nearly all its authority during the last century, an unfortunate cultural lapse (we can now see). More rationalist procedures, thematically focused, worked to unhinge us from the physique of the literary experience that comes through so much more clearly in performative recitation.

Literary works can be, have been, performed in a variety of interpretive ways. "Did you ever read one of her Poems backwards . . . ? A something overtakes the Mind" (Johnson 3: 916; prose fragment 30). That is Emily Dickinson's remarkable proposal for a recitation-based method of radical reinterpretation. William Morris's Kelmscott Press editions—for example, of Geoffrey Chaucer, John Keats, Rossetti, and of his own works, perhaps especially *The Earthly Paradise*—are acts of reinterpretation executed as bibliographic performances. Johanna Drucker's analysis of the different types of white space that function on a single page of the Kelmscott Chaucer—she distinguishes some twenty kinds—is a dramatic demonstration of the critical-interpretive potentials of bibliographic coding.

Such work bears a close functional resemblance to the interpretive performance of linguistic translation. In each case a target work is recast into another medium. If literary works were fundamentally data and information corpora, then translation—bibliographic or linguistic—would aspire to as much literal transparency as possible. This transparency is the working assumption guiding the practice of most information-technology approaches to literary works, such as TEI (the Text Encoding Initiative). But literary works covet a precision of heteronomy: they are machines that aspire to the multiplication of particular meaning, and adequate translations are obliged to reflect that quality.

One of the great acts of English language translation, Sir Thomas Urquhart's 1653 *The Works of Mr. Francis Rabelais*, perfectly illustrates what is called for. Rabelais is "now faithfully translated into English," we are informed on Urquhart's title page. But to be faithful in such a case is not to be literal, and if one compares Urquhart's work with his Rabelais original, one is struck by the astonishing freedom of his translation considered in a literal sense. Indeed, Urquhart's work often resembles a jazz performance in the riffs it plays off the Rabelaisian riffs it is responding to. Algernon Swinburne's translations of the "Dies Irae" or of François Villon

(409, 171), like Rossetti's translation of Dante's *Vita Nuova* (in Rossetti, *Early Italian Poets*), are great because they exhibit the quality of original works. All are also critical and interpretive acts—as we see, for example, in T. S. Eliot's recoil from Rossetti's work, which approaches Dante in a spirit utterly inimical to Eliot's twentieth-century Anglo-Catholicism.

Like Swinburne, Rossetti was well aware of the critical function his work was undertaking: "a translation," he observes in his introduction to his book of translations *The Early Italian Poets*, "involving as it does the necessity of settling many points [of interpretation] without discussion . . . , remains perhaps the most direct form of commentary" (*Dante Gabriel Rossetti* 239). We would add only that bibliographic design and literary recitation are equally direct forms of commentary, as are pastiche, hoax, and parody. Brilliant examples of the critical use of such forms are plentiful from Edgar Allan Poe and Oscar Wilde through Alfred Jarry and Jorge Luis Borges. So far as scholarly interpretation is concerned, we have good recent examples of the critical potential of such models. The vigorous discussion that followed the hoax essay published in 1996 by Alan Sokal in *Social Text* is a succinct illustration of the critical power of the hoax form ("Transgressing"; see also Sokal, "What the *Social Text* Affair"), as the two books of Pooh parodies issued by Frederick Crews (in 1963 and 2001) illustrate the critical power of parody.

Those kinds of critical acts are humane and unnatural, which is why they are so common in the humanities and so rare in the objective sciences, where the focus is trained on what is normative and natural (natural: that is to say, nonhuman, including the nonhuman aspects of human being). Acts of interpretation get invested with ludic elements in order to raise their level of self-critical awareness, on one hand, and on the other to dramatize the fact that meanings are made and made for particular reasons. Philology's nineteenth-century turn to science for procedural models often obscures the subjectivity that is essential for literary and aesthetic interpretation. In science per se, objective norms are functional requirements. They are not in the arena of aesthetic inquiry. For us, even aggressively normative modes of interpretation—let us say, for instance, Dr. Samuel Johnson's or Laura Riding's—are proposed and argued and therefore always in question and at issue, Riding's explicitly so (*Anarchism* and *Progress*). Johnson would have thought William Blake's interpretation of John Milton and *Paradise Lost* reprehensible, perhaps even mad, and certainly not true. We may read Johnson with a similar critical freedom and construct (let us say) a Pooh parody of him. That could be a useful interpretive act. It could not be done well, however, without bringing into play a fair amount of scholarly expertise, both procedural and informational. You can't parody what you haven't closely studied.

SCHOLARLY INTERPRETATION

We commonly associate the interpretation of literature and culture with institutional apparatuses that develop and maintain certain rules and standards—the Church, the university and its educational affiliates, professional organizations that monitor the literary law (that is to say, the arts and procedures for the accurate preservation of the works of culture). These social formations comprise what Stanley Fish called "interpretive communities." Subcommunities are continually emerging and further subdividing, within those larger "ideological apparatuses," as they were famously named by Louis Althusser. The evolution of psychoanalytic or historicist studies—their rich, not to say wild, proliferation of distinct microgroups—perfectly illustrates the special character of interpretive communities in the twentieth century.

In those institutional orbits—where this book, I, and you are located—a host of interpretational activities are sanctioned and executed, and in recent years they have proliferated at a rate that many find alarming. These procedures are most familiar when they coalesce under specialized headings that stand for methods of reading and critical exegesis: New Criticism, Hermeneutics (in various forms), Historicism (again, in various forms), Theory (which develops in many metatheoretical and interpretive subspecies like Feminist, Narrative, Queer, Psychoanalytic, etc.), Narratology, Cognitive Poetics, Marxist Criticism, Literary Pragmatics, and so forth. Observed in a professional frame of reference like the one we inhabit, these activities fairly represent the varieties of current interpretational experience, the phenomena of interpretation.

In the heavens of interpretation are many mansions. Because all those superstructures are "of the earth, earthy" (1 Cor. 15.47), we pursue their readerly devotions on the common ground they share with one another: the sociohistorical environment that licenses and shapes their interpretive possibilities.

So the scholar urges his friend the reader to begin the quest of interpretation "in the foul rag-and-bone shop of the heart" (129). William Butler Yeats's famous line reminds us that all literature's ladders start with the materials, means, and modes of textual production. If you are after flesh and blood in interpretation, if you mean to be serious, you begin with what the scholar calls the history of a work's production on one hand and the history of a work's reception on the other. Those two historical strands together compose the double helix from which the many forms of culture develop. Acts of interpretation, themselves coded by this double helix, typically select a particular aspect or view of our cultural inheritance for investigation. Whatever our governing interpretive specialization, we necessarily pursue our studies under the horizon of this double and codependent set of sociohistorical determinants. The works we examine have all been shaped by that double helix, and so have all our critical reflections on them.

One caveat should be kept in mind. Certain interpreters focus their work on such technical issues—metrical and prosodic studies, for instance, or analytic and descriptive bibliography—that they often do not consider the foundational

interpretive frames of reference and agencies for the issues. Interpretation always negotiates a compromise between the demands of procedural rigor and the call for critical reflection. These kinds of technical studies remind us that an engineer and a theologian live and work inside even the most nuanced reflexive interpreter—Roland Barthes (*Critical Essays* and *S/Z*), say, or Umberto Eco. There is a foul rag-and-bone shop of the brain too, after all. To the degree that an interpretive procedure makes an ideological engagement with its subject, however, to that degree it will be forced to engage with the codependent pair of historical determinants (production history and reception history) and to reflect critically on its own place in those histories.

Given those general considerations, we can construct a model for works of cultural interpretation that would be organized like the model we have for the genetic code. It too is a double helix with one strand composed of a work's production history and the other of its reception history. From this model we may elaborate—as in the example given just below—an analytic outline of interpretation's essential subjects and topics. The specific subjects and topics placed under each categorical heading call us to clarify their circumstantial character—that is, they call us to make a sociohistorical analysis. These specific analyses, interrelated, constitute an analytic presentation of the category, and the adequacy of any interpretive act in that category will be a function of the range of discourse materials that are brought out for critical examination.

An interpretive investigation ranged under categories A and B constitutes a theoretically finished sociohistorical program. Such a program gains a properly critical character when the material ranged under category C gets incorporated into the analysis.

> **Interpretation always negotiates a compromise between the demands of procedural rigor and the call for critical reflection.**

A. The Originary Discursive Moment

1. Author
2. Other persons, groups, and agents in-

vested in the initial process of cultural production

3. The institutional frameworks of cultural production (ideological and material)
4. The material and cultural inheritances that can be shown to shape, positively or otherwise, these three factors
5. The temporal phases that supply a coherent expository organization for analyzing each of those four factors

B. Secondary Moments of Discursive Production and Reproduction (Individual and Related Sequences)

Discursive fields (or any portion of those fields) are dynamic and pass through processes of transformation engineered by the agencies that act in and on those fields. The fields are what Humberto Maturana and Francesco Varela have called autopoietic systems—that is, systems devoted to self-maintenance through processes of self-transformation. So the five dimensions composing the originary discursive moment all undergo a continual process of dynamic transformation and reconstruction. An author for example, will get re-viewed and reshaped over time by different people operating in the framework, material as well as ideological, of different classes, institutions, and groups. The number of Byron biographies illustrates the point, as it also shows that different cultural materials exert different levels of influence. Those reconstructive agencies themselves have to be studied and analyzed in terms of the five dimensions that characterize the originary discursive moment.

Discourse fields comprise specifiable works that emerge in certain concrete and specific forms along a series of equally concrete and specific avenues. Specifying the dynamic interplay of the field elements constitutes the interpretational event. In an interpretive move, one can take as one's object of interest either some work or set of works in the field or the discourse field itself (or some part or aspect of it). Veronica Forrest-Thomson's readings of various poems from Shakespeare to the present exemplify a move of the first kind; Friedrich Kittler's Foucauldian work is a move of the second kind.

The example of documentary transmission illustrates the general dynamical character of discourse fields. Literary documents bear in themselves the evidence of their own making, as McKenzie and others have shown, and those evidentiary marks solicit an interpretation of their meaning and significance. Historical patterns are literalized in the interpretation of a transmission history's documentary record.

Categories A and B are to be studied under interpretation's milder (and preliminary) rubric: What does this mean? Value judgments—political, ethical, aesthetic—remain after such a question is posed. Indeed, the question of the meaning of some feature of a discursive field must itself be ready for judgment, for the significance of an interpreter's questions cannot be taken for granted.

C. The Immediate Moment of Interpretation

The immediate moment of interpretation proposes an analysis of the interpreter's critical purposes. This analysis is probably the most demanding of all interpretive tasks, since it involves a critical reflection on acts of interpretation as they are in the process of development.

This moment appears as a specific interpretive action that may get located in a particular essay or book, imaginative or otherwise, or in a particular constellation of such works. What is important to realize is that interpreters may approach their subject matter critically (categories A and B) without ever subjecting their critical work to interpretive reflection. The heuristic model for such an event (i.e., for reflection only at levels A and B) would be, for example, the production of a scholarly edition by a technically skilled editor as a set task or the production of an interpretive essay or book from a standpoint assumed to be objective or in some fashion privileged with enlightenment. Paul de Man's importance in the recent history of literary studies was a function of his acute critical sympathy with the blindness that accompanies the insight of most critical and interpretive acts.

Models for an interpretive action that positively seeks to approach a task from an inner standpoint—that is, models that solicit level C—

would be Thucydides's *History of the Peloponnesian War* or Leon Trotsky's *History of the Russian Revolution*. Models from current literary studies would be Susan Howe's *My Emily Dickinson* or Charles Bernstein's *My Way*, in particular his remarkable essay "The Revenge of the Poet-Critic; or, The Parts Are Greater than the Sum of the Whole."

Works that exhibit a high degree of expertise in this third world of interpretation will almost inevitably assume a controversial position. Such Such works will also exhibit, probably by necessity, more or less serious deficiencies in their interpretive grasp of their given subjects (categories A and B). This interpretive *felix culpa* follows from the decision to lay the act of interpretation open to question as the act is going on. Such interpretations succeed by exposing their own limits.

Professional interpretive essays customarily organize their evidence in order to make a case for what they advance. They wait on other acts of interpretation for quality control. To that extent, such works can never seriously address questions of value: Is this interpretive understanding good or bad, is it right or wrong, and why does one arrive at such judgments?

INTERPRETATION BY INDIRECTION

Weil regarded questions of value as essential, and they haunt every interpretive act, whether the act deliberately seeks to raise them or not. They are questions that can only be addressed (and readdressed), for they are open questions; they do not have answers. The touchstone of critical and interpretive adequacy, then, follows from this question: How much has the subject or problem been opened out by the critic's intervention?

Such a question (it too is open) can't be usefully engaged if the scholar or critic does not begin with a clear understanding that every interpretation is an abstract reduction drawn out of

Every interpretation is an abstract reduction drawn out of the original work or object of attention.

the original work or object of attention. Scholars murder to dissect when their interpretations rather than the works they are seeking out come to occupy the center of interest. Every critical performance is in this sense a deformance— but a useful deformance, if self-consciously undertaken.

The great Italian scholar Galvano Della Volpe developed a lucid explanation of how this critical procedure functions. He gives a practical demonstration of his ideas in his *Critique of Taste* (1960), which develops what he calls a realist view of interpretation. Because Della Volpe's ideas were shaped in a period dominated by the ideas of New Critics like Cleanth Brooks, his interpretive demonstrations typically focus on a single work. As is very clear even from René Wellek and Austin Warren's influential handbook of New Critical theory and method, Della Volpe's procedures are applicable to any kind of discursive formation, from the localized poem or story up to complex discourse fields like those studied by Michel Foucault (*Madness* and "Order") and his many followers.

Like Dante and in contrast to, say, Samuel Coleridge or Friedrich von Schlegel, Della Volpe sees imaginative literature as a type of discourse whose rationality—*ragionamento*—consists in its exploitation of the polysemous dimensions of language, whose structures are no more (and no less) difficult or even mysterious than processes of logical deduction and induction. For Della Volpe, intelligibility is as much a feature of poiesis as of scientia.

Interpretation is the application of scientia to poiesis or the effort to elucidate one discourse form in terms of another. Furthermore, the effort is directed not toward establishing general rules or laws but toward explaining a unitary, indeed a unique, phenomenon. A doubled gap thus emerges through the interpretive process itself, and it is the necessary presence of this gap that shapes Della Volpe's critical thought. We may usefully recall here that when poets and artists use imaginative forms to interpret other such forms, they pay homage to this gap by throwing it into relief. Rossetti's famous sonnets for pictures, like all such works, from those of Guido Cavalcanti to those of John Ashbery, do not so much translate the originals as construct imaginative paraphrases. Rossetti's theory of translation, as we see in *The Early Italian Poets* (1861), follows a similarly paraphrastic procedure.

Della Volpe's theory of interpretation runs along the same intellectual salient. When he argues that "critical paraphrase" should ground interpretive method, he is consciously installing a non-Hegelian form of dialectical criticism. In place of "a *circular* movement of negation and conservation of an original meta-historical unity of opposites," Della Volpe offers "a dialectic of expressive facts"—in his case, the facts of the discrete poem and its discrete paraphrase—in which "neither of the elements of the relation can be reduced absolutely to the other . . . for . . . they . . . circulate only *relatively* within each other, in the *diversified unity of an historical movement*" (200). Interpretation for Della Volpe, whatever its pretensions, always displays a gap between the work being examined and the student. But this gap does not represent a failure of criticism or even a mysticism of poiesis. It locates the source and end and test of the art being examined. Della Volpe calls the gap a "quid," which comes into play as soon as the critic develops some "philosophical or sociological or historical equivalent of the poetic text," that is to say, the "paraphrase . . . of the poetic thought or . . . content." Because this paraphrase will necessarily constitute "a reduction" of the original, "a comparison will necessarily be instituted between this paraphrase and the poetic thought or 'content' which it paraphrases" (193).

Critical interpretation develops out of an initial moment of the originary work's "degradation" through "uncritical paraphrase":

for in the case of the poetic, polysemic text, paraphrase—the *regression* to current linguistic use . . . constitutes the premise of an internal *progression* of thought . . . , an internal variation and development of meanings, which is disclosed . . . in

a . . . philological comparison . . . of the paraphrase with that which is paraphrased.   (133)

Interpretation, then, is a constellation of paraphrases that evolve dialectically from an uncritical to a critical moment, from "regression" to "progression." The interpretive constellation develops as the "uncritical" features of each critical turn get exposed—as new turns are taken, as the paraphrase is successively rephrased. One moves from degradation to degradation, from deformance to deformance. Thus paraphrastics becomes "the *beginning* and *end* of a whole process" of comparative explorations that get executed across the quid or gap that a process of interpretation brings into being. Again, the process is open-ended not because the poem itself possesses some mysterious, inexhaustible meaning but because its originary semiotic determinations must repeatedly be discovered in the historical space defined by the Della Volpian quid, where distantiation licenses "the method . . . of experimental analysis" (199).

Della Volpe carefully separates his theory of interpretation from the dialectics we associate with Hegel and especially Heidegger. The latter involves a process of thought refinement: through conversation or internal dialogue, we clarify our ideas to ourselves. We come to realize what we didn't know we knew. This kind of reflection traces itself back to the idea of Platonic anamnesis. Della Volpe, by contrast, follows an Aristotelian line of thought, a "method . . . of experimental analysis." This method develops a process of non-Hegelian historical reflection. Interpretive moments stand in nonuniform relations with each other so that the interpretation unfolds in fractal patterns of continuity and discontinuity. Besides realizing, perhaps, what we didn't know we knew, we are led to imagine what we never knew.

The deformative examples set forth in the previous section are conceived as types of a Della Volpean experimental analysis. Being a philologist, Della Volpe pursues this kind of analysis through a series of searching historicist paraphrases of the texts he chooses to consider. To attempt a sociohistorical paraphrase is to exper-iment with the poetical work, to subject it to a hypothesis of its meanings. As in any scientific experiment, the engagement with the originary phenomenon inevitably exposes the limits of the hypothesis and returns us to an even more acute sense of what we desire to understand. So it is with Della Volpe's paraphrases. By contrast, our experimental analyses place primary emphasis on the preconceptual elements of text. We do this because social and historical formations seem to us far less determinate, far more open to arbitrary and imaginative construction, than they appear in Della Volpe's Marxist frame of reference.

If we follow Della Volpe's method, then, we feel ourselves closer in spirit to the thought of, say, Blake when he remarks on the difference between the intelligence of art and the intelli-gence of philosophy: "Cunning & Morality are not Poetry but Philosophy the Poet is Indepen-dent & Wicked the Philosopher is Dependent & Good" (634). Our deformations do not flee from the question, or the generation, of meaning. Rather, they try to demonstrate—the way one demonstrates how to make something or do something—what Blake here assertively proposes: that meaning in imaginative work is a secondary phenomenon, a kind of metadatum, what Blake called a form of worship "Dependent" on some primary poetical tale. This point of view explains why, in our deformative maneuvers, in-terpretation represents a thought experiment we play with the primary materials. In the experi-ment of interpretation, meaning is initially im-portant as a catalyst in the investigative action. When the experiment has (for the nonce) fin-ished, meaning reappears in a new form, as the residues left behind for study and analysis. Meanings emerge then not as explanations of the poem but as evidence for judging the effective-ness of the experiment we undertook.

One could do worse than to recall, even in this special aesthetic frame of reference, Karl Marx's last thesis on Ludwig Feuerbach. Only philosophers try to understand art. The point is to change it. (Editorial efforts to preserve our cul-tural inheritance are themselves types, perhaps

arche-types, of the changes we make when we try to preserve that inheritance.) Our actions on these works, our deformations, help us under-stand our thinking about them. To essay a more direct application of interpretation to imagina-tive work runs the risk of suggesting that inter-pretation can be adequate to poiesis. It cannot; it can only run a thematic experiment with the work, enlightening it by inadequacy and indi-rection. Like the artworks it explores, interpre-tation is what Ford Madox Ford called "a game that must be lost" (83).

In a hermeneutic age like our own, illusions about the sufficiency of interpretative meaning before the work of art are especially strong. At such a historical moment, one might rather look for interpretations that flaunt their subjectivity and arbitrariness, interpretations that increase their value by offering themselves at a clear discount.

To deliberately accept the inevitable failure of interpretive adequacy is to work toward discov-ering new interpretive virtues, somewhat as Lyn Hejinian claims that the supposed "inadequacy" of language "is merely a disguise for other vir-tues" (278). Interpretive works that parody or ironize themselves are especially useful—works like Jacques Derrida's *The Post Card* or Laura Rid-ing's remarkable *Anarchism Is Not Enough*. Rid-ing's attitude toward the process of critical think-ing is helpful:

> our minds are still moving, and *backward* as well
> as *forward*; the nearest we get to truth at any given
> moment is, perhaps, only an idea—a dash of truth
> somewhat flavouring the indeterminate substance
> of our minds.   (*Progress* 10)

This thought calls for a critical method intent on baring its own devices. We take it seriously be-cause it makes sure that we do not take it too seriously. Examples of such critical approaches are legion: we just need to remember to look for them and, perhaps, how to look for them.

NOTE

This essay, commissioned by the MLA for this volume, has appeared, in slightly different form, in the author's *The Scholar's Art: Literary Studies in a Managed World*

(Chicago: U of Chicago P, 2006) as the chapter "Interpretation as a Game That Must Be Lost" (135–47), © 2006 by The University of Chicago. All rights reserved.

WORKS CITED AND SUGGESTIONS FOR FURTHER READING

Acker, Kathy. *Blood and Guts in High School*. New York: Grove, 1978.

Althusser, Louis. "Ideology and Ideological State Apparatuses." *"Lenin and Philosophy" and Other Essays*. Trans. Ben Brewster. London: New Left, 1971. 129–86. 19 June 2006 <http://ptb.sunhost.be/marx2mao/Other/LPOE70ii.html#s5>.

Barber, Stephen L., and David L. Clark, eds. *Regarding Sedgwick: Essays on Queer Culture and Critical Theory*. New York: Routledge, 2002.

Barthes, Roland. *Critical Essays*. Trans. Richard Howard. Evanston: Northwestern UP, 1972.

———. *S/Z*. Trans. Richard Howard. New York: Hill, 1975.

Bennett, Tony. *Formalism and Marxism*. London: Methuen, 1979.

Bernstein, Charles. *My Way: Speeches and Poems*. Chicago: U of Chicago P, 1999.

Bible: King James Version. Humanities Text Initiative. U of Michigan. 18 Feb. 1997. 22 Feb. 2006 <http://www.hti.umich.edu/k/kjv/>.

Blake, William. *The Complete Poetry and Prose*. Ed. David V. Erdman. Rev. ed. Berkeley: U of California P, 1988.

Bleicher, Josef. *Contemporary Hermeneutics: Hermeneutics as Method, Philosophy, and Critique*. London: Routledge, 1980.

Bloom, Harold, et al. *Deconstruction and Criticism*. London: Routledge, 1979.

Brooks, Cleanth. *The Well-Wrought Urn*. New York: Harcourt, 1947.

Bruns, Gerald. *Hermeneutics Ancient and Modern*. New Haven: Yale UP, 1992.

Cohen, Philip, ed. *Texts and Textuality: Textual Instability, Theory, and Interpretation*. New York: Garland, 1997.

Coltman, Rod. *The Language of Hermeneutics: Gadamer and Heidegger in Dialogue*. Albany: State U of New York P, 1998.

Crews, Frederick. *The Pooh Perplex: A Freshman Casebook*. New York: Dutton, 1963.

———. *Postmodern Pooh*. New York: North Point, 2001.

Dargan, Joan. *Simone Weil: Thinking Poetically*. Albany: State U of New York P, 1999.

Della Volpe, Galvano. *Critique of Taste*. Trans. Michael Caesar. London: New Left, 1978.

de Man, Paul. *Blindness and Insight: Essays in the Rhetoric of Contemporary Criticism*. New York: Oxford UP, 1971.

Derrida, Jacques. *The Post Card: From Socrates to Freud and Beyond*. Trans. Alan Bass. Chicago: U of Chicago P, 1987.

Drucker, Johanna. "Graphical Readings and Visual Aesthetics of Textuality." *Text* (2003): forthcoming. 19 June 2006 <http://www.people.virginia.edu/~jrd8e/research/01_papers/Graphical%20ReadingsSTS.doc>.

Eco, Umberto. *The Limits of Interpretation*. Bloomington: Indiana UP, 1990.

Fish, Stanley. *Is There a Text in This Class? The Authority of Interpretive Communities*. Cambridge: Harvard UP, 1980.

Ford, Ford Madox. *Rossetti. A Critical Essay on His Art*. Chicago: Rand McNally, 1916.

Forrest-Thomson, Veronica. *Poetic Artifice: A Theory of Twentieth-Century Poetry*. Manchester: Manchester UP, 1978.

Foucault, Michel. *Madness and Civilization: A History of Insanity in the Age of Reason*. New York: Random, 1965.

———. "The Order of Discourse." Trans. Ian McLeod. *Untying the Text: A Poststructuralist Reader*. Ed. Robert Young. London: Routledge, 1982. 48–78.

Genette, Gerard. *Paratexts: Thresholds of Interpretation*. Trans. Jane Lewin. Fwd. Richard Macksey. Cambridge: Cambridge UP, 1997.

Halliwell, Stephen, ed. *Aristotle's Poetics*. Chicago: U of Chicago P, 1998.

Harari, Josue, ed. *Textual Strategies: Perspectives in Poet-Structuralist Criticism*. Ithaca: Cornell UP, 1979.

Heidegger, Martin. *Elucidations of Hölderlin's Poetry*. Introd. and trans. Keith Hoeller. Amherst: Humanity, 2000.

Hejinian, Lyn. "The Rejection of Closure." *Writing/Talks*. Carbondale: Southern Illinois UP, 1985. 270–91.

Hirsch, E. D. *The Aims of Interpretation*. Chicago: U of Chicago P, 1976.

Howe, Susan. *My Emily Dickinson*. Berkeley: North Atlantic, 1985.

Iser, Wolfgang. *The Range of Interpretation*. New York: Columbia UP, 2000.

Johnson, Thomas H., ed. *The Letters of Emily Dickinson*. 3 vols. Cambridge: Harvard UP, 1958.

Kittler, Friedrich A. *Discourse Networks, 1800/1900*. Trans. Michael Metteer. Stanford: Stanford UP, 1990.

Lawrence, D. H. *Complete Poems*. Penguin Twentieth-Century Classics. New ed. New York: Penguin, 1994.

Mailloux, Steven. *Interpretive Conventions: The Reader in the Study of American Fiction*. Ithaca: Cornell UP, 1982.

Marx, Karl. *Theses on Feuerbach*. 1845. Trans. W. Lough. Marx/Engels Internet Archive. 1995. 23 Feb. 2006 <http://www.marxists.org/archive/marx/works/1845/theses/theses.pdf>.

Maturana, Humberto, and Francesco Varela. *Autopoiesis and Cognition*. Dordrecht, Neth.: Reidel, 1980.

McGann, Jerome. *The Beauty of Inflections: Literary Investigations in Historical Method and Theory*. Oxford: Clarendon, 1985.

———. "Herbert Horne's *Diversi Colores* (1891): Incarnating the Religion of Beauty." *New Literary History* 34 (2003): 535–52.

———. *The Textual Condition*. Princeton: Princeton UP, 1991.

McGann, Jerome, and Lisa Samuels. "Deformance and Interpretation." *Radiant Textuality: Literature after the World Wide Web*. By McGann. New York: Palgrave, 2002. 105–36.

McKenzie, D. F. *Bibliography and the Sociology of Texts*. London: British Lib., 1986.

———. *Making Meaning: "Printers of the Mind" and Other Essays*. Amherst: U of Massachusetts P, 2002.

Morris, William. *The Earthly Paradise: A Poem*. 8 vols. Hammersmith, Eng.: Kelmscott, 1896–97.

Nagy, Gregory. *Poetry as Performance*. Cambridge: Cambridge UP, 1996.

Richards, I. A. *Principles of Literary Criticism*. New York: Harcourt, 1928.

Riding, Laura. *Anarchism Is Not Enough*. Ed. Lisa Samuels. Berkeley: U of California P, 2001.

———. *Progress of Stories*. New York: Persea, 1994.

Robbins, Ruth. *Literary Feminisms*. New York: St. Martin's, 2000.

Rossetti, Dante Gabriel. *Dante Gabriel Rossetti: Collected Poetry and Prose*. Ed. Jerome McGann. New Haven: Yale UP, 2000.

———. "The Stealthy School of Criticism." Rossetti, *Dante Gabriel Rossetti* 335–42.

Said, Edward. *The World, the Text, and the Critic*. London: Faber, 1983.

Sokal, Alan D. "Transgressing the Boundaries: Towards a Transformative Hermeneutics of Quantum Gravity." *Social Text* 46–47 (1996): 217–52.

———. "What the *Social Text* Affair Does and Does Not Prove." *A House Built on Sand: Exposing Postmodernist Myths about Science*. Ed. Noretta Koertge. New York: Oxford UP, 1998. 9–22.

Showalter, Elaine. *The New Feminist Criticism: Essays on Women, Literature, and Theory*. London: Virago, 1986.

Suleiman, Susan R., and Inge Crossman, eds. *The Reader in the Text: Essays on Audience and Interpretation*. Princeton: Princeton UP, 1980.

Swinburne, Algernon Charles. *Major Poems and Selected Prose*. Ed. Jerome McGann and Charles Sligh. New Haven: Yale UP, 2004.

Thucydides. *History of the Peloponnesian War*. Trans. Rex Warner. Ed. M. I. Finley. Penguin Classics. Rev. ed. New York: Penguin, 1972.

Trotsky, Leon. *History of the Russian Revolution*. New York: Pathfinder, 1980.

Urquhart, Thomas, trans. *The Works of Mr. Francis Rabelais*. By François Rabelais. New York: Rarity, 1932.

Veeser, H. Aram, ed. *The New Historicism*. London: Routledge, 1989.

Weil, Simone. *The Need for Roots: Prelude to a Declaration of Duties toward Mankind*. Trans. Arthur Wills. New York: Putnam, 1952.

Wellek, René, and Austin Warren. *Theory of Literature*. 1949. New York: Harcourt, 1970.

Yeats, William Butler. "The Circus Animals' Desertion." *Yeats's Poetry, Drama, and Prose*. Ed. James Pethica. Norton Critical Ed. New York: Norton, 2000. 128–29.

∼ Historical Scholarship

CATHERINE GALLAGHER

It is generally acknowledged that there was a historical turn in literature departments in the 1980s, which continued to gyrate throughout the 1990s and into the current decade. Annabel Patterson's prediction, in her account of historical scholarship for the 1992 edition of this volume, that "the new historical criticism of the 1990s will likely be situated mostly within the territory of social and cultural [rather than intellectual, political, or strictly literary] history," was borne out, and the result has been more than a broadening of the range of topics allowable or the inclusion of issues that once seemed remote from literary study ("Historical Scholarship" 184). When Patterson wrote of the changes that literary-historical scholarship underwent in the 1980s, she stressed that critics were extending the range of the texts they treated; were applying techniques of literary analysis to extraliterary works and documents; and were analyzing cross-textual discursive patterns that linked literature to larger political, social, and cultural formations. They were not only exploring previously disregarded contexts but also challenging the legitimacy of the text/context distinction. The historical turn in literary studies entailed posing new kinds of historical questions about literary works as well as attempting to answer historical

questions with literary evidence and critical analytic tools.

The expansionist tendencies of the 1980s have continued, but they have also been accompanied by a more introspective focus. Indeed, the interest in history has come home to literary studies in several important respects, leading us increasingly to ask historical questions about the underlying premises of our discipline and its overall organizing categories. Patterson surveyed the changes in historical scholarship by progressing through the established subfields of the profession, which have been formed by slicing national literatures into historical periods (English Renaissance literature, early modern French literature, etc.), but the very formation of those subdivisions was insistently placed under scrutiny in the last decade, as scholars turned their attention to the construction of authorship, canons, reading practices, nationhood, and the idea of the literary. Despite the waning of theoretical discourse in literature departments in the 1990s, many historical scholars deepened the self-reflective explorations that had characterized their work in the 1980s by studying the creation of these fundamental disciplinary categories, as well as by continuing to explore the past of our own profession and its relation to the growth of

professional culture generally. Debate about historical
theories and methodologies,
moreover, was met by paradoxical attempts to historicize
and render problematic the
very concept of history while continuing to analyze its literary character.

Attention to the cultural field as the historical object has led critics to confront the relatively recent appearance of the differentiated entity we call literature.

The internal dynamic of historical criticism
has been partly responsible for these developments. "Always historicize," Fredric Jameson's
famous 1981 slogan, emphatically demands to
be historicized, even though Jameson himself
called it a "trans-historical imperative" (9). The
historicisms that became prevalent in the 1980s
and 1990s were antifoundationalist in the sense
that they explicitly rejected the premise that literary history is merely an epiphenomenon of underlying economic or geopolitical circumstances.
Aligning with the cultural turn in the discipline
of history, historical critics during the last two
decades have increasingly sought to regard history not as an extratextual set of events or a dynamic process of cause and effect powered by a
constant set of material forces but rather as a field
for the investigation of chronological cultural
differences, which are not only expressed but
also generated in part by literary works. (For reflections on the cultural turn in history, see "Review Essays.") This attention to the cultural field
as the historical object has led critics to confront
the relatively recent appearance of the differentiated entity we call literature and hence to attempt explanations for its emergence. Critics in
the 1980s and 1990s often tried to straddle
rather than choose between the two paths Jameson claimed historicization might take: "the
path of the object and the path of the subject,
the historical origins of the things themselves
and that more intangible historicity of the concepts and categories by which we attempt to understand those things" (9).

But the internal development of current historicisms do not entirely explain the self-
reflectiveness of some of their most influential
practitioners. A contributing factor has been ongoing controversies surrounding new histori-

cisms. Despite their obvious
gains in the last two decades,
new trends in historical criticism have met considerable
resistance, and the self-
searching of critics can be
partially attributed to the fact that traces of their
earlier polemical self-assertions, which were
noted in Patterson's essay, are still to be found,
often softened into self-explanations. No longer
a minority movement, historical criticism has
had to shoulder the responsibilities of success,
which include articulating its relation to other
critical endeavors and its role in theoretical and
methodological developments. Historical critics
who are interested in literary theory have responded to its challenges partly by historicizing
the competition. And of course they have continued to disagree with one another. Among the
many competing kinds of historical work now
prevalent in literature departments, what counts
as history has not been settled, and disagreement
over a range of other methodological issues has,
like pressure from critics who object to the historical turn altogether, helped create the climate
for self-examination.

In this essay, I concentrate on attempts to
historicize the organizing categories of literary
study—especially "author," "text," "reader," "literature," and "national." I try as well to outline
some of the theoretical and methodological controversies that attend such attempts, but I want
to remark at the outset that most actual historical
criticism conforms only loosely to these models.
Some scholars have made interrogating our disciplinary coordinates their main objective, but
most historical scholars do not engage in meta-
criticism even when their work finds inspiration
there. So although I concentrate on "the path of
the subject," I also keep an eye on "the path of
the object": the attempts at writing an ever fuller
and more accurate history of modern literatures
(however we may be using those terms). Indeed,
new ways of organizing the historical study of
literature have been driven as much by technological advances, empirical curiosity, and demands for representational inclusion by previ-

ously excluded groups as by methodological self-consciousness. Although unable to do justice in the present essay to the intricate interplay of these motives, I try to indicate some of the most prominent instances of their mutual reinforcement.

AUTHOR

The author is a modern figure, a product of our society insofar as, emerging from the Middle Ages with English empiricism, French rationalism and the personal faith of the Reformation, it discovered the prestige of the individual, of, as it is more nobly put, the "human person." It is thus logical that in literature it should be this positivism, the epitome and culmination of capitalist ideology, which has attached the greatest importance to the "person" of the author.

—Roland Barthes

To those who were already doing historical scholarship in the 1970s, perhaps the most controversial thing about emerging postmodern historicisms was their relative indifference to an author's biography, for it had been generally assumed that an author was the primary historical agent connecting a literary work to its shaping environment of production. As R. S. Crane categorically put it in 1935:

> A literary history . . . is a narrative of the changing habits, beliefs, attitudes, tastes, and purposes of individual persons and groups or organizations of persons living in particular times and places; it is not a history of literature but of literary men.
> (7)

The gist of this statement would have seemed quite uncontroversial up through the 1960s: the historical nature of literature results from historical differences among its authors. Nor was this necessarily a naively held assumption, for a great deal of theoretical energy went into articulating the relations among authors, their works, and their formative institutions and ideologies; complicated notions of mediation, alienation, and reification had been elaborated to discuss these issues. Furthermore, those who looked (and look) to the life of the author for most historical evidence could not confidently be said to languish in the toils of ideological bourgeois individualism, for much of the most sophisticated work along these lines was produced by Western Marxists. Author-centered, contextualizing historical criticism was no monolithic dogma, but it was the prevailing modus operandi before the new historicisms of the 1970s and 1980s announced themselves, and it may now be returning in revised forms.

The new historicisms that broke this consensus came in several overlapping kinds, which included: discursive criticism derived primarily from Michel Foucault but influenced also by the French *Annales* school of historians and other anthropologically oriented thinkers (the new historicism that took root first in English Renaissance studies); renovated ideology critique influenced by Marxist structuralists, such as Louis Althusser and Pierre Macherey (the new historicism prevalent in English Romantics criticism); and the cultural poetics inspired by Raymond Williams and the *Annales* school (prevalent in Britain rather than the United States but so closely tied to the emergence of cultural studies in this country that its impact has been durable under that name). These new critical approaches deemphasized not only the independent shaping power of the author but also the concentric circles of contextual embedding that had previously been thought to connect as well as separate the literary work from the surrounding historical field. For example, those influenced by Foucault tended to cut across generic boundaries, connecting texts, other kinds of representations, and behavior into discursive practices that were unauthored. Discourse (i.e., modes of thought, action, and communication in a given institution) pulsates through texts, indeed is pumped along by them, carving out individual subjectivities and carrying the effects of social power into the most seemingly secluded recesses of consciousness. The notion that discourse creates consciousness (instead of independent minds creating discourse) does not require Foucauldian critics to ignore individual writers (indeed, Foucault himself was fascinated by personal lives), but it undoubtedly makes them seem less active as the ultimate historical cause or source of a literary work. A similar analysis could be made of the fate of authors under the weight of ideology in structuralist Marxism or the weight of culture in cultural studies.

Most important, as the quotation from Roland Barthes at the head of this section illustrates ("Death" 1467), these movements tended to historicize the category of authorship itself as part of a larger attempt to destabilize the idea of the subject. The critique of the subject, which was undertaken by French intellectuals in the wake of existentialism, assumed the dominance in Western culture of either a Lockean empirical self or a German idealist notion of human consciousness (deriving from Kant and Fichte), and it affirmed the primacy of acts of epistemological and ethical agency. The attack on those models was mounted from various sides: deconstructionists asserted that the subject is both made and unmade as a textual phenomenon, and Lacanian psychoanalytic theorists also claimed it as an effect of language, while Althusserians added that the modern subject was called into being, or interpellated, by ideological apparatuses of the state. Barthes's essay "Death of the Author" visits all these ideas, lighting only briefly on the philosophical and social developments—empiricism, rationalism, Protestantism, and capitalism— that presided over the birth of the author. But the very fact that Barthes could refer with such casual ease to the modernity of the phenomenon indicates that the historical nature of authorship was already widely understood in France in the late 1960s. In the English-speaking world, the implications of the idea were explored over the last quarter of the twentieth century.

Terry Eagleton made perhaps the most influential poststructuralist attempt of the 1970s to systematize a mode of literary history that would render the authorial subject problematic. In an elaborate application of Althusser's theory of ideology (ideology is one's imaginary relation to the historical real ["Ideology"]), Eagleton argued that texts are the overdetermined results of multiple

causes, only one of which is the authorial ideology (also referred to as the AuI and defined as "the mode of insertion of the author into the GI" [general ideology]) (*Criticism* 58). The literary historian's task would be to uncover how the text configures and reveals the various, overlapping, and often contradictory ideologies informing it, including not only the AuI and the GI but also the GMP (general mode of production), the LMP (literary mode of production), and the AI (aesthetic ideology). This stringent Althusserianism, with its scientific-sounding acronyms, never quite caught on in the United States, but a somewhat softer version, in which the author remained essentially an ideological nexus, resonated with both the native anti-intentionalism of New Criticism and the prevalent antifoundationalism of deconstruction.

Among American scholars of English Romanticism, especially, such a critique of the subject became intimately connected not only with making individual writers properly historical objects but also with asserting the historical specificity of the author. Writers, the argument went, began making absolute claims for the primacy of their individual consciousnesses during the Romantic period (approximately when Kant and Fichte were also validating subjectivity), and later literary scholars, believing the Romantic writers' assertions of autonomy and universality, followed suit by celebrating the authors' triumphs over their historical determinants. Jerome McGann's seminal 1983 *The Romantic Ideology* describes the process by which Romantic idealism put the lone authorial consciousness at the center of the work as a displacement of history: "In the [Intimations Ode], objective history has disappeared. The poem annihilates its history, biographical and sociohistorical alike, and replaces these particulars with a record of pure consciousness" (90). The Romantic model of authorship was thus rendered antihistorical in its essence because it not only displaced history but also came into existence precisely to accomplish that displacement. Literary historians, McGann recommended, should free both themselves and the works from this ideology by reading for the traces of elision:

> If Wordsworth's poetry elides history, we observe in this "escapist" or "reactionary" move its own self-revelation. It is a rare, original, and comprehensive record of the birth and character of a particular ideology–in this case, one that has been incorporated into our academic programs.
>
> (91)

The form of the literary work, in other words, contains the residue of the effort of displacement, and consequently only close reading, rather than broad contextualization, will restore the specific nature of its historical mode of being. No matter how fervently (or successfully) writers work to gather the poem's totality into the confines of their consciousness, the poem itself, as a record of the struggle, testifies against the author effect and in favor of a suppressed history. Although McGann disclaimed the influence of Althusserianism on his thinking, his close reading of poems for the traces of their elisions is certainly reminiscent of Macherey's contention that literary form makes ideology recognizable through internal distantiation.

A related example is Marjorie Levinson's *Wordsworth's Great Period Poems* (1986), which shows the influence of Althusserianism more explicitly. Dwelling like McGann on writers' attempts to assert full authorial control by excluding the contradictions that made them—"My object was to explain the particular and particularly constrained manner in which Wordsworth sought figurally, mythically, or formally to resolve those conflicts which were his *ideés fixes* . . . his ideological knowledges." Levinson also argues that the historical dissonances are "muffled" by the "amassing harmonies" of the authorial voice (3).

In short, this school of Romantic scholars undertook the historicization of authorship, but it also opposed the authorship it studied to every other kind of history; Wordsworth's authorial effect was, they argued, the erasure of his history. To be sure, they did not leave working empirical writers out of account, but neither did they attribute to them the conscious, autonomous production even of the effect called Romantic authorship—for that, like everything else about the poem, was shown to be overdetermined, the result of factors too dissimilar to be ranked in order of their importance. The idea was congruent with Paul de Man's attack on the "aesthetic ideology," in which aesthetics represented the smoothing over of gaps, fissures, pain, and discontinuity.

For these new historicists, the author as supreme subject, an autonomous and noncontingent consciousness, was a similarly spurious ideological formation, but whereas de Man's name for the potentially disruptive forces opposing ideology was *textuality* (or sometimes *literariness*), the new historicists called them *history*. This difference in terms led to some logical as well as methodological confusions. On the one hand, the new historicists used *history* to name the process by which ideologies (especially antihistorical ideologies) formed; on the other hand, they used it as "a non-identity factor," controverting "often by fracturing, the centered, totalizing, and rational subject." *History* was less an order than an "uncoordinated and nonlinear field of contradiction and contingency" or "an excess precipitated by social processes of making and ordering" (Levinson, "Romantic Poetry" 185). Often, like Jacques Lacan's *real*, *history* seemed categorically unspecifiable, which perhaps accounts for the fact that these new historicists leaned heavily on the sublime effect of a single historical rupture—the French Revolution—as the ungraspable trauma from which the Romantic subject was trying to recover. In more mature stages, this movement developed a broader concept of history, but it continued to disclose the operations of that force primarily through close readings of canonical texts.

There were, of course, other ways of historicizing authorship. Stephen Greenblatt's *Renaissance Self-Fashioning* appeared three years before McGann's *Romantic Ideology*. Notoriously eclectic in its method but characterized by extensive reading across various sorts of contemporary texts as well as by intensive attention to textual detail, it eschewed theoretical metadiscourse in favor of a reading practice. *Renaissance Self-Fashioning* nevertheless drew on a range of thinkers who had "called the subject into question," as the language of the era tended to put it. Althusserianism was a prominent part of the mix; to describe the effect of Thomas Wyatt's lyrics, for example, Greenblatt quoted Althusser's "Letter on Art": they "give us a 'view' of the ideology to which their work alludes and with which it is constantly fed, a view which presupposes a retreat, an internal distantiation from the very ideology from which [they] emerged" (153).

The modern subject that Greenblatt thought emerged in the Renaissance (the placement is closer to Barthes's than was McGann's) did not, however, greatly resemble the bourgeois model of a bounded, stable, and noncontingent consciousness. Instead it was a radically improvisational self, one that could easily tolerate nonidentity and whose effectiveness derived precisely from its ability to exploit its understanding of the other. Iago's "I am not what I am" (*Oth.* 1.1.65), rather than William Wordsworth's "egotistical sublime" (Keats), was the slogan of modern selfhood and, by extension, of authorial self-consciousness. This formulation manifested the influence of Foucault, whose contention that subjectivity was a historically malleable conduit of power came to inform Greenblatt's thinking, and that of other new historicists, increasingly in the 1980s.

Foucauldian new historicism resembled the other new historicisms in its desire to denaturalize authorial subjectivity, but it departed from them in refusing to privilege nonidentity as a subversive alternative to Kantian agency. The Foucauldians, who were primarily Renaissance scholars, Victorianists, and Americanists, sought to demonstrate instead that the gaps, fissures, ruptures, and slippages cherished by Althusserians and deconstructionists could just as easily be in the service of power as opposed to it. The author was not one monolithic Renaissance, En-

lightenment, or Romantic invention but an endlessly labile self that could be "fashioned," to use Greenblatt's resonant word, for a variety of discursive purposes.

Thus Foucault's highly influential article "What Is an Author?" labeled "the death of the author" merely another of the author's reincarnations, "a kind of enigmatic supplement of the author beyond his own death" (1625). Foucault posited instead the existence of an "author function," which defines how the names of individual writers operate in various discourses, of which the literary is only one. All that can be said of the author function in general is that "it is tied to the legal and institutional systems that circumscribe, determine, and articulate the realm of discourses" (1631). Even in the modern period, some publications are authored and some are not. The varieties of modern literary authorship, for example, proceeded from the juridical need to hold individuals responsible for certain kinds of publications, and the same exigency has been established differently in other discourses. For example, a paper coming out of a physics laboratory with sixty signatories is not authored in the same sense that this article is. Foucault thus made the concept a variable in a vast field of discursive practices, encouraging literary historians to look across kinds of production, exploring the mutual determinations of author function in not only literary and nonliterary writing but also "painting, music, technical fields, and so forth" (1631).

None of this argument rules out attention to the lives of writers; but instead of assuming that writers express themselves (however those selves are formed) in published works, new attention focuses on how—under certain legal constraints and opportunities, inside certain ideologies and discourses, within the rules of certain institutions, and with the help of certain productive forces—they make themselves into authors. What Greenblatt and McGann had in common was an understanding of the author not as a starting place but as a product. The writer is only

> **The author was not one monolithic Renaissance, Enlightenment, or Romantic invention but an endlessly labile self.**

one of the things that goes into the making of an author.

The legal history of authorship has become a primary focus of interest. Foucault's identification of the state's need to hold individuals responsible for their writing as a primary factor in the creation of authorship gave a new impetus to scholarship on censorship and suppression of all kinds. Dozens of studies have appeared analyzing the relation between censorship and the appearance of modern authorship in early modern England alone. In addition to Greenblatt's work, one might name Patterson's *Censorship and Interpretation* (1984), Richard Dutton's *Licensing, Censorship, and Authorship in Early Modern England* (2000), the Shakespeare chapter of Jonathan Dollimore's *Sex, Literature, and Censorship* (2001), and Janet Clare's *"Art Made Tongue-Tied by Authority": Elizabethan and Jacobean Dramatic Censorship* (1999).

Once scholars began conceiving of censorship as a force in the making, rather than just the suppression, of authors, the topic moved from the periphery of literary history to its core and has become so popular in studies of early modern work that it has spawned its own research guide, Dorothy Auchter's *Dictionary of Literary and Dramatic Censorship in Tudor and Stuart England* (2001). Nor did the authorizing and deauthorizing activities of censorship end in Britain with the cessation of open hostilities between religious factions and between the Crown and Parliament, as the numerous studies by scholars in later periods of British literature reveal (Manning; Marsh; and Gilmartin). Beyond work on British literature, the interactions between censorship and authorship in Europe generally have been explored by both cultural and literary historians, as we see later in this essay when we canvass the scholarship produced in two relatively new fields, the history of the book and the history of reading.

The discovery that an author is a legal as well as a literary artifact has also inspired a stream of historical studies dealing with the constitution of authors as proprietors of their texts. For example, Martha Woodmansee (*Author*) and Mark

Rose both draw on Foucault's claim that modern notions of authorship are shaped by the imperative to attribute texts to individuals, an imperative that writers captured for their own benefit in the creation of copyright in the eighteenth and nineteenth centuries. Woodmansee, whose work centers on German literature, links the proprietary claims of writers at the end of the eighteenth century to the construction of Romantic authorship and thereby gives greater legal and economic specificity to the claims earlier made by new historicists for the invention of modern authorship in that period. Rose, concentrating on British literature, locates the transition approximately a century earlier. It has always been widely known that Britain had the earliest copyright law (1710), enabled by its advanced financial and legal institutions and its relatively lax controls on publication. But the appearance of the author-proprietor as early as 1710 also entitled scholars of eighteenth-century Britain to proclaim their period as the beginning of modern authorship, and several studies have followed up on that lead. Carla Hesse's recent article "The Rise of Intellectual Property" cautions, however, against regarding the proprietary author as a sudden, unprecedented invention. Her warning might apply, as well, to the whole issue of when the modern author came into being, since even this cursory examination of recent studies of the legal history places that nativity anywhere from the early modern period to the nineteenth century.

In addition to demonstrating how authorship was created in legal categories, scholars have examined its formation in economic relations. It was only a short, inevitable step from studying the author as proprietor to studying the author as both economic agent and commodity. Not content with earlier, vaguer claims that the modern author function was a product of bourgeois social relations, scholars sought the specific authorial modes of a variety of literary economies. Once again this effort often entailed the search for a beginning, and some studies looked to the growth in what has come to be called print culture in the early modern period—especially the widening availability of printed commodities, the growth of the public sphere, and the opening possibilities of making one's living by letters—as the nexus out of which modern authorship emerged. The works of several cultural and intellectual historians fed this enterprise: Jürgen Habermas's *Structural Transformation of the Public Sphere* (which appeared in 1962 but was translated into English only in 1989), J. G. A. Pocock's *Virtue, Commerce, and History* (1985), and John Brewer's *The Sinews of Power: War, Money, and the English State, 1688–1783* (1988) directed the attention of literary critics to the birth of new public discourses, institutions, and reconfigurations of public and private life in eighteenth-century Britain and also to the vast economic changes wrought by the late-seventeenth-century revolution in credit. Authorship was also linked to economics in the eighteenth century by literary historians like Peter De Bolla, whose *The Discourse of the Sublime: Readings in History, Aesthetics, and the Subject* (1989) drew on the new economic criticism to explore the similarities in the dynamics of economic and literary exchange. And the status of the modern author has been placed as a specific (although also anomalous) instance of the general rise of the professional classes in Europe and America in the eighteenth and nineteenth centuries (Collini; Kittler; Robbins; Siskin). Economic development broadly conceived is thus taken as a condition of the emergence of the author, an intersecting system of exchange providing many of the terms in which literary interaction was conceived, and a force field for the professional division of literary labor.

Ironically, the burden of many of these studies is that authorship may have been created by literary commodification but was also threatened by that process, so that the model of an autonomous and perfectly self-expressive author developed as a reaction to the conditions of textual production. When critics specify exactly which aspect of authorial identity was thus threatened, it often turns out to be masculinity, and hence the submerged topic of the historical gender of authorship arises. Studies in the history of authorship that attend to its gendered variations are certainly a continuation of the feminist project of recovering the history of women writers. But instead of assuming, as had most gynocritics, that women always aspired to literary fame and were only prevented from fulfilling their ambitions by prohibition or prejudice, these later studies ask what brought women into the business of letters in particular times and places and what the solicitation of their works tells us about the general state of authorship in that period. For example, my study of the economics of five women's careers spanning the period from the Restoration through the early nineteenth century, *Nobody's Story*, traces how alternative models of authorship were developed to create internal hierarchies as well as to promote the impressions of disinterestedness and moral superiority. Authorship, at least in that period, often took on decidedly feminine qualities, while it also helped contour the outlines of the very idea of femininity. Margaret Cohen comes to similar conclusions about French authorship in a later period in her *The Sentimental Education of the Novel* (1999).

Equivalent claims were made in other studies of what has come to be called minority authorship: instead of taking the authorial persona for a simple expression of a marginalized or suppressed subjectivity, critics have asked how and why certain writers created textual effects of minority consciousness and how those effects, in turn, helped support, even as they seemed to press against, the norm of an unhyphenated generic authorship. David Lloyd's *Nationalism and Minor Literature* (1987), for example, combined with the *The Nature and Context of Minority Discourse*, an anthology Lloyd coedited with Abdul JanMohamed in 1990 (JanMohamed and Lloyd), introduced this new historical approach to minority authorship, which has subsequently been applied to numerous other literatures. Regenia Gagnier's survey of nineteenth-century British working-class autobiography, *Subjectivities*, further disputed the claim that authorship is a technique for the production of bourgeois subjects; Gagnier revealed the great diversity of subjective characteristics in Victorian life writing.

These investigations into the varieties of authorship have made Barthes's equation of the author with the sovereign subject seem rather old-fashioned, and hence the hostility that propelled the historicization of authorship in the first place has now evaporated. After the competition for historical priority has subsided (Was Augustine the first modern author? Shakespeare? Montaigne? Goethe? Wordsworth?), the conditions of the author's appearance have been debated, and the author's empirical varieties have been enumerated, is the project of historicizing the category of authorship itself ending? If the interest in the history of authorship was stimulated by the discipline's need to interrogate the subject, what does it continue to contribute now that the subject has lost its sinister hegemony?

First, we are only beginning to assemble an adequately detailed and accurate picture of authorship in different times and places, so that we can write deeper histories, which take into account the many different ways in which writers and readers have learned to relate themselves to texts. Second, when we center a history on writers, we have learned to specify the paradigms of authorship available to them and to explore what kinds of ambition, despair, or cynicism those paradigms fostered in specific people. The historicization of authorship is becoming an integral part even of that activity once considered its antithesis, literary biography, for attending to individual self-constructions yields the microhistories of the phenomenon. Young scholars who are planning to do historical studies of authors should know that they have a rich variety of theoretical and critical methods before them. Denaturalizing authorship invites potential literary biographers to explore a deeply historical dimension of their subject, but the question remains open of exactly how to write authors' lives while exploring the fluidity of authorship.

TEXT

The Text is plural.

—Roland Barthes

The fundamental categories of the profession—author, text, reader, literature, and so on—are so deeply interconnected that rooting around in the history of any of them necessarily disturbs them all. If, as Barthes and Foucault claimed, the author was a technique for ordering texts, then how could the universe of texts be conceived without authors? Indeed, there is a prior question: What is a text? Barthes's well-known distinction between *text* (an open-ended network or weave of signifiers or a methodological field) and *work* (a closed system that seems to convey a definite intention) did not exactly clarify the meaning of the word. His usage directly contravened the previous sense of *text* for most literary historians:

> The wording adopted by an editor as (in his opinion) most nearly representing the author's original work; a book or edition containing this; also, with qualification, any form in which a writing exists or is current, as a *good, bad, corrupt, critical, received text.* ("Text")

But even for textual editors of the old school, a text was not just anything written by an author; it had to be something significant enough to warrant editing. Moreover, the vast number of writings that have been treated as texts in that sense—edited, modernized, published, canonized—with only that wisp of an author function known as Anonymous to help determine their identities does somewhat problematize the claim that the death of the author would liberate the text (assuming we know what one is) from semantic restriction.

The cause of textual plurality and indeterminacy was ultimately advanced less by the theoretical attack on the author than by the intensely scholarly work of a new breed of textual historians, who were paying close attention to the materiality of written artifacts: their versions, modes of production, preservation, and dissemination. In the early 1980s a few influential studies appeared that looked at the history of how our profession has fixed its textual objects, and the subfield of textual-historical scholarship came into being. Noticing how heavily we all rely on a separate group of technically trained scholar-editors to produce the texts we use, these literary historians mounted an investigation of the presuppositions of the editors and placed them in historical perspective.

If the notion that a text is constructed by its modes of transmission and dissemination came as a revelation to some literary critics in the 1970s, it was hardly surprising to editors, who had been consigned the job (as they often saw it) of retrieving, from all that indeterminacy, the actual configuration of signs that the rest of us would unhesitatingly call *Hamlet* or *Ulysses*. As Lee Patterson and Jerome McGann pointed out in the early 1980s, that central operation of the discipline—supplying the rest of us with the texts we read and teach—was invented as a deeply historical discipline itself in the eighteenth and nineteenth centuries:

> To edit ancient texts required, first, that the entire cultural and historical context of the original work be recovered; second, that the entire critical history be explored and elucidated; and finally, that the work itself be reconstituted for the present in terms of these two historical matrices.
>
> (McGann, *Critique* 117)

McGann objected to the application of this method to the solution of all textual problems, on the grounds that it narrowed the field of possible historical questions about texts. The concentration on an author's final intentions and the production of a single text expressive of them tended to hide the variety of texts available as well as the history of the text's production, dissemination, and reception. Similarly, Patterson pointed out that the thorough historicization of texts tends to dissolve them, so that in the history of textual criticism the recourse to authorial intention has been a necessary way of protecting the concept of text from the heterogeneity that historical criticism would produce if left entirely to itself.

The 1990s saw a large increase in the number of historical critical books that retrieved and celebrated the heterogeneity of texts instead of determining their historically true variants. The theoretical questioning typical of the essays collected in McGann's seminal 1985 collection *Tex-*

The enthusiasm for regarding texts not as finished entities . . . motivated an unprecedented interest in the material production of literature.

tual Criticism and Literary Interpretation may have receded into the background, but it continues to enliven historical research. Textual historical criticism made its deepest impression in medieval and early modern studies, where it launched the movement called the new philology, which emphasizes the fundamental variability in the transmission of manuscripts and attempts to gauge the effect of such textual instability on the culture of the period. Textual historical criticism has also proved indispensable in our understanding of the development of print culture (see, e.g., Orgel; Warren), of the making of modern authorship (see, e.g., Manning; McGann, *Romantic Ideology*) and of its gendering (see, e.g., Silver). Textual variation has also been recovered in order to understand more fully nineteenth- and twentieth-century conditions of production and dissemination. Although many of these studies stop far short of overtly questioning the very notions of author and text, they nevertheless instance how open and plural our idea of text has become and how many mediating factors have come into play for us between texts and authors.

The enthusiasm for regarding texts not as finished entities but as ongoing processes has also motivated an unprecedented interest in the material production of literature. The field referred to as the history of the book, which used to seem as hidebound as its objects, is now an indispensable component of a properly materialist criticism for those working in modern and early modern literatures. But a knowledge of book history would be only a minimal qualification for understanding the variety that has overtaken our canonical texts. Some technical knowledge of the history of printing or of manuscript transmission is necessary to the diligent pursuit of variation, but so are (depending on individual cases) histories of theater, oral performance, illustration, photography, religious customs, formal and informal censorship, licensing, libraries, markets, coteries, paper making, taxation, international copyright, university curricula, film, television, the Internet, and so on. Textual historical criticism has sometimes merged with media studies, as the essays in *Reimagining Textuality: Textual Studies in the Late Age of Print* indicate (Loizeaux and Fraistat).

Unearthing the history of the profession's methods of textual construction, practicing literary history from the starting point of textual fluctuation, and opening literary history to the history of media—these are some of the principal ways in which the pressure on text has been registered by literary historians. They are gradually working their way into our pedagogy as they inspire variorum teaching editions and an array of digital presentations, such as CD-ROM hypertexts, online texts with links to variations and adaptations, or the hypermedia archive invented by McGann.

The fluidity of the concept of text emerging from these new studies has, moreover, permitted the continuation of a tendency that was already establishing itself in the early 1970s: to read across works, to construct and analyze systems, such as the supratextual entities we sometimes call discourses or ideologies, that we hypothesize as having been operative in the past. Since textual scholars now themselves participate in scoring the edges of the once self-contained literary entities, it becomes all the easier to concatenate them into larger objects of study, which range far beyond traditionally literary territory. This is merely to repeat what has so often been remarked in the last thirty years: that the difference between text and context is often purposely collapsed. The amalgamation of such discursive texts has also produced appropriate pedagogical tools in the last decade. Just as new textual studies were disseminated in publishing and digital projects during the 1990s, new experiments in exploring the dynamics of discursive intertextuality also began to appear in the form of textbooks and electronic hypertexts.

Paradoxically, the imaging and digital technologies that have made this rich textual material available also tend to change our experience of space and time, the coordinates of the historical imagination. Representing all media from all times and places in a single dimension and a single ghostly material form, the digital technologies, like postmodernism in general, might be accused of replacing our previous experience of history as chronological sequence, in which loss and change occur, with a more superficial experience of synchronic juxtapositions. As both teachers and scholars, we face the challenge of how to present the history of our texts without flattening them onto a new plane of permanent presentness. The task will not be simply to reinstate historical sequence but also to think about its implications more extensively. Why should we, for example, periodize works according to the dates of their production only?

READER

The historicity of literature rests not on an organization of "literary facts" that is established post festum, but rather on the preceding experience of the literary work by its readers.

—Hans Robert Jauss

The texts that issue out of the new textual studies are often uncanny: their matter, their time and place, their boundaries tending toward uncertainty and suggesting that the "history" in literary history may be a more problematic word than we suppose. Hans Robert Jauss, in his famous "Literary History as a Challenge to Literary Theory," formulated the problem this way:

> The *Perceval* of Chrétien de Troyes, as a literary event, is not "historical" in the same sense as, for example, the Third Crusade, which was occurring at about the same time [*Perceval* was composed]. . . . The historical context in which a literary work appears is not a factical, independent series of events that exist apart from an observer.
>
> (1553)

Perceval happens whenever and wherever it is read; the historical text is, in the words of Wolfgang Iser, Jauss's Konstanz school colleague, the virtual text of the reading process and is thus multiple in time and place. To literary theorists with a positivist notion of history, this insight seemed to disqualify textuality from historical specification altogether, and the idea of the reader was similarly abstracted from all coordinates. "The reader is without history, biography, psychology; he is simply that *someone* who holds together in a single field all the traces by which the written text is constituted," wrote Barthes ("Death" 1469). But to others it opened the challenging new field of the history of reading, which attends to the differences between, for example, the way a thirteenth-century manuscript reader would have interacted with a text of *Perceval* and the way a student in a French literature course interacts with one now. Their "horizons of expectation" (Jauss 1554) or "interpretive communities" (Fish) would be utterly dissimilar. The thirteenth-century reader would not only view it as a poetic wonder and a dazzling object but also use it as a guide to courtly deportment and decode it as commentary on near contemporaries; the twenty-first-century student would be likely to approach it as an unfinished classic to be understood in aesthetic and historical terms. Moreover, their social and material relations to the text would contrast sharply. The thirteenth-century reader would be confronted with a singular manuscript, probably associated with a particular place and so rare that the difference between the physical artifact and an ideational abstraction existing between versions would not easily come to mind; to own it, maintain it, preserve it, copy it, would be to keep the poem itself alive. Contemporary students, on the other hand, have no such sense of participation in the life of the poem. They own one of thousands of identical, mass-produced, and largely disposable copies, unattached to a place and easily replaceable. They also have access to various translations electronically and to digital pictures of the earlier manuscripts; they can experience the text in the multiform diversity of what textual scholars call its versioning. These various conditions of reading place quite disparate demands on readers and result in a variety of virtual texts in Iser's sense. *Perceval* may be ongoing, but it does not always go on in the same way, and specifying the history of its readings (its actualizations and

fragmentations) would give us, in effect, the history of *Perceval*.

There is nothing strikingly new about reception history in general, but theoretical claims in the 1970s—that texts simply are their readings, that literary canons are made by readers, and that the nature of human subjectivity is radically altered by different kinds of literacy—inspired a new attention to historical differences in reading and other reception practices. To German reception theory was added American reader-response criticism, French cultural history, and a newly reenergized discipline of bibliography that was paying attention to how the physical text (the book) and other material, social, and political conditions shape reading (see, e.g., McKenzie's *Bibliography and the Sociology of Texts*).

As a field, the history of reading tends to nest within the history of the book, and its rapid development in the 1990s has been traced to Robert Darnton's seminal essay "First Steps toward a History of Reading" (*Kiss* 154–87). Using Darnton's terms, David Finkelstein and Alistair McCleery note in *The Book History Reader* that the history of reading has lately moved from the empirical inquiries of who, what, where, and when people read to the more substantive questions of why and how they read, which have increasingly attracted the interest of literary critics (290). Why and how were audiences, readers, patrons, buyers, or viewers called into existence in different times and places? Why and how did those readers, in turn, actively shape the texts they consumed? Unsurprisingly, this project has been most robust in fields that study large transitions from one technology to another: from orality to writing, from manuscript to print, from hand press to industrial printing. Much of the foundational work in the history of reading, for example, was done by cultural historians who studied the impact of print in early modern Europe: Michel de Certeau, Natalie Davis, Roger Chartier (*Cultural History*, *Culture*, and *Order*), Darnton (*Kiss* and *Great Cat Massacre*), and François Furet and Jacques Ozouf on early modern France; both Carlo Ginzburg and Anthony

Grafton on early modern Italy; both Keith Thomas and Patterson (*Censorship* and "Historical Scholarship") on early modern England; and Elizabeth Eisenstein on Europe generally.

Throughout the 1990s, scholars continued to debate various theses about the profundity of the immediate impact of print. They questioned the rate at which print consumption became the reading norm and displaced older reading habits and earlier orientations toward texts, and they questioned the extent to which the printing press, rather than the introduction of new kinds of manuscripts in the late medieval period, produced not just a different sort of reader but a different sort of person. Most recent scholarship has emphasized continuity between late manuscript and early print culture, and studies of later periods have also stressed that even a fully established print culture contains significant residues of earlier reading protocols (see, e.g., Febvre; Love; Marotti; and Ezell.) Even in the same historical period, these studies indicate, a particular individual may be more than one reader—receiving and processing, for example, manuscripts in one way and printed works in another. The one constant in the scholarship is the reiteration that the meaning of a text depends on its reading and its reading depends on its material and cultural conditions: "Reading is not a solely abstract intellectual operation; it involves the body, is inscribed within a space, and implies a relationship to oneself or to others" (Cavallo and Chartier 4).

A large proportion of this scholarship tries to establish the nature of the "relationship[s] to oneself or to others" implied by various kinds of reading. It analyzes the modes of political and social interaction that take place through texts. It contains lively debates over social agency and authority, as the contending arguments in books such as Guglielmo Cavallo and Roger Chartier's *A History of Reading in the West*; James Raven, Helen Small, and Naomi Tadmor's *The Practice and Representation of Reading in England*; and David D. Hall's *Cultures of Print* demonstrate. In the field as a whole, one line of thought, which goes

back at least to Richard Hoggart's *The Uses of Literacy* (1957) and was reinforced by both Foucault's and Pierre Bourdieu's writings (see Bourdieu, *Distinction*), has suspected popular literacy of political manipulation and pacification, of implanting the recessive subjectivity and self-discipline required by the modern state, or of maintaining the distinctions of habitus. (As used by Bourdieu, *habitus* is a culturally specific way of perceiving, thinking, and behaving, which is regarded as natural by those inhabiting it [*Outline* 82–83]. It is the necessary starting point for action and shared understanding.)

These suspicions have been countered by an opposing line of argument with a more positive valuation of literacy's social and political role. Numerous studies in the 1990s laid emphasis on the independence of readers and on their tendency to mold texts to their own purposes. These studies showed that women, political and social rebels, workers, and other disempowered readers subverted, reworked, and otherwise energetically appropriated texts instead of passively assimilating them. The modern reading subject can thus be seen as practicing forms of social self-consciousness that enable resistance to oppression and exploitation. Instead of assuming that texts have the same effects on all readers, effects that can be studied in the texts themselves, scholars have employed empirical techniques to discover readerly activity. Diaries, journals, and autobiographies have been indispensable records for reception historians, as have library records, sales records, adaptations, sequels, prequels, parodies, piracies, and—increasingly—marginalia (see Flint; Sharpe; Zwicker; Davidson; D. Brewer; and Hutson).

Insofar as the history of reading has been a history of readers, it has gravitated toward the same questions that dominate the history of authorship, to which it is obviously closely connected. What is the relation between the modern subject and various forms of textuality? When does the relation between a text and a person become individual, private, and appropriative? What are the relations of power between texts and persons and between persons through texts? Moreover, the history of reading, like the history of authorship, seems to have a somewhat repetitive plot. Judging from Cavallo and Chartier's *A History of Reading in the West*, which has essays that range from ancient Greece to contemporary France, a certain set of transitions seems to occur in each period under consideration: from communal to private consumption; from reading aloud to reading silently; from books with continuous unbroken text to books with texts divided for readerly convenience; from intensive reading of few texts to extensive reading of many; from large unwieldy texts to smaller, more portable ones; from relatively homogeneous, learned readerships to mass readerships. In short, the privatization and individualization of increasing numbers of subjects that take place through the growth of literacy and differentiation of kinds of reading matter seem to be a steady tendency that is never completed, just as the author subject seems continually to be emerging on the other side of the text.

Like the history of authorship, the history of reading has a twist at the end, when the reader, like the author, after centuries of getting consolidated, suddenly comes apart into fragments or altogether disperses into a digital vapor. The author subject and the reader subject both seem to have depended on a certain stage of textual production, at which print was the primary medium of public communication and its most prestigious form was the book intended for private consumption. Books are certainly not disappearing, but, the argument goes, they are undergoing transformations in their environment of visual and electronic communication that change the nature of authors and readers. All through the twentieth century books were obviously being displaced from the center to the margins of communication, and the current digitization of their texts causes thoroughgoing change in the perceptions of their separateness and integrity, which entails as well the collapse of the separateness and integrity of the positions of reader and writer.

> **The history of reading has a twist at the end, when the reader . . . after centuries of getting consolidated, suddenly comes apart.**

As Cavallo and Chartier point out, readers who access a text instantaneously can also change it radically, and yet such readers seem to be more a technological function than actual people. Their appearance nevertheless betokens the advent of the third great "revolution in reading":

> The move from the [book form] to the screen is just as great a change as the shift from the roll to the codex. It challenges the entire order of books familiar to the men and women of Western Europe since the earliest centuries of the Christian era. (28)

In this time of disorienting transition, it is hardly surprising that book-bred literary historians, like Minerva's owl setting out at sunset, would want to survey the history of our leading concepts, which are perhaps becoming unrecognizable in this twilight of the order of books. Younger scholars, who grew up reading from the screen, will be better equipped to assess the magnitude of the current change and understand past transitions from its vantage point.

LITERATURE

As the philosophers might say, "literature" and "weed" are functional rather than ontological terms: they tell us about what we do, not about the fixed being of things. They tell us about the role of a text or a thistle in a social context, its relations with and differences from its surroundings, the ways it behaves, the purposes it may be put to and the human practices clustered around it.

　—Terry Eagleton

When Terry Eagleton asked the question, "What is Literature?," and answered with, "There is no 'essence' of literature whatsoever" (*Literary Theory* 8), few literary historians were surprised. It was becoming commonplace by 1983 to cite, for example, Raymond Williams's discussion of the late-eighteenth-century provenance of our specialized usage of the word *literature* to mean certain kinds of texts rather than just anything written (183–87), and it is now certainly old hat to point out that our concept of the literary is relatively modern. Nevertheless, many questions regarding the history of the concept of literature remain open. If, as Eagleton claimed, it is a "functional" concept, then what have its functions been and what are the conditions of its emergence, reproduction, and maintenance? If *literature* refers to a peculiarly modern distinction, might it be merely the latest in a long history of functionally equivalent categories previously called by other terms?

Much of the historical work addressing these questions was pursued in the context of the canon wars of the 1980s, when it seemed important just to prove that literary canons were constructed according to certain assumptions about the nature of literary value that they were then used to reinforce. Jane Tompkins's *Sensational Designs: The Cultural Work of American Fiction, 1790–1860*, for example, claimed that the "fluctuating reputations" of antebellum authors "illustrate how changing definitions of literary value, institutionally and socially produced, continually refashion the literary canon to suit the culture's needs" (34). Many of these histories were polemically directed both against various formalist attempts inside the profession to establish transhistorical, objective criteria of literariness (e.g., linguistic estrangement, self-referentiality, disclosure of textuality) and against those outside the profession who were determined to undo the revisions of the canon that had been going on since the 1970s. For the purposes of these histories, it seemed sufficient simply to document the widely divergent criteria that had been invoked for recognizing the texts in the category and to demonstrate that canons are always being made and unmade. Revisionists, who had access through microfilm and other technologies to much larger textual samples than previous generations of critics did, were simultaneously retrieving obscure writers

> **Overlapping phenomena—the public sphere, national identity, capitalism, and the print market— have now been quite firmly established as a nexus in which literariness differentiated itself.**

(especially women and minority writers) for inclusion in a vastly expanded canon and writing the history of their exclusion. The concept of literariness, in various historical costumes, emerged as a culprit. The first answer to the question about the historical function of the idea of literature, therefore, tended to be exclusion, especially the exclusion of the texts of certain categories of writers in order to produce the hegemony of a dominant group.

Given the attention to the period in which *literature* begins to take on its modern meaning and to the link between that usage and canon formation, it is not surprising that eighteenth-century scholars and Romanticists took up the topic of the history of the concept of literature, often combining it with the history of authorship. Indeed, many of the studies I've already cited on the history of authorship are also relevant here, for the claim has been repeatedly made that the modern idea of literature emerges with the proprietary author. During the 1990s, the exclusionist thesis was perpetuated in studies of the long eighteenth and early-nineteenth centuries and frequently linked to gendered models of authorship. (For example, see studies by Kucich; Goldsmith; and Mellor. In *Romanticism and Gender*, Mellor blames the imposition of a modernist literariness for the absence of Romantic women writers from the canon.)

But as the mere exposure of the role of literariness in maintaining male (or white, or European) hegemony became a cliché, it was subjected to more detailed and sophisticated historical analyses. Jonathan Kramnick's 1999 *Making the English Canon* investigates the emergence of the idea of literary tradition out of, as the book's flyleaf puts it, "a prolonged engagement with the institutions of cultural modernity, from the public sphere and national identity to capitalism and the print market." Laura C. Mandell's *Misogynous Economies* examines misogyny and literariness as reactions to literary commodification. Those overlapping phenomena—the public sphere, national identity, capitalism, and the print market—have now been quite firmly established as a nexus in which literariness differentiated itself.

Several important studies view this subject through the lenses of particular genres, exploring their social and cultural meanings as well as the dynamics of their receptions. Observing that *literature* came to be applied not only to certain styles of language but also to certain categories of works (poetry, plays, novels, etc.), the history of the organization of those styles and categories into canons, their differentiation as genre, their competition for cultural preeminence, and their increasing complexity have all been investigated. The inclusion of the novel into the ranks of literature has been seen as a standard operation in the making of national literary canons, and recent studies of the stages of the novel have also investigated the consolidation of the category of fiction (see McKeon; L. Davis; and Gallagher). Henry Zhao traces the origins of that concept in twentieth-century China, relating it to changes in the form of the nation. But poetic genre making has also been placed in the context of the development of special literary institutions. Stuart Curran argued that Romanticism as a European phenomenon was stimulated by the recovery of past vernacular literatures by late-eighteenth-century histories and, further, that the British Romantic poets were the first to have a truly wide knowledge of the history of poetry in English and the first to aspire to join the ranks of a long vernacular tradition (*Poetic Form*).

The single most important book in this field gathered several of these themes but took the analysis in a somewhat different direction. John Guillory's *Cultural Capital: The Problem of Literary Canon Formation* uses Bourdieu's argument that aesthetic production emerged as a relatively autonomous field of cultural activity in the eighteenth century, the differentiation of literature playing an important part in that emergence. Only the relative autonomy of literature, Guillory stresses, allows it to be accrued and exchanged as "cultural capital," and the disputes over its value are ultimately irreducible to other kinds of social competition. He formulates the functions of literariness in these terms:

> [T]he production of literary texts cannot be reduced to a specific and unique social function, not even the ideological one. Authors confront a monumentalized textual tradition already immersed as speakers and writers in the social condition of linguistic stratification that betrays at every level the struggle among social groups over the resources of language, over cultural capital in its linguistic form.   (63)

Imagining these struggles as the mere reflexes of other conflicts, viewing their function simply as the maintenance of certain social exclusions that are already in place, actually trivializes the literary phenomena under analysis. Moreover, he overcomes the historical shortsightedness that led others to claim literary language as an epiphenomenon of the eighteenth-century book market. Drawing on the work of a number of theorists and historians in addition to Bourdieu (Auerbach, Bakhtin, the sociolinguist Charles Ferguson, Michel Beaujour, and Renée Balibar and Dominique Laporte), Guillory gives a succinct yet subtle account of the forms of literary language that have appeared in Europe since antiquity, the continuities and differences in their functions, and the institutions that gave rise to the distinctive shapes such language took in the last two centuries.

Among those institutions is one that received too little attention from historians of literariness prior to Guillory: the schools and universities. Although canon formation was certainly often on their minds, the pedagogical use of the canon as curriculum had received less attention. Guillory's analysis of the different functions of the canons of standard and higher education is too complicated to summarize here; suffice it to say that it adds new layers of complexity to discussions of literariness and brings the history of the phenomenon into intimate connection with the history of the institution, academic literary criticism, which is our peculiar habitus. Historical studies of the profession by Eagleton (*Criticism*), Gerald Graff, Jonathan Culler, Chris Baldick, Gauri Viswanathan, and Nancy Armstrong began appearing in the 1980s and continued throughout the 1990s. The recent appearance of anthologies that assemble essays on the making of the literary, the uses of canons in pedagogy, and the profession of criticism is a further sign that these interests are coalescing into a field with a canon of its own.

The critique of the concept of the literary seems also to have undergone a disciplinary normalization, as evidenced by its acquisition of a introductory textbook all to itself, by Peter Widdowson in the New Critical Idiom series, which

> offers a concise history of the constitution of a canonic concept of "literature" from its earliest origins to the orthodoxies that occurred through the later nineteenth-century to the middle of the twentieth. It also traces its dismantling from the late-60s onward.

But, the jacket copy reassures us, "the book attempts to recuperate a notion of 'the literary' by way of a series of readings of diverse texts." The circularity of this formulation is remarkable: the literary can always be recuperated by performing certain kinds of readings, because the literary is largely produced by such readings in the first place. We seem to have arrived at a slightly revised premise that allows us to assert the value of what we do: the literary may be a historical construct, which has served a variety of interests in the past, but it is nevertheless a reality basic to the discipline, and we renew it daily in our critical practices, even when we are denaturalizing the idea of the literary.

NATION, RACE, EMPIRE

Investigations into the history of the literary and its institutions revealed the intricate connections between those phenomena and the development of modern nations, encouraging research into the subjective dimensions of the formation of national, subnational, and supranational polities. The major historical events of the late 1980s and the 1990s—the end of the cold war; the sudden and unexpected collapse of the Soviet Union and of Yugoslavia; the resurgence of latent national identities and rivalries throughout central and

eastern Europe; the drastic reorganization of national politics in that region and in South Africa; the maturation of supranational political organizations such as the European Union; and the acceleration of those processes grouped under the term *globalization*, including massive emigration—all fostered a new and urgent desire to understand the making and unmaking of political and social institutions and identities, both currently and throughout history, including national literatures. Moreover, since states and regimes that had recently appeared solid were manifestly melting into air in the wake of apparently nonviolent upheavals of consciousness as well as infrastructural collapse, and since relatively homogeneous nation-states were fast becoming multicultural, the role played by culture and imagination in binding and dissolving collectivities, in forming empires and in defining enclaves, came more insistently into the foreground.

Benedict Anderson's *Imagined Communities: Reflections on the Origin and Spread of Nationalism* and the essays collected by Homi Bhabha in *Nation and Narration* began a flood of studies investigating both the role of nations in making literary canons and the role of literature in making nations. A search for variations on the word *nation* in the MLA Bibliographies between 1970 and 1985 and then between 1986 and 2002 showed that the word was used in only 143 titles in the MLA Bibliography volume devoted to literatures in the English language during the earlier fifteen-year period, but it was used in 1,797 titles in the following sixteen-year period. A somewhat less dramatic jump was observed in the non-English-language volume: from 55 to 386. Many of these thousands of critical works listed, including many already mentioned in this essay, are concerned primarily with the consolidation of national literary canons: the selection and dissemination of a certain set of past texts supposedly expressive of a national genius or character. The essays collected by Haruo Shirane and Tomi Suzuki in *Inventing the Classics: Modernity, National Identity, and Japanese Literature* (2001), for example, make the argument that the Japanese assembled a canon of classic texts only as Japan built itself into a modern nation. The same basic argument about the nationalistic motivations for designating a set of vernacular classics has been made for English, French, German, and Russian literatures. If the main point of such studies is that the student of, for example, Japanese literature should take neither *literature* nor *Japanese* for granted but instead study their mutual insemination, a secondary benefit has been the recovery of a large number of philological traditions, the scholarly legacy of the nineteenth century, as well as intriguing variations on the nation-building theme. Ian Duncan points out that the project of preserving a Scottish cultural heritage allowed for the abandonment rather than the pursuit of Scottish national political ambitions.

What contradictions appear when countries in the throes of national liberation struggles must write in the languages of the very empires they seek to overthrow?

Following more directly in the footsteps of Anderson, a second strand of research in this field examines not the retrospective creation of national literary classics but rather the production of modern literatures in conjunction with nation making. Several important studies concentrating on particular genres (as Anderson concentrated on the novel) have appeared. Guillory's chapter "Mute Inglorious Miltons: Gray, Wordsworth, and the Vernacular Canon" examines Gray's "Elegy," its textual history and reception, as a case study in the politics of poetic diction and the separation of literary language from standard polite usage that accompanied and troubled the project of national education. Other influential studies in national genres are Doris Sommer's *Foundational Fictions: The National Romances of Latin America* and Katie Trumpener's *Bardic Nationalism: The Romantic Novel and the British Empire*, both of which argue for the importance of allegorical romances to the national imaginary. They draw as well on the thesis, promulgated in the anthology *Nationalisms and Sexualities* (Parker, Russo, Sommer, and Yaeger), that national and sexual identities mutually constitute each other through particular literary forms.

Anderson, Sommer, Trumpener, and Duncan demonstrate as well the intrinsic relation between the national discourses of the last two and a half centuries and the growth and disintegration of European empires, a topic that raises several important complications for those who would posit a simple correlation between literariness and nationalism. How, for example, do polities like Great Britain, with its linguistic and cultural variety, relate to English as a language and England as a subnational category? How, when Britain is itself a conglomeration of nations, does it in turn distinguish its parts from the subject nations of its empire, even as it uses its literary canon (as opposed to its religious beliefs) to create British subjects abroad? To what extent is the very idea of Britishness a creation of empire? The ends of formal empire pose equally urgent questions. What contradictions appear when countries in the throes of national liberation struggles must write in the languages of the very empires they seek to overthrow, or when they narrate their national longings in the genres and according to the national models of the imperialists? How is postcolonial nationalism affected by the aesthetic education of the classes that led the national liberation struggles? And how were literatures in the last half of the twentieth century inflected by transnational ideologies, such as Marxism and pan-Arabism, or by the exigencies of a global literary market? What is the effect of national literatures written in exile? To what extent can we continue, in a time of widespread migration, to categorize literatures by the national affiliations of authors?

Historians of the relation between literature and the making of United States national consciousness have been in a somewhat anomalous position for the last dozen years because the topic was by no means new to them. Works by Ernest Tuveson, Henry Nash Smith, F. O. Matthiessen, and other founders of the field in the 1950s and 1960s had closely examined the ambition of mid-nineteenth-century writers to create a nation through literature. It was precisely against their work that the revisionist new American studies was directed, for the national tradition identified by the older generation was found to have naively taken the idea of the nation for granted even while investigating the nation's literary composition. The idea of a single cultural tradition, native to New England Protestants and spreading gradually westward, was, for example, attacked as woefully inadequate, as was the account of discursive nation making limited to a handful of texts. Taking a cue from Habermas, Michael Warner rewrote the history of the colonial American public sphere, and other critics revised the cultural history of the American Renaissance, which had once been the centerpiece of the national canon and proof that America was a distinct nation by the mid–nineteenth century (see Spillers).

Literary history is more than just a technique for rendering our terms problematic.

Most American revisionists, however, tended to concentrate on the racial and gender exclusions constituting the national canon, that product of white middle-class males, who only appeared to have a distinct and unified tradition because so much writing, even their own, had been left out. Thus a critique of the unified national model went hand in hand with the projects of canon revision, aiming to remake the national literary repository as a multiracial and multigendered representation of the population (see Gordon; Kerkering; and Kanneh). Eric Sundquist's influential *To Wake the Nations: Race in the Making of American Literature* (1993) attempted to save the idea of a distinctively American literary tradition by recovering its biracial nature. Yet many historical studies traced the literary development of separate racial identities, almost in isolation, which sometimes relied on the nationalist model. For example, since the concept of African Americans as a nation within the nation was already available in black nationalist ideology, several historians turned their attention to the linguistic creation of that identity.

The more radical historical claim of the 1990s, though, was not that the United States is

racially or even nationally multiple or divided but that its various races are themselves historical constructions. According to this view, the nation is a constantly changing system of racial differences rather than a mere agglomeration of identities formed in genetically based enclaves. The critique of identity in general that had accompanied the attack on the subject was extended to racial and ethnic identity, which was seen to operate as one of three crucial coordinates (race, class, gender) of social distinction, the systematic interactions of which must be traced historically. The stage of scholarship continues in which critics broke the national literary heritage into hyphenated subdivisions, requiring that each group be represented in literary histories, but it also coexists uneasily with the demand to be skeptical about the subdivisions and write the history of how we became a nation obsessed with hyphens.

Even as they have subjected the concept of national literature to severe pressure, literary historians have also examined, and wondered at, the depth of the sentiments it engenders and conveys. We have not yet answered Anderson's intriguing question about why a phenomenon as relatively new as nationalism is so often experienced as archaic, native, originary. It remains a mystery how people come not only to imagine themselves as part of the horizontal fraternity of a nation but also to feel that bond so profoundly that they are willing to die for it. To specify the role played by the media generally and literature specifically in instilling such emotions, critics are now beginning to undertake the daunting task of exploring the history of affect, but that investigation is still in its infancy. Perhaps as the history of national sentiment becomes less polemically invested in attacking or defending the phenomenon, we will be able to grasp the affective dimensions of cultural difference in their complexity.

~

It would be appropriate to end this essay with a section on our attempts to historicize the writing of history itself, and there has been a strong interest in tracing the development of history as a discipline, a category of consciousness, a method of defining periods, and a narrative practice. But even the briefest survey of that vast topic would take this essay far beyond its assigned limits. Moreover, no amount of historicizing will ever sufficiently answer the critique of historical practice made by theorists such as Hayden White, F. R. Ankersmit, and Dominick La Capra in the skeptical poststructuralist mood of the 1970s. The new historicisms were adaptations to the antifoundationalism of that critique. Living in the shadow of the ruins of History with a capital H and trying hard to avoid the *grands récits* of the nineteenth century, they developed methods of synchronic analysis—writing, for example, on single years, juxtaposing different moments to heighten contrast, concentrating on ruptures and avoiding narratives of transition. Some scholars have even seen these techniques as retrievals of premodern methods of representing the past. But to make such a claim, one must assume the prerogative of the historian who claims to know the stages of the development of history writing. In short, one may be able to problematize or unsettle the category of author by uncovering its historical multiplicity, but the concept of history cannot be challenged in the same way, for its historicization tends to reinstate it as the ground on which everything finds its proper place.

With this recognition that our self-questioning has limits, that there is no vantage point beyond the profession from which it can be viewed, should come the salutary reminder that literary history is more than just a technique for rendering our terms problematic. Even as we've engaged in metacritiques of literary study, we've also managed to produce an impressive amount of durable literary-historical scholarship that will continue to be valuable even when the self-questioning takes different forms. In the last fifteen years, the profession's introspective tendencies have emphasized the path of the subject in historical scholarship, and yet the interest in the history of our organizing concepts has also reinvigorated old fields and opened altogether new ones along the path of the object.

WORKS CITED AND SUGGESTIONS FOR FURTHER READING

Althusser, Louis. "Ideology and Ideological State Apparatuses: Notes toward an Investigation." Althusser, *"Lenin"* 127–87.

———. *"Lenin and Philosophy" and Other Essays*. Trans. Ben Brewster. New York: Monthly Rev., 1971.

———. "A Letter on Art in Reply to André Daspre." Althusser, *"Lenin"* 221–28.

Anderson, Benedict. *Imagined Communities: Reflections on the Origin and Spread of Nationalism*. New York: Verso, 1991.

Ankersmit, F. R. *A New Philosophy of History*. Chicago: U of Chicago P, 1995.

Armstrong, Nancy. *Desire and Domestic Fiction: A Political History of the Novel*. New York: Oxford UP, 1987.

Ashcroft, Bill, Gareth Griffiths, and Helen Tiffin, eds. *The Empire Writes Back: Theory and Practice in Postcolonial Literatures*. New York: Routledge, 2002.

Auchter, Dorothy. *Dictionary of Literary and Dramatic Censorship in Tudor and Stuart England*. Westport: Greenwood, 2001.

Baldick, Chris. *The Social Mission of English Criticism, 1848–1932*. Oxford: Oxford UP, 1987.

Barthes, Roland. "The Death of the Author." Leitch et al. 1466–70.

———. *Image, Music, Text*. Ed. and trans. Stephen Heath. New York: Noonday, 1977.

Baucom, Ian. *Out of Place: Englishness, Empire, and the Locations of Identity*. Princeton: Princeton UP, 1999.

Berlant, Laurent. *The Anatomy of National Fantasy: Hawthorne, Utopia, and Everyday Life*. Chicago: U of Chicago P, 1991.

Bhabha, Homi K., ed. *Nation and Narration*. New York: Routledge, 1990.

Bourdieu, Pierre. *Distinction: A Social Critique of the Judgement of Taste*. Trans. Richard Nice. Cambridge: Harvard UP, 1984.

———. *Outline of a Theory of Practice*. Trans. Richard Nice. Cambridge: Cambridge UP, 1999.

Brewer, David. *The Afterlife of Character, 1726–1825*. Philadelphia: U of Pennsylvania P, 2005.

Brewer, John. *The Sinews of Power: War, Money, and the English State, 1688–1783*. New York: Knopf, 1989.

Busby, Keith, ed. *Towards a Synthesis? Essays on the New Philology*. Atlanta: Rodopi, 1993.

Cavallo, Guglielmo, and Roger Chartier. *A History of Reading in the West*. Amherst: U of Massachusetts P, 1994.

Certeau, Michel de. "Reading as Poaching." *The Practice of Everyday Life*. Berkeley: U of California P, 1984. 165–76.

Chartier, Roger. *Cultural History: Between Practices and Representations*. Trans. Lydia G. Cochrane. Ithaca: Cornell UP, 1988.

———, ed. *The Culture of Print: Power and the Uses of Print in Early Modern Europe*. Trans. Lydia G. Cochrane. Princeton: Princeton UP, 1989.

———. *The Order of Books*. Stanford: Stanford UP, 1994.

Clare, Janet. *"Art Made Tongue-Tied by Authority": Elizabethan and Jacobean Dramatic Censorship*. New York: St. Martin's, 1999.

Cohen, Margaret. *The Sentimental Education of the Novel*. Princeton: Princeton UP, 1999.

Colley, Linda. *Britons: Forging the Nation, 1707–1837*. New Haven: Yale UP, 1992.

Collini, Stefan. *Public Moralists: Political Thought and Intellectual Life in Britain, 1850–1930*. Oxford: Clarendon, 1991.

Crane, R. S. "History versus Criticism." *"The Idea of the Humanities" and Other Essays Critical and Historical*. Vol. 2. Chicago: U of Chicago P, 1967. 3–24.

Culler, Jonathan. *Framing the Sign: Criticism and Its Institutions*. Norman: U of Oklahoma P, 1988.

Curran, Stuart. *Poetic Form and British Romanticism*. New York: Oxford UP, 1986.

———. "Romantic Poetry: Why and Wherefore?" *The Cambridge Companion to British Romanticism*. Ed. Curran. New York: Cambridge UP, 1993. 216–35.

Darnton, Robert. *The Great Cat Massacre and Other Episodes in French Cultural History*. New York: Vintage, 1984.

———. *The Kiss of Lamourette: Reflections in Cultural History*. New York: Norton, 1990.

Davidson, Cathy, ed. *Reading in America: Literature and Social History*. Baltimore: Johns Hopkins UP, 1989.

Davis, Lennard. *Factual Fictions: The Origins of the English Novel*. New York: Columbia UP, 1983.

Davis, Natalie. "Printing and the People." *Society and Culture in Early Modern France*. Stanford: Stanford UP, 1975. 189–226.

De Bolla, Peter. *The Discourse of the Sublime: Readings in History, Aesthetics, and the Subject*. New York: Blackwell, 1989.

de Man, Paul. *Aesthetic Ideology*. Minneapolis: U of Minnesota P, 1996.

Dollimore, Jonathan. *Sex, Literature, and Censorship*. Malden: Blackwell, 2001.

Duncan, Ian. "Authenticity Effects: The Work of Fiction in Romantic Scotland." *South Atlantic Quarterly* 102 (2003): 93–116.

Dutton, Richard. *Licensing, Censorship, and Authorship in Early Modern England*. New York: Palgrave, 2000.

Eagleton, Terry. *Criticism and Ideology: A Critical Investigation*. Chicago: U of Chicago P, 1983.

———. *Literary Theory: An Introduction*. 2nd ed. Minneapolis: U of Minnesota P, 1996.

Eisenstein, Elizabeth. *The Printing Press as an Agent of Change: Communications and Cultural Transformations in Early Modern Europe*. New York: Cambridge UP, 1979.

Ezell, Margaret. *Social Authorship and the Advent of Print*. Baltimore: Johns Hopkins UP, 2003.

Febvre, Lucien. *The Coming of the Book: The Impact of Printing, 1450–1800*. Trans. D. Gerard. London: NLB, 1976.

Finkelstein, David, and Alistair McCleery, eds. *The Book History Reader*. New York: Routledge, 2002.

Fish, Stanley. *Is There a Text in This Class? The Authority of Interpretive Communities*. Cambridge: Harvard UP, 1980.

Flint, Kate. *The Woman Reader, 1847–1914*. New York: Oxford UP, 1993.

Foucault, Michel. "What Is an Author?" Trans. Donald F. Bouchard and Sherry Simon. Leitch et al. 1622–35.

Furet, François, and Jacques Ozouf. *Reading and Writing: Literacy in France from Calvin to Jules Ferry*. New York: Cambridge UP, 1982.

Gagnier, Regenia. *Subjectivities: A History of Self-Representation in Britain, 1832–1920*. New York: Oxford UP, 1991.

Gallagher, Catherine. *Nobody's Story: The Vanishing Acts of Women Writers in the Marketplace, 1670–1820*. Berkeley: U of California P, 1994.

Gates, Nathaniel, and Benjamin N. Cardozo, eds. *Cultural and Literary Critiques of the Concept of Race*. New York: Garland, 1997.

George, Rosemary. *The Politics of Home: Postcolonial Relocations and Twentieth-Century Fiction*. New York: Cambridge UP, 1996.

Gilmartin, Kevin. *Print Politics: The Press and Radical Opposition in Early Nineteenth-Century England*. New York: Cambridge UP, 1997.

Ginzburg, Carlo. *The Cheese and the Worms: The Cosmos of a Sixteenth-Century Miller*. Baltimore: Johns Hopkins UP, 1980.

Goldsmith, Steven. *Unbuilding Jerusalem: Apocalypse and Romantic Representation*. Ithaca: Cornell UP, 1993.

Gordon, Dexter. *Black Identity: Rhetoric, Ideology, and Nineteenth-Century Black Nationalism*. Carbondale: Southern Illinois UP, 2003.

Graff, Gerald. *Professing Literature: An Institutional History*. Chicago: U of Chicago P, 1987.

Grafton, Anthony. "Renaissance Readers and Ancient Texts: Comments on Some Commentaries." *Renaissance Quarterly* 38 (1985): 615–49.

Greenblatt, Stephen. *Renaissance Self-Fashioning: From More to Shakespeare*. Chicago: U of Chicago P, 1980.

Guillory, John. *Cultural Capital: The Problem of Literary Canon Formation*. Chicago: U of Chicago P, 1993.

Habermas, Jürgen. *The Structural Transformation of the Public Sphere: An Inquiry into a Category of Bourgeois Society*. Cambridge: MIT P, 1991.

Hall, David D. *Cultures of Print: Essays in the History of the Book*. Amherst: U of Massachusetts P, 1996.

Hesse, Carla. *Publishing and Cultural Politics in Revolutionary Paris, 1789–1810*. Berkeley: U of California P, 1991.

———. "The Rise of Intellectual Property, 700 B.C.–A.D. 2000: An Idea in the Balance." *Daedalus* (Spring 2002): 6–45.

Hoggart, Richard. *The Uses of Literacy: Changing Patterns in English Mass Culture*. Fair Lawn: Essential, 1957.

Holub, Robert. *Crossing Borders: Reception Theory, Post-*

structuralism, Deconstruction. Madison: U of Wisconsin P, 1992.

Howard, Jean. *Engendering a Nation: A Feminist Account of Shakespeare's English Histories.* New York: Routledge, 1997.

Hunter, Ian. *Culture and Government: The Emergence of Literary Education.* Houndmills, Eng.: Macmillan, 1988.

Hutson, Lorna, ed. *Feminism and Renaissance Studies.* New York: Oxford UP, 1999.

Iser, Wolfgang. *The Act of Reading: A Theory of Aesthetic Response.* Baltimore: Johns Hopkins UP, 1980.

Jameson, Fredric. *The Political Unconscious: Narrative as a Socially Symbolic Act.* Ithaca: Cornell UP, 1981.

JanMohamed, Abdul, and David Lloyd, eds. *The Nature and Context of Minority Discourse.* New York: Oxford UP, 1990.

Jauss, Hans Robert. "Literary History as a Challenge to Literary Theory." Excerpt. Leitch et al. 1550–64.

Kanneh, Kadiatu. *African Identities: Race, Nation, and Culture in Ethnography, Pan-Africanism, and Black Literatures.* New York: Routledge, 1998.

Keats, John. Letter to Richard Woodhouse. 27 Oct. 1818. 2 Mar. 2006 <http://www.john-keats.com/briefe/271018.htm>.

Kerkering, John D. *The Poetics of National and Racial Identity in Nineteenth-Century American Literature.* New York: Cambridge UP, 2003.

Kittler, Friedrich A. *Discourse Networks, 1800/1900.* Trans. M. Metteer. Stanford: Stanford UP, 1990.

Kramnick, Jonathan. *Making the English Canon: Print Capitalism and the Cultural Past, 1700–1770.* New York: Cambridge UP, 1998.

Kucich, Greg. "Gendering the Canons of Romanticism: Past and Present." *Wordsworth Circle* 27.2 (1997): 95–102.

La Capra, Dominick. *Writing History, Writing Trauma.* Baltimore: Johns Hopkins UP, 2000.

Larsen, Neil. *Determinations: Essays on Theory, Narrative, and Nation in the Americas.* New York: Verso, 2001.

Leitch, Victor B., et al., eds. *The Norton Anthology of Theory and Criticism.* New York: Norton, 2001.

Levinson, Marjorie. "Romantic Poetry: The State of the Art." *Modern Language Quarterly* 54 (1993): 183–214.

———. *Wordsworth's Great Period Poems: Four Essays.* New York: Cambridge UP, 1986.

Liu, Alan. *Wordsworth, the Sense of History.* Stanford: Stanford UP, 1989.

Lloyd, David. *Nationalism and Minor Literature: James Clarence Mangan and the Emergence of Irish Cultural Nationalism.* Berkeley: U of California P, 1987.

Loizeaux, Elizabeth Bergman, and Neil Fraistat, eds. *Reimagining Textuality: Textual Studies in the Late Age of Print.* Madison: U of Wisconsin P, 2002.

Love, Harold. *Scribal Publication in Seventeenth-Century England.* New York: Oxford UP, 1993.

Macherey, Pierre. *A Theory of Literary Production.* Boston: Routledge, 1978.

Mandell, Laura C. *Misogynous Economies: The Business of Literature in Eighteenth-Century Britain.* Lexington: UP of Kentucky, 1999.

Manning, Peter. *Reading Romantics: Texts and Contexts.* New York: Oxford UP, 1990.

Marotti, Arthur F. *Manuscript, Print, and the English Renaissance Lyric.* Ithaca: Cornell UP, 1995.

Marsh, Joss. *Word Crimes: Blasphemy, Culture, and Literature in Nineteenth-Century England.* Chicago: U of Chicago P, 1998.

McGann, Jerome. *A Critique of Modern Textual Criticism.* Charlottesville: UP of Virginia, 1983.

———. *The Romantic Ideology: A Critical Investigation.* Chicago: U of Chicago P, 1983.

———, ed. *Textual Criticism and Literary Interpretation.* Chicago: U of Chicago P, 1985.

McKenzie, D. F. *Bibliography and the Sociology of Texts.* Panizzi Lectures. London: British Lib., 1986.

McKeon, Michael. *The Origins of the English Novel, 1600–1740.* Baltimore: Johns Hopkins UP, 2002.

Mellor, Anne. *Romanticism and Gender.* New York: Routledge, 1993.

Moretti, Franco. *Atlas of the European Novel, 1800–1900.* New York: Verso, 1998.

Ohmann, Richard. *English in America: A Radical View of the Profession.* New York: Oxford UP, 1976.

Orgel, Stephen. *The Authentic Shakespeare: And Other Problems of the Early Modern Stage.* New York: Routledge, 2001.

Parker, Andrew, Mary Russo, Doris Sommer, and Patricia Yaeger, eds. *Nationalisms and Sexualities.* New York: Routledge, 1992.

Patterson, Annabel. *Censorship and Interpretation: The Conditions of Writing and Reading in Early Modern England.* Madison: U of Wisconsin P, 1984.

———. "Historical Scholarship." *Introduction to Scholarship in Modern Languages and Literatures.* 2nd ed. Ed. Joseph Gibaldi. New York: MLA, 1992. 183–201.

Patterson, Lee. "The Logic of Textual Criticism." McGann, *Textual Criticism* 55–91.

Pocock, J. G. A. *Virtue, Commerce, and History: Essays on Political Thought and History, Chiefly in the Eighteenth Century.* New York: Cambridge UP, 1985.

Raven, James, Helen Small, and Naomi Tadmor, eds. *The Practice and Representation of Reading in England.* New York: Cambridge UP, 1996.

"Review Essays: Beyond the Cultural Turn." *American Historical Review* 107 (2002): 1475–520.

Robbins, Bruce. *Secular Vocations: Intellectuals, Professionalism, Culture.* New York: Verso, 1993.

Rose, Mark. *Authors and Owners: The Invention of Copyright.* Cambridge: Harvard UP, 1993.

Saldívar, José David. *Border Matters: Remapping American Cultural Studies.* Berkeley: U of California P, 1997.

Samuels, Shirley. *Romances of the Republic: Women, the Family, and Violence in the Literature of the Early American Nation.* New York: Oxford UP, 1996.

Sauerberg, Lars Ole. *Intercultural Voices in Contemporary*

British Literature: The Implosion of Empire. New York: Palgrave, 2001.

Scholes, Robert. *The Rise and Fall of English: Reconstructing English as a Discipline*. New Haven: Yale UP, 1998.

Scott-Childress, Reynolds J., and Renee Childress, eds. *Race and the Production of Modern American Nationalism*. Wellesley Studies in Critical Theory, Lit. History, and Culture. New York: Garland, 1999.

Sharpe, Kevin. *Reading Revolutions: The Politics of Reading in Early Modern England*. New Haven: Yale UP, 2000.

Shirane, Haruo, and Tomi Suzuki, eds. *Inventing the Classics: Modernity, National Identity, and Japanese Literature*. Stanford: Stanford UP, 2001.

Shumway, David R., and Craig Dionne, eds. *Disciplining English: Alternative Histories, Critical Perspectives*. Albany: State U of New York P, 2002.

Silver, Brenda. "Textual Criticism as Textual Practice." *Representing Modernist Texts: Editing as Interpretation*. Ed. George Bornstein. Ann Arbor: U of Michigan P, 1991. 193–222.

Simpson, David. *Romanticism, Nationalism, and the Revolt against Theory*. Chicago: U of Chicago P, 1993.

———. *Wordsworth's Historical Imagination: The Poetry of Displacement*. New York: Methuen, 1987.

Siskin, Clifford. *The Work of Writing: Literature and Social Change in Britain, 1700–1830*. Baltimore: Johns Hopkins UP, 1998.

Sommer, Doris. *Foundational Fictions: The National Romances of Latin America*. Berkeley: U of California P, 1993.

Spillers, Hortense J., ed. *Comparative American Identities: Race, Sex, and Nationality in the Modern Text: Essays from the English Institute*. New York: Routledge, 1991.

Streeby, Shelley. *American Sensations: Class, Empire, and the Production of Popular Culture*. Berkeley: U of California P, 2002.

Sundquist, Eric. *To Wake the Nations: Race in the Making of American Literature*. Cambridge: Harvard UP, 1993.

Szeman, Imre. *Zones of Instability: Literature, Postcolonialism, and the Nation*. Baltimore: Johns Hopkins UP, 2003.

"Text." Def. 1d. *The Oxford English Dictionary*. 2nd ed. 1989.

Thomas, Keith. "The Meaning of Literacy in Early Modern England." *The Written Word: Literacy in Transition*. Ed. Gerd Baumann. New York: Oxford UP, 1986. 97–131.

Tiffin, Chris, and Alan Lawson, eds. *De-scribing Empire: Post-colonialism and Textuality*. New York: Routledge, 1994.

Tompkins, Jane. *Sensational Designs: The Cultural Work of American Fiction, 1790–1860*. New York: Oxford UP, 1985.

Trumpener, Katie. *Bardic Nationalism: The Romantic Novel and the British Empire*. Princeton: Princeton UP, 1997.

Viswanathan, Gauri. *Masks of Conquest: Literary Study and British Rule in India*. New York: Oxford UP, 1998.

Warner, Michael. *The Letters of the Republic: Publication and the Public Sphere in Eighteenth-Century America*. Cambridge: Harvard UP, 1990.

Warren, Michael. *The Parallel King Lear, 1608–1623*. Berkeley: U of California P, 1990.

White, Hayden. *Metahistory: The Historical Imagination in Nineteenth-Century Europe*. Baltimore: Johns Hopkins UP, 1975.

Widdowson, Peter. *Literature*. New Critical Idiom. New York: Routledge, 1999.

Wiegman, Robyn. *American Anatomies: Theorizing Race and Gender*. Durham: Duke UP, 1995.

Williams, Jeffrey, ed. *The Institution of Literature*. Albany: State U of New York P, 2002.

Williams, Raymond. *Keywords: A Vocabulary of Culture and Society*. New York: Oxford UP, 1976.

Woodmansee, Martha. *The Author, Art, and the Market: Rereading the History of Aesthetics*. New York: Columbia UP, 1994.

———, ed. *The Construction of Authorship: Textual Appropriation in Law and Literature*. Durham: Duke UP, 1994.

Zhao, Henry. *The Uneasy Narrator: Chinese Fiction from the Traditional to the Modern*. New York: Oxford UP, 1995.

Zwicker, Steven. *Reading, Society, and Politics in Early Modern England*. New York: Cambridge UP, 2003.

⁓ Comparative Literature

J. MICHAEL HOLQUIST

DEFINITION, PHILOSOPHY, ASSUMPTIONS

Previous editions of *Introduction to Scholarship* did not include an essay on comparative literature. The former editors were perhaps made uncertain by the complex status of comparative literature as a profession. It is a discipline that has undergone a number of sea changes, and the editors might justifiably have wondered which of various definitions that evolved was definitive.

There is still widespread disagreement about just what comparative literature is. It is to be expected, then, that definitions of comparative literature constitute a genre in their own right. While such definitions often contradict one another, as a genre they share rules that give them a certain unity. The first of these rules is to make clear that there is no definition of comparative literature, or at least none comprehensive enough, to cover all the kinds of work done under that sign in the past and present. A second rule follows from the first: the history of comparative literature is the story of succeeding attempts to define what it is. A third rule is to declare the present moment a period of crisis. From squabbles among its practitioners in the 1830s in France through the emergence of a dis-

tinctively American version of comparative literature, there has been an uninterrupted series of manifestos and warnings, in the modern period from René Wellek's "Crisis of Comparative Literature" (1959) through the anxious surveys of the profession issued every ten years by the American Comparative Literature Association (ACLA) and continuing into the present moment. Indeed, a preliminary definition of comparative literature might well be a profession in which identity crisis is the norm.

At this belated stage in the profession, it is not uncommon for people in it to reject the very name of comparative literature. The relatively conservative Claudio Guillén begins a book on the subject by declaring comparative literature "a conventional and not very enlightening label" before going on to express the opinion that comparative literature "is more a yearning than an object" (3–4). Charles Bernheimer (in "The Bernheimer Report," a statement authorized by and issued in the name of the ACLA) declared comparative literature to be an "anxiogenic" discipline, forever in search of a legitimizing self-definition ("Introduction" 1). In 1993, the official statement of the ACLA questioned both components of its disciplinary name: "comparative," it noted with a certain satisfaction, was being increasingly replaced on campuses across the country by "cultural." And as far as "literature" is concerned,

> Literary phenomena are no longer the exclusive focus of our discipline . . . literary texts are now being approached as one discursive practice among many others in a complex, shifting and often contradictory field of cultural production.
> ("Bernheimer Report" 42)

Of course other disciplines composing the academic study of literature have also gone through intense periods of self-examination. But from its inception as a scholarly profession in the early nineteenth century, comparative literature has had more than its share of disciplinary self-fashionings.

Ambiguity in the definition of comparative literature resulted in a certain fuzziness in how it was institutionalized on different campuses. The field assumes a wide variety of organizational forms. Unlike faculty in disciplines that are characteristically organized as departments, such as English or French, comparative literature faculty comes together in several different groupings. Comparative literature is commonly organized as a program; as an adjunct of a larger unit, such as English (at Columbia); or as an amalgam of foreign language units (at Rutgers). There are, of course, departments of comparative literature, but they represent only a small portion of work being done in the field.

This ambivalence of comparative literature in academic structure is reflected in the challenges and opportunities students of comparative literature face both at the beginning and at the end of their training. On completion of their studies, students in English departments assume they will go on to jobs in a department of English. Graduates of French or Slavic departments can likewise expect that they will end up in a department that will have the same name as the one they are leaving. There is an institutional correspondence between their training and the jobs they will enter.

For comparatists, things are not so simple. There is no comparative literature out there that can legitimize comparative literature in the academy, in the way that English is out there for English department graduates. Therefore students who get doctorates in comparative literature shape their training with a double intention: they must be prepared to compete for jobs that come open in any given year in a comparative literature department; they must also be prepared to hold their own with other contenders for the more numerous jobs in national language departments, and most of those contenders will have prepared in just such a language department. It is not unusual for a student to get a degree in comparative literature, but work in, say, a French or English department—or, increasingly, in a cultural or media studies unit. Nevertheless, comparative literature graduate students have done quite well in the changing job market. According to the 2001 MLA survey of PhD placement, the 135 comparative literature candidates did at least as well as the 673 foreign language and 976 English candidates. Specifically, 41.5% of students who were seeking jobs found a tenure-track position (Laurence).

It is reasonable to think that the identity problem of the profession would be less vexed on the relatively small number of campuses where comparative literature operates as a distinct department. But where such entities exist, there is no less contention about the identity of comparative literature than at campuses where there is merely a loose cross-departmental aggregation or no separate entity at all. Where comparative literature departments exist, the constant question hangs over them: Why are some people in them, while others who seem to have an equal claim to being comparatists are not? There will always be comparatists who are not in the comparative literature department—and some will have degrees in comparative literature. There will always be comparatists in the department (some of whom without degrees in comparative literature) who are perceived by outsiders as not really doing comparative literature. Why are people who work on relations between, say, texts from the United States and South America in departments of Spanish, while those who work on theoretical questions as they have been posed primarily by French thinkers get included in the comparative literature department? And isn't any one who does early modern studies necessarily a comparatist? Why then are they often in separate units called Renaissance studies, English, and so on?

The ambiguous nature of the field makes comparative literature demanding, but it is also the source of the excitement most comparatists feel in their work. The ambiguity provides an unusual degree of freedom—but an unusual order of commitment for graduate students entering the field (there are few undergraduate programs in comparative literature). Aspirants face language requirements far beyond those posed in most other doctoral programs in literature. Typically, the incoming graduate student is expected to have competence (usually defined as the ability to take an advanced course taught in the language) in two foreign languages, plus the ability to read a classical language. It was considered a liberalization of comparative literature studies in the 1980s, when many departments loosened their demand for Greek or Latin and accepted other languages to meet this requirement: classical Chinese, Biblical Hebrew, classical Arabic, Sanskrit, Old Church Slavonic, and so on. Few American-trained BAs can meet these rigorous demands, unless they have from a very early stage prepped for a comparative literature degree in the way that, say, premed students do as undergraduates—that is, by specializing from the beginning of their undergraduate training. As a result, a portion of the typical cohort in a serious comparative literature graduate program will be students from abroad, where foreign language training is built into the secondary and even primary levels of education.

Although I have dwelt on aspects of comparative literature that resist any attempt to formulate a late a conventional definition of it, there is enough agreement on certain features of comparative literature to give it many of the marks of institutional presence found in other disciplines. It has a national and

an international professional association. The ACLA has a quarterly journal, has an annual national meeting, and is a member of the American Council of Learned Societies. There are academic departments of comparative literature at many universities. Professional appointments are made in the field (usually cross-listed with some other field). What, then, for all of comparative literature's ambiguities, are the agreed-on characteristics that ground it as an institutional presence?

First of all, comparative literature is unusually plastic, free of the external constraints (admittedly those constraints have grown less normative) that limit the work in other literary departments; confinement to a single language, to a canon, and so on. Unconstrained by the geographic, political, or generic definitions that govern work in most other literature departments, comparatists must establish the guidelines of their work. They experience a kind of vertigo of liberty (Sartre). They face both the freedom and the necessity of motivating connections that in most other literary disciplines are rationalized by preexisting criteria.

It is not by chance, then, that comparatists have been drawn to theory from the outset of their discipline: some structure is needed to provide a basis for their work, a basis that in other departments already inheres in preexisting definitions of the profession. Or such, at least, was the case until recently. As other disciplines have confronted their own crises of professional identity, they too have found it useful to rationalize their readings through an appeal to one or another theoretical base. English departments sometimes speculate about the need for comparative literature units on their campus, because, as one English chair put it, "Now that we have absorbed theory, they are no longer necessary." Naturally, few comparatists would agree, but such a challenge points to the continuing need for comparatists to legitimize their profession's identity.

Comparative literature is a profession, then, that has historically evolved in the very

> **[Comparatists] face both the freedom and the necessity of motivating connections that in most other literary disciplines are rationalized by preexisting criteria.**

conditions that professions devoted to national literatures now confront as new challenges. The very porosity of its borders may be its most defining feature. It is well known in most comparative literature programs (and to all academic administrators) that they are frequently conceived to be either a dumping ground or a wind tunnel. As a dumping ground, they are convenient places to stash appointments of people who are otherwise unclassifiable, such as philosophers who are rejected by philosophy departments or literary scholars whose specialty is not recognized by departments representing better-defined disciplines. The dark side of this tendency is seen in the growing institutional role comparative literature is called on to play as an umbrella under which can be gathered an amalgamation of formerly separate national literature departments when their enrollments begin to decline. When such an arrangement works (as it sometimes does), the result can be a productive synergy among specialists who were formerly more sharply divided by nation than had been many of the authors they study. As a wind tunnel, comparative literature units are places where all kinds of experiments can be conducted. For instance, the comparative literature program is often where administrations have recently turned when they sought to initiate new courses in world literature or other curricular experiments in globalism. There is increasingly a productive relation between comparative literature and emerging media studies programs.

Lest approaching comparative literature by a *via negativa* seem invidious, it might be well to remember that in his *Conflict of the Faculties* (*Streit der Fakultäten*), Immanuel Kant defined the privilege of the despised philosophical faculty precisely by the fact that the philosophers had nothing to offer but questions about the other existing faculties, each of which was defined by the positive agenda it fulfilled for the state (i.e., medicine produced doctors who had as their subject the human body, theology produced pastors who had as their subject Holy Writ, and law produced attorneys who had as their subject the legal code). The difficulty of

defining itself continues to be the profession's greatest opportunity as well as its greatest challenge.

HISTORY

Foundations in Nineteenth-Century Romanticism

Ultimately, comparative literature, like other disciplines devoted to the study of modern literature (i.e., nonclassical texts), derives from the ancient discipline of philology. But the descent from philology to a modern science has been more tortuous for comparative literature than for most other disciplines. For instance, those who study Italian literature are at end of a gradual development from the hegemony of Latin to the emergence of another, descendant language that differed from other offshoots of Latin as they evolved in Italy as opposed to France or Spain. The uniqueness of a distinctively Italian language, historically present as a series of texts dating from at least Dante and Petrarch, was for centuries blurred by its incorporation into a larger and more cosmopolitan theory of poetics.

Classical norms still governed the study and practice of literature for a long time even after Latin divided into distinct national languages. As a result, if you observed the statutory demands of the genre as laid down in Latin, it mattered not that your poem was written in Italian or French. An ode was judged more by how closely it followed the classical norm of the ode than it was by the distinctiveness of its Italian or English. The criteria were extralinguistic, insofar as most students assumed a body of definitions laid down in the distant past that could be modified to judge later works no matter what the language in which the works were composed.

Sometime in the early modern period, things began to change, both in the history of literature and in the political history that lay outside it, culminating finally—in the late eighteenth, early nineteenth century—in a complete revolution in standards for judging whether a work was successful or not. Before national literatures could emerge, a different understanding of literature itself had to come into being. The conventional way to mark this revolution is to call it Romantic. As is well known, after the French Revolution, and under the influence of thinkers such as Johann Gottfried von Herder and the Jena school, there emerged a new filiation among national languages, national literature, and international politics. Novel values for judging and studying literature came into existence, most clearly present in the new phenomenon of national poets, such as Johann Wolfgang von Goethe, Aleksandr Pushkin, Adam Mickiewicz (and the renewed perception of Shakespeare that occurs about this time). Works able to express a connection among a particular language, a specific set of sociopsychological characteristics, and a political entity in which the state manifested itself as a nation now came to the fore as defining acts of culture, indeed, as producers of history.

German scholars played a large role in developing non-Germanic national philologies.

This Romantic revolution (here obviously caricatured in the service of economy) coincided with a new chapter in the institutional history of universities, marked most dramatically in the foundation of the University of Berlin in 1810. As literature was discovered to be both the record of the nation's integrity through the ages and its guarantor of authentic identity in the present and future, higher education came to be perceived as the seedbed of citizenship, the preeminent institution for inculcating patriotism. As a result of this coincidence, university curricula all over Europe expanded beyond the four traditional faculties deriving from the medieval university. New courses were added that went beyond classical philology (which had, in any case, been confined to the philosophy or more often theology faculty). Classes in the national language and its literature were now introduced all over Europe.

European scholars now began to mine the national past to form their own philological tradition as universities adopted the German model in one form or another to study each national language and literature. In 1810, its first year of operation, the University of Berlin appointed Friedrich von der Hagen as a junior professor of German language and literature. After their dismissal from Göttingen in 1837, the Brothers Grimm received a government stipend and moved to Berlin also, where they continued to be active in the Berlin Academy. But it was the great New Testament scholar Karl Lachmann more than any other who developed *Germanistik* as a university subject from 1825 on. His publication of classical Middle High German texts such as the *Nibelungenlied*, *Walter von der Vogelweide*, and *Parsifal* were foundational texts. In 1835 Georg Gottfried Gervinus published his five-volume *Geschichte der poetischen Nationalliteratur der Deutschen*, which further strengthened the move to a new national philology (see Rüegg 430–31).

Often German scholars played a large role in developing non-Germanic national philologies. The holder of the chair in the history of medieval and modern literature at the newly founded University of Bonn from 1823 was Friedrich Diez, who is sometimes called the inventor of Romance studies because of the courses he gave not only in Old High German but in French, Italian, Spanish, and Portuguese as well (Rüegg 433). At the end of the nineteenth and beginning of the twentieth century, the Germans would play a leading role even in the formation of Romance philology, resulting in Wilhelm Meyer-Lübke's great four-volume grammar of the Romance languages (1890–1902) and his thirteen-volume etymological dictionary (1911–20). In 1849 the University of Vienna appointed Franz von Miklosich to a chair in Slavonic philology, and Berlin named the other great Slavist of the age, Vratoslav Jagič, to its new chair in 1874.

In the United States, scholars such as George Ticknor (who trained at Göttingen) also now came to be appointed to chairs in postclassical languages and literature. The remarkable Francis March produced a number of books on the history of the English language, causing the *New*

York Times to write in 1859, "We shall be disappointed if [March's lectures at Columbia] do not prove the means of making a systematic study of the English language an essential part of the American Collegiate course hereafter" (Franklin 360). The history of March's various titles constitutes a short history of the arrival of English as a subject in American academe. When first appointed at Lafayette College, the name of March's chair was Professor of Rhetoric and Evidences of Christianity; this title was changed in 1856 to Adjunct Professor of Belles Lettres and English Literature; a year later it was changed to Professor of English Language and Comparative Philology, the first in the United States.

Comparative literature is an epiphenomenon of this history in Europe and the new world. A freshly evolved national consciousness, together with its attendant institutions, gave rise in several countries to new academic programs. Germany introduced new courses in German literature, Russia initiated programs in Russian literature, and so on. It was the existence of such clearly demarcated schools of literature, each going out of its way to dramatize its uniqueness, that brought into being another level of study: once you had many different literatures (instead of a single European tradition deriving from Greek and Latin examples), the question arose of how these new (or newly discovered or posited) entities related to one another. Quite simply, you had to have more than one literature before you could compare them. (The existence of non-European canons would play a role only somewhat later, the European prejudice being that they did not yet constitute literatures.)

The death of a unitary poetics and the rise of modern national literatures coincided in the 1830s with the birth of a new (and inevitably parasitic) profession. Probably the first academic chair in comparative literature was given to the Irishman H. M. Posnett at the University of Auckland. From 1877 to 1888, Hugo Meltzl, professor of German at Klausenburg University (now Babes-Bolyai University in Cluj, Rumania) edited a remarkable series called Acta Comparationis Litterarum Universarum, dealing in twenty-one languages and involving one hundred and thirty colleagues on five continents.

These events were undoubtedly significant in clearing the way for comparative literature. But they unfolded at the periphery of what were then the reigning European cultural centers. The very peripherality of comparative literature's founders can be advanced as an argument for the impulse in the profession from the first to transcend traditional boundaries, to study not just comparative but world literature. But the most immediate effect Meltzl or Posnett had in the nineteenth century was complicated by events unfolding in the capitals of western Europe.

The first chair in comparative literature would not be established in France until 1896 (for Joseph Texte [1865–1900] at the University of Lyons). But decades earlier the profession had established a profile for itself in the scholarship of men such as Abel François Villemain (1790–1870), who is generally credited with coining the term *littérature comparée*; Philarète Chasles (1798–1873); and Jean-Jacques Ampère (1800–64).

The Romantic insistence on originality combined with a new appreciation for the value of folk tradition initiated a search in each nation for features of its culture that were distinctive to it alone. It is only apparently paradoxical that the first chairs in local literatures were founded precisely in those countries that had least confidence in their national identity. Thus, while chairs in English were established at Oxford and Cambridge only in 1894 and 1916, respectively, chairs in English were present in the United States from 1857. And the first Russian literature chair was created as early as 1835.

These institutional details in their totality make clear that, early or late, the study of national literatures was an inexorable tide in the nineteenth century. This localization of literature into national domains had the effect of creating a new need to understand the difference among competing canons as they came on line in universities all across Europe. The more pronounced the differences that emerged, the more urgent became the necessity for some kind of program that could systematize them. Texte put it very well:

> [Romantic criticism] on the one hand has given rise to a movement of each people toward their origins, an awakening of the collective consciousness, a concentration of their sparse or scattered forces on the creation of truly autochthonic works. It has provoked, on the other hand, by a contrast to be expected, a lowering of frontiers, a freer communication between neighboring peoples, a more complete knowledge of foreign works. It has been, in one sense, an agent of *concentration*, and in another, an agent of *expansion*.
> (qtd. in Guillén 28)

It might be argued that comparative literature is still historically best conceived as an unintended (if inevitable) consequence of Romanticism.

The rise of comparative literature was also hastened by the split that occurred in the early nineteenth century in philology: instead of the combined study of language and literature, which had always been the hallmark of the rhetorical and philological traditions, the study of language and of literature now separated into two new and distinct disciplines. On the one hand, the study of literature became the study of national literatures, as we have seen. But perhaps more radically, such study was transformed by the defection from within its ranks of professional students of language, who now broke off to form their own discipline, *Sprachwissenschaft* or linguistics. This breakup of the twin concerns of ancient philology created the need for new synthetic methodologies and a whole new objective foundation for the study of literary works, after they ceased to be regarded as textual records of the history of language.

Literaturwissenschaft, the new professional study of literature that resulted when linguists broke off to found their separate discipline, now more than ever focused on questions of theme and character, with a noticeably diminished interest in formal analysis. Different national traditions wrestled with these pan-European developments differently. The French variant proved defining for the fledgling discipline of comparative literature in the years before World War II.

The French School

As a discipline, then, comparative literature derives from many different strands in nineteenth-century intellectual, institutional, and political history. But the version of comparative literature that had the largest later influence is a French invention of the nineteenth century, though greatly beholden in its contours to earlier developments in German Romanticism.[1] For decades French scholars continued to define the profession. They shared a vision based on an unquestioning belief in the existence of distinct national literatures. Consequently, comparison was always between works chosen as the most characteristic representatives of different national traditions. Motivated frequently by a more or less explicit patriotism, comparative studies tended to concentrate on influence: how one's literature enriched another literature.

Such later figures as Fernand Baldensperger (1871–1958) at the Sorbonne sought a less partisan basis for comparison, demonstrating, as in his study of Goethe's influence all over Europe, a greater cosmopolitanism. This generation emphasized a more inclusive European intellectual history, as in Paul Hazard's (1878–1944) 1934 *Crise de la conscience européenne, 1680–1715*. The canonical French vision of comparative literature as a study of influence by one great writer on others is found in its purest expression in the pages of *Revue de littérature comparée*, founded in 1921 by Baldensperger and Hazard. In 1931 Paul Van Tieghem (1871–1948) published an influential manual of comparative literature that went through four editions by the 1950s. Before the 1940s, these were the names and the ideas that dominated the still fledgling study of comparative literature in the United States.

The Emergence of an American School

Today comparative literature is perhaps more strongly ensconced in the United States university system than in any other country in the world. But its beginnings were rather wobbly. The birth of a distinctive brand of comparative literature in the United States can be traced back to the catholic interests of such nineteenth-century intellectuals as Washington Irving and Henry Wadsworth Longfellow, culminating in George Edward Woodberry's (1855–1930) founding of the first program of comparative literature at Columbia University in 1899, followed soon by his (short-lived) scholarly review, the *Journal of Comparative Literature* (1903; not to be confused with *Comparative Literature*, published since 1948). Harvard and Berkeley also established early programs (resp., in 1904 and 1912).

But it was not until some decades later, under the influence of a remarkable wave of refugees from Europe, that a discipline emerged in the United States that was strong and clearly distinct from the French model of Baldensperger and Van Tieghem.

The repression of fascism and Stalinism during the 1930s and 1940s drove a gifted generation of scholars to the United States, where they virtually reinvented comparative literature. René Wellek (1903–95), after studying at Charles University in Prague, where he was associated with Roman Jakobson's (1896–1982) Prague Linguistic Circle, found himself in London as the Germans invaded his homeland. He managed to get to the United States, where (after a brief sojourn at the University of Iowa) in 1946 he settled at Yale. He initiated a new department of comparative literature; it was belated by comparison with such established programs as those at Columbia, but it had the virtue of being organized around new principles and different priorities, which turned out to have long-lasting effects on the discipline.

Instead of deriving directly from the French tradition of *littérature comparée*, the new departments found their inspiration in an Eastern Eu-

ropean tradition that had for decades conceived the study of literature as grounded in close attention to details of individual works. Instead of comparing works to see what they might reveal about different national tendencies, the Russian formalists and Czech aestheticians such as Jan Mukařovský (1891–1975) were interested in isolating those qualities in a work that made it precisely literary. Comparison was between the systematic attributes of texts in different discursive modes. Wellek was deeply influenced by the Russians but had a more philosophical view of the subject than they (his first book was on Kant's influence in England [*Immanuel Kant*]); like others in the Prague Linguistic Circle, he was deeply read in phenomenology, particularly as it was practiced by Edmund Husserl's Polish disciple, Roman Ingarden.

Wellek's vision (canonized in *Theory of Literature*, written with Austin Warren [1947]) had at its center the aim of revealing the literariness of literary works. Assuming a deep knowledge of several literatures and their histories, exiles such as Wellek, and later Erich Auerbach (1892–1957) at Yale and Leo Spitzer (1887–1960) at Johns Hopkins, concentrated on large issues in the study of literature, such as how to organize a scientific history of literature not confined to any particular nation's version of its tradition. This approach meant an intense concentration on particular texts, an emphasis that coincided (especially at Yale, where Robert Penn Warren [1905–89], William Wimsatt [1907–75], and Cleanth Brooks [1906–94] taught) with the rise of the so called New Criticism in English departments across the country—a movement that also called for close reading, if on somewhat different principles.

This emphasis on close—or, as it was called in Russian, slow—reading of particular texts might at first glance appear to be at odds with comparative literature, which up to this point had defined itself precisely by its consideration of more than one text. The refugees showed that better comparison depended on deeper analysis of textual components. Instead of comparing questionable thematic attributes (such as Frenchness or Englishness), they directed their attention now to formal details in the texts compared. This new turn brought in its train a fresh need for the discipline's theoretical underpinning. Wellek argued that closer attention to the formal details of literary works required a general theory able to give significance to what otherwise were isolated minutiae.

A paradox emerged: the closer a reading was, the more it demanded theorization. A new tension was established between theory of literature and close reading, which resulted in the inevitability of comparison. No matter what theory you invoked, its robustness depended on its applicability across a wide spectrum of texts. This fact, combined with attention to the primordial linguistic base of literature that for critics such as Spitzer and Auerbach was normative, meant that advocacy of any particular theory implied it should be applicable to readings from different languages. Comparative literature in the 1940s and 1950s defined itself in the United States as a liberal, pluralistic, and cosmopolitan discipline. Like the earlier émigré anthropologists from Europe—Franz Boas, for example—the exiles who created comparative literature in American universities saw themselves as combating parochialism and the nationalistic excesses that had led to the horrors of totalitarianism in their homeland.

Increasingly during the 1950s and 1960s, theory became a subject in its own right. The almost monopolistic hold on theory that was the privilege of most comparative literature units (largely through their members' holding shared appointments in French) served to give new energy to comparative literature.

The Age of Theory

Readers of this volume will be familiar with the rise and fall of theory in the recent history of literary study, so I allude only to those aspects of both that bear on comparative literature as a discipline. The sources of theory's hegemony during the 1960s and 1970s are various, but from the distinctive point of view of comparative literature they can be seen as the logical outcome of the profession's twin origins in France and Eastern Europe. We saw how figures such as Baldensperger and Wellek defined different stages in the rise of comparative literature in the United States before the 1960s. After the 1960s, general questions arose about virtually every aspect of the study of literature, to the point where the understanding of literature itself underwent change.

While theory of some kind has always been a part of the academic study of literature, in the 1970s and 1980s the sheer amount of emphasis on theory increased exponentially. Many began to fear it would eclipse the study of literature itself. Elaine Showalter sums up those years very well in her account of an interview with a prospective candidate for a job in the Princeton English department in the 1980s. The candidate described his dream course as one that would be "theory and nontheory." When asked what "nontheory" was, the candidate promptly replied, "You know, poems, stories, plays."

Because comparative literature was born in the nineteenth century as a child of European scholars, it felt natural for students and professors in other departments, often uncomfortable with the bizarre new ideas that had been swept under the conceptual rug of theory in the 1970s and 1980s, to assume their comparative literature colleagues somehow knew how "to do theory." Comparative literature units began offering literary theory surveys that attracted students from many other sectors of the university. Schools of theory emerged at campuses such as Yale, Irvine, Hopkins, Buffalo, and Cornell, and these schools were frequently defined by local teachers who might be in an English or French department but who more often than not held a joint appointment in comparative literature.

> **The almost monopolistic hold on theory . . . served to give new energy to comparative literature.**

It would be inappropriate to examine here the causes that led to the demise of high theory in the late 1970s. But it is impossible to understand the changes in comparative literature's fortunes that occurred at that time without recognizing that a more or less exclusive focus on literature that had been characteristic of earlier theory (such as formalism and structuralism) was now expanded to include new and more immediately engaged topics. These were—and continue to be—highly various but have in common a greater concern for theme than form. Literary texts came more frequently to be read as only one of several sources of historical, social, political, and religious data that could be mined for a better understanding of issues that were of general, not merely academic, concern.

Several consequences flowed from this new demand that literature be relevant beyond the narrow confines of its former scholarly borders. An immediate effect was perceptible in foreign language departments: since close reading of literary texts previously felt to embody the spirit of the nation that produced them was no longer fashionable, it was less necessary to have command of the language in which those texts were originally written. German departments started to change into German studies programs, Slavic into Slavic studies, and so on. The flight of students from traditional language courses was compensated by the introduction of new courses, invariably taught in English, on topics such as the Nazi film industry or the importance of bread making in French history. Even where courses were still taught in foreign languages, previously unstudied texts were now introduced. One read not only metropolitan French or peninsular Spanish literature. A fresh canon was discovered in francophone works, written by authors in French colonies, or in texts from Latin America. Even English departments, always able to depend on a predictable enrollment, began to emphasize anglophone works from Africa or the Caribbean. Indian writers of English novels opened up vast new territory.

Some irony attaches to the fact that the origin of such programs can be traced back to academic departments that had earlier adopted a studies model of their subject. Many departments of classical languages had met enrollment decline by introducing a classical studies model, focusing on the culture of the Greeks and Romans. Courses in Greek may have languished, but courses in Greek mythology taught in English flourished. American studies, set up originally to study anglophone literature as it evolved in the United States, began to study inter- and intra-American texts: Afro-American, Asian American, and so on.

Since comparative literature units are always in some kind of symbiotic relation with the English and foreign language departments, these developments could not help but have an effect on comparative literature as a discipline. If literature had changed in the eyes of society at large, so had comparative literature changed in the eyes of the academy.

The Current Scene

At the present time, comparative literature can best be grasped as a spectrum of activities, all of which seek to bring order into the welter of new definitions of how geographic space is organized politically in the world outside the university, as those changes reflect themselves in boundary shifts among disciplines in the academy. There has been a blurring of the traditional humanitites with the social sciences. The spectrum includes at least three different tendencies, the internationalist voice of each in a somewhat different timbre: world literature, globalism, and cultural studies. Of course, something like these tendencies are present in other academic departments as well, but comparative literature shades them in its own way.

The two most important extra-academic forces influencing change in comparative literature units can be charted at different levels of abstraction. At the highest level are changes in how international politics has recently reconceived the globe as a series of existing or potential nation-states. The assumption, prevalent at least since Kant's late essays on universal history and perpetual peace, that the natural order of an enlightened world is a balance of power among nation-states seems increasingly to be hopelessly optimistic. After World War I, a search began for new ways to conceive the international order. An inevitable direction such thinking has taken is a quest for units of organization less fraught with parochialism than the nationalisms of the past. This impulse has resulted in a number of different tendencies that collectively have resulted in several versions of world literature, globalism, and cultural studies.

Tectonic shifts outside the academy have had powerful influence in universities all over the world but especially in the United States. Comparative literature has been deeply affected. Beginning as a discipline that sought to reach beyond the boundaries of narrowly defined national literary canons, it nevertheless took for granted the reality of those canons. Comparatists such as Baldensperger and Van Tieghem relied on the prior work of such national canon builders as Hippolyte Taine. Thus comparatists in their own parasitic way were just as dependent on the construct of autonomous national canons as those who forged that construct. They might be critical of it, but they did not question the existence of parthenogenetically evolved national literatures.

Even so, comparative literature in the past asked many of the questions about the autonomy of national literary canons that the national language departments were forced to confront only recently. While Goethe clearly did not in 1827 mean by *Weltliteratur* what is now called world literature (Damrosch, "Introduction"), his very coinage of such a term points to a dawning recognition among the more cosmopolitan members of the Romantic international intelligentsia and their heirs (among whom the parents of comparative literature are to be counted) that national literature was perhaps an invention of patriots. In any case, it was theoretically inadequate.

WORLD LITERATURE

It is not by chance, then, that on many campuses it is the comparative literature faculty members who initiate courses in and write textbooks for the many new programs in world literature that have already or are about to come into existence. Comparatists have found authorization not in devotion to theory but in the cosmopolitanism that their discipline has mandated from its inception. Representative of this trend in current comparative literature is the enormous *Norton Anthology of World Literature*, with its sixteen editors (among whom Wellek is still listed) (Mack et al.). The anthology is typically for survey courses, the more ambitious of which may begin with Gilgamesh and end with Toni Morrison. Such survey courses represent a challenge to comparitists not only because they must depend on scholarship outside their specialty but also because they perforce teach most texts in translation.

Franco Moretti at Stanford and the Columbia comparatist David Damrosch are perhaps the leading figures now in this version of comparative literature. Damrosch is author of a magisterial book that seeks to provide a new definition of world literature (*What Is*) and editor of a *Longman Anthology of World Literature* that is even more comprehensive than the Norton (Damrosch et al.). He has articulated a vision of comparative literature's subject as not just postcolonial but also postcanonical. His subtle and useful point is that canons directing curricula have not disappeared; given that there are only so many authors who can be crowded into even the most generous syllabus, canons never will disappear. But the old list of agreed-on masterpieces has morphed into a new structure comprising at least three levels. After studying recent scholarly publication, Damrosch breaks current trends in the academy into a hypercanon, composed of former giants still dominating the field, such as William Shakespeare and James Joyce; a countercanon, composed of new figures from subaltern literatures or minor languages in great power areas of dominance, such as Lu Xun and, preeminently, Salman Rushdie; and a shadow canon, composed of authors who were once much studied but have begun to slip into obscurity (but who may later be resuscitated), such as William Hazlitt and John Galsworthy.

Moretti has recently undertaken numerical studies of different genres of the novel as they have been published at different periods and in different parts of the globe, including Nigeria and Japan. He has theorized the importance of cartography and statistics for large-scale investigation in literary history. He has provided detailed maps of literary London and Paris in the nineteenth century as they relate to novels of the period (*Atlas*). His recent work contains graphs and tree diagrams charting evolutionary cycles of novel types.

In what served as a kind of manifesto for study of world literature, published in *New Left Review* in 2000, Moretti—drawing on world systems theory as pioneered by Immanuel Wallerstein—advocated that comparative literature break with its tradition of close reading of particular texts ("Conjectures"). The philological hangover of close reading (especially in the United States) has hindered perception of our true subject, he argues: the "planetary system" of literary texts from everywhere (54). As Auerbach asked in his own (more restrained) manifesto on this subject ("Philologie"), how, in the midst of so huge a topic, is one to find a place to begin (an *Ansatzpunkt*)? Moretti's answer is to begin with a genre, in his case the novel, and then to read not exclusively original texts (how could one?) but translations and even scholarship on texts one will never read. This "distant reading" is the price a responsibly comprehensive take on world literature must pay (57).

While Moretti has aroused criticism from those in the profession who still feel emphasis should be put on close reading of individual texts (a skill he himself possesses, as he has demonstrated on other occasions), he has inspired a number of scholars to reconceive their subject. While highly original, his work in some ways is a continuation of the old formalist dream of conceiving literature as a system—a project that only a comparative literature perspective can entertain.

Globalism as it is present in contemporary versions of comparative literature is not to be confused with world literature, although there are of course overlaps between the two. For one thing, globalists usually include more political history and are more oriented toward the modern period than their colleagues in world literature. An early leader of this later wave of global awareness was Edward Said, whose 1978 *Orientalism* eloquently laid out the case against the parochialism of Western scholarship when confronting non-European cultures. The eloquence of his style and his charismatic personal force demonstrated once again the ability of comparative literature's wider view to influence other disciplines.

Said's colleague at Columbia, Gayatri Spivak, has been another inspired leader of this trend. As Said, she demonstrates the important place that outsiders have played in the formation of comparative literature in the United States. Her first degree was from Calcutta; she then studied at Cornell and wrote a dissertation under (a pre-Derridean) Paul de Man on Yeats. While teaching at Iowa, her 1976 version of Jacques Derrida's *Of Grammatology* with its magisterial translation and performative preface helped initiate the age of theory. In a long series of publications since then, Spivak has carved out the subdiscipline of postcolonialism, although she describes herself as a "para-disciplinary, ethical philosopher" (Interview 25).

Emily Apter of New York University has shown new ways that literatures influence one another, through subtle readings that are inflected by unexpected historical and political insights. The famous sojourn of Spitzer and, later, Auerbach in Turkey during their exile from Nazism was often perceived as a kind of regrettable interruption in their careers before they settled in the United States. Apter shows on the contrary that the encounter with Turkish traditions and intellectuals had a determining effect on Spitzer's later work and his activity in Istanbul in the 1930s might be considered the origin of globalism as it is now conceived ("Global *Translatio*"). Current work in postcolonialism, such as Elleke Boehmer's *Empire, the National, and the Postcolonial*, can deal with texts that are primarily in English but that range over South Asian, Irish, and South African sources. Another figure who has done much to demonstrate the richness of previously unexplored global connections is Dudley Andrew, through his work on French and Japanese films (*Mists* and *Kenji Mizognchi*) and more recently in his Moretti-inspired search for the various places on the world map where cinema has experienced unusual spikes of creativity.

All work in cultural studies, no matter how defined, is ineluctably affiliated with comparative method, but certain professors of comparative literature have done a great deal to advance particular strands in cultural studies. Expanding Freudian psychoanalysis has been of special interest to comparatists such as Sander Gilman, Shoshana Felman (*Jacques Lacan* and *Juridical Unconscious*), Cathy Caruth (*Trauma* and *Unclaimed Experience*), and Peter Brooks (*Reading* and *Troubling Confessions*). They have engaged a wide array of topics, including differing conceptions of the body, anti-Semitism, and the workings of the law. Felman recently used her deep knowledge of Freudian and Lacanian theory to reread a number of famous legal battles, from O. J. Simpson's trial to Hannah Arendt's account of the Eichmann trial (*Juridical Unconscious*). She emphasizes what might be called the poetics of witnessing. Trauma theory plays a particularly large role in her work, as it does in that of Caruth, both in her own books (*Empirical Truths*) and in the influential anthologies she has edited (*Trauma*). Brooks, whose earlier work on narrative theory made powerful and original use of Freudian theory, also recently turned his attention to literature in the law and the law in literature. His work, particularly his study of confessional modes, has proved influential not only among humanist scholars but with practicing lawyers as well (*Troubling Confessions*).

∼

As this brief survey makes clear, comparative literature today is a neighborhood in transition—but then, when was it not? The obvious fact of its expansion into new fields—film studies, legal studies, gender, identity studies, and many

All work in cultural studies, no matter how defined, is ineluctably affiliated with comparative method.

more—should not obscure an even more fundamental change that has occurred in recent years: the breakout from comparative literature's former condition of terminal Eurocentrism. The expansion of languages that now characterizes work done in comparative literature programs and departments will have enormous consequences for future study. In the years following World War II, when comparative literature was being formed in this country by European refugees, it was only natural that European languages should have dominated the profession. For all its ideological commitment to cosmopolitanism, comparative literature in the United States from the 1950s to the 1990s focused almost exclusively on the literatures of Europe. Auerbach's *Mimesis* is perhaps as close to a defining act of comparative literature scholarship as has ever been published—and yet it covers only west European texts (with the exception, of course, of the Bible), ignoring even texts from Eastern Europe.

Happily, things are changing rapidly, and the one prediction that can be made with assurance is that comparative literature units will be much more broadly based in the languages they serve. This trend has been particularly apparent among scholars devoted to Chinese culture. Stephen Owen has written extensively on Chinese poetry, but always from a perspective that included deep knowledge of Western aesthetics and literary history. His work on Chinese literary theory demonstrates the rich possibilities available to those who can expand their horizons to include knowledge of previously disparate traditions. Pauline Yu and Kang-i Sun Chang (currently coeditor of the forthcoming *Cambridge History of Chinese Literature* [Owen and Chang]) have also both demonstrated the virtues of knowing Western theory and history in their readings of classical Chinese poetry. Younger scholars such as Lydia Liu and Haun Saussy have taken the interchange between Eastern and Western traditions, using insights gained from their deep knowledge of ancient Greek, modern French, and Italian literature to interpret Chinese culture for Western audiences.

In sum, the future of comparative literature would seem to be immense. As it increasingly turns to world literature as its subject, the entire world is literally before it. There are enormous rewards to be had for those who have the languages, the energy, and vision to pursue an autonomous life of learning.

NOTE

1. Part of the explanation is to be found in the unique shape that French reforms in higher education assumed after Napoléon closed the universities.

WORKS CITED AND SUGGESTIONS FOR FURTHER READING

Amer. Comparative Lit. Assn. Official statement. 1993.

Ampère, Jean-Jacques. *Histoire de la formation de la langue française pour server de complement à l'histoire de la France.* 2nd ed. Paris: Didier, 1869.

Andrew, Dudley. *Kenji Mizoguchi: A Guide to References and Resources.* Boston: Hall, 1981.

———. *The Mists of Regret: Culture and Sensibility in Classic French Film.* Princeton: Princeton UP, 1995.

Apter, Emily. *Continental Drift: From National Characters to Virtual Subjects.* Chicago: U of Chicago P, 1999.

———. "Global *Translatio*: The 'Invention' of Comparative Literature, Istanbul, 1933." *Critical Inquiry* 29 (2003): 253–81.

Auerbach, Erich. *Mimesis: The Representation of Reality in Western Literature.* 1946. Trans. Willard Trask. Princeton: Princeton UP, 1953.

———. "Philologie der Weltliteratur." 1952. *Gesammelte Aufsätze zur romanischen Philologie.* Bern: Francke, 1967. 301–10. Trans. as "Philology and Weltliteratur." Trans. Maire Said and Edward Said. *Centennial Review* 13 (1969): 1–17.

Baldensperger, Fernand. *Goethe en France: Étude de littérature comparée.* 2nd ed. Paris: Hachette, 1920.

Bernheimer, Charles, ed. *Comparative Literature in the Age of Multiculturalism.* Baltimore: Johns Hopkins UP, 1995.

———. "Introduction: The Anxieties of Comparison." Bernheimer, *Comparative Literature* 1–7.

"The Bernheimer Report, 1993." Bernheimer, *Comparative Literature* 39–50.

Boehmer, Elleke. *Empire, the National, and the Postcolonial, 1890–1920.* Oxford: Oxford UP, 2002.

Brooks, Peter. *Reading for the Plot: Design and Intention in Narrative.* New York: Knopf, 1984.

———. *Troubling Confessions: Speaking Guilt in Law and Literature.* Chicago: U of Chicago P, 2000.

Caruth, Cathy. *Empirical Truths and Critical Fictions: Locke, Wordsworth, Kant, Freud.* Baltimore: Johns Hopkins UP, 1991.

———, ed. *Trauma: Explorations in Memory.* Baltimore: Johns Hopkins UP, 1995.

———. *Unclaimed Experience: Trauma, Narrative, and History.* Baltimore: Johns Hopkins UP, 1996.

Chasles, Philarète. *Questions du temps et problèmes d'autrefois: Pensées sur l'histoire, la vie sociale, la littérature.* Paris: Baillière, 1867.

Damrosch, David. "Introduction: Goethe Coins a Phrase." Damrosch, *What Is* 1–38.

———. *What Is World Literature?* Princeton: Princeton UP, 2003.

Damrosch, David, et al., eds. *Longman Anthology of World Literature.* New York: Longman, forthcoming.

Felman, Shoshana. *Jacques Lacan and the Adventure of Insight: Psychoanalysis in Contemporary Culture.* Cambridge: Harvard UP, 1985.

———. *Juridical Unconscious: Trials and Traumas in the Twentieth Century.* Cambridge: Harvard UP, 2002.

Franklin, Phyllis. "English Studies: The World of Scholarship in 1883." *PMLA* 99 (1984): 356–70.

Gervinus, Georg Gottfried. *Geschichte der poetischen Nationalliteratur der Deutschen.* 5 vols. Leipzig, 1835–42.

Gilman, Sander. *Freud, Race, and Gender.* Princeton: Princeton UP, 1993.

Guillén, Claudio. *The Challenge of Comparative Literature.* Trans. Colin Franzen. Cambridge: Harvard UP, 1993.

Hazard, Paul. *La crise de la conscience européenne.* Paris: Livre de Poche, 1994.

Kant, Immanuel. *The Conflict of the Faculties / Die Streit der Fakultäten.* Ed. and trans. Mary J. Gregor. Lincoln: U of Nebraska P, 1979.

Lachmann, Karl, ed. *Die Gedichte Walthers von der Vogelweide.* Berlin: Reimer, 1827.

———, ed. *Der Nibelunge Not mit der Klage: In der ältesten Gestalt mit den Abweichungen der gemeinen Lesart.* Berlin, 1826.

———, ed. *Parzival.* By Wolfram von Eschenback. Berlin, 1833.

Laurence, David. E-mail to the author. 19 July 2005.

Levin, A., ed. *The Legacy of Philarète Chasles.* Chapel Hill: U of North Carolina P, 1957.

Liu, Lydia. *Translingual Practice: Literature, National Culture, and Translated Modernity.* Stanford: Stanford UP, 1995.

Mack, Maynard, et al., eds. *The Norton Anthology of World Literature.* 2 vols. New York: Norton, 1995.

Meyer-Lübke, Wilhelm. *Grammatik der romanischen Sprachen.* 4 vols. Leipzig: Reisland, 1890–1902.

———. *Romanisches etymologisches Wörterbuch.* Heidelberg: Winter UP, 1992.

Moretti, Franco. *Atlas of the European Novel, 1800–1900.* 1977. New York: Verso, 1999.

———. "Conjectures on World Literature." *New Left Review* 1 (2000): 54–68.

Owen, Stephen. *Traditional Chinese Poetry and Poetics*. Madison: U of Wisconsin P, 1985.

Owen, Stephen, and Kang-i Sun Chang, eds. *Cambridge History of Chinese Literature*. 2 vols. Cambridge: Cambridge UP, forthcoming.

Rüegg, Walter. "Theology and the Arts." *A History of the University in Europe: Universities in the Nineteenth and Twentieth Centuries* Vol.3. Ed. Rüegg. Cambridge: Cambridge UP, 2004. 424–46.

Said, Edward. *Orientalism*. New York: Pantheon, 1978.

Sartre, Jean-Paul. *Being and Nothingness*. New York: Washington Square, 1992.

Saussy, Haun. *Great Walls of Discourse*. Cambridge: Harvard U Asia Center, 2001.

Showalter, Elaine. "A Champion of Cultural Theory?" *Chronicle of Higher Education* 23 Jan. 2004, Chronicle Review: B9. 15 Mar. 2006 <http://chronicle.com/free/v50/i20/20b00901.htm>.

Spivak, Gayatri Chakravorty. *Death of a Discipline*. New York: Columbia UP, 2003.

———. Interview with Sara Danius and Stefan Jonsson. *Boundary 2* 20.2 (1993): 24–50.

———, trans. *Of Grammatology*. By Jacques Derrida. Baltimore: Johns Hopkins UP, 1976.

Texte, Joseph. *Études de la littérature européene*. Paris: Colin, 1898.

Van Tieghem, Paul. *La littérature comparée*. Paris: Colin, 1931.

Villemain, Abel François. *Mélanges historiques et littéraires*. 3 vols. Paris: Ladvocat, 1827.

Wallerstein, Immanuel. *The Modern World-System: Capitalist Agriculture and the Origins of the European World-Economy in the Sixteenth Century*. New York: Academic, 1976.

Wellek, René. "The Crisis of Comparative Literature." *Proceedings of the Second International Congress of Comparative Literature*. Ed. W. P. Friedrich. Vol. 1. Chapel Hill: U of North Carolina P, 1959. 148–56.

———. *Immanuel Kant in England, 1793–1838*. Princeton: Princeton UP, 1931.

Wellek, René, and Austin Warren. *Theory of Literature*. 1947. 3rd ed. San Diego: Harcourt, 1984.

Yu, Pauline. *Reading of Imagery in the Chinese Poetic Tradition*. Princeton: Princeton UP, 1987.

⁓ Cultural Studies

JEAN FRANCO

Several factors account for the emergence of cultural studies: the cultural turn in the social sciences, the interest in subcultures, the media and everyday life, the perceived elitism of literary studies, and the increasing fluidity of boundaries among disciplines. At its most innovative, cultural studies offers a democratic view of culture and embraces a spectrum of methodologies. At present, there is little agreement on what precisely is involved in cultural studies, nor is there much understanding of its many regional variations. One Web entry describes it as a "simmering stew of ideas, voices and lives of people all over the world" (*Cultural Studies Central*). The field is linked to communications studies, media studies, postcolonial studies, feminist studies, ethnic studies, and urban studies. There are journals of European cultural studies and Latin American cultural studies as well as nationally focused journals—for example, devoted to American cultural studies, Irish cultural studies, and Australian cultural studies.

Because it is not underpinned by any particular theory or methodology, the interpretation of what counts as cultural studies is highly variable. In the introduction to *A Companion to Cultural Studies*, Toby Miller sees cultural studies as

a tendency across disciplines, rather than a discipline itself. This is evident in practitioners' simultaneously expressed desires to resist definition, insist on differentiation, and sustain departmental credentials. . . . Cultural studies' continuities come from shared concerns and methods: the concern is the reproduction of culture through structural determinations on subjects versus their own agency, and the method is historical materialism. Cultural studies is animated by subjectivity and power—how human subjects are formed and how they experience cultural and social space. ("What It Is" 1)

At the very least, the approach suggests "a remapping of the humanities as a whole around new contents, new canons, new media, and new theoretical and methodological paradigms" (Bathrick 320). Not surprisingly, the editors of an early anthology of essays on cultural studies opted for total serendipity. Cultural studies

> has no guarantees about what questions are important to ask within given contexts or how to answer them; hence no methodology can be privileged or even temporarily employed with total security and confidence, yet none can be eliminated out of hand.
>
> (Nelson, Treichler, and Grossberg 2)

Cultural studies pastures on a variety of disciplines.

209

All this variability is complicated by the fact that cultural studies pastures on a variety of disciplines:

> It takes its agenda and mode of analysis from economics, politics, media and communication studies, sociology, literature, education, the law, science and technology studies, anthropology, and history, with a particular focus on gender, race, class, and sexuality in everyday life, commingling textual and social theory under the sign of a commitment to progressive social change.
>
> (Miller, "What It Is" 1)

The *Cultural Studies* anthology, edited by Lawrence Grossberg, Cary Nelson, and Paula Treichler, lists "textual analysis, semiotics, deconstruction, ethnography, interviews, phonemic analysis, psychoanalysis, rhizomatics, content analysis, survey research" as methodologies (Nelson, Treichler, and Grossberg 1). As if this were not enough, some Web sites use material

> inherited from traditional academia, archiving texts written long before the digital revolution . . . institutionalizing at least something of a canon, offering readily accessible information and relatively easy publication to the aspiring scholar . . . [while others are] decidedly counter-disciplinary and even counter-academic structures that erode the barriers between subjects, levels of authority, practices of academic writing, and writers and readers.   (Vieth 431)

Paul Smith has criticized the "propensity in cultural studies to avoid offering up any especially firm definition or methodologically suggestive view of what culture really is." He goes on to warn that this lack of definition is the "not inconsiderable price of rendering cultural studies an at best eclectic, at worst unprincipled intellectual endeavor" (333). Certainly an opportunistic element enters both into the proliferation of cultural studies in the academy, especially in Britain and the United States, and into its eager embrace by publishers. Penguin helped finance the Centre for Contemporary Cultural Studies (CCCS) at the University of Birmingham, and Hutchinson published some of the early work. In the United States, Routledge has played a major role in publishing and disseminating cultural

studies, and the University of Minnesota Press has a Cultural Studies of the Americas series. But what, if anything, has given a certain coherence to the field is the political agenda of many of its practitioners and a constantly renewed effort to redefine its contexts. Indeed, it is argued that "context is everything and everything is context for cultural studies; cultural studies is perhaps best seen as a contextual theory of contexts as the lived milieux of power" (Grossberg, "Cultural Studies, Modern Logics" 7–8).

Because the field seems virtually unlimited, a guide to scholarship must necessarily impose its own boundaries. I have chosen to trace the development of cultural studies historically in two influential environments—Britain and the United States (despite the risk of prioritizing Britain)—but also in an area, Latin America, where cultural studies emerged from quite a different intellectual tradition. In conclusion, I examine the challenge of globalization to cultural studies.

CULTURAL STUDIES IN BRITAIN

The 1964 inauguration of the Centre for Contemporary Cultural Studies in Birmingham by Richard Hoggart is generally regarded as a foundational moment, although this opinion has also been hotly contested. It was even suggested that the genealogy of cultural studies could be traced to a variety of sources in Africa, the West Indies, and Russia (Wright 34). Hoggart was the author of the influential book *The Uses of Literacy,* in which he gave an account of working-class culture and habits—a culture that, in the postwar world, was undergoing rapid change under the impact of mass culture. He believed "that the remnants of what was at least in parts an urban culture 'of the people' are being destroyed; and that the new mass culture is in some important ways less healthy than the often crude culture it is replacing" (23–24). One of the novelties of his book was the focus on culture as the key to understanding the changes in postwar Britain.

Hoggart was not alone in making this move. E. P. Thompson also focused on culture in his influential *Making of the English Working Class* (1963). Raymond Williams who, like Hoggart, came from a working-class background and was associated with the New Left, monitored changes that "we now point to as distinctively modern in situation and feeling." The relation between these elements is comprehended in the word "culture "with all its complexity of idea and reference" (*Culture* xv). Williams would elaborate on the social definition of *culture* in *The Long Revolution*, in which he described it as "a description of a particular way of life, which expresses certain meanings and values not only in art and learning but also in institutions and ordinary behavior" (41). He went on to describe the analysis of culture as inclusive of historical criticism

> but [it] will also include analysis of elements that to followers of other definitions are not "culture" at all: the organization of production, the structure of the family, the structure of institutions which express or govern social relationships, the characteristic forms through which members of society communicate.   (42)

In *Television, Technology and Cultural Form*, Williams wrote an interesting analysis of the way the programming of television affected the notion of temporality. He returned to a discussion of culture in *Marxism and Literature*, taking issue with Marxism's view of cultural history as

> dependent, secondary, "superstructural": a realm of "mere" ideas, beliefs, arts, customs, determined by the basic material history. . . . Thus the full possibilities of the concept of culture as a constitutive social process, creating specific and different "ways of life," which could have been remarkably deepened by the emphasis on a material social process, were for a long time missed, and were often in practice superseded by an abstracting unilinear universalism.   (19)

He argued that Antonio Gramsci's theory of hegemony

> includes and goes beyond two powerful earlier concepts: that of "culture" as a "whole social process," in which men define and shape their whole

lives, and that of "ideology," in any of its Marxist senses, in which a system of meanings and values is the expression or projection of a particular class interest.   (108)

Williams's preoccupation with a broader development of culture had its roots outside the academy, in the expansion of further education, especially through organizations such as the Workers Education Association, and in the New Left's critique of traditional Marxism. This background helps explain the overtly political thrust of the CCCS especially after Stuart Hall, who had been editor of *New Left Review*, took over as acting director in 1969. With Williams, he contributed to the May Day Manifesto (1968), which challenged the Labor Party and set out a program of social transformation. Hall acknowledged that many of the key questions he tackled arose from "working within shouting distance of Marxism, working on Marxism, working against Marxism, working with it, working to try to develop Marxism" ("Cultural Studies" 279).

In the early years, the center existed precariously: many of the papers prepared by its members were distributed on mimeographed paper, and research was often a collective endeavor. I stress these details because they also point to a conscious desire on the part of CCCS to separate itself from the elite academy.

Important in the early years was the need to account for the changes in postwar life particularly among the working class, changes that were being reconfigured by immigration from the West Indies, India, and Pakistan as well as by access to consumer culture and greater educational options. Although Hall himself came from a family of West Indian immigrants, the early focus was not on immigration but on what was termed, after the Italian Marxist Gramsci, the "national popular" as a force for resistance and control (Rojek 108–16). The emergence of youth groups such as the Teddy boys (who dressed in Edwardian dress), the mods, and the rockers, who identified themselves according to style and musical tastes, challenged Marxist assumptions about class consciousness, exposing its omission of subjectivity and identification. During the

1970s, the subculture group of CCCS focused on these youth groups; the title of the collected papers, *Resistance through Rituals* (Hall and Jefferson), underscores both the focus on dissidence and the then predominantly ethnographic approach.

Greatly influenced by the work of Phil Cohen, who had argued that subcultures expressed and resolved "albeit magically, the contradictions which remain hidden or unresolved in the parent culture (i.e., working-class culture)" (78), the subculture group examined lifestyles—clothing, rituals, and behavior that created maps of meaning or social texts and bonded their members. "Not only did they negotiate with or oppose the dominant culture, but in many cases they actively appropriated and transformed (and thus subverted) dominant meanings" (Turner 90). Dick Hebdige's *Subculture: The Meaning of Style* elaborates on this research and shows how style can significantly interrupt the process of hegemonic normalization. For the cultural studies practitioner, the

> task becomes . . . to discern the hidden messages transcribed in code on the glossy surfaces of style to trace them out as "maps of meaning" which obscurely re-present the very contradictions they are designed to resolve or conceal.   (18)

In a later study, *Hiding in the Light* (1988), Hebdige modified his view of subculture as resistance and, drawing on the work of Michel Foucault, asserted:

> The "subcultural response" is neither simply affirmation nor refusal, neither "commercial exploitation" nor "genuine revolt." It is neither simply resistance against some external order nor straightforward conformity to the parent culture. It is both a declaration of independence, or otherness, of alien intent, a refusal of anonymity, of subordinate status. It is an insubordination. And at the same time it is also a confirmation of the fact of powerlessness, a celebration of impotence.   (35)

The mention of Gramsci, Roland Barthes, and Foucault in the description of the work of CCCS clearly suggests what became a trend in cultural

Culture is central to both the consolidation of hegemony as well as to the formation of emergent groups dedicated to change.

studies work: to take whatever was necessary from contemporary theorists. The established disciplines, especially philosophy and English, were during the 1970s and 1980s in Britain quite resistant to Continental theory. Not so cultural studies. In CCCS in the 1970s, the problems were twofold: how to explain working-class negotiations with and acceptance of the dominant culture and how to read cultural formations. For the first problem, CCCS turned to Gramsci and the French Marxist Louis Althusser; for the second, it turned to semiotics.

Hall would list what he learned from Gramsci as

> immense amounts about the nature of culture itself, about the discipline of the conjunctural, about the importance of historical specificity, about the enormously productive metaphor of hegemony, about the way in which one can think questions of class relations only by using the displaced notion of ensemble and blocs.
>
> ("Cultural Studies" 280)

Gramsci complicated the traditional Marxist view of the rise of the proletariat by arguing that relations among politics, ideology, the state, political parties, and civil society were never fixed, always shifting. In this panorama, the ruling bloc exercises its hegemony not by repression or propaganda but through a consensus, a tacit agreement as to what constitutes common sense and the norm—that is, those unrecognized forms of acceptance of the status quo that are rooted in the unconscious. Culture is central to both the consolidation of hegemony as well as to the formation of emergent groups dedicated to change. The interest of CCCS in popular culture was generally motivated by this broader political undertow.

Hall emphasized the difference between CCCS and academic departments by attempting to make its researchers into "organic intellectuals" (another Gramscian term)—that is, intellectuals aligned with an emerging historical movement. But he also acknowledged:

> We were organic intellectuals without any organic point of reference; organic intellectuals with a

nostalgia or will or hope (to use Gramsci's phrase from another context) that at some point we would be prepared in intellectual work for that kind of relationship, if such a conjuncture ever appeared.   (281)

The work of Althusser would add precision to this social theory by suggesting, against orthodox Marxism, that a complex of determinations (including the law, family, the education system as well as economic factors) operate on social experience and that it is ideology "that produces, not knowledge, but a recognition of the things we already knew" (Hall, "Rediscovery" 75). Ideology viewed as the "imaginary relation of individuals to the real conditions of existence" substantially enriched Gramsci's "common sense" (Althusser 162–77).

The French connection was extraordinarily important to cultural studies in the 1970s and 1980s (although the French have never responded with enthusiasm to cultural studies itself), for it appropriated not only Althusser's theory of ideology but also elements of semiotics, as developed by Ferdinand de Saussure and by Barthes, whose *Mythologies* and *Système de la mode* theorized cultural practices and the making of the social text without needing the label of cultural studies. Two of the most influential British texts—*Policing the Crisis: Mugging, the State, and Law and Order* (Hall, Critcher, Jefferson, Clarke, and Roberts) and Hall's "Encoding/Decoding"—illustrate this cross-fertilization. The first text, written in response to the fear of being mugged, which allowed the conservative government to win over a substantial portion of the middle-class population in its support, illustrates a thoroughgoing attempt to apply a Gramscian analysis to the political situation. The second text was a challenge to mass communications research that had been largely based on functionalism. Hall distinguishes various codes that operate in this struggle: the dominant or hegemonic code; the professional code (i.e., techniques of construction and transmission); and the negotiated code that allows for interpretation on the basis of lived experience: "the mismatches between the hegemonic code and the situated logic of lived experience potentially expose the hiatus

between fact and bias which ideology labours to disguise" (Rojek 98). Finally there is the oppositional code by which messages are read against the grain. Hall's "Encoding/Decoding" stimulated both criticism and detailed research. Two of the best known books reflecting that research are Judith Williamson's *Decoding Advertisements* and John Fiske and John Hartley's *Reading Television*.

The turn of British cultural studies in the direction of discourse theory owes a great deal to Ernesto Laclau and Chantal Mouffe, whose influential book *Hegemony and Socialist Strategy* (1985) was radically antifoundational. According to their theory, identities are partially constituted through networks of power that are consolidated in discourse though never totally fixed. All social relations, including class, are characterized by contingency. Although Hall himself did not accept the full consequences of this idea, he was receptive to those aspects of discourse theory that underpinned his own view of politics as a strugggle over representation. His work also looked beyond the academy and sought to be an intervention in politics. During the Thatcher years, he was an influential critic of Margaret Thatcher's policies and a member of the Commission on the Future of Multi-ethnic Britain, which published the Parekh Report (2000) that affirmed the ethnically diverse nature of the nation (Rojek 182).

The Centre for Contemporary Cultural Studies was never monolithic; several of its researchers reacted against a narrowly ideological approach. Hebdige's *Subculture* had pointed out that semiosis was not always constrained by ideologies, and Paul Willis diverged even further from the center's core tendencies when he identified what he called "profane culture," that is to say a culture that is embodied and sensuous and beyond the reaches of ideology.

Hall left CCCS in 1979 to become professor of sociology at the newly founded Open University, where working men and women receive the opportunity to study for degrees in their free time. Cultural studies now became available to a new population of students who took a course like Culture, Media and Identities. The conversion of polytechnics into full-fledged universities, thereby opening a space for less conventional disciplines, also stimulated the development of cultural studies.

Two areas neglected in the early years of cultural studies, feminism and race, came to the fore in the late 1970s and early 1980s. In *Women Take Issue: Aspects of Women's Subordination* (Centre), women participants in CCCS chafed against the "masculine domination of both intellectual work and the environment in which it was carried out" (Turner 203). *Off-Centre: Feminism and Cultural Studies* (Franklin, Lury, and Stacey) argued for the centrality of gender in cultural studies and its absence in, for instance, Hall's analysis of Thatcherism. *The Empire Strikes Back* (1982), written like *Women Take Issue* to show up critical absences in cultural studies, underscored the absence of blacks in studies of the working class (Centre). Paul Gilroy's well-known book *There Ain't No Black in the Union Jack* attacked the "morbid celebration of England and Englishness from which blacks are systematically excluded" (12). In *The Black Atlantic: Modernity and Double Consciousness* Gilroy, in a radical gesture that rejected the cultural nationalism that hitherto had characterized cultural studies, proposed that "cultural historians could take the Atlantic as one single, complex unit of analysis in their discussions of the modern world and use it to produce explicitly transnational and intercultural perspective" (15). Gilroy's notion of a compound culture, composed of elements of different cultures, resonates with Latin American theories of hybridity and breaks with the national focus of British cultural studies, although Hall, increasingly focused on race, was engaged by the question of what Britishness meant, given the new ethnicities ("Occupying"). With the increasing concern with globalization, new problems—particularly those of consumption and citizenship—came to the fore. The publication of *Back to Reality* (McRobbie) charted the meeting of cultural studies with globalization.

The influence of British cultural studies has been widespread, thanks to the fact that several of the members of the Birmingham center went on to teach and work in other countries. Tony Bennett, John Fiske, and John Hartley developed cultural studies in Australia, and Gilroy, Lawrence Grossberg, and Hazel Carby now teach in the United States.

CULTURAL STUDIES IN THE UNITED STATES

In the United States, there was no substantial Marxist basis for cultural studies. Indeed, it has been argued that Marxist cultural theory had little effect on American cultural studies (Denning 171), which was rapidly incorporated into the academy. Furthermore, as John Hartley, one of the editors of the anthology *American Cultural Studies* (Hartley and Pearson), pointed out, the dominant position of the United States in the world cast a shadow, especially as America figured as both democratic ideal and imperial foe. Mass commodification was further advanced in the United States than elsewhere, and its products were exported throughout the world.

The genealogy of American cultural studies is not easy to trace. One might begin with the Chicago school of sociology and their research into the working class, including the writing of Studs Terkel, or with the intellectual debates on popular and mass culture in which Dwight McDonald and others participated and that are documented by Andrew Ross in *No Respect: Intellectuals and Popular Culture* (1989). Ross places these debates in the context of the cold war, which fostered the pessimistic view of cultural decline on both left and right. Without describing his work as cultural studies, Ross argues for the "respectful contestation of popular meanings which this book finally seeks to endorse" (210) and justifies academic work as a form of intervention.

While not usually mentioned in connection with American cultural studies, the members of the Frankfurt school can also be numbered among the precursors. Not only were Theodor Adorno, Herbert Marcuse, and Siegfried Kracauer (all immigrants to the United States) interested in the politics of culture but Kracauer was also a pioneer student of mass culture. His book *The Mass Ornament* (1963), though dealing with the Weimar Republic, included essays on best sellers, travel, dance, and hotel lobbies. In his essay on the mass ornament, Kracauer argued that the Tiller Girls—products of the American "distraction factory"—"are no longer individual girls, but indissoluble girl clusters whose movements are demonstrations of mathematics" (75–76). As such the girls become abstractions whose performance could without difficulty be transferred to India, Africa, or Europe. Kracauer is suggesting here a form of deterritorialization whereby culture can be freed from local and national roots and exported internationally—a phenomenon that would become important with the advent of globalization.

Adorno and Marcuse were critical of mass culture, but Walter Benjamin, who died while escaping from Vichy France in 1944, was also an influence on cultural studies. His *Arcades Project* became an influential pioneer text that traced the links among streets, arcades, and the behavior and cultural life of the modern city's inhabitants. His essay "The Work of Art in the Age of Mechanical Reproduction" argued that the aura of the work of art is no longer sustainable in an industrial society that can reproduce images ad infinitum so that they are no longer unique. This argument is crucial, since the loss of aura has dissolved the borderline that separated high from mass culture. Benjamin's writing (and that of Barthes mentioned above) underscored the increasing domination of images through advertisement, signs, photography, and cinema. This domination became one of the themes of cultural studies, along with consumption and everyday life. The theme of everyday life was formulated thanks to the French critic Michel de Certeau, who was interested in how the "procedures and ruses of consumers compose the network of an antidiscipline" (xv).

In the 1970s, the media were usually studied in communications departments that, although highly empirical in their approach, spawned a critical opposition from within—a group of ac-

ademics, notably Herbert Schiller, who were interested in mapping corporate control. In Canada, Marshall McLuhan's controversial but widely disseminated *The Gutenberg Galaxy: The Making of Typographic Man* offered a dazzling promise of postprint culture. One of its main tenets was that the new electronic interdependence re-creates the world in the image of a global village and that the electronic media's reliance on the image is creating a nonliterary culture. McLuhan's books, amply illustrated, were best sellers that popularized mass-culture theory. Michael Denning traces the genealogy of United States cultural studies back to the 1930s and 1940s and to writers and critics such as Kenneth Burke, Constance Rourke, F. O. Matthiessen, Oliver Cromwell Cox, and Carey McWilliams—all of whom shared "a socialist or social-democratic politics, an interest in the popular arts, a desire to rethink notions of race and ethnicity, nation and people, and a concern for cultural theory" (139–40).

In the 1960s, the challenges posed by youth to all conventional standards, the explosion of the drug culture, and the new journalism made culture a central element in contesting the status quo and the exclusionism of high culture. Journalists like Hunter S. Thompson and Tom Wolfe and writers like Norman Mailer and Joan Didion "abandoned the standard of journalistic 'objectivity' to engage in radically subjective critiques of cultural trends and change" (Hartley and Pearson 20). Although not usually mentioned in relation to cultural studies, one should certainly take note of Fredric Jameson's work, especially *Postmodernism*. One of the complications suggested by Jameson is that postmodernism and cultural studies are not easily distinguished. This observation resonates with Ross's description of postmodernism's "profusion and appropriation of the meanings that are then redefined to different ends and contexts whose meanings can be appropriated and applied to different ends and, more importantly, different causes" (*Universal Abandon?* xi). Indeed, several contributors to Ross's anthology of postmodernism—Grossberg ("Putting"), George Yúdice ("Marginality"),

Meaghan Morris ("Tooth")—are associated with cultural studies.

Denning describes cultural studies in the United States as "an immigrant, a travelling theory, adopting its name from British cultural studies, which was itself something between an academic discipline and an intellectual movement of the New Left" (136–37). Nevertheless, one feature of cultural studies in the United States was its rapid incorporation into the academy in the 1980s and 1990s at a time when both feminism and ethnic studies were challenging the standard curriculum, demanding that it take account of multiculturalism; gender; and the hitherto ignored contributions of African American and Latino intellectuals, writers, and artists. The cultural wars of the 1980s over issues such as the changes in the Stanford freshman curriculum in order to accommodate texts outside the Western canon and over art exhibitions held to be indecent were symptomatic of a crisis over what constituted knowledge and culture.

Houston Baker outlined the defense tactics of those who claimed to defend humanities thus:

> Conserving the definite article *the* for humanities conceived only in selective Western terms is the first move in the dance. Backward glances to a glorious past—one free of colonial expansion, racism, sexism, and self-interested imperialism—a past that never was—is the second move. The third and decisive move is—in a telecommunal age—to couch the crisis of *the* humanities in bookish terms, as though reading and writing were not mere technologies that favored an order of privileged ascendency and effective power and ideological control known even to Thoth and his King long ago.   (188)

Whether this hitherto marginalized or excluded material was best examined from the point of view of gender (women's studies), race (ethnic studies), or cultural studies was not easy to determine. It is true that women's studies, queer studies, and ethnic studies have been centrally concerned with theorizing gender and race and with the politics of inclusion and exclusion. Insofar as cultural studies focuses on "interrelationships between supposedly separate cultural domains" and "on understanding social transformation and cultural change" (Nelson, Treichler, and Grossberg 11), questions of identity and representation could not be ignored. Probably the most challenging theoretical contribution to this debate, however, has come not from cultural studies practitioners but from Judith Butler's critique of feminist theory in *Gender Trouble* and her argument that gender is a habitus that is constituted and subversively reconstituted through performance. Most cultural studies contributions to the understanding of identity focus on difference, hybridity, and diaspora—all approaches criticized by Grossberg, who emphasizes agency and a "belonging without identity" ("Identity" 119).

Because of the indeterminate reach of cultural studies in the North American context, I limit my discussion to the meshing of cultural studies with feminism and race and to the political agenda of cultural studies. I speak of meshing because women's and ethnic studies departments are often places where cultural studies is practiced although not necessarily named as such. Studies of masculinity, of male and female fantasy, and of queerness often explore mass culture—film, romance, the imagery of advertisements, and so on—in search of creative responses that resignify mass-media messages or resistance to conventional forms of identity construction. Feminists have strongly opposed the view that women are passive consumers held totally in the thrall of mass culture. Janice Radway's *Reading the Romance* (1984) was a key contribution to this debate. Radway argued for the positive aspects of the Harlequin romance that allowed women to reexperience the pleasurable early childhood experience of nurturing. She drew on literary criticism, ethnography, and psychoanalysis in her book, which exemplifies the importance to cultural studies of examining reception and agency. Although her work was criticized for not taking into account the subversive potential of fantasy (Penley), it is symptomatic of the focus on reception as the place where alternative and often subversive readings of the social text are performed.

Many African Americans and Latinos were incorporated into the academy in departments of ethnic and black studies, where studies of popular culture—especially music—were important innovations. Minorities had in the words of Baker "given birth to energetic expressive forms such as postmodern hip-hop, interventionist film culture, and radical scholarship into gender, class and race determinants of power and knowledge in the world we inhabit" (189). "Rapping" is, in his view, "a challenging form of creativity that converts oppression and lack into a commercial and communal success" (192). This is also the thesis of Juan Flores's work on Latino identity.

Ethnic studies and gender studies often draw on material that they have in common with cultural studies. One common interest is the question of identity and representation; another is agency—that is, the ability to act in defense of one's interests in the various frameworks and constraints set by society. Language and the acquisition of interpretive power are all important tools to this end, as is illustrated by the word *black*, which after being a negative marker was turned into a positive sign during the civil rights movement of the 1960s. What has become central is precisely the struggle for interpretive power and a resistance to stereotyped identities. Although these issues are not confined to the United States, they take on a local aspect in an environment in which the media are proactive in the constitution of identities so that assumptions about generalized Latinos, Hispanos, blacks, women, Native Americans, and queers must be challenged constantly. The need to challenge has led Yúdice to argue that performativity that deploys fantasy and imagination is both constitutive of identity and a tool for challenging scripted identities ("Comparative Cultural Studies Traditions").

Migration and cultural hybridity raise the issue of globalization and America's place in the world. Hartley's introductory essay to *American Cultural Studies,* rejecting the notion of American cultural imperialism, argues that American culture, even as it is disseminated throughout the world in film, television, advertisement, and music, has itself been influenced and shaped by its contact with other cultures (11). The "American way of life," Eva Vieth argues, "embraces both free speech and free enterprise capitalism, modernity through ideology and modernity through technology, and a 'manifest destiny' to shape the future" (427). Denying the validity of theories that attribute the global domination of American exports to direct imperial force, Hartley argues:

> Transparency, hybridity, mutual attraction, and dialogue—these terms seemed better suited to the international traffic of the semiosphere, rather than the paranoid Cold War terminology of conventional social and political science. (11)

This revisionist argument suggests that the once intoxicating brew of a politically interventionist cultural studies has been superseded, although "mutual attraction" and "dialogue" hardly address the inequalities that exist between powerful United States research institutions, with their infrastructure of publishing and Internet activities, and universities and research institutions on the periphery.

Given the protean nature of the university, cultural studies has become fissiparous—as departments now promote visual culture, material culture, and cinema studies that often cover ground similar to the ground covered by cultural studies. Clearly, there is a sales pitch in such promotions as teachers try to slant their courses in ways that will attract students, so that under the rubric of cultural studies something like entertainment creeps into the curriculum. At the other extreme, there is what Hall calls "theoretical fluency," by which everything—politics, race, class, gender, subjugation, domination, exclusion, marginality, otherness, and so on—comes to be textualized, so that "there are ways of constituting power as an easy floating signifier which just leaves the crude exercise and connec-

Migration and cultural hybridity raise the issue of globalization and America's place in the world.

tions of power and culture altogether emptied of any signification" ("Cultural Studies" 286).

LATIN AMERICAN CULTURAL STUDIES

While the term *cultural studies* is not commonly used in Latin America, its scholars have made some important contributions to theory as well as significant critiques of American cultural studies. In order to understand the source of this critique, we should remind ourselves of the historic preoccupation of Latin Americans with the notion of copying: the fear that Latin American thought and culture has generally been secondhand, a reflection of or a reaction to what was thought and done elsewhere. Historically the lettered intelligentsia played an important role in formulating definitions of national character and utopian projects of liberation from the yoke of dependency. On the other hand, what the culture critic Angel Rama termed "the lettered city" owed its prestige and its pedagogical intention to its difference from the illiterate masses.

Public intellectuals in Latin America are often writers of fiction or poetry who also write on political, social, and general cultural issues. Twentieth-century modernization along with mass culture brought about a transformation in this relation when, under the influence of new technologies and the media, literacy was no longer the one path to culture and responsible citizenship. Up to that point, cultural change had been monitored in the novel, in poetry, and in the essays of *pensadores* ("thinkers") such as José Martí, José Vasconcelos, Gilberto Freyre, José Carlos Mariátegui, and Fernando Ortíz.

One of the main concerns of the literary intelligentsia was the incorporation of the popular classes and different racial constituencies into the nation, especially as populist governments adapted elements of popular culture to identify the nation and drew on national dress, music,

[In Latin America] it was the social scientists who first took on debates on postmodernism and cultural studies.

and dance as emblems of national specificity. Interestingly it was Laclau, an Argentine scholar and political scientist who taught mostly in Britain and has been a major influence on British cultural studies, whose examination of populism radically transformed notions of resistance and opposition. Laclau, in collaboration with the French critic Mouffe, modified in important ways the Gramscian theory of hegemony and counterhegemony. Laclau and Mouffe dismantled the binarisms of traditional and modern, progressive and reactionary, by showing that multiple interests and cultures were at play in any moment. They used the term *articulation* to describe "a relation among resources that modifies identity." They understood *discourse* as "the structured totality reproduced and constituted through articulatory practices" (Rojek 125). Agency is an effect of articulation and therefore contingent, and identity is at best precarious. The Latin American context of populism as a discursive formation, though less of an influence on Latin American cultural critique, propelled Laclau's argument.

Given the reluctance of writers and literary critics to deal with mass culture, it was the social scientists who first took on debates on postmodernism and cultural studies. During the period of the military governments in the Southern Cone, privately funded research centers became involved in the analysis of the media (CEDES [Centro de Estudios de Estado y Sociedad] in Argentina, CENECA [Centro de Indagación y Expresión Cultural y Artística] and FLACSO [Facultad Latinoamericana de Ciencias Sociales] in Chile), an analysis that was grounded mainly in sociology. The context in which these groups worked was particularly fraught. In the 1960s and 1970s, faced with insurrection from guerrilla bands and with social unrest, military governments seized control of the Southern Cone countries. In Central America there was civil war; in Mexico, the one-party system stifled democratic process. It was in this grim environment that the media expanded their hold. The right-wing domination of the media during the political struggles that preceded the military coup in Chile prompted Ariel Dorfman and Armand Mattelart to write the widely noted *How to Read Donald Duck*, an analysis of comic books that revealed the imperialist message under apparently innocent cartoon characters. Dorfman and Mattelart argued that the comics manipulated readers—especially in the most vulnerable sectors of the population.

But theories of manipulation did not begin to weigh the complexity and ambiguities of reception, especially when, in the wake of the military governments, Latin America fully entered the era of globalization and postmodernism. It was postmodernism rather than cultural studies that opened up the debates over the end of totalizing systems and utopias. As the political scientist José Joaquín Brunner wrote:

> The sensation of the permanent crisis of everything, of the economy, institutions, political regimes, universities, art, public services, private enterprise, the armed forces, poorly and barely hides the fact that we live and think in the middle of a modernity in the process of construction, whose dynamic is increasing the heterogeneities of our very perceptions, knowledges and information. (309)

In other words, the great totalizing narratives that had sustained Latin American culture—national autonomy, continental specificity, and utopianism—no longer had any purchase.

What was now apparent was dispersion and the coexistence and interaction of different social and cultural fragments, interests, and identities. It was not cultural studies as such that captured this change so much as the *crónica* ("chronicle"), which was often written for newspapers and which became the privileged and most flexible form of monitoring and commenting on social change. The foremost practitioner is the Mexican critic Carlos Monsiváis, whose writing registers every aspect of change in Mexico and especially the culture of the megacity. For Monsiváis, the very fragmentation and dispersal of contemporary urban life make it difficult for the dominant classes to impose an ideology. Everywhere the sheer heterogeneity of the crowd defies authoritarian order.

TRANSCULTURATION AND HYBRIDITY

Since the Conquest (and even before), Latin America had experienced conflicts of cultures. The violent imposition of Spanish culture on indigenous peoples never totally eliminated indigenous cultures, which subtly entered into that of the dominant group. Latin American scholars in the 1920s began to refer to this two-way traffic between black, indigenous, and mestizo populations as transculturation. In Cuba, Fernando Ortíz used the term to describe the contact and cultural transformations as black culture filtered into that of the elite (see *Fernando Ortíz*). The Uruguayan critic Rama appropriated the term *transculturation* for the bleeding of indigenous culture into Andean cultures and their mutual appropriations.

By the 1980s many of the cultures formerly considered traditional were undergoing intense change under the impact of modernization as governments increasingly pursued neoliberal policies that opened countries to consumer societies and as peasants immigrated en masse to the cities, altering their profile. In the past, European taste had influenced high culture; now it was American pop culture from rock music to *The Virginian* that was not only pervasive but also impugned by many as destroying traditional cultures and undermining national values. Against pessimistic assessments of cultural imperialism, the Spanish critic Jesús Martín Barbero, a resident of Colombia, undertook studies of reception that focused on the mediations that accounted for different readings and on genres such as melodrama that transformed an older form into the modern setting of the *telenovela*.

The globalization of culture was described by the Brazilian critic Renato Ortiz as "mundialização" ("worlding"). The culture that was emerging, according to Ortiz, was an international popular culture, abstracted from roots and constantly resignified in its travels throughout the world.

Nestor García Canclini's *Transforming Modernity: Popular Culture in Mexico*, published in 1982 and based on ethnographic studies and on the work of Claude Lévi-Strauss and Pierre Bourdieu, changed the whole tenor of debate. García Canclini argued that in indigenous communities there was a two-way traffic, for while villagers increasingly bought mass-produced clothes instead of producing their own textiles, they also had access to new markets for their artisan products and creatively adapted their production to accommodate the tastes of tourists. This development is seen not merely as commercialization but also as a readaptation that involves new forms of self-expression and reinforces local communities. In addition, he demonstrated that responses to modernization varied from village to village, a heterogeneity that theories of manipulation or cultural imperialism simply did not account for.

García Canclini's *Hybrid Cultures* stimulated widespread debate and also became one of the key texts of Latin American cultural studies, once and for all refuting the notion that Latin American culture was a mere copy or imitation. Under the rubric of modernization, this book (first published in 1990) takes the reader on a Mexican journey that encompasses cultural changes of all kinds. What happens to elite culture when Jorge Luis Borges and Octavio Paz appear on television? What is the mass appeal of the Picasso exhibition in Mexico City? How do we assess the massive urban immigration of people born into different cultural contexts? How is Mexican history and multiculturalism displayed in museums? How do we read the culture of a frontier town like Tijuana? For García Canclini, culture is a network in which different temporalities intersect and allow for multiple positions and responses. Instead of the death of traditional cultural forms, they become articulated with modern forms ("Cultural Conversion").

García Canclini's political project is very different from that of British cultural studies, which, at least in its early days, was focused on resistance. His emphasis is on democratization

and citizenship, on the ways that hierarchies and authoritarian structures are being dismantled by the foot traffic of the populace of the contemporary city. Appropriating from Gilles Deleuze and Félix Guattari the term *deterritorialization*, which refers to the process of abstraction and uprootedness characteristic of advanced capitalism, García Canclini refuses to idealize the popular as necessarily contestatory. He argues that the constant processes of interpretation and cultural mixing cannot be classified, in the Gramscian manner, as hegemonic and subaltern, modern and traditional. He writes:

> High, popular and mass are no longer to be found in their familiar places. The tradition and the modern are mixed together all the time, even in cities where the disposition of neighborhoods and institutions has been governed by criteria of social strata. Artisans sell weavings and native pottery in front of art museums. Painters who might once have been classified as elite incorporate quotes from comic strips in the works, or work in industrial design.   ("Cultural Conversion" 30–31)

"Reconversion" contributes to this process:

> To reconvert cultural capital means to transfer symbolic patrimony from one site to another in order to conserve it, increase its yield and better the position of those who practice it. . . . [Reconversion] questions the notion that popular sectors achieve emancipation and are integrated into modernity by means of the socialization of hegemonic cultural assets through education and mass dissemination.   (32–33)

All aspects of cultural life are undergoing rapid change. Technology allows for the distant consumption of serially produced goods, and these agents of cultural production and dissemination have changed from states to "financial institutions, cultural foundations and chains of art galleries related to finance capital or high-tech industries." Traditional opinion makers have given way to those who now control the symbolic market, and "big business now competes with state cultural administration, artistic movements and traditional entrepreneurs and sponsoring organizations" (35–36).

García Canclini's *Consumers and Citizens* focuses on "the concrete conditions in which cultural practices develop in different countries, on the interaction of globalizing projects and the specific multicultural social arrangements obtaining in given regions" (4). Consumption is usually deplored by critics as a manipulation of desire, but for García Canclini it can be a "means of thinking" that opens the way to new forms of citizenship and a different kind of political culture, though he is careful to separate *consumption* from its usual associations with "useless expenditures and irrational impulses" and reconceptualize it so that it includes "access to housing, health, education and access to other goods" (5). His emphasis is on negotiation and citizenship and the need for cultural studies to engage in policy with the aim of constructing "a democratic multiculturalism from its foundation in civil society and with the participation of the state" (161). Clearly this approach implies not an authoritarian or corrupt state but one that allows a variety of local interests to be negotiated.

Yúdice has noted García Canclini's increasing involvement in cultural politics ("From Hybridity" xvi). Yúdice's own work focuses on citizenship that answers the need to create public institutions that respond to popular demand and whose policies may be formulated by representatives of nongovernmental organizations. In this he departs radically from the oppositional attitude that had characterized British cultural studies. In *The Expediency of Culture* he offers a view of culture as actively managed and administered through corporations and foundations that are independent of the state and that provide new social spaces for performing citizenship and for resignifying the social text.

Latin American cultural criticism strongly resists United States academic models. The Argentine critic Beatriz Sarlo, while admitting the need for a new Latin American cultural studies, argues that it "has an object that has yet to take shape in terms of theory but whose material and social existence should be recognized" (341). The Franco-Chilean critic Nelly Richard, while recognizing that cultural studies has helped democratize the academy, nevertheless be-

lieves that many practitioners accept academic standards of verisimiltude and only describe social change "without ever questioning the disruptive effect of such change on the very language itself" (157; my trans.). Instead of *cultural studies* she uses the term *crítica cultural* ("cultural criticism") to describe an approach that could involve examining how particular forms of knowledge have been incorporated into the academy.

~

Has cultural studies lost its way in the era of globalization? Has it come to terms with the vast changes in cultural production and relations? A decade or so ago, critics from the periphery tended to be wary of theories and rhetoric developed in the United States. Morris, an Australian scholar who has worked outside the academic context, raises some crucial issues when she asks if *international*

> comes to work in cultural studies as it does in the film and record industries—as a euphemism for a process of streamlining work to be "interesting" to American and European audiences. . . . [This kind of internationalism], may foster the "strategic" adoption in cultural studies of saleable rhetorics with tenuous links indeed to Australian social conditions.   ("On the Beach" 456)

In the early days of the boom in cultural studies, Morris had already criticized what she termed the "romantic inheritance of cultural studies" on the grounds that cultural studies works to create a "fraught space" of ethical grandiloquence, in which massive, world-historical problems are debated on such a level of generality that they cannot possibly be solved and are posed in ways that do not, will not, and cannot ever connect to agencies by which actual social futures may be given a "definite shape" (466). Certainly there is considerable tension among national, regional, and international forms of cultural studies that is as yet unresolved.

This essay by no means exhausts the subject of cultural studies or recognizes all its practitioners. Those hostile to

There are strong arguments for a field that is avowedly political in its confrontation with the rapidly changing conditions of modern life.

cultural studies find it presentist—that is, too concerned with the contemporary. It has been criticized for its shallow or nonexistent concept of history and for its scant respect for native languages and the delicate politics of translation (Spivak, *Critique* 376–77). It is quite possible that in the future, certain projects and interests of cultural studies will scatter to be absorbed into ancillary fields. Yet despite its insecurities, there are strong arguments for a field that is avowedly political in its confrontation with the rapidly changing conditions of modern life. Gayatri Chakravorty Spivak's agenda for the future of cultural studies looks daunting:

> The point is to negotiate between the national, the global, and the historical as well as the contemporary diasporic. We must both anthropologize the West, and study the various cultural systems of Africa, Asia, Asia-Pacific, and the Americas as if peopled by historical agents. ("Scattered Speculations" 278)

At the very least, such an agenda calls for returning to one of the initial practices of the Birmingham center—namely, collective research and teaching—though it is important to reach out beyond national agendas to comprehend the questions, doubts, and differences that have emerged in contexts other than our own.

WORKS CITED AND SUGGESTIONS FOR FURTHER READING

Althusser, Louis. *"Lenin and Philosophy" and Other Essays.* Trans. Ben Brewster. New York: Monthly Rev., 1971.

Baker, Houston. "Handling Crisis: Great Books, Rap Music, and the End of Western Homogeneity: Reflections on the Humanities in America." Hartley and Pearson, *American Cultural Studies* 186–97.

Barbero, Jesús Martín. *Communications, Culture and Hegemony: From the Media to Mediations.* London: Sage, 1993.

Barthes, Roland. *Mythologies.* Paris: Seuil, 1957.

———. *Système de la mode.* Paris: Seuil, 1967.

Bathrick, David. "Cultural Studies." *Introduction to Scholarship in Modern Languages and Literatures.* Ed. Joseph Gibaldi. New York: MLA, 1992. 320–40.

Benjamin, Walter. *The Arcades Project.* Trans. Howard Eiland and Kevin McLaughlin. Cambridge: Harvard UP, 1999.

———. "The Work of Art in the Age of Mechanical Reproduction." *Illuminations.* Trans. Harry Zohn. London: Cape, 1970. 219–53.

Bennett, Tony. "Intellectuals, Culture, Policy: The Practical and the Critical." Miller, *Companion* 357–74.

———. "Putting Policy into Cultural Studies." Grossberg, Nelson, and Treichler 23–34.

Brunner, José Joaquín. "Notes on Modernity and Postmodernity in Latin American Culture." *The Latin American Cultural Studies Reader.* Ed. Ana del Sarto, Alicia Ríos, and Abril Trigo. Durham: Duke UP, 2004. 291–309.

Butler, Judith. *Gender Trouble: Feminism and the Subversion of Identity.* New York: Routledge, 1999.

Centre for Contemporary Cultural Studies. *The Empire Strikes Back: Race and Racism in 70s Britain.* London: Hutchinson, 1982.

———. *Women Take Issue: Aspects of Women's Subordination.* London: Hutchinson, 1978.

Certeau, Michel de. *The Practice of Everyday Life.* Berkeley: U of California P, 1988.

Cohen, Phil. "Subcultural Conflict and Working-Class Community." Hall, Hobson, Lowe, and Willis 78–87.

Commission on the Future of Multi-ethnic Britain. *The Report.* Runnymeade Trust. 2003. 20 Mar. 2006 <http://www.runnymedetrust.org/projects/meb/report.html>.

Cultural Studies Central. 1996–2000. 17 Mar. 2006 <www.culturalstudies.net>.

Curran, James. "Rethinking Mass Communications." *Cultural Studies and Communications.* Ed. Curran, David Morley, and Valerie Walkerdine. London: Arnold, 1996. 119–65.

Deleuze, Gilles, and Félix Guattari. *Anti-Oedipus: Capitalism and Schizophrenia.* Trans. Robert Hurley, Mark Seem, and Helen R. Lane. Minneapolis: U of Minnesota P, 1983.

Denning, Michael. *Culture in the Age of Three Worlds.* London: Verso, 2004.

Dorfman, Ariel, and Armand Mattelart. *How to Read Donald Duck: Imperialist Ideology in the Disney Comic.* Ed. and trans. David Kunzle. New York: Intl. General, 1991.

Fernando Ortiz on the Phases of Transculturation. Comp. J. A. Sierra. Historyofcuba.com. 21 Mar. 2006 <http://www.historyofcuba.com/history/race/Ortiz-2.htm>.

Fiske, John, and John Hartley. *Reading Television.* London: Methuen, 1978.

Flores, Juan. *From Bomba to Hip-Hop: Puerto Rican Culture and Latino Identity.* New York: Columbia UP, 2000.

Franklin, Sarah, Celia Lury, and Jackie Stacey, eds. *Off-Centre: Feminism and Cultural Studies.* New York: Harper, 1991.

García Canclini, Nestor. *Consumers and Citizens: Globalization and Multicultural Conflicts.* Trans. and ed. George Yúdice. Minneapolis: U of Minnesota P, 2001.

———. "Cultural Conversion." *On Edge: The Crisis of*

Contemporary Latin American Culture. Ed. George Yúdice, Jean Franco, and Juan Flores. Minneapolis: Minnesota UP, 1992. 29–43.

———. *Hybrid Cultures: Strategies for Entering and Leaving Modernity*. Trans. Christoper L. Chiappari and Silvia L. López. Minneapolis: U of Minnesota P, 1995.

———. *Transforming Modernity: Popular Culture in Mexico*. Austin: U of Texas P, 1993. Trans. of *Las culturas populares en el capitalismo*. 1982.

Gilroy, Paul. *The Black Atlantic: Modernity and Double Consciousness*. London: Verso, 1993.

———. *There Ain't No Black in the Union Jack*. London: Hutchinson, 1997.

Gramsci, Antonio. *Prison Notebooks*. Vol. 1. Ed. Joseph A. Buttigieg. New York: Columbia UP, 1991.

Grossberg, Lawrence. "Cultural Studies: Crossroads Blues." *European Journal of Cultural Studies* 1 (1998): 65–82.

———. "Cultural Studies, Modern Logics and Theories of Globalisation." McRobbie 7–35.

———. "Identity and Cultural Studies: Is That All There Is?" Hartley and Pearson, *American Cultural Studies*. 114–21.

———. "Putting the Pop Back into Postmodernism." Ross, *Universal Abandon?* 167–90.

Grossberg, Lawrence, Cary Nelson, and Paula Treichler, eds. *Cultural Studies*. New York: Routledge, 1991.

Hall, Stuart. "Cultural Studies and Its Theoretical Legacies." Grossberg, Nelson, and Treichler 277–94.

———. "Encoding/Decoding." Hall, Hobson, Low, Willis 128–38.

———. "Occupying Britishness and Entrenching Change." *Runnymeade Bulletin* 325 (2001): 17–19.

———. "The Rediscovery of 'Ideology': The Return of the 'Repressed' in Media Studies." *Culture, Society and the Media*. Ed. Michael Gurevich, Tony Bennett, James Curran, and Janet Woollacott. London: Methuen, 1982. 56–90.

Hall, Stuart, Chas Critcher, Tony Jefferson, John Clarke, and Brian Roberts. *Policing the Crisis: Mugging, the State, and Law and Order*. London: Macmillan, 1978.

Hall, Stuart, Dorothy Hobson, Andrew Lowe, and Paul Willis, eds. *Culture, Media, Language*. London: Routledge, 1992.

Hall, Stuart, and Tony Jefferson, eds. *Resistance through Rituals: Youth Subcultures in Post-war Britain*. London: Hutchinson, 1976.

Handel, K. Wright. "Dare We De-center Birmingham? Troubling the 'Origin' and Trajectories of Cultural Studies." *European Journal of Cultural Studies* 1 (1998): 33–56.

Hartley, John. "Cultural Exceptionalism: Freedom, Imperialism, Power, America." Hartley and Pearson, *American Cultural Studies* 1–13.

Hartley, John, and Roberta E. Pearson, eds. *American Cultural Studies: A Reader*. London: Oxford UP, 2000.

———. Introduction to "The New Journalism and Its Legacy." Hartley and Pearson, *American Cultural Studies* 19–21.

Hebdige, Dick. *Hiding in the Light: On Images and Things*. London: Routledge, 1988.

———. *Subculture: The Meaning of Style*. London: Methuen, 1979.

Hoggart, Richard. *The Uses of Literacy*. New York: Oxford UP, 1970.

Jameson, Fredric. *Postmodernism; or, The Cultural Logic of Late Capitalism*. Durham: Duke UP, 1991.

Kracauer, Siegfried. *The Mass Ornament: Weimar Essays*. Trans. and ed. Thomas Y. Levin. Cambridge: Harvard UP, 1995.

Laclau, Ernesto, and Chantal Mouffe. *Hegemony and Socialist Strategy: Towards a Radical Democratic Politics*. Trans. Winston Moore and Paul Cammack. London: Verso, 1985.

McLuhan, Marshall. *The Gutenberg Galaxy: The Making of Typographic Man*. Toronto: U of Toronto P, 1962.

McRobbie, Angela, ed. *Back to Reality: Social Experience and Cultural Studies*. Manchester: Manchester UP, 1997.

Miller Toby, ed. *A Companion to Cultural Studies*. Malden: Blackwell, 2001.

———. "What It Is and What It Isn't: Introducing . . . Cultural Studies." Miller, *Companion* 1–19.

Monsiváis, Carlos. *Mexican Postcards*. Ed. and trans. John Kraniauskas. London: Verso, 1997.

Morris, Meaghan. "On the Beach." Grossberg, Nelson, and Treichler 450–78.

———. "A Question of Cultural Studies." McRobbie 36–57.

———. "Tooth and Claw: Tales of Survival and *Crocodile Dundee*." Ross, *Universal Abandon?* 105–27.

Nelson, Cary, Paula A. Treichler, and Lawrence Grossberg. "Cultural Studies: An Introduction." Grossberg, Nelson, and Treichler 1–22.

Ortiz, Renato. *Mundialização e cultura*. São Paulo: Brasiliense, 1994.

Penley, Constance. "Feminism, Psychoanalysis, and the Study of Popular Culture." Grossberg, Nelson, and Treichler 479–500.

Radway, Janice. *Reading the Romance: Women, Patriarchy, and Popular Literature*. Chapel Hill: U of North Carolina P, 1984.

Rama, Angel. *The Lettered City*. Ed. and trans. Charles Chasteen. Durham: Duke UP, 1996.

Richard, Nelly. *Residuos y metáforas: Ensayos de crítica cultural sobre el Chile de la transición*. Santiago: Cuarto Propio, 1998.

Rojek, Chris. *Stuart Hall*. Cambridge: Polity, 2003.

Ross, Andrew. *No Respect: Intellectuals and Popular Culture*. New York: Routledge, 1989.

———, ed. *Universal Abandon? The Politics of Postmodernism*. Minneapolis: U of Minnesota P, 1988.

Sarlo, Beatriz. "Cultural Studies: Reworking the Nation, Revisiting Identities." *Journal of Latin American Cultural Studies* 11 (2002): 333–42.

Schiller, Herbert I. *Mass Communications and American Empire*. Boston: Beacon, 1971.

Smith, Paul. "Looking Backwards and Forwards at Cultural Studies." Miller, *Companion* 331–40.

Spivak, Gayatri Chakravorty. "Can the Subaltern Speak." *Marxism and the Interpretation of Culture*. Ed. Lawrence Grossberg and Cary Nelson. Minneapolis: U of Minnesota P, 1988. 271–313.

———. *A Critique of Postcolonial Reason: Toward a History of the Vanishing Present*. Cambridge: Harvard UP, 1999.

———. "Scattered Speculations on the Question of Culture Studies." *Outside in the Teaching Machine*. New York: Routledge, 1993. 255–84.

Thompson, E. P. *The Making of the English Working Class*. New York: Vintage, 1966.

Turner, Graeme. *British Cultural Studies: An Introduction*. 3rd ed. New York: Routledge, 2003.

Vieth, Eva. "The Future Is Present: American Cultural Studies on the Net." Hartley and Pearson 427–36.

Williams, Raymond. *Culture and Society, 1780–1950*. New York: Harper, 1958.

———. *The Long Revolution*. New York: Columbia UP, 1961.

———. *Marxism and Literature*. London: Oxford UP, 1977.

———. *Television: Technology and Cultural Form*. London: Fontana, 1974.

Williamson, Judith. *Decoding Advertisements: Ideology and Meaning in Advertising*. London: Boyars, 1978.

Willis, Paul. *Profane Culture*. London: Routledge, 1978.

Wright, Handel K. "Dare We De-centre Birmingham?" *European Cultural Studies* 1.1 (1998): 33–56.

Yúdice, George. "Comparative Cultural Studies Traditions: Latin America and the US." Miller, *Companion* 217–31.

———. *The Expediency of Culture: Uses of Culture in the Global Era*. Durham: Duke UP, 2003.

———. "From Hybridity to Policy: For a Purposeful Cultural Studies." García Canclini, *Consumers* ix–xxxviii.

———. "Marginality and the Ethics of Survival." Ross, *Universal Abandon?* 214–36.

～ Feminisms, Genders, Sexualities

ANNE DONADEY WITH FRANÇOISE LIONNET

During the past two decades, feminist humanities scholarship has undergone a series of transformations due in part to the consolidation of interdisciplinary women's studies programs, from which much of the scholarship originates. The explosion of interest in cultural studies, dwindling publication outlets for literary criticism, and an ever-growing enthusiasm for the study of visuality and performativity have further limited feminist engagement with the world of the literary. As a result, this essay is much less focused on literature than Naomi Schor's corresponding essay in the second edition of this book. In the 1990s, feminist studies had already begun to heed the call of feminists of color for intersectional analyses taking into account the interlocking factors of race, class, nation, gender identity, and sexuality, thus preparing the terrain for the transnational perspectives that have now become one of the most fruitful sites of inquiry for the humanities, as the push to internationalize the curriculum accelerates.

The boundaries among "feminisms, genders, sexualities," "race and ethnicity," "migrations, diasporas, and borders," and "cultural studies" have become more and more porous, and the corresponding essays in this book are most productively read in dialogue with one another. Feminism as we conceptualize it is as much about race and colonialism as it is about gender and sexuality. The paradigm shift feminists of color required of the field in the 1980s, from a "monist" (gender or sexuality only) to a "multiplicative" (race, class, and gender) approach continues to structure the field and to allow it to grow by including other elements into the matrix, such as colonialism, ability, age, religion, and nationality (King 84, 80). It is not just a matter of adding new elements to the mix. These new concepts, which had not been foregrounded before, in turn force feminism to reconceptualize itself and contribute to more sophisticated theories for understanding our world.

Feminism as we conceptualize it is as much about race and colonialism as it is about gender and sexuality.

Another general development in humanities scholarship has been the move away from essentialist perspectives (Afrocentric, woman-only, lesbian-only) and the concomitant rising dominance of models of hybridity and borders. The paradigm-shifting work of Paul Gilroy and Gloria Anzaldúa in the late 1980s and early 1990s contributed to a reformulation of black studies as black Atlantic studies and of Chicano/a studies as border studies. The influence of these two scholars' works went far beyond ethnic or feminist studies; their works contributed to profound reorientation in many areas of humanities research. Intersectional perspectives, black Atlantic, border, cultural, and postcolonial studies have ushered in the ascendancy of the hybrid or migrant subject as a central object of study. Poststructuralist perspectives have been productively transformed through postcolonial, border, and queer studies. Finally, to the emphasis on theory has been added an increasing interest in personal criticism and memoir writing.

It is of course impossible to provide a cartography of the field at any given moment. There will always be blind spots, elements that fall off the map. This essay can be best understood as in process, as a still photograph of objects in motion, some of which may be outside the frame entirely. In other words, we offer this survey of the recent evolution in feminism and sexuality studies without claiming comprehensiveness. We recognize that our location as United States–based scholars with special interests in interdisciplinary postcolonial feminist studies necessarily colors our approach. For instance, our focus on the self-representation of marginalized groups means that we are not giving much space to other important projects such as whiteness studies, masculinity studies, or postcolonial feminist reassessments of colonial discourse. This essay is a point of departure for multiple redefinitions, not a final accounting of the state of the field.

"US THIRD WORLD FEMINISMS"

"US Third World feminism" is the term Chela Sandoval and others select over "women-of-color feminism" in order to highlight the presence of the Third World in the First and the coalitional potential of the work of feminists of color worldwide (41). Sandoval's long-awaited *Methodology of the Oppressed* is one of the most thought-provoking examples of humanities scholarship in the last fifteen years. She defines her concept of "differential consciousness" as the trickster ability to shift among various tactics and theoretical positions depending on the context (58). She sees differential consciousness as a specific theoretical contribution of US Third World feminism, exemplified in Gloria Anzaldúa's "conciencia de la mestiza." She interfaces this concept with Jacques Derrida's "*différance*," Roland Barthes's semiology, Trinh T. Minh-ha's "inappropriated otherness," Gayatri Spivak's "strategic essentialism," Audre Lorde's "house of difference," Patricia Hill Collins's "outsider/within," and Henry Louis Gates, Jr.'s, "signifyin' " (153, 202n29). In doing so, she maps out the similarities and differences among various intellectual projects that all evince a commitment to social justice.

As a solution to Fredric Jameson's Marxist despair over the difficulty of maintaining revolutionary positions in a fragmented postmodern society and to Barthes's poststructuralist feelings of being the lone critical voice in the desert of ideology, Sandoval suggests that the postmodern subject should look to "the survival skills, theories, methods, and the utopian visions" of "the historically-decentered citizen subject: the colonized, the outsider, the queer, the subaltern, the marginalized" (27). She creatively positions Barthes and the Martinican theorist of decolonization Frantz Fanon as possible precursors to feminist theory and ethnic studies (131). Sandoval's work exemplifies the fruitful nature of border crossings in the theoretical field, what other critics such as Françoise Lionnet and Shumei Shih now call the "creolization of theory" (see Creolization of Theory Conf.). The impact of Anzaldúa's border work can also be felt in Valerie Smith's *Not Just Race, Not Just Gender*, a book that centers on literary, filmic, and cultural sites where "conventional binarisms (black/white, male/female, gay or lesbian/heterosexual) are called into question" (xxi).

The ascendancy of nonessentialist, transnational black Atlantic and border studies paradigms has been a major development in the field, a position clearly articulated by Smith and bemoaned by Elizabeth Cook-Lynn (35, 178). Smith argues that black feminism is characterized by its intersectional focus rather than by the race and gender of the person writing the analysis; it is a mode of reading that may be detached from the identity of the critic (*Not Just Race* xv–xvi). She recognizes that one danger of this position is that it may absent black women entirely (xvi). Given that the academic community has been more successful at racially diversifying its curriculum than its personnel in the last fifteen years, such a concern should be taken seriously (Carby, "Race and the Academy" 96; duCille 596–600; Matsuda 128–29). The current dismantling of affirmative action in many states only compounds the problem. Collins's definition of black feminist thought as being produced by various constituencies working together, yet needing to have actual black women as its center, is a way of responding to this dilemma (*Black Feminist Thought* 35–38). Influenced by critiques of essentialist positions, Collins significantly revised her *Black Feminist Thought* between 1990 and 2000. Whereas the first edition positioned black feminist thought at the intersection of feminist and Afrocentric standpoints, the second edition evinces a clear distancing from Afrocentric perspectives. (An analysis of the book's index demonstrates that Afrocentrism was a central concept in the 1990 version, occurring on forty-three pages; allusions to it appear in only three pages in the 2000 revision.)

Collins also responded to 1990s calls to internationalize the curriculum by adding a new chapter on transnational connections between American and African women's issues. Such comparative and transnational perspectives have become central to United States Third World studies. In *Feminism on the Border*, Sonia Saldívar-Hull brings together a study of Chicana writers and Latin American testimonials written by women, highlighting the transnational alliances between both sets of texts. She delineates the evolution of Chicana feminisms "from ethnic identity to global solidarity" (27). Like Saldívar-Hull, Amy Kaminsky links the writings of Latinas in the United States to those of Latin American women in her *After Exile*. Saldívar-Hull focused mostly on the former group, but Kaminsky's book is primarily devoted to the latter.

The field of Asian American studies has always been transnational and comparative, dealing with issues of immigration, racism, diaspora consciousness, cultural identity, and coalitional formations from the start. For example, Lisa Lowe's superb *Immigrant Acts* demonstrates the extent to which cultural perceptions of Asian Americans as foreigners are entangled with United States immigration policies that specifically denied citizenship to Asian immigrants in the second half of the nineteenth and first half of the twentieth century (4–7, 13). Lowe also shows that United States immigration policies were deeply gendered as well as racialized, as they denied immigration rights to Chinese women and stripped American women (but not men) of United States citizenship for marrying an "alien ineligible for citizenship" (11).

American Indian studies has struggled for recognition of the continuing lack of full sovereignty of Native nations in the North American context and has sought to establish a distinction between the status of Native peoples and that of ethnic Americans. A focus on tribal sovereignty, land rights, and physical and cultural survival has meant that many American Indian women have had a vexed relation to feminism as a movement that failed to take a stand on these issues. As a result, these women have sought to define their activism differentially (Mihesuah). A transnational, comparative perspective has become central to indigenous studies. For example, by comparing Native and African issues in decolonization in her study of United States museum representations of Africans and Native Americans, Patricia Hilden moves American Indian issues outside an ethnic American context (which too often tends to subsume issues of colonization and tribal sovereignty under issues of racism and access to full United States citizenship) and into a framework of decolonization ("Race"). Similarly, Cook-Lynn positions American Indian issues as related to Third World—especially African—decolonization movements rather than as ethnic assimilation into a multicultural America (45, 182). Finally, Leslie Marmon Silko insists on a continuity of indigenous resistance throughout the Americas, linking Native resistance in North America to indigenous guerrilla movements in Chiapas and Guatemala (123). This linkage, in turn, leads us to a consideration of transnational paradigms in feminist scholarship. Although United States ethnic feminisms and postcolonial studies initially clashed over questions of theory and history, their mutual focus on diasporic communities led to a common concern with international and global issues.

POSTCOLONIAL AND TRANSNATIONAL FEMINISMS IN AN AGE OF GLOBALIZATION

Postcolonial studies, a field of research devoted to illuminating the colonial experience and its aftermath for both colonized and colonizer cultures, developed in the 1980s and created by the 1990s a recognized subfield, postcolonial feminism. The work of scholars such as Gayatri Spivak (*Critique*), Chandra Mohanty ("Under Western Eyes"), and Trinh T. Minh-ha was central to the consolidation of the field. By the mid-1990s, the field had expanded to include the work of Anne McClintock, Ann Laura Stoler, Ella Shohat and Robert Stam, Mary Louise Pratt, and Rey Chow (*Writing*).

Globalization refers to the operations of transnational capital in the postmodern world, with new networks of production and consumption extending beyond national boundaries and creating new forms of social, economic, and political control. A transnational framework is often used to mediate "between nationalism and globalization, becoming a way to designate the claims of minoritarian languages and cultures and of diasporic communities" (Apter 70). Postcolonial frameworks have been employed primarily in the humanities, but globalization discourses first flourished in the social sciences. However, the humanities show a growing interest in approaches to globalization, and in 2001 special issues of both *PMLA* (Gunn) and *Comparative Literature* (Li) were entirely devoted to this topic. Globalization seems to be primarily of interest to

scholars who are eager to find a way to talk about countries' relations to one another outside a framework of colonization, either because the scholars shy away from the political implications of the topic or because colonization is not appropriate to the context (Ong 36).

The gay studies scholar Dennis Altman succinctly notes the close relation among globalization, colonialism, capitalism, and imperialism: "In a sense, globalization is capitalist imperialism writ large. . . . What was once accomplished by gunships and conquest is now achieved via shopping malls and cable television" (31). Similarly, Chow and others equate globalization with Western imperialism and argue that late capitalism's globalizing technologies are on a continuum with the "globalizing" of the world ushered in by Christopher Columbus in 1492 (Chow, "How" 69; Coursil and Perret 195; Shohat and Stam 15–18; Trouillot 8). Finally, several scholars prefer to avoid the vagueness and drawbacks associated with postcolonial studies by replacing the term with the words *transnational* or *transcolonial* (Grewal and Kaplan; Lionnet, "Transnationalism"; Lionnet and Shih).

Regardless of their term of choice, scholars analyzing literature from postcolonial-transnational-global perspectives tend to focus on some similar issues, such as the relation of women to the nation and the links between historical trauma and fictional rewriting. As Kaminsky points out in the Latin American context:

> The use of gendered metaphors in developing the idea of nation has been well rehearsed by feminist scholars, from Annette Kolodny's wonderfully titled *The Lay of the Land*. . . . Francine Masiello adds to this body of research and theory with her discussions of the ways women and nation are intertwined in the Argentine case. . . . Masiello is more conscious of the racial component of this discourse. . . . Masiello has argued elegantly and persuasively that from the beginnings of the nation in the nineteenth century through the 1930s, Argentine women writers graph a response to what it means to be conscripted to the national project as symbol rather than subject, wresting back a subject position from which they write a more complex story of nation that depends on internal fracture and difference.   (24, 31)

Winifred Woodhull and others have argued that postcolonial nationalist projects have also imagined women as metaphors for a nation needing to be protected by its active, male citizenry. A consequence of this representation has been to facilitate men's access to citizenship and to make women's access to citizenship symbolically more difficult, since it is hard to conceptualize someone as being both the nation and an active agent of the nation (Woodhull 2–3, 16–24). Authors such as the francophone Algerian Assia Djebar respond to these representations by both drawing attention to such overdetermined representations of women and inserting women as agents of resistance into their narratives (Donadey xxx).

Scholars have also demonstrated how postcolonial feminist writers like Djebar have produced complex palimpsests of colonial and postcolonial history in their fiction. Postcolonial feminist writers weave autobiographical narratives in texts that seek to bring out the voices and agency of colonized people, women and men, who were silenced in colonial and postcolonial historiographies. Like many Holocaust writers, they insist on the need to rewrite history in order to bring to light the violent traumas of genocide and exploitation so as to prevent the past from repeating itself. Postcolonial feminist fictional rewritings of history rarely feature coherent counternarratives. As Anne Anlin Cheng discusses in her analysis of *Dictée*, by the Korean American writer Theresa Hak Kyung Cha, such texts tend to be nonlinear narratives that rewrite a "history of foreign invasions" (142). Cha both reconstructs Korean history and critiques that reconstruction through the use of fragmented form. Like Djebar, Cha refuses to fall into the traps of "national nostalgia," "reification" or "reappropriation" of historical narrative (Cheng 144–47).

The question of history and memory takes on a somewhat different valence in the context of postdictatorship countries in Latin American literature, especially Southern Cone countries. Following Ariel Dorfman's lead, Kaminsky suggests that "while remembering is crucial to that process [of reestablishing a national community], amnesty is the price of peace. Amnesty, of course, is quite literally the opposite of memory" (21). In other words, the danger is that in exhuming too much of the violence of the past, the country may be destabilized and the opportunity for dictatorship to reinstate itself reactivated (20, 37). Whereas in postcolonial or North American contexts, the danger is that the past will repeat itself if not remembered, in Latin America, the danger seems to be that the past will repeat itself if remembered too much. For example, Kaminsky analyzes the concept of active forgetting in works by the Argentine writer Luisa Valenzuela. In particular, she focuses on Valenzuela's metaphor of writing as erasure and of the writer's notebook as erased palimpsest. If for the Argentine woman writer, "writing itself depends on the power to choose what to forget" (77), in contrast, Djebar and other postcolonial writers constantly return to the haunted spaces of a (post) colonial history under erasure, turning their novels into historical palimpsests (Rosello; Khanna; Donadey).

Part of the difference between the two contexts may be related to the different time frames in which they operate. As Doris Sommer points out, there is often a necessary time lag in the process of telling trauma (179). Postcolonial responses to historical trauma, like postdictatorship ones, tend to begin with silence, as speaking about the past at first threatens to split the individual psyche as well as the national body. It seems to take a few decades before that initially protective silence becomes traumatic and the need to take stock of the past asserts itself. Djebar's 1980 short story "Femmes d'Alger dans leur appartement" charts this passage from silence about the violence of the Algerian war of decolonization from the French to the need to speak about the consequences of that war on women. The main character, Sarah, a former freedom fighter who was tortured by the French and is described throughout the story as someone who has "problems with words," emerges at the end

> **Postcolonial nationalist projects have also imagined women as metaphors for a nation needing to be protected by its active, male citizenry.**

of the short story as an advocate for women's dialogue as the only solution to the blocked situation of contemporary Algerian women (61).

Revisiting the sites of historical haunting and trauma has also been central to African American literature, and there is room for generative comparative scholarship in this area. Like Djebar, who unearths historical and literary traces of brutalized Algerians, especially women, Toni Morrison describes her fictional project as a "literary archaeology" (302). In the African American context, the critic Ashraf Rushdy describes contemporary, fictional slave narratives by African American women writers as palimpsestic texts, a term Anne Donadey applies to literature written by francophone postcolonial women writers. For instance, there are clear similarities in the historiographic and fictional literary projects of the African American writers Octavia E. Butler (*Kindred*) and Morrison and in that of Djebar. Using the concepts of *métissage* and of diaspora literacy, respectively, Lionnet in *Autobiographical Voices* and VèVè Clark in "Developing Diaspora Literacy" pioneered such black Atlantic comparative feminist criticism. Feminist critics like Spivak, Shohat, Lionnet, and Shih are currently calling for more comparative studies between postcolonial-transnational-global-area studies and ethnic, feminist, and comparative literary studies.

FEMINISMS AND SEXUALITY STUDIES

In the early and mid 1990s, the term "queer studies" appeared with more and more frequency. First suggested by Teresa De Lauretis in 1991 ("Queer Theory"), the term soon began to replace the earlier "gay and lesbian." This change was due to a convergence of at least two reasons: as other sexual minorities such as bisexuals, transgendered people, and transsexuals fought for inclusion in the lesbian and gay movement, *queer* could become an umbrella term to cover current and future groups seeking recognition; *queer* was also a shortcut to lesbian, gay, bi-

sexual, transgender, and questioning—or to LGBTQ. The rise of *queer* nomenclature also corresponded to a new way of doing theory in sexuality studies, based on the rising hegemony of poststructuralist frameworks in academia and the desire for the field to consolidate itself academically. Michel Foucault became the anointed father of the newly reconfigured field; its leading figures were Judith Butler and Eve Kosofsky Sedgwick; and its subjects of analysis were most often gay males, which ran the risk of marginalizing lesbian existence and lesbian feminist perspectives (L. Garber 183, 189; Zimmerman, "Placing" 270–71). This risk is ironic given that Butler, Sedgwick, and other queer theorists are also major feminist theorists (Turner 5). One of the appeals of the term *queer* for its practitioners was its fluidity and lack of clear referentiality (Turner 35; see also J. Butler). Yet, as William Turner notes (basing his argument on the work of Evelynn Hammonds and Laura Alexandra Harris), that very strength—the ability to "launch critiques of ideal identity categories"—was also a source of weakness, as "the very definitional instability of the term 'queer' could become the gender-and-race blind utopia of white males" (171, 168).

According to Lisa Duggan, the contribution of queer theory, starting from the paradigmatic work of Eve Sedgwick, was that it extended the purview of gay and lesbian studies in

> at least two directions: taking queer questions and knowledges into the domain of mainstream theoretical paradigms, and bringing the formulations of feminist, Marxist, postmodernist and poststructuralist theories to bear on issues of queer culture and politics.   ("Making" 168)

In contrast, Donald Morton strongly criticizes queer studies (and especially Sedgwick) for eliding Marxist frameworks and replicating liberal pluralist models of individual freedom. Gay and queer studies scholars have taken up similar topics from various angles, such as questions of race and sexuality and responses to the AIDS crisis (Alonso and Koreck; Edelman; D. Miller; Patton; Warner).

Critics agree that the genealogies of feminist, gay, lesbian, queer, and transgender studies intersect, although to what extent and how much remains open for (sometimes fierce) debate. There seems to be a critical consensus that the lesbian-feminist sex wars of the 1980s, which pitted women promoting egalitarian sexual relationships against women seeking to legitimate practices such as S and M, nonmonogamy, pornography, and sex work, morphed in the 1990s as many in the latter group aligned with queer studies, attracted in part by queer theory's intense focus on the transgressive potentialities of nonnormative sexual pleasure. Despite the sex-positive aspect of queer theory, Leo Bersani cautions that the move from gay and lesbian to queer terminology risks "[d]egaying gayness," "self-erasure," and "*desexualizing* discourses" (5).

In *Identity Poetics*, Linda Garber reconfigures the field's history. Whereas queer theory has tended to present itself as a postmodernist reaction against the essentialism of gay and lesbian studies, she rejects the writing of the field's intellectual history as a generational gap between early lesbian thinkers—especially working-class lesbians and lesbians of color, who are ignored in this debate—and queer postmodern theory (1–3; see also Duggan, "Discipline Problem" 197; Martin 71–72; Rubin with Butler 95–96; Zimmerman, "Placing" 269, 274). Garber first establishes that lesbian feminism was not as essentialist as some queer theorists make it out to be. In particular, in the 1970s and 1980s, lesbianism was often presented as a political choice rather than as something one was born with, as the work of Adrienne Rich attests ("Compulsory Heterosexuality"). Garber shows how lesbian feminists self-consciously created a lesbian identity and history through poetry and went through their own essentialist-versus-constructionist debate in the 1970s (11, 17–18). Unfortunately, by the early 1980s, lesbian feminist essentialism had solidified and did not particularly welcome intersectional analyses, especially around race and class, despite the centrality of both working-class lesbians and lesbians of color in the movement (19–21, 27).

In particular, Garber recenters the works of Audre Lorde and Gloria Anzaldúa for the field of sexuality studies. She highlights the fact that "the work of working-class/lesbians of color prefigures postmodern insights about positionality, coalition, and multiply located, shifting 'identity' " (185), a point that bell hooks also made about black women writers (*Remembered Rapture* 200), Wahneema Lubiano about African Americans and American Indians (156), Sandoval about subaltern groups (27), and Lionnet about women writers from colonized backgrounds ("Spaces" 169). Garber analyzes the lesbian feminist *and* queer aspects of poetry and prose by Lorde, Anzaldúa, and Rich, among others, through close readings of their major works.

Building on the work of Zimmerman, Lillian Faderman (*Odd Girls*), Barbara Christian, De Lauretis, and others, Garber demonstrates the extent to which queer theory has its roots in the earlier formulations of gay and lesbian studies (esp. the work of lesbians of color on difference) but sought to highlight a more academically valued genealogy—solidly Continental, white, and male (176–77, 204–08; see also Duggan, "Discipline Problem" 206; De Lauretis, "Fem/Les Scramble" 45; Zimmerman, "Confessions" 166; Case 209–11; Faderman, Afterword 225). Lesbian feminism was not the only area of scholarship whose insights were erased by the ascendancy of a queer studies paradigm: Turner points out that the earlier work of gay social constructionist historians of sexuality such as that of Jonathan Ned Katz and Jeffrey Weeks was also paradoxically displaced and reframed in Foucauldian terms (62–82). Yet, even as Turner seeks to reestablish the significance of lesbian-queer feminist and gay male historical scholarship in his brilliant genealogy of queer theory, his book keeps returning to Foucault, ironically recentering queer theory around the towering figure of Foucault and topics in gay male sexuality.

One aspect of sexuality that began to receive some attention in the 1990s is bisexuality. In the early 1990s, several anthologies were published on the topic. Yet neither gay and lesbian studies nor queer studies has really incorporated bisexuality into its frameworks, as many bisexuality studies scholars, such as Stacey Young, point out (65). Bisexual issues have been elaborated primarily in sociological perspectives or personal narratives; they do not appear to have affected the field of literary criticism very much. One exception is Marjorie Garber, whose *Vice Versa* highlights the following paradox: although many famous authors such as Oscar Wilde, Virginia Woolf, Claude McKay, and Langston Hughes were in fact bisexual, they have been rendered invisible as such (105). Garber reads literature for the figure of the bisexual or for bisexual plots in works by authors such as Henry James, James Baldwin, Ernest Hemingway, Lillian Hellman, and Tennessee Williams.

Amanda Udis-Kessler explains biphobia in the gay and lesbian community in the following terms: because many gays and lesbians linked bisexual existence to a social constructionist model of sexuality and because their politics were based on somewhat essentialist identity claims, they felt that both bisexuality and social constructionist models of sexuality threatened the ground they stood on (352–53). In other words, because bisexual existence raises questions about stable sexual identity for people who self-identify either as heterosexual or homosexual, bisexuals undermine the hetero-homo binary opposition and force others to ask themselves uncomfortable questions about their own sexual identity (355–56). Along similar lines, Young argues that the silence surrounding bisexuality has to do with gay and lesbian scholars' avoidance of the fact that sexuality rarely fits in established categories. To recognize bisexuality might open the door to the recognition that the categories of gay, bisexual, and lesbian are more porous than the hetero-homo binary dichotomy accounts for. In this process, "bisexuality is made to stand in for multiplicity and complexity, and is then banished together with all of that multiplicity in order to restore the appearance of a stable, binary world" (61). A similar process of banishment and inclusion has been at work with respect to feminist, gay, lesbian, and queer responses to transsexual and transgender activism.

Feminism can be said to have been both an enabling and a disabling point of departure for much transgender and transsexuality studies. People who do not identify as being one of two genders or whose birth sex is different from their gender expression are referred to as transgendered. People whose gender identity is at odds with their sexual characteristics are characterized as transsexuals. Transgender and transsexuality studies developed in part as a corrective to a 1970s radical feminist consolidation of the dual gender system and its equation of male-to-female transsexuals with men seeking to usurp women's place (Raymond). For example, the concept of women-only "safe spaces" became a site of struggle over whether male-to-female (MTF) transsexuals should be included in lesbian communities. More recent incarnations of this radical-lesbian feminist position portray the self-identification of some butch lesbians as female-to-male transsexuals as a threat to lesbian existence (Jeffreys). In response to such views, transgender and transsexual activists and scholars have been calling, since the early 1990s, for a paradigm shift around feminist and lesbian conceptions of gender. Ironically for people who sought to argue for female liberation by refusing biological arguments about women's roles, feminists' responses to claims of recognition on the part of transgendered or transsexual people have too often based themselves on a retrenchment behind biological conceptions of sexual difference (Raymond).

Transsexual scholars and their allies have called for lesbians-feminists to modify our understanding of gender to include the concept of gender identity. Gender identity refers to how one defines or views oneself as male, female, or other. One's psychological sense of one's gender

Feminism can be said to have been both an enabling and a disabling point of departure for much transgender and transsexuality studies.

identity may or may not correspond to one's physical sexual characteristics. Like Gayle Rubin reformulating the sociological binary concepts of biological sex and cultural gender into the sex/gender system ("Traffic"), transgender and transsexual scholars have politicized the medical model of gender identity, thereby providing a powerful way to theorize (from) their experience by adding another important concept to the list of interlocking forms of difference. Most people's physical sexual characteristics are aligned with their gender identity. Most of us, then, are in a position of privilege with respect to gender identity. As with other forms of social oppression based on gender, race, sexuality, or other factors, people whose gender identity is not aligned with their sexual characteristics and with their gender attribution (the way others read us as male or female) have a right to be respected and included in our coalitions. Just as white or male allies in the fight against racism or sexism need to take stock of their privilege, so must people whose gender identity is unproblematically aligned with other characteristics (see Feinberg, *Trans Liberation* 118).

Judith Shapiro proposes a view of transsexuals that highlights the transgressive potential of their gendering: transsexuals make explicit the process of becoming gendered. The existence of transsexuals reminds all of us that gender is socially constructed (see also Stryker 250). Shapiro's interpretation of MTF transsexuals takes the opposite perspective from that of Janice Raymond: Shapiro proposes that MTF transsexuals could be seen as "defectors from male status" (275), which is the preferred one in our culture. This perception, according to her, makes MTFs a threat to the established hierarchy, because they intentionally move down in the system (270). Perhaps her most compelling and eye-opening insight is the suggestion that we apply the citizenship model to transsexuals, who could be viewed as "naturalized women and men," like foreigners who become naturalized citizens and have (almost all) the same rights (259–60). MTF transsexual feminist scholars such as Kate Born-

stein, Sandy Stone, Riki Anne Wilchins, and Susan Stryker argue that transsexuals should be out as transsexuals and refuse to disappear into the categories of man or woman.

The presence of female-to-male (FTM) scholars, while even more recent than that of MTF ones, has also opened up important new avenues for research and theorizing. In particular, following Rubin's argument in "Of Catamites and Kings," several scholars have shown the border between FTM transsexuals and butch lesbians to be porous and have highlighted the need to respect various groups' specificity and to create intergroup alliances (Hale 340). For example, C. Jacob Hale critiques lesbian and feminist interpretations of the hate-crime victim Brandon Teena as a lesbian. While these moves attempted to be inclusive, their effect was to erase transgender and potentially transsexual subjectivities (313). Hale and the queer theorist Judith Halberstam provide an excellent example of scholarly intergroup alliance in their works, which build on each other in a rich, respectful dialogue analyzing the FTM and butch lesbian border zones from different perspectives.

Halberstam's masterful book *Female Masculinity* provides an important contribution to feminist, lesbian, queer, and transgender studies. In it, she defines and theorizes the concept of female masculinity, or masculinity without its norm—(white) men. Making an argument similar to that of Shapiro on transsexualism, she says that female masculinity is subversive; she interprets it not as mimicry but as affording us "a glimpse of how masculinity is constructed as masculinity" and as a multiple position that explodes "compulsory gender binarism" (1, 27). In particular, Halberstam writes against the 1970s lesbian feminist view of the butch as someone who internalizes and replicates patriarchal concepts of gender. In her view, female masculinity is a site for "a queer subject position that can successfully challenge hegemonic models of gender conformity" (9). Joan Nestle and others similarly argue that both butches and femmes deconstruct rather than repeat the binary gender system ("Flamboyance" 14). Halberstam unearths the presence of female masculinity in literary works and the visual arts. In particular, she revisits the character of Stephen Gordon in Radclyffe Hall's lesbian classic *The Well of Loneliness*, arguing "that Stephen represents something more than the 'mannish lesbian': she embodies a sexual and gender identity that is not fully contained by the term 'lesbian' " (97).

Embodying the border zone among transgender, transsexual, and butch lesbian identities has been the trailblazing writer Leslie Feinberg, whose moving, autobiographically inspired novel *Stone Butch Blues* first gave voice to "the differences and continuities between transsexual, transgender, and lesbian masculinities" (Halberstam 142). Feinberg's inspiring collection of essays, *Trans Liberation*, exemplifies the breadth of "hir" (his/her) coalition politics. Like other queer studies scholars, s/he also includes issues of intersexuality (formerly referred to as hermaphroditism) in "hir" discussion of coalitional politics. Feinberg personally identifies as transgendered because "my birth sex—which is female—appears to be in social contradiction to my gender expression—which is read as masculine. I defend my right to that social contradiction" (69). The concept of gender expression (in which Feinberg includes drag) is crucial to an understanding of the transgender category. As Feinberg indicates, gender expression should not be confused with sexuality. For instance, masculine females may or may not be lesbians, and butch lesbians have to deal with very specific forms of violence and discrimination that have more to do with their gender expression than their sexuality (59). The concepts of gender identity and gender expression, developed to provide theoretical frameworks with which to better comprehend transsexual and transgender experiences, represent significant recent contributions to a more sophisticated feminist understanding of gender.

Overall, most sexuality studies focus on the United States and Europe, and several include considerations of queer people of color and of the difference race makes to understandings of

sexuality (Feinberg; Hammonds; Lugones; Mercer; Rodriguez). One of the areas black feminists have recently sought to explore revolves around issues of sexuality. Hammonds argues that black lesbians' general silence over black lesbian desire (with a few major exceptions such as the work of Audre Lorde, in particular her "biomythography" *Zami*) should be related to two major factors that overdetermine the politics of that silence: on the one hand, the erasure of race as a critical concept in the formulation of lesbian, gay, and queer theory; on the other hand, the Western stereotypes of black female sexuality as immoral, hyperaggressive, and deviant, which have sometimes caused black communities to enforce sexual conformism as a gateway to acceptance. The black British cultural studies scholar Kobena Mercer shows that black gay men have to deal with a related pressure from black communities to perform tough black masculinity (137).

Collins opens up an analysis of African Americans' sexuality in its overdetermined context in *Black Sexual Politics*. Like other black feminists such as hooks in *We Real Cool*, Hazel Carby in *Race Men*, and Michael Awkward in *Negotiating Difference*, Collins moves from an analysis of black women to an analysis of racialized gender, including issues of masculinity. She also attempts to respond to the call to incorporate issues of lesbian and gay sexuality into her analytic model of race, class, and gender, discussing the need for black communities to move beyond homophobia and exploring links between racism and heterosexism (95–97).

In the Asian American context, stereotypes feminizing Asian men have also contributed to cultural nationalist reconfigurations of martial Asian men that reinforce "compulsory heterosexuality with all its attendant misogyny and homophobia" (Eng, "Out Here" 35). In his *Racial Castration*, David Eng analyzes works such as David Henry Hwang's play *M. Butterfly*. Using a psychoanalytic approach informed by "feminist, queer, postcolonial, and critical race" frameworks, he explores the ways in which white male America projects its anxiety over masculinity onto Asian American men by feminizing and queering them (2). He thus demonstrates how psychic castration is intimately linked to racial processes and focuses on Asian American literary reworkings of and responses to such stereotypes. In Eng's analysis, Hwang's intertextual refiguration of Puccini's opera *Madama Butterfly* highlights "failures of conventional white masculinity" as well as deconstructs orientalist stereotypes of passive, self-sacrificing Asian women and feminized Asian men (144).

There have been a few attempts at documenting the lives and representations of queer people in other cultures. Such undertakings usually also provide reconceptualizations of terms such as *gay, lesbian, homosexual,* and *transgender* (Altman; Swarr and Nagar). In the Latin American and Latino contexts, scholars all emphasize that the meanings attached to homosexuality are different from what they are in United States queer studies. Jorge Salessi suggests that at the turn of the century in

> Argentina the medicolegal category of homosexuality did not seem to replace the category of sexual inversion. . . . The persistent distinction between an active and a passive role in male-male sex—as well as in a relationship between two passive uranist women . . . was a residue of a Mediterranean concept and representation of sex.
> (86–87)

The work of other scholars such as José Piedra, Tomás Almaguer, and Alonso and Koreck testifies to the continuing relevance of this concept today. In male-male relationships, as evidenced both in literature and sociological research, only the partner who is the recipient of the sexual act is considered homosexual and is consistently feminized. Robert Richmond Ellis thus insists that "male homoeroticism is subsumed within gender" because of its association with the passivity traditionally attached to women (6). As Paul Julian Smith and Emilie Bergmann summarize it, queer studies in the Latin American and Latino contexts illuminates "a founding distinction which is not that of hetero and homo but rather insertive and receptive" (4).

Another important aspect of the literature has been its focus on the overdetermined nature of the queer experience, especially in postcolonial contexts where the expression of that existence is circumscribed on the one hand by the predominance of a Western (especially United States–based), upper-middle-class model of sexuality and on the other hand by nationalist rewritings of local queer practices as degenerate, colonialist Western impositions (Hawley, Introd. 5). In response to such nationalist positions, Gaurav Desai insightfully suggests that

> one could argue that at least in some African contexts, it was not *homosexuality* that was inherited from the West but rather a more regulatory *homophobia* [through the influence of Christianity and] colonially inherited legal discourses.
> (148–49)

Recently, a few scholars have begun to conceptualize the connections among disability, feminism, and queer studies. For example, one may argue that Feinberg's concept of gender expression productively intersects with that of "appearance impairments," which Rosemarie Garland-Thomson includes as part of a broad redefinition of disability in her review essay "Feminist Disability Studies" (1558, 1579). Like Feinberg, Garland-Thomson makes a place for intersexuality in her writings (1558, 1580). Further, taking the work of the feminist Rich as his starting point, Robert McRuer argues that not only is "the system of compulsory able-bodiedness that produces disability . . . thoroughly interwoven with the system of compulsory heterosexuality that produces queerness" but also each system is contingent on the other (89). This observation leads us to a discussion of the connections between feminism and disability studies.

FEMINIST DISABILITY STUDIES

Inspired by the advances made by ethnic and women's studies, scholars interested in issues of disability have argued in favor of abandoning the three most common models of disability—

medical, personal tragedy, and charity—in order to embrace a civil rights approach to understanding disability as a social phenomenon (Morris, *Pride* 176, 180). In the 1990s, disability studies established itself as a vibrant and diverse area of inquiry, recognized in the humanities by a 2002 MLA publication (Snyder, Brueggemann, and Garland-Thomson). The field has productively intersected with feminism, in particular thanks to the work of the philosopher Susan Wendell and the literary scholar Garland-Thomson. Special issues of *Hypatia* (Kittay, Silvers, Wendell, and Schriempf) and *NWSA Journal* (K. Hall) have focused on feminism and disability studies.

Wendell and Garland-Thomson respond to earlier feminist reformulations of the definition of *women* to argue for the need to expand the subject of feminism to disabled women. Like feminists of color before them, they contest the "theoretical invisibility" of disabled people in feminist studies (King 76). Many of their arguments are indebted to and build on the intersectional analyses of feminists of color. Disability scholars all insist on the disabling effect of a society that marginalizes disabled people and denies them the resources that would allow for their societal integration. The distinction between (material) impairment and (social) disability is central in disability studies, where some compare it with the central categories of sex and gender in feminism. Feminist disability scholars such as Alexa Schriempf and others have called for a less binary way of conceptualizing the material and the social. As early as 1989, Wendell proposed that we use only the term *disability* to "emphasize that disability is socially constructed from biological reality" (107). Similarly, Garland-Thomson argues that the disabled body is constructed in culture but is also marked by bodily, biological issues. Therefore, the social constructionist argument is of limited value for disabled people, who cannot afford not to take the materiality of the body into account (*Extraordinary Bodies* 22–25). More recently, Elizabeth Donaldson sug-

> **The social constructionist argument is of limited value for disabled people, who cannot afford not to take the materiality of the body into account.**

gests that, instead of focusing on the distinctions between impairment and disability, it may be more insightful to conceive of the impairment/disability system, on the model of Rubin's sex/gender system (111). Eli Clare also points out that the distinction between disability and impairment "makes theoretical and political sense but misses important emotional realities" (7).

For Garland-Thomson, feminist and disability studies cannot afford not to take each other's insights into account because "[f]emininity and disability are inextricably entangled in patriarchal culture" and because "a firm boundary between 'disabled' and 'nondisabled' women cannot be meaningfully drawn" (*Extraordinary Bodies* 27). Wendell adds other reasons: "more than half of disabled people are women and approximately 16% of women are disabled." Further, disability scholars confront similar philosophical issues as feminist scholars do, such as "sameness vs. difference," "integration vs. separatism," and ambivalent beliefs about the body (105, 106, 112–13).

Similar to the ways in which feminists of color reconceptualized feminism's understandings of work and the family in the 1980s and 1990s (Collins, *Black Feminist Thought*), Garland-Thomson draws attention to three ways in which disability theory can fruitfully revise such central feminist concepts as the sexualized gaze, compulsory motherhood, and the liberal belief in the search for female autonomy. She shows that whereas most females are subjected to a patriarchal, sexualized gaze, women with disabilities are subjected to a desexualizing stare as if they were a grotesque spectacle. Instead of compulsory motherhood, women with disabilities tend to have to face prohibited motherhood; instead of proscribed abortion, prescribed abortion. Finally, theorizing from the standpoint of women who need structures for assisted living allows us to question the liberal feminist framework that views independence and autonomous individuality as an ideal (*Extraordinary Bodies* 25–26). Because of these productive intersections, Garland-Thomson has proposed to rename this area of research feminist disability studies ("Integrating" 1).

Feminist disability studies sometimes extends the multiplicative approach to include postcolonial concerns (LaCom), LGBTQ issues (Clare; McRuer; McRuer and Wilkerson), and questions of race (Morris, *Pride*; Garland-Thomson, *Extraordinary Bodies*; Clare). For instance, the last chapter of Garland-Thomson's foundational book is devoted to an exploration of disabled African American female figures in texts by African American women writers, especially Morrison's. These disabled figures are not presented as deviant; here, the disabled body "bears the etchings of history" and signals both oppression and agency (105): "These women's bodies *re-member*: they recall and reconstitute history and community" (122). Garland-Thomson insists that these disabled figures should not simply be read as metaphors for racial oppression. Instead, Morrison presents a revaluation of "bodily uniqueness and personal history" (125). Thinkers like Clare see the connections between the largest number of overlapping and interlocking frames; "hir" focus is on disability, sexual violence, queerness and transgender issues, as well as environmental destruction, social class, and rural issues.

THE AUTOBIOGRAPHICAL TURN

It is clear from this overview that subfields of feminist and sexuality studies are diverse and multiplying. One characteristic they all seem to share has been the move toward academic memoir writing; in some ways, we have witnessed a major realignment of the field from poststructuralist theory to personal criticism. Since the early 1990s, there has been memoir fever among academics publishing in the United States as well as abroad (Cixous; Mernissi). Memoirs are traditionally thought of as the recollections of famous political men who, at retirement, look back on their careers and justify their actions. The memoir as a genre thus privileges a public

figure's participation in his time, in history making. Memoirs are typically full of gaps when it comes to the private life of the public man. Perhaps because of this feature, female academics, novelists, and activists, as well as academics from the postcolonial world and gay and lesbian scholars, many of whom never before wrote about the self, have lately experimented with the memoir genre (Ahmed; Awkward, *Scenes*; Duberman; Dworkin; Faderman, *Naked*; Friedan, *Life*; Hilden, *When Nickels*; Lim; McDowell; N. Miller, *Bequest*; Nafisi; Suleiman, *Budapest Diary*; Suleri, *Meatless Days*; Tompkins).

Memoir as a genre brings together the historical and the personal, history and autobiography. Perhaps because of the turn to personal criticism in feminist theory of the 1990s (Nancy K. Miller, Susan Rubin Suleiman, bell hooks), many female academics have been publishing memoirs since the early 1990s (Gilmore 16). Memoirs are a genre in which the overlapping and interlocking frames of postcolonialism, postmodernism, feminism, sexuality studies, and United States ethnic studies come together in particularly interesting ways. These texts run the gamut from childhood memoir to personal criticism; some are scholarly volumes primarily composed of philosophical or critical essays shot through with autobiographical content.

Suleiman proposes that the development of personal writing among academics is due to two main phenomena, "the demise of structuralism and the growth of a politically self-conscious feminist criticism, intent on confirming that 'the personal is political' " (*Risking* 1; see also hooks, *Remembered Rapture* 66). Feminist criticism always focused on the importance of theorizing from experience (MacKinnon; Hartsock; Scott). Feminists of color in the 1980s and 1990s showed that theorizing is not a disconnected, abstract practice but that it exists in a dialectical relation to experience (Collins, *Black Feminist Thought*; Christian; hooks, *Yearning*). In her memoir *Wounds of Passion*, hooks rightly points to Lorde's "biomythography" *Zami* as a precursor to current memoirs (xix). Feminists of color redefined critical writing for 1980s feminism in books and essays mixing nonfiction writing, poetry, and theory. Such collections of essays by Lorde (*Sister/Outsider*), Anzaldúa, Cherríe Moraga, and Rich (*Blood*) are the precursors to Bornstein's *Gender Outlaw*, Clare's *Exile and Pride*, Nancy Miller's *Getting Personal*, Aurora Levins Morales's *Medicine Stories*, and Suleiman's *Risking Who One Is*, among others. This influence has extended to the legal field where, since the 1990s, critical race feminism has been applying tools of literary analysis to legal case studies and encouraging the use of personal narrative to develop a legal approach that incorporates issues of race, class, and gender (Matsuda; Williams; Wing, *Critical Race Feminism* and *Global Critical Race Feminism*).

Over the past twenty years, critics have become more and more aware of the need to recognize one's situatedness. It has become commonplace for them now to explicitly acknowledge personal locations and partial standpoints in order to avoid universalizing assumptions in scholarship. For many critics, such statements may be an entry into or an encouragement to continue autobiographical writing. It can also be argued that memoir writing, which generates memoir reading, may in turn trigger the reader's desire to write about the self (N. Miller, *Getting Personal* 135).

The 1990s literary critics' move toward memoir writing ironically underscores the importance of identity politics to many poststructuralist theorists who previously attacked identity politics for its essentialism and unreconstructed simplifications (Suleiman, *Risking*; Suleri, "Woman"). Typical of the antiessentialist position is Sara Suleri's talk of being turned into "an otherness machine" in the United States (*Meatless Days* 105). Perhaps another reason for the growth of academic memoir writing lies in the fact that the direction of theory over the last decade dovetails with the interests of many of the critics' memoirs. For instance, Alice Kaplan's *French Lessons* documents theory's shift from the height of deconstruction in the 1970s and 1980s to a focus on the status of history, memory, ethics, subjectivity, race, class, gender, and sexuality in the 1980s and 1990s. Such issues are foregrounded in most academic memoirs. In this respect, it is interesting to note that all the memoirists mentioned above insist to a greater or lesser degree on their racial, sexual, ethnic, hybrid, or ethnoreligious identities—be it as African Americans, women of color, Indian, Arab, Jewish, lesbian, gay, or transgendered persons.

The current popularity of memoir writing may have also been triggered by the need to "write with feeling" (Kaplan 219) in an academic world that still tends to reject the possible contributions of emotions to knowledge. Here again, the primary forerunners in this area have been feminists, especially women of color (Christian; Jaggar; Narayan). Also, the importance of psychoanalysis in literary criticism may have provided critics familiar with psychic processes and the talking cure with a model and a desire to write about the self (Gilmore 2). For instance, hooks mentions in *Remembered Rapture* that *Bone Black* began as part of her therapy (90). Further, she notes that "[t]he growing body of confessional writing by women coincided with the proliferation in mass culture of the talk show as a place for personal confession" (60).

There seems to be a difference between the desire to reach a larger public exhibited by the feminists of the 1980s, especially women of color, and the motivation of many of the more recent critics who write in a personal vein. The purpose of the former was primarily political in nature (to change the world by reaching as many readers as possible); the purpose of the latter stems more from the wish to take stock of one's life while moving away from the dry constraints of academic writing. This difference in purpose is consistent with the institutionalization of feminism, which at first was located primarily in radical grass-roots movements, then entered the academy and became somewhat coopted in the process. Some critics have characterized this change as going from "the personal is political" to "the political is personal." There are many notable exceptions, such as Hilden's uncompromising *When Nickels Were Indians*, which politicizes the personal story by placing it in the larger framework of American Indian history.

The literary critic Leigh Gilmore points out the influence of the market:

> market demand currently encourages marketing practices such as subtitling an author's first book "a memoir" when in previous years it might have been classified as fiction, or selecting for publication a memoir by someone whose story would not have previously been expected to appeal to a so-called general audience. (17)

These remarks are illustrated in the experience of Meena Alexander, who was invited to write her memoir, *Fault Lines*, for publication in the Feminist Press's memoir series (1).

Finally, one may wonder whether the turn to memoir writing by literary critics isn't linked to the crisis in academic publishing that started in the late 1980s. As universities began to lose federal and state funding, university libraries stopped purchasing books that were considered nonessential, and many university presses must now rely on reduced subsidies. A consequence of this situation has been that most university presses began to slash their humanities lists, especially in literary criticism. This cut could not have happened at a worse time: the ratcheting up of tenure and promotion expectations for faculty research everywhere meant that the pressure to publish more was on in most universities, at the same time as it was becoming increasingly difficult for faculty members in the modern languages to find a publisher.

Memoir writing is a chance for scholars to get away from the specialized audiences of university presses and to move into the larger-scale world of trade publishing with presses such as Random House and Knopf (Lionnet, "Questions" 9). Some university presses such as Chicago take memoir publishing as the very serious business that it is. As a result, the well-established division between literary criticism and creative writing in English departments is becoming more porous, in part because of the state of the publishing industry. In turn, this porosity reflects a general interest in interdisciplinary work in academia today.

〜

Because the baby boomers (who are primarily responsible for academic feminism) are now an aging group, it is to be expected that feminist aging studies will rise to prominence in the next decade. The 1970s feminist leaders Betty Friedan (*Fountain*), Germaine Greer, and others have published their reflections on aging in the last ten years or so. Feminist scholars such as Margaret Cruikshank, Margaret Morganroth Gullette, Kathleen Woodward, and others have begun the task of theorizing feminist aging studies. Since all disability scholars emphasize the links between old age and disability, there is room for many connections among feminism, disability studies, and aging studies in the next decades, although as Friedan cautions, one of the challenges for more productive views on aging must involve decoupling aging and illness (*Fountain* 415).

The multiply overlapping frames discussed in this essay all share a dual goal: on the one hand, they theorize the experiences of women, LGBTQ people, people of color, postcolonial people, women with disabilities, and so on. On the other hand, they seek to redefine and unsettle the corresponding hegemonic categories of masculinity, heterosexuality, whiteness, the West, and ability, therefore attempting to undermine the binary system itself.

NOTE

Many thanks to the people who assisted us with their suggestions for this piece: Edith Benkov, Susan Cayleff, Elizabeth Colwill, Oliva Espín, Patricia Huckle, Kathleen B. Jones, Irene Lara, Esther Rothblum, Deboleena Roy, Bonnie Kime Scott, Maria-Barbara Watson-Franke, and Jane Winston.

WORKS CITED AND SUGGESTIONS FOR FURTHER READING

Abelove, Henry, Michèle Aina Barale, and David M. Halperin, eds. *The Lesbian and Gay Studies Reader*. New York: Routledge, 1993.

Ahmed, Leila. *A Border Passage: From Cairo to America—a Woman's Journey*. New York: Farrar, 1999.

Alexander, Meena. *Fault Lines: A Memoir*. New York: Feminist, 1993.

Almaguer, Tomás. "Chicano Men: A Cartography of

Homosexual Identity and Behavior." Abelove, Barale, and Halperin 255–73.

Alonso, Ana Maria, and Maria Teresa Koreck. "Silences: 'Hispanics,' AIDS, and Sexual Practices." Abelove, Barale, and Halperin 110–26.

Altman, Dennis. "Rupture or Continuity? The Internationalization of Gay Identities." Hawley, *Postcolonial* 19–41.

Anzaldúa, Gloria. *Borderlands / La Frontera.* San Francisco: Aunt Lute, 1999.

Apter, Emily. Introduction. "World Borders, Political Borders." By Etienne Balibar. *PMLA* 117 (2002): 68–71.

Awkward, Michael. *Negotiating Difference: Race, Gender, and the Politics of Positionality.* Chicago: U of Chicago P, 1995.

———. *Scenes of Instruction: A Memoir.* Durham: Duke UP, 1999.

Bergmann, Emilie L., and Paul Julian Smith, eds. *¿Entiendes? Queer Readings, Hispanic Writings.* Durham: Duke UP, 1995.

Bersani, Leo. *Homos.* Cambridge: Harvard UP, 1995.

Bornstein, Kate. *Gender Outlaw: On Men, Women, and the Rest of Us.* New York: Vintage, 1994.

Butler, Judith. "Critically Queer." *Bodies That Matter: On the Discursive Limits of "Sex."* New York: Routledge, 1993. 223–42.

Butler, Octavia E. *Kindred.* Boston: Beacon, 1988.

Carby, Hazel V. "Race and the Academy: Feminism and the Politics of Difference." *Cultures in Babylon: Black Britain and African America.* London: Verso, 1999. 93–99.

———. *Race Men: The W. E. B. Du Bois Lectures.* Cambridge: Harvard UP, 1998.

Case, Sue-Ellen. "Toward a Butch-Feminist Retro-Future." Heller 205–20.

Cha, Theresa Hak Kyung. *Dictée.* New York: Tanam, 1982.

Cheng, Anne Anlin. *The Melancholy of Race.* Oxford: Oxford UP, 2000.

Chow, Rey. "How (the) Inscrutable Chinese Led to Globalized Theory." *PMLA* 116 (2001): 69–74.

———. *Writing Diaspora: Tactics of Intervention in Contemporary Cultural Studies.* Bloomington: Indiana UP, 1993.

Christian, Barbara. "The Race for Theory." *Making Face, Making Soul / Haciendo Caras: Creative and Critical Perspectives by Feminists of Color.* Ed. Gloria Anzaldúa. San Francisco: Aunt Lute, 1990. 335–45.

Cixous, Hélène. *Les rêveries de la femme sauvage.* Paris: Galilée, 2000.

Cixous, Hélène, and Mireille Calle-Gruber. *Hélène Cixous: Photos de racines.* Paris: Des Femmes, 1994.

Clare, Eli. *Exile and Pride: Disability, Queerness, and Liberation.* Cambridge: South End, 1999.

Clark, VèVè A. "Developing Diaspora Literacy: Allusion in Maryse Condé's *Heremakhonon.*" *Out of the Kumbla: Caribbean Women and Literature.* Ed. Carole Boyce

Davies and Elaine Savory Fido. Trenton: Africa World, 1994. 303–19.

Collins, Patricia Hill. *Black Feminist Thought: Knowledge, Consciousness, and the Politics of Empowerment.* 2nd ed. New York: Routledge, 2000.

———. *Black Sexual Politics: African Americans, Gender, and the New Racism.* New York: Routledge, 2004.

Cook-Lynn, Elizabeth. *Anti-Indianism in Modern America: A Voice from Tatekeya's Earth.* Urbana: U of Illinois P, 2001.

Coursil, Jacques, and Delphine Perret. "The Francophone Postcolonial Field." *Postcolonial Theory and Francophone Literary Studies.* Ed. H. Adlai Murdoch and Anne Donadey. Gainesville: UP of Florida, 2005. 193–207.

Creolization of Theory Conf. Transnational and Transcolonial Studies Multicampus Research Group. U of California, Los Angeles. 5–6 May 2006.

Cruikshank, Margaret. *Learning to Be Old: Gender, Culture, and Aging.* Lanham: Rowman, 2003.

De Lauretis, Teresa. "Fem/Les Scramble." Heller 42–48.

———. "Queer Theory: Lesbian and Gay Sexualities: An Introduction." *Differences: A Journal of Feminist Cultural Studies* 3.2 (1991): iii–xviii.

Desai, Gaurav. "Out in Africa." Hawley, *Postcolonial* 139–64.

Djebar, Assia. "Femmes d'Alger dans leur appartement." *Femmes d'Alger dans leur appartement.* Paris: Des Femmes, 1980. 13–70.

Donadey, Anne. *Recasting Postcolonialism: Women Writing between Worlds.* Portsmouth: Heinemann, 2001.

Donaldson, Elizabeth J. "The Corpus of the Madwoman: Toward a Feminist Disability Studies Theory of Embodiment and Mental Illness." *NWSA Journal* 14.3 (2002): 98–119.

Duberman, Martin. *Midlife Queer: Autobiography of a Decade, 1971–1981.* New York: Scribner's, 1996.

duCille, Ann. "The Occult of True Black Womanhood: Critical Demeanor and Black Feminist Studies." *Signs* 19 (1994): 591–629.

Duggan, Lisa. "The Discipline Problem: Queer Theory Meets Lesbian and Gay History." Duggan and Hunter 194–206.

———. "Making It Perfectly Queer." Duggan and Hunter 155–72.

Duggan, Lisa, and Nan D. Hunter, eds. *Sex Wars: Sexual Dissent and Political Culture.* New York: Routledge, 1995.

Dworkin, Andrea. *Heartbreak: The Political Memoir of a Feminist Militant.* New York: Basic, 2002.

Edelman, Lee. *Homographesis: Essays in Gay Literary and Cultural Theory.* New York: Routledge, 1994.

Ellis, Robert Richmond. Introduction. *Reading and Writing the Ambiente: Queer Sexualities in Latino, Latin American, and Spanish Culture.* Ed. Susana Chávez-Silverman and Librada Hernández. Madison: U of Wisconsin P, 2000. 3–18.

Eng, David L. "Out Here and Over There: Queerness

and Diaspora in Asian American Studies." *Social Text* 52–53 (1997): 31–52.

———. *Racial Castration: Managing Masculinity in Asian America*. Durham: Duke UP, 2001.

Faderman, Lillian. Afterword. Heller 221–29.

———. *Naked in the Promised Land*. Boston: Houghton, 2003.

———. *Odd Girls and Twilight Lovers: A History of Lesbian Life in Twentieth-Century America*. New York: Columbia UP, 1991.

Feinberg, Leslie. *Stone Butch Blues: A Novel*. Ithaca: Firebrand, 1993.

———. *Trans Liberation: Beyond Pink or Blue*. Boston: Beacon, 1998.

Friedan, Betty. *The Fountain of Age*. New York: Simon, 1993.

———. *Life So Far*. New York: Simon, 2000.

Garber, Linda. *Identity Poetics: Race, Class, and the Lesbian-Feminist Roots of Queer Theory*. New York: Columbia UP, 2001.

Garber, Marjorie B. *Vice Versa: Bisexuality and the Eroticism of Everyday Life*. New York: Simon, 1995.

Garland-Thomson, Rosemarie. *Extraordinary Bodies: Figuring Physical Disability in American Culture and Literature*. New York: Columbia UP, 1997.

———. "Feminist Disability Studies." *Signs* 30 (2005): 1557–87.

———. "Integrating Disability, Transforming Feminist Theory." *NWSA Journal* 14.3 (2002): 1–32.

Gilmore, Leigh. *The Limits of Autobiography: Trauma and Testimony*. Ithaca: Cornell UP, 2001.

Gilroy, Paul. *The Black Atlantic: Modernity and Double Consciousness*. Cambridge: Harvard UP, 1993.

Greer, Germaine. *The Change: Women, Aging, and the Menopause*. New York: Knopf, 1992.

Grewal, Inderpal, and Caren Kaplan, eds. *Scattered Hegemonies: Postmodernity and Transnational Feminist Practices*. Minneapolis: U of Minnesota P, 1994.

Gullette, Margaret Morganroth. *Declining to Decline: Cultural Combat and the Politics of the Midlife*. Charlottesville: UP of Virginia, 1997.

Gunn, Giles, ed. *Globalizing Literary Studies*. Spec. issue of *PMLA* 116 (2001): 16–188.

Halberstam, Judith. *Female Masculinity*. Durham: Duke UP, 1998.

Hale, C. Jacob. "Consuming the Living, Dis(re)membering the Dead in the Butch/FTM Borderlands." *GLQ* 4.2 (1998): 311–48.

Hall, Kim Q., ed. *Feminist Disability Studies*. Spec. issue of *NWSA Journal* 14.3 (2002): vii–xiii, 1–221.

Hall, Radclyffe. *The Well of Loneliness*. New York: Anchor, 1990.

Hammonds, Evelynn. "Black (W)holes and the Geometry of Black Female Sexuality." Weed and Schor 136–56.

Harris, Laura Alexander. "Queer Black Feminism: The Pleasure Principle." *Feminist Review* 54 (1996): 3–30.

Hartsock, Nancy C. M. "The Feminist Standpoint: Developing the Ground for a Specifically Feminist Historical Materialism." *Discovering Reality: Feminist Perspectives on Epistemology, Metaphysics, Methodology, and Philosophy of Science*. Ed. Sandra Harding and Merrill B. Hintikka. Boston: Reidel, 1983. 283–310.

Hawley, John C. Introduction. Hawley, *Postcolonial* 1–18.

———, ed. *Postcolonial, Queer: Theoretical Intersections*. Albany: State U of New York P, 2001.

Heller, Dana, ed. *Cross-Purposes: Lesbians, Feminists, and the Limits of Alliance*. Bloomington: Indiana UP, 1997.

Hilden, Patricia Penn. "Race for Sale: Narratives of Possession in Two 'Ethnic' Museums." *TDR: The Drama Review: A Journal of Performance Studies* 44.3 (2000): 11–36.

———. *When Nickels Were Indians: An Urban, Mixed-Blood Story*. Washington: Smithsonian Inst., 1995.

hooks, bell. *Bone Black: Memories of Girlhood*. New York: Henry Holt, 1996.

———. *Remembered Rapture*. New York: Henry Holt, 1999.

———. *We Real Cool: Black Men and Masculinity*. New York: Routledge, 2004.

———. *Wounds of Passion: A Writing Life*. New York: Henry Holt, 1997.

———. *Yearning: Race, Gender, and Cultural Politics*. Boston: South End, 1990.

Hwang, David Henry. *M. Butterfly*. New York: Plume, 1989.

Jaggar, Alison M. "Love and Knowledge: Emotion in Feminist Epistemology." *Gender/Body/Knowledge: Feminist Reconstructions of Being and Knowing*. Ed. Jaggar and Susan R. Bordo. New Brunswick: Rutgers UP, 1989. 145–71.

Jeffreys, Sheila. *Unpacking Queer Politics: A Lesbian Feminist Perspective*. Cambridge, Eng.: Polity, 2003.

Kaminsky, Amy K. *After Exile: Writing the Latin American Diaspora*. Minneapolis: U of Minnesota P, 1999.

Kaplan, Alice Yeager. *French Lessons: A Memoir*. Chicago: U of Chicago P, 1993.

Katz, Jonathan Ned. *Gay American History: Lesbians and Gay Men in the USA: A Documentary*. New York: Crowell, 1976.

Khanna, Ranjana. *Dark Continents: Psychoanalysis and Colonialism*. Durham: Duke UP, 2003.

King, Deborah K. "Multiple Jeopardy, Multiple Consciousness: The Context of a Black Feminist Ideology." *Feminist Theory in Practice and Process*. Ed. Micheline R. Malson, Jean F. O'Barr, Sarah Westphal-Wihl, and Mary Wyer. Chicago: U of Chicago P, 1990. 75–105.

Kittay, Eva, Anita Silvers, Susan Wendell, and Alexa Schriempf, eds. *Feminism and Disability*. Spec. issue of *Hypatia: Journal of Feminist Philosophy* 16.4 (2001): vii–xii, 1–160; 17.3 (2002): 45–253.

Kolodny, Annette. *The Lay of the Land: Metaphor as Experience and History in American Life and Letters*. Chapel Hill: U of North Carolina P, 1975.

LaCom, Cindy. "Revising the Subject: Disability as 'Third Dimension' in *Clear Light of Day* and *You Have Come Back*." *NWSA Journal* 14.3 (2002): 138–54.

Li, David Leiwei, ed. *Globalization and the Humanities*. Spec. issue of *Comparative Literature* 53.4 (2001): 275–461.

Lim, Shirley Geok-lin. *Among the White Moon Faces: An Asian-American Memoir of Homelands*. New York: Feminist, 1996.

Lionnet, Françoise. *Autobiographical Voices: Race, Gender, Self-Portraiture*. Ithaca: Cornell UP, 1989.

———. "Questions de méthode: Itinéraires ourlés de l'autoportrait et de la critique." *Postcolonialisme et Autobiographie: Albert Memmi, Assia Djebar, Daniel Maximin*. Studies in Compar. Lit. 20. Ed. Alfred Hornung and Ernstpeter Ruhe. Amsterdam: Rodopi, 1998. 5–20.

———. "Spaces of Comparison." *Comparative Literature in the Age of Multiculturalism*. Ed. Charles Bernheimer. Baltimore: John Hopkins UP, 1995. 165–74.

———. "Transnationalism, Postcolonialism or Transcolonialism? Reflections on Los Angeles, Geography, and the Uses of Theory." *Emergences* 10.1 (2000): 25–35.

Lionnet, Françoise, and Shu-mei Shih, eds. *Minor Transnationalism*. Durham: Duke UP, 2005.

Lorde, Audre. *Sister/Outsider: Essays and Speeches*. Freedom: Crossing, 1984.

———. *Zami: A New Spelling of My Name*. Trumansburg: Crossing, 1982.

Lowe, Lisa. *Immigrant Acts: On Asian American Cultural Politics*. Durham: Duke UP, 1996.

Lubiano, Wahneema. "Shuckin' Off the African-American Native Other: What's 'Po-Mo' Got to Do with It?" *Cultural Critique* 18 (1991): 149–86.

Lugones, María. "El Pasar Discontínuo de la Capachera/Tortillera del Barrio a la Barra al Movimiento / The Discontinuous Passing of the Capachera/Tortillera from the Barrio to the Bar to the Movement." *Pilgrimages/Peregrinajes: Theorizing Coalition against Multiple Oppressions*. Lanham: Rowman, 2003. 167–80.

MacKinnon, Catharine A. *Toward a Feminist Theory of the State*. Cambridge: Harvard UP, 1989.

Martin, Biddy. "Sexualities without Genders and Other Queer Utopias." *Femininity Played Straight: The Significance of Being Lesbian*. New York: Routledge, 1996. 71–94.

Masiello, Francine. *Between Civilization and Barbarism: Women, Nation, and Literary Culture in Modern Argentina*. Lincoln: U of Nebraska P, 1992.

Matsuda, Mari J. *"Where Is Your Body?" and Other Essays on Race, Gender, and the Law*. Boston: Beacon, 1996.

McClintock, Anne. *Imperial Leather: Race, Gender, and Sexuality in the Colonial Conquest*. New York: Routledge, 1995.

McDowell, Deborah E. *Leaving Pipe Shop: Memories of Kin*. New York: Norton, 1996.

McRuer, Robert. "Compulsory Able-Bodiedness and Queer/Disabled Existence." Snyder, Brueggemann, and Garland-Thomson 88–99.

McRuer, Robert, and Abby L. Wilkerson, eds. *Desiring Disability: Queer Theory Meets Disability Studies*. Spec. issue of *GLQ: A Journal of Lesbian and Gay Studies* 9.1–2 (2003): 1–330.

Mercer, Kobena. *Welcome to the Jungle: New Positions in Black Cultural Studies*. New York: Routledge, 1994.

Mernissi, Fatima. *Dreams of Trespass: Tales of a Harem Girlhood*. Reading: Addison, 1994.

Mihesuah, Devon Abbott. *Indigenous American Women: Decolonization, Empowerment, Activism*. Lincoln: U of Nebraska P, 2003.

Miller, D. A. "Sontag's Urbanity." Abelove, Barale, and Halperin 212–20.

Miller, Nancy K. *Bequest and Betrayal: Memoirs of a Parent's Death*. New York: Oxford UP, 1996.

———. *Getting Personal: Feminist Occasions and Other Autobiographical Acts*. New York: Routledge, 1991.

Mohanty, Chandra Talpade. "Under Western Eyes: Feminist Scholarship and Colonial Discourses." *Third World Women and the Politics of Feminism*. Ed. Mohanty, Ann Russo, and Lourdes Torres. Bloomington: Indiana UP, 1991. 51–80.

———. " 'Under Western Eyes' Revisited: Feminist Solidarity through Anticapitalist Struggles." *Feminism without Borders: Decolonizing Theory, Practicing Solidarity*. Durham: Duke UP, 2003. 221–73.

Moraga, Cherríe. *Loving in the War Years: Lo que nunca pasó por sus labios*. Boston: South End, 1983.

Moraga, Cherríe, and Gloria Anzaldúa, eds. *This Bridge Called My Back: Writings by Radical Women of Color*. New York: Kitchen Table, 1983.

Morales, Aurora Levins. *Medicine Stories: History, Culture, and the Politics of Integrity*. Cambridge: South End, 1998.

Morris, Jenny. "Impairment and Disability: Constructing an Ethics of Care That Promotes Human Rights." *Hypatia* 16.4 (2001): 1–16.

———. *Pride against Prejudice: A Personal Politics of Disability*. London: Women's, 1991.

Morrison, Toni. "The Site of Memory." *Out There: Marginalization and Contemporary Cultures*. Ed. Russell Ferguson, Martha Gever, Trinh T. Minh-Ha, and Cornel West. New York: New York Museum of Contemporary Art, 1990. 299–305.

Morton, Donald. "The Politics of Queer Theory in the (Post)Modern Moment." *Genders* 17 (1993): 121–50.

Nafisi, Azar. *Reading* Lolita *in Tehran: A Memoir in Books*. New York: Random, 2003.

Narayan, Uma. "Working Together across Difference: Some Considerations on Emotions and Political Practice." *Hypatia* 3.2 (1988): 31–47.

Nestle, Joan. "Flamboyance and Fortitude: An Introduction." Nestle, *Persistent Desire* 13–20.

———, ed. *The Persistent Desire: A Femme-Butch Reader.* Boston: Alyson, 1992.

Ong, Aihwa. *Flexible Citizenship: The Cultural Logics of Transnationality.* Durham: Duke UP, 1999.

Patton, Cindy. "From Nation to Family: Containing African AIDS." Abelove, Barale, and Halperin 127–38.

Piedra, José. "Nationalizing Sissies." Bergmann and Smith 370–409.

Pratt, Mary Louise. *Imperial Eyes: Travel Writing and Transculturation.* London: Routledge, 1992.

Raymond, Janice G. *The Transsexual Empire: The Making of the She-Male.* Boston: Beacon, 1979.

Rich, Adrienne. *Blood, Bread, and Poetry: Selected Prose, 1979–1985.* New York: Norton, 1986.

———. "Compulsory Heterosexuality and Lesbian Existence." Rich, *Blood* 23–75.

Rodriguez, Juana María. *Queer Latinidad: Identity, Practices, Discursive Spaces.* New York: New York UP, 2003.

Rosello, Mireille. *France and the Maghreb: Performative Encounters.* Gainesville: UP of Florida, 2005.

Rubin, Gayle. "Of Catamites and Kings: Reflections on Butch, Gender, and Boundaries." Nestle, *Persistent Desire* 466–82.

———. "The Traffic in Women: Notes on the 'Political Economy' of Sex." *Feminist Frameworks: Alternative Theoretical Accounts of the Relations between Women and Men.* 2nd ed. Ed. Alison M. Jaggar and Paula S. Rothenberg. New York: McGraw, 1984. 155–71.

Rubin, Gayle, with Judith Butler. "Sexual Traffic: Interview." Weed and Schor 68–108.

Rushdy, Ashraf H. A. *Remembering Generations: Race and Family in Contemporary African American Fiction.* Chapel Hill: U of North Carolina P, 2001.

Saldívar-Hull, Sonia. *Feminism on the Border: Chicana Gender Politics and Literature.* Berkeley: U of California P, 2000.

Salessi, Jorge. "The Argentine Dissemination of Homosexuality, 1890–1914." Bergmann and Smith 49–91.

Sandoval, Chela. *Methodology of the Oppressed.* Minneapolis: U of Minnesota P, 2000.

Schor, Naomi. "Feminism and Gender Studies." *Introduction to Scholarship in Modern Languages and Literatures.* 2nd ed. Ed. Joseph Gibaldi. New York: MLA, 1992. 262–87.

Schriempf, Alexa. "(Re)Fusing the Amputated Body: An Interactionist Bridge for Feminism and Disability." *Hypatia* 16.4 (2001): 53–79.

Scott, Joan W. "Experience." *Feminists Theorize the Political.* Ed. Judith Butler and Scott. New York: Routledge, 1992. 22–40.

Sedgwick, Eve Kosofsky. *Epistemology of the Closet.* Berkeley: U of California P, 1990.

Shapiro, Judith. "Transsexualism: Reflections on the Persistence of Gender and the Mutability of Sex." *Body Guards: The Cultural Politics of Gender Ambiguity.* Ed. Julia Epstein and Kristina Straub. New York: Routledge, 1991. 248–79.

Shih, Shu-mei. *Visuality and Identity: Sinophone Articulations across the Pacific.* Berkeley: U of California P, forthcoming.

Shohat, Ella. "Area Studies, Gender Studies, and the Cartographies of Knowledge." *Social Text* 72 (2002): 67–78.

Shohat, Ella, and Robert Stam. *Unthinking Eurocentrism: Multiculturalism and the Media.* London: Routledge, 1994.

Silko, Leslie Marmon. *Yellow Woman and a Beauty of the Spirit: Essays on Native American Life Today.* New York: Simon, 1996.

Smith, Paul Julian, and Emilie L. Bergmann. Introduction. Bergmann and Smith 1–14.

Smith, Valerie. *Not Just Race, Not Just Gender: Black Feminist Readings.* New York: Routledge, 1998.

Snyder, Sharon L., Brenda Jo Brueggemann, and Rosemarie Garland-Thomson, eds. *Disability Studies: Enabling the Humanities.* New York: MLA, 2002.

Sommer, Doris. *Proceed with Caution, When Engaged by Minority Writing in the Americas.* Cambridge: Harvard UP, 1999.

Spivak, Gayatri Chakravorty. *A Critique of Postcolonial Reason: Toward a History of the Vanishing Present.* Cambridge: Harvard UP, 1999.

———. *Death of a Discipline.* New York: Columbia UP, 2003.

Stoler, Ann Laura. *Carnal Knowledge and Imperial Power: Race and the Intimate in Colonial Rule.* Berkeley: U of California P, 2002.

Stone, Sandy. "The Empire Strikes Back: A Posttranssexual Manifesto." *Camera Obscura: A Journal of Feminism and Film Theory* 29 (1992): 150–76.

Stryker, Susan. "My Words to Victor Frankenstein above the Village of Chamounix: Performing Transgender Rage." *GLQ* 1.3 (1994): 237–54.

Suleiman, Susan Rubin. *Budapest Diary: In Search of the Motherbook.* Lincoln: U of Nebraska P, 1997.

———. *Risking Who One Is: Encounters with Contemporary Art and Literature.* Cambridge: Harvard UP, 1994.

Suleri, Sara. *Meatless Days.* Chicago: U of Chicago P, 1989.

———. "Woman Skin Deep: Feminism and the Postcolonial Condition." *Colonial Discourse and Postcolonial Theory: A Reader.* Ed. Patrick Williams and Laura Chrisman. New York: Columbia UP, 1994. 244–56.

Swarr, Amanda Lock, and Richa Nagar. "Dismantling Assumptions: Interrogating 'Lesbian' Struggles for Identity and Survival in India and South Africa." *Signs* 29 (2004): 491–516.

Tompkins, Jane P. *A Life in School: What the Teacher Learned.* Reading: Addison, 1996.

Trinh T. Minh-ha. *Woman, Native, Other: Writing Post-coloniality and Feminism.* Bloomington: Indiana UP, 1989.

Trouillot, Michel-Rolf. "The Perspective of the World: Globalization Then and Now." *Beyond Dichotomies: Histories, Identities, Cultures, and the Challenge of Globalization.* Ed. Elisabeth Mudimbe-Boyi. Albany: State U of New York P, 2002. 3–20.

Turner, William B. *A Genealogy of Queer Theory.* Philadelphia: Temple UP, 2000.

Udis-Kessler, Amanda. "Present Tense: Biphobia as a Crisis of Meaning." *Bi Any Other Name: Bisexual People Speak Out.* Ed. Loraine Hutchins and Lani Kaahumanu. Boston: Alyson, 1991. 350–58.

Valenzuela, Luisa. *Simetrías.* Buenos Aires: Sudamericana, 1993.

Warner, Michael, ed. *Fear of a Queer Planet: Queer Politics and Social Theory.* Minneapolis: U of Minnesota P, 1993.

Weed, Elizabeth, and Naomi Schor, eds. *Feminism Meets Queer Theory.* Bloomington: Indiana UP, 1997.

Weeks, Jeffrey. *Coming Out: Homosexual Politics in Britain, from the Nineteenth Century to the Present.* London: Quartet, 1977.

Wendell, Susan. "Toward a Feminist Theory of Disability." *Hypatia* 4.2 (1989): 104–24.

Wilchins, Riki Anne. *Read My Lips: Sexual Subversion and the End of Gender.* Ithaca: Firebrand, 1997.

Williams, Patricia J. *The Alchemy of Race and Rights.* Cambridge: Harvard UP, 1991.

Wing, Adrien K., ed. *Critical Race Feminism: A Reader.* New York: New York UP, 1997.

———. *Global Critical Race Feminism: An International Reader.* New York: New York UP, 2000.

Woodhull, Winifred. *Transfigurations of the Maghreb: Feminism, Decolonization, and Literatures.* Minneapolis: U of Minnesota P, 1993.

Woodward, Kathleen, ed. *Figuring Age: Women, Bodies, Generations.* Bloomington: Indiana UP, 1999.

Young, Stacey. "Dichotomies and Displacements: Bisexuality in Queer Theory and Politics." *Playing with Fire: Queer Politics, Queer Theories.* Ed. Shane Phelan. New York: Routledge, 1997. 51–74.

Zimmerman, Bonnie. " 'Confessions' of a Lesbian Feminist." Heller 157–68.

———. "Placing Lesbians." *The New Lesbian Studies: Into the Twenty-First Century.* Ed. Zimmerman and Toni A. H. McNaron. New York: Feminist, 1996. 269–75.

⌒ Race and Ethnicity

KENNETH W. WARREN

Since 1985, when Henry Louis Gates, Jr., introduced *"Race," Writing, and Difference* with the complaint that "except for aberrant moments in the history of criticism, race has not been brought to bear upon the study of literature in any apparent way," the picture has changed dramatically (2). Indeed, it is now almost de rigueur for literary scholars and cultural critics to declare their intent to take race into account when reading texts and analyzing culture. To take one example not quite at random, in 1994 Lawrence Rainey and Robert von Hallberg launched the journal *Modernism/Modernity* by devoting the first two issues to race, "a subject crucial both to modernism and to the social transformations of modernity." They justify devoting two issues to the topic by explaining that "we want to hold this focus long enough to suggest how the history of modernism might look if we took race as an originating concern of modernism." In asserting race's centrality to the major aesthetic movement of the twentieth century, Rainey and Hallberg confirm that this topic, long of interest primarily to scholars of minority literatures (and even then, to scholars of a sociological bent), has taken its place among the organizing concepts of literary and aesthetic inquiry. Equally significant, though, the journal could treat race at length because the famine of race-inflected critical inquiry

described by Gates in the mid-1980s had become, in the intervening years, a scholarly feast. "We have had no difficulty finding fascinating work on this topic," the editors assure their readers (2).

In this essay, I seek to account for and critique the appeal of race to literary critics over the past two decades and to suggest reasons we ought to modify or resist aspects of that appeal. The racial turn in literary scholarship occurred just as mainstream cultural scholarship was reiterating the truth that biology provides no justification for dividing up the human population into racial groups. Race is a social construction. To be sure, the falsity of basing race in biology was old news even by the 1930s and 1940s, when scholars such as Ralph Bunche and Oliver Cromwell Cox published significant studies affirming the economic, political, and social bases of racialization. And W. E. B. Du Bois, struggling in 1940 to come up with a response to the question, "But what is this group; and how do you differentiate it; and how can you call it 'black' when you admit it is not black?," answers simply, "I recognize it quite easily and with full legal sanction; the black man is a person who must ride 'Jim Crow' in Georgia" (*Dusk* 666).

In the intervening decades, however, a number of factors have acted in concert to stall the effort to discredit biologist or metaphysical justifications of racial difference. First, and somewhat paradoxically, in attempting to counter sociologically based explanations of black behavior and society as a mostly pathological reaction to slavery, segregation, and poverty, writers and scholars from Ralph Ellison in the 1940s and 1950s through the black aestheticians of the 1960s posited a more or less autonomous, self-reproducing black culture that, though not genetically determined, had the capacity to endure and re-create itself over time. Second, the persistence of disproportionate poverty among blacks after the civil rights victories of the 1960s prompted neoconservative scholars to insist that something other than racial discrimination must account for the persistence of black/white difference. And finally, the development of sociobiology as a field in the mid-1970s gave new life to the idea that the sphere of human activity governed by our DNA was much larger than had been previously acknowledged. If moral virtues like altruism could be tracked to the configuration of one's genetic code, then why not entertain the possibility that race was a biological reality as well. This idea became quite visible with the publication in 1994 of Richard Herrnstein and Charles Murray's *The Bell Curve: Intelligence and Class Structure in American Life*, whose claim for a racial basis to IQ differences received a more favorable reception than its argument warranted. Likewise, Steven Pinker's *The Blank Slate: The Modern Denial of Human Nature* (2002), after a variety of qualifications, concludes, "some racial distinctions thus may have a degree of biological reality, even though they are not exact boundaries between fixed categories" (144).

Kwame Anthony Appiah, then, is hardly restating the obvious in "The Uncompleted Argument: Du Bois and the Illusion of Race," when he insists that races are social creations, not biological givens. Appiah writes:

> Differences between peoples in language, moral affections, aesthetic attitudes, or political ideology—those differences which most deeply affect

Attacking essentialism and embracing social constructivism appeared a necessary first step in dismantling an unjust social order.

> us in our dealings with each other—are not biologically determined to any significant degree.
>
> (22)

His critique of biologism embraces what had become by the late 1980s and early 1990s in cultural scholarship a full-scale assault on essentialism, a term denoting the belief that shared innate and heritable biological or metaphysical characteristics underwrite racial, gendered, or sexual identities. Eschewing biology for antiessentialism or social constructivism, Appiah urged scholars to focus instead on the contingent array of economic, political, and social forces and actions that had produced identities as ascriptive categories. Given that assigning racial designations or gender roles on the basis of presumed innate characteristics has been crucial to constructing political and social hierarchies, attacking essentialism and embracing social constructivism appeared a necessary first step in dismantling an unjust social order.

Yet even as some scholars sought to make the assault on essentialism synonymous with both antiracism and a broad opposition to the political status quo, others raised questions about the wisdom, or even the possibility, of doing away with race altogether. The scholars voicing these objections did not constitute a particularly cohesive group and perhaps should not be designated as a group at all, inasmuch as the reasons for skepticism about antiessentialism derived from a variety of concerns and worries. Nonetheless most of these reservations centered on a tight constellation of questions: Was race unavoidably essentialist? If so, was essentialism necessarily a bad thing? And correspondingly, was antiessentialism always a good thing? In regard to the last question, many black female writers and critics—among them, Toni Morrison, Joyce Ann Joyce, and Barbara Christian—expressed varying degrees of suspicion about the implications of poststructuralist critical theory when it came to race, noting that the attack on the legitimacy of race as a social and aesthetic category had seemed to gather momentum just as black writers and scholars were enjoying unprecedented visibility in the field. In Christian's words, the exclusive language of critical theory had "surfaced, interestingly enough, just when the literature of peoples of color, black women, Latin Americans, and Africans began to move to the 'the center' " (283).

In this view, the broadly democratic pretensions of critical theory were also belied by its specialized and difficult-to-master jargon and by its identification for the most part with a handful of elite institutions and a group of highly paid, predominantly male, scholars. According to this demurral, while race was indeed a technology of domination, it had also been the means through which subordinated groups maintained their cohesiveness and mounted an insurgency against white supremacy. In the light of this history, Joyce writes, "It is insidious for the Black literary critic to adopt any kind of strategy that diminishes or . . . negates his blackness" (341). Identity apparently had become an effective political tool that one should consider carefully before relinquishing.

Sharing the suspicion that dismissing race is a risky political strategy (albeit for reasons not inimical to literary theory) have been cultural studies and poststructuralist scholars like Stuart Hall, Howard Winant, Gayatri Chakravorty Spivak, and critical race theorists like Kimberle Crenshaw (see Crenshaw, Gotanda, et al.). Although all these scholars agree that essentialism is a problem, they also agree that the advocacy of nonracialism as a remedy for inequality is a suspect strategy, because for all the ills wrought by the concept of race, it has not only done some good but has also remained for nonelites a way of grounding collective resistance and oppositional identities. Hall's widely cited "Race, Articulation, and Societies Structured in Dominance" explains the dual political valence of race as follows:

> Racist interpellations can become themselves the sites and stake in the ideological struggle, occupied and redefined to become the elementary forms of an oppositional formation—as where "white racism" is vigorously contested through the symbolic inversions of "black power." The ideologies of racism remain contradictory structures, which can function both as the vehicles for the imposition of dominant ideologies, and as the elementary forms for the cultures of resistance. Any attempt to delineate the politics and ideologies of racism which omits these continuing features of struggle and contradiction wins an apparent adequacy of explanation only by operating a disabling reductionism.   (57)

In Hall's view a die-hard antiessentialism would toss out the baby of resistance and opposition with the bathwater of white domination. And while one might be tempted to argue that losing both sides of the equation would not be such a bad bargain given that the demise of white racism would seem to obviate the need for resistance to racism, Hall, Winant, and others warn that to yield to this temptation would be a mistake, at least at present, because white domination now works precisely by disavowing race as a force in creating and maintaining inequality. Winant makes his case clearly when he writes:

> In the twenty-first century, race will no longer be invoked to legitimate the crucial social structures of inequality, exploitation, and injustice. Appeals to white superiority will not serve, as they did in the bad old days. Law, political and human rights, as well as concepts of equality, fairness, and human difference will therefore increasingly be framed in "race-neutral" terms. Yet the race-concept will continue to work at the interface of identity and inequality, social structure and cultural signification. The rearticulation of (in)equality in an ostensibly color-blind framework emphasizing individualism and meritocracy, it turns out, preserves the legacy of racial hierarchy far more effectively than its explicit defense.   (35)

The largely successful efforts by right-wing political activists during the waning decades of the twentieth century to outlaw or restrict race-conscious programs in college admissions, hiring, and allocating public contracts, coupled with persistent gaps between blacks and whites in income, wealth, educational achievement, and quality of life, as measured by statistical aggregates, suggest that disparate social outcomes are produced not merely despite but now crucially because of the apparent disappearance of race as a legitimate social category.

Left-of-center critics also worried that as academics discredited the analytic validity of race, oppressed minority groups would continue to press their political demands in explicit identitarian terms resulting in a gulf between theory and practice. In several venues Spivak warns that essentialism is not so easily dispensed with if one's goal is to link antiessentialist cultural theory inside the academy with essentialist and identitarian political praxis outside it. As a remedy she recommends that "radical intellectual[s] in the West" learn to read the subaltern "as *strategically* adhering to the essentialist notion of consciousness" and to follow such a course themselves (206–07). That is, critics should not attack essentialist statements emanating from putative allies outside the academy but operate as if both the radical scholar and the subaltern activist were adopting a kind of studied duplicity regarding matters of racial identity, treating identity as a necessary even if not ontologically true statement about the subject. Spivak warns that to fail to take the strategic turn would force the radical intellectual to grant "to the oppressed either that very expressive subjectivity which s/he criticizes, or a total unrepresentability" (209). Were radical scholars to abjure essentialism as a strategy, they would likely end up either as intellectual foes of the subaltern or conspirators in the silencing of the subaltern.

But Spivak's strategic essentialism would be unnecessary if it were somehow possible to produce a nonessentialist account of race. That is, can we underwrite the solidarity presumably enjoyed by subordinated racial groups with something other than discredited intellectual justifications of race? Might we not want to have race if racism didn't come along with it? It is questions like these that Winant and critical race theorists explore in sociology and legal scholarship, respectively. For example, the introduction to the 1995 flagship anthology of critical race theory describes the collective's "project as an effort to construct a race-conscious and at the same time anti-essentialist account of the processes by

Might we not want to have race if racism didn't come along with it?

which law participates in 'racing' American society" (Crenshaw, Gotanda, et al. xxvi). The goal here is not to unrace American society but rather to race it differently so that we can retain the ability to identify specific effects of domination on discrete population groups—the way that, say, poor black women do not seem to be benefiting from existing social policies presumably enacted on behalf of black people generally.

Without this degree of specificity these scholars fear that existing inequalities will be perceived, even by those suffering the effects of injustice, as the expression of innate human differences. And these same people will face such injustice without being able to affirm their links to a historical community that might sustain them in their resistance to domination.

Citing the influence of critical race theory on his work, Winant remarks that a big part of the problem we currently face is that "race is still largely perceived as a problem, rather than as a flexible dimension of human variety that is valuable and permanent" (xiv). Of course, in highlighting the idea of race as a permanent feature of human existence, he accedes to the logic of racism, which is any "*signifying practice that essentializes or naturalizes human identities based on racial categories or concepts.*" By contrast, the notion of race that Winant wants to hold on to is

> a concept that signifies and symbolizes sociopolitical conflicts and interests in reference to different types of human bodies. Although the concept of race appeals to biologically based human characteristics (so-called phenotypes), selection of these particular human features for purposes of racial signification is always and necessarily a social and historical process. There is no biological basis for distinguishing human groups along the lines of "race," and the sociohistorical categories employed to differentiate among these groups reveal themselves, upon serious examination, to be imprecise if not completely arbitrary.   (317)

In other words, although race appeals to observable human features that are biologically determined, it must be understood not to derive from those features. For Winant what makes it potentially valuable to preserve race but reprehensible to engage in racism is that while grouping and treating people on the basis of ascribed biological differences is indefensible, it is important to recognize that across time and space those who have been thus treated have constructed cultures and lifeworlds on the basis of those differences, cultures that have embedded in themselves opposition to the unjust assumptions of a white-supremacist order.

Yet the difficulty of parsing Winant's commitment to defining race as a nonessential component of human existence that is yet somehow permanent and inherently valuable helps explain why some scholars have argued that the essentialist/antiessentialist debate is itself the problem. Diana Fuss's *Essentially Speaking* argues, "in and of itself, essentialism is neither good nor bad, progressive nor reactionary, beneficial nor dangerous" (xi). Instead, "the radicality or conservatism of essentialism depends, to a significant degree, on *who* is utilizing it, *how* it is deployed, and *where* its effects are concentrated." In terms that seem to address Winant's dilemma, Fuss argues that constructivist critiques of essentialism do not end up repudiating essentialism but rather "rerouting and dispersing it through a number of micropolitical units or sub-categorical classifications, each presupposing its own unique interior composition or metaphysical core" (20). That is, we tend to essentialize even when we don't mean to, so that instead of trying to avoid the inevitable, we'd be better off attending to and evaluating the effects of differing essentialist practices.

There is more than a little to be said for Fuss's claim in a general sense. In his recent critique of postmodernism, Terry Eagleton agrees with Fuss in saying that essentialism

> is not necessarily a characteristic of the political right, or anti-essentialiam an indispensable feature of the left . . . [largely] because we need to know among other things which needs are essential to humanity and which are not. Needs which are essential to our survival and well-being . . .

can then become politically critical: any social order which denies such needs can be challenged on the grounds that it is denying our humanity, which is usually a stronger argument against it than the case that it is flouting our contingent cultural conventions. (100, 104)

The question left unanswered is whether or not the forms of collective identity compatible with race can be understood as necessary to our humanity. If race cannot be discerned biologically, it is visible only culturally—that is, as a pattern of behaviors and activities deemed appropriate to the group one happens to be a part of. Are the specific elements that constitute my culture then also essential to my humanity in ways that make them politically critical? To this, Eagleton answers:

> What culture you inhabit is not definitive of your humanity, in the sense that beings of different cultures are not creatures of different species. To be *some* kind of cultural being is indeed essential to our humanity, but not to be any particular kind. (101)

A popular emendation of Eagleton's formulation holds that you cannot claim indifference to the culture you happen to inhabit—first, because you are born into it (even if not destined to remain in it); second, because important consequences ensue from committing yourself to one cultural identity instead of another. Fuss suggests that for historical reasons it might be important to ask whether "the relationship of Afro-American subjectivity to social text [is] fundamentally the same or different from Anglo-American subjectivity" (95). Behind such a question is the idea that the particular cultural identity you inhabit seizes you so early in your development that it constitutes the very subjectivity through which you regard and cognitively process the world around you. As Hortense Spillers writes:

> The individual in the collective traversed by "race"—and there are no exceptions, as far as I can tell—is covered by it before language and its differential laws take hold. It is the perfect affliction, if by that we mean an undeniable setup that

not only shapes one's views of things, but demands an endless response from him.   (378)

It would seem that while biology does not destine us to be raced and gendered in the way that we are, history does.

The common warrant for framing the question of black identity along the lines suggested by Fuss and Spillers is found in the paragraphs addressing "double consciousness" in Du Bois's 1903 classic *The Souls of Black Folk*. In words that are now quite well known, Du Bois observes:

> After the Egyptian and Indian, the Greek and Roman, the Teuton and Mongolian, the Negro is a sort of seventh son, born with a veil, and gifted with second-sight in this American world, — a world which yields him no true self-consciousness, but only lets him see himself through the revelation of the other world. It is a peculiar sensation, this double-consciousness, this sense of always looking at one's self through the eyes of others, of measuring one's soul by the tape of a world that looks on in amused contempt and pity. One ever feels his two-ness,—an American, a Negro; two souls, two thoughts, two unreconciled strivings, two warring ideals in one dark body, whose dogged strength alone keeps it from being torn asunder. The history of the American Negro is the history of this strife,—this longing to attain self-conscious manhood, to merge his double self into a better and truer self. In this merging he wishes neither of the older selves to be lost.   (*Writings* 364–65)

This passage has proved broadly generative of varying permutations of postmodern and post-structural accounts of subject formation, accounts that embrace fragmentation rather than wholeness as a way of freeing subjects from social strictures. And yet, because the trajectory outlined by Du Bois's formulation runs counter to that of postmodernism (i.e., starting from contingency and fragmentation rather than moving toward them), this assimilation has allowed for a simultaneous assertion of black difference on a couple of fronts. That is, in supporting the idea that black subjectivity and white subjectivity are constituted differently, Du Boisian double consciousness can appear either as a precocious postmodernism, in which the black individual becomes the quintessential postmodern subject

operating in fragmentation and self-division, or as a standing critique of the idea that the dissolution of the human subject necessarily leads to liberation, with figures in black providing the elements of a cautionary tale.

Spillers, in essays such as "Mama's Baby, Papa's Maybe: An American Grammar Book" and " 'All the Things You Could Be by Now, If Sigmund Freud's Wife Was Your Mother': Psychoanalysis and Race," argues that historically imposed social limits have produced processes of subject formation for African Americans that make it problematic to assume that current left-inflected critiques of gendering and psychoanalysis have the same beneficial effects on blacks as on whites when considered in the light of history of slavery and racism. That black women have been systematically denied the opportunity to define themselves as women might affect how one assesses the erasure of gender distinctions as a political goal. Although she cites Spillers only in passing, Claudia Tate likewise insists that the idealization of marriage in late-nineteenth-century black women's fiction tended to challenge rather than capitulate to social conventions. Institutions like marriage often offered "the recently emancipated an occasion for exercising political self-definition in fiction at a time when the civil rights of African Americans were constitutionally sanctioned but socially prohibited" (7). That black writers found themselves sometimes insisting on upholding the social norms of dominant society and sometimes contesting those norms affirms for Tate the utility of Du Bois's double consciousness conceit (230).

Perhaps the most influential of the Du Boisian inflected efforts to chart a course between or around the essentialist/antiessentialist binary during the 1990s has been Paul Gilroy's *The Black Atlantic: Modernity and Double-Consciousness* (1993), which opens with the declaration, "Striving to be both European and black requires some specific forms of double consciousness" (3). Gilroy finds his "ground" for reconciling essentialist and contingent accounts of black identity on and beneath the waters of the Atlantic Ocean, the pathway of the Atlantic slave trade. Repudiating the antiessentialist conclusion that "the pursuit of any unifying dynamic or underlying structure of feeling in contemporary black cultures is utterly misplaced" (80), he adduces a shared structure of feeling among the black subjects across the globe, putatively latent in the sounds of a worldwide black music that finds its origins in the experience of blacks victimized by the slave trade. Arguing that slavery is a modern rather than a premodern form of exploitation, Gilroy then describes the cultural response to it as a nonverbal, prerational form of utopian politics. Art and music

> became the backbone of the slaves' political cultures and of their cultural history. It remains the means through which cultural activists even now engage in "rescuing critiques" of the present by both mobilizing memories of the past and inventing an imaginary past-ness that can fuel their utopian hopes.   (57)

Although the concept of the Atlantic world as a domain of study was in circulation, particularly among historians, well before the publication of *The Black Atlantic*, Gilroy's notion of a black transatlantic and transhistorical lifeworld sutured by a collective memory that finds expression in the sound of black music has proved quite evocative for scholars seeking a means to step outside approaches to culture that remain confined within national boundaries. The particular community Gilroy has in mind also seems helpfully described as a diaspora, a term that was also enjoying widespread usage before *The Black Atlantic* was published, in order to denote the condition of black persons around the globe.

From its earlier use as a term for the dispersal of Jews beyond Palestine, *diaspora* has come to be applied to any population group with substantial numbers who are seen as living outside of, but retaining ties to, an ancestral homeland. It is, of course, the nature of these ties that lies at the center of diasporic accounts, and for those scholars seeking to downplay biology as the tie that binds, the more tenuous links among these populations have proved most enabling. Diasporas cannot be assumed; they must be made

through actions: mnemonic, physical, and aesthetic. And the production of a critical memory capable of forging a scattered population into a people stands as the most prized (and most problematic) outcome of these activities. If memory is the way we connect past and present, the problem presented by the slave trade is the absence of continuity, the lack of an unbroken line between old world and new. Day-to-day cultural practices viewed as constitutive of identity for most blacks in the Americas differ significantly from day-to-day practices on the African continent. Nonetheless, the desire to find evidence of continuity in the deep structure of cultural practices has shaped such volumes as Genevieve Fabre and Robert O'Meally's *History and Memory in African American Culture* (1994), which orbits around the idea that if the dominant mode of American culture is premised on forgetting the past in favor of making the world new, African American culture, conscious of having been bereft of an official past, is "[s]purred on by a will to remember—by a conscious effort to limit forgetfulness" (7). Music, imaginative literature, and dance provide the occasion for acts of memory that create and shape diasporic consciousness.

Ian Baucom's 2001 special issue of *South Atlantic Quarterly*, which focuses on Atlantic genealogies, credits Gilroy for having identified modernity with the black Atlantic. Baucom praises *The Black Atlantic* as "undoubtedly the most influential and field defining" study of the work done on the Atlantic world ("Introduction" 6), and he presents his special issue as a demonstration of the in-it-but-not-entirely-of-it relation of black culture to Western modernity that Gilroy posits as distinctive of the black Atlantic. Baucom writes:

> An Atlantic discourse can perhaps most fully perform the double labor of articulating itself as a counterdiscourse in and on modernity while, simultaneously, discovering in its fragmentary, heterogeneous protocols of assemblage and disassemblage an Atlantic genealogy of the modern.
> (8)

The intent here is to make central to historical inquiry those discourses and experiences that

Diasporas cannot be assumed; they must be made through actions: mnemonic, physical, and aesthetic.

have been exiled to the periphery without, in the process, erasing the processes that produced marginalization in the first place. One can also see that nestled in these processes of memorializing, assembling, and disassembling the past is once again the question of whether or not the concept of race subtends the Atlantic genealogies under construction.

Gilroy emphasizes that black identity in Britain has come to comprise South Asians and Arabs as well as the descendants of sub-Saharan blacks, brought together not by shared ancestry but a shared appreciation for the music deriving mostly from United States African American sources. Even so, the literature addressed in *The Black Atlantic* consists largely of texts taught in standard African American studies courses, and the language of the black Atlantic remains English. The essays in Baucom's special issue, however, discuss authors as disparate as Olaudah Equiano, Edmund Spenser, and Samuel Beckett, indicating that the boundaries of the black Atlantic are not to be seen as coterminous with those of race. Nonetheless the challenge posed for these scholars lies in correlating the central atrocity of the transatlantic slave trade, an atrocity visited on a specific population, with the experiences of others across space and time without losing the specific in its translation to the general.

Brent Edwards's *The Practice of Diaspora: Literature, Translation, and the Rise of Black Internationalism* (2003) takes on the problem of linking disparate texts across linguistic traditions, first, by considering black francophone texts alongside anglophone texts and, second, by placing the act of translation at the center of diasporic practice. Edwards does continue Gilroy's privileging of music, concluding his study with the observation, "Black internationalism . . . is less like a sturdy edifice or a definitive program than like the uncertain harmony of a new song" (318). He connects black diasporic texts with one another through a concept he calls décalage, a term adapted from Leopold Senghor to suggest both the connectedness and the discontinuity in the black diaspora. Edwards writes:

Décalage is the kernel of precisely that which cannot be transferred or exchanged, the received biases that refuse to pass over when one crosses the water. It is a changing core of difference; it is the work of "difference within unity," an unidentifiable point that is incessantly touched and fingered and pressed.   (14)

Although his theory is attractive precisely for its refusal to flatten out or ignore differences in language or geography in diasporic populations, the unity in which these differences matter appears to be that of race. Black internationalism, too, presumes at least the rudimentary coherence of race as a category.

In fact what links virtually all the neo–Du Boisian accounts mentioned thus far is the desire to match the acknowledgment that race cannot be reduced to phenotype with the claim that some version of race remains a necessary good or evil. Against Appiah's warning that "there is nothing in the world that can do all we ask 'race' to do for us" (34), scholars persist in thinking there must be some way for race to do at least some of the oppositional things they ask of it.

Some commentators have held out the possibility that the concept of ethnicity as well as the terms often associated with it—pluralism and multiculturalism—might prove capable of resolving some of the dilemmas presented by race. In denoting an amalgam of inherited practices and beliefs, ethnicity seems less dependent on the latent biological essentialism associated with race. In the American context, Irish, Italian, Jewish, Chicano, Puerto Rican, and many other similar terms designate the idea that different groups retain some orientation toward their country of origin no matter how long ago their ancestors emigrated. Scholars of ethnicity generally acknowledge Horace Kallen's 1920s writings as the key source for the idea that ethnic pluralism provided a more accurate and politically beneficial description of the United States than did the concept of the nation as a melting pot. Nonetheless, most scholars note that it was not until the late 1960s and early 1970s, in the wake of the civil rights and black power movements, that the concept came to wield the sway of a ruling idea.

At that point social critics claimed that contrary to expectations, Americans were not increasingly viewing themselves as rootless individualists. Rather, their status as descendants of immigrants remained a significant point of orientation for political and social affiliation. Nathan Glazer and Daniel Patrick Moynihan's *Beyond the Melting Pot* (1970) and Michael Novak's *The Rise of the Unmeltable Ethnics* (1971) made this argument forcefully. At about the same time, Harold Cruse's *The Crisis of the Negro Intellectual* sounded the same note in castigating black elites for having bought into an integrationist model of social advancement while failing to recognize that their erstwhile allies, in particular Jewish liberals, had clung to an ethnic group model.

The evidence supporting the strengthening of ethnic ties during these decades is not persuasive. Stephen Steinberg, in *The Ethnic Myth: Race, Ethnicity, and Class in America* (2001), argues that "the ethnic revival was a 'dying gasp' " and did not "signify a genuine revitalization of ethnicity, but rather was symptomatic of the atrophy of ethnic cultures and the decline of ethnic communities" (51). Adolph Reed argues that the emerging emphases on ethnic and racial particularism mark a transformation in the dynamics of consumer capitalism and is better seen as part of a process of the depoliticization of rather than a strengthening of grassroots political movements.

However inaccurate ethnicity may have been as a term of analysis for what was happening on the American political scene outside the academy, the study of literature and history in the academy often overlooked or undervalued the writings of nonwhites as well as that of white women. This lack made ethnicity and multiculturalism, along with feminism, effective tools for exposing the bias and inadequacy of American literary study. The rise of black studies, fueled by the Black Arts Movement's claim that the study of black texts required employing protocols from within a black tradition, ignited a rush to produce anthologies that helped define discrete literary canons. A group of writers headed by Frank Chin published in 1974 *Aiiieeeee! An Anthology of Asian-American Writers*, and in the early 1980s Cherríe Moraga and Gloria Anzaldúa edited *This Bridge Called My Back: Writings by Radical Women of Color*. One could easily add dozens of titles here, but other features are perhaps worthier of note—for example, that the organizing identities that scholars and anthologists employed were more inclusive than their communities of origin. Asian replaced Chinese, Japanese, Korean, and so on; Latina/Latino replaced Mexican American, Puerto Rican, or Cuban. In some instances "people of color" became a term of art.

Behind the preference for these midlevel terms of identification lay the suspicion that merely to insist on the inclusion of immigrant traditions was to accede to rather than challenge the dominant social order. If the goal was to make ethnic identities oppositional to, or at least resistant to, neoliberal society, then insisting on recognition from dominant institutions was not enough. Lisa Lowe has written:

> Rather than attesting to the absorption of cultural difference into the universality of the national political sphere as the "model minority" stereotype would dictate, the Asian immigrant—at odds with the cultural, racial, and linguistic forms of the nation—emerges in a site that defers and displaces the temporality of assimilation.   (6)

What differentiates Lowe's formulation from the 1970s version of ethnic pluralism was the insistence that identity is not a way of operating within the prevailing social order but instead a way of producing an alternative to it.

Another feature of the turn to identity in the 1980s and 1990s was the desire not to lose sight of the inequalities that still plague United States society. Even if one agrees that all ethnic traditions are equally deserving of study, there remains the fact that granting canonical equality to writers of color does not automatically produce equivalent political and socioeconomic dividends, a point John Guillory makes. According to some scholars, also contributing to the disparate socioeconomic fates of ethnic groups is that the boundary between a dominant whiteness and ethnic identity has shifted and been revised repeatedly over the past century and a half. The attempt to address these shifts and revisions has led to the emergence of whiteness studies as one of the more visible facets of racial study in the literary academy in the 1990s.

As with the turn to race generally, whiteness studies is underwritten by the social constructivist consensus across the humanities and social sciences. A number of historians, led by David Roediger and Noel Ignatiev, have argued that not only is whiteness made and constantly being remade but also that many of the people currently regarded as white were not always so regarded. The title of Ignatiev's 1995 book, *How the Irish Became White*, became, mutatis mutandis, the refrain for numerous accounts of the evolving status of a variety of social groups in the Americas and Europe as they went from being described in the terms of otherness we tend to see as usually reserved for blacks, Native Americans, and Asians to being accorded an unremarkable sameness (albeit a sameness that sometimes allowed for ethnic differentiation) that made them available for full assimilation into white society. By exposing claims to white identity as an ever-shifting process, scholars of whiteness seek to undermine the power of the term to do its work surreptitiously.

This project of exposure may claim too much for itself. In assessing the shortcomings of the whiteness movement, Eric Arnesen notes that here too a formulation by Du Bois has proved particularly suggestive. As indicated by such titles as Roediger's *The Wages of Whiteness: Race and the Making of the American Working Class* (1991) and Cheryl I. Harris's "Whiteness as Property," many of these writers have taken their cue from Du Bois's observation in *Black Reconstruction* that being white constituted "a sort of public and psychological wage" that granted even downtrodden working-class whites "public

The social and material benefits of whiteness accrue to individuals regardless of their intent to claim the advantages accorded them by identity.

deference and titles of courtesy because they were white" (700). Immigrant groups were led quite quickly to believe that despite the material interests they shared with black Americans it was more beneficial to forestall identification along class lines in favor of a commitment to white supremacy. Similar findings have echoed in work by the philosophers Charles Mills and Lucius Outlaw, as well as by the cultural studies critic George Lipsitz, and by the critical race theory scholars Harris and Kimberle Crenshaw, to name a few.

Mills proposes a "racial contract" subtending the idea of the theoretical social contract by which governments were constituted to secure the rights and establish the responsibilities of its signatories. It is Mills's claim that throughout Western societies the polities constituted by this social contract have entailed a sometimes tacit, sometimes explicit agreement that eligibility to become a signatory rests on one's whiteness. The social and material benefits of whiteness accrue to individuals regardless of their intent to claim the advantages accorded them by identity, a structural privileging that has operated even in politically progressive constituencies. The felt need to address this privileging of whiteness accounts in part for the emergence of critical race theory from critical legal theory. It has also led to a hyperattentiveness among scholars to the racism that has plagued the labor movement for the last century and more recently has justified critics' attending to the subject position and race of other critics in assessing their work. Patricia Hill Collins and Michael Awkward have cautioned black scholars about failing to consider the unconscious will to white and male power that may operate when self-conscious white scholars venture into the precincts of African Americanist critique. Hazel Carby's analysis of the emergence of the black woman novelist proceeds from a similarly cautionary observation about the ways in which hegemonic control of dominant classes has been secured at the expense of sisterhood. . . . For women this has meant that many of their representative organizations have been disabled by strategies and struggles which have been race-specific, leading to racially divided movements like the temperance and suffrage campaigns. No history should blandly label these organizations "women's movements."   (18)

Correspondingly, privileged scholars working in racially defined fields have often drawn attention to and taken account of their subject position as they launch their readings of black texts and authors. Dana J. Nelson concludes her preface to *The Word in Black and White: Reading "Race" in American Literature, 1638–1867* by confessing:

All "whites" (myself included) benefit from institutionalized racism in the United States, and this means that all "whites" (myself included) must take responsibility for the effects *and* the elimination of racism. As an Anglo-American, an academic, an educator, I realize that there is no vantage from which I can speak or know or act outside of the "contamination" of power.   (xiii)

In his turn Kenneth Mostern—invoking Robyn Wiegman's *American Anatomies*—concludes his study of race, autobiography, and identity politics by reminding his fellow white scholars, "We continue to need the honesty to objectify ourselves in the mirror of our particular others, and to choose our ethical battles in the context of the reality of those objectifications" (216). Even Awkward in his forays into black feminist theory calls attention to the limitations that being "a biological male" impose on his intended contributions (45).

Among the chief effects, then, of attending to whiteness in critical studies has been the validation of the autobiographical-confessional mode as a critical strategy, for critics of color and particularly for dominant-group scholars moving into nontraditional fields. The white critics' visible struggle with their subject position becomes a point of departure for the effort to divest them-

selves of the advantages of white identity. There is a problem here, however. No matter how admirable one considers this attempt (and to be fair, most of these critics explicitly disavow any claim to kudos for their critical self-awareness), the individualist and hortatory solution to what has been defined as a systemic problem produces a lack of correspondence between diagnosis and remedy. Arnesen observes that a "recurring hero in some versions of whiteness studies is the 'antiracist' or 'race traitor,' who essentially 'just says no' to membership in the 'club' that is the 'white race' " (7). Mills in fact dedicates *The Racial Contract* to race traitors who have refused to become parties to the racial contract.

But if the fundamental claim of whiteness studies is that people's consciousness of themselves as a racial subject is an effect caused by specific social structures and historical processes, a solution that focuses on individual psychology and moral heroism can only be an argumentative non sequitur. The reading of history, both literary and social, then becomes a morality play in which social movements, imaginative writers, and literary texts are lauded or faulted for resisting or succumbing to the racial orthodoxy of their historical moment. Nelson tells us that while Lydia Maria Child's *A Romance of the Republic*

is highly critical of individual misuses of capital in both the North and South, it complacently accepts a system that ultimately guarantees both individual misuses and institutionalized class/race prejudices. We must acknowledge this important limitation.   (89)

At issue here is not Nelson's observations that Child's novel is a creature of its moment (which it obviously could not help but be) but the implication that we should see and judge Child for having been limited in troubling ways. What we are being enjoined to do, in effect, is to look to literature for the politically exceptional, the heroic, even as we are cautioned to be aware of the shortcomings of our would-be heroes.

To be sure, the attempt to flush out

unacknowledged or perhaps unconscious commitments to whiteness has produced interesting and provocative readings of literary works. Morrison's *Playing in the Dark: Whiteness and the Literary Imagination* hypothesizes that much of canonical white literature has been shaped by its response "to a dark, abiding, signing Africanist presence" (5). Authorial decisions about plotting, characterization, and even sentence structure can be seen as effects caused by an encounter with this presence. For example, in reading a particularly awkward passage from Ernest Hemingway's *To Have and Have Not*, Morrison suggests that Hemingway's tortured syntax results from his attempt "to avoid a speaking black" in his narrative (72). Morrison's extended essay helpfully draws attention to the need to be more attentive to the possibility that few white American writers have been able to avoid the problem of representing racial difference, but she describes this "Africanist presence" as a fixed, almost metaphysical entity whose force operates virtually the same across the whole of American history. That is, while the Africanist presence depends on the historical reality of an enslaved and exploited black population, Africanism in Morrison's text is a metaphor that seems to float ghostlike through the consciousnesses of all American writers.

Nonetheless, *Playing in the Dark* is symptomatic of a turn in literary scholarship to considering black and white literary texts as mutually constitutive. In American literary scholarship, this turn, as described by Shelley Fisher Fishkin, was in many respects a return to Ralph Ellison's contention that "the Negro" lies at the center of the American imagination (579). Fishkin herself, in *Was Huck Black?*, contends persuasively that Mark Twain's little known sketch "Sociable Jimmy," which features the voice of a young black boy, provided the model and inspiration of the vernacular phrasings of Huck Finn's distinctive voice. Eric J. Sundquist's *To Wake the Nations: Race in the Making of American Literature* pairs "minor" texts by white canonical authors with texts by African American writers "to suggest that neither perspective is by itself adequate

to account for the ongoing crisis over race in American cultural and political life" (7). George Hutchinson, in *The Harlem Renaissance in Black and White*, set out to counter assessments that the Harlem Renaissance had failed largely as a result of the inability of black writers to free themselves of the influence of white writers and patrons. Instead, he urges us to see the interactions between black and white writers as a successful interracialism in American letters. And to return to the context of modernism with which this essay began, Michael North's *The Dialect of Modernism* draws attention to the extensive play with black dialect voice and characterization by T. S. Eliot, Ezra Pound, and Wallace Stevens in order to make a case that the dialect was essential to the linguistic challenge that modernist poets were able to mount against standard authoritative language. In effect, North argues, the literary avant-garde's success at remaking the language of modern poetry depended on acts of racial ventriloquism. Correspondingly, North notes that "the success of the white avant-garde made life more difficult for Afro-American and Afro-Caribbean writers" for whom dialect verse constituted a racist convention more difficult (but as the career of Langston Hughes demonstrates, not impossible) to refashion into a challenge to cultural standardization (195).

Notwithstanding North's linguistic focus, his work—like those of Fishkin, Sundquist, Hutchinson—remains subject-centered in having committed at some level to the idea that different racial points of view make distinct contributions to a richer national or global vision. The implicit framework for these and many similar studies is multicultural and pluralistic, endorsing both tacitly and explicitly, if often inadvertently, Du Bois's belief, as expressed in "The Conservation of Races," that "the Negro people, as a race, have a contribution to make to civilization and humanity, which no other race can make" (*Writings* 825). In North's study we learn, if the white avant-garde experienced lasting success in renovating American poetic language, "much of the credit must also go to the culture that inspired and led them" (195). Broadly reflective of efforts across the academy to justify affirmative action policies by emphasizing racial and ethnic diversity as an educational good, multiculturalist scholarship puts forward either the idea that many of the cultural projects we currently enjoy derive at least some of their power from abjected cultures they disavow or the notion that our current critical biases have contributed to a failure to appreciate the quality of work produced by members of subaltern groups. We must learn, that is, to locate and appreciate difference.

There is also a strain of scholarship, which includes my work as well as that of Adolph Reed and Walter Benn Michaels, that attempts to account historically for race in the production of American literary and intellectual life without giving way to an anachronistic tendency to praise or blame historical figures for having anticipated or failed to realize current concerns. In varying ways this work critiques the commitment to identity, tradition, and canon building in contemporary critical practice, not so much for what that work does but for the ways in which scholars engaged in these enterprises explain and describe their critical interventions. My *Black and White Strangers*, for example, seeks to reveal how the aesthetic commitments of writers like Henry James and William Dean Howells contributed inadvertently to trends and forces that worked against the drive for political equality for black freedmen in the late nineteenth century. The point here is not to condemn either writer for having been a part of this process but rather to understand the contingencies and interrelations that shaped both the aesthetic fate of realism in the 1880s and 1890s and the political fate of black freedmen during these same decades.

The potential political value of this sort of literary historical study stems from its disarticulating literary genres and modes from any specific politics. A commitment to realism or sentimentalism means nothing inherently but derives its political force from specific and time-bound considerations. Likewise the varying political appropriations of Ellison's work during the post-segregation era exposes how the speaking-for-the-Negro mantle assumed by black writers

during the Jim Crow era (when so many black Americans were denied access to the franchise) has continued to prove attractive to black intellectuals as a way of validating their work even when the political realities shaping the day-to-day realities of blacks have changed significantly.

Reed has provided the most penetrating critique of the Du Boisian roots of recent African Americanist work on race in his *W. E. B. Du Bois and American Political Thought: Fabianism and the Color Line*. He demonstrates that the emergence of double consciousness as Du Bois's most-discussed concept has been of relatively recent vintage and "tells us more about contemporary black intellectual life than about Du Bois" (129). This "contemporary black intellectual life" has been dominated by the literary scholarship of Houston Baker and Henry Louis Gates, who despite their differences have been as one in seeking to establish an authentic, black tradition—an enterprise that by its very nature collapses, ignores, or dubiously resolves the differences among writers and thinkers and in the name of speaking for the collective advances the interests of a particular class fraction. Reed writes:

> The idea of a reified black tradition and the imagery of double-consciousness connect particularly with the middle-class stratum that operates in largely integrated career environments, especially those professional milieux—including elite colleges and universities—in which work and social networks overlap.   (165)

If there seems to be some overlap with the critiques of poststructuralism leveled by Joyce and Christian, the overlap is at most partial. As Reed points out, the power of the double-consciousness trope "presumes a model of identity constructed from monads such as femaleness, blackness, whiteness, gayness, and the like" (165), and the demurral voiced by Joyce and Christian is not prompted by a dissent from the idea of monadic identity but comes from the concern that Baker and Gates betray the very tradition and identity they seek to represent.

Perhaps the most controversial and challenging work in this vein has been that of Michaels, who in *Our America: Nativism, Modernism, and*

Pluralism and *The Shape of the Signifier* has argued that while considerations of race and identity have indeed been central to the formal experimentation of American modernism and have moved to the center of major theoretical shifts in the American literary academy of the last three decades, the effects have largely been opposite that of what many critics intended. Advocates of pluralism, multiculturalism, and antiessentialism have sought to produce progressive accounts of identity that do not depend on ideas of race they regard as discredited, but Michaels counters that no such updating is possible:

> Any notion of cultural identity that goes beyond the description of our actual beliefs and practices must rely on race (or something equivalent, say, sex) in order to determine which culture is actually ours. Hence the idea of cultural identity—despite the fact that in recent years it has customarily been presented as an alternative to racial identity—is in fact, not only historically but logically, an extension of racial identity.
> ("*Our America*" 121)

Culture can define who we are and distinguish us from others only if we already know who we are. And the only thing that can tell us which culture and which history is ours is a prior commitment to some form of identity.

Given Michaels's argument that the work of modernism was the work of racializition ("I don't think you can understand modern identitarianism without understanding literary modernism" [125]), it was no surprise that after having devoted its first two issues to race, *Modernism/Modernity* would also find it necessary to take up Michaels's challenge, using another issue to reprint the proceedings of a panel discussion devoted to *Our America* ("*Our America*"). The participants in this panel defined Michaels's challenge in various ways, but the greatest worry in the scholarly turn to race concerns the political significance of this scholarly enterprise. There is no gainsaying that an accurate consideration of the aesthetics and politics of the modern era demands that we attend to the ways

The cultural politics of race has gained salience largely because the discussion of social inequality has skewed toward questions of representation, questions that matter greatly for literature.

that race emerged from and has figured into the processes by which inequalities have been created and maintained. There is also no gainsaying that attention to race has been the effect of greater numbers of people of color entering the academy over the past thirty years. But here's the rub: the cultural politics of race has gained salience largely because the discussion of social inequality has skewed toward questions of representation, questions that matter greatly for literature. Knowing more about the production of race as an ideology and a discourse enables us to understand better literary history and the panoply of texts that constitute that history. This knowledge does not and should not be expected to give us tools to fix current inequalities.

WORKS CITED AND SUGGESTIONS FOR FURTHER READING

Appiah, Anthony Kwame. "The Uncompleted Argument: Du Bois and the Illusion of Race." Gates 21–37.

Arnesen, Eric. "Scholarly Controversy: Whiteness and the Historians' Imagination." *International Labor and Working-Class History* 60 (2001): 3–32.

Awkward, Michael. *Negotiating Difference: Race, Gender, and the Politics of Positionality*. Chicago: U of Chicago P, 1995.

Baucom, Ian. "Introduction: Atlantic Genealogies." *South Atlantic Quarterly* 100.1 (2001): 1–13.

———. "Specters of the Atlantic." *South Atlantic Quarterly* 100.1 (2001): 61–81.

Bunche, Ralph. *A World View of Race*. Washington: Assocs. in Negro Folk Educ., 1936.

Carby, Hazel. *Reconstructing Womanhood: The Emergence of the Afro-American Woman Novelist*. New York: Oxford UP, 1987.

Chin, Frank, ed. *Aiiieeeee! An Anthology of Asian-American Writers*. Washington: Howard UP, 1974.

Christian, Barbara. "The Race for Theory." *African American Literary Theory: A Reader*. Ed. Winston Napier. New York: New York UP, 2000. 280–89.

Collins, Patricia Hill. *Black Feminist Thought: Knowledge, Consciousness, and the Politics of Empowerment*. London: Harper, 1990.

Cox, Oliver Cromwell. *Caste, Class, and Race: A Study in Social Dynamics*. New York: Modern Reader, 1948.

Crenshaw, Kimberle, Neil Gotanda, et al., eds. *Critical Race Theory: The Key Writings That Formed the Movement*. New York: New, 1995.

Cruse, Harold. *The Crisis of the Negro Intellectual*. New York: New York Rev., 2005.

Du Bois, W. E. B. *Black Reconstruction in America*. New York: Simon, 1995.

———. *Dusk of Dawn: An Essay toward an Autobiography of a Race Concept*. Du Bois, *Writings* 549–802.

———. *Writings*. Ed. Nathan Huggins. New York: Lib. of Amer., 1986.

Eagleton, Terry. *The Idea of Culture*. Malden: Blackwell, 2000.

Edwards, Brent. *The Practice of Diaspora: Literature, Translation, and the Rise of Black Internationalism*. Cambridge: Harvard UP, 2003.

Ellison, Ralph. "What America Would Be like without Blacks." *The Collected Essays of Ralph Ellison*. Ed. John F. Callahan. New York: Modern Lib., 1995. 577–84.

Fabre, Genevieve, and Robert O'Meally, eds. *History and Memory in African American Culture*. New York: Oxford UP, 1994.

Fishkin, Shelley Fisher. *Was Huck Black? Mark Twain and African-American Voices*. New York: Oxford UP, 1993.

Fuss, Diana. *Essentially Speaking: Feminism, Nature, and Difference*. New York: Routledge, 1989.

Gates, Henry Louis, Jr., ed. *"Race," Writing, and Difference*. Chicago: U of Chicago P, 1992.

Gilroy, Paul. *The Black Atlantic: Modernity and Double-Consciousness*. Cambridge: Harvard UP, 1993.

Glazer, Nathan, and Daniel Patrick Moynihan. *Beyond the Melting Pot: The Negroes, Puerto Ricans, Jews, Italians, and Irish of New York City*. Cambridge: MIT P, 1970.

Guillory, John. "Canonical and Non-canonical: A Critique of the Current Debate." *ELH* 54 (1987): 36–54.

Hall, Stuart. "Race, Articulation, and Societies Structured in Dominance." *Black British Cultural Studies: A Reader*. Ed. Houston A. Baker, Jr., Manthia Diawara, and Ruth H. Lindeborg. Chicago: U of Chicago P, 1996. 16–60.

Harris, Cheryl I. "Whiteness as Property." *Harvard Law Review* 106 (1993): 1709–91.

Herrnstein, Richard J., and Charles Murray. *The Bell Curve: Intelligence and Class Structure in American Life*. New York: Free, 1994.

Hutchinson, George. *The Harlem Renaissance in Black and White*. Cambridge: Harvard UP, 1995.

Ignatiev, Noel. *How the Irish Became White*. New York: Routledge, 1995.

Joyce, Joyce A. "The Black Canon: Reconstructing Black American Literary Criticism." *New Literary History* 18 (1986): 335–44.

Kallen, Horace M. *Culture and Democracy in the United States*. New York: Boni, 1924.

Lipsitz, George. *The Possessive Investment in Whiteness: How White People Profit from Identity Politics*. Philadelphia: Temple UP, 1998.

Lowe, Lisa. *Immigrant Acts : On Asian American Cultural Politics*. Durham: Duke UP, 1996.

Michaels, Walter Benn. *Our America: Nativism, Modernism, and Pluralism*. Durham: Duke UP, 1995.

———. *The Shape of the Signifier: 1967 to the End of History*. Princeton: Princeton UP, 2004.

Mills, Charles W. *The Racial Contract*. Ithaca: Cornell UP, 1997.

Moraga, Cherríe, and Gloria Anzaldúa, eds. *This Bridge Called My Back: Writings by Radical Women of Color*. New York: Kitchen Table; Women of Color, 1983.

Morrison, Toni. *Playing in the Dark: Whitenesss and the Literary Imagination*. Cambridge: Harvard UP, 1992.

Mostern, Kenneth. *Autobiography and Black Identity Politics: Racialization in Twentieth-Century America*. New York: Cambridge UP, 1997.

Nelson, Dana J. *The Word in Black and White: Reading "Race" in American Literature, 1638–1867*. New York: Oxford UP, 1992.

North, Michael. *The Dialect of Modernism: Race, Language, and Twentieth-Century Literature*. New York: Oxford UP, 1994.

Novak, Michael. *The Rise of the Unmeltable Ethnics: Politics and Culture in the 1970s*. New York: Macmillan, 1973.

"*Our America* and Nativist Modernism: A Panel." *Focus on American Modernism*. Spec. issue of *Modernism/Modernity* 3.3 (1996): 97–126.

Outlaw, Lucius, Jr. *On Race and Philosophy*. New York: Routledge, 1996.

Pinker, Steven. *The Blank Slate: The Modern Denial of Human Nature*. New York: Viking, 2002.

Rainey, Lawrence, and Robert von Hallberg. Introduction. *Modernism/Modernity* 1.1 (1994): 1–3.

Reed, Adolph, Jr. *W. E. B. Du Bois and American Political Thought: Fabianism and the Color Line*. New York: Oxford UP, 1997.

Roediger, David R. *The Wages of Whiteness: Race and the Making of the American Working Class*. London: Verso, 1991.

Spillers, Hortense. *Black, White, and in Color*. Chicago: U of Chicago P, 2003.

Spivak, Gayatri Chakravorty. *In Other Worlds: Essays in Cultural Politics*. New York: Routledge, 1987.

Steinberg, Stephen. *The Ethnic Myth: Race, Ethnicity, and Class in America*. Boston: Beacon, 2001.

Sundquist, Eric. *To Wake the Nations: Race in the Making of American Literature*. Cambridge: Harvard UP, 1993.

Tate, Claudia. *Domestic Allegories of Political Desire: The Black Heroine's Text at the Turn of the Century*. New York: Oxford UP, 1996.

Warren, Kenneth W. *Black and White Strangers: Race and American Literary Realism*. Chicago: U of Chicago P, 1993.

Wiegman, Robyn. *American Anatomies: Theorizing Race and Gender*. Durham: Duke UP, 1995.

Winant, Howard. *The World Is a Ghetto: Race and Democracy since World War II*. New York: Basic, 2001.

~ Migrations, Diasporas, and Borders

SUSAN STANFORD FRIEDMAN

Identity is changed by the journey.

> —Madan Sarup, "Home and Identity"

Living on borders and in margins, keeping intact one's shifting and multiple identity and integrity, is like trying to swim in a new element, an "alien" element.

> —Gloria Anzaldúa, *Borderlands / La Frontera*

Out of Africa the human species came, dispersing across the globe over the eons. The transnational Genome Project, involving scientists from all over the world, is the mark of the times, the science of human beings constantly on the move, creating contact zones of genes and more than genes—cultures; ways of being in the world; ways of creating; ways of hating; ways of conquering and being conquered; ways of surviving, enduring, and resisting. The anthropologist James Clifford calls it "traveling cultures" and invites us to look not only to the cultures of dwellings and fixed places but also to the cultures of mobility, of those who travel, migrate, and bring differences into contact with one another to make new cultural formations based on exchange and intermingling—an intermingling that is sometimes creatively reciprocal, sometimes oppressively brutal, and often a complex mixture of the two (*Routes* 17–46). Nomads, once thought to exist at the irrelevant fringe of "civilization," are being newly understood as the impressarios of cultural traffic in goods, ideas, peoples, and practices (Khazanov; Weatherford). Great transcontinental patterns of travel and intercultural contact have shaped every period in history and every part of the globe. Movement, whether forced or sought out, is the foundation of human evolution and the history of change on a global landscape.

Migrations, diasporas, and borders are nothing new; they have shaped human cultures from time immemorial. But as areas of inquiry in literary studies, they are relatively new, developing out of the past two and a half decades of innovation in the humanities. Rooted in the departures from New Criticism and from traditional forms of literary history in the 1970s, the study of migration, diasporas, and borders gathered momentum in the late 1980s and 1990s, emerging preeminently from postcolonial studies, the rising interest in travel writing, and the interdisciplinary fields centered on questions of identity—race and ethnic studies, gender studies, sexuality studies. This study has been also influenced by the analysis of textual language,

> **Great transcontinental patterns of travel and intercultural contact have shaped every period in history and every part of the globe.**

discursive regimes, and systems of representation developed during the heyday of poststructuralist theory in the 1980s. But its widespread impact on mainstream literary scholarship starts with the return to history and the rise of interdisciplinary cultural studies beginning in the early 1990s.

Literary scholarship on migration, diaspora, and borders has not evolved as a single field; each subject has its own complex history of formation and institutional expression in the academy. Moreover, each is particularized in reference to the languages, national literatures, and particular geographies under study. But the cultural theory of these distinct fields has become increasingly interwoven and mutually constitutive in literary studies. They cohere, without having the coherence of a single school, whether in theoretical, methodological, or institutional terms. Vast in scope and disparate in design, they pose an enormous challenge for anyone attempting an overview, a challenge compounded by the new mandate in literary studies for planetary thinking and the decline of the nation-state model. This essay represents a preliminary mapping, and although I strive to be inclusive, it no doubt reflects my roots in the field of twentieth- and twenty-first-century literary studies and cultural theory, predominantly in English.

Why now—the naming of migrations, diasporas, and borders as a field? In a word, *globalization*, a term with shifting meanings that spawn debate about its politics, its utopian possibilities, and its dystopic realities.[1] For some, like Fredric Jameson and Masao Miyoshi, globalization refers solely to the contemporary period, often associated with late capitalism. For others, including me, globalization is not a new phenomenon, although the naming of it is new, indicating heightened awareness of what has been there all along. The routes of ceaseless intercultural exchange among different societies—what Philip Curtin and others have called the global ecumene—developed as a constitutive element of human civilization, involving the dispersion of peoples, the formation of vast trade routes and interconnecting metropoles, and the conquest

and inequities that accompanied the rise and fall of numerous empires worldwide. What is different is the particular form that globalization began to take by the end of the twentieth century: a highly accelerated form of the global ecumene in which technologies of travel, information, media, exchange, and violence have intensified the patterns, mechanisms, and degrees of interconnectedness. This contemporary phase of globalization is distinctive at least in part because the new technologies of the so-called information revolution are primarily representational in nature, enabling (in a way the steam engine did not) radically new forms of knowledge production, dissemination, surveillance, and communication in the virtual realities of cyberspace.[2]

The anthropologist Arjun Appadurai, a founder of the influential journal *Public Culture*, has theorized that the intensified global flow of money, goods, people, and media in this period of late modernity (or postmodernity, as some term it) has led to a worldwide network of cultural traffic and a global ethnoscape that has broken down seemingly fixed differences among national cultures, ethnicities, and races (*Modernity* 48; see esp. 48–66). Massive movements of people as refugees and migrants in a world filled with ethnic and religious violence, national conflicts, and widening divisions among rich and poor countries have swelled the cities of the world with peoples from many locales, setting in motion radical juxtapositions of different languages and cultural practices. Cosmopolitanism, once thought to be the privilege of metropolitan elites, travelers, and expatriate artists, is newly understood to include those who move in search of a more secure or better life at the most basic level of survival, even those whose migration is only ambiguously voluntary or decidedly involuntary.[3]

Blurring the boundaries between home and elsewhere, migration increasingly involves multiple moves from place to place and continual travel back and forth instead of journeys from one location to another. The Internet has transformed the diasporic experience of many through the formation of virtual communities connecting the far-flung with those still back home. Many migrants and diasporics associate home not with a particular geographic location but with an "imaginary homeland" (Rushdie, *Imaginary Homelands* 9–21), with the experience of being perpetually in between cultures, or with an affiliation based on a communal identification that crosses national boundaries (e.g., religion, gender, queerness, indigeneity).[4] The writing of home has become in a variety of ways, from the literal to the metaphoric, increasingly deterritorialized.[5] Globalization has not eliminated the power of nationalism as a global force. But transnational mass media, economies, cultural practices, and peoples have reshaped national institutions and identities and made for new forms of interplay (both creative and destructive) between the global and the local.

One effect of this newest phase in globalization has been increased attention to transnationalism in literature and language, a change marked by a special issue of *PMLA*, *Globalizing Literary Studies*, edited by Giles Gunn in 2001. The articles in that issue contrast sharply with the 1992 edition of the MLA's *Introduction to Scholarship*, which included an overview essay on border studies, as well as essays on feminist and gender studies, ethnic and minority studies, and cultural studies (Gibaldi).[6] Implicitly framing all these earlier essays was the overriding significance of the nation-state as the entity within which these issues played out in literary studies. Greater attention to nationalism, national identity, and geopolitics in literary studies in the past decade or so has paradoxically led to the opposite: greater understanding of the porousness of the cultural borders of the nation-state; how the history of empire and (post)colonialism binds the literatures of different parts of the world together; how national literatures are formed in conjunction with the literatures of other nations; and how interconnected and mutually constitutive the cultures of the world have always been— and will continue to be in ever-intensified ways, because of the new technologies of knowledge and communication.

Instead of focusing exclusively on a national literature *within* the boundaries of a single nation-state, literary scholarship has shifted dramatically toward a transnational perspective: literatures written in a common language in different parts of the globe. Postcolonial studies dominated by the literature and culture of the British Empire and the new nations that emerged from its demise has transformed British and Commonwealth literary studies by providing a new theoretical framework for analysis; expanding the canon to include literatures in English throughout the anglophone world; and highlighting the significance of the colonies for the formation of literature in Britain, including British literature not written in English.[7] Latin American and United States Latino/a literary and cultural studies has rapidly expanded in Spanish departments, often quite separate from the study of Iberian Spanish literature and reflecting long-overdue attention to the Spanish literatures of the Americas since the early days of contact through the present (Alley; Anderson and Kuhnheim; R. Johnson; McClennen; Mignolo, *Darker Side* and *Local Histories*; Pratt). The study of Portuguese literature, typically located in departments that originally focused on the Iberian Peninsula, has now broadened to become lusophone studies, encompassing literatures produced in Portugal's former colonies in South America, Africa, and Asia in the world's sixth most common language (see, e.g., *Lusophone Studies*). The francophone world, especially in the Caribbean and Africa, has blended with postcolonial studies to become a significant new area in French literary studies, even as the status of French as the world's lingua franca has yielded to English (Forsdick and Murphy; Jack). The breakup of the Soviet Union into many nations has necessitated the development of transnational analysis in Slavic and central Asian studies (Moore). Where American studies used to focus on the formation of the United States and its cultures as distinct from Europe and other lands of immigrant origins, the field is now decidedly transnational in emphasis, reconstituting itself along north-south and east-west axes to incorporate examination of indigenous and migratory cultures from every continent as these have shaped the literatures of the United States.[8]

The new globalization has also reshaped comparative literature, undermining the discipline's early emphasis on European culture capitals, extending the bases of comparison to non-Western literatures, and fostering the development of translation studies (Apter; Bassnett; Lionnet and Shih; Saussy, *Comparative Literature*; Spivak, *Death*). Race and ethnicity studies have moved toward the examination of transnational and intranational diasporas: tracking the forced or voluntary migration of peoples across continents and within national boundaries, tracing the meanings of shifting borders for indigenous peoples, and identifying the formation of new ethnicities over time and space.[9]

The rapid emergence of transnationalism and globalization as pervasive categories in literary studies helps explain the new significance of migration, diaspora, and borders as a cross-departmental and cross-speciality field of inquiry in the study of modern languages. What brings together the three areas of interest in this field is underlying questions about identity in motion on a transnational landscape—not only identity as it is changed by the journey, to echo the epigraph from Madan Sarup, but also identity as it is in a continual process of (re)formation in relation to changing spaces and times. The feminist critic Carole Boyce Davies terms these phenomena "migrations of the subject."[10] As the geographers Michael Keith and Steve Pile argue, "identity and location [are] inseparable: knowing oneself [is] an exercise in mapping where one stands" (26). Or, in the widely cited words of the feminist poet and social critic Adrienne Rich, we need "to understand how a place on the map is also a place in history" (212). The geographies of identity articulated in the field reflect new attention to space (and embodiment in given locations) as a constitutive component of human experience and culture. In a prescient lecture given in 1967, appearing in English in 1986 and

now widely cited, Michel Foucault predicted, "The present epoch will perhaps be above all the epoch of space. We are in the epoch of simultaneity: we are in the epoch of juxtaposition, the epoch of the near and far, of the side-by-side, of the dispersed" (22). Migrations, diasporas, and borders heighten the meanings for literature of juxtaposition, near and far, side by side, and dispersion not only in themes explored but also in the forms of literary embodiment.

Geography has been rapidly acquiring a new significance for literary studies and remains an essential interdiscipline for migration, diaspora, and border studies. History has long been important for literary studies and will surely remain so, at the very least for the historical contextualization of writers and literary texts, for historical narratives of literary movements and genres, and for identification of change and continuity over time. But geography is gaining a compensatory presence, providing concepts for thinking about the literary meanings of location, movement, simultaneity, juxtaposition, and interactions of sameness and difference.

The work of such geographers as Henri Lefebvre, Edward Soja, Linda McDowell, and Doreen Massey variously establishes ways in which space is conceived not as empty or neutral—the backdrop of history—but rather as full: generative of situation, relation, and social being; marked by formations of power and resistance. Not a static essence, space in these terms is a location of historical overdetermination, a site for the production of communal and individual identities. In short, geography is providing literary studies with a new form of contextualization—a specifically spatial one that complements the long-standing methodologies of historicization. For migration, diaspora, and border studies in particular, the new geography often provides conceptual tools for thinking about the multiple spatialities of identities in motion.

Anthropology has been as important for migration, diaspora, and border studies as geography—not the structuralist anthropology that influenced Northrop Frye's archetypal criticism in the 1950s–60s, and only partially the theoretical anthropology pervasive in the new historicism in the 1980s (e.g., Claude Lévi-Strauss, Victor Turner, Mary Douglas, etc.). Rather, the anthropologies of cultural identity that developed in conjunction with area studies, postcolonial studies, gender and sexuality studies, race and ethnicity studies, and (post)modernity studies have shaped criticism on the literatures of writers and communities defined by movement and intercultural encounter. Anthropologists such as Clifford, Appadurai, Lila Abu-Lughod, Ruth Behar (Behar and Gordon), Kirin Narayan, Renato Rosaldo, Michael Taussig, Michel-Rolph Trouillot, Kamala Visweswaran, and Neil Whitehead have served as a rich source of concepts useful for literary studies—culture, hybridity, ethnoscape, intercultural transaction, transculturation, cultural mimesis, cultural traffic, fetish, primitivism, and so forth. In turn, literary studies and the turn to theory (esp. postmodern or poststructuralist theory) have influenced these anthropologies, with increased attention to the effects of the ethnographer's standpoint, subjectivity, and writing on transcultural acts of representation.

DIFFERENCES: BACKGROUNDS AND ISSUES

Migration, diaspora, and borders as distinct interest areas in literary studies initially developed in conjunction with interdisciplinary postcolonial, gender, race, multicultural, and queer studies. Like these fields, it emerged most extensively from scholars working in the modern period, roughly from the late nineteenth century, through the twentieth century, and into the current century. They have gradually come to influence those working in earlier historical periods, a process analogous to the beginnings of new historicism in Renaissance studies and its eventual spread to other periods. A brief overview of each area is instructive for the way they have more recently come to interweave, collaborate, and to some extent cohere.

Migration

The movement of peoples from one place to another around the globe is a history of dislocation and relocation, displacement and emplacement, losing homes and making new homes, living in a limbo between worlds and adapting over time to new ways, being changed by and also changing the culture of the adopted land. As a term, *migration* encompasses a plethora of distinct migrants, sometimes subtly and sometimes vastly different from one another in relation to structures of power and privilege and to issues of agency: refugees, cosmopolitans, exiles, diasporics, pilgrims, nomads, settlers, asylum seekers, evacuees, émigrés, displaced persons, strangers, guest workers, migrant workers, travelers, tourists, and so forth. Migration has been a powerful stimulant to literary expressions of identity in motion and the self-fashioning that new homelands require. To my knowledge, few scholars have attempted to theorize the discursive field of migration literature per se or to identify structural patterns of migration literature beyond generalizations about the literature of distinctive cultural groups or comparisons among them.[11] But migration has long been a staple for those who study the national literatures of nation-states or regions built predominantly through massive waves of immigrants from different parts of the world (e.g., the Americas, Australia, New Zealand, South Africa). Narratives of assimilation; cultural clashes; hyphenated identities; generational conflict; intermarriage; and competing national, ethnic, or religious loyalties have been explored for decades, especially in American studies.[12]

In the past decade or so, however, the national and ethnic paradigms for studying migration literature have yielded to transnational models emphasizing the global space of ongoing travel and transcontinental connection. Examples are the literary-cultural scholarship of the Pacific Rim (e.g., Lowe; Bow; Ma), the circum-Atlantic (e.g., Gilroy; Appiah, *In My Father's House* and *Cosmopolitanism*), the North-South axis (e.g., Gikandi, *Maps*; Pratt; Ramos), and cultures of the Indian Ocean (e.g., Ghosh). Another major shift in migration studies has come from what many see as a significant change in global migration patterns in the second half of the twentieth century, leading to what is widely termed the new migration. The rise to economic and military power of the United States after World War II and the 1965 Immigration Act, which effectively opened the door that had been shut in 1924, have made the United States a magnet for those from the Caribbean, Latin America, Africa, and Asia who seek to escape repression or poverty. Economic and political asymmetries between European nations and their former colonies in the postcolonial period (starting in the late 1940s) have led to the migration of millions from Africa, Asia, the Caribbean, and Latin America into Britain and Europe. Racism, religious differences, class disparities, and fears about changes in national identity produced through immigration have produced intense conflict, even violence, and pressure to enact restrictive citizenship laws. Not all migration has been between the so-called First and Third Worlds, however. Political instability, ethnic cleansing, and economic disparities have led to refugee and labor migrations from India to the Gulf States, for example; from the Philippines to the Middle East, Europe, and the Americas; from one part of Africa to another; from one former Soviet state to another; and from rural to urban areas in China and India.

> **Migration has been a powerful stimulant to literary expressions of identity in motion and the self-fashioning that new homelands require.**

New technologies of travel and communication also contribute to the new migration. The speed of migration (airplane vs. ship) and transcontinental contact (e-mail and telephone vs. sea mail) have increased for many the frequency of circular migration, ongoing visits back home, and connection with the home culture—all of which has made the radical rupture of migration less fixed for many, especially the more affluent.

The criticism of the new-migration literature has tended to follow the example of prior decades by focusing on the experience and writings of single ethnic, national, or racial groups or by initiating some comparative study across different groups. Criticism on migration narratives in the United States still predominates, with some postcolonial criticism of migration narratives in Britain and Europe now appearing as well. Alpana Sharma Knippling's *New Immigrant Literatures in the United States* is an invaluable sourcebook presenting introductions to the history, culture, and literature of post–World War II migrants into the United States from twenty-two countries and regions of the world—Finnish, Korean, Arab, Armenian, Sephardic Jewish, Greek, Czech, and Mexican, to name a few. Critics like Paul Heike in *Mapping Migration*, Gilbert Muller in *New Strangers in Paradise*, Katherine Payant and Toby Rose in *The Immigrant Experience in North American Literature*, Eleanor Ty and David C. Goellnicht in *Asian North American Identities*, Louis Mendoza and S. Shankar in *Crossing into America*, and Carine Mardorossian in "From Literature of Exile to Migrant Literature" stress a major shift in North American migration narratives away from the assimilationist model, which centers on the plot of Americanization in earlier narratives like Mary Antin's *The Promised Land* or Anzia Yezierska's *Bread Givers*. Instead, they see in the post-1965 migration narratives more fluidity of identity, more heterogeneity, more resistance to assimilation, more bilingualism and hybridity, and less willingness on the part of American society in general to integrate these newly racialized immigrants.

As Matthew Frye Jacobson describes in *Whiteness of a Different Color*, many groups coming into the United States on earlier waves of immigration were not considered white at first—especially the Irish, Jews, Italians, and Slavs. However, they gradually acquired the privileged status of whiteness in opposition to black, Native, and Asian populations, who remained racial others, perpetually marginalized, legally segregated, and not fully American.

Despite tensions between new immigrants to the United States and older racialized communities, the new migrants have more often joined the ranks of people of color than those of white America. Tensions over race, religion, and culture are reflected in such contemporary migration narratives and poetry as Meena Alexander's *The Shock of Arrival*, Diana Abu-Jaber's *Arabian Jazz*, Mohja Kahf's *E-Mails from Scheherazad*, Junot Díaz's *Drown*, Loida Maritza Pérez's *Geographies of Home*, Gish Jen's *Mona in the Promised Land*, Leila Ahmed's *Border Passage*, and Pamela Mordecai's *Certifiable*. Cultural critics of the United States like Ali Behdad in *A Forgetful Nation* and Kevin Johnson in *The Huddled Masses Myth* add important historical contexts to this literature of the new migration, arguing that the American national imaginary has celebrated the country as a nation of immigrants at the same time that it has repressed memories of compulsory migrations, conquest, and nativist movements.

Migration within the United States and Canada has also become a focus of study. The Great Migration of African Americans from the South to the North in the twentieth century, the internal migrations of Native peoples forced from their homelands, and the internment of Japanese Americans during World War II—to cite a few prominent examples—have inspired both literature and literary studies.[13] The expressive culture of the Great Migration—literature, music, the arts, folk culture, and so on—has been in particular the subject of several sustained studies. Farah Jasmine Griffin's *"Who Set You Flowin'?"* Lawrence R. Rodgers's *Canaan Bound*, and David G. Nicholls's *Conjuring the Folk* variously explore the forms of expression that record the drive to migrate north, the shock of the urban landscape for predominantly rural folk, the formation of northern black urban culture, the experiences of racial invisibility and alienation, and the continued presence of the South in the arts and culture of the transplanted African Americans in the North.

Other nations and continents have experienced massive migration, of course, and their literatures reflect its significance, especially in fiction, autobiography, and other forms of life writing. Some of these migrations have involved searches for a better life, especially in Canada, Australia, France, and Spain. But for others, involuntary migration, political exile, ethnic cleansing, genocide, refugeeism, and perpetual guest worker status meant suffering and homelessness. Past history of colonial migration underlies the new migration of the late twentieth century. Settlers from the British Isles moved in large numbers not only to the United States, Canada, Australia, and New Zealand but also to India and Africa, especially southern and eastern Africa, established as small minorities with economic and political hegemonies based on racist ideology—a history that Doris Lessing explores in settler novels like *The Grass Is Singing*.

In turn, the postcolonial era contains a vast reverse migration into the once imperial metropoles of Britain and Europe. This migration of largely brown or black people into the heart of whiteness has challenged the underlying racial basis of European national imaginaries. As Bruce King points out in *The Internationalization of English Literature*, the new migration from the former colonies has internationalized English literature in Britain, introducing narratives of migratory nostalgia and self-fashioning, back-and-forth movement, mixed-race identities, conflict around gender and sexuality, and tension among the different cultural groups often homogenized under the derogatory label *black* in their new home.

The identity of English literature and its writers has itself become migratory, a notion that writers like Hanif Kureishi, Buchi Emecheta, Ben Okri, and Salman Rushdie (*Satanic Verses*) both embody and narrativize. For example, Rushdie writes as a cosmopolitan—born a Muslim in Bombay, separated from his family in Pakistan by the aftermath of partition, now a British citizen and living in the United States. Should he be called an Indian, English, British, or American writer? Is his oeuvre part of English, British, American, Indian, or South Asian literature? Even the term "English literature" in Britain is an ambiguous designation: alternately linguistic, ethnic, or geopolitical at a time when literature in Britain is increasingly micronational (e.g., Scottish, Welsh, English), multicultural, multiracial, and even multilingual. Other European countries face similar ambiguities. Are the Muslim girls in France who insist on wearing a *hijab* to public school denying their Frenchness? Or can Frenchness be separated from its historical ties to the universalist discourse of republican France so as to institute a new, multicultural understanding of *French*? As Azade Seyhan points out, the literature of Turkish guest workers in Germany, some of it reflecting several generations of life in Germany, exists in a kind of legal and cultural in-between, since even the children of these workers born in Germany do not have access to German citizenship.[14]

Although few studies attempt to theorize migration literature beyond the patterns evident in the literatures of specific groups, migration studies in the social sciences has developed a considerable theoretical body of scholarship that would greatly benefit literary studies. As Caroline Bretell and James F. Hollifield note in *Migration Theory: Talking across the Disciplines*, social scientists have developed some key terminology for migration, such as *sending* and *receiving cultures*; *push* and *pull factors*; *out-migration* and *in-migration*; *host-newcomer relations*; *networked migration*; *enclave migration*; and various terms with distinctive and nuanced meanings for cultural change—*assimilation, acculturation, enculturation, deculturation, transculturation, cultural hybridity, hyphenization*, and so forth.[15] They have also developed complex typologies of migration, including such categories as seasonal, temporary nonseasonal, recurrent, continuous, permanent, yo-yo, commuter, shuttle, return, and brightlight (rural to urban). Bretell warns against typology as a homogenizing practice that tends to erase contradictions and tensions within any given migration, especially those produced by gender (Bretell and Hollifield 109–13).[16]

Modeling migration in the social sciences has drawn on different kinds of social theory, from modernization theory to historical-structuralist theory and newer transnational paradigms. Modernization theory, Bretell suggests, tends to be microlevel, focused on individual reasons for migration, agency and decision making, and the attraction of modernity as an advance over tradition (Bretell and Hollifield 102–06). The historical-structuralist models are macrolevel analysis of world systems that emphasize systemic forces and the lack of choice. Transnational models deal with the new globalization, theorizing the effects of deterritorialization, new modes of travel and communication, and the issues of national borders and citizenship.

Some social science theory on migration makes a particular effort to bridge the gap between social theory and literary-language studies of migration and is therefore of particular use to future literary migration studies. In *The Turbulence of Migration*, the sociologist Nikos Papastergiadis links the study of the "new migration" to modernity studies, arguing that "the dynamic of displacement is intrinsic to migration and modernity" (12). He notes that "the metaphor of the journey, the figure of the stranger and the experience of displacement have been at the centre of many of the cultural representations of modernity," as in the work of James Joyce (11). The "restless dynamism in modern society" and the "movement of people and the circulation of symbols" characterize late-twentieth-century modernity, so much so that cultural displacement is experienced even by those who are not migrating (15). Papastergiadis critiques the old sociological models of migration as water-pump models, too mechanistic and static, whether the neoliberal voluntarist model based on push-out or pull-up forces or the Marxist world-systems model. He posits a model of turbulence that takes into account subjectivity and agency and places concepts of cultural translation—including linguistic and aesthetic practices—and the semiotics of hybridity at the center of analysis.

Migrancy has functioned at the level of lyrical speculation and postmodern philosophy as well, at times removed from the literal meanings of *migration* in material space and time but nonetheless evocative and influential in literary studies as a way of unmooring the subject from illusory certainties of language, representation, and being. In *Nomadic Subjects*, for example, the feminist philosopher Rosi Braidotti deterritorializes nomadism and adapts the term as a metaphor for epistemological migrancy, which she defines as a critical consciousness that is "transmobile," "transnational," and attuned to the

> axes of differentiation such as class, race, ethnicity, gender, age, and others [as they] intersect and interact with each other in the constitution of subjectivity. . . . The nomad is my own figuration of a situated, postmodern, culturally differentiated understanding of the subject in general and of the feminist subject in particular.   (4)

The interdisciplinary cultural critic Iain Chambers in *Migrancy, Culture, Identity* regards migration, "together with the enunciation of cultural borders and crossings," as the primary concept underlying "the itineraries of much contemporary reasoning" (2). Adapting a rhetoric of mobility, Chambers advocates the journey as "the form of a restless interrogation," a sort of perpetual questioning that privileges displacement and the need

> for a mode of thinking that is neither fixed nor stable. . . . For the nomadic experience of language, wandering without a fixed home, dwelling at the crossroads of the world, bearing our sense of being and difference, is no longer the expression of a unique tradition or history. . . . Thought wanders. It migrates, requires translation. . . . This inevitably implies another sense of 'home,' of being in the world. It means to conceive of dwelling as a mobile habitat.   (4)

Treating migration as a lyrical signifier emptied of reference to the real of mobility in geo-historical space and time carries its own risk, but such slippage between the metaphorics of migration and the literary representations of migrating people is common in contemporary criticism and can be richly suggestive.[17]

Diaspora

By definition, diaspora involves migration—but specific kinds of migration that set in motion particular longings for a lost homeland. Diaspora is migration plus loss, desire, and widely scattered communities held together by memory and a sense of history over a long period of time. Frequently, but not always, this history has involved oppression against a whole people and thus an attachment to community based on a sense of shared suffering and the richness of the community's minority traditions. *Diaspora*, as the sociologist Robin Cohen points out in *Global Diasporas*, is a Greek word that means the sowing or dispersion of seed (*speiro*, is "to sow," *dia*, is "over"), and it was used by the ancient Greeks to refer to migrations of colonizing Greeks who formed settlements throughout the Mediterranean world, extending the economic, political, and cultural power of those who remained "at home" (ix).[18] But as the term developed in literary and cultural studies of the past decade or so, it was associated with collectivities of the expelled, the exiled, or the forcibly removed rather than with the colonizing settlers of imperial powers. Thus *diaspora* is bound up with notions of a once-territorial homeland to which dispersed communities remain emotionally attached even as their relation to it is a form of perpetual deterritorialization, a consciousness of collective rather than individual exile.

Diasporas are "imagined communities," to adapt the influential term Benedict Anderson developed to describe the role of collective consciousness in the formation of the nation-state. The continuation of diasporas is related not to the fate of the nation-state but to a diasporic consciousness, an imagined community of the scattered held together by their shared sense of a distinct history and culture as a people and by obstacles to full assimilation in diverse host countries. Some diasporas are long-standing, like the two-thousand-year diaspora of the Jews or the five-hundred-year African diaspora; others are more recent, yet insistently claimed, such as the Armenian (after World War I) or the Palestinian (after 1947).

In recent years diasporic consciousness has developed around other migrations that are less clearly tied to compulsory loss of homeland. Impoverished laborers from India, for example, fanned out to the Americas, the Caribbean, Africa, and Southeast Asia in the nineteenth and early twentieth centuries, with many remaining as large and sometimes prosperous communities, as in Trinidad, Fiji, and eastern and southern Africa. A second wave of South Asian migration began after Indian independence and partition, particularly to the former colonial center in Britain, both political and economic reasons fueling that demographic implosion. Yet a third wave of South Asian migration in the past thirty years is complexly layered: Indians expelled from Uganda going to Britain and the United States, laborers going to the Gulf States and Southeast Asia for jobs, intellectuals and highly trained engineers and computer experts going to the West, and so forth. Often differing in religion, language, caste, class, and nation(s) of origin, these South Asians are newly constituting themselves as the South Asian Diaspora, claiming the term, producing literatures, and engaging in other cultural practices that reflect a newly imagined community dispersed around the globe.[19]

Much debate in diaspora studies has been devoted to definitional questions, represented usefully in Jana Evans Braziel and Anita Mannur's *Theorizing Diaspora*.[20] What is a diaspora? What groups and kinds of experiences can justifiably be called diasporic? How does diaspora relate to exile? Is it negative or positive? utopian or dystopian? What are its politics? What is the relation of diaspora to nation, nationalism, the nation-state, (de)territorialization, transnationalism? How does gender complicate diasporic consciousness and community? In founding the journal *Diaspora: A Journal of Transnational Studies* in 1991, Khachig Tölölyan calls for an expansive understanding of the term and points to how discourses of diaspora and nation are thoroughly entangled. *Diaspora*'s mission

> is concerned with the ways in which nations, as real yet imagined communities . . . , are fabulated, brought into being, made and unmade, in culture and politics, both on land people call their own and in exile. Above all, this journal will focus on

such processes as they shape and are shaped by the infranational and transnational Others of the nation-state.   (3)

The "semantic domain" of *diaspora* "includes words like immigrant, expatriate, refugee, guestworker, exile community, overseas community, ethnic community. This is the vocabulary of transnationalism" (4–5).

Other definitional approaches have been less inclusive, especially the typological ones. William Safran's "Diasporas in Modern Societies" is a structuralist identification of six characteristics of diasporas based on a center/periphery model that sets in opposition the lost point of origin, the margins of dispersion, and the promise of return. Safran uses the Jewish diaspora as an ideal type and recognizes that many historical diasporas do not share all six defining elements. Arguing against the use of any one diaspora as a prototype, Cohen identifies five different kinds of diaspora: victim, labor and imperial, trade, nationalist, and culturalist. He emphasizes that diasporas change over time, often leading to communities with great stability and creative interactions with host societies.

Clifford advocates a "relational" and "lateral" approach that focuses on tensions or contradictions that an array of different diasporic formations share (*Routes* 244–78). The main tension is encapsulated in the homonym *roots-routes*, which he introduced in his 1992 essay "Traveling Cultures" (*Routes* 17–46). Diasporic cultures are products of the interplay between their "roots" in consciousness of common community, past, and original homeland and their "routes," that is, their migration(s) and relocations into new societies. "Diaspora cultures," he writes, "thus mediate, in a lived tension, the experiences of separation and entanglement, of living here and remembering/desiring another place" (255). Diasporas involve "a loosely coherent, adaptive constellation of responses to dwelling-in-displacement," a liminal and hybrid space in between separatist and assimilationist movements (254). Diasporas induce a form of

Diaspora is migration plus loss, desire, and widely scattered communities held together by memory and a sense of history over a long period of time.

cosmopolitanism and "double consciousness" based in both accommodation to the dominant culture and an ongoing tie to a homeland elsewhere. They involve "feeling global" in a locale that is both home and not quite home (257).

Like Clifford, Avtar Brah in *Cartographies of Diaspora* centers her theory in the fundamental contradictions of diaspora—for example, the concepts of home as "a mythic place of desire" and as "the lived experience of a locality" (182); diasporas as reminders of trauma and as "sites of hope and new beginnings" (193). "Paradoxically," she writes, "diasporic journeys are essentially about settling down, about putting roots 'elsewhere' " (182). Moreover, any given diaspora embodies the contradiction of establishing a "we" out of heterogeneity. "All diasporas are differentiated," not only from other diasporas but also by the impact of dispersion itself. As people from a single diaspora settle in different lands, they indigenize at the same time as they hold on to a sense of common diasporic culture (184). Another dimension of differentiation for Brah is the "intersectionality" of national identity with gender, race, religion, sexuality, class, and so forth (10). Using diaspora as a conceptual tool for analyzing complex identities, she foregrounds the "multi-axial" dimensions of any given diaspora, refusing metanarratives of diasporic home and centers of origin (189).

Despite the widening applications of *diaspora*, especially in reference to contemporary globalization, two particular affliction diasporas continue to play a normative role in diaspora studies, serving as a kind of theoretical touchstone for the field. These are the Jewish and African diasporas, entangled not only as theoretical models but also as historical phenomena, since the biblical narratives and exilic experiences of the Jewish diaspora often functioned as symbolic analogues for people in the African diaspora engaged in the formation of their own diasporic consciousness.

As prototype, the Jewish diaspora has functioned as a story of perpetual wandering based

The Jewish and African diasporas [are] entangled not only as theoretical models but also as historical phenomena.

on multiple expulsions or re-diasporizations: from Israel, in the Babylonian captivity starting in 587 BCE, then with the destruction of the second temple in Jerusalem in 70 CE; from Spain, Portugal, and their colonies in the Americas in 1492 as part of the Inquisition; from Eastern Europe with the pogroms of the nineteenth and early twentieth centuries; from Europe with the Holocaust; and from Arab lands after World War II. Scattered to every continent of the globe, the Jews retained a sense of themselves as a people with shared cultural practices (if not beliefs), a shared history, global networks of affiliation, and attachment to the imagined homeland of Israel— a place that for some was an actual territory and for others a spiritual site for the union of a people with its god. In this type of diaspora, communal identity is bound up with consciousness of affliction and minority status, both the pain of and pride in difference, both the desire for and the continual threat of assimilation. With the establishment of the state of Israel in 1947, the Jewish diaspora entered a new and more controversial phase as the reterritorialization of the dispersed through the law of return for Jews anywhere involved the creation of a new diaspora of Palestinians expelled not from their own nation-state but from their lands, which had been ruled by the Ottomans and the Europeans for generations.

In Jewish studies, the meanings of diaspora and exile have been the subject of widespread debate, belying the idea of a fixed prototype. There is disagreement about the significance of the nation-state of Israel. Howard Wettstein argues that the term *exile* is too "hauntingly negative" and that the Jewish diaspora does not exclusively represent anguish and forced homelessness; it also incorporates "a positive" notion of a "people of the Book" whose "homeland resides in the text" (2). This alternative view recognizes that "diasporic communities were often stable" and desired for the benefits of widespread intercultural exchange and trade; they were often chosen destinations (3). Jonathan Boyarin, a critical legal scholar, and Daniel Boyarin, a specialist in Talmudic culture, further argue that the association of identity with the exclusive control of territory is ultimately destructive. They suggest that Jewish identity began with Abraham outside Israel, not in a territorial homeland. They insist that the creative and positive aspects of the Jewish diaspora be acknowledged as well as how the diaspora has empowered some at the expense of others. "Evaluating diaspora," they write, "entails acknowledging the ways that such identity is maintained through exclusion and oppression of internal others (especially women) and external others," including other diasporas (7–8). They favor a comparative approach to diasporas that explores the Jewish diaspora not in isolation, not as an unchanging essence justifying the claim on biblical lands, but as phenomena in a changing landscape of history, filled with problems and possibilities.[21]

The discourse of the African diaspora, the second main prototype, often self-consciously adapts the Jewish model to the specificities of systemic racism, colonialism, and the affiliation of many scattered peoples of African descent around the concepts of blackness and the lost homeland of Africa, a place without the geographic specificity of biblical Israel but a generalized location of home nonetheless. Although becoming current in scholarly circles in the past fifteen years, the notion of the black diaspora has deep historical roots in the history of slavery, the Marcus Garvey and Rastafarian "back to Africa" movements of the 1920s and 1930s, the negritude movement and pan-African movements from the 1930s through the 1960s, and the civil rights and black nationalist movements of the 1950s through the present in various countries. The Middle Passage—some three hundred and fifty years of the transatlantic slave trade—is the defining moment of this diaspora, the traumatic theft from sub-Saharan Africa and the sale of populations on a massive scale to and in the Americas. With languages and local cultural groupings often lost in the face of deliberate dispersions of the enslaved, such cultural practices as the oral tradition, religious and spiritual com-

munities, political organizations, and expressive forms in the arts provided the basis for the imagined communities of blackness. As a continent rather than a country, Africa functioned as a source of spiritual rootedness and affirmative identity drawn on to counter the sorrows and lamentations of a brutalizing diaspora and ongoing racism.

The initial focus in black studies on race in a single nation (e.g., the United States, Britain, France) or region (e.g., the Caribbean) has since the 1990s increasingly shifted toward attention to a transnational African diaspora. The Department of Afro-American Studies at Harvard University, for example, became in 2002–03 the Department of African and African American Studies. Underlying this shift is not only the growing transnationalism of literary and cultural studies but also a debate over the meanings of diaspora that parallels the opposing views in Jewish studies. For some, like a leading voice in Afrocentrism, Molefi Asante, the African diaspora coheres around an essential and inherent blackness that goes back to the ancient dynasties of Egypt and descends through the great kingdoms of black Africa (e.g., Asante and Fulani empires in West Africa, Great Zimbabwe of the Shona people, and Zululand). But for others, like Paul Gilroy and Stuart Hall, the African diaspora is a relatively new ethnicity in the making, a formation that underlines how the modernities of Europe, Africa, and the Americas were mutually constitutive, with the enslavement of millions as the initial dislocation in that construction. In his influential book *The Black Atlantic: Modernity and Double Consciousness*, Gilroy attacks Afrocentric "ethnic absolutism" (2) and argues that the "black Atlantic" connecting Europe, Africa, and the Americas has always been a hybrid space of cultural exchange and the interplay of sameness and differentiation.[22]

New claims to the term *diaspora* have diffused the exclusive force of the prototypical Jewish and African diasporas and affliction diasporas in general. A sampling of books from the past decade or so demonstrates the global range and variety of migrations laying claim to the word: Nicholas

Van Hear's *New Diaporas*, on refugeeism; Shahnaz Kahn's *Aversion and Desire: Negotiating Muslim Female Identity in the Diaspora*; R. Radhakrishnan's *Diasporic Mediations*; Amy Kaminsky's *After Exile: Writing the Latin American Diaspora*; Azade Seyhan's *Writing outside the Nation*; Martin Manalansan's *Global Divas: Filipino Gay Men in the Diaspora*; Kandice Chuh and Karen Shimakawa's *Orientations: Mapping Studies in the Asian Diaspora*; Anuradha Dingwaney Needham's *Using the Master's Tools: Resistance and the Literature of the African and South Asian Diasporas*; Rebecca Walsh's special issue of *Interventions, Global Diasporas*. In queer and gender studies, the concept of diaspora deals with sexual exile and outcast status as well as the transnational circuits of sexuality and culture (Cruz-Malavé and Manalansan; Joseph; Manalansan; Patton and Sánchez-Eppler). For others, the discourse and experience of exile has blended with the concept of diaspora, as in Edward Said's *Out of Place* and "Reflections on Exile," Nico Israel's *Outlandish: Writing between Exile and Diaspora*, André Aciman's *Letters of Transit: Reflections on Exile, Identity, Language, and Loss*, and Michael Hanne's *Creativity in Exile*.

The conceptual border between diaspora and other forms of migration such as travel, exile, expatriatism, immigration and emigration, nomadism, and refugeeism has become ever more porous. In part, this definitional flexibility emerges out of a growing awareness of the complexity of diaspora and the differences among diasporas. But it also reflects that many of the pioneering theorists of diaspora are intellectuals living and working outside their native lands. Diasporas, everyone seems to agree, involve whole communities, not just individuals. But it remains true that the most eloquent articulations of contemporary diaspora come from diasporic intellectuals and writers, from individuals whose migrancy is often chosen or ambiguously compelled and whose ties to communal diaspora are heavily mediated by class. Amitava Kumar's *Passport Photos*, to cite one example, is an ambitious critical, theoretical, autobiographical, photographic meditation on the modalities of migra-

tion that embodies this new intellectual thread. With its chapters organized around the categories of the passport—from "Language," "Photograph," and "Name" to "Nationality," "Sex," and "Identifying Marks"—this hybrid text moves through the geohistorical landscapes of diaspora with its commingling of shame, abjection, hope, despair, and desire as linguistic, aesthetic, and philosophical border crossings.

Universities, especially in the West, have increasingly become transnational crossroads for highly educated cosmopolitans, who often travel back and forth across multiple borders, feeling fully at home nowhere as they move through contact zones where race, religion, gender, class, and national origin constitute their identity differently. At times attacked for their relative privilege, they also experience alienating forms of othering, particularly racism. In *Writing Diaspora*, Rey Chow turns a critical eye on "third world intellectuals," including herself, insisting that they be attuned to the conditions of their own articulation. She worries that diasporic intellectuals can too easily hide behind or inside their "victim" status in the West, not taking into account their own positions as elites in both old and new "homes" (99–119). Her critique notwithstanding, many of these migrants from Asia, Latin America, Africa, and the Caribbean embody the paradoxes of diaspora, the simultaneous rooting and routing of situated identities in different cultural terrains. Their diasporic theorizing often effectively incorporates what Brah terms "the technologies of autobiography" or what Meena Alexander calls "alphabets of flesh": a narrativizing and metaphorizing of individual diasporic experience as communal voice.[23] As May Joseph puts it, "Cultural citizenship is a nomadic and performative realm of self-invention" (358), and diasporic intellectuals are an avant-garde of perpetual dislocation and relocation.

Borders and Borderlands

Border studies begins with attention to the material borders among nation-states, the technologies of enforcement, the controls and markers of citizenship, and the structures of inclusion and exclusion that are enabled by borders as lines on a map backed by armies and law. But border studies has also developed in the past fifteen years across a spectrum of divergent issues and fields in literary studies, ranging well beyond the geopolitical to exploration of the metaphoric dimensions of borders and borderlands as tropes for regulative and transgressive patterns in the cultural and social order. Underlying these spatialized modes of critical thought is the basic contradiction embedded in both the material and figurative meanings of *border*.

Borders are fixed and fluid, impermeable and porous. They separate but also connect.

Borders are fixed and fluid, impermeable and porous. They separate but also connect, demarcate but also blend differences. Absolute at any moment in time, they are always changing over time. They promise safety, security, a sense of being at home; they also enforce exclusions, the state of being alien, foreign, and homeless. They protect but also confine. They materialize the law, policing separations; but as such, they are always being crossed, transgressed, subverted. Borders are used to exercise power over others but also to empower survival against others. They regulate migration, movement, travel—the flow of people, goods, ideas, and cultural formations of all kinds. They undermine regulatory practices by fostering intercultural encounter and the concomitant production of syncretic heterogeneities and hybridities. They insist on purity, distinction, difference but facilitate contamination, mixing, creolization.

Geographic borderlands are related to but distinct from borders. Borders are imaginary lines of separation with real effects, as in a geopolitical boundary between nation-states. From the American Southwest to other parts of the world like Alsace-Lorraine, the Caribbean, South Asia, the Balkans, Iraq-Iran, China-Tibet, and Israel-Palestine, borderlands are ambiguously demarcated areas with complicated histories, where different peoples and cultures have intermingled over time, often in the context of competing state powers and institutional regulation. Borderlands have been the sites of hatred and murderous acts, akin to the grating of continental tectonic plates and their occasional violent eruptions. They can also be locations of utopian desire, reconciliation, and peace. Borderlands are a "contact zone"[24] where fluid differences meet, where power is often structured asymmetrically but nonetheless circulates in complex and multidirectional ways, where agency exists on both sides of the shifting and permeable divide.

While the geographic and geopolitical basis of border studies has remained compelling, borders and borderlands have also taken on broad theoretical dimensions as spatial metaphors for the liminal space in between, the interstitial site of interaction, interconnection, and exchange across all kinds of differences: psychological, spiritual, sexual, linguistic, generic, disciplinary. A frontier between differences also operates figuratively as a conceptual space for performative identities beyond the fixed essentialisms of fundamentalist or absolutist identity politics. It has functioned as a tropic space of play and interplay, of representational transgression and postmodern experimentation, of fluidity and utopian possibility. Such expansive and figural work in border theory moves far beyond the economic, political, material, and even cultural realities of the peoples who live on both sides of a geopolitical border, which are the focus of scholars working in more empirically based fields in border studies. The metaphorization of borders in cultural and literary theory remains a point of considerable tension in the field.[25]

Gloria Anzaldúa's *Borderlands / La Frontera: The New Mestiza* has been a touchstone text for border studies, often cited, taught, and critiqued as both literature and theory across the disciplines. Published in 1987, this collage of prose and poetry, English and Spanish (six kinds of Spanish, according to Anzaldúa), history and theory starts from the bitter history of the geopolitical borderlands of the American Southwest and moves on to psychological, spiritual, and sexual borders as figural representations of regulation and transgression. As a self-identified Chicana feminist and lesbian, Anzaldúa explores the pain and pleasures of *mestizaje* in the history of pre-Contact Meso- and Southwest America, the Spanish conquest and Mexican independence, the Mexican-American war and its aftermath, and twentieth-century Chicano/a experience.[26]

The importance of Anzaldúa's *Borderlands / La Frontera* for border studies highlights the centrality of the Mexican–United States border culture (including California), Central America, and Latin America in general for the formation of the field. What Néstor García Canclini calls the "hybrid cultures" of Latin America and its borders in the north have been a primary generator of border theory. Adapting the work of Gilles Deleuze and Félix Guattari on "minor" literature, deterritorialization, and Kafka (*Kafka*), Emily Hicks theorizes the significance of biculturalism and bilingualism for the production of multidimensional models of border writing and border crossers between self and other in Latin American literature. *Criticism in the Borderlands*, edited by Héctor Calderón and José David Saldívar, calls for a new Pan-American studies that recognizes how the United States conquest of Mexican lands in 1848 created a borderlands culture mixing Hispanic, Indian, white, and other traditions. Saldívar suggests that this border culture breaks the pattern of linear migration, substitutes bi- or multiculturalism for assimilation, and highlights the intercultural and transnational nature of popular and high cultural forms of linguistic and aesthetic expression (*Border Matters*). Debra Castillo and María Socorro Tabuenca Córdoba challenge the mainstream notions of border culture produced in Chicano/a studies and explore women writers on both sides of the Mexican–United States border in a comparative methodology that resists homogenization.[27]

With the spread of border theory, other border regions of the world have become subjects of literary study. Rachel Brenner examines the literature of Israeli and Arab Jews in Israel to see how writers who dissent from the prevailing exclusionary discourses of both Israel and Palestine create a borderland of dialogue between the victors and the vanquished. An explosion of partition literature in South Asia in recent years, for example, has led to studies on violence, religion, identity, gender, and memory in the context of the cataclysmic sectarian violence that erupted with the splitting of India into Pakistan and India at the end of the British raj in 1947–48. The role of fiction, life writing, testimony, and the oral tradition has been the subject of many interdisciplinary books and conferences in South Asian studies that examine the repressions, hauntings, and attempts to remember that accompany collective trauma and its aftermath in the contemporary period (e.g., Bhalla, *Partition Dialogues* and *Stories*; Butalia; Menon and Bhasin; Kaul; and Saint and Saint). The particular suffering and silences of women who experienced rape, disgrace, and widowhood during the partition, with the massive migrations of millions (esp. Hindus, Muslims, and Sikhs) across the new borders has been a rich area for feminist research. As Mary Layoun points out in reference to other intensely divided border regions in Greece, Cyprus, and Beirut, nationalisms often resort to highly gendered tropes of nation to expel the other and enforce exclusionary borders. With woman as metaphor for nation, actual women often experience the displacements of nationalism with competing loyalties that reflect the intersecting identities of gender, nation, class, religion, and sexuality.[28]

Border as geographic metaphor has been especially prevalent in postcolonial studies for its suggestive overtones of in-betweenness and liminality, which are particularly suited to characterize subjectivities on the move between cultures; palimpsestically layered by formative experiences in different locations; hybridically blended out of different cultural strands; and often caught up in the dynamics of past and present, tradition and modernity, self and other.

Homi Bhabha is the preeminent theorist of the interstitial, of the examination of culture in the "moment of transit," and of the "borders" and "borderposts" that are crossed in the "articulation of cultural differences" (*Location* 1).[29] For Bhabha, the interstitial is a border space that exists over time but gains its most resonant meaning as metaphor for postmodernity. The concept is basic to his notion of "colonial mimicry" (120), the imitation in the contact zone between colonizer and colonized that denaturalizes the colonizer's assumed superiority by highlighting the constructedness of cultural practices. But the interstitial also captures for Bhabha the particular conditions of postmodernity, with what he calls the demography of the "new internationalism": "the history of postcolonial migration, the narratives of cultural and political diaspora, the major social displacements of peasant and aborigine communities, the poetics of exile, the grim prose of political and economic refugees." The discourse of "boundary" or "border" signifies the continual "displacement and conjunction" that characterizes the physical and psychological existence of people caught up in the new internationalism (5).

Less sanguine about the utopian possibilities of border liminality than Bhabha, the Latin Americanist Walter D. Mignolo has developed an alternative theory of "border thinking," what he calls "border gnosis," one that takes as its framework Immanuel Wallerstein's world-systems theory and his emphasis on post-1500 European imperialism as structural force of inequality that produces border gnoseology. Akin to Pratt's concept of the contact zone as a product of the asymmetrical power relations of colonialism, Mignolo's border gnosis represents a critical stance toward colonialism, one developed as a form of subaltern resistance. It involves

> absorbing and displacing hegemonic forms of knowledge into the perspective of the subaltern. This is not a new form of syncretism or hybridity, but an intense battlefield in the long history of colonial subalternization of knowledge and legitimation of the colonial difference.
>
> (*Local Histories* 12)

Border thinking is inherently critical, a form of "colonial semiosis" that expresses the resistance of the colonized (14).[30]

Border theory across the spectrum of identity studies draws on the geographic roots of the metaphor but goes well beyond this spatial terrain. As lines that divide and join, borders function figuratively as the point of connection and disconnection between differences. They also trope the borderlands in between various binary oppositions: male/female, white/black, heterosexual/homosexual, self/other, and so forth.[31] For Julia Kristeva, such states of liminality are sites of abjection, thereby exerting a deconstructive force on the symbolic order (*Powers*, esp. 207–10). The rhetoric of borders often accompanies the adaptations of deconstruction to social and cultural analysis of identity in fields such as women's studies, race and ethnicity studies, postcolonial studies, and queer studies. Consequently, the language of borders pervades works that examine the regulative and resistant discourses that insist on identity differences as well as discourses that suggest imitation, sameness, and hybridity. As Rosaldo writes:

> Our everyday lives are crisscrossed by border zones, pockets, and eruptions of all kinds. Social borders become salient around such lines as sexual orientation, gender, class, race, ethnicity, nationality, age, politics, dress, food or taste.... Such borderlands should be regarded not as analytically empty transitional zones but as sites of creative cultural production that require investigation.
>
> (207–08)

COMMONALITIES: SHARED CONCERNS

While migration, diaspora, and border studies have developed along separate tracks, they have also converged around several core issues that underlie the location and movement of people in space over time.

Culture and Identity

How do individuals and collectivities of people change through their intercultural contacts with others? What are the effects of those changes? How do they reflect structures of power? To think about intercultural exchange, do we need some kind of consensus on what we mean by *culture*? What is the relation between culture as forms of creative expressivity and the culture of everyday life? Zygmunt Bauman notes, "The idea of culture was itself a historical invention," one that has produced endless philosophical and political debate (*Culture* xiv). Two opposing notions have been particularly significant for issues of migration, diaspora, and border in literary studies: "culture as the activity of the free roaming spirit, the site of creativity, invention, self-critique and self-transcendence" and "culture as a tool of routinization and continuity—a handmaiden of social order" (xvi). But complicating this binary has been the assertion that the culture of creativity can also be complicit with the social order and that the culture of everyday life can disrupt it—all the more so in communities of people on the move.[32]

The interaction of cultures on the move or existing in border areas ensures that no one culture will exist in pure form: each is influenced by all the others to which it is exposed. But what is the nature of this influence? Terms like *assimilation*, *acculturation*, *deculturation*, and *accommodation* suggest what Rosaldo calls a "cultural stripping away," a loss of culture as minority individuals or communities become absorbed into the mainstream (209). The United States image of the melting pot for national identity originated with Israel Zangwill's 1908 play *The Melting-Pot*. The play was opposed to the insistence of Anglo-Americans like the prominent sociologist Henry Pratt Fairchild that immigrants fully assimilate to American culture by the abandonment of their home cultures.[33] But over time, the trope of the melting pot morphed into its opposite and has become the center of critique as an ideological rhetoric veiling an imposed assimilation, with Americanization meaning the loss of past language, culture, and identity of origin.

Images of diversity—the mosaic, stir-fry, salad, stew, callaloo, rainbow, quilt, and so on—have developed as a rhetoric of resistance to mainstream groups determined to exclude the foreign, racial, or otherwise othered subordinate groups who do not want to lose their distinctive cultures. The "glorious mosaic" in particular suggests that the assimilation model is neither desirable nor accurate as a descriptor for national identity in the face of migration, diaspora, and border cultures. The mosaic rhetoric of pluralism, however, tends toward an understanding of culture as a patchwork of fixed differences, of a proliferation of unchanging minorities who remain forever marginalized from the center, from the cultures of privilege and power.

Transculturation is a term used for an approach to intercultural interaction that emphasizes the reciprocal influences across borders of all kinds. Immigrant and diasporic cultures not only change in relation to their new locations but the cultures in which they settle also transform as a result of the presence of the outsiders in their midst. As a concept developed in the new ethnography, transculturation in particular acknowledges the agency of marginalized, subjugated, or foreign peoples. As Pratt puts it in *Imperial Eyes*, while such people "cannot readily control what emanates from the dominant culture, they do determine to varying extents what they absorb into their own, and what they use it for" (6). She discusses transculturation in the context of imperialism, but the concept has much wider applications in both cultural and literary theory.[34] Taussig, for example, theorizes in *Mimesis and Alterity* that the drive to imitate is as basic to human (and animal) culture as the need to differentiate. As a word associated with both representation and imitation, *mimesis* foregrounds the way aesthetic and cultural forms develop as a form of border crossing in the praxis of culture. The diasporic Caribbean poet and critic Édouard Glissant theorizes the "*flood of convergences*" unleashed by

Instead of assuming complete cultural erasure, transculturation posits continual circuits of cultural mixing, often in settings of unequal power relations.

intercultural encounters as the dynamic, relational, and chaotic "processes of circular nomadism," as "the immeasurable intermixing of cultures," and as an "aesthetic of rupture and connection" (45, 137, 138, 151).

Transculturation assumes the existence of cultural hybridity or syncretism as a defining issue for analysis. Instead of assuming complete cultural erasure, transculturation posits continual circuits of cultural mixing, often in settings of unequal power relations. Also termed *creolité* (especially in Caribbean studies), *métissage* (in French and francophone studies), *métizaje* (in Spanish and Latino/a studies), and *tahjien* (in Arabic studies), cultural hybridity is much debated as to its meaning and politics. At times, hybridity means the fusion of cultural differences into the production of an entirely new cultural form; at times, it means the interplay of differences that retain their cultural distinctiveness; and at still other times, it means the mixing of the already syncretic. For some, hybridity is endemic to culture itself, always present in an ordinary, routine fashion as the process of cultural development; for others, hybridity is inherently destabilizing, transgressive, parodic, and creative, a strategy adopted to resist tyrannies of social and discursive orders.

The politics of hybridity, fiercely debated, is sometimes condemned as ideological, obscuring power relations and ignoring the need for communal solidarities; sometimes attacked as naively utopian; sometimes valorized as nonsectarian or antifundamentalist; and sometimes recognized for its potentially positive and negative formations depending on location and period of history.[35] Moreover, cultural hybridity is not just a product of interculturalism; it is also a process that takes on various forms of cultural translation, transplantation, adaptation, and indigenization. Cultural traffic on a global scale, to invoke Appadurai's discussion of the global ethnoscape in *Modernity at Large*, involves the praxis of cultural formation, deformation, and reformation—transformations in which aesthetic expressions have a particularly important role to play.

Intersectionalism

Identities within a cultural group are not homogeneous, however much they are imagined to be. Generalizations about the African diaspora, Mexican immigrants, overseas Chinese, the Islamic *ummah* (global community), the NRI (nonresident Indians), and so forth often obscure the divisions within such groups, especially divisions based on gender, sexuality, class, religion, and caste. The imagined community of nation or culture frequently assumes a normative or defining identity that all too easily ignores hierarchical distributions of power within the group.

Working against these homogenizing tendencies in migration, diaspora, and border studies has been the development of intersectionalism as the analysis of multiple axes of power and difference as they intersect, mediate, and articulate one another. Feminists have pioneered this analysis, particularly in the area of nation and gender studies.[36] Women on the move often experience competing patriarchies and internal conflicts between loyalty to their cultural traditions and desire to change the ones that imprison. Advocating change in their cultural group often opens them to charges of betrayal and inauthentic Westernization. As Uma Narayan writes in *Dislocating Cultures*:

> Feminists all over the world need to be suspicious of locally prevalent pictures of "national identity" and "national traditions," both because they are used to privilege the views and values of certain parts of the heterogeneous national population, and because they are almost invariably detrimental to the interests and political standing of those who are relatively powerless within the national community. . . . If nations are "imagined communities," then bigoted and distorted nationalism must be fought with feminist attempts to *reinvent* and *reimagine* the national community as more genuinely inclusive and democratic.   (35)

The need for intersectional analysis of migrant groups is not restricted to gender. As Avtar Brah points out, diasporic communities dispersed throughout the globe are themselves heterogeneous (esp. 10–16). South Asians in Britain, Fiji, Trinidad, Guyana, South Africa, the Gulf States, and the United States—to name a few prominent migrant locations of the far-flung South Asian diaspora—differ greatly from one another because of their varying degrees of integration into their new homelands. Moreover, the South Asian diaspora reflects the diversity and hybridity of the subcontinent to begin with, including sharp religious, caste, linguistic, class, and regional or national differences. Sexuality can be a flash point for conflict in diasporic, border, and migrant communities, often producing individual exile and rebellion against communal mores. Intermarriage, love matches (as opposed to arranged marriages), and queer sexualities often result in generational conflict, alienation, or expulsion from the community, and an uneasy relation with the new homeland. Given the role of the marriage plot, family conflict, and *Bildung* in the history of the novel, narratives of such intersectional issues have proliferated in diasporic, migrant, and border writing.

Memory and Desire

"Memory is a phenomenon of conceptual border zones," writes Seyhan. "It is an intersection and an interdiction. It dwells at the crossroads of the past and the present" (31). Moreover, "it is embedded in the past and will have to be retrieved in symbolic action. Memory marks a loss. It is always a re-presentation, making present that which once was and no longer is" (16). Memory—and its partner, forgetting—define the consciousness of migration, diaspora, and borders. The act of remembering—past lives, past homelands, past ways of being—is symbolic, that is, a process of meaning making that is dependent on narrative and figuration. Whether memories are silently experienced, told in oral and communal form, or written down, they exist as a form of storytelling resonant with metaphor. What has been forgotten can often return in the form of hauntings, ghostly traces of the past, longings that don't quite dare direct ex-

pression, mournings for what once was and is now lost. Memory and forgetting, as Sigmund Freud theorized, are psychodynamic processes that play out desire and the repression of desire in a symbiotic dance of creative forms (*Interpretation* and "Repression"). For the migrant, the diasporic, and the border crosser, memory is the point of transit between old and new, past and present, there and here. It is the funnel, the channel, the technology of contact. Communities in transit develop a culture of collective memory, mechanisms for passing on a heritage through the generations. Oral and written traditions—especially storytelling and literature—play a central role in articulating that collective memory and reensuring the continued existence of the community over time.[37]

Attention to memory in migration, diaspora, and border studies foregrounds the function of desire and longing in the production and continuation of distinctive communities of people with crossroads identities and bi- or multilinguistic imaginations. Desire, especially as theorized in psychoanalysis, represents a state of lack—once sated, it no longer exists. Especially for migrants and diasporics, home is often the perpetual object of desire, a longing that is never fulfilled in the ambiguity of existence caught between a consciousness of roots elsewhere and the realities of routes, of life shaped by movement through different locations that are never quite home. Desire crossed by diaspora often produces nostalgia and its discontents. In her study of nostalgia and immigrant identity, Andreea Deciu Ritivoi discusses nostalgia as a form of homesickness (*nostos* means "return"; *algia* means "pain") that can both hinder and enable individual adaptation to a new homeland (15). She writes, "nostalgia is a genuine *pharmakos*, both medicine and poison: It can express alienation, or it can replenish and rebutress our sense of identity by consolidating the ties with our history" (39). Kumar, in contrast, stresses the illusionary constructions of nostalgic desire:

> Why do we so easily replace our material past with a mythical one, pure and glorious—and then shed blood, ours and that of others, to protect

that unreal, entirely illusory sense of ourselves? After all, the India of our pasts has historically been a place of cultural mixing. This process has continued in the diaspora, where our roots have given way to routes. (*Bombay* 31)

Desire in the borderlands and diaspora can also fuel hope, serve as the drive for change, opportunity, freedom, the embrace of the new—and, of course, love of all kinds. Desire is double-edged, motivating rigidity on the one hand and adaptability on the other. Like memory, desire finds its most resonant forms in acts of the imagination, in the symbolic representations of culture. In "Reflections on Exile," Said points especially to "the lyrics of loss," poems in which "the pathos of exile is in the loss of contact with the solidity and the satisfaction of earth: homecoming is out of the question" (179). Rushdie notes:

> Exiles or emigrants or expatriates, are haunted by some sense of loss, some urge to reclaim, to look back. . . . But if we do look back, we must also do so in the knowledge . . . that we will not be capable of reclaiming precisely the thing that was lost; that we will, in short, create fictions . . . imaginary homelands, Indias of the mind.
> (*Imaginary Homelands* 10)

Desire in the borderlands between self and other oscillates between the dystopic and utopic, with perhaps a benign curiosity existing somewhere in the middle. Such fluctuations have inspired writing in all modes, from the lyric, narrative, and dramatic to the ironic, tragic, and comic. Desire for the other can involve the fascination for the stranger as alien, exotic, fearful, primitive, stigmatized, fetishized, and an assumed absolute difference. Such fascination often combines disgust and attraction, projecting repressed aspects of the self onto the other. As Kristeva writes in *Strangers to Ourselves*, "The foreigner is the other of the family, the clan, the tribe" (95). And as Sarup points out, this sense of the other's strangeness is inseparable from the idea of "*strangeness within the self*" (99).

For Trouillot, the other occupies the "savage slot" in a symbolic field that appropriates subjectivity and heterogeneity for the self and its tribe, not for the other. He counters this total-izing narrative of "us and all of them binary" by insisting, "There is no Other, but multitudes of others," that is others who have historically and geographically specific forms of difference, not ontological or ideological ones (39). As the "savage slot," the other can be the racial or ethnic other, but also the other by gender, sexuality, religion, class, and a host of other ways in which human beings separate themselves into distinct communities. Migrants, however, are often culturally marked as the stranger—in legal terms, aliens policed at geopolitical borders and potentially harassed by the laws of citizenship; in cultural terms, aliens whose speech, clothes, food, festivals, religion, and so forth separate them from the mainstream into which they may or may not want to assimilate. As Trinh T. Minh-ha describes it in *Woman, Native, Other*, "It is as if everywhere we go, we become someone's private zoo" (82).

But desire in the borderlands can take utopic forms, the longing for mixing with others in creative interplay, stimulating fusions, and the hope for understanding across difference, for reconciliation, coexistence, or peace. The innovative playwright and actor Anna Deveare Smith crosses the borders of cultural difference by traveling to and inhabiting the other's body in performance, inhabiting the actual speech and mannerisms of different sides in the racial-ethnic conflicts of Crown Heights, Brooklyn, in 1992 and Los Angeles after the Rodney King incident. "The spirit of acting," she explains, "is the *travel* from the self to the other" (xxvi). Contrasting her theory of performance with the Stanislavsky method of expressing the other by thinking about the self, she writes, "To me the search for character is constantly in motion. It is a quest that moves back and forth between the self and the other" (xxvi–xxvii). In her attempt as writer and performer to heal cultural divisions, Smith's utopian dramas embody what S. P. Mohanty advocates in his discussion of the potentially utopic epistemology of the borderlands. To cross the divide between "us" and "them," he writes, we must begin with the assumption of the subjectivity of the other.

Language, Multilingualism, and Cultural Translation

Is there a mother tongue, a single language learned in the intimacy of the family and held dear as the core signature of one's culture? Has the mother tongue been forbidden, forced into extinction or near loss? Or are there multiple mother tongues, different languages learned through exposures in a variety of settings, signaling the multilayered and interwoven complexities of community and communal identities for people in diaspora, the borderlands, or multilingual societies? How do such language options encode the history of migrations, of colonialisms past and present? As a result of the old British Empire and the new American hegemony, English has supplanted French as the global language and is now the most common second language around the world.[38] But for many people, Spanish, French, Portuguese, Mandarin, Hindi, and Arabic are the linguistic entryways into economic and cultural literacy, no matter the attachment to mother tongue(s) or the need for English in an age of intensified globalization. Language issues are at the heart of the larger cultural translation that movement from one culture into another necessarily entails. For migrant or nomadic writers and intellectuals, the question of language is central. In what language should they write? For which audiences? How do the institutions of production, dissemination, and reception in print culture affect their linguistic choices? Whatever choice they make, geopolitical histories and realities overdetermine their decisions, making the linguistic act frought with past histories and potentially conflicting desires.

Bilingualism and multilingualism are key markers of transit; of the refusal to assimilate completely; and of the insistence on retention of the past, other homes, and other cultural identities. Generational differences intensify the significance of language: first-generation migrants both need and resist the language of the host-land, and subsequent generations retain, lose, or hybridically combine the old with the new. For the Chicana writer Ana Castillo (*Massacre of the Dreamers*), the "poetics of self-definition" begins with language:

> As mestizas, we must take a critical look at language, *all* our languages and patois combinations, with the understanding that language is not something we adopt and that remains apart from us. Explicitly or implicitly, language is the vehicle by which we perceive ourselves in relation to the world.   (qtd. in Seyhan 106)

The hybridity of Spanglish, Chinglish, and other creole combinations embodies the blending of cultures that accompanies migration and life in the borderlands (on Spanglish, see Stavans).

Itineraries of multiple migrations create a linguistic hybridity of a different kind, a sort of geographic palimpsest with linguistic aftereffects created over time. Meena Alexander, for example, grew up with Hindi, Malayalam, English, French, and Arabic and is now awash in the different Englishes and Spanishes of New York City. Her family home is in Kerala, where Malayalam is the mother tongue, but she first learned Hindi because she was born in Allahabad. Growing up with North African French and then the Arabic of Khartoum, she was later educated in Britain and moved to the States. She never learned to read or write in Malayalam, although the "rhythms of the language first came to me, not just in lullabies or in the chatter of women in the kitchen . . . but in the measured cadences of oratory and poetry, and nightly recitations from the Bible and the epics" ("Alphabets" 145). For Alexander, language is supercharged, a multiplicity of places and identities.

FUTURE DIRECTIONS

Growth areas and issues for migration, diaspora, and border studies are diverse. I outline here a few of the most relevant for literary studies.

Bilingualism and multilingualism are key markers of transit; of the refusal to assimilate completely; and of the insistence on retention of the past, other homes, and other cultural identities.

Genre and Textuality

Literary scholarship in migration, diaspora, and border studies has focused heavily on the narrative genres of travel writing, autobiography, novel, and testimony. This attention to fiction and life writing may reflect a foregrounding of culture, identity, and politics and an unexamined need for modes of writing that are more easily assimilated, especially across cultural borders, and that are more conventionally tied to the real. Poetry translates less easily than narrative and fiction—both linguistically and culturally. Drama, too, relies heavily on culturally specific forms and norms for performance. Jahan Ramazani has called for more attention to postcolonial poetry; Tejumola Olaniyan writes extensively on drama in the African diaspora; and criticism on experimental diasporic writers such as Theresa Hak Kyung Cha (author of the long poem *Dictée*) is now developing.[39] This trend needs to expand, in my view, with greater attention in general to issues of textualization and form as well as to less-studied genres and modes of writing.

History

The recent compensatory turn to geography and spatialized thinking has been fruitful for literary studies in general and a central feature of migration, diaspora, and border studies. However, the field's predominant focus on the twentieth and twenty-first centuries is too limiting and belies the way that any spatial location contains the palimpsestic layers of history that overdetermine the present and help shape the future. Literary studies of earlier periods is now fruitfully taking up questions of migration, travel, and intercultural contact (e.g., the Arabic, European, and African exchanges in the medieval world; travel writing in the age of European discoveries; colonialism and Romanticism). Basem Ra'ad considers questions of the "legacies of Canaan and Etruria" for the history of writing and literature in later periods. Amitov Ghosh's *In an Antique Land* has been widely read for its combination of medieval scholarship, contemporary ethnography, and life writing in his exploration of cultural, economic, and religious traffic across Arabic Spain, North Africa, and into Persia and India. Nabil Matar's *Turks, Moors, and Englishmen in the Age of Discovery* attests to the largely ignored presence of Muslims in England and its significant impact on Elizabethan literature; his *In the Lands of the Christians: Arabic Travel Writing in the Seventeenth Century* shows how Arabs in turn represented Europeans. John Archer's *Old Worlds: Egypt, Southwest Asia, India, and Russia in Early Modern English Writing* brings questions of intercultural contact into Renaissance studies, as does Whitehead's edition of Walter Raleigh's *Discoverie of the Large, Rich and Bewtiful Empyre of Guiana*, which blends ethnohistory, analysis of travel writing, and anthropological perspectives on the ecumene. Saree Makdisi examines the complicity between the rise of Romanticism and Western imperialism. The expansion of this work will add vital historical depth to the understanding of globalization and to the literatures of migration, diaspora, and borders.[40]

Comparatism, World Literature, and Institutional Issues

Migration, diaspora, and border studies—with their enhanced attention to geopolitics on a global landscape—have led to a new comparatism: one less centered on European literatures and their diffusion or on the literatures of different nation-states; one more global in scope, more interested in creative agencies outside Europe and the United States, more likely to consider transnational literatures in a single language across national boundaries, and more attuned to traveling and transplanted cultures.

This new comparatism challenges center/periphery and diffusionist models that privilege the literatures and languages of the West and consign the Rest to marginality and pale imitation. It assumes different nodal centers of aesthetic production and agency around the globe and examines the effects of transnational contact zones, traveling ideas and forms, reciprocally constitutive formations, and hybridic processes of transplantation and indigenization. Simon Gikandi's *Maps of Englishness*, for example, examines how English identity and literature from Anthony Trollope and Thomas Carlyle through Graham Greene and Salman Rushdie are formed through their interactions with colonial others. His *Writing in Limbo* looks at the uneasy engagements of writers in the Caribbean with modernism and modernity. Rob Nixon's *Homelands, Harlem, and Hollywood* explores the travels back and forth across the Atlantic, taking up the impact of the Harlem Renaissance and Hollywood on the Sophiatown writers in South Africa; the exiles and boycotts of apartheid; and the formation of the new South Africa in the wake of the cold war, the fall of Communism, and the wars in the Balkans.[41] These and other instances of the new comparatism look to the interpenetration of the global and the local and work to bridge the divide between global studies and area studies. The thick description of local knowledge that the anthropologist Clifford Geertz advocated in *The Interpretation of Cultures* (esp. 3–30) and *Local Knowledge* (esp. 4, 55–72) is combined in the new comparatism with attention to cultural theory across borders and to the impact of cultural traffic on a global landscape at the local level.

This trend is likely to continue, and it should be encouraged. Surely, in the world after the end of the cold war, 9/11, and the United States invasion of Iraq, one of the most important growth areas for the new comparatism in literary studies should and will be the Muslim literatures and cultures in conjunction with those of other religious and cultural groups and in connection with the issues of migration and diaspora. Barbara Fuchs's and Matar's work on the early modern period, Brenner's *Inextricably Bonded*, Ken Seigneurie's collection *Crisis and Memory: The Representation of Space in Modern Levantine Narrative*, and Amin Malak's *Muslim Narratives and the Discourse of English*—to cite just a few examples—are paving the way for criticism on migration, travel, diaspora, and exile across the religious and cultural borders that are shaping the twenty-first century.

Additionally, the institutional issues that this new comparatism raises need further discussion and thought. As fields encouraging comparative methodologies, migration, diaspora, and border studies implicitly transgress the institutional structures that often separate literature and language studies by nation and region. They develop a comparatism that in part borrows from the discipline of comparative literature and in part fosters new forms of comparative work in all literature and language departments. Some scholars welcome porous boundaries among disciplines; others resist them. At stake is more than the enrichment of interdisciplinary work. Some of the smaller departments—comparative literature and languages other than English, Spanish, and French, for example—fear being swallowed up in the new institutional move toward the support of global languages. The question of ownership of literature-in-translation courses at times provokes a tug-of-war, with the issue of institutional survival in the air.[42]

Migration, diaspora, and border studies also sit at the crossroads of important debates about the newly reconfigured field of world literature, monolingualism versus multilingualism, and literature in translation. As Spivak argues in *Death of a Discipline*, the new comparatism needs to move beyond the privileging of European languages, resist the homogenizing tendencies of monolingualism, and foster the study of multiple languages in which literatures are written. At the same time, I believe, the field needs to acknowledge the power and impact on literature of transnational languages such as English, Spanish, French, Portuguese, and Mandarin, whatever their past relations to imperialism and empire. English literary studies is no longer the study of literature in Britain and the United States; it incorporates literatures in English of Africa, Asia, and the Caribbean. Spanish literary studies now includes Latin America. French literature in Africa is now regularly part of French departments. And so forth. Moreover, world literature as a field needs greater

Some scholars welcome porous boundaries among disciplines; others resist them.

theoretical examination of its parameters, its relation to language and translation, its connection to notions of traveling cultures and circulation, its newer methods of juxtaposition that are replacing older Eurocentric diffusionism. The dangers of Western appropriation of non-Western literatures also need to be examined.[43] Migration, diaspora, and border studies highlight these institutional changes because their literatures involve people on the move across geopolitical and continental borders.

~

A retrospective and prospective look at the exploding fields of migration, diaspora, and border studies is inevitably filled with omissions and gaps. The sheer scope and interdisciplinarity of the fields makes a mockery of any attempt at mastery. Rather, I have attempted to name some of the many lines of inquiry; the pathways of exploration; the kinds of questions people have been pursuing; and the spectrum of concerns from material and political to metaphoric and psychological, cultural, and aesthetic.

The focus has been on literary studies, informed by other disciplines and interdisciplinary fields. But I close with an appeal made by geographers to their fellow social scientists, to pay attention to the literature of migration and diaspora. In *Writing across Worlds: Literature and Migration*, Russell King, John Connell, and Paul White complain that social scientists seldom capture the "ambivalence" at the core of migration experience; social science "fails to portray nostalgia, anomie, exile, rootlessness, restlessness" (x), precisely the nuanced psychological dimensions of migration so often explored in literature. They ask social scientists to draw more directly on the rich literary archive of migration, from "fully-fledged creative literatures" in all genres and films to more ephemeral migration writing in ethnic newspapers, newsletters, magazines, diaries, songs, oral narratives, and reportage, often in "mother tongues" (xii–xiii). They ask, in short, for their colleagues to look at the data that are the main subject of our work in the modern literatures and languages—namely, the realms of aesthetic and creative production,

of representation and meaning making. I have asked in turn that we literary scholars turn to the social sciences for assistance in theorizing migrancy. Perhaps a fitting end for this overview is a blending of the humanities and the social sciences evident in the geographers' characterization of what they have learned from the rich literatures of migration, diaspora, and borders:

> Migrant literature is individual, subjective, diverse: it reflects but also may exaggerate or even invert the social experience that drives it. . . . For some groups, migration is not a mere interval between fixed points of departure and arrival, but a mode of being in the world—"migrancy." . . . The migrant voice tells us what it is like to feel a stranger and yet at home, to live simultaneously inside and outside one's immediate situation, to be permanently on the run, to think of returning but to realize at the same time the impossibility of doing so, since the past is not only another country but also another time, out of the present. It tells us what it is like to traverse borders like the Rio Grande or "Fortress Europe," and by doing so suddenly become an illegal person, an "other"; it tells us what it is like to live on a frontier that cuts through your language, your religion, your culture. It tells of long-distance journeys and relocations, of losses, changes, conflicts, powerlessness, and of infinite sadness that severely test the migrant's emotional resolve. It tells of new visions and experiences of the familiar and unfamiliar. For those who come from elsewhere, and cannot go back, perhaps writing becomes a place to live.
>
> (King, Connell, and White xv)

"Living in a state of psychic unrest in a Borderland," writes Anzaldúa, "is what makes poets write and artists create. It is like a cactus needle embedded in the flesh" (73). The displacements produced by migration, diaspora, and borders create a poetics of their own.

NOTES

For their assistance in my attempts to cross borders of history, geography, and language, I am particularly grateful to Alda Blanco, Leslie Bow, Bahareh Lampert, Nellie Y. McKay, John D. Riofrio, Aliko Songolo, Sean Teuton, and Susanne Wofford and to my tireless and skilled assistants John Bradley, Megan Massino, Kristin Matthews, and Elizabeth Schewe. Rebecca Walkowitz's suggestions for revision were invaluable.

1. For a sampling of debate about globalization particularly influential in or relevant to literary studies, see Appadurai, *Modernity* and *Globalization*; Bauman, *Globalization*; Breckenridge, Pollock, Bhabha, and Chakrabarty; F. Buell; Frank; Friedman and Randeria; Gunn; Hodgson; Hulme; Jameson and Miyoshi; Mudimbe-Boyi; Muller, *New World Reader*; Radhakrishnan, *Theory*; Sanderson; Wallerstein; Waters.

2. The late twentieth century has even been dubbed "the age of migration" (Castles and Miller).

3. Contemporary debates about the nature and politics of cosmopolitanism are a significant part of migration, diaspora, and border studies. For a sampling, see Appiah, *Cosmopolitanism*; Archibugi; Berman; Breckenridge, Pollock, Bhabha, and Chakrabarty; Brennan; Cheah and Robbins; Clifford, *Routes* 17–47 and *Predicament*; Dharwadker; Kaplan, esp. 101–42; Nussbaum; Vertovec and Cohen, *Conceiving*; Walkowitz.

4. Intellectual diasporics and exiles are particularly likely to articulate such multifaceted belongings. See for example Alexander, "Alphabets"; Appiah, *In My Father's House*; Bammer; Bhabha, *Location*; Braidotti; Chambers, *Border Dialogues* and *Migrancy*; Chen; Friedman, "Bodies"; Hanne; Israel; Kumar, *Passport Photos*; U. Narayan; Radhakrishnan, *Diasporic Mediations*; Rushdie, *Imaginary Homelands*; Said, "Reflections"; Sarup.

5. Initiated by Gilles Deleuze and Félix Guatarri in the 1970s–1980s (*Kafka* and *Thousand Plateaus*), the concept of deterritorialization and its related notion of nomadism have gained great currency in literary studies, with widely divergent meanings and debates centered particularly on how much to link these concepts to geohistorical conditions. See for example Braidotti; JanMohamed and Lloyd; Kaplan, esp. 65–100; Lionnet and Scharfman.

6. Paula Gunn Allen wrote the volume's essay on border studies and focused particularly on women of color as writers and critics in the United States. The border she explored was racial more than geopolitical as she called for more attention to the intersections of gender and color in the writing of women (" 'Border' Studies"). See the recent collection of her own border essays in *Off the Reservation*.

7. Postcolonial studies on British and anglophone literatures and cultures are too vast to properly reference here, but for some influential texts and useful collections, see Said, *Orientalism* and *Culture*; Spivak, *In Other Worlds*; Ashcroft, Griffiths, and Tiffin; Chambers and Curti; Gandhi; Gikandi, *Maps and Writing*; McClintock; Olaniyan; Radhakrishnan, *Diasporic Mediations* and *Theory*; Ramazani; Williams and Chrisman.

8. There is a fast-growing literature on the new transnational emphasis in American literature and cultural studies. See L. Buell; Dimock, "Literature" and *Shades*; Edwards; Grewal; Jay, "Beyond Discipline?"; Kadir; Kaplan and Pease; Madsen; Pease and Wiegman; Rowe, *New American Studies* and *Postnationalist American Studies*; Saldívar, *Dialectics*; Spillers, *Comparative American Identities*; Walters.

9. See Gilroy; Hall, "New Ethnicities"; M. Jacobson; Sollors, *Invention*; Olaniyan; and note 13.

10. The terms *identity* and *subject* are not identical, coming as they do out of different philosophical, political, and national traditions. In using *identity*, I do not align myself with essentialist identity politics; presume a self that exists outside language; or assume an unchanging collective identity of groups by race, gender, nation, and so on. Nor do I accept a view often associated with poststructuralism that the subject is fully determined by preexisting discursive regimes. I use *identity* in the context of a cultural constructivism that assumes a dialectical relation between determinism and agency as part of a historical process existing in specific locations. See Friedman, *Mappings*, esp. 3–104; Alcoff, Hames-García, Mohanty, and Moya.

11. A few exceptions include Rosemary Marangoly George's "Traveling Light," which identifies immigrant literature as a genre characterized by narrative repetition and echoes, metaphors of baggage (spiritual and material), and a link with colonialism. William Q. Boelhower's "The Immigrant Novel as Genre" is a structuralist analysis of immigrant narrative patterns with examples drawn from United States literature. Thomas Ferraro's *Ethnic Passages* similarly draws only on the United States example, but Ferraro presents a useful genealogy of literary criticism on migration narratives and argues against the common marginalization of migration literature from the American canon. He suggests that the genre contains across ethnic differences a core concern with the writer's personal negotiation between being American and being alien: "An aspiring writer from an immigrant background feels damned on the one side for having become too American and damned on the other side for not being able to become American enough" (10).

12. See Takaki, *Different Mirror*; Boelhower, *Through a Glass*; Sollors, *Multilingual America*; Stephan; and Simone's annotated bibliography in *Immigrant Experience*.

13. See, for example, on the Great Migration, Griffin; Nicholls; Rodgers; on the Japanese internment, Kogawa; Yamada; Lowe, esp. 48–51; Weglyn; on Native American migration, Aldama; Ehle; Hale; Harjo; Hogan; Jahoda; Luna-Firebaugh; McCall; Rozema.

14. For more discussions of migration, culture, and literature in countries other than the United States, see Aciman; Adelson; Appadurai, *Modernity*; Bammer; Corkhill; Ghosh; Gilroy; Hanne; Hargreaves; Huyssen; Ireland and Proulx; Kaminsky; King,

Connell, and White; Parmar and Somaia-Carten; Sherman; Ty and Goellnicht.

15. *Migration Theory*, edited by Bretell and Hollifield, contains overviews of migration theory in history, economics, sociology, anthropology, law, and political science. For other theories of migration in the social sciences, see Bretell; Friedman and Randeria; King, Connell, and White; D. Jacobson; Meilaender; Papastergiadis, "Restless Hybrids" and *Turbulence*; Suárez-Orozco, Suárez-Orozco, and Qin-Hilliard, *Interdisciplinary Perspectives* and *New Immigration* (Marcelo Suárez-Orozco and Carola Suárez-Orozco are codirectors of the Harvard Immigration Project); publications of the International Library of Studies on Migration, a series edited by Robin Cohen, esp. Vertovec and Cohen, *Conceiving* and *Migration*; Willis and Yeoh. For genealogies of and debates about the term *assimilation* in American historiography, see Alba and Nee; Kazal; Suárez-Orozco.

16. For feminist criticism on gender in migration narratives, see Ahmed, Castaneda, and Fortie; Alexander, "Alphabets"; Danquah; Davies; Friedman, "Bodies"; Grewal; Heike; Irving; Parmar and Somaia-Carten; and Zaborowska.

17. Migration has no doubt influenced the figurations of both Braidotti and Chambers. Braidotti was born in Italy, immigrated to Australia, was educated in France, and currently teaches in the Netherlands; Chambers has lived in many countries and was teaching in Naples at the time of his book's publication. See also Janet Wolff's theorizing of women as alien strangers.

18. Philip Curtin's *Cross-Cultural Trade in World History* implicitly evokes the Greek roots of *diaspora* in his global history of trade diasporas.

19. For the South Asian Diaspora, see Appadurai, *Modernity*; Brah; Grewal; Kumar, *Bombay, Passport Photos*, and *Away*; U. Narayan; Needham; Radhakrishnan, *Diasporic Mediations* and *Theory*; Shukla; Tambiah. The term *diaspora* is also increasingly being used in relation to Chinese outside the mainland of China, people who have been known as overseas Chinese for centuries. See Anderson and Lee; Chow; Chuh and Shimakawa; Lowe; Ty and Goellnicht; and Cohen's discussion of the overseas Chinese as a "trade diaspora" (83–104).

20. Braziel and Mannur's collection includes many of the most significant contemporary theoretical essays on diaspora. Their introduction and that of the anthropologists Lavie and Swedenburg in their *Displacement, Diaspora, and Geographies of Identity* are particularly useful overviews.

21. For recent discussions of Jewish and Israeli diasporic literature, see Brenner; Shreiber; Weber.

22. For recent discussions of black diasporan literature, film, and culture in the Americas, see Edwards; Foster; Gilroy; Spillers, "Introduction"; Walters.

23. Brah 9; Alexander, "Alphabets" and *Shock* 13–16.

See Friedman, "Bodies." For other blendings of autobiography and diasporic theory, see Bhabha, "Frontlines" and *Location*; Chow; Davies; Chen; Frankenberg and Mani; Kumar, *Away*, *Passport Photos*, and *Bombay*; U. Narayan; Radhakrishnan, *Diasporic Mediations* and *Theory*; Sarup; Said, "Reflections"; Seyhan; and Spivak, *Post-colonial Critic*. Said's "Reflections on Exile" and Rushdie's "Imaginary Homelands" predate the use of the term *diaspora* in cultural theory but have been influential autobiographical theory in diaspora studies.

24. Pratt introduced the term "contact zone," which she defines in *Imperial Eyes* as "social spaces where disparate cultures meet, clash, and grapple with each other, often in highly asymmetrical relations of domination and subordination—like colonialism, slavery, or their aftermaths as they are lived out across the globe today" (4).

25. See Stallybrass and White on transgression of high and low borders; JanMohamed on the specular "homelessness-as-home" of "border intellectuals"; Welchman's *Rethinking Borders*, which extends border theory in multimedia, interdisciplinary, and theoretical ways; Trinh's "An Acoustic Journey," for the move from refugees to philosophic borderlands. For a critique of the erasure of empirical scholarship in border theory and literature, see the sociologist Pablo Vila's *Ethnography at the Border*, esp. 306–41.

26. See "Theories and Methodologies . . . Anzaldúa," devoted to Anzaldúa's work and legacy; Friedman, *Mappings*, 93–101. The poems, critical writings, and carnivalesque performance art of Guillermo Gómez-Peña have also been influential in both Mexico and the United States (e.g., *The New World Border*). See Fregoso for discussions of Chicanas and "meXicanas" in the production of American and Mexican border culture in film, literature, and popular culture.

27. See also Polkinhorn, Di-Bella, and Reyes; Jay's overview of border studies, "Myth." For acknowledgment of the formative influence of the American Southwest on border theory and an insistence that border theory move beyond its regional origins, see Michaelsen and Johnson; Welchman.

28. Geographic borders under examination in border studies are not always contiguous. The so-called civilizational divide between East and West has led to work particularly in comparative literature examining the cultural exchanges and fruitful juxtapositions of European and East Asian literary and aesthetic cultures; see for example Hayot; Saussy, *Great Walls* and *Problem*; L. Zhang; Y. Zhang.

29. See also Chambers, *Border Dialogues*; Trinh, "Acoustic Journey." For discussions of border issues, cultural politics, and narrative, see Egerer; Fregoso; Friedman, *Mappings* 132–78; Izzo and Spandri; Stallybrass and White.

30. In "The Many Faces of Cosmo-polis," Mignolo links border thinking to "critical cosmopolitanism" and sees colonial modernities as distinct from Enlightenment modernity. See also his *Darker Side of the Renaissance*.

31. Bhabha uses the rhetoric of borders to discuss the breakdown of minority identities based on a single identity category and the development of intersectional analysis of the multiple constituents of identity ("Frontlines"). For border rhetoric and fetishism, see Spyer.

32. For other influential discussions of culture as concept, see Bourdieu; Certeau; Rosaldo; Hall, "Cultural Identity"; Hannerz, esp. 3–39; Manganaro; Stallybrass and White.

33. See Alba and Nee; Kazal; Zangwill's passionate defense of "melting-pot" America as a national identity built on diversity in his afterword to the 1914 edition of *The Melting-Pot*; Fairchild's attack of Zangwill and Anglocentric rationale for assimilation in *The Melting-Pot Mistake*; the attempt to resurrect the original meaning of the trope in Jacoby's *Reinventing the Melting Pot*; Schreibersdorf; and Wilson on this early-twentieth-century debate.

34. The Cuban sociologist Fernando Ortíz coined the term *transculturation* in the 1940s (Pratt 228n4). See Rosaldo's broader definition of transculturation as the "creative processes" of "improvisation" in the borderlands (215–16).

35. For overviews of debate about cultural hybridity, see Friedman, *Mappings* (82–93); Kalra, Kaur, and Hutnyk; Papastergiadis, "Restless Hybrids"; Pieterse; Purdom; Werbner and Modood; Young.

36. See, for example, Friedman, "Feminism," "Locational Feminism," and *Mappings*; Grewal; Grewal and Kaplan; Kaplan, Alarcón, and Moallem; Layoun; U. Narayan; Yuval-Davis.

37. See in particular Said, "Reflections"; Rushdie, *Imaginary Homelands*; Alexander, "Alphabets"; and Seyhan, esp. 23–64.

38. On global English, see McArthur; for hybridic Englishes, see Ch'ien. For the relation of current globalization and language, see especially Artega.

39. See Lowe 128–53; Kim and Alarcón; and Friedman, "Modernism."

40. See also Fuchs; Kadir; Mignolo, *Darker Side* and *Local Histories*; Vitkus, *Piracy* and *Three Turk Plays*; Singh; and Hulme. Said's *Orientialism* is an important precursor to this trend; see also his *Culture and Imperialism*. For historians of early intercultural contact, see especially J. Abu-Lughod; Frank; Sanderson.

41. For critiques of Eurocentrism in comparative literature, see Lanser; Lionnet and Shih; Spivak, *Death*; Saussy, *Comparative Literature*.

42. See esp. Saussy, *Comparative Literature* for debates about the new comparatism and institutional implications. For the impact of current globalization

on institutional structures in the academy, see Jay, "Beyond Discipline?"

43. For examples of this new debate on world literature, see Apter; Bassnett; Casanova; Damrosch; Dimock, "Literature"; Lionnet and Shih; Moretti; "Theories and Methodologies: Comparative Literature"; Saussy, *Comparative Literature*; Spivak, *Death*; L. Zhang; Y. Zhang.

WORKS CITED AND SUGGESTIONS FOR FURTHER READING

Abu-Jaber, Diana. *Arabian Jazz*. New York: Norton, 1993.

Abu-Lughod, Janet L. *Before European Hegemony: The World System, A.D. 1250–1350*. New York: Oxford, 1989.

Abu-Lughod, Lila, ed. *Remaking Women: Feminism and Modernity in the Middle East*. Princeton: Princeton UP, 1998.

Aciman, André, ed. *Letters of Transit: Reflections on Exile, Identity, Language, and Loss*. New York: New York Public Lib., 1999.

Adelson, Leslie A. *The Turkish Turn in Contemporary German Literature: Toward a New Critical Grammar of Migration*. Basingstoke, Eng.: Palgrave-Macmillan, 2005.

Ahmed, Leila. *A Border Passage: From Cairo to America, a Woman's Journey*. New York: Farrar, 1999.

Ahmed, Sara, Claudia Castaneda, and Anne-Marie Fortie, eds. *Uprootings/Regroupings: Questions of Home and Migration*. Oxford: Berg, 2004.

Alba, Richard, and Victor Nee. "Rethinking Assimilation Theory for a New Era of Immigration." Suárez-Orozco, Suárez-Orozco, and Qin-Hilliard, *New Immigration* 35–66.

Alcoff, Linda Martín, Michael Hames-García, Satya P. Mohanty, and Paula M. L. Moya, eds. *Identity Politics Reconsidered*. New York: Palgrave-Macmillan, 2006.

Aldama, Arturo J. *Disrupting Savagism: Intersecting Chicano/a, Mexican Immigrant, and Native American Struggles for Self-Representation*. Durham: Duke UP, 2001.

Alexander, Meena. "Alphabets of Flesh." Shohat 143–54.

———. *The Shock of Arrival: Reflections on Postcolonial Experience*. Boston: South End, 1996.

Allen, Paula Gunn. " 'Border' Studies: The Intersection of Gender and Color." Gibaldi 303–19.

———. *Off the Reservation: Reflections on Boundary-Busting Border-Crossing Loose Canons*. Boston: Beacon, 1998.

Alley, David C. "Integrating Afro-Hispanic Studies into the Spanish Curriculum: A Rationale and a Model." *Afro-Hispanic Review* 13.2 (1994): 3–8.

Anderson, Benedict. *Imagined Communities: Reflections on the Origin and Spread of Nationalism*. London: Verso, 1991.

Anderson, Danny J., and Jill S. Kuhnheim, eds. *Cultural Studies in the Curriculum: Teaching Latin America.* New York: MLA, 2003.

Anderson, Wanni W., and Robert G. Lee, eds. *Displacements and Diasporas: Asians in the Americas.* New Brunswick: Rutgers UP, 2005.

Antin, Mary. *The Promised Land.* 1912. New York: Penguin, 1999.

Anzaldúa, Gloria. *Borderlands / La Frontera: The New Mestiza.* San Francisco: Aunt Lute, 1987.

Appadurai, Arjun, ed. *Globalization.* Durham: Duke UP, 2001.

———. *Modernity at Large: Cultural Dimensions of Globalization.* Minneapolis: U of Minnesota P, 1996.

Appiah, Anthony. *Cosmopolitanism: Ethics in a World of Strangers.* New York: Norton, 2006.

———. "Cosmopolitan Patriots." Cheah and Robbins 91–116.

———. *In My Father's House: Africa in the Philosophy of Culture.* Oxford: Oxford UP, 1993.

Apter, Emily. *The Translation Zone: A New Comparative Literature.* Princeton: Princeton UP, 2006.

Archer, John. *Old Worlds: Egypt, Southwest Asia, India, and Russia in Early Modern English Writing.* Stanford: Stanford UP, 2001.

Archibugi, Daniele, ed. *Debating Cosmopolitics.* London: Verso, 2003.

Artega, Alfred. *An Other Tongue: Nation and Ethnicity in the Linguistic Borderlands.* Durham: Duke UP, 1994.

Asante, Molefi. *Afrocentricity: The Theory of Social Change.* Buffalo: Amulefi, 1980.

Ashcroft, Bill, Gareth Griffiths, and Helen Tiffin, eds. *The Post-colonial Studies Reader.* London: Routledge, 1995.

Bammer, Angelika, ed. *Displacements: Cultural Identities in Question.* Bloomington: Indiana UP, 1994.

Bassnett, Susan. *Comparative Literature: A Critical Introduction.* Oxford: Blackwell, 1993.

Bauman, Zygmunt. *Culture as Praxis.* 1973. Rev. ed. London: Sage, 1999.

———. *Globalization: Its Human Consequences.* New York: Columbia UP, 1998.

Behar, Ruth, and Deborah A. Gordon, eds. *Women Writing Culture.* Berkeley: U of California P, 1995.

Behdad, Ali. *A Forgetful Nation: On Immigration and Cultural Identity in the United States.* Durham: Duke UP, 2005.

Berman, Jessica. *Modernist Fiction, Cosmopolitanism, and the Politics of Community.* Cambridge: Cambridge UP, 2003.

Bhabha, Homi K. "Frontlines/Borderposts." Bammer 269–72.

———. *The Location of Culture.* London: Routledge, 1994.

Bhalla, Alok. *Partition Dialogues: Memories of a Lost Home.* New York: Oxford UP, 2006.

———, ed. *Stories about the Partition of India.* New Delhi: Harper, 1999.

Boelhower, William Q. "The Immigrant Novel as Genre." *MELUS* 8.1 (1981): 3–13.

———. *Through a Glass Darkly: Ethnic Semiosis in American Literature.* Oxford: Oxford UP, 1987.

Bourdieu, Pierre. *The Logic of Practice.* 1980. Trans. Richard Nice. Stanford: Stanford UP, 1990.

Bow, Leslie. *Seduction and Other Acts of Subversion: Feminism, Sexual Politics, Asian American Women's Literature.* Princeton: Princeton UP, 2001.

Boyarin, Jonathan, and Daniel Boyarin. *Powers of Diaspora: Two Essays on the Relevance of Jewish Culture.* Minneapolis: U of Minnesota P, 2002.

Brah, Avtar. *Cartographies of Diaspora: Contesting Identities.* London: Routledge, 1996.

Braidotti, Rosi. *Nomadic Subjects: Embodiment and Sexual Difference in Contemporary Feminist Theory.* New York: Columbia UP, 1994.

Braziel, Jana Evans, and Anita Mannur, eds. *Theorizing Diaspora.* Oxford: Blackwell, 2003.

Breckenridge, Carol A., Sheldon Pollock, Homi K. Bhabha, and Dipesh Chakrabarty, eds. *Cosmopolitanism.* Durham: Duke UP, 2002.

Brennan, Timothy. *At Home in the World: Cosmopolitanism Now.* Cambridge: Harvard UP, 1997.

Brenner, Rachel Feldhay. *Inextricably Bonded: Israeli Arab and Jewish Writers Re-Visioning Culture.* Madison: U of Wisconsin P, 2003.

Bretell, Caroline B. *Essays on Transnationalism, Ethnicity, and Identity.* Oxford: AltaMira, 2003.

Bretell, Caroline B., and James F. Hollifield, eds. *Migration Theory: Talking across the Disciplines.* London: Routledge, 2000.

Buell, Frederick. *National Culture and the New Global System.* Baltimore: Johns Hopkins UP, 1994.

Buell, Lawrence, ed. *Postcolonial Theory and the United States: Race, Ethnicity, and Literature.* Jackson: UP of Mississippi, 2000.

Butalia, Urvashi. *The Other Side of Silence: Voices from the Partition of India.* New Delhi: Viking, 1998.

Calderón, Héctor, and José David Saldívar, eds. *Criticism in the Borderlands: Studies in Chicano Literature, Culture, and Ideology.* Durham: Duke UP, 1991.

Casanova, Pascale. *The World Republic of Letters.* 1999. Trans. M. B. DeBevoise. Cambridge: Harvard UP, 2004.

Castillo, Debra A., and María Socorro Tabuenca Córdoba. *Border Women: Writing from La Frontera.* Minneapolis: U of Minnesota P, 2002.

Castles, Stephen, and Mark J. Miller. *The Age of Migration: International Population Movements.* 3rd ed. New York: Guildford, 2003.

Certeau, Michel de. *The Practice of Everyday Life.* 1974. Trans. Steven Rendall. Berkeley: U of California P, 1984.

Chambers, Iain. *Border Dialogues: Journeys in Postmodernity.* London: Routledge, 1990.

———. *Migrancy, Culture, Identity.* London: Routledge, 1994.

Chambers, Iain, and Lidia Curti, eds. *The Post-colonial Question: Common Skies, Divided Horizons.* London: Routledge, 1996.

Cheah, Pheng, and Bruce Robbins, eds. *Cosmopolitics: Thinking and Feeling beyond the Nation.* Minneapolis: U of Minnesota P, 1998.

Chen, Kuan-Hsing. "The Formation of a Diasporic Intellectual: An Interview with Stuart Hall." Morley and Chen 484–503.

Ch'ien, Evelyn Nien-Ming. *Weird English.* Cambridge: Harvard UP, 2004.

Chow, Rey. *Writing Diaspora: Tactics of Intervention in Contemporary Cultural Studies.* Bloomington: Indiana UP, 1993.

Chuh, Kandice, and Karen Shimakawa, eds. *Orientations: Mapping Studies in the Asian Diaspora.* Durham: Duke UP, 2001.

Clifford, James. *The Predicament of Culture: Twentieth-Century Ethnography, Literature, and Art.* Cambridge: Harvard UP, 1998.

———. *Routes: Travel and Translation in the Late Twentieth Century.* Cambridge: Harvard UP, 1997.

Clifford, James, and George E. Marcus, eds. *Writing Culture: The Poetics and Politics of Ethnography.* Berkeley: U of California P, 1986.

Cohen, Robin. *Global Diasporas: An Introduction.* Seattle: U of Washington P, 1997.

Corkhill, Annette Robyn. *The Immigrant Experience in Australian Literature.* Melbourne: Academia, 1995.

Cruz-Malavé, Arnaldo, and Martin F. Manalansan IV, eds. *Queer Globalizations: Citizenship and the Afterlife of Colonialism.* New York: New York UP, 2001.

Curtin, Philip D. *Cross-Cultural Trade in World History.* Cambridge: Cambridge UP, 1984.

Damrosch, David. *What Is World Literature?* Princeton: Princeton UP, 2003.

Danquah, Meri Nana-Ama, ed. *Becoming American: Personal Essays by First Generation Immigrant Women.* New York: Hyperion, 2000.

Davies, Carole Boyce. *Black Women, Writing and Identity: Migrations of the Subject.* London: Routledge, 1994.

Deleuze, Gilles, and Félix Guattari. *Kafka: Towards a Minor Literature.* 1975. Trans. Dana Polan. Minneapolis: U of Minnesota P, 1986.

———. *A Thousand Plateaus: Capitalism and Schizophrenia.* 1980. Trans. Biran Massumi. Minneapolis: U of Minnesota P, 1987.

Dharwadker, Vinay, ed. *Cosmopolitan Geographies: New Locations in Literature and Culture.* London: Routledge, 2000.

Díaz, Junot. *Drown.* New York: Riverhead, 1996.

Dimock, Wai Chee. "Literature for the Planet." *PMLA* 116 (2001): 173–88.

———. *Shades of the Planet: American Literature as World Literature.* Princeton: Princeton UP, 2007.

Edwards, Brent Hayes. *The Practice of Diaspora: Literature, Translation, and the Rise of Black Internationalism.* Cambridge: Harvard UP, 2003.

Egerer, Claudia. *Fictions of (In) Betweenness.* Gothenburg Studies in English 68. Göteborg, Swed.: Acta Universitatis Gothoburgensis, 1996.

Ehle, John. *Trail of Tears: The Rise and Fall of the Cherokee Nation.* New York: Anchor, 1997.

Emecheta, Buchi. *The Family.* New York: Brazilier, 1989.

Fairchild, Henry Pratt. *The Melting-Pot Mistake.* Boston: Little, 1926.

Ferraro, Thomas J. *Ethnic Passages: Literary Immigrants in Twentieth-Century America.* Chicago: U of Chicago P, 1993.

Forsdick, Charles, and David Murphy, eds. *Francophone Postcolonial Studies: A Critical Introduction.* New York: Oxford UP, 2003.

Foster, Gwendolyn Audrey. *Women Filmmakers of the African and Asian Diaspora: Decolonizing the Gaze, Locating Subjectivity.* Carbondale: Southern Illinois UP, 1997.

Foucault, Michel. "Of Other Spaces." 1984. Trans. Jay Miskowiec. *Diacritics* 16.1 (1986): 22–27.

Fox, Richard G., ed. *Recapturing Anthropology: Working in the Present.* Sante Fe: School of Amer. Research, 1991.

Frank, André Gunder. *ReOrient: Global Economy in the Asian Age.* Berkeley: U of California P, 1998.

Frankenberg, Ruth, and Lata Mani. "Crosscurrents, Crosstalk: Race, 'Postcoloniality,' and the Politics of Location." Lavie and Swendenburg 273–94.

Fregoso, Rosa Linda. *MeXicana Encounters: The Making of Social Identity on the Borderlands.* Berkeley: U of California P, 2003.

Freud, Sigmund. *The Interpretation of Dreams.* Trans. James Strachey. New York: Avon, 1965.

———. "Repression." 1915. *General Psychological Theory.* Ed. Philip Rieff. New York: Collier, 1963. 104–16.

Friedman, Jonathan, and Shalini Randeria, eds. *World on the Move: Globalization, Migration, and Cultural Security.* New York: Palgrave, 2004.

Friedman, Susan Stanford. "Bodies on the Move: A Poetics of Home and Diaspora." *Tulsa Studies in Women's Literature* 23.2 (2004): 189–212.

———. "Feminism, State Fictions, and Violence: Gender, Geopolitics, and Transnationalism." *Communal/Plural* 9.1 (2001): 111–29.

———. "Locational Feminism: Gender, Cultural Geographies, and Geopolitical Literacy." *Feminist Locations: Global and Local, Theory and Practice.* Ed. Marianne DeKoven. New Brunswick: Rutgers UP, 2001. 13–36.

———. *Mappings: Feminism and the Cultural Geographies of Encounter.* Princeton: Princeton UP, 1998.

———. "Modernism in a Transnational Landscape: Spatial Poetics, Postcolonialism, and Gender in Césaire's *Cahier/Notebook* and Cha's *Dictée.*" *Paideuma* 32.1–3 (2003): 39–74.

Frye, Northrup. *Anatomy of Criticism: Four Essays.* Princeton: Princeton UP, 1957.

Fuchs, Barbara. *Mimesis and Empire: The New World, Islam, and European Identities.* Cambridge: Cambridge UP, 2004.

Gandhi, Leela. *Postcolonial Theory: A Critical Introduction.* 1998. New York: Columbia UP, 2005.

García Canclini, Néstor. *Hybrid Cultures: Strategies for Entering and Leaving Modernity.* Trans. Christopher L. Chiappari and Silvia L. López. Minneapolis: U of Minnesota P, 1995.

Geertz, Clifford. *The Interpretation of Cultures.* New York: Basic, 1973.

———. *Local Knowledge: Further Essays in Interpretive Anthropology.* New York: Basic, 1983.

George, Rosemary Marangoly. "Traveling Light: Of Immigration, Invisible Suitcases, and Gunny Sacks." *Differences* 4.2 (1992): 72–99.

Ghosh, Amitov. *In an Antique Land: History in the Guise of a Traveler's Tale.* New York: Vintage, 1993.

Gibaldi, Joseph, ed. *Introduction to Scholarship in Modern Languages and Literatures.* 2nd ed. New York: MLA, 1992.

Gikandi, Simon. *Maps of Englishness: Writing Identity in the Age of Colonialism.* New York: Columbia UP, 1997.

———. *Writing in Limbo: Modernism and Caribbean Literature.* Ithaca: Cornell UP, 1992.

Gilroy, Paul. *The Black Atlantic: Modernity and Double Consciousness.* Cambridge: Harvard UP, 1993.

Glissant, Édouard. *Poetics of Relation.* 1990. Trans. Betsy Wing. Ann Arbor: U of Michigan P, 2000.

Gómez-Peña, Guillermo. "Bilingualism, Biculturalism, and Borders." *English Is Broken Here: Notes on Cultural Fusion in the Americas.* Ed. Coco Fusco. New York: New, 1995. 147–58.

———. *The New World Border: Prophecies, Poems, and Loqueras for the End of the Century.* San Francisco: City Lights, 1996.

Grewal, Inderpal. *Transnational America: Feminisms, Diasporas, Neoliberalisms.* Durham: Duke UP, 2005.

Grewal, Inderpal, and Caren Kaplan, eds. *Scattered Hegemonies: Postmodernity and Transnational Feminist Practices.* Minneapolis: U of Minnesota P, 1994.

Griffin, Farah Jasmine. "*Who Set You Flowin'?* The African-American Migration Narrative.* New York: Oxford UP, 1995.

Gunn, Giles, ed. *Globalizing Literary Studies.* Spec. issue of *PMLA* 116 (2001): 16–188.

Hale, Janet Campbell. *Bloodlines: Odyssey of a Native Daughter.* Tucson: U of Arizona P, 1998.

Hall, Stuart. "Cultural Identity and Difference." Williams and Chrisman 392–403.

———. "New Ethnicities." Morley and Chen 441–49.

Hanne, Michael, ed. *Creativity in Exile.* New York: Rodopi, 2004.

Hannerz, Ulf. *Cultural Complexity: Studies in the Social Organization of Meaning.* New York: Columbia UP, 1992.

Hargreaves, Alex G. *Immigration and Identity in Beur Fiction: Voices from the North African Immigrant Community in France.* New York: Oxford UP, 1997.

Harjo, Joy. *How We Became Human: New and Selected Poems, 1975–2001.* New York: Norton, 2004.

Hayot, Eric. *Chinese Dreams: Pound, Brecht,* Tel Quel. Ann Arbor: U of Michigan P, 2003.

Heike, Paul. *Mapping Migration: Women's Writing and the American Immigrant Experience from the 1950s to the 1990s.* Heidelberg, Ger.: Winter, 1999.

Hicks, D. Emily. *Border Writing: The Multidimensional Text.* Minneapolis: U of Minnesota P, 1991.

Hodgson, Marshall. *Rethinking World History: Essays on Europe, Islam, and World History.* Cambridge: Cambridge UP, 1993.

Hogan, Linda. *Solar Storms.* New York: Scribner's, 1995.

Hulme, Peter. *Colonial Encounters: Europe and the Native Caribbean, 1492–1797.* London: Methuen, 1986.

Huyssen, Andreas. "Diaspora and Nation: Migration into Other Pasts." *New German Critique* 88 (2003): 147–64.

Ireland, Susan, and Patrice J. Proulx, eds. *Immigrant Narratives in Contemporary France.* Westport: Greenwood, 2001.

Irving, Katrina. *Immigrant Mothers: Narratives of Race and Maternity, 1890–1925.* Urbana: U of Illinois P, 2000.

Israel, Nico. *Outlandish: Writing between Exile and Diaspora.* Stanford: Stanford UP, 2000.

Izzo, Donatella, and Elena Spandri, eds. *"Contact Zones": Rewriting Genre across the East-West Border.* Naples, IT.: Liguori, 2003.

Jack, Belinda. *Francophone Literatures: An Introductory Survey.* New York: Oxford UP, 1996.

Jacobson, David, ed. *The Immigration Reader.* Oxford: Blackwell, 1998.

Jacobson, Matthew Frye. *Whiteness of a Different Color: European Immigrants and the Alchemy of Race.* Cambridge: Harvard UP, 1998.

Jacoby, Tamar, ed. *Reinventing the Melting Pot: The New Immigrants and What It Means to Be American.* New York: Basic, 2004.

Jahoda, Gloria. *The Trail of Tears: The Story of the American Indian Removals, 1813–1855.* 1975. San Antonio: Wings, 1995.

Jameson, Fredric, and Masao Miyoshi, eds. *The Cultures of Globalization.* Durham: Duke UP, 1998.

JanMohamed, Abdul R. "Worldliness-without-World, Homelessness-as-Home: Toward a Definition of the Specular Border Intellectual." *Edward Said: A Critical Reader.* Ed. Michael Sprinker. Cambridge: Cambridge UP, 1992. 96–120.

JanMohamed, Abdul R., and David Lloyd, eds. *The Nature and Context of Minority Discourse.* Oxford: Oxford UP, 1990.

Jay, Paul. "Beyond Discipline? Globalization and the Future of English." *PMLA* 116 (2001): 32–47.

———. "The Myth of 'America' and the Politics of Location: Modernity, Border Studies, and the Literature of the Americas." *Arizona Quarterly* 54.2 (1998): 165–92.

Jen, Gish. *Mona in the Promised Land.* New York: Vintage, 1996.

Johnson, Kevin R. *The Huddled Masses Myth: Immigration and Civil Rights*. Philadelphia: Temple UP, 2003.

Johnson, Roberta. "Twentieth-Century Spanish Literature and the Humanities Today." *ADFL Bulletin* 33.1 (2001): 12–14.

Joseph, May. "Transatlantic Inscriptions: Desire, Diaspora, and Cultural Citizenship." Shohat 357–59.

Kadir, Djelal, ed. *America: The Idea, the Literature*. Spec. issue of *PMLA* 118 (2003): 9–113.

Kahf, Mohja. *E-Mails from Scheherazad*. Gainesville: UP of Florida, 2003.

Kahn, Shahnaz. *Aversion and Desire: Negotiating Muslim Female Identity in the Diaspora*. Toronto: Women's, 2002.

Kalra, Virinder, Raminder Kaur, and John Hutnyk. *Diaspora and Hybridity*. London: Sage, 2005.

Kaminsky, Amy K. *After Exile: Writing the Latin American Diaspora*. Minneapolis: U of Minnesota P, 1999.

Kaplan, Amy, and Donald Pease, eds. *Cultures of United States Imperialism*. Durham: Duke UP, 1993.

Kaplan, Caren. *Questions of Travel: Postmodern Discourses of Displacement*. Durham: Duke UP, 1998.

Kaplan, Caren, Norma Alarcón, and Minoo Moallem, eds. *Between Women and Nation: Nationalisms, Transnational Feminism, and the State*. Durham: Duke UP, 1999.

Kaul, Suvir. *The Partitions of Memory: The Afterlife of the Division of India*. Bloomington: Indiana UP, 2002.

Kazal, Russell A. "Revisiting Assimilation: The Rise, Fall, and Reappraisal of a Concept in American Ethnic History." *American Historical Review* 100 (1995): 437–71.

Keith, Michael, and Steve Pile, eds. *Place and the Politics of Identity*. London: Routledge, 1993.

Khazanov, Anatoly M. *Nomads and the Outside World*. Trans. Julia Crookenden. Cambridge: Cambridge UP, 1984.

Kim, Elaine H., and Norma Alarcón, eds. *Writing Self, Writing Nation: Essays on Theresa Hak Kyung Cha's* Dictée. Berkeley: Third World Women's, 1994.

King, Bruce. *The Internationalization of English Literature*. Oxford: Oxford UP, 2004.

King, Russell, John Connell, and Paul White, eds. *Writing across Worlds: Literature and Migration*. London: Routledge, 1995.

Knippling, Alpana Sharma, ed. *New Immigrant Literatures in the United States: A Sourcebook to Our Multicultural Literary Heritage*. Westport: Greenwood, 1996.

Kogawa, Joy. *Obasan*. 1981. Boston: Godine, 1984.

Kristeva, Julia. *Powers of Horror: An Essay on Abjection*. Trans. Leon Roudiez. New York: Columbia UP, 1982.

———. *Strangers to Ourselves*. Trans. Leon Roudiez. New York: Columbia UP, 1991.

Kumar, Amitava, ed. *Away: The Indian Writer as an Expatriate*. London: Routledge, 2004.

———. *Bombay, London, New York*. London: Routledge, 2002.

———. *Passport Photos*. Berkeley: U of California P, 2000.

Kureishi, Hanif. *The Buddha of Suburbia*. New York: Penguin, 1990.

Lanser, Susan Sniader. "Compared to What? Global Feminism, Comparatism, and the Master's Tools." *Reconfigured Spheres: Feminist Explorations of Literary Space*. Ed. Margaret R. Higonnet and Joan Templeton. Amherst: U of Massachusetts P, 1994. 280–300.

Lavie, Smadar, and Ted Swedenburg, eds. *Displacement, Diaspora, and Geographies of Identity*. Durham: Duke UP, 2001.

Layoun, Mary N. *Wedded to the Land? Gender, Boundaries, and Nationalism in Crisis*. Durham: Duke UP, 2002.

Lefebvre, Henri. *The Production of Space*. Trans. Donald Nicholson-Smith. Oxford: Blackwell, 1991. Trans. of *Production de l'espace*. 1974.

Lessing, Doris. *The Grass Is Singing*. 1950. New York: Harper, 2000.

Lionnet, Françoise, and Ronnie Scharfman, eds. *Post/ Colonial Conditions: Exiles, Migrations, and Nomadisms*. Spec. issue of *Yale French Studies* 82–83 (1993): 1–233.

Lionnet, Françoise, and Shu-mei Shih, eds. *Minor Transnationalism*. Durham: Duke UP, 2005.

Lowe, Lisa. *Immigrant Acts: On Asian American Cultural Politics*. Durham: Duke UP, 1996.

Luna-Firebaugh, Eileen M. "The Border Crossed Us: Border Crossing Issues of the Indigenous Peoples of the Americas." *Wicazo Sa Review* 17.1 (2002): 159–81.

Lusophone Studies. Spec. issue of *Portuguese Studies Review* 6.1 (1997): 11–189.

Ma, Sheng-mei. *Immigrant Subjectivities in Asian American and Asian Diaspora Literatures*. Albany: State U of New York P, 1998.

Madsen, Deborah L., ed. *Post-colonial Literatures: Expanding the Canon*. London: Pluto, 1999.

Makdisi, Saree. *Romantic Imperialism: Universal Empire and the Culture of Modernity*. Cambridge: Cambridge UP, 1998.

Malak, Amin. *Muslim Narratives and the Discourse of English*. New York: State U of New York P, 2003.

Manalansan, Martin F., IV. *Global Divas: Filipino Gay Men in the Diaspora*. Perverse Modernities. Durham: Duke UP, 2003.

Manganaro, Marc. *Culture, 1922: The Emergence of a Concept*. Princeton: Princeton UP, 2002.

Mardorossian, Carine M. "From Literature of Exile to Migrant Literature." *Modern Language Studies* 32.2 (2002): 15–33.

Massey, Doreen. *Space, Place, and Gender*. Minneapolis: U of Minnesota P, 1994.

Matar, Nabil I., ed. and trans. *In the Lands of the Christians: Arabic Travel Writing in the Seventeenth Century*. London: Routledge, 2003.

―――. *Turks, Moors, and Englishmen in the Age of Discovery*. New York: Columbia UP, 1999.

McArthur, Tom. *Oxford Guide to World English*. Oxford: Oxford UP, 2002.

McCall, Sophie. "The Forty-Ninth Parallel and Other Borders: Recent Directions in Native North American Literary Criticism." *Canadian Review of American Studies* 34.2 (2004): 205–20.

McClennen, Sophia A. "After Civilization: The Theory and Practice of Introducing Latin American Culture." *ADFL Bulletin* 34.2 (2003): 6–14.

McClintock, Anne. *Imperial Leather: Race, Gender, and Sexuality in the Colonial Context*. London: Routledge, 1995.

McDowell, Linda. *Gender, Identity, and Place: Understanding Feminist Geographies*. Minneapolis: U of Minnesota P, 1999.

Meilaender, Peter C. *Toward a Theory of Immigration*. New York: Palgrave, 2001.

Mendoza, Louis, and S. Shankar, eds. *Crossing into America: The New Literature of Immigration*. New York: New, 2003.

Menon, Ritu, and Kamla Bhasin. *Borders and Boundaries: Women in India's Partition*. New Brunswick: Rutgers UP, 1998.

Michaelsen, Scott, and David E. Johnson, eds. *Border Theory: The Limits of Cultural Politics*. Minneapolis: U of Minnesota P, 1997.

Mignolo, Walter D. *The Darker Side of the Renaissance: Literacy, Territoriality, and Colonization*. Ann Arbor: U of Michigan P, 1995.

―――. *Local Histories / Global Designs: Coloniality, Subaltern Knowledges, and Border Thinking*. Princeton: Princeton UP, 2000.

―――. "The Many Faces of Cosmo-polis: Border Thinking and Critical Cosmopolitanism." Breckenridge, Pollock, Bhabha, and Chakrabarty 157–88.

Mohanty, S. P. "Between 'Us' and 'Them': On the Philosophical Bases of Political Criticism." *Yale Journal of Criticism* 2.2 (1989): 1–31.

Moore, David Chioni. "Is the Post- in Postcolonial the Post- in Post-Soviet? Toward a Global Postcolonial Critique." *PMLA* 116 (2001): 111–28.

Mordecai, Pamela. *Certifiable*. Toronto: Goose Lane, 2001.

Moretti, Franco. "Conjectures on World Literature." *New Left Review*. 2nd ser. 1 (2000): 54–68.

Morley, David, and Kuan-Hsing Chen, eds. *Stuart Hall: Critical Dialogues in Cultural Studies*. London: Routledge, 1996.

Mudimbe-Boyi, Elisabeth, ed. *Beyond Dichotomies: Histories, Identities, Cultures, and the Challenge of Globalization*. Albany: State U of New York P, 2003.

Muller, Gilbert H. *New Strangers in Paradise: The Immigrant Experience and Contemporary American Fiction*. Lexington: UP of Kentucky, 1999.

―――, ed. *The New World Reader: Thinking and Writing about the Global Community*. Boston: Houghton, 2005.

Narayan, Kirin. "How Native Is a 'Native' Anthropologist?" *American Anthropologist* 95 (1993): 671–86.

Narayan, Uma. *Dislocating Cultures: Identities, Traditions, and Third World Feminism*. London: Routledge, 1997.

Needham, Anuradha Dingwaney. *Using the Master's Tools: Resistance and the Literature of the African and South Asian Diasporas*. New York: St. Martin's, 2000.

Nicholls, David G. *Conjuring the Folk: Forms of Modernity in African America*. Ann Arbor: U of Michigan P, 2000.

Nixon, Rob. *Homelands, Harlem, and Hollywood: South African Culture and the World Beyond*. London: Routledge, 1994.

Nussbaum, Martha C. *For Love of Country: Debating the Limits of Patriotism: Martha Nussbaum with Respondents*. Ed. Joshua Cohen. Boston: Beacon, 1996.

Okri, Ben. *The Famished Road*. New York: Doubleday, 1992.

Olaniyan, Tejumola. *Scars of Conquest / Masks of Resistance: The Invention of Cultural Identities in African, African-American, and Caribbean Drama*. Oxford: Oxford UP, 1995.

Papastergiadis, Nikos. "Restless Hybrids." *Third Text* 32 (1995): 9–18.

―――. *The Turbulence of Migration: Globalization, Deterritorialization and Hybridity*. Cambridge: Polity, 2000.

Parmar, Prabhjot, and Nila Somaia-Carten, eds. *When Your Voice Tastes like Home: Immigrant Women Write*. Toronto: Second Story, 2003.

Patton, Cindy, and Benigno Sánchez-Eppler, eds. *Queer Diasporas*. Durham: Duke UP, 2000.

Payant, Katherine B., and Toby Rose, eds. *The Immigrant Experience in North American Literature: Carving out a Niche*. Westport: Greenwood, 1999.

Pease, Donald E., and Robyn Wiegman, eds. *The Futures of American Studies*. Durham: Duke UP, 2002.

Pérez, Loida Maritza. *Geographies of Home*. New York: Viking, 1999.

Pieterse, Jan Nederveen. "Globalization as Hybridization." *Global Modernities*. Ed. Mike Featherstone, Scott Lash, and Roland Robertson. London: Sage, 1995. 45–68.

Polkinhorn, Harr, José Manuel Di-Bella, and Rogelio Reyes, eds. *Borderlands Literature: Towards an Integrated Perspective*. San Diego: Inst. for Regional Studies of the Californias, 1990.

Portes, Alejandro, and Min Zhou. "The New Second Generation: Segmented Assimilation and Its Variants." Suárez-Orozco, Suárez-Orozco, and Qin-Hilliard, *New Immigration* 85–104.

Pratt, Mary Louise. *Imperial Eyes: Travel Writing and Transculturation*. London: Routledge, 1992.

Purdom, Judy. "Mapping Difference." *Third Text* 32 (Autumn 1995): 19–32.

Ra'ad, Basem L. "Primal Scenes of Globalization: Legacies of Canaan and Etruria." *PMLA* 116 (2001): 89–110.

Radhakrishnan, R. *Diasporic Mediations: Between Home and Location.* Minneapolis: U of Minnesota P, 1996.

———. *Theory in an Uneven World.* Oxford: Blackwell, 2003.

Ramazani, Jahan. *The Hybrid Muse: Postcolonial Poetry in English.* Chicago: U of Chicago P, 2001.

Ramos, Julio. *Divergent Modernities: Culture and Politics in Nineteenth-Century Latin America.* Trans. John D. Blanco. Durham: Duke UP, 2001.

Rich, Adrienne. "Notes toward a Politics of Location." *Blood, Bread, and Poetry: Selected Prose, 1979–1985.* New York: Norton, 1986. 210–31.

Ritivoi, Andreea Deciu. *Yesterday's Self: Nostalgia and the Immigrant Identity.* Lanham: Rowman, 2002.

Rodgers, Lawrence R. *Canaan Bound: The African American Great Migration Novel.* Urbana: U of Illinois P, 1997.

Rosaldo, Renato. *Culture and Truth: The Remaking of Social Analysis.* Rev. ed. Boston: Beacon, 1993.

Rowe, John Carlos. *The New American Studies.* Minneapolis: U of Minnesota P, 2002.

———, ed. *Post-nationalist American Studies.* Berkeley: U of California P, 2000.

Rozema, Vicki. *Voices from the Trail of Tears.* Winston-Salem: Blair, 2003.

Rushdie, Salman. *Imaginary Homelands: Essays and Criticism, 1981–1991.* London: Penguin, 1991.

———. *The Satanic Verses.* New York: Viking, 1989.

Safran, William. "Diasporas in Modern Societies: Myths of Homeland and Return." *Diaspora* 1.1 (1991): 83–99.

Said, Edward W. *Culture and Imperialism.* New York: Vintage, 1994.

———. *Orientalism.* New York: Vintage, 1978.

———. *Out of Place: A Memoir.* New York: Vintage, 1999.

———. "Reflections on Exile." 1984. *"Reflections on Exile" and Other Essays.* Cambridge: Harvard UP, 2002. 173–86.

Saint, Ravikant, and Tarun K. Saint. *Translating Partition.* New Delhi: Katha, 2001.

Saldívar, José David. *Border Matters: Remapping American Cultural Studies.* Berkeley: U of California P, 1997.

———. *The Dialectics of Our America: Genealogy, Cultural Critique, and Literary History.* Durham: Duke UP, 1991.

Sanderson, Stephen K., ed. *Civilization and World Systems: Studying World-Historical Change.* London: Sage, 1995.

Sarup, Madan. "Home and Identity." *Travellers' Tales: Narratives of Home and Displacement.* Ed. George Robertson, Melinda Mash, Lisa Tickner, Jon Bird, Barry Curtis, and Tim Putnam. London: Routledge, 1994. 93–104.

Saussy, Haun, ed. *Comparative Literature in an Age of Globalization.* Baltimore: Johns Hopkins UP, 2006.

———. *Great Walls of Discourse and Other Adventures in Cultural China.* Cambridge: Harvard U Asia Center, 2001.

———. *The Problem of a Chinese Aesthetic.* Stanford: Stanford UP, 1995.

Schreibersdorf, Lisa. "Hyphens on the Home Front: Imagining American Culture through the German-American Hyphen, 1911–1919." Diss. U of Wisconsin, Madison, 2005.

Seigneurie, Ken, ed. *Crisis and Memory: The Representation of Space in Modern Levantine Narrative.* Wiesbaden, Ger.: Reichert, 2003.

Seyhan, Azade. *Writing outside the Nation.* Princeton: Princeton UP, 2001.

Sherman, Joseph. *Constructing Immigrant Identity: The "Kaffireatnik" in South African Yiddish Literature.* Johannesburg: Inst. for Advanced Social Research, U of the Witwatersrand, 1997.

Shohat, Ella, ed. *Talking Visions: Multicultural Feminism in a Transnational Age.* Cambridge: MIT P, 1999.

Shreiber, Maeera Y. "The End of Exile: Jewish Identity and Its Diasporic Poetics." *PMLA* 113 (1998): 273–87.

Shukla, Sandhya. *India Abroad: Diasporic Cultures of Postwar America and England.* Princeton: Princeton UP, 2003.

Simone, Roberta. *The Immigrant Experience in American Fiction: An Annotated Bibliography.* Metuchen: Scarecrow, 1994.

Singh, Jyotsna. *Colonial Narratives / Cultural Dialogues: "Discoveries" of India in the Language of Colonialism.* London: Routledge, 1996.

Smith, Anna Deveare. *Fires in the Mirror: Crown Heights, Brooklyn, and Other Identities.* New York: Doubleday, 1994.

Soja, Edward W. *Postmodern Geographies: The Reassertion of Space in Critical Social Theory.* London: Verso, 1989.

Sollors, Werner. *The Invention of Ethnicity.* New York: Oxford UP, 1989.

———, ed. *Multilingual America: Transnationalism, Ethnicity, and the Languages of American Literature.* New York: New York UP, 1998.

Spillers, Hortense J., ed. *Comparative American Identities: Race, Sex, and Nationality in the Modern Text.* New York: Routledge, 1991.

———. "Introduction: Peter's Pans: Eating in the Diaspora." *Black, White, and in Color: Essays on American Literature and Culture.* Chicago: U of Chicago P, 2003. 1–64.

Spivak, Gayatri Chakravorty. *Death of a Discipline.* New York: Columbia UP, 2003.

———. *In Other Worlds: Essays in Cultural Politics.* London: Methuen, 1987.

———. *The Post-colonial Critic: Interviews, Strategies, Dialogues.* Ed. Sarah Harasym. London: Routledge, 1990.

Spyer, Patricia, ed. *Border Fetishisms: Material Objects in Unstable Spaces.* London: Routledge, 1998.

Stallybrass, Peter, and Allon White. *The Politics and Poetics of Transgression.* Ithaca: Cornell UP, 1986.

Stavans, Ilan. *Spanglish: The Making of a New American Language.* New York: Rayo, 2003.

Stephan, Halina, ed. *Living in Translation: Polish Writers in America*. New York: Rodopi, 2003.

Suárez-Orozco, Marcelo M. "Everything You Ever Wanted to Know about Assimilation but Were Afraid to Ask." Suárez-Orozco, Suárez-Orozco, and Qin-Hilliard, *New Immigration* 67–84.

Suárez-Orozco, Marcelo, Carola Suárez-Orozco, and Desirée Qin-Hilliard, eds. *Interdisciplinary Perspectives on the New Immigration*. 6 vols. London: Routledge, 2001–05.

———. *The New Immigration: An Interdisciplinary Reader*. London: Routledge, 2005.

Takaki, Ronald. *A Different Mirror: A History of Multi-cultural America*. Boston: Little, 1993.

———. *Strangers from a Different Shore: A History of Asian Americans*. New York: Penguin, 1989.

Tambiah, Stanley J. "Transnational Movements, Diaspora, and Multiple Modernities." *Daedalus* 129.1 (2000): 163–94.

Taussig, Michael. *Mimesis and Alterity: A Particular History of the Senses*. London: Routledge, 1993.

"Theories and Methodologies: Comparative Literature." *PMLA* 118 (2003): 326–41.

"Theories and Methodologies: Gloria Anzaldúa." *PMLA* 121 (2006): 225–94.

Tölölyan, Khachig. "The Nation-State and Its Others: In Lieu of a Preface." *Diaspora* 1.1 (1991): 3–7.

Trinh T. Minh-ha. "An Acoustic Journey." Welchman 1–17.

———. *Woman, Native, Other: Writing Postcoloniality and Feminism*. Bloomington: Indiana UP, 1989.

Trouillot, Michel-Rolph. "Anthropology and the Savage Slot: The Poetics and Politics of Otherness." Fox 17–44.

Ty, Eleanor, and David C. Goellnicht, eds. *Asian North American Identities: Beyond the Hyphen*. Bloomington: Indiana UP, 2004.

Van Hear, Nicholas. *New Diasporas: The Mass Exodus, Dispersal, and Regrouping of Migrant Communities*. Seattle: U of Washington P, 1998.

Vertovec, Steven, and Robin Cohen, eds. *Conceiving Cosmopolitanism*. Oxford: Oxford UP, 2002.

———, eds. *Migration, Diasporas and Transnationalism*. Cheltenham, Eng.: Elgar Reference Collection, 1999.

Vila, Pablo. "Conclusion: The Limits of American Border Theory." Vila, *Ethnography* 306–42.

———, ed. *Ethnography at the Border*. Minneapolis: U of Minnesota P, 2003.

Visweswaran, Kamala. *Fictions of Feminist Ethnography*. Minneapolis: U of Minnesota P, 1994.

Vitkus, Daniel J., ed. *Piracy, Slavery, and Redemption: Barbary Captivity Narratives from Early Modern England*. New York: Columbia UP, 2001.

———, ed. *Three Turk Plays from Early Modern England*. New York: Columbia UP, 2000.

Walkowitz, Rebecca. *Cosmopolitan Style: Modernism beyond the Nation*. New York: Columbia UP, 2006.

Wallerstein, Immanuel. *The End of the World As We Know It: Social Science for the Twenty-First Century*. Minneapolis: U of Minnesota P, 1998.

Walsh, Rebecca, ed. *Global Diasporas*. Spec. issue of *Interventions: International Journal of Postcolonial Studies* 5.1 (2003): 1–158.

Walters, Wendy. *At Home in Diaspora: Black International Writing*. Minneapolis: U of Minnesota P, 2005.

Waters, Malcolm. *Globalization*. London: Routledge, 1995.

Weatherford, Jack. *Genghis Khan and the Making of the Modern World*. New York: Three Rivers, 2004.

Weber, Donald. *Haunted in the New World: Jewish American Culture from Cahan to* The Goldbergs. Bloomington: Indiana UP, 2005.

Weglyn, Michi. *Years of Infamy: The Untold Story of America's Concentration Camps*. Rev. ed. Seattle: U of Washington P, 1996.

Welchman, John C., ed. *Rethinking Borders*. Minneapolis: U of Minnesota P, 1996.

Werbner, Pnina, and Tariq Modood, eds. *Debating Cultural Hybridity: Multi-cultural Identities and the Politics of Anti-racism*. London: Zed, 1997.

Wettstein, Howard, ed. *Diasporas and Exiles: Varieties of Jewish Experience*. Berkeley: U of California P, 2002.

Whitehead, Neil L., ed. *The Discoverie of the Large, Rich and Bewtiful Empyre of Guiana*. By Walter Ralegh. Norman: U of Oklahoma P, 1998.

Williams, Patrick, and Laura Chrisman, eds. *Colonial Discourse and Post-colonial Theory: A Reader*. New York: Columbia UP, 1994.

Willis, Katie, and Brenda Yeoh, eds. *Gender and Migration*. Cheltenham, Eng.: Elgar Reference Collection, 2000.

Wilson, Sarah. "Modernism and the Melting Pot." Modernist Studies Assn. Annual Conf. Chicago Marriott Downtown, Chicago. 3 Nov. 2005.

Wolff, Janet. *Resident Alien: Feminist Cultural Criticism*. New Haven: Yale UP, 1995.

Yamada, Mitsuye. *Camp Notes and Other Writings*. 1976. New Brunswick: Rutgers UP, 1998.

Yezierska, Anzia. *Bread Givers*. 1924. New York: Persea, 1999.

Young, Robert J. C. *Colonial Desire: Hybridity in Theory, Culture and Race*. London: Routledge, 1995.

Yuval-Davis, Nira. *Gender and Nation*. London: Sage, 1997.

Zaborowska, Magdalena J. *How We Found America: Reading Gender through East-European Immigrant Narratives*. Chapel Hill: U of North Carolina P, 1995.

Zangwill, Israel. *The Melting-Pot: Drama in Four Acts*. 1909. Rev. ed. New York: Macmillan, 1920.

Zhang, Longxi. *Allegoresis: Reading Canonical Literature East and West*. Ithaca: Cornell UP, 2005.

Zhang, Yingjin, ed. *China in a Polycentric World: Essays in Chinese Comparative Literature*. Stanford: Stanford UP, 1998.

⁓ Translation Studies

LAWRENCE VENUTI

THEORIES AND PRACTICES

Since the 1950s translation has gradually emerged as an area of instruction and research in the Americas as well as elsewhere. Yet in comparison with academic trends in such other regions as Europe and Asia, American translation studies remains very much a fledgling discipline that has not developed to the same degree or in the same manner in every place. This situation is due partly to the global dominance of English, to its status as the language that is the most translated worldwide but relatively little translated into. Contributing factors specific to academic institutions include the greater value assigned to literary criticism and linguistic research than to translation practice and the widespread reliance on foreign language pedagogies that privilege direct communication and therefore preempt or subordinate translation. As a result, translation studies has thrived in American cultures in which Spanish or Portuguese is the native language or in which French has achieved an ascendancy that rivals the power of English. Programs designed to train translators are located primarily in South American countries and Canada, not in the United States, where relatively few colleges and universities have instituted curricula for translation practice and instruction in

translation occurs predominantly in isolated courses offered in foreign language departments and creative writing programs (see Caminade and Pym [periodically updated at www.fut.es/~apym]; Harris).

When we turn to the issue of research, these uneven developments are further complicated by disciplinary divisions. Because translation research is scattered across various institutional sites, including not only applied linguistics but also foreign languages and literatures, English, comparative literature, philosophy, and anthropology, it is fragmented among diverse and conflicting methodologies. Hence, although degrees and concentrations in translation research have been created in American graduate programs, they reveal different emphases that answer to specializations and trends in particular disciplines as well as to the expertise of current faculty members, and a uniform or even a core curriculum has yet to materialize. Methodological fragmentation is in fact characteristic of translation studies around the world, and it appears in various guises. Perhaps the most crucial distinction is that between theory and practice.

These two categories are remarkably close for translation, interrelated and reciprocal in their effects, much more so than for such fields as literary criticism and composition as they are now configured. Innovative research in translation, whether theoretically or historically oriented, can lead to new translation practices, at once inspiring and justifying different ways to translate; innovative practices, whether spurred by a specific cultural situation, the appearance of a unique text type, or the invention of a communications medium, can lead to new theoretical concepts and research projects. Such interrelations between theory and practice are not only typical of translation today; they actually date back to classical antiquity. Among the most influential cases is Cicero's recommendation of free translating as a pedagogical exercise for the orator: his brief remarks in *De optimo genere oratorum* (46 BC) inaugurate a long tradition of sense-for-sense translation (stressing the capture of meaning over the imitation of word order and other formal properties), which is variously conceptualized and implemented by such different figures as Jerome and Luther, D'Ablancourt and Dryden, Matthew Arnold and Eugene Nida. In humanistic disciplines, theory can take various and sometimes eclectic forms, even in the same discipline, and these forms will reflect the sites where the research is carried out. Translation is no exception.

> **Interrelations between theory and practice are not only typical of translation today; they actually date back to classical antiquity.**

Not unexpectedly, translation research that issues from training programs has emphasized the practical application of theoretical concepts as students are prepared for employment in the translation market. In 1958 Jean-Paul Vinay and Jean Darbelnet published an extremely influential work, *Stylistique comparée de français et de l'anglais*, which initiated and in many ways remains typical of this prevailing trend: using the findings of comparative stylistics, they codified various methods or procedures for translating between French and English (for a more recent example, see Hervey and Higgins). The practical approach to research foregrounds linguistic analysis of the foreign and translated texts while examining the relations between them with an eye toward solving translation problems. Subsequent research in this vein has incorporated theoretical

concepts from various branches of linguistics, including systemic-functional linguistics, discourse analysis, and pragmatics. Basil Hatim and Ian Mason's *The Translator as Communicator* (1997) deploys an array of such concepts, taking into account style, genre, and ideology in a broad range of languages and text types (see also Nord, *Text Analysis*; Baker, *In Other Words*).

In institutional sites where translation research has lacked a direct connection to training, the most widely adopted approaches have been less linguistic than literary and cultural, philosophical and political. Consequently, practical applications have not been consistently emphasized. In 1955, while writing his own English translation of Aleksandr Pushkin's verse novel *Eugene Onegin*, Vladimir Nabokov assessed previous versions and described the sources and prosody of the Russian text so as to argue for the most literal translation method supplemented by extensive annotations. By the 1980s, however, after absorbing European theoretical discourses for more than two decades, translation research had taken a more speculative turn. Walter Benjamin's philosophical essay "The Task of the Translator" (1923) assumed unprecedented importance, attracting several critical commentaries that used poststructuralist styles of thinking to interpret Benjaminian notions like the "pure language" released by translation (see Jacobs; Derrida, "Des tours"; de Man; A. Benjamin; Johnston). The prevailing trend in this line of research relies on poststructuralism, remaining on the level of theoretical speculation, or synthesizes it with varieties of Marxism, feminism, and psychoanalysis to develop projects that are historically oriented or politically engaged or both. Translation thus becomes a cultural practice that enables a consideration of such issues as nationalism, colonialism and postcolonialism, gender and sexual identity, and globalization (see Cheyfitz; Niranjana; Bhabha; Simon; Cronin). Here linguistic analysis is minimized and in some cases excluded in favor of formulating theoretical concepts, reconstructing social situations and historical moments, and performing ideological critiques.

One might wonder whether the different strands of translation studies are fated to autonomous development or susceptible to productive syntheses. At present, the greatest divide in research methodologies lies between varieties of linguistics-based approaches, on the one hand, and approaches informed by literary and cultural studies, on the other. Although it seems possible to demarcate areas where they complement each other, such an effort is potentially oversimplifying and misleading because of the disparities between their theoretical traditions and conceptual discourses. It can, however, be illuminating to juxtapose different treatments of the same problems, submitting their concepts and methods to an interrogation that exposes strengths and limitations.

In this essay, I take three sets of problems that are central to recent developments in translation research—equivalence and shifts, cultural systems and norms, ethics and politics—and consider the work of leading scholars who have significantly influenced our thinking about them. The focus throughout is on interlingual translation, rewriting in a different language, which has so far received less attention in the United States than forms of translation that are intralingual—rewriting or rewording in the same language, as often happens in textual interpretation—or intersemiotic, transformation into a different sign system, as in film adaptations of literary or dramatic texts (these distinctions rely on Jakobson). Largely for reasons of space I set aside interpreting, or oral translation, a practice that in the Americas as elsewhere is widely performed in various social settings and institutions, including academic conferences and law courts, refugee hearings and social service agencies. Although interpreting is receiving more and more attention from scholars, the bulk of the research has addressed issues of practice and pedagogy, regardless of the problems it shares with written translation (for a survey of the research, see

Pöchhacker and Shlesinger). The field deserves a separate treatment.

EQUIVALENCE AND SHIFTS

By *equivalence* I mean the varying concepts of adequacy, correspondence, fidelity, identity, or resemblance that have been proposed to describe the relation between the foreign and translated texts and to determine translation accuracy or correctness. Most translation theory has assumed that translating is primarily communicative of the form and meaning of the foreign text, an assumption that makes equivalence an essential goal of every translation even if the precise significance assigned to the concept can vary widely. "Translation equivalence," states the linguist J. C. Catford, "occurs when a SL [source language] and a TL [target language] text or item are relatable to (at least some of) the same features of substance," where "substance" can signify a definite range of linguistic levels and categories as well as an unlimited series of cultural situations (50). Substance is usually defined in terms that are grammatical and lexical, stylistic and generic, but it may also be functionalist, defined by the purpose that the translation is designed to serve in the receiving culture (see Koller, *Einführung*; Reiss, *Möglichkeiten*). The sheer number of possible definitions shows that equivalence cannot be ascertained merely by comparing the foreign and translated texts; a third, metalinguistic term must be applied to establish and specify a basis of comparison between them. This third term, moreover, is interpretive: not only does it reflect the concepts and methods of a particular discipline, more often than not a branch of linguistics, but also on application it fixes an invariant in the foreign text that is subsequently used to indicate the existence and degree of equivalence. Thus it is potentially normative, likely to be used to prescribe a translation method or choice.

Any concept of equivalence must also take into

Shifts are inevitable . . . because of the structural differences between languages and the cultural differences between audiences.

account translation shifts or deviations from the foreign text. In fact, an analysis that establishes a relation of equivalence will simultaneously reveal points of deviation distributed throughout the translation. Shifts are inevitable features of translations because of the structural differences between languages and the cultural differences between audiences. As a result, they cannot be simply labeled as translation errors. On the contrary, some theorists have suggested that shifts are designed to secure equivalence at a higher level than the word, phrase, or sentence. Anton Popovič argues that "shifts do not occur because a translator wishes to 'change' a work, but because he strives to reproduce it as faithfully as possible and to grasp it in its totality, as an organic whole" (80).

Shifts have accordingly been understood as a means of solving translation problems that result from the irreducible linguistic and cultural differences of the foreign text. A shift may compensate for a formal or semantic loss. A typical compensation is the insertion of a brief explanation for terms and allusions that are unfamiliar to the projected readership of the translation, especially features that are deeply rooted in the foreign culture. Compensations may also include free renderings or substitutions intended to produce an effect that the translator could not produce in the translation at precisely the same place that it occurs in the foreign text (see Harvey).

Far from putting into question the concept of equivalence, the inevitability of shifts has actually led to reformulations that validate free, paraphrastic translating. This development can be seen in the highly influential work of Nida, who in the 1960s consolidated centuries of translation theory and practice by distinguishing between "formal" and "dynamic" equivalence and generally recommending the latter. For Nida, "formal equivalence focuses attention on the message itself, in both form and meaning," and is usually reserved for scholarly translations, whereas dynamic equivalence

> is based upon "the principle of equivalent effect." In such a translation one is not so concerned with matching the receptor-language message with the source-language message, but with the dynamic relationship, that the relationship between receptor and message should be substantially the same as that which existed between the original receptors and the message. A translation of dynamic equivalence aims at complete naturalness of expression, and tries to relate the receptor to modes of behavior relevant within the context of his own culture. . . . One of the modern English translations which, perhaps more than any other, seeks for equivalent effect is J. B. Phillips' rendering of the New Testament. In Romans 16:16 he quite naturally translates "greet one another with a holy kiss [*philemati agioi*]" as "give one another a hearty handshake all around." (159)

The obvious differences between a "holy kiss" and a "hearty handshake" suggest that dynamic equivalence depends on reducing the foreign text to a semantic core, an extremely simplified form of the meaning, which is then reconstructed in a form that is culturally relevant to the receptors. As Nida later made explicit, the underlying linguistic theory is generally based on Noam Chomsky's transformational generative grammar: the foreign text is seen as containing a structural kernel that the translator abstracts through a reductive analysis and then restructures in the translating language (Nida and Taber).

Nonetheless, one may doubt whether this process actually results in equivalence. If the translator assimilates the foreign text to "modes of behavior" in the receiving culture, the effect can be regarded as equivalent only if linguistic and cultural differences are not seen as constitutive of meaning, only if universals are assumed to exist at some deeper level to enable communication. It can be argued that Nida's very example exposes insurmountable differences. Because a kiss, no matter how holy, is patently not a handshake, Phillips's translation has not so much communicated an invariant meaning as inscribed the Pauline epistle with a different set of cultural values, a squeamishness, possibly a prudery—even a masculinism, if we regard a handshake as a distinctively masculine form of greeting at the time he was translating: Phillips began his version of the New Testament in the

1940s. In his foreword to the complete translation, Phillips himself recognized the "gulf" between the two phrases, but he viewed his task as effacing it: "to introduce such an expression [as 'a holy kiss'] into a modern English translation immediately reveals the gulf between the early Christians and ourselves, the very thing which I as a translator am trying to bridge" (ix–x). Here any equivalence is compromised by the "sensibilities of modern English readers" for whom Phillips wrote, and translation functions as acculturation, even as an affirmation of those readers' sensibilities in view of the enormous cultural authority of the foreign text (ix).

In linking dynamic equivalence to "complete naturalness of expression," Nida is prescribing a particular translation strategy, a fluency or easy readability that relies on current standard usage, the most familiar dialect, or in Phillips's practice "modern English." The effect of this strategy is to ensure that the inscription of receiving cultural values becomes invisible to the reader. A translation that appears natural is likely to pass as transparent or seemingly untranslated during the reading experience, as a text originally written in the translating language, even as the foreign original. And indeed Phillips asserted that the first "test" of a "good" translation "is simply that it must not sound like a translation at all. If it is skillfully done, and we are not previously informed, we should be quite unaware that it is a translation, even though the work we are reading is far distant from us in both time and place" (vii). Dynamic equivalence thus produces a peculiar illusion for the reader: not only does it displace what is foreign about the foreign text and substitute values that are accepted in the receiving culture but it simultaneously conceals the very act of displacement and substitution while implying that the receiving values communicate the truth of that text.

Both Nida and Phillips underestimate—in fact fail to consider—the economy of loss and gain in the translation process. Translating is radically decontextualizing: the linguistic structures that constitute the foreign text are dismantled, if not entirely jettisoned, whereby that text is stripped of its connotations and intertextual

connections, the linguistic, literary, and cultural contexts that make it meaningful to native readers who have read widely in their language and literature. At the same time, in the move to the translating language, the foreign text is recontextualized: the translator creates different structures laden with different connotations and connections, which are intended to be imitative of the foreign text, to be sure, but which always add formal and semantic dimensions because they signify in the receiving language and culture. The loss of foreign contexts, both intratextual and intertextual, is irreparable and casts doubt on the possibility of an equivalent response, on the notion that a reader of a translation can respond to it in the same way that the foreign reader responds to the foreign text. A scholarly apparatus can help restore the foreign contexts, but only at the cost of restricting the audience to academic readers, who in many cases were not the foreign author's projected readership.

To take into account the simultaneous loss and gain in translation, we might turn to poststructuralist thinking about language and textuality. Jacques Derrida, for example, uses translation to illustrate his concept of iterability, the fact that the meaning of any sign can change because a sign "can break with every given context and engender infinitely new contexts in an absolutely nonsaturable fashion" ("Signature" 320). Hence the recontextualizing work of translation transforms the foreign text, although any transformation is guided fundamentally by the structural differences between languages.

Philip E. Lewis draws on contrastive linguistics to describe more specifically the "deplorable impasse" with which iterability confronts the translator. He observes:

> Translation has to move whatever meanings it captures from the original into a framework that tends to impose a different set of discursive relations and a different construction of reality. When English rearticulates a French utterance, it puts an interpretation on that utterance that is built into English. (35)

Lewis acknowledges, like Nida, that this process involves a "double interpretation," an analysis of the foreign text and of the translating language.

Unlike Nida, however, he avoids any analytic reduction to a core meaning and instead argues that the two interpretations are "mutually exclusive" (36). Poststructuralist thinkers like Derrida and Lewis have brought a greater awareness of the inscriptive force of language, challenging any simplistic notion of translation as the communication of a univocal meaning inherent in the foreign text.

Yet this awareness does not lead Lewis to abandon the concept of equivalence; rather, he reformulates it as "fidelity to much more than semantic substance, fidelity also to the modalities of expression and to rhetorical strategies," to the chain of signifiers, to syntax and discourse (41). He terms this sort of equivalence "abusive": the translator seeks to reproduce whatever features of the foreign text abuse or resist dominant values in the foreign language and culture, yet this reproductive effort requires the invention of analogous means of signification that are doubly abusive, that resist dominant values in the translating language and culture while exceeding and even "directing a critical thrust back toward" the foreign text (43). Thus if Phillips's translating had been governed by abusive fidelity instead of dynamic equivalence, he might have resorted to the close rendering he refused, "a holy kiss," already unusual in the Greek text for its paradoxical combination of eroticism with Christian piety. Such a rendering would not only reproduce the startling effect of the phrase but also exaggerate it in Phillips's own, much more morally conservative, situation in the 1940s. This exaggeration might in turn question the laconic nonchalance with which Paul uses it in addressing the Roman Christians.

Lewis's concept of equivalence is just as prescriptive as Nida's. But whether abusive fidelity can be generally applied to translation, whatever the text type, remains unclear (for an attempt at a more general application, see Venuti, *Translator's Invisibility*). Lewis in fact formulated it for the express purpose of describing and evaluating an English translation of Derrida's essay "La mythologie blanche," a piece that is typical of the philosopher's stylistically inventive writing. No such qualification needs to be made regarding Nida's concept of dynamic equivalence: fluent, acculturating translation continues to be the dominant strategy worldwide, regardless of the language and culture. It is hardly limited to Indo-European languages and Christian cultures. During the twentieth century, for instance, Arabic translators revised Shakespeare's plays to make them acceptable to Muslim audiences, not only deleting offensive words and phrases but also inserting allusions to the Qur'an (Amin-Zaki).

CULTURAL SYSTEMS AND NORMS

Too often theories of equivalence have risked an ahistorical comparison between the foreign and translated texts without fully considering the various cultural and social forces that shape translation at any historical moment. During the 1970s a group of theorists began to address this limitation by developing the work of the Russian formalists and the Prague Linguistic Circle (this pioneering research first appeared in Even-Zohar, *Papers*; Toury, *In Search*; and Hermans). Jurij Tynjanov's concept of literature as a "system of the functions of the literary order which are in continual interrelationship with other orders" (72) lies behind Itamar Even-Zohar's more general concept of culture as a semiotic "polysystem—a multiple system, a system of various systems which intersect with each other and partly overlap, using concurrently different options, yet functioning as one structured whole, whose members are interdependent" (*Polysystem Studies* 11). For Even-Zohar, translated literature itself constitutes one such system, and its precise nature is defined by its "function," that is to say, its interrelation with the values, forms, and practices that comprise the "repertoire" of the literary system as a whole (10, 39–40, 45–46). Just as Tynjanov observed that "a system is not an equal interaction of all elements but places a group of elements in the foreground—the 'dominant' " (72), Even-Zohar insists on the hierarchical arrangement of values, forms, and practices, distinguishing between the "canonized" and the "non-canonized" or between the "center" and the "periphery" in a polysystem as well as in each of its constituent systems (13–17). Hence, any literary system is heterogeneous and dynamic; change occurs through oppositional interactions between its centers and peripheries. Translation, like other cultural practices, can precipitate systemic change or maintain the status quo. In Even-Zohar's view, it is the position of translation in a literary system that determines whether it is "innovatory," active in the creation of a new repertoire, or "conservatory," active in reinforcing a dominant repertoire and the hierarchy in which it is situated (46–48).

Crucial to polysystem theory is the concept of norms, the values that inform cultural production. Gideon Toury's work has done much to illuminate the sense in which translation is a "norm-governed activity." Toury offers a typology of the various norms that affect every stage in the translation process, from the selection of foreign texts to the development of discursive strategies to translate them (*Descriptive Translation Studies* 53–69). Although he assumes that "translation behaviour within a culture tends to manifest certain *regularities*," he is nonetheless careful to point out that the norms governing a body of translations or even a particular translation may be multiple and conflicting (56). As a result, studying translation norms requires both a close analysis of the translated text and a detailed reconstruction of the cultural situation in which it was produced. The analysis can include shifts: textual features where the translation deviates from the foreign text are likely to reveal the pressure of linguistic, literary, and cultural norms that can then be inferred from the particular shift. The most decisive norms for translation thus become the diverse values circulating in the receiving system. For Even-Zohar and Toury, translation studies calls for a "target" orientation, treating translations "as facts of the culture that hosts them, with the concomitant assumption that whatever their function and identity, these are constituted within that same culture and reflect its own constellation" (Toury, *Descriptive Translation Studies* 24).

Polysystem theory marks a significant advance over primarily linguistics-based attempts to theorize translation equivalence. By establishing translation as a fact of the target culture, Even-Zohar and Toury have delimited the translated text as an object of study in its own right, relatively autonomous from the foreign text. They have thereby set new agendas for translation studies, including not only the examination of large corpora of translations but also speculative research that derives its methodology from linguistics. Toury's work on norms underlies the discourse analyst Shoshana Blum-Kulka's effort to discern what is unique about the language of translated texts by concentrating on such discursive features as cohesion and coherence. Through analyses of shifts and their impact on the meaning of translated texts in various genres, literary and nonliterary, Blum-Kulka formulated an "explicitation hypothesis," in which she "postulates an observed cohesive explicitness from SL to TL texts regardless of the increase traceable to differences between the two linguistic and textual systems involved" (19). Explicitation can be seen in a larger number of cohesive devices, such as conjunction, repetition, and substitution, which increase the semantic unity of the translation, although it can also take the form of an expansive rendering that adds precise details or even an explanatory phrase (see Halliday and Hasan).

Blum-Kulka suggests that explicitation might be "a universal strategy inherent in the process of language mediation, as practiced by language learners, non-professional translators and professional translators alike" (21). Yet in taking this universalist turn, she actually departs from the fundamentally historicist method of polysystem theory. Toury's response to her claim is telling: he argues that it needs to be qualified according to various factors—including the agents who perform the explicitation, whether language learners or translators; the kinds of translating during which it is performed, whether oral or written; and the cultural system in which it occurs, "cultures that assign centrality to translating and translations vs. cultures where they

> **The norms governing a body of translations or even a particular translation may be multiple and conflicting.**

are marginalized" (*Descriptive Translation Studies* 227).

Polysystem theory demands a rigorous contextualization that demonstrates the historical variability of the very nature of translation. During the seventeenth and eighteenth centuries, for example, English and French translators display a preference for free rewriting that would not be described as translation today. Yet although Alexander Pope's version of the Homeric epics (1715–26) and the Abbé Prévost's version of Samuel Richardson's *Pamela* (1760) contain significant revisions of the foreign texts, both the translators and many of their readers regarded the results as accurate translations. Prévost, while reducing seven English volumes to four in French, still asserted:

> I have not changed anything pertaining to the author's intention, nor have I changed much in the manner in which he put that intention into words, and yet I have given his work a new face by ridding it of the flaccid excursions, the excessive descriptions, the useless conversations, and the misplaced musings.   (qtd. in Lefevere, *Translation/History/Culture* 39)

To brand such work merely as adaptation is anachronistic, imposing on a remote historical period a set of norms that did not fully emerge until the twentieth century.

Perhaps the greatest advance of polysystem theory is to have presented a more historically grounded way of thinking about translation equivalence. Toury draws an important distinction between the "adequacy" and the "acceptability" of a translation: "whereas adherence to source norms determines a translation's *adequacy* as compared to the source text, subscription to norms originating in the target culture determines its *acceptability*," where the criterion of acceptability may be source-oriented or target-oriented and therefore encompass different concepts of equivalence (*Descriptive Translation Studies* 56–57). Ultimately, Toury concludes that "it is norms that determine the (type and extent of) equivalence manifested by actual translations" (61). Concepts of equivalence can vary with the changing norms of the receiving culture and should not be limited to a fixed range of possible relations or assume that the foreign text will be interpreted in the same way by every readership in every period.

George Steiner's sensitively nuanced readings of translations in *After Babel* (1975) make precisely this assumption. Although Steiner notes how a translation might reflect the linguistic and literary values of its moment, he describes and judges it according to its adequacy, expecting it to reproduce the distinctive stylistic features of the foreign text as he interprets them. Yet it is Toury, not Steiner, who enables us to understand how French translators in the eighteenth and twenty-first centuries might claim that their very different versions of the same foreign text are accurate. Prévost defined an accurate translation as conforming to the foreign author's "intention" and verbal "manner" or style, which he evidently regarded as essences to be carved out of accidental defects. A French translator today might likewise base a claim of accuracy on such categories as authorial intention and style, yet the claim would assume such a different understanding of them as to entail the translation of every word that the foreign author included in the foreign text.

Polysystem theory also clarifies how canons of foreign literatures are formed in translation. Toury remarks that translation inevitably involves at least two languages and two cultural traditions—that is, at least two sets of norm systems on each level. Thus the value behind a translation may be described as consisting of two major elements:

> (1) being a text in a certain language, and hence occupying a position, or filling in a slot, in the appropriate culture, or in a certain section thereof;
> (2) constituting a representation in that language/culture of another, pre-existing text in some other language, belonging to some other culture and occupying a definite position within it.
> (*Descriptive Translation Studies* 56)

The "position" that translation occupies in the receiving culture, its interrelations with the norms in the literary system, might be seen as determining the "representation" that it constructs, not only of an isolated foreign text but also of an entire foreign literature. Insofar as translation is always a selective practice and a foreign literature is never translated in its entirety, a pattern of choosing foreign texts for translation may take shape, resulting in a canon that differs so widely from the texts canonized in the foreign literature as to amount to a reductive or stereotypical representation of it. André Lefevere has explored this topic through his notion of translation as "refraction" or "rewriting" (see his "Mother Courage's Cucumbers" and *Translation, Rewriting*). Although working within the parameters of polysystem theory, Lefevere introduces such other factors as patronage and poetics to study the partial representation of foreign literatures in anthology selections as well as the transformative operations to which a foreign text might be subjected if it deviates significantly from target-culture norms.

Polysystem theory is not without its conceptual problems. It follows linguistics in taking the physical sciences as its model for research. Toury conceives of translation studies as an "empirical science," objectively "descriptive" instead of normative in judging and prescribing forms of translation practice; its goal is "the formulation of general laws of translational behaviour, which would be probabilistic in nature" and would enable "justifiable predictions" (*Descriptive Translation Studies* 1–2, 69, 267; see Even-Zohar, *Polysystem Studies* 9; Lefevere, "Mother Courage's Cucumbers" 5). Yet if polysystem theory requires a detailed contextualization of translation practices, embedding them in particular cultural situations at particular historical moments, would not that contextualization take on a specificity that militates against the formulation of laws that are so generalized as to apply to translation in other times and places?

When we consider the translation laws put forth by Even-Zohar and Toury, it seems possible to cite cases that do not simply necessitate the inclusion of a missing cultural or social factor but in fact amount to an invalidation. One such law asserts that the more peripheral the cultural position occupied by translation, the more conservative it will be and the more it will adhere to

dominant values. "In such a situation," states Even-Zohar, translation "is modelled according to norms already conventionally established by an already dominant type in the target literature" (*Polysystem Studies* 49; see also Toury, *Descriptive Translation Studies* 271). Yet although translation is peripheral in twentieth-century American poetry, ranked significantly lower than original composition in cultural prestige and increasingly less practiced by poets during the century, we nonetheless find a veritable tradition of translation experimentalism, starting with Ezra Pound's versions of Guido Cavalcanti and Arnaut Daniel and including such remarkably inventive works as Louis Zukofsky and Celia Zukofsky's Catullus and Paul Blackburn's Provençal troubadours.

Might the inverse of the law hold—namely, that the more central the position of translation, the more innovative it will be in developing new literary values, forms, and practices (Even-Zohar, *Polysystem Studies* 47)? In the early eighteenth century, when Pope was translating Homer, translation was central to British literature: it had acquired enormous prestige from the translation practices and commentary of a distinguished poet like John Dryden, and it was contributing to the rise of the novel (see Cohen and Dever). Yet Pope's Homer cannot be called innovative: not only is it cast in the dominant prosodic form of the period, the heroic couplet, but it is also inscribed with the dominant cultural and social values of Hanoverian Britain, perhaps most visible in Pope's transformation of the Achaean tribal chiefs into monarchs. The search for translation laws seems to suppress the very historical differences that translation studies should be considering.

Polysystem theory also lacks a concept of agency that allows for the full complexity of human behavior in such cultural practices as translation (for a similar criticism, see Berman, *Pour une critique* 59–60). Toury follows Jan Mukařovský's distinction between a norm and its codification in regarding translation norms as largely unformulated and applied by the translator without self-conscious reflection. Just as Mukařovský defines a norm as "a regulating energetic principle" that "makes its presence felt as a limitation on the freedom of [the individual's] action" (49–50), so Toury views translation norms as "sociocultural constraints" (*Descriptive Translation Studies* 54–56). The translator's subjectivity is thus collapsed into the values of the receiving culture. The conscious intentions that motivate and monitor translation choices are minimized, if not discounted altogether, as are the relations between intentionality and such unconscious factors as the unacknowledged conditions and unanticipated consequences of translation. To mediate between the personal and the social, the psychological and the ideological, translation studies needs a more sophisticated concept of action as at once intentional and determinate (see, e.g., Giddens; Simeoni; Gouanvic; Venuti, "Difference" and "Retranslations").

Finally, polysystem theory has not sufficiently conceptualized the relations between translation and the social formation in which it functions. The social relations of literary production have long been regarded as a blind spot in formalist theories (see Bennett). Tynjanov admitted the "prime significance of major social factors," while arguing that "it must be elucidated to its full extent through the problem of the evolution of literature," that is, "the evolutionary interactions of functions and forms" in the literary system (77). Even-Zohar never takes up this issue, instead assuming that the "relations between literature and society" are "homologous" and that the "hierarchies" of the literary system are "isomorphic" with class divisions (*Polysystem Studies* 23).

Such views show that polysystem theory developed apart from the various Marxist and cultural materialist theories of literature that were formulated in the 1980s. In these theories, literary texts exist in a differential or disjunctive relation to social developments, capable of offering no more than interested representations because literary form is ideologically coded (see, e.g., Jameson). Translations too might be seen as ideological in their imitation of foreign texts and in their production of social effects, encoding values, beliefs, and representations that serve the interests of social groups and form cultural and social identities. But whenever the term *ideology* appears in the work of polysystem theorists, it lacks the conceptual rigor and sophistication given to it by such influential thinkers as Louis Althusser and seems to mean simply values, as in Even-Zohar's glance at "literary ideologies" (*Polysystem Studies* 23), as in Lefevere's reference to "the ideological, economic, and aesthetic constraints" that determine the selection of translations for anthologies ("Mother Courage's Cucumbers" 10).

ETHICS AND POLITICS

Whereas polysystem theory has sought a value-free research methodology to describe translation practices, other theorists developed evaluative principles that have taken the form of a translation ethics. For the most part, these ethical reflections have been deontological, citing duties that a translator ought to perform in keeping with contractual obligations. Hans Vermeer, for example, sees the *skopos* or purpose of a translation as an important factor in determining the translator's accountability: the *skopos* can be stipulated in a client's commission and thus transformed into a criterion for evaluating the translator's work ("Skopos" 186). Christiane Nord introduces the notion of loyalty into Vermeer's functionalism: agreeing with him that the intended purpose of the translation should take priority over its fidelity to the foreign text, she argues that the translator is nonetheless obligated to cooperate with the parties involved in a project, the readers of the translation as well as the foreign author. This obligation means that the translator should explain the reasons for any shift from the foreign text ("Skopos").

It would seem that Vermeer and Nord have in mind mostly pragmatic text types, such as advertisements and business correspondence, instruction manuals and tourist brochures, software packages and Web pages, which may require substantial rewriting so that the translation fulfills their generic function in a different language and culture. Hence any ethical value is first of all a matter of fair dealing in a commercial transaction, satisfying a client's interest in maintaining or increasing sales, for example, as well as a reader's interest in using a product or service. Yet both theorists also address projects where the values at stake are less economic than cultural: Vermeer includes literary translations, such as the interlingual adaptation of a foreign classic for children ("Translation" 100), and Nord considers a Bible translation on which she herself collaborated ("Loyalty").

Here the attempt to join the functionalism of *Skopostheorie* with ethical reflection raises problems that go unnoticed by these theorists. In translating the Bible, Nord asserts:

> Loyalty can be achieved by making the translation strategies explicit in a preface, by adopting clear choices at points of source-text ambiguity, and by using the most advanced theological and philological scholarship to ensure loyalty to the source-text author's intentions.   ("Loyalty"; abstract)

If loyalty is equated with these actions, the purpose of the translation has in effect been defined as the clear and explicit application of a certain variety of scholarship. Treating translation as a matter of reproducing a communicative intention, Nord overlooks not only that various interpretive acts intervene between the foreign text and the reader of the translation but also that any interpretation constructs meaning according to values, forms, and practices that can transform any notion of loyalty into a mystification of particular cultural and social interests.

With a historically remote sacred text whose interpretation has long been informed by divergent theological concepts, scholarship cannot determine the foreign author's intentions but only produce another interpretation, which is anachronistically governed by academic institutions at a later moment. In applying this scholarship in the translation, the translator enacts yet

Because a functionalist approach neglects the relation between the translation and the foreign text, it leaves itself exposed to the charge that its so-called ethics is merely commercial expediency or cultural factionalism.

another interpretation that expresses a loyalty, not so much to the foreign text or to its author as to the translator's own religious and scholarly values while excluding values held by other cultural constituencies. Nord in fact dismisses negative reviews of her translation as "based on absolutist conceptions of [the reviewers'] own subjective theories" ("Loyalty"; abstract), unaware that she herself has no means, except through the validation of an academic institution, to privilege her competing theory.

Because a functionalist approach neglects the relation between the translation and the foreign text, it leaves itself exposed to the charge that its so-called ethics is merely commercial expediency or cultural factionalism. It is precisely the question of the foreign that Antoine Berman makes the basis of his translation ethics. For Berman, bad translation is at once "ethnocentric," in assimilating the foreign text to values in the receiving culture, and "hypertextual," in "deforming" that text so as to effect the assimilation ("Traduction et la lettre" 29–30; my trans.). "Generally under the guise of transmissibility," states Berman, it "carries out a systematic negation of the strangeness of the foreign work" (*Experience* 5). Good translation limits this negation by staging "an opening, a dialogue, a crossbreeding, a decentering" whereby it forces the receiving language and culture to register the foreignness of the foreign text (4). Berman follows Walter Benjamin's notion of "inferior translation" as "the inaccurate transmission of an inessential content" (70), arguing that, "more than communicate," translation "reveals, manifests": "it is, in its very essence, animated by the *desire to open its own linguistic space to the Foreign insofar as it is Foreign*" (Berman, "Traduction et la lettre" 75–76; my trans.). Berman's view of translation is fundamentally agonistic, encapsulated in his use of the term *épreuve*, which might be rendered here as "trial": not only does the foreign text undergo a trial in that it is inevitably transformed during the translation process, "uprooted from its own *language-ground*," but also the translating language is "profoundly modified," developed by the translator's effort to imitate the linguistic and cultural differences of the foreign text (Berman, "Traduction comme épreuve" 67, 81).

Berman's project involves a recovery of the German translation tradition, notably nineteenth-century commentators like Goethe and Friedrich Schleiermacher who distinguish between domesticating and foreignizing strategies and see the latter as the highest form of translation. Schleiermacher's famous pronouncement actually gives the interlingual translator only two options: "Either the translator leaves the author in peace as much as possible and moves the reader toward him; or he leaves the reader in peace as much as possible and moves the author toward him" (49). Just as Schleiermacher argues that foreignizing translation requires literalism—"the more precisely the translation adheres to the turns and figures of the original, the more foreign it will seem to its reader" (53)—so Berman asserts that "the ethical aim of translation, precisely because it intends to welcome the Foreign in its fleshly corporeality, can only be attached to the *letter* of the work" ("Traduction et la lettre" 77).

Berman's ethics amounts to a philosophical approach to translation: it is designed to challenge the Western metaphysical tradition, particularly Platonism, which for more than two millennia has valued sense-for-sense over word-for-word translation, the spirit over the letter. His concept of the letter, however, resembles less Schleiermacher's close adherence to the foreign text than Martin Heidegger's recommendation of "poetizing" instead of ordinary language to translate early Greek thinking: the German philosopher favors the use of archaisms, which he submits to etymological interpretations (19). Thus whereas ethnocentric translation "must be written in a *normative* language—more normative than that of a work written directly in the translating language"—and whereas it "must not *offend* with any lexical or syntactical 'foreignness,' " ethical translation experiments with deviations

from current standard usage so as to imitate the "multiple concrete signs of foreignness" in the foreign text (Berman, "Traduction et la lettre" 35, 76). As examples of these deviations Berman cites not only the use of regional dialects, archaisms, and neologisms but also the ways in which translators like Friedrich Hölderlin, Chateaubriand, and Pierre Klossowski allow foreign syntactical constructions to imprint the translating language. In its labor on the letter, then, ethical translation noticeably seeks to re-create the signifying process of the foreign text, while ethnocentric translation aims to communicate a clear meaning in familiar language and thereby winds up producing a text that seems untranslated.

Berman's translation ethics rests on a method of textual analysis that elucidates a range of "deforming tendencies" in the translated text, including "clarification" or "explicitation," "ennoblement," and the "destruction of linguistic patternings" ("Traduction et la lettre" 52–68). He is careful to distinguish these tendencies from historically variable norms as Toury defines them. Berman points out that although "literary, social, cultural" norms "partly govern the translating act in every society," they are not specific to translation and can shape various writing practices, whereas his analytic method "focuses on the universals of deformation inherent in translating as such" ("Traduction comme épreuve" 80). Consequently, his affiliation of ethnocentric translation with Western metaphysics must be revised to encompass translation traditions in every language. At the beginning of the twentieth century, during the late Qing dynasty, the translator Yan Fu described several criteria for producing a good translation—fidelity (*xin*), clarity or comprehensibility (*da*), and elegance or fluency (*ya*)—which also appeared in ancient Chinese translation theory, specifically in translations of Buddhist scripture during the third century AD (see Venuti, *Scandals* 181–82). These criteria resemble Berman's deforming tendencies to some extent; they were also applied in sinicizing translations of Western literary and philosophical texts. The universal dominance of ethnocentric translation may well reflect not so much a Western philosophical tradition as the millennia-long dominance of metaphysical thinking in human cultures, a privileging of the semantic spirit over the formal letter in language.

One may question whether Berman's ethics is too narrowly conceptualized to judge translation practices in different cultures at different historical moments. Indeed, although the sinicizing projects of Chinese translators like Yan Fu sought to reinforce dominant values such as the classical literary language, they unexpectedly precipitated cultural innovation and change by introducing Western ideas and forms into China. Even ethnocentric translation can signal the foreign, depending on the nature of the foreign text and the receiving cultural situation (see Venuti, *Scandals* 186–89).

Berman later qualified his thinking, suggesting that the key question is not whether a translation is thoroughly domesticating or incorporates foreignizing tendencies but whether it resorts to "trumpery" by concealing its "manipulations" of the foreign text or shows respect for it by "offering" a "correspondence" that "enlarges, amplifies, and enriches the translating language" (*Pour une critique* 92–94). Yet here too it seems important to broaden his idea of the letter or signifying process to take into account varieties of intertextuality that might be constructed by the translator to register the foreignness of the foreign text and thereby develop the translating language. Pound, for example, advocated translations that created an analogue with literary forms in the receiving culture: to render Cavalcanti's poetry, he drew on what he called "pre-Elizabethan English," the work of poets like Sir Thomas Wyatt and Henry Howard, earl of Surrey, because he felt that they "were still intent on clarity and explicitness" and therefore useful in mimicking distinctive features of the Italian texts (Anderson 250). There remains the question of whether such strategies would work with every audience or, more generally, whether foreignizing translation can be appreciated by

every cultural constituency or only an elite minority who can bring to their reading experience a specialized knowledge of literary traditions and an openness to linguistic experiments. Berman's ethical reflection might be productively joined to a theory of literary taste that can make intelligible different forms of reception and assess the prospects for cultural change presented by a translation project (for an effort to explore these issues, see Venuti, *Scandals* 9–20).

In distinguishing between normative and innovative translation, Berman's ethics carries political implications. His concept of ethnocentric translation originates in such thinkers as Friedrich Nietzsche, who described how Roman poets like Horace and Propertius appropriated the texts of their Greek predecessors, removing names, geographic markers, and cultural references and rewriting those texts in Latin. Nietzsche linked the suppression of difference, historical as well as cultural, with imperialism. The Roman poets, he writes, "did not know the delights of the historical sense; what was past and alien was an embarrassment for them; and being Romans, they saw it as an incentive for a Roman conquest" (137). Henri Meschonnic similarly calls attention to the political function of translations that perform a work of "annexation" by "transpos[ing] the so-called dominant ideology" under the "illusion of transparency" (308; my trans.). Extending both Nietzsche and Meschonnic, Berman criticizes the use of translation in Christian evangelism from the Apostles to Nida, a consultant for the American Bible Society—Nida's concept of dynamic equivalence was in fact derived from the "principles and procedures involved in Bible translating" (Nida). In Berman's view,

> The evangelizing impulse of Christianity is superimposed on the translating impulse of pagan Rome bent on forming its own culture by looting, borrowing, and annexation: it is necessary that every people might hear the Word of God, it is necessary to translate. This is translation *for* more than translation *by*, and the enterprise has not ceased, it is the same as that of a Nida in the

United States; and as in antiquity the evangelizing impulse was joined to the Roman annexationist impulse, Nida's translating evangelism is today joined to North American cultural imperialism.

("Traduction et la lettre" 33)

Berman's concept of ethical translation is equally political, not only in its promotion of cultural innovation and change but also in its historical origins. In recovering the German translation tradition, Berman was adapting theories of cultural development (*Bildung*) that enlisted foreignizing translation in a nationalist movement to free Prussia from French cultural domination during the Napoleonic wars (Venuti, *Translator's Invisibility* 110–16). Here too translation appropriates the foreign for an agenda that is specific to the receiving situation, it is "translation *for*," although with the proviso that German culture cannot develop without signaling the foreignness of the texts it translates. Berman does not examine this contradiction.

From the 1980s onward, especially in North America, scholars increasingly devised projects that illuminated the politics of translation. The concerns of the emerging discipline of translation studies thus began to overlap with current trends in literary and cultural theory, notably the spate of research into colonialism and postcolonialism. Vicente Rafael's pioneering study of Spanish colonizers in the Philippines shows how the close relations between empire and evangelism depended on translation between Castilian and Tagalog. Rafael observes:

> For the Spaniards, translation was always a matter of reducing the native language and culture to accessible objects for and subjects of divine and imperial intervention, [whereas] for the Tagalogs translation was a process less of internalizing colonial-Christian conventions than of evading their totalizing grip by repeatedly marking the differences between their language and interests and those of the Spaniards. (213)

In colonial situations, translation becomes an arena of contest: it is used by the colonizers to form a subjugating identity for the colonized, which is necessarily hybrid, at once metropolitan and indigenous, and therefore unstable; at the same time, translation is used by the colonized to resist and tamper with the processes of identity formation imposed by the colonizers.

Some of the most productive research in this area has synthesized various theoretical discourses and analytic tools to offer incisive examinations of translation practices at specific historical moments. Annie Brisset's study of Québécois drama translation between 1968 and 1988 draws on polysystem theory, Henri Gobard's analysis of linguistic functions, and Berman's concept of ethnocentrism to consider how writers, lexicographers, and translators "elevate[d] a dialect to the status of a national and cultural language" (165). The work of canonical playwrights such as Shakespeare, August Strindberg, Anton Chekhov, and Bertolt Brecht was translated into Québécois French in order to transform this dialect from what Gobard calls a "vernacular," a native or mother tongue, into a "referential" language, the vehicle of a national literature, investing the dialect with cultural authority so it could compete against the domination of Parisian French and North American English. Brisset exposes not only the nationalism inherent in this project but also the formation of a cultural identity that was exclusionary and repressive: "In the name of distinctness, the salvation of the Québécois identity, all forms of alterity must be automatically ejected from the group, confined to their own differences" (172).

Maria Tymoczko similarly draws on polysystem theory to study English versions of medieval Irish literature made by Irish translators during the nineteenth and twentieth centuries. Yet she joins it with discourse analysis and postcolonial theory to consider how this "translation movement found ways to resist and challenge English stereotyping and English cultural spoliation" (20–21). The Irish translations, like the Québécois, were designed to form a cultural identity in the service of a nationalist agenda, and Tymoczko's nuanced analyses examine both textual strategies and their social effects. She discriminates carefully among the various ideological determinations of the translations to argue that they constituted

> one of the discursive practices that contributed to freeing Ireland from colonialism, a discursive practice that took its place among other discursive practices that shaped Ireland's resistance to England and led eventually to political action and physical confrontation.   (15)

In projects such as Brisset's and Tymoczko's, the political functions of translation are tied closely to the analysis of linguistic forms in detailed historical contexts.

FUTURE DIRECTIONS

I have surveyed the recent history of translation studies in a way that is necessarily selective, given my decision to focus on key problems and the contributions of leading scholars. Nonetheless, the result does provide a basis for suggesting some of the paths that further research might take in order to advance the field. These suggestions strike me as possibilities that particularly recommend themselves at this juncture, when the boundaries between translation studies and such other fields as linguistics, literary theory and history, and cultural studies continue to be permeable and opportunities for crossfertilization have yet to be exploited.

It seems clear that the most productive research will be the most interdisciplinary, not only in straddling the different languages, literatures, and cultures that are brought together in a translation or body of translations but also in combining theoretical discourses and analytic tools from different disciplines. The development of translation studies since the 1950s shows beyond a doubt that when the analysis of translated texts is divorced from their cultural situations and social functions or when these situations and functions are considered apart from textual analysis, the object of study ceases to be translation and instead becomes language or dis-

course, culture or society, allowing the research methodology of a particular discipline to dominate and limit the scope and findings of the project. Thus linguistics-based approaches have tended to stress textual analysis at the cost of the social effects and philosophical implications of translation, while approaches informed by cultural studies have tended to stress ideological critique and philosophical speculation at the cost of textual analysis (see Venuti, "Translating Derrida"). Interlingual translation is a cultural practice, but its linguistic basis and its cultural functioning are reciprocally determining, and neither can be studied without sophisticated theories of both language and culture.

Yet the point is not simply to combine linguistic and cultural approaches but to conceptualize their interrelations and implement them in studying the production and reception of translations. Hence translation studies must be grounded in research into specific cultural situations and historical moments, into the diverse factors that play into the publication and reviewing, the reading and teaching of translated texts. Only archival research can yield the data to make clear the ideological determinations and social effects of translation. But once the scholar turns to the archive, existing literary canons are unsettled: the number of translations and translators we find there is truly staggering, demonstrating that for centuries translation has been a highly important practice in most languages and literatures, but its role continues to be minimized (or simply omitted) in many literary histories or defined solely in relation to canonical authors who have also written translations. Joan DeJean's groundbreaking study of the "fictions" of Sappho is exemplary in joining traditions of translation and classical philology with original compositions, taking into consideration figures who have fallen into neglect (see also Prins). Translation studies should be carrying out similarly wide-ranging and detailed historical contextualizations. The focal point of the research, however, must be not only canonical

Interlingual translation is a cultural practice, but its linguistic basis and its cultural functioning are reciprocally determining.

authors but also particular periods in the history of a language and literature when evaluations of foreign texts may well differ from the canons in place in the scholar's moment.

Attention to translation ultimately redefines the very concept of the literary and requires research to encompass a wider group of texts, genres, and media. David Damrosch's answer to the question "What is world literature?" tellingly replaces Goethe's notion of a stable canon of literary texts with modes of reception that acknowledge both that national literatures are "refracted" as they travel to different cultures and that, when translated, a specific text "gains" in meaning and cultural force (281). Translation studies can build on this insight by exploring the gamut of humanistic disciplines, not only literature as traditionally defined but also religion, philosophy, history, sociology, and anthropology, where translated texts likewise reveal significant gains that exert an enormous influence on academic and other cultural institutions worldwide. Yet because translation also plays a powerful role in the current geopolitical economy, we must go even further to study popular cultural forms such as best sellers in various genres, children's literature, and film and video, as well as pragmatic texts like advertisements and travel guidebooks. The globalized flow of capital could not continue without these and other kinds of translation, which inevitably influence the cultures where they circulate as well as the cultures that they represent. As translation begins to achieve a surer foothold in the American academy, it stands to make a unique contribution in the study of languages, literatures, and cultures, present as well as past. We should define its range of possibilities broadly.

WORKS CITED AND SUGGESTIONS FOR FURTHER READING

This bibliography contains not only works cited in the text but also English translations of foreign works of scholarship. Several of these translations are included in my *Translation Studies Reader*. The student of translation might also find helpful the following works of reference: Shuttleworth and Cowie's *Dictionary of Translation Studies*, Baker's *Routledge Encyclopedia of Translation*

Studies, and France's *Oxford Guide to Literature in English Translation*.

Althusser, Louis. *Essays on Ideology*. Trans. Ben Brewster. London: Verso, 1984.

Amin-Zaki, Amel. "Religious and Cultural Considerations in Translating Shakespeare into Arabic." *Between Languages and Cultures: Translation and Cross-Cultural Texts*. Ed. Anuradha Dingwaney and Carol Maier. Pittsburgh: U of Pittsburgh P, 1995. 223–43.

Anderson, David, ed. *Pound's Cavalcanti: An Edition of the Translations, Notes, and Essays*. Princeton: Princeton UP, 1983.

Baker, Mona. *In Other Words: A Coursebook on Translation*. London: Routledge, 1992.

———, ed. *Routledge Encyclopedia of Translation Studies*. London: Routledge, 1998.

Benjamin, Andrew. *Translation and the Nature of Philosophy*. London: Routledge, 1989.

Benjamin, Walter. "The Task of the Translator." *Illuminations*. 1923. Ed. Hannah Arendt. Trans. Harry Zohn. New York: Schocken, 1968. 69–82.

Bennett, Tony. *Formalism and Marxism*. London: Methuen, 1979.

Berman, Antoine. *L'épreuve de l'étranger: Culture et traduction dans l'Allemagne romantique*. Paris: Gallimard, 1984. Trans. as *The Experience of the Foreign: Culture and Translation in Romantic Germany*. Trans. S. Heyvaert. Albany: State U of New York P, 1992.

———. *Pour une critique des traductions: John Donne*. Paris: Gallimard, 1995.

———. "La traduction comme épreuve de l'étranger." *Texte* 4 (1985): 67–81.

———. "La traduction et la lettre, ou l'auberge du lointain." *Les tours de Babel: Essais sur la traduction*. Mauvezin: Trans-Europ-Repress, 1985. Paris: Seuil, 1999. 31–150.

Bhabha, Homi. *The Location of Culture*. London: Routledge, 1994.

Blum-Kulka, Shoshana. "Shifts of Cohesion and Coherence in Translation." *Interlingual and Intercultural Communication: Discourse and Cognition in Translation and Second Language Acquisition Studies*. Ed. Juliane House and Blum-Kulka. Tübingen, Ger.: Narr, 1986. 17–35.

Brisset, Annie. *Sociocritique de la traduction: Théâtre et altérité au Québec (1968–1988)*. Longueuil: Le Préambule, 1990. Trans. as *A Sociocritique of Translation: Theatre and Alterity in Quebec, 1968–1988*. Trans. Rosalind Gill and Roger Gannon. Toronto: U of Toronto P, 1996.

Caminade, Monique, and Anthony Pym. *Les formations en traduction et interprétation: Essai de recensement mondial*. Paris: Société Française des Traducteurs, 1995.

Catford, J. C. *A Linguistic Theory of Translation: An Essay in Applied Linguistics*. London: Oxford UP, 1965.

Cheyfitz, Eric. *The Poetics of Imperialism: Translation and Colonization from* The Tempest *to* Tarzan. New York: Oxford UP, 1991.

Cicero, Marcus Tullius. *De inventione. De optimo genere oratorum. Topica.* Trans. H. M. Hubell. Cambridge: Harvard UP, 1949.

Cohen, Margaret, and Carolyn Dever, eds. *The Literary Channel: The Inter-national Invention of the Novel.* Princeton: Princeton UP, 2001.

Cronin, Michael. *Translation and Globalization.* London: Routledge, 2003.

Damrosch, David. *What Is World Literature?* Princeton: Princeton UP, 2003.

DeJean, Joan. *Fictions of Sappho, 1546–1937.* Chicago: U of Chicago P, 1989.

de Man, Paul. " 'Conclusions': Walter Benjamin's 'The Task of the Translator.' " *The Resistance to Theory.* Minneapolis: U of Minnesota P, 1986. 73–105.

Derrida, Jacques. "Des tours de Babel." Trans. Joseph Graham. Graham 165–248.

———. "Signature Event Context." *Margins of Philosophy.* Trans. Alan Bass. Chicago: U of Chicago P, 1982. 307–30.

Even-Zohar, Itamar. *Papers in Historical Poetics.* Tel Aviv: Porter Inst. for Poetics and Semiotics, 1978.

———. *Polysystem Studies.* Spec. issue of *Poetics Today* 11.1. (1990): 1–270.

France, Peter, ed. *Oxford Guide to Literature in English Translation.* Oxford: Oxford UP, 2000.

Giddens, Anthony. "Agency, Structure." *Central Problems in Social Theory: Action, Structure, and Contradiction in Social Analysis.* Berkeley: U of California P, 1979. 49–95.

Gouanvic, Jean-Marc. "A Bourdieusian Theory of Translation; or, The Coincidence of Practical Instances: Field, 'Habitus,' Capital, and 'Illusio.' " *Translator* 11.2 (2005): 147–66.

Graham, Joseph, ed. *Difference in Translation.* Ithaca: Cornell UP, 1985.

Halliday, M. A. K., and Ruqaiya Hasan. *Cohesion in English.* London: Longman, 1976.

Harris, Brian, ed. *Translating and Interpreting Schools.* Amsterdam: Benjamins, 1997.

Harvey, Keith. "A Descriptive Framework for Compensation." *Translator* 1.1 (1995): 65–86.

Hatim, Basil, and Ian Mason. *The Translator as Communicator.* London: Routledge, 1997.

Heidegger, Martin. *Early Greek Thinking.* Ed. and trans. David Farrell Krell and F. A. Capuzzi. New York: Harper, 1975.

Hermans, Theo, ed. *The Manipulation of Literature: Studies in Literary Translation.* London: Croom Helm, 1985.

Hervey, Sándor, and Ian Higgins. *Thinking Translation: A Course in Translation Method, French to English.* London: Routledge, 1992.

Jacobs, Carol. "The Monstrosity of Translation." *MLN* 90 (1975): 755–66.

Jakobson, Roman. "On Linguistic Aspects of Translation." *On Translation.* Ed. Reuben A. Brower. Cambridge: Harvard UP, 1959. 232–39.

Jameson, Fredric. *The Political Unconscious: Narrative as a Socially Symbolic Act.* Ithaca: Cornell UP, 1981.

Johnston, John. "Translation as Simulacrum." *Rethinking Translation: Discourse, Subjectivity, Ideology.* Ed. Lawrence Venuti. London: Routledge, 1992. 42–56.

Koller, Werner. *Einführung in die Übersetzungswissenschaft.* Heidelberg: Quelle, 1979.

———. "Equivalence in Translation Theory." *Readings in Translation Theory.* Ed. and trans. Andrew Chesterman. Helsinki: Oy Finn Lectura Ab, 1989. 99–104.

Lefevere, André. "Mother Courage's Cucumbers: Text, System and Refraction in a Theory of Literature." *Modern Language Studies* 12.4 (1982): 3–20.

———, ed. and trans. *Translation/History/Culture: A Sourcebook.* London: Routledge, 1992.

———. *Translation, Rewriting, and the Manipulation of Literary Fame.* London: Routledge, 1992.

Lewis, Philip E. "The Measure of Translation Effects." Graham 31–62.

Meschonnic, Henri. *Pour la poétique II.* Paris: Gallimard, 1973.

Mukařovský, Jan. "The Aesthetic Norm." *Structure, Sign, and Function: Selected Essays.* 1937. Ed. and trans. John Burbank and Peter Steiner. New Haven: Yale UP, 1978. 49–56.

Nabokov, Vladimir. "Problems of Translation: *Onegin* in English." *Partisan Review* 22 (1955): 496–512.

Nida, Eugene. *Toward a Science of Translating, with Special Reference to Principles and Procedures Involved in Bible Translating.* Leiden: Brill, 1964.

Nida, Eugene, and Charles Taber. *The Theory and Practice of Translation.* 1969. Leiden: Brill, 1982.

Nietzsche, Friedrich. *The Gay Science.* 1882. Trans. Walter Kaufmann. New York: Vintage, 1974.

Niranjana, Tejaswini. *Siting Translation: History, Poststructuralism, and the Colonial Context.* Berkeley: U of California P, 1992.

Nord, Christiane. "Loyalty Revisited: Bible Translation as a Case in Point." *Translator* 7.2 (2001): 185–202.

———. "Skopos, Loyalty, and Translational Conventions." *Target* 3 (1991): 91–109.

———. *Textanalyse und Übersetzung: Theoretische Grundlagen, Methode und didaktische Anwendung einer Übersetzungsrelevanten Textanalyse.* 2nd ed. Heidelberg: Groos, 1991.

———. *Text Analysis in Translation.* Amsterdam: Rodopi, 1991.

Phillips, J. B., trans. *The New Testament in Modern English.* London: Macmillan, 1959.

Pöchhacker, Franz, and Miriam Shlesinger, eds. *The Interpreting Studies Reader.* London: Routledge, 2001.

Popovič, Anton. "The Concept of 'Shift of Expression' in Translation Analysis." *The Nature of Translation.* Ed. James S. Holmes, Frans de Haan and Popovič. The Hague: Mouton, 1970. 78–87.

Prins, Yopie. *Victorian Sappho*. Princeton: Princeton UP, 1998.

Rafael, Vicente. *Contracting Colonialism: Translation and Christian Conversion in Tagalog Society under Early Spanish Rule*. Ithaca: Cornell UP, 1988.

Reiss, Katharina. *Möglichkeiten und Grenzen der Übersetzungskritik: Kategorien und Kriterien für eine sachgerechte Beurteilung von Übersetzungen*. München: Hueber, 1971.

———. *Translation Criticism: The Potentials and Limitations: Categories and Criteria for Translation Quality Assessment*. Trans. E. F. Rhodes. Manchester: Saint Jerome, 2000.

Schleiermacher, Friedrich. "On the Different Methods of Translating." 1813. Trans. Susan Bernofsky. Venuti, *Translation Studies Reader* 43–63.

Shuttleworth, Mark, and Moira Cowie. *Dictionary of Translation Studies*. Manchester: Saint Jerome, 1997.

Simeoni, Daniel. "The Pivotal Status of the Translator's Habitus." *Target* 10.1 (1998): 1–39.

Simon, Sherry. *Gender in Translation: Cultural Identity and the Politics of Transmission*. London: Routledge, 1996.

Steiner, George. *After Babel: Aspects of Language and Translation*. 3rd ed. Oxford: Oxford UP, 1998.

Toury, Gideon. *Descriptive Translation Studies and Beyond*. Amsterdam: Benjamins, 1995.

———. *In Search of a Theory of Translation*. Tel Aviv: Porter Inst. for Poetics and Semiotics, 1980.

Tymoczko, Maria. *Translation in a Postcolonial Context: Early Irish Literature in English Translation*. Manchester: Saint Jerome, 1999.

Tynjanov, Jurij. "On Literary Evolution." 1927. *Readings in Russian Poetics: Formalist and Structuralist Views*. Ed. Ladislav Matejka and Krystyna Pomorska. Cambridge: MIT P, 1971. 66–78.

Venuti, Lawrence. "The Difference That Translation Makes: The Translator's Unconscious." *Translation Studies: Perspectives on an Emerging Discipline*. Ed. Alessandra Riccardi. Cambridge: Cambridge UP, 2002. 214–41.

———. "Retranslations: The Creation of Value." *Translation and Culture*. Ed. Katherine Faull. Lewisburg: Bucknell UP, 2004. 25–38.

———. *The Scandals of Translation: Towards an Ethics of Difference*. London: Routledge, 1998.

———. "Translating Derrida on Translation: Relevance and Disciplinary Resistance." *Yale Journal of Criticism* 16.2 (2003): 237–62.

———, ed. *The Translation Studies Reader*. 2nd ed. London: Routledge, 2004.

———. *The Translator's Invisibility: A History of Translation*. London: Routledge, 1995.

Vermeer, Hans. "Skopos and Commission in Translational Action." *Readings in Translation Theory*. Trans. and ed. Andrew Chesterman. Helsinki: Oy Finn Lectura Ab, 1989. 173–87.

———. "Translation als 'Informationsangebot.'" *Lebende Sprachen* 27.3 (1982): 97–101.

Vinay, Jean-Paul, and Jean Darbelnet. *Comparative Stylistics of French and English: A Methodology for Translation*. Trans. and ed. Juan C. Sager and M.-J. Hamel. Amsterdam: Benjamins, 1995.

———. *Stylistique comparée du français et de l'anglais: Méthode de traduction*. Paris: Didier, 1958.

⌒ Epilogue: The Scholar in Society

BRUCE ROBBINS

"Marx famously said that our job is not to interpret the world, but to change it. In the academy, however, it is exactly the reverse: our job is not to change the world, but to interpret it." Stanley Fish presents this argument (in an op-ed contribution to the *New York Times*) as a minority opinion. The majority of his colleagues, he says, would "most likely resist the injunction to police the boundary between academic work and political work." If Fish is right that his opinion is unrepresentative, as I suspect he is, it becomes interesting to speculate on why he should be right—why the majority view of the scholarly vocation from within should involve not merely interpreting society but also trying to change it, why the majority would hold itself to a much higher and more strenuous standard than Fish's commonsensical injunction to do your job, your whole job, and nothing but your job.[1]

Your job, according to Fish, sits there before you, waiting to be done. Feeling a touch guilty, perhaps, you may wonder why you are reading this essay instead of getting on with it. But consider—as a reason for continuing to read and for continuing to reflect on the scholar's affiliations with society—that the existence of your job cannot in fact be taken for granted. I mean this in several senses, none of them trivial. You or I may well be uncertain about whether we personally will get a job, for example, or whether our friends will. These questions, though seemingly private and subtheoretical, are peremptory and endlessly unnerving. They have a way of working themselves into the sort of thinking we do when we write and teach. They matter, and not just to ourselves. The same holds for anxiety as to whether an opening will even be advertised for which we might be tempted to apply, and for the routine seasonal suspense as to whether a given job, once advertised, will eventually turn out to be funded or not. Those of us who are lucky enough to have jobs, but jobs that are not permanent or tenure-track, will be aware of the contingency of employment in a different but no less acute fashion. And so on. These various sources of individual unease, which the reigning ideology encourages us to channel into solitary self-doubt, can be more usefully understood as elements of a cumulative, collective, profession-wide experience: the experience of uncertainty about how committed our society is to the continuing existence of any jobs in departments of literature.

There is no secret about the downward trend in the public funding of higher education, whether it is dated from the end of the cold war or (more accurately) from the early 1970s. We have seen this trend painfully reflected in the merging and closing down of foreign literature departments; in the wholesale replacement of full-time faculty positions with cheaper, benefit-less, conveniently flexible adjunct positions; and in the causal chain that leads from parsimonious state budgets to slashed library acquisitions, from slashed library acquisitions to diminished opportunities of publishing monographs on subjects that are suddenly declared to have only narrow appeal, and from diminished publishing opportunities to a redistribution of career op-portunities, such as they are. Given such exam-ples, which could of course be multiplied, a blithe assurance that the job as we know it will persist indefinitely, deciding now and for all time the proper shape and limits of our professional energies, would seem unrealistic and perhaps even irresponsible. What guarantee do we have that future scholars will not look back with some mixture of envy, nostalgia, and astonishment on the days when (so the histori-ans tell us) provision seemed to be made for these curious disciplinary slots or corners, each of them furnished with at least a minimum of salary, students, and office space as well as opportunities for pub-lication and eventual job security, and each de-voted to teaching and research in some tradi-tionally defined literature, period, or genre?

The uncertainty of public support appears to be a long-term feature of the humanities in America—in other words, less a momentary crisis than a persistent structural weakness.

The familiar phrase "crisis of the humanities" captures the genuine urgency here, the need to find some way of fending off a civic subversion that, if not immediately life-threatening for the profession as a whole, at the very least threatens many humanists and would-be humanists with a major scaling back of their professional pros-pects. But to call this a crisis of the *humanities* risks exaggerating the specificity of the victim, and to call it a *crisis* risks exaggerating the uniqueness of the historical moment. On the one hand, the defunding of the humanities is only one particular aspect of a general movement to delegitimate and privatize a wide range of public services. There is a crisis, but the humanities are not alone in suffering from it. On the other hand,

if we take a more distant perspective on this ten-dency, as the proposed ten-year shelf life of this volume suggests, the uncertainty of public sup-port appears to be a long-term feature of the humanities in America—in other words, less a momentary crisis than a persistent structural weakness.

In his contribution to the 1992 edition of this volume, Gerald Graff began with a quotation from David Lodge describing their shared "his-torical moment" as one in which literary scholars "most needed to justify their existence" ("Scholar" 343). The open assault on the hu-manities that set off the so-called culture wars of the 1980s and 1990s, an offensive that can be thought of in retrospect as intended to clear the way for the downsizing or dismantling of various programs of government support, happily no longer seems an inevitable focus for an essay on the scholar in society. For the moment at least, things seem to have calmed down. Yet this relative calm has not done away with the felt imperative to justify our exis-tence. Far from being an emer-gency expedient seized on in an unusual moment of danger, self-justification, I would sug-gest, can now be seen as a demand dating back to the profession's precarious and still recent be-ginnings and extending forward into the foresee-able future (see also Graff, *Clueless*).

Why should this be? As the French sociologist Loic Wacquant points out, American academics

> have instituted as the regulative norm of their practice the figure of the *professional*—physician, lawyer, or expert possessed of a neutral body of knowledge reduced to its technical dimension—in preference to that of the European-style *intel-lectual* as crystallized around the Dreyfus Affair . . . and defined by the unstable alloying of (sci-entific or artistic) autonomy and (political) en-gagement.   (21)

As Wacquant does not point out, attempts to alloy or balance scientific or artistic autonomy with some sort of political engagement are not restricted to the intellectual; nothing could be more characteristic of American-style profession-alism. In order to establish and sustain them-selves, most professions have had to supplement the familiar claim to autonomy, based on tech-nical expertise alone, with some larger claim to speak for or to the good of society as a whole.

Sociologists of the American professions teach that when public support for a given pro-fession is in doubt, which is to say when a par-ticular line of work is either striving for the priv-ileges of professional status or seeking to defend such privileges in the face of their possible re-striction or retraction, the profession will address the public in self-defense, seeking for itself greater public legitimacy. University teachers of vernacular literature have never enjoyed the sort of unquestioned public legitimacy that was long associated with doctors and lawyers—a legiti-macy that even doctors and lawyers must now of course defend, undermined in their autonomy as both groups have been by recent exposure to the open-market pressures of the bottom line. Far more exposed, however, and for far longer, academic humanists have always had to be aware, on some level of professional conscious-ness, that the existence of their jobs cannot be taken for granted. They have worried, privately and publicly, about the relevance of their work to society at large, however they define that rel-evance, if only because—should other motives be lacking—the willingness of society at large to allocate resources to the work of the humanities has been open to doubt. To say that humanists have been in the habit of seeking legitimation is to say only that they have had to demonstrate, and therefore to contemplate, what the French call their "reason for being." Humanists seek le-gitimation when they declare to anyone who will listen that they build moral character, train the whole mind, fashion citizens, guide or shore up the national culture, or whatever—in short, that they change the world, however gradually and indirectly, rather than merely interpret it.

The newer statements of purpose in the hu-manities, which name or hint at such goals as student self-problematization, the exploration of how knowledge itself has been constituted, the

recognition of multicultural diversity, and the critique of American imperial power, are often seen as more political. Such statements often presume the desirability of changing the world more radically or rapidly. And they often try to hold scholarship accountable to a different, more inclusive version of society. (More on this be-low.) But from the viewpoint of rhetorical func-tion, they are absolutely consistent with the older projects of character building and citizenship training. All these projects, old as well as new, are political—all claim to change the world rather than merely interpret it. And all do so at least partly in oblique answer to the legitimizing imperative: society's demand to know what ben-efits it receives from the money it spends on higher education, especially higher education's less profitable sectors. However vague and un-persuasively sonorous some of these claims may appear, they belong to a rhetorical practice that is indispensable: academics providing to non-academics a rationale for the existence of the academy.[2]

When Fish suggests that we give up trying "to alter the world by forming moral character, or fashioning democratic citizens, or . . . anything else," he implies that no answer is needed to the question of why, if we merely did the work be-fore us instead of offering society something it wants, society should continue to spend good money on us. It's as if there always have been academic jobs, and there always will be.[3] So why worry? Since universities in general and literary study in particular are not self-sustaining Pla-tonic essences but social institutions requiring a social mandate, however, the real question is not whether we should aim to change the world or not. Whatever our political preferences and commitments as individuals, collectively speak-ing we cannot afford not to make claims to some sort of social value or purpose and to back up those claims as convincingly as possible. The question that must be debated is which claims—which legitimizing statements or strategies we scholars should choose to adopt, which of these extremely different projects of change deserve or deserves our allegiance.

We are already in effect debating that question. In literary circles, the term *legitimation* has a somewhat exotic ring; it does not instantly conjure up an activity that has to be performed on Tuesday morning, like grading a stack of papers or leading a class discussion of triangular desire in Stendhal. It is most recognizable, alas, in the often embarrassing form of high-minded statements pronounced on special occasions by highly placed university officials, statements like those Fish cites and rejects in his op-ed piece: "helping students 'realize the values and skills of a democratic society,'" or teaching them "the knowledge and commitments to be socially responsible citizens." But it would be a mistake to think of legitimation as a vulgar if necessary defensive struggle carried on for us, as it were, by a mercenary army of administrators stationed on the university's ramparts in order that life inside the citadel can go on unperturbed. The fortress metaphor, like the more familiar metaphor of the ivory tower and others suggesting monastic seclusion, underestimates the many ways in which the university is already inside society and society is already inside the university. Legitimation, one of these ways, is particularly fascinating because it reveals an alien social presence at the intimate core of intellectual work: how the job we do on Tuesday morning is defined and redefined by implicit reference to the values and viewpoints of distant strangers.

Long-standing debates over, say, the representativeness of historical anecdotes; the interpretive value of authorial biography; or the preference for popular, nonliterary texts in cultural studies can be described more abstractly as debates over the proper definition of the discipline's object of knowledge. They can also be considered, more abstractly still, as debates about the sort of social function scholars propose to perform, the sort of social contribution they claim to offer. Indeed, nothing better reveals how deep into the discipline's inner workings the influence of the legitimizing imperative extends.[4]

Why is it that the discipline of literary criticism should possess not one but two objects of knowledge: literature, which is distinctive to it, and culture, which is shared with other disciplines like anthropology, history, and fine arts? Why is literature not enough? Though literature is a subset of culture, it is also distinct from culture in that it puts a stronger and more consistent emphasis on the aesthetic. The aesthetic, whether considered as noninstrumental imagination, defamiliarization, the deliberate intensification of already existing indeterminacy, or whatever, is always defined by its distance from the ordinary workings of society, which are seen by contrast as pragmatic and instrumental. Culture, on the other hand, even in its highest, Arnoldian formulations, always to some degree refers to the ordinary, nonaesthetic ways and means by which ordinary people live, to a whole way of life or culture in the anthropological sense. (Matthew Arnold offers the newspaper sentence "Wragg is in custody" [15] both as a judgment on England's existing small *c* culture and as a demand for more culture in the high, capital *C* sense.) In other words, culture is always at least somewhat continuous with the ordinary, instrumental workings of society.

Overstating for a moment the distinction between literature and culture, one could say that literature always struggles to distinguish itself from society, while culture never quite escapes from being society. Thus culture promises to have a direct effect on society, to be able to change it, and literature promises to withdraw from it and thus interpret it critically. The legitimating logic of the doubleness is clear. Literature offers critics a more or less distinct body of materials to work on, materials that jar us loose from unexamined modes of social action and membership. Yet literary critics need the supplement of culture in order to explain how this social distance returns to society, as it were, in the form of some more or less palpable benefit.[5]

This is, as I said, an overstatement. The tension I've described between literature and culture is also reproduced in each term. The other side of the story of culture is told in Raymond Williams's classic *Culture and Society*, which argues that the concept rose to prominence not because it seemed to represent society but because it could be understood as a counterweight to society, a critical standard by which society can be judged. The working assumption in many acts of literary criticism seems to be that literature is set apart from ordinary discourse by virtue of its ability to frustrate or exceed direct, normal, instrumental communication, to do something other or more than merely express or represent. Yet the most effective working rationale that has been proposed for literary criticism by sympathetic outsiders (e.g., Martha Nussbaum) remains the notion of literature as a vehicle for preserving, transmitting, and interpreting the experience of individuals and groups distanced from us in time or space.

Literature must be valued, saved, and taught (and must not be displaced from the secondary school curriculum, as has been proposed, in favor of reading and writing skills) because, the argument goes, it makes the experience of others available—in short, because it does the work of representation. Literature is social experience, and literature is also the dissolution or evasion or problematizing of social experience. There seems no way around the paradox. The idea that literature can honor the experience of others with proper scrupulousness only by showing that experience to be unrepresentable or by showing the limits of any representation of it, a position that has gained much ground since the late 1990s, cleverly if not entirely satisfactorily combines these two rationales, thereby confirming the unconscious strength of the legitimizing imperative.

No thesis about the literary scholar in society can be convincing across the disciplines if it does not acknowledge both the strength and the breadth of this imperative. Literary critics sometimes speak as if literature's difference from other discourses, its seemingly infinite potential to proliferate meanings, its autonomy vis-à-vis the demands of everyday accuracy and instrumentality—made it uniquely mysterious, eliciting critical interest solely and precisely because it re-

fuses the rational laws governing nonaesthetic phenomena. But a side glance at other, contiguous objects of disciplinary knowledge—rhetoric (for composition), society (for sociology), culture (for anthropology), politics (for political science), or space (for geography)—quickly reveals that these other disciplines, too, are obliged to stake out and defend a large zone of inscrutability, if only in order to guarantee continuing work for the discipline's practitioners.[6]

All disciplines seem to resemble literary criticism in the sense that they too exist in an unstable and precarious relation to a shifty object of knowledge that they can never fully possess or master, an object of knowledge that, like literature, sustains their work only by perpetually threatening to escape from their possession and undermine that work. Though critics like to think that they are blessed or cursed—it hardly matters—by the uniquely obscure and recalcitrant nature of what they work on, a wandering, undefinable object of uncertain borders is not in fact a deviation from some supposed disciplinary norm. And yet the wandering and the inscrutability can never be unlimited or uncontrolled. Like the objects of other fields, literature must satisfy two opposing exigencies: one, the mystery of distinctness; two, the impulse toward clarity, closure, and constraint that accompanies what Derek Attridge calls the "power to intervene in the ethical and political life of a community" (1). In order to show that they are not merely of interest to amateurs, eccentrics, and antiquarians, all disciplines must submit themselves to some criteria of urgency, ethical concern, general usefulness. In other words, they must render some account of their social significance.

Framing the issue of the scholar in society in terms of a transdisciplinary need for legitimation might seem to entail remaining meekly and ineffectually agnostic on the question described above as crucial: namely, how the world most needs changing, or which particular version or versions of social significance literary criticism should properly aspire to. It is true that the

All disciplines must submit themselves to some criteria of urgency, ethical concern, general usefulness.

framework sketched out thus far cannot hope to decide this all-important question. But it can bring a certain clarity to some of the competing answers that have been proposed. For example, it offers grounds for agreeing with Fish that "advocacy" is not the best term for our discipline's collective aspiration.

There is advocacy of a quiet but compelling sort merely in positing the range of topics to be discussed, the kinds of argument that will be acceptable, and how much discussion time will be allotted to any given topic. If "having an agenda"—one phrase of choice for those who seek to discourage advocacy—means putting some items at the top of the list and some lower down and always leaving many items off, then there is no production of knowledge that does not have an agenda. The very object of knowledge (which is always also an object of controversy) is constituted by politics. Without some desire to change the world, we wouldn't know which of the world's infinite parts were worth singling out for interpretation in the first place. On this level, scholars cannot *not* be advocates.

The same statement applies to teaching, or to effective teaching. The slice of society with which most scholars are most directly involved on a day-to-day basis is students. Students in the humanities demand, quite rightly, to be inspired. They want a demonstration that the mountain of material before them is not merely, like Everest, to be climbed because it is there but worth studying because it is significant. One might say that, in teaching, scholars practice their legitimizing outreach to the professionally unconverted. In another vocabulary, teachers stand up for something they believe, attesting by their investment of time, energy, and emotion that to them, personally, the subject matter matters. Mark Oppenheimer writes:

> If academics truly believed that the proper reading of Austen or Cather is of ultimate concern, they should have the courage to convince their students, not just their colleagues. I generally assume that the average mail carrier has a dash of Newman in him (Newman being the *Seinfeld*

character who megalomaniacally declared, "He who controls the mail controls everything!"). He believes that his job matters, a lot. Professors should feel the same thing.   (B9)

Teachers deemed successful at their job tend to communicate just this feeling.

But how much should one's job matter? Claims to control everything through the pursuit of one's gainful occupation will provoke mirth and even perhaps cast doubt on the claimant's sanity. When scholars claim, like Newman, to be uniquely placed by virtue of their disciplinary object so as to be able to change the world, what is to keep students from giggling and taking some other course? Literary criticism has clearly flirted with Newman's mail-centric perspective. Like the mail, culture could claim from the beginning to stand outside and above the usual particularism enforced by the division of labor. In recent scholarship, that claim has been broadened and amplified. Literary and cultural critics have of course tended to blur the border between the aesthetic and the instrumental, claiming in effect (I put this more crudely than it deserves) that nothing is merely pragmatic or instrumental and everything is therefore aesthetic or cultural. Culture *is* society. To change the one is therefore to change the other. This connection to everything embodies a large claim to social significance.[7] It has given criticism a distinctive political edge.[8] Does this edge cut into the status quo too deeply or not deeply enough? Mightn't it cut at the wrong place or the wrong angle?

More could be said here about the program of constructionism (the practice of demonstrating that X, which looks like a natural, unproblematically serviceable term, is actually a social or cultural construct) considered as a strategy of legitimation. Continuous with previous strategies, it obviously extends and politicizes the reach of the literary imagination. Less obviously, it also flatters the public that the social world remains open to the American dream of social mobility, in this sense paralleling the earlier promise of a literary education to provide aspiring social climbers with cultivated taste. It can do so, of course, only because it rejects the notion of society as something apart from itself. By dissolving or digesting, as it were, the hard otherness of the society to which it might be held accountable, it allows the dark and persistent political antagonisms from which critics might otherwise take their bearings to fade from view. No less dramatically, it undermines the model of legitimation itself. I return to this point below.

The argument for scholarship as political advocacy has recently been articulated by Francis Mulhern in *Culture/Metaculture* (2000). Controversies setting a supposedly radical cultural studies against a supposedly conservative literary criticism, Mulhern suggests, are misguided and politically insignificant. For cultural studies, like criticism, reposes on the foundation of culture, and it too has been severely hampered in its proper political aspirations by dependence on this object of knowledge (see also Collini). Though the concept of culture endowed literary criticism with a spectacularly persistent discipline-wide hostility to capitalist modernity (a feat whose magnitude has not always been adequately appreciated), it also inspired its devotees to reject with disgust two indispensable components of anticapitalist politics: mass democracy and political instrumentality. Elitist and aestheticist, the concept of culture insidiously installed a depoliticizing tendency in the heart of the very discourse on which social critics have depended to define their presumed subversiveness. It is still having this effect, Mulhern continues, on cultural studies. The cultural studies formula that everything is political (which derives from culture's seemingly infinite expansiveness) leaves nothing political in a usefully specifiable sense. Politics in this more precise, specialized sense is defined by action. "It is normally deliberative in character, governed by the question, What is to be *done?*" (170). Culture has been able to serve as a conceptual umbrella offering equal shelter to Marxists and to romantic reactionaries, along with other otherwise divergent groups and interests, because it refuses to divide, as politics must, along the definitive axis of what is to be done.

This tight, eloquent argument, which will elicit grateful recognition from those who doubt that politics can ever be everything, nonetheless runs up against a serious obstacle, even for readers attuned to Mulhern's own politics. The institution from which Mulhern is demanding united political action is the university. But universities cannot aim at the goal of unity, least of all unity that passes the test of joint political action. Departments and disciplines lodged in universities are structurally obliged to do precisely what Mulhern accuses the concept of culture of doing: accommodating divergent values, identities, and interests, even seemingly incompatible ones, in a structure of continuing controversy. (I would argue that political parties and movements do the same thing—hence the strange-bedfellows principle—if not to the same degree. But this is not the place for that argument.)[9] No scholarly discipline can be unanimous.

It's not that the discipline should not, for ethical reasons, demand consensus but that it literally cannot subsume internal differences without ceasing to function as a discipline. These internal differences are indeed limited, directed into certain channels rather than others. So it is not nonsense to talk about particular disciplines having a distinctive political character, as criticism arguably does. But the formal need to allow for unending controversy, to provide space for and indeed provoke substantive argument, means that there are severe limits to the political force and focus that can be demanded of any discipline.

Culture, which has done so much to make literary criticism's case for social significance, has limited the politics of critics working in its ambit even while giving many of them a politics in the first place. But if culture were to be replaced by some other term, like *discourse* or *signifying practices* or *political action*, that term too would limit—not in precisely the same way, granted, but to more or less the same extent. Like culture, the new term would have to allow for controversy. It would also have to explain to society, as culture did, why society should sponsor its study; and it would have to do so in a way that society could accept.

By these criteria, the candidacy of political action as an academic raison d'être is a non-starter. Universities cannot be treated as if they were pressure groups or political parties. Let us translate back into the more familiar term *advocacy*: a pedagogy that champions a particular political cause, organizing all readings and discussions on one side of that cause and demanding student adherence as a prerequisite for admission or successful completion. Advocacy of this hypothetical and perhaps extreme sort represents a version of political commitment that cannot recognize or adapt itself to the constraints of being located in a university department, constraints not all of which are open to renegotiation. Such advocacy therefore doesn't belong in a university department.[10] The humanities, for all their encouragement of activism and revolutionary thought, cannot reasonably expect to rename themselves activist studies or revolution studies.

Max Weber, whose two great lectures "Politics as a Vocation" and "Scholarship as a Vocation" famously articulated a strong version of the no-politics position, can also point us toward a more nuanced and more persuasive version.[11] In "Scholarship as a Vocation," which remains the ideal type for reflections on the scholar in society, Weber depicts the scholar's life as one of existential heroism. Scholars must have the courage, the modesty, and the dignity to pursue the truth without any self-flattering illusions—Weber is sure they are illusions—about the truth making anyone free or changing society for the better. Yet in both lectures, he also insisted that a choice between the seductive call of political commitment, to which he was not deaf, and the attractions of scholarship, which he chose for himself, made sense only in the light of those existing social institutions that would shape and delimit each option. The political party and the university, each of which

he discusses in great historical detail, are at once the social vehicle and the social obstacle on their respective paths.[12] It was what Weber had to say about these institutions that grounded his judgment about the superiority of the scholarly to the political path, and for that matter about the distinctness of the two paths.

Since Weber, both institutions have changed considerably. And a range of others have been added to them. Some—like the United Nations, the European Union, Amnesty International, and Doctors without Borders—characteristically combine in some degree a state-like claim to political effectiveness with a university-like claim to humanistic or humanitarian neutrality. In Weber's own terms, then, it would seem that we cannot speak responsibly about the scholar's proper relation to society without refreshing our sense of the particular institutions and levels of society that mold the options available to our moment and that scholarship would occupy or shun, support or subvert.

Let me put this in another way. Every description of the scholar, critic, or intellectual presupposes a particular social terrain. To focus on an individual type in close-up is almost necessarily to blur the view behind and around that type. Yet the ethical demands and recommendations addressed to this figure, which is to say exhortations to the reader to go and do likewise, can be properly evaluated only in relation to the implicit backdrop. Every ethics presupposes a sociology. Intellectual portraits presuppose social landscapes. Terms like *society* and *civil society* arose—were invented or constructed, as we now say—as landscape terms, hypotheses about the nature of power in a given time and place and about how power might (or might not) be challenged. In order to know what sort of scholar or intellectual you want to be, first you have to know what sort of social landscape you will be operating in, what sorts of remediable injustice it harbors, and what sorts of remedy it is in your power to deliver. The

In order to know what sort of scholar or intellectual you want to be, first you have to know what sort of social landscape you will be operating in.

courtier, for example, implies monarchy. The dissident implies totalitarianism. The boundary-crossing Zola-like intellectual, invented around the period of the Dreyfus Affair, implies both a newly specialized division of labor in which the writer, the academic, and the politician are expected to follow separate tracks and the possibility of transcending that division.

The more recent phrase "public intellectual" arises at a moment when the honor of being an intellectual is widely accorded to American academics working in their assigned areas of specialization. It is also a moment when ordinary specialized scholarship—presumably the work of private intellectuals, the contrastive phrase that is implied but never pronounced—is also widely seen as leaving something to be desired from the point of view of wider vision and adversarial inspiration. Hence the need for a more honorific term, registering the politically and epistemologically inhibiting effects of being expected to attend first and foremost to one's own occupational business (this is why *Seinfeld's* megalomaniacal mail carrier is not simply an object of mockery) and offering publicness as a higher, more strenuous goal.[13]

The division of labor, which is confronted with much the same defiance by Mulhern's action as by the usual culture, seems a crucial example of such landscapes. Should scholars who want to change the world indignantly reject their specialized location in the division of labor? Or on the contrary should they resign themselves to it, choosing instead to repose on this foundation and to act against something else? In his essay "Resignation," a companion piece to his critique of Sartrean *engagement*, Theodor Adorno doubts whether political action is the inevitable and proper measure of worth for those who, like himself, work on cultural materials while also deriving their commitment to that work from outrage at injustice. Thus he has become notorious for what Cornel West calls his "political impotence" (168). Adorno's prize doctoral student Hans-Jürgen Krahl was one of many in the late 1960s who charged that Adorno "was not able to translate his private compassion for the

wretched of the earth into a . . . theory for liberation of the oppressed" (165). Adorno answers, in effect, by questioning a culture-based understanding of action that sets action, like culture itself, against the division of labor. Though appalled by what the division of labor hides, he is resigned to living in it, but living in the division of labor is not the same as giving up all grounds or means of action against injustice.

Adorno writes:

> The purpose that has fallen to [theoretical thinkers] in a society based on the division of labor may be questionable; they themselves may be deformed by it. But they are also formed by it; of course they could not by sheer will abolish what they have become.   (289)

I don't share Adorno's high esteem for pure thought, as in the closing formula "thought is happiness" (293). Nor do I share the vision of a totally administered society that seems to make this idealization of thought necessary. But what Adorno says about the division of labor seems to break open his otherwise totalizing view of society. Consider his essay's next reference to the division of labor. This reference comes under the heading of "pseudo-activity," defined as an attempt to rescue "enclaves of immediacy in the midst of a thoroughly mediated and rigidified society":

> The disastrous model of pseudo-activity is the *"do-it-yourself"* [*Mach es selber*]: activities that do what has long been done better by the means of industrial production only in order to inspire in the unfree individuals, paralyzed in their spontaneity, the assurance that everything depends on them. The nonsense of do-it-yourself in the production of material goods, even in the carrying out of many repairs, is patently obvious.   (291)

In describing action as a version of "do-it-yourself," this passage does not exactly endorse the division of labor, but it implies several things in its favor: first, that the division of labor carries on the necessary business of production better than individuals could on their own; second, that "spontaneity" is at least as much a source of unfreedom as the division of labor itself; and third, that the division of labor embodies a social interdependence that needs to be refashioned but cannot be done away with.

To try to do away with social interdependence as such is to opt for action that can only be incoherent, and incoherent action is the theme of Adorno's next allusion to the division of labor. It is dangerous to idolize spontaneity, he argues, citing Schiller's *Wilhelm Tell*. For if one does, "the axe in the house that never saves the carpenter will smash in the nearest door, and the riot squad will be at the ready." As the translator's note suggests, this line refers to Schiller's self-sufficient mountaineer hero, who says, as he finishes his repair work, "an axe in the house will save a joiner's labor" (3.1.1512). Adorno says it won't. This is a false economy. Hire a specialist. In saying this, he is both defending theory as a specialization and taking his distance from the German Romantic tradition, which makes anti-specialization the centerpiece of its social critique, hence also (here this gets close to home for us) the basis of aesthetics. As Fredric Jameson puts it (approvingly) in *Marxism and Form*:

> Schiller's profound originality . . . was . . . to have transferred the notion of the division of labor, of economic specialization, from the social classes to the inner functioning of the mind, where it assumes the appearance of . . . a spiritual deformation which is the exact equivalent of the economic alienation in the social world outside. (87)

Adorno's contention, and my own, is that though the division of labor has served to naturalize the enormous inequality of resources and possibilities that we see increasing around us every day, it should not be confused with either spiritual deformation or the source or reason for social inequality—let's say, with class structure itself. As Andrew Sayer and Richard Walker argue in their book on the division of labor, there would be a highly developed division of labor under any conceivable socialist substitute for capitalism. To imagine that we could do without one not only fritters away our limited energies in a fruitless quest for an unavailable state of *Ge-*

meinschaft, but it also stops us from changing what we can and must change about the *Gesellschaft*-like state of affairs that we will continue to inhabit.[14]

So why has this faulty diagnosis continued to seem so plausible? One of the strangest things about words like *action* and *activism*, at least as they are currently used in the humanities, is their functional equivalence to apparently distant words like *culture*, *intellectual*, and *art*, each of which is accorded the privilege of transcending the division of labor. Even when what is meant is not revolutionary action, action must be seen as the latest in a series of terms that, for reasons that go back to our own disciplinary formation or deformation, we have asked to stand for the magical resolution of social contradictions; for the ideal unities; for the antidotes to the state of division, fragmentation, reification, and so on that we imagine reigning outside, thereby justifying our disciplinary existence. If we actually look at what is happening outside, politically speaking, it is immediately clear that action is no such thing; possesses no such impossible powers; has less to do with art than with politics in the de-idealized, messy, even door-smashing sense: the art of the possible.

The humanities already possess a discourse suggesting the desirability of teaching political action that does not directly challenge the division of labor: the discourse of citizenship. One important turn in the discourse of legitimation over the past decade has been a resurgence of interest, sponsored in part by the influence of Michel Foucault, in action at or near the level of the state, what has come to be called governmentality. Logically enough, the championing of governmentality as an implicit discourse of legitimation has proceeded in step with the critique of aesthetics (and of aesthetics's own implicit discourse of legitimation). For Ian Hunter, literary criticism has made the mistake of surrendering in advance its claim to political significance in this other, citizenly sense. It has done so by defining itself in terms of literariness or the aesthetic, which translates (again in the language of legitimation) into a claim to social externality, or what Hunter, after Immanuel Kant, calls critique. Critique is a practice of self-problematization, a habit of mistrusting experience that includes both the aesthetic and so-called critical thinking. It claims, falsely for Hunter, to be free of dogmatism; worse, it discourages us from recognizing how much freedom is there to be found and made use of in ordinary social institutions. Hunter's proposal is thus for a return to the rhetorical tradition of training for governance or civil life that used to be associated with the classics—a training that does not insist on a prior distance from or hesitation before the existing institutions of civil life.

This proposal may be premature—it certainly is premature in the United States, where the chance for liberal-minded people to do successful and self-fulfilling work in government bureaucracies is not quite as great as it is in Hunter's Australia. But it remains useful to reflect, with Hunter, on the hypothesis that the freedom we have associated with critique is also to be found in the institutions we have seen solely as objects of critique, that we have seen these institutions as lacking in freedom not because we have studied them in detail but because we needed a foil for the freedom of the aesthetic, something to define it against.

The risk involved in this hypothesis is abandoning an intellectual default setting of suspicion and critical distance, a predisposition that has perhaps deformed our habitual judgments but has done so, so to speak, on the progressive side, by keeping a certain amount of intellectual energy automatically flowing in the direction of social change. (There is nothing in Hunter's argument that would prevent criticism from being refashioned, for example, into some sort of management training.) I believe that this risk is worth running. The advantage of abandoning the default setting is that we would have to specify the values we are supporting both in our literary and in our political judgments, including some values that are already there in the institutions we occupy, like the university. We would certainly be more persuasive to outsiders in our critiques of capitalism, say, once those critiques

were no longer built into the premises of our argument.

Hunter's proposed return to rhetoric as citizenship training faces another problem of timing. Recent scholarly common sense tends to insist on a comparativist and transnational view of its object of knowledge. The nation-state, to which the concept of citizenship has traditionally been attached, is widely perceived to be in decline. How strong a case can be made for the pedagogical ideal of citizenship in the so-called era of globalization?

Since culture too has been attached to the nation-state, this question has an even deeper resonance. Is it still possible to speak concretely and responsibly about the scholar's role in society? What society are we talking about? Skepticism on this subject has been fueled on the one hand by a pervasive free-market individualism, as represented for example by Margaret Thatcher's famous declaration, "There is no such thing as society," and on the other hand by cultural high theory, as represented for example by Ernesto Laclau's declaration that society is impossible. This challenge to any attempt at the legitimation of scholarship, which as I noted above follows from the general premises of constructionism, has been articulated most forcefully by Bill Readings in his influential book *The University in Ruins* (1996). Readings argues that culture defined and legitimated the work of the humanities in the era of the nation-state. But in subverting the nation-state, globalization has put an end to that rationale and indeed to any rationales that depend on a consensual, community-like society. After globalization, there is no society, hence no university based on or responsible to society. That is why the university is in crisis, or in ruins.

What has replaced the previous national-cultural rationale, Readings argues, is an abstract, content-neutral ideal of excellence, which adapts the university to the exigencies of global capitalism through the quantifying language of corporate management.[15] Readings blasts the new rationale with blistering and well-deserved anger. Yet on second glance, there is something strange about his critique. Excellence, he says, offers the university a "unifying principle" (22), and what it unifies is an otherwise unmanageably diverse assortment of intellectual enterprises, divided for example as scientific versus humanistic, and then subdivided endlessly. Excellence fails because it can unify only by becoming so abstract as to be empty: "the general application of the notion is in direct relation to its emptiness" (23). The objection is in the name of particulars as opposed to abstractions: "An excellent boat is not excellent by the same *criteria* as an excellent plane" (24).

The problem is that this charge could be directed with equal force at the earlier rationale. *Nation, culture, the public* (society conceived as capable of collective self-representation), and *society* itself—all these terms, whether national or postnational, are constructs that offer themselves up for deconstruction; all are large abstractions that impose themselves on a diversity of particulars. Readings's preferred idea of the university is what he calls "the community of dissensus" (ch. 12), which is to say diversity writ large. In his view, the initial particulars of identity must be fixed and preserved, as if sacred and untouchable. All commonality between them must be forbidden. Thus Readings opposes the idea of a national public. For by definition, publics put pressure on the diverse identities in them, attempting to impose at least some degree of reciprocal translation. It is disingenuous of him, therefore, to mourn the loss of the idea of national culture or to blame that loss on global capitalism. By his logic, globalization continues at a transnational level the nefarious, homogenizing work that the national public was already doing, but it also helpfully undoes that work. If globalization had not happened and national publics still flourished, they would have to be resisted just as strenuously as globalization and again in the name of the incalculable otherness of singular identities. In this sense global capitalism, by breaking down the nation-state and liberating its particular identities from bondage, is actually Readings's ally, conveniently doing his deconstructing of the national culture for him and making his pro-

diversity point. If global capitalism didn't exist, he would have had to invent it.

Hence Readings's surprising congruence with Thatcher, who sets the supposed unreality of society against the unquestioned reality of individual consumers much as Readings plays off false abstraction against real particulars. If we can see society as no more and no less real than the particulars with which it is contrasted, if its supposed nonexistence is revealed as an ideological prejudice rather than an empirical discovery, then we are no longer prevented from observing that existence at various scales, whether national, subnational, or transnational. We can also see criticism's new attention to the transnational, which as Readings says accompanies its turn to cultural studies, not as a sudden and abject kowtowing to global capital but as continuous with criticism's earlier and honorable interests in literature and culture. It should be clear that both these overlapping objects of knowledge now exist on a transnational scale. Why should the same not be true of the society to which criticism holds itself accountable in studying them?[16] Again, shifts in legitimation proceed hand in hand with shifts in scholarly perspective. Society remains that to which we must hold ourselves accountable only because it is acknowledged to have expanded, only to the extent that it can successfully claim to include and represent the expanded field of cultural and national particulars that are now the objects of scholarly attention.

If terms like *society* and *culture* have meaning at the scale of the nation, which conspicuously transcends what is held to be the firmer reality of face-to-face encounters, then there is no reason to think *society* and *culture* cannot also be meaningful at still larger, transnational scales. In an article in *PMLA* entitled "Beyond Discipline? Globalization and the Future of English," Paul Jay declares that although the nation-state persists,

the rapid circulation of cultural commodities . . . has come at the expense of the nation-state's ability to control the formation of national subjectivities and ideologies. . . . Culture is now being defined in terms less of national interests than of a shared set of global ones.   (32)

In short, those subjectivities and ideologies are now being formulated on a global scale, and literary critics have no choice but to track them at the same transnational scale. The discipline called English already seems to be separating itself from its origins in the United Kingdom. While properly anxious over whether its new aspiration to globality might signify (like globalization itself) a covert nationalist recentering on the United States, it is drifting in the direction of world literature in translation.

Further evidence is all around us. Why else would the late Edward W. Said be described, in Giles Gunn's words, as "the conscience of our profession"? Said, Gunn writes, "knew that there is nothing strictly speaking innocent either about the act of writing or the act of reading" (71). Since our profession often implies that it acts as a sort of collective conscience to the society around it, this guilty knowledge would make Said a sort of quintessence of conscientiousness. How did he manage it? While speaking out publicly and passionately on issues far removed from his professional training, he did something less obvious: in the academy, he discovered a new reason for guilt, a new accusation that our already conscientious, indeed obsessively self-castigating profession had not yet applied to itself or the materials it works on. This new standard of good and evil was, roughly speaking, the welfare of the world as a whole. Henceforth nations outside Europe would be counted as equals with the supposed center of civilization.[17] Scholarship would be held accountable to a society imagined to include people from anywhere and everywhere on earth. Scholars would still be asked to be citizens and to form students into citizens, but the relevant citizenship had been stretched to worldly or cosmopolitan proportions. Said held a limited, Eurocentric humanism to its theoretical promise of being genuinely universal. Narrower loyalties, whether national or civilizational, would henceforth be punishable by loss of scholarly credit.

Said's own theory of intellectuals, on the

> **Subjectivities and ideologies are now being formulated on a global scale, and literary critics have no choice but to track them at the same transnational scale.**

other hand, is all portrait, no landscape. Said does not speculate, for example, on why his accusation should have taken, why the profession should have allowed itself to be judged guilty by this new and seemingly alien standard. For to inquire into matters of reception would lead inescapably to some theory of how scholars are embedded in society. Such a theory might allude to how Said's extended sense of society had already been Americanized, for better or worse—how decades of capitalist globalization talk had prepared Americans, both inside and outside the academy, to look with some favor on the standard of accountability to the world as a whole. It might mention the fact that, in accepting Said's accusation, the humanities were also accepting an enormous and lucrative contract for further work to be done.

From the perspective of postcolonial studies, the accusation was also a gift. Perhaps out of modesty, Said omits any generalizable grounds like these that would help explain why his ideas were greeted as they were. Instead, he champions the individual "speaking truth to power" and thus exemplifying a lonely, inexplicable heroism. But the exhortation to speak truth to power is responsible only if there is some reason to believe that the particular sort of power addressed can perhaps be made to listen—if there is some source of authority residing in the words, the position of the speaker, or the circumstances of the speech, or perhaps in the combination thereof, such that the speakers cannot be retrospectively described as merely posturing or offering themselves up in fruitless self-sacrifice. Profoundly suspicious of what he calls system, Said cannot take the just measure of the individual's heroism by taking the measure both of what it is up against in its given society and what it has going for it.[18]

The lonely hero speaking truth to power is only with difficulty imagined feeding the baby, taking out the trash, or for that matter grading a stack of papers, even if he or she in fact does all those things. Intellectuals have been persistently imagined as masculine precisely because they have been imagined as ideal instances of a more generally valued self-reliance. Unless we are content to assume that someone else, probably female, is doing all the work necessary to the maintenance of biological and familial life, that intellectuals will have no children or will enjoy the financial means to hire servants for child rearing and other menial activities, it seems desirable to pay less attention to scholarly portraits and more to social landscapes. In a review of Robert Putnam's *Bowling Alone*, one of many recent books that have bemoaned the decline of grass-roots political activism and other forms of voluntary civic engagement, Margaret Talbot points out that "the large-scale entrance of women into the labor market" is crucial in explaining this decline, and certainly more crucial than the factors Putnam prefers: television and the dying off of a generation formed by "wartime patriotism":

> The very women who are now working the longest hours—educated professional women—are the same group who in the past founded the benevolent societies and filled the ranks of the social movements that virtually defined America's civil society.   (12)

So we return to the issue of jobs and the consequences of having them or not having them. As this example suggests, these consequences are often unpredictable and averse to clear alignment on a progressive-conservative axis. Unless they are factored in, however, discussion of the scholar's role in society remains an exercise in empty idealization.

We speak of scholars and intellectuals so as to remind ourselves from time to time of an ideal that's visibly higher than our everyday chores and annoyances and that animates them, at least in principle, even while it tends to be obscured by them. In order to respect that ideal, we would have to add to the considerable housekeeping work involved in merely maintaining the daily life of the university the further work of improving it. There is much to be done. Simply turning one's attention to one's workplace would already lay out an ambitious program of social reform.

The university is an employer and as such must be held to fair and reasonable standards of wages, benefits, and working conditions for all its employees. The university is a landlord and a neighbor and as such must respect the rights of its tenants and those affected by its use of its land. The university is a large-scale purchaser of food and clothing and as such has a responsibility to ensure that it does not barter away the right to offer healthy food at the behest of some powerful corporate sponsor and that apparel sporting its logo is not produced in sweatshops. Many universities are also large investors and as such must ensure, in the bounds of the possible, that its investments do not contribute directly to military aggression and massive human rights violations. Meanwhile, the struggle for wider and more diverse access to higher education is far from over. With the university more and more pressured to regress to a pre–GI Bill model, opening its gates only for those upper-middle-class families who have the considerable funds necessary, we can be sure that there are more and more Jude the Obscures out there with no more hope of getting into Cornell than Jude had of getting into Christminster.

Making changes in these aspects of university life is not inconceivable—there are encouraging signs on more than one front—but it will not be easy. It will require more than political work in the university. If we apply, to the university, norms of conduct more rigorous than those of the capitalist marketplace, the reason is that the university was historically a not-for-profit institution. Ironically but characteristically, the university's early history of restricted access, in gentleman's club style, was the source of standards that now, in the era of for-profit universities with no check but consumer satisfaction on the credentials they trade in, offer a useful moral friction against the prevailing corporate ethos, including the present ethos of most university administrations. Yet would-be reformers of the university, like scholars seeking both to interpret and to change the wider world, also have to seek a wider social legitimation. Too much self-righteous "city on a hill" talk will risk driving away much-needed allies. Michael Bé-rubé writes:

> In an economy where the average worker changes jobs eight times in a career and is never assured of health insurance or paid vacations, university faculty are an easy target for resentment, and to date very few observers outside the universities seem to want to acknowledge or reflect on the fact that 45 percent of college professors are now part-time employees (usually working without benefits). The institution of tenure has a lot to do with that resentment—and with the lack of attention to part-time labor. We are already witnessing the *de facto* eradication of tenure in the wholesale conversion of full-time positions to adjunct positions.
>
> ("Public Perceptions" 14–15; see also Bradley)

Resentment seems inevitable if we humanists defend ourselves by claiming too much for ourselves—an effect we tend to produce indirectly by setting unreasonably high standards for ourselves. The ethical injunction to speak truth to power, for example, sounds as if it assumes that everyone has tenure, or should have it. How else could the implied object of the injunction be expected to act with such exceptional freedom and confidence? This assumption does not square with the working conditions of most actual academics, and it also tends to alienate those nonacademics who know how far removed they are from such privileged speech and job security. "No bad jobs" is a more realistic slogan than "tenure for all," especially when addressed to academics and nonacademics alike, and yet it is already quite an ambitious slogan. To fight for the rights of part-time workers in the academy may thus also be the key to winning support from part-time workers outside the academy and indeed support from society at large. Many observers drew just this conclusion from the success of the Teamsters 1997 strike against United Parcel Service, which highlighted UPS's treatment of its part-timers.

The scholarship we undertake also affects public support. Though the legitimation of cultural studies has stressed its analysis of popular culture, there are large sectors of society that would not be displeased if cultural and literary critics were to turn their attention away from Madonna and toward—I quote Bérubé's metrically memorable line—"Enron, Clear Channel, Halliburton, Fox" ("What"). Scholarly conferences featuring demonstrations that there is no such thing as a free market, arguments in favor of protecting consumers by means of genuine regulation and oversight (rather than more Foucauldian complaints that oversight means surveillance), and attention to stock-market fraud as a zone of imaginative self-fashioning might just make for a different sort of coverage in the press than the profession is in the habit of receiving.

Public appearances in the media are of course one way in which scholars and scholarship exercise a certain world-changing power. Media appearances by humanists like Said, Fish, Martha Nussbaum, and Cornel West have no doubt affected public perceptions of what humanists are and do. But it would be a mistake to focus exclusively on political performance in the domain of print and electronic media. As John Guillory argues, there are losses as well as gains when politics is "routed through the publicity system, with its regnant principle of celebrity" (110). We should not forget that ordinary scholarship also communicates broadly, if by slower and less visible channels whose small, capillary outflowings are harder to measure. A noteworthy example of such communication is the success of constructionism as a broad, extra-academic version of common sense. The formula "X is a construct," which is now applied somewhat indiscriminately in various contexts, will probably strike even sympathetic academic practitioners as somewhat alien—a slight mistranslation, not quite what they meant to say. Yet this feeling of slight alienness probably accompanies all political accomplishments, even the most satisfying. To go on to say that society at large is itself a construct is not to do

The ethical injunction to speak truth to power . . . sounds as if it assumes that everyone has tenure.

away with the sense of accomplishment. First, because if we call society a social construct, then we simultaneously recognize the existence of an agent called society that did the constructing. Second, because in so doing we only reassure ourselves that since all social agents and objects are fragments, we need not mourn the inevitable failure to achieve any complete political transformation. We can therefore feel a bit better about the fragmentary victories that have been and can be achieved.

Constructionism probably cannot be made to coincide perfectly with the program for the defense of the humanities sketched above, which calls for joining up with other providers of social services on the basis of a common concern for the long-term welfare of society as a whole. In other words, seeing our work in the somewhat alien context of the welfare state. Constructionism would mean refusing to put all our emphasis on our distinctness, as if we were practicing a sort of humanities identity politics—by suggesting, for example, that we are the only ones who know that everything is a social construct. Instead, we should mix a proper respect for that distinctness with an equally proper and necessary consciousness of grounds for our legitimation that are also shared with others.

But there is no avoiding the messiness of divided loyalties here. When we try to make common cause with nonacademic, nonprofessional workers while also trying to hold on to the special value of our professional credentials, we must expect some falling away from the credentials, from the alliance, or from both.[19] Declaring that support for what we do is functionally inextricable from support for the welfare state means attaching our destiny as humanists to just that sense of national culture and national solidarity that Readings and others declare lost forever, destroyed by globalization. I don't think this sense of national solidarity has been lost or lost beyond recall. But it's true that when national solidarity asserts itself, it can sometimes conflict with international solidarity. International solidarity, as I noted above, has been a crucial guide for recent scholarship in the hu-

manities. Indeed, this is one area in which universities have lately risen above other social institutions—for example, in their brave defense of unpopular internationalist perspectives since the attacks of September 11, 2001, and the wars in Afghanistan and Iraq that followed them.

The contradiction Readings indicates between nationalism and (non-Eurocentric) humanism is a very real contradiction. But this contradiction is not an argument against efforts to resolve it, both by the university in general and by humanists in particular—efforts to mediate as best one can between the claims of the welfare state at home and a newly strenuous engagement with knowledges and loyalties abroad.[20] It's only by embracing this contradiction that scholarship can mark its responsibility to society in the various contradictory senses of society and thus reinvent itself for the decades to come.

NOTES

1. One hypothesis, rendered inevitable by its pervasive and fatal appeal to the press, focuses on the generation of 1960s and 1970s activists, a generation that managed (so the story goes) to jump through the university's customary hoops with its ideals intact and thus became a cohort of tenured radicals, its influence visible in the succeeding cohorts it has trained in something like its own image. But this hypothesis puts too much weight on historical accident and too little on the university as the stage of these movements. The movements of the 1960s were characteristically incubated by the university, more than by some other site or institution, because many of the values that inspired them were characteristic of the university. The activist students were often asking universities to do no more than live up to the values they were teaching.

2. Given the idealism and implied disinterestedness that characterize so many of our proclamations, the suggestion that high-minded rationales for literary study are produced in response to the pressures of public legitimation may seem cynical. That is not how it is intended. Self-interest is an aspect of all politics; scholars have no reason to hide their face in shame. After all, they are not socially unlocatable, outside the constraints and determinations that affect all other social actors. Collective, sustained, institutionalized outbursts of eagerness to change the social system do not come from nowhere; they cannot be treated as pleasant but random mysteries, even when they come from people who are not the

most direct sufferers from the system. The idea that political commitments are personal in some exclusive sense, that we bring them with us fully formed when we enter professions and disciplines, having acquired them in our prior life by means that have to do only with our identities, families, geographies, and so on, is manifestly untrue to the experience of professional and disciplinary socialization. We have all seen the means, subtle and not so subtle, by which commitments are encouraged and even demanded as prerequisites for the accomplishing of professional-level work in a given field or subfield. People with no personal experience of American slavery or European colonialism must in effect project themselves into strong affective identification with the victims of both in order to know how and where to put the proper emphasis in an act of critical interpretation of Shakespeare's *Tempest* or Morrison's *Beloved*. The fact that disciplines like English offer to convert some of the pregiven identities of their practitioners into a form of cultural capital, a source of epistemological authority or—what is just as good, from the practitioner's point of view—a site of controversy over that authority, should not be allowed to conceal the much more pervasive fact that disciplinary socialization creates identity-like political investments.

3. Fish's argument could perhaps be construed as suggesting that if we stop making large claims for ourselves and instead treat the existence of literary scholarship as natural, inevitable, and therefore in no need of defense, the public will be subliminally urged to adopt our view and will fund us generously on no other grounds than the fact that literature exists. Literature is a distinct, indeed a unique object, and because it exists, criticism too must exist. However, a moment of reflection about any university's list of departments, even the largest and most inclusive list, will reveal that many hypothetical or potential objects of knowledge—upholstery and necromancy, bombing and beekeeping, animals that from a long way off look like flies—do not possess departments of their own. A defense of departments of literature cannot repose, therefore, on the mere existence or distinctness of literature.

4. I develop this argument further in *Secular Vocations*.

5. A counterargument might be elaborated here to the effect that literature's very externality to society, which makes it critical of society, has served as a real if paradoxical legitimizing claim. This claim would of course throw a more favorable light on Fish's back-to-literature position.

6. This paragraph and the next two are adapted from my "Pretend."

7. The concept of culture has negotiated between romantic creativity, seen as the domain of individual freedom (hence also individual responsibility), on the one hand, and on the other hand the social and historical weight of collective representativeness, a whole way of life that is largely inherited and resists violation by rational choice or external imposition. You see both sides of the culture concept persisting into the present in the form of constructionism, or the formula, "X is not natural but a construct." Constructionism is arguably almost hegemonic these days, and all the more so because of its inconsistencies. What about the agents—social? cultural?—that do the constructing? Are they also constructs? The regress is infinite. But that need not stop us from peddling our spicy mixture of free self-invention and social constraint. And it mainly doesn't.

8. Note that Newman's advocacy of his job requires that he know much more than that job. In order to praise the mail to those who are not postal workers, he must make the case that the mail is connected to everything else.

9. Is there any politics that escapes the particular vices of cultural studies populism, which (in Mulhern's description) promiscuously accommodates seemingly incompatible extremes, bringing divergent groups and identities together in a perpetually unstable alliance that perfectly represents the interests of none of them? "Populism, for all its attachment to the great simplicities of people and nation, is often confusing as a political phenomenon (some would say, always and intrinsically so) . . . Its varieties have extended from left to extreme right" (135). It's unclear whether revolutionary politics can serve, as Mulhern implicitly asks it to, as the simplifying, single-minded exception to this confusion. And even if it can, the question remains of what politics might be if revolution is not on the agenda.

10. Culture has worked because, within limits, it has incited differences that have been considered worth arguing over. Its replacement would have to do the same. Any call to political action that points beyond the university, for example—and as I have been arguing, that is something legitimation not only can do but must do—also has to compromise with certain givens of the university.

11. I have amended the translation of the German *Wissenschaft* from "science" to "scholarship."

12. Weber, who thought so long and hard about legitimation, ironically saw no need to offer a legitimating rationale for value-free scholarship like his own.

13. This is not to remove the goal of publicness from proper critical scrutiny. In the media-dominated landscape of the twenty-first century, it is arguable that calling attention to oneself is no longer the risky confrontation with censoring power that it was, say, to Sartre under the regime of de Gaulle. It's now at least as much a means of acquiring the power of celebrity. See Guillory for a brilliant elaboration.

14. *Gesellschaft* and *Gemeinschaft* are usually translated as "society" and "community," respectively.
15. Readings's vision of excellence is translated back into the language of legitimation in the work of the anthropologist Marilyn Strathern and her colleagues, which deals with the application to the university of accounting's audit model.
16. For Readings, internationalization "means the rupture of any . . . link between a given University and the society around it" (180). The United Nations, which could be conceived as an effort to bring an international public sphere into existence, is a mistake. Yet his reasons for calling it a mistake have nothing to do with the observable consequences or possibilities of internationalization and everything to do with his a priori sacralization of the particular. The United Nations "seeks to resolve the contradiction between nationalism and the ideal of human community" (182). The contradiction seems worth resolving, and resolving it might even be described as one of the tasks recently set for itself by the university. But we must not seek to resolve it, Readings says. One must not presume communicability, or even seek it. To discover, heaven forbid, that communication is possible across national borders would be to violate Readings's one ethical imperative: particulars must be left untouched.
17. If Said was critical of European representations of non-Europe without setting against them non-European self-representations, at least in *Orientalism*, the implicit standard there and everywhere remained for him that of global equality.
18. Much the same might be said of the otherwise inspiring work of Pierre Bourdieu, whose description of scholarship in terms of fields and cultural capital again omits a general theory of how the fields relate to one another as well as whether or not cultural capital is convertible into economic capital—in short, a theory of society.
19. Thanks to Jeffrey Wallen for spelling this out to me.
20. The growing popular enthusiasm for regulating and overseeing global corporations; for instituting standards of corporate transparency and accountability; for making corporations worry about things like human rights, subcontracting to sweatshops, and leaving their employees without pensions would seem for example to count undecidably both as internationalism and as nationalism.

WORKS CITED AND SUGGESTIONS FOR FURTHER READING

Adorno, Theodor W. "Resignation." *Critical Models: Interventions and Catchwords.* Trans. Henry W. Pickford. New York: Columbia UP, 1998. 289–94.

Arnold, Matthew. *The Function of Criticism at the Present Time.* 1864. Whitefish: Kessinger, 2004.

Attridge, Derek. *Peculiar Language: Literature as Difference from the Renaissance to James Joyce.* London: Methuen, 1988.

Bérubé, Michael. "Public Perceptions of Universities and Faculties." *Academe* July-Aug. 1996: 10–17.

———. "What Would Gramsci Do?" Cultural Studies Assn. Founding Conf. Wyndham Garden Hotel, Pittsburgh. 5 June 2003.

Bourdieu, Pierre. *Homo Academicus.* Trans. Peter Collier. Stanford: Stanford UP, 1988.

Bradley, Gwendolyn. "Contingent Faculty and the New Academic Labor System." *Academe* Jan.-Feb. 2004: 28–31.

Collini, Stefan. "On Variousness." *New Left Review* 27 (2004): 65–97.

Fish, Stanley. "Why We Built the Ivory Tower." *New York Times* 21 May 2004: A23.

Graff, Gerald. *Clueless in Academe: How Schooling Obscures the Life of the Mind.* New Haven: Yale UP, 2003.

———. "The Scholar in Society." *Introduction to Scholarship in Modern Languages and Literatures.* Ed. Joseph Gibaldi. New York: MLA, 1992. 343–62.

Guillory, John. "Literary Critics as Intellectuals: Class Analysis and the Crisis of the Humanities." *Rethinking Class: Literary Studies and Social Formations.* Ed. Wai Chee Dimock and Michael T. Gilmore. New York: Columbia UP, 1994. 107–49.

Gunn, Giles. "On Edward W. Said." *Raritan* 23.4 (2004): 71–78.

Hunter, Ian. "Aesthetics and Cultural Studies." *Cultural Studies.* Ed. Lawrence Grossberg, Cary Nelson, and Paula Treichler. New York: Routledge, 1992. 347–72.

Jameson, Fredric. *Marxism and Form: Twentieth-Century Dialectical Theories of Literature.* Princeton: Princeton UP, 1971.

Jay, Paul. "Beyond Discipline? Globalization and the Future of English." *PMLA* 116 (2001): 32–47.

Krahl, Hans-Jürgen. "The Political Contradictions of Adorno's Critical Theory." *Telos* 21 (1974): 164–67.

Laclau, Ernesto. *New Reflections on the Revolution of Our Time.* London: Verso, 1990.

Mulhern, Francis. *Culture/Metaculture.* London: Routledge, 2000.

Nussbaum, Martha C., *Poetic Justice: The Literary Imagination and Public Life.* Boston: Beacon, 1995.

Oppenheimer, Mark. "In Praise of Passionate, Opinionated Teaching." *Chronicle of Higher Education* 21 May 2004: B7–9.

Putnam, Robert D. *Bowling Alone: The Collapse and Revival of American Community.* New York: Simon, 2000.

Readings, Bill, *The University in Ruins.* Cambridge: Harvard UP, 1996.

Robbins, Bruce. "Pretend What You Like: Literature under Construction." *The Question of Literature: The Place of the Literary in Contemporary Theory.* Ed. Liz Beaumont Bissell. Manchester: U of Manchester P, 2002. 190–206.

————. *Secular Vocations: Intellectuals, Professionalism, Culture*. London: Verso, 1993.

Said, Edward. *Orientalism*. New York: Pantheon, 1978.

Sayer, Andrew, and Richard Walker. *The New Social Economy: Reworking the Division of Labor*. Oxford: Blackwell, 1992.

Schiller, Johann Christoph Friedrich von. *Wilhelm Tell*. Trans. and ed. William F. Mainland. Chicago: U of Chicago P, 1972.

Strathern, Marilyn, ed. *Audit Cultures: Anthropological Studies in Accountability, Ethics, and the Academy*. London: Routledge, 2000.

Talbot, Margaret. "Who Wants to Be a Legionnaire?" *New York Times Book Review* 25 June 2000: 11–12.

Thatcher, Margaret. "AIDS, Education and the Year 2000." *Woman's Own* 31 Oct. 1987: 8–10.

Wacquant, Loic J. D. "The Self-Inflicted Irrelevance of American Academics." *Academe* July-Aug. 1996: 18–23.

Weber, Max. *From Max Weber: Essays in Sociology*. Trans. and ed. H. H. Gerth and C. Wright Mills. New York: Oxford UP, 1946.

West, Cornel. *Keeping Faith: Philosophy and Race in America*. New York: Routledge, 1993.

Williams, Raymond. *Culture and Society, 1780–1950*. New York: Columbia UP, 1983.

⌐ Notes on Contributors

DAVID BARTHOLOMAE is professor and chair of the Department of English at the University of Pittsburgh. He has served on councils and committees of the MLA, the National Council of Teachers of English, the Conference on College Composition and Communication, and the Association of Departments of English. He has published six books and over forty articles on composition. CCCC honored his work with a Braddock Award and the "Exemplar" Award. His *Writing on the Margins: Essays on Composition and Teaching* won the 2005 MLA Mina Shaughnessy Award.

CHARLES BERNSTEIN is Donald T. Regan Professor of English, University of Pennsylvania. Among his books are *Girly Man* (2006), *Shadowtime* (2005), *With Strings* (2001), *Republics of Reality, 1975–1995* (2000), *My Way: Speeches and Poems* (1999), *A Poetics* (1992), and *Content's Dream: Essays, 1975–1984* (1986, 1994).

HEIDI BYRNES is George M. Roth Distinguished Professor of German at Georgetown University. Her recent edited and coedited books dealing with the acquisition of advanced levels of ability in a second or foreign language are *Advanced Foreign Language Learning: A Challenge to College Programs* (2004), *Educating for Advanced Foreign Language Capacities: Constructs, Curriculum, Instruction, Assessment* (2006), *Advanced Language Learning: The Contribution of Halliday and Vygotsky* (2006), and *The Longitudinal Study of Advanced L2 Capacities* (forthcoming).

ANNE DONADEY is associate professor of European studies and women's studies at San Diego State University. She is author of *Recasting Postcolonialism: Women Writing between Worlds* (2001) and coeditor, with H. Adlai Murdoch, of *Postcolonial Theory and Francophone Literary Studies* (2005).

JEAN FRANCO is professor emerita of the Department of English and Comparative Literature at Columbia University and one of the editors of the series Cultural Studies of the Americas (Univ. of Minnesota Press). She is also general editor of the Library of Latin America series (Oxford Univ. Press). Among her books are *The Modern Culture of Latin America: Society and the Artist* (1967), *Plotting Women: Gender and Representation in Mexico* (1989), and *The Decline and Fall of the Lettered City: Latin America and the Cold War* (2001). For lifetime achievement she received awards from PEN and the Latin American Studies Association.

SUSAN STANFORD FRIEDMAN is Virginia Woolf Professor of English and Women's Studies at the University of Wisconsin, Madison. She is the author of *Psyche Reborn: The Emergence of H. D.* (1981), *Penelope's Web: Gender, Modernity, H. D.'s Fiction* (1990), and *Mappings: Feminism and the Cultural Geographies of Encounter* (1998). Her edited books include *Signets—Reading H. D.* (1990), *Joyce: The Return of the Repressed* (1993), and *Analyzing Freud: Letters of H. D., Bryher, and Their Circle* (2001). She has published a number of articles on diaspora and transnationalism and is at work on a book entitled "Planetary Modernism and the Modernities of Empire, Nation, and Diaspora."

CATHERINE GALLAGHER is Eggers Professor of English Literature at the University of California, Berkeley. Her books include *The Industrial Reformation of English Fiction: Social Discourse and Narrative Form, 1832–67* (1985), *Nobody's Story: The Vanishing Acts of Women Writers in the Literary Marketplace* (1994), *Practicing New*

Historicism (with Stephen Greenblatt; 2000), and *The Body Economic: Life, Death, and Sensation in Political Economy and the Victorian Novel* (2005).

J. MICHAEL HOLQUIST is professor emeritus of Slavic and comparative literature at Yale University. He is author of *Doestoevsky and the Novel* (1977, 1986), *Mikhail Bakhtin* (with Katerina Clark), and *Dialogism* (1990, 2002). He translated or edited a number of Bakhtin's works. He is a member of the Society of Senior Scholars at Columbia's Heyman Center for the Humanities. His current project concerns the influence of Kant and Wilhelm von Humboldt in twentieth-century Russian literary theory.

PAUL J. HOPPER holds the Paul Mellon Distinguished Chair of Humanities at Carnegie Mellon University. He is the coauthor, with Elizabeth Traugott, of *Grammaticalization* (2003). His research centers on microrhetoric and the interface between grammar and discourse.

SUSAN C. JARRATT is campus writing coordinator and professor of comparative literature at the University of California, Irvine. She is author of *Rereading the Sophists: Classical Rhetoric Refigured* (1991), coeditor of *Feminism and Composition Studies: In Other Words* (1998) with Lynn Worsham, and coeditor of the forthcoming *Norton Anthology of Rhetoric and Writing*.

FRANÇOISE LIONNET is professor of French, francophone studies, and comparative literature at the University of California, Los Angeles. She is author of *Autobiographical Voices: Race, Gender, Self-Portraiture* (1989) and *Postcolonial Representations: Women, Literature, Identity* (1995). She is coeditor of *Minor Transnationalism* (2005) and several journal special issues, including *Signs: Journal of Women in Culture and Society* (1995 and 2004).

LEAH S. MARCUS is Edwin Mims Professor of English at Vanderbilt University. She is author of *Childhood and Cultural Despair* (1978), *The Politics of Mirth* (1986), *Puzzling Shakespeare* (1988), and *Unediting the Renaissance* (1996). She has coedited the *Works of Queen Elizabeth I*

(with Janel Mueller and Mary Beth Rose) and edited *The Merchant of Venice* for Norton (2006). She is presently working on an Arden edition of *The Duchess of Malfi*.

JEROME McGANN is the John Stewart Bryan University Professor at the University of Virginia. His most recent books are *The Scholar's Art: Literary Studies in a Managed World* (2006) and *The Point Is to Change It: Poetry and Criticism in the Continuing Present* (2006). His *Radiant Textuality* (2002) received the MLA's James Russell Lowell Award.

DAVID G. NICHOLLS is director of book publications for the Modern Language Association of America. He is author of *Conjuring the Folk: Forms of Modernity in African America* (2000) and editor of *Harlem Calling: The Collected Stories of George Wylie Henderson* (2005).

BRUCE ROBBINS is professor of English and comparative literature at Columbia University. He is author of *Feeling Global: Internationalism in Distress* (1999), *The Servant's Hand: English Fiction from Below* (1986), *Secular Vocations: Intellectuals, Professionalism, Culture* (1993), and *Upward Mobility and the Common Good* (2007) and coeditor of the *Longman Anthology of World Literature* (2003). He edited *Intellectuals: Aesthetics, Politics, Academics* (1990) and *The Phantom Public Sphere* (1993) and coedited *Cosmopolitics: Thinking and Feeling beyond the Nation* (1998).

DORIS SOMMER is Ira and Jewell Williams Professor of Romance Languages and Literatures and director of the Cultural Agents Initiative at Harvard University. She edited *Cultural Agency in the Americas* (2006) and *Bilingual Games* (2004). Her developed proposal for the arts and ethics associated with bilingualism is *Bilingual Aesthetics: A New Sentimental Education* (2004).

LAWRENCE VENUTI is professor of English at Temple University. He is author of *The Translator's Invisibility: A History of Translation* (1995) and *The Scandals of Translation: Toward an Ethics of Difference* (1998) and editor of *Rethinking*

Translation: Discourse, Subjectivity, Ideology (1992) and *The Translation Studies Reader* (2004). His translations from the Italian include Antonia Pozzi's *Breath: Poems and Letters* (2002), *Italy: A Traveler's Literary Companion* (2003), and Massimo Carlotto's novel *The Goodbye Kiss* (2006).

KENNETH W. WARREN is Fairfax M. Cone Distinguished Service Professor in the Department of English at the University of Chicago. He is author of *So Black and Blue: Ralph Ellison and the Occasion of Criticism* (2003) and *Black and White Strangers: Race and American Literary Realism* (1993).

Index of Titles

～ Index of Names